Wealth, Commerce, and Philosophy

WEALTH, COMMERCE, AND PHILOSOPHY

Foundational Thinkers and Business Ethics

Edited by Eugene Heath and Byron Kaldis
with a Foreword by Deirdre N. McCloskey

The University of Chicago Press
Chicago and London

The University of Chicago Press, Chicago 60637
The University of Chicago Press, Ltd., London
© 2017 by The University of Chicago
Published 2017
Printed in the United States of America

26 25 24 23 22 21 20 19 18 17   1 2 3 4 5

ISBN-13: 978-0-226-44371-3 (cloth)
ISBN-13: 978-0-226-44385-0 (paper)
ISBN-13: 978-0-226-44399-7 (e-book)
DOI: 10.7208/chicago/9780226443997.001.0001

Library of Congress Cataloging-in-Publication Data

Names: Heath, Eugene, editor. | Kaldis, Byron, editor. | McCloskey, Deirdre N., writer of
    foreword.
Title: Wealth, commerce, and philosophy : foundational thinkers and business ethics /
    edited by Eugene Heath and Byron Kaldis ; with a foreword by Deirdre N. McCloskey.
Description: Chicago : The University of Chicago Press, 2017. | Includes index.
Identifiers: LCCN 2016033178| ISBN 9780226443713 (cloth : alk. paper) |
    ISBN 9780226443850 (pbk. : alk. paper) | ISBN 9780226443997 (e-book)
Subjects: LCSH: Business ethics—Philosophy. | Business ethics—History.
Classification: LCC HF5387 .W422 2017 | DDC 174/.4—dc23 LC record available at
    https://lccn.loc.gov/2016033178

♾ This paper meets the requirements of ANSI/NISO Z39.48-1992 (Permanence of
Paper).

CONTENTS

Foreword: "While Conforming to . . . Law and . . . Ethical Custom":
How to Do Humanomics in Business Ethics   *vii*
   Deirdre N. McCloskey

Introduction   1
   Eugene Heath and Byron Kaldis

1   Wealth and Commerce in Archaic Greece: Homer and Hesiod   11
   Mark S. Peacock

2   Aristotle and Business: Friend or Foe?   31
   Fred D. Miller Jr.

3   Confucian Business Ethics: Possibilities and Challenges   53
   David Elstein and Qing Tian

4   The Earthly City and the Ethics of Exchange: Spiritual, Social,
   and Material Economy in Augustine's Theological Anthropology   75
   Todd Breyfogle

5   Thomas Aquinas: The Economy at the Service of Justice
   and the Common Good   95
   Martin Schlag

6   The Ethics of Commerce in Islam: Ibn Khaldun's *Muqaddimah* Revisited   115
   Munir Quddus and Salim Rashid

7   Hobbes's Idea of Moral Conduct in a Society of Free Individuals   135
   Timothy Fuller

8   John Locke's Defense of Commercial Society: Individual Rights,
   Voluntary Cooperation, and Mutual Gain   157
   Eric Mack

9 As Free for Acorns as for Honesty: Mandevillean Maxims
   for the Ethics of Commerce   *179*

   Eugene Heath

10 "Commerce Cures Destructive Prejudices": Montesquieu
   and the Spirit of Commercial Society   *201*

   Henry C. Clark

11 Hume on Commerce, Society, and Ethics   *221*

   Christopher J. Berry

12 The Fortune of Others: Adam Smith and the Beauty of Commerce   *241*

   Douglas J. Den Uyl

13 Why Kant's Insistence on Purity of the Will Does Not Preclude
   an Application of Kant's Ethics to For-Profit Businesses   *263*

   Norman Bowie

14 Tocqueville: The Corporation as an Ethical Association   *283*

   Alan S. Kahan

15 J. S. Mill and Business Ethics   *301*

   Nicholas Capaldi

16 Karl Marx on History, Capitalism, and . . . Business Ethics?   *321*

   William H. Shaw

17 Friedrich Hayek's Defense of the Market Order   *341*

   Karen I. Vaughn

18 The Power and the Limits of Milton Friedman's Arguments
   against Corporate Social Responsibility   *359*

   Alexei Marcoux

19 Beyond the Difference Principle: Rawlsian Justice, Business Ethics,
   and the Morality of the Market   *381*

   Matt Zwolinski

20 Commitments and Corporate Responsibility: Amartya Sen on
   Motivations to Do Good   *401*

   Ann E. Cudd

Contributors   *421*

Index   *423*

"While Conforming to . . . Law and . . . Ethical Custom": How to Do Humanomics in Business Ethics

Deirdre N. McCloskey

The title of Milton Friedman's famous, or infamous, article in the *New York Times Magazine* in 1970—"The Social Responsibility of Business Is to Increase Its Profits"—was crafted by a clever headline writer from the *first* clause of a sentence early in the piece. My title here is from the *second* clause in the same sentence, which reverses what economists and their enemies have supposed Friedman was saying—that we students and practitioners of business don't need to learn about ethics. Friedman was saying the opposite (such as about the ethics of stewardship).

And so too does the present book. A problem with business ethics is that it is not serious about ethics. Another is that it is not serious about business. After *Wealth, Commerce, and Philosophy* there will be no excuse, on either count.

I want to recommend the book under a novel rubric, "humanomics," which is to say the study of business with the humans, and the humanities, left in. The humanities deal with the categories of meaning that humans regard as important, such as business ethics vs. political ethics, corporation vs. partnership, red giants vs. white dwarves, viruses vs. bacteria, citizens vs. illegals, ugly vs. beautiful, dignity vs. pleasure, good vs. bad. You need to know the meaning of a category before you can count its members, which is why the humanistic sciences—the Germans call them *die Geisteswissenschaften*, the "spirit sciences"—must always precede the quantitative sciences, whether social or physical. Meaning is scientific, as Niels Bohr among many have noted, because scientists are humans with human questions on their lips.

So too here, the "spirit science" of philosophy is applied to the business world. True, it is not *only* technical philosophy among the humanities that can illuminate the business of ordinary life. You can learn from the plays of Henrik Ibsen or Arthur Miller about the meaningful categories in a bourgeois life—such as that a Master Builder fears entry by the young; or that respect must be paid even to the unsuccessful salesman. You can learn from Milton—John, not Friedman—that "Evil be thee my good" is a clever fool's plan for a life, even an angelic one, as is also an aristocratic or peasant or bourgeois plan such as "He who dies with the most toys wins." You can learn from linguistics, or from the *Dilbert* cartoon, that the surface rhetoric of a manager's declaration can have the opposite pragmatic or illocutionary force. You can learn from the existence theorem of mathematics beloved in highbrow economic theory—itself part of the humanities, not the quantitative sciences—that there might exist a category of spillovers in free markets that might justify massive intervention by a hypothetically perfect government of benevolent philosopher kings. The categories themselves of spillover (any effect whatever?), justified intervention (shooting polluters?), government (monopoly of violence?), benevolent (toward whom?), and philosopher (not rhetorician?) are themselves appropriate subjects for a humanistic inquiry.

The experimental economist Bart Wilson, who coined the term "humanomics," recently used the philosopher Ludwig Wittgenstein (1889–1951) to locate the sense of justice not merely in the utility functions of individuals but in the language game they play.[1] He is the only economist to use Wittgenstein deeply. I myself have begun to use the philosopher John Searle (1932–) to bring the study of economic institutions up to philosophical and literary speed in the matter of categories to count.[2] Such a game pays off scientifically. That is, you can learn the categories of human meaning, the first step in a science, by getting to know, on all the matters that most concern us, "the best which has been thought and said in the world" by a variety of philosophers, from Confucius (Kongzi, Kung the Teacher) to Amartya Sen. The guides in the present book are expert and reliable, telling you what was said by such men. (I note, alas, the absence of women. The philosophers Elizabeth Anscombe, Philippa Foot, and Martha Nussbaum on virtue ethics could teach business ethics, too.)[3] The book's message is the following: Read the best philosophers, read their very texts, and see how they can be of use in a commercial society.

The second step, the test of usefulness in understanding and practicing in a commercial society, is crucial, because, as is shown here repeatedly, until the Bourgeois Era, and indeed well into it (in Marx and Rawls and even Sen), the philosophers seldom escaped from the antibusiness prejudices of their societies, especially of the intellectual elite. Fred Miller in his essay, for example, has the difficult task of making aristocrat-loving Aristotle useful for business ethics. He does it with what the Greeks called an *elenchus*, a judo move, one worthy of Socrates himself. Nicholas Capaldi rescues Mill's utilitarianism from vulgarity by showing that Mill's core value was human dignity. The move raises the study of business ethics above the utilitarianism of adding up the costs and benefits of stakeholders. Likewise Douglas Den Uyl argues that in the Blessed Adam Smith "commerce . . . promises only fittingness and progress, not personal happiness." The poor boy who strives, for example, may deform his character by doing so. Yet, Den Uyl argues, Smith saw beauty—yes, beauty—in the commercial whole, "the obvious and simple system of natural liberty." "Smith can reasonably claim," Den Uyl writes, "that one can have unfavorable attitudes toward many of the actors within a commercial setting ['People of the same trade seldom meet together . . .'] while still being favorably disposed toward commerce generally," because in Montesquieu's words (see Henry Clark's characteristically lucid essay) it softens and civilizes. I myself would observe that the deformation of the poor boy's character by commerce is perhaps no worse than deformation of the little lord toward arrogance and deformation of the novitiate toward monkish vices. In the mass it may be better.

Consider another example of the scientific gain to philosophical sophistication, from Fr. Martin Schlag's essay on what would seem a hard case, the Divine Doctor, Saint Thomas Aquinas—whose orthodoxy among Roman Catholics sometimes gives nonbelievers an excuse to ignore this most brilliant of philosophers. Aquinas is not, Schlag points out, a methodological individualist. He justifies private property by its social consequences, for the common good. As is often the case, Aquinas thought notably more clearly than many of his successors. The Lockean notion many centuries later of justifying property by the mixing of labor with the land is hopelessly ambiguous. Ask: Does the labor of one's first-grade teacher justify her getting a share of your property? Did you build that? By contrast the social usefulness of a system of business is plain to see. *Someone* must own the land if it is to be used properly, and leaving it to oxymoronic "public ownership" does not do the job.

Aquinas and his teacher Albert the Great, Schlag writes, "overcame the somewhat negative attitude toward private property predominant in the tradition that preceded them. . . . Thomas's arguments for property aim at the better functioning of the whole." "Better functioning" is a matter of *teloi,* ends, the consideration of which, as Schlag also points out, is supposed to be forbidden to modern social scientists. No discussion of ends, please: we're social engineers. Yet the individualism of a libertarian such as the economist Murray Rothbard—and Mill (as Capaldi points out) and Hayek (as Karen I. Vaughn points out)—did in fact consider the ends of human flourishing.[4] Schlag puts Thomas in a middle position, "too concentrated upon his rejection of greed to accept the inner logic and positive consequences of international [and for that matter local] commerce based on profit." And so are many students of business and theology to this day, too concentrated on rejecting greed to see that greed is not peculiar to commerce.

Not all the writers here escape from such antieconomic prejudices in their philosophers. Todd Breyfogle is correct to quote Saint Augustine: "We must use this world and not enjoy it"—that is, use it to attain true and proper ends, above all spiritual ends, not for mere pleasure. Ice cream again. Yet what Augustine fails to understand, and with him Pope Francis I, is that riches come in a virtuous commercial society overwhelmingly from service to others. The mistake is to look only at the balance sheet of the entrepreneur, asking whether she gives some of her net wealth to the Salvation Army, and not noticing what she creates for others in her income statement down in the marketplace. The urban monks of the thirteenth century such as Saints Albert and Aquinas and Francis noticed the creative side, analogizing the business-person's to God's creative work. As Montesquieu said, as Henry Clark reminds us, at that point the "theologians were obliged to curb their principles, and commerce . . . returned . . . to the bosom of integrity."

One way to use the philosophers of olden days is to shift their emphasis on political philosophy to the philosophy of corporate governance and economic regulation. David Elstein and Qing Tian, for example, use Confucius (Kongzi) and Mencius (Mengzi) on the government as models for corporate behavior, noting that in ancient China a citizen dissatisfied with one ruler could decamp to another. (Alan Kahan appropriates Tocqueville in the same way, a business being a voluntary association for pursuit of goals in a society of equals.) Yet Confucianism, Elstein and Tian argue, can sometimes overemphasize individual ethics, in contrast to Western political and economic thought overemphasizing formal law. "The Confucian ideal is to be motivated by intrinsically following the Way. . . . Coercive measures alone [it said] are not enough." That the Confucians emphasized ethics as against compelled law is news to me, and useful as a corrective to the a-ethical inadequacies of neoinstitutional orthodoxy these days in economics: "Add institutions—compelled rules of the game, new laws, fresh constitutions—and stir."

Some economists want to reduce ethics to incentives. The tactic assumes that incentives will work so as to make it unnecessary for anyone actually to have ethics. The corresponding error, common in recent thinking about ethics, even in business ethics, is to suppose that ethics is only about grand issues such as murder or abortion or outright fraudulence in accounting, the instances of television dramas, one might say. But it is also about daily goodwill and one's identity as a professional, such as an accountant doing as well as she can or a professor earnestly trying to tell the truth or a New Orleans police officer not abandoning the city during Katrina.

Hobbes famously wrote, Timothy Fuller reminds us, that "the force of words being (as I have formerly noted) too weak to hold men to the performance of their covenants, there are . . . but two imaginable helps, . . . either a fear of the consequences . . . or a glory or pride in appearing, . . . [which]

latter is a generosity too rarely to be found to be presumed on." Hobbes was quite mistaken in this, and set political philosophy off in the wrong direction of ignoring rhetoric and attending only to interest.

Hobbes was also mistaken in supposing that the government can easily apply the rod to interest. Two centuries prior, Ibn Khaldun wrote of a *muhtasib* (the "powerful market supervisor," in the words of Munir Quddus and Salim Rashid) who "sees to it that the people act in accord with the public interest in the town." Yet even the Romans had been suspicious of such an economic deus ex machina, asking, "Who supervises the very supervisor?" The saints required to run central-planning socialism of the Oscar Lange sort described in Karen Vaughan's essay are not in ample supply. As Matt Zwolinksi notes, it was assumed during John Rawls's 1960s, in the bright dawn of social engineering (I remember it well, with a certain fondness), that the "technocratic state" could easily surpass in justice and efficiency a liberal market order.

So, in short, conform to law and ethical custom, and read here the ethical and political philosophers, and then sit and think about our lives in business.

NOTES

1. Bart J. Wilson, "Social Preferences Aren't Preferences," *Journal of Economic Behavior & Organization* 73 (2010): 7–82.

2. Deirdre N. McCloskey, "Max U versus Humanomics: A Critique of Neo-Institutionalism," *Journal of Institutional Economics* (Spring 2015): 1–27, doi:10.1017/S1744137415000053; and Larry Arnhart, "Lockean Liberalism as Symbolic Niche Construction: Locke's Mixed Modes and Searle's Institutional Facts," *Darwinian Conservatism* (blog), June 11, 2015, http://darwiniancon servatism.blogspot.com/2015/06/lockean-liberalism-as-symbolic-niche.html2015.

3. Elizabeth Anscombe, "Modern Moral Philosophy," *Philosophy* 33 (1958): 1–19; Philippa Foot, *Virtues and Vices and Other Essays in Moral Philosophy* (Berkeley: University of California Press, 1978); and Martha Nussbaum, *The Fragility of Goodness: Luck and Ethics in Greek Tragedy and Philosophy* (Cambridge: Cambridge University Press, 1986).

4. Gerard Casey, *Murray Rothbard* (New York: Continuum, 2010), 42.

Eugene Heath and Byron Kaldis

In the discipline of business ethics, scholars examine the foundations of markets, the moral basis of exchange, the practices of business (including the nature of the corporation), the conditions for the production and distribution of wealth, the social responsibilities of corporations, and the consequences of commerce, whether local or global. The academic discussion of these subjects assumes and implies concepts and principles whose compass is moral, political, economic, social, and legal. Obviously, such subjects have deep and broad roots, yet in many instances, the insights and contributions of notable philosophers, social theorists, and political economists remain untapped or represented schematically. This volume seeks to reinvigorate and widen business ethics scholarship so that the discipline will be informed more fully and deeply by the perspectives of significant philosophers and thinkers. In this way, this volume will serve as a salient and resourceful reminder that the morality of economic exchange, the ethics of markets and business, and the production or uses of wealth are subjects that have been examined and debated by a long history of writers, theorists, and philosophers. The works of these thinkers merit careful attention because of their relevance and depth, not to mention their surprising and sometimes unrecognized insights.

The essays gathered here offer original interpretations of foundational thinkers. Given the crescendo of interest in business ethics, it is surprising that there is no single work devoted to scholarly essays on great thinkers and their relevance to the ethics of commerce and wealth. This collection remedies that lacuna by providing clear, accurate, and compelling accounts of how the ideas and arguments of significant thinkers relate to commerce, wealth, and markets. In so doing, the volume aims to encourage, within the discipline of business ethics, a richer and more philosophical approach that enlivens debate, illuminates perspectives ignored or forgotten, and informs discussion through fresh approaches. At the same time it reminds us of the need for a critical and interpretative stance to address certain philosophical ideas or theses that are otherwise employed, in business ethics scholarship, rather uncritically or routinely. In this way, the inquiries of business ethics will incorporate and confront principles and ideas that not only resonate beyond the topical and current but in many instances have been ignored, misunderstood, or sidelined by entrenched interpretations.

The significance of these ideas can hardly be doubted. After all, trade lies at the center of civilization. The exchange of goods and services, which itself presupposes activities of creative and productive labor, serves to connect individuals and to bridge distinct societies. Moreover, a desire for wealth has been one of the principal motive forces in the constitution of the social world. Given the importance, therefore, of these activities and aspirations it should not be surprising that moralists and philosophers, especially those interested in the foundations of human nature and the appropriate contours of social interaction, would have something compelling to say on the activities of trade and commerce or on the uses of wealth. Their insights, arguments, and perspectives should prove relevant and essential to any thoughtful examination of the morals of commerce and wealth. Perhaps it is in this sense that Samuel Johnson's conclusion rings true: "There is nothing which requires more to be illustrated by philosophy than trade does."[1]

This volume aims to fulfill Johnson's dictum. However, its success must be weighed in light of the methods and tasks of business ethics as currently conceived. In their analyses of some topic or problem, business ethicists often employ ethical and legal principles, sometimes with an explicit appeal to a theoretical conception of the market (such as the economic model of perfect competition). In some cases scholars also invoke general, even tacit, considerations about the nature of the business firm or the culture of business more generally. However, when scholars apply ethical theories to some particular problem or to circumstances of commerce or corporate life, they draw, typically, from the works of major philosophers—Aristotle, Immanuel Kant, and John Stuart Mill in particular. In such contexts, the ideas of these thinkers serve as paradigms of specific normative positions. For example, business ethicists may deploy the moral principle of Kant (to treat others as ends in themselves), the virtues of Aristotle (such as generosity or honesty), or a standard of utility in order to examine questions of advertising and marketing, human resources and hiring, management obligations, or responsibilities to the natural environment, as well as to arbitrate ethical issues arising in specific areas of business, such as corporate governance, finance, or accounting. On numerous other occasions, ethical analyses derive less from the application of a general normative theory than from outlooks specific to business ethics. In these instances, theories of corporate social responsibility or normative stakeholding provide the moral filters by which to assess some aspect of the conduct of business or of businesspersons.

Other than Aristotle, Kant, and Mill, the insights and contributions of notable philosophers, social theorists, and political economists often remain untapped or are utilized merely to illustrate some moral point. As a consequence, the field of business ethics loses connection with a larger tradition of thought. Dispossession from this grander field of ideas may thwart innovative analyses and constructive criticisms. Taking into account that business ethics is also an expanding and evolving field, with new avenues of exploration and seemingly novel problems to confront, it is all the more imperative that the discipline maintain linkages to notable philosophers and thinkers (even if the primary focus of such figures rests on fields other than commercial ethics).

Of course, it could be argued that business ethics is, in significant part, an applied discipline in which, accordingly, there must be some sacrifice of abstract elements of moral and social theory if there is to be any bridge between thought and practice. By this argument, to render the discipline of business ethics relevant to the institutions and conduct of commercial life, its orientation must incline not to the theoretical but the specific—those problems and challenges that arise within the life of the corporation or in business more generally. However, this perspective mistakes a practical emphasis for practical justification: practical justification requires a serious sifting of concepts, institutions, and possibilities if a normative evaluation is to have relevance and moral value. Such an examination is necessary because the business ethicist approaches the circumstances and agents of commerce with a set of prior understandings, whether of human beings, society, or the business firm and its engagements. These prior understandings, which incorporate abstract questions of concept, practice, and belief, cannot be fully set aside so as to move immediately to the practical application; rather, these tacit assumptions must be considered, understood, explored, and weighed. In fact, many of these prior understandings or conceptual foundations may possess a rigorous articulation in the writings of philosophers and thinkers who grappled with moral, social, and economic questions. Their theses and perspectives suggest applications, direct and indirect, as well as points of instruction valuable to business ethicists, even when the latter are working on issues that seem, at first sight, remote from so-called abstract philosophical reasoning. Given that business ethicists do not always agree on how to confront, evaluate, or resolve an issue, the points of difference may rest in these deeper comprehensions. Once these assumptions are set forth clearly, divergences no longer obscured may enter into the debate; a more nuanced reflective understanding may even diminish disagreements.

This collection of essays reveals a rich variety of thought on the nature of human aspiration and economic life, the benefits and costs of trade and prosperity, the role of self-interest and the common good, the interaction between commercial activity and moral improvement, the responsibilities of the corporation, the relation between markets and equality, the place of knowledge in society and economy, and the links between a generalized liberty and the freedom to believe and to act, to produce and to exchange. The thinkers taken up in this volume include some expected names (Aristotle, Kant, Mill) but also some unexpected ones (Homer, Hesiod, Augustine, Ibn Khaldun, Bernard Mandeville, Montesquieu, Alexis de Tocqueville, Karl Marx, and Amartya Sen, among others). An underlying concern inspiring the conception of this volume has been our belief that certain important thinkers have been ignored or not sufficiently acknowledged in the reflections of contemporary business ethicists.

The criteria for selection include both the significance of the person's thought and the extent to which its content conveys insights, arguments, or concepts relevant to an inquiry into business ethics, whether understood in terms of the morals (and moral effects) of commerce and commercial societies or in terms of conduct, individual or corporate, within business itself. These criteria, of significance and relevance, generated obvious candidates for inclusion (Aristotle and Adam Smith, for example), but they also suggested a greater number of thinkers than one volume could contain. In general we have inclined, as the title suggests, toward *foundational* thinkers whose work both orients and resonates forward. Given the limits of a single volume, we have tried to avoid any repetition of perspective (so to include John Locke, as a foundational defender of rights and freedom, we decided against Robert Nozick). We have also avoided the inclusion of theologians, even as we incorporated thinkers whose perspectives are, to say the least, informed by belief. With all of this said, each of the editors can name thinkers whom we would have preferred to have included, given sufficient space: G. W. F. Hegel, Émile Durkheim, James M. Buchanan, and the previously noted Nozick all come to mind immediately.

Each chapter is an original essay authored by a scholar (or scholars) with specialization in the work of that thinker *and* knowledge of commercial ethics. Given the variety of themes, the essays manifest two broad emphases: the morals of commerce in general and the ethics of business conduct, whether that of the individual or the firm. Some essays (those of Peacock, Miller, Quddus and Rashid, Mack, Clark, Berry, Shaw, Vaughn, and Zwolinski) reveal how a variety of writers and thinkers have elaborated concepts and arguments related to the institutions, principles, or practices that should inform or govern markets and commerce. Other essays (as in the case of Breyfogle, Elstein and Tian, Den Uyl, Bowie, Kahan, Capaldi, Marcoux, and Cudd) hinge on how a theorist's ideas pertain to the conduct of individuals within a market or to the operation of the firm or of corporations more specifically. Still others (the essays of Schlag, Fuller, and Heath) indicate how a thinker's concerns bear on both the institutions of commerce and individual conduct.

Despite these broad categories, the essays are arranged chronologically, even though thematic comparisons and conversations emerge in more complex pairings and patterns. In the first essay, Mark S. Peacock amends a prevailing view about early Greek thought, pointing out that Homer and Hesiod, unlike classical philosophers such as Plato or Aristotle, did not regard the commerce of their epoch as inimical to a noble life. Neither poet regarded (manual) labor as a degrading activity. However, Plato would later reckon that wealth and goodness were opposites, and Aristotle would maintain that our everyday pursuits must be subordinate to a higher end. Yet, as Fred D. Miller, Jr., contends, the moral theory of Aristotle, contrary to his own inferences, does not yield conclusions opposed to trade or to usury. Challenging customary understandings of the implications of Aristotle's conception of virtue, Miller explains how basic commercial activities, and the concerns of contemporary business ethics, can be accommodated within the contours of an Aristotelian virtue ethics. In classical China, Kongzi (Confucius) and Mengzi (Mencius) did not reject either wealth or the pursuit of profit. As David Elstein and Qing Tian explain, the contemporary corporation bears a rough resemblance to the competing states of ancient China. After offering some cautionary remarks on both the identification of Confucianism with Chinese culture and the challenges of interpreting classical texts, Elstein and Tian employ this analogy to elicit some general themes relevant to commercial ethics, including the idea that some Confucian virtues (such as reciprocity and understanding) may prove similar to the conception in contemporary management theory of "organizational citizenship."

From the late Roman era to the modern period, many thinkers addressed the question of production and trade through the lens of explicit religious and philosophic belief. Todd Breyfogle points out how Augustine condemns neither property nor wealth but counsels that attachment to earthly goods, including the improper love of wealth, should not occur in defiance of the spiritual. Property and commercial exchange are conventional not natural; the responsible enjoyment of wealth demands prudent understanding of the goods necessary for human beings. Such a perspective sets the stage for something akin to a version of social responsibility—the spiritual economy shall restore the wholeness or unity of the natural human person otherwise undone within a purely material economy. Though naturally distanced from modern economics, Thomas Aquinas's thought on commercial matters does not present a rigid system but one of reasoned argument, as Martin Schlag explains. Thomas's ethical analyses of specific economic phenomena (e.g., just pricing, interest-bearing loans, or unproductive hoarding) exhibit a depth that renders his judgments germane to aspects of contemporary business ethics. For Thomas, wealth possesses instrumental value and property is justified by natural law insofar as ownership contributes to the common good. It is welcome to discover that Thomas's writings reveal a wider spectrum of interest on economic and business matters than the often jejune views commonly attributed to him (e.g., on the prohibition of usury). For Thomas, a decent profit is no different from a decent wage; a just price engenders obligations on both the seller *and* the customer; and the common good relates to justice, a pivotal linkage that recalls Augustine's embrace of a concept often eclipsed in modern debates, that of social unity. The Muslim thinker Ibn Khaldun regards commerce as an essential part of the cycle of civilization. However, as Munir Quddus and Salim Rashid indicate in their refreshing reassessment of this neglected theorist, the wealth generated by commerce encourages the ruling class to impose ever higher taxes so that they might indulge in frivolous luxuries. The result is moral and civilizational decline. Yet against these larger events Ibn Khaldun maintains that commercial trade, although exhibiting elements of "cunning," is both productive and natural.

Writing toward the middle of the seventeenth century, Thomas Hobbes was well aware of an emerging commercial order. Timothy Fuller counters the simplified view that Hobbes is but the architect of a theory of the sovereign and describes, instead, how Hobbes offers a portrait of the moral imagination that shows the compatibility of business and ethics. As Fuller's account testifies, an essential route for the study of business ethics lies in the study of the self, the very sort of inquiry that Hobbes invokes in his *Leviathan*. The upshot of Fuller's portrayal is the revelation, surprising in itself, that in Hobbes's work one finds exemplified one of the signal aims of this volume: a reconsideration of how business ethics may be placed within a larger philosophical foundation informed by precepts of moral theory, as well as philosophy, moral psychology, and political theory. In his essay, Eric Mack draws widely and deeply from John Locke's work—utilizing Locke's political essays as well as his letters on toleration and his *Second Treatise of Government*—to show that a principle of liberty serves as the ground for Locke's account of property and of commerce. Indeed, Mack reveals how, for Locke, the institutions of economic liberty, such as property and contract, also provide a philosophical and practical basis for religious freedom and toleration.

A burgeoning commerce, a stronger division of labor, the development of increasingly organized modes of production, as well as a nascent comprehension that wealth is not so much finite as an effect of creative or productive activity—these are marks of the modern society emerging more fully in the eighteenth century. One of the first to grapple with these changes was Bernard Mandeville. Regarded by his contemporaries as a defender of egoism and amorality, Mandeville proves to be a social theorist of some importance. Eugene Heath elaborates Mandeville's provocative account of the conditions for prosperity, the evolutionary growth of society, and a pluralist view of ends. From Mandeville's varied works, Heath gleans three maxims relevant to the contemporary study of business and society: the importance of unintended outcomes, the significance of practical knowledge to ethics, and the necessity to weigh the compatibility of ideals prior to issuing normative recommendations. Like Mandeville, Montesquieu recognizes the public benefit of self-interested acts. Henry C. Clark delineates Montesquieu's historical approach to commerce (and its consequences) and points out that unlike Mandeville, the Baron of La Brède accepts the reality of virtue in everyday life. Clark illuminates how the qualities of humanity and justice provide the frame of a genuine business ethic. In fact, these virtues are not external to markets but gain their footing in the interactions characteristic of commerce. David Hume also attests to the benefits, material and moral, of commerce, as Christopher J. Berry describes. Hume criticizes the reigning prejudices against luxury and contends that a vice such as avarice should be channeled toward industry. A commercial society not only generates prosperity, which improves the conditions of the poor, but also helps to maintain liberty. Such a society, Berry suggests, demands both an impartial administration of justice and, by implication, a purely voluntary conception of corporate social responsibility. Adam Smith is known for his defense of a "system of natural liberty," but, as Douglas J. Den Uyl elucidates, Smith also suggests that a significant appeal of commercial society rests not in its prosperous outcomes but in the way in which it allows individuals to reconcile in the imagination their aims, interactions, and moral norms. This reconciliation constitutes an "aesthetic" justification of commercial society and reveals it to have a "fittingness" or beauty that links the imaginative life to everyday commercial practice. Although Immanuel Kant had an appreciation for Smith's moral theory, his own principles diverged from those of eighteenth-century moralists such as Hume and Smith. As Norman Bowie recounts, it is sometimes maintained that Kant's central moral imperative—resting on the idea of a good will—is incompatible with the pursuit of profit. However, Bowie argues against such a naïve understanding of Kant, and elaborates how the manager of a corporation has a moral obligation to pursue profit, a duty born of a promise to shareholders. Bowie proposes that this duty is compatible with duties of corporate beneficence.

In the nineteenth century, the idea that commerce is a natural component of democracy reappears in the work of Alexis de Tocqueville, a thinker overlooked by business ethicists. For Tocqueville, not unlike Montesquieu, business contributes to the ethical life of a democratic society and, more concretely, as Alan S. Kahan shows, the corporation can be seen as a source of democratic ethics. Tocqueville employs the idea of association, including that of the corporation, to counter any tendency to withdraw into a private world of self and family, forsaking any larger concerns or broader self-interest.

Kahan then assesses both stakeholder and shareholder theories in light of Tocqueville's principles of association, enlightened self-interest, collective individualism, and freedom from government and the tyranny of the majority. Nicholas Capaldi challenges the widespread view that J. S. Mill is a straightforward utilitarian and that his ethical theory is, somehow, independent of his social and economic concerns. As Capaldi points out, a notion of human dignity plays a crucial role in Mill's overall outlook. Indeed, liberty of action finds justification on grounds of autonomy and self-development, not in terms of rights or the pursuit of pleasure. Capaldi proceeds to provide provocative accounts of how Mill's views relate to salient topics of business ethics, including the nature of the firm and corporate governance. Karl Marx might seem an unlikely authority on the morals of capitalism, especially since Marx regarded his work as scientific not ethical. However, William H. Shaw explores how it may be possible to generate an ethics of business that, at the least, conveys the Marxist spirit. In so doing, the theorist could address a topic in terms of the imperatives of class or capitalism, the perspective of the disadvantaged, or in light of how circumstances affect and determine behavior.

The market need no longer be a specific place, as in the agora of ancient Athens, but an abstract idea that may be variously described and employed so as to generate conclusions and hypotheses about the myriad actions and transactions that allow for production and constitute the exchange of goods or services. Within the contemporary era, broadly conceived, some of the most interesting implications for business ethics have arisen from twentieth-century economists who challenge in one way or another some of the prevailing models and perspectives on the economy. Three of these, all winners of the Nobel Prize in Economics, are included in the last section of the collection, along with one of the major political philosophers of the past century. As Karen I. Vaughn points out, F. A. Hayek defends the market order, in part, in terms of epistemic challenges to centralized economic planning. Hayek criticizes the static model of perfect competition often invoked by economists (and business ethicists) and elaborates the connections between freedom and prosperity. As Vaughn illuminates, free societies function well not because their members share some collective purpose or ranking of ends but because rules (of property and contract, as well as other traditions of conduct) render social interactions predictable and peaceful, allow for experimentation and discovery, and permit risk taking and responsibility. Known in economics for his monetary theory, Milton Friedman's arguments against corporate social responsibility often serve business ethicists as a (moving) target whose bull's-eye is vaguely restated, perhaps the better to catch the arrows of criticism, as routine as they are blunt. In his careful reexamination, Alexei Marcoux corrects the received view by distinguishing between (evolving) kinds of corporate social responsibility. He explains how Friedman's original arguments convey both practical and normative concerns, the former focusing on epistemic and technocratic questions, the latter on fiduciary and jurisdictional responsibilities. Despite the power of these arguments, they may not hold against socially responsible endeavors that benefit both society and the bottom line. Many would contend that the philosopher John Rawls's theory of justice runs counter to market principles or classical liberal views. But Matt Zwolinski submits that business ethicists focus on but one of Rawls's two principles of justice, the egalitarian difference principle, and on only one of his works, *A Theory of Justice*. Zwolinski maintains that the basic liberties of the first principle of justice require economic liberties (which themselves possess intrinsic value). Moreover, a successful application of the second and egalitarian principle may require the sort of incentives available only in a free market society, itself emblematic of the pluralism embraced by Rawls in his later work, *Political Liberalism*. In the last essay of the collection, Ann E. Cudd explores how Amartya Sen's work in economic theory and on human motivation situates him against what she calls the "instrumental" model of business agency and its imperative to maximize profit or self-interest. Cudd attempts to forge a link between Sen's thought on ethical motivation (and its principal social effect, trust) and the normative question central to much of business ethics: whether firms ought to have social or moral responsibilities. In suggesting that individuals and thus corporations may have ends other than the creation or acquisition of wealth, Sen revises and broadens the notion of self-interest, challenges the behaviorist view of revealed preference theory, and offers a motivational model that incorporates commitments as well as desires. Therefore, Cudd attests, Sen's arguments provide reasons to set aside Friedman's constrained view of corporate social responsibility.

The analyses in these essays not only enrich our understanding of contemporary issues in the moral life of business but exhibit how the history of ideas shows itself indispensable to our comprehension and amelioration of concerns of the present. A business ethics that is both rich and richly informed must include the perspectives of thinkers whose insights prove not only relevant but foundational. The essays assembled here remind us of the contributions of a variety of thinkers whose work merits both a renewed attention and a broader appreciation from business ethicists.

ACKNOWLEDGMENTS

The idea for this collection was originally devised, several years ago, at a business ethics conference in Athens. For her assistance and patience in seeing this project through to its end, we thank Elizabeth Branch Dyson, our editor at the University of Chicago Press. For another kind of support and encouragement, tacit and explicit, steady and sustaining, we thank Reva Wolf and Katia Papadaki, along with little Christos Gabriel, whose future, we hope, will be improved by better thinking about business, ethics, and society.

NOTE

1. Samuel Johnson, Saturday, March 16, 1776, in James Boswell, *Life of Johnson*, ed. R. W. Chapman (Oxford: Oxford University Press, 1980), 682–83.

CHAPTER 1

Wealth and Commerce in Archaic Greece: Homer and Hesiod

Mark S. Peacock

Throughout much of history, wealth and commerce have had a dubious moral status, and those who accumulate wealth or pursue commerce have often been vilified. Many scholars assume that all thinkers of early Greece were, like Plato, wary of activities linked with trade or commerce. This essay reassesses this assumption in the context of archaic Greece (ca. 800–500 BCE), for which Hesiod's *Works and Days* and Homer's epics are the most important literary sources. Homer and Hesiod invoke notions—wealth, trade, and labor—essential to the ethical evaluation of commerce; their considerations provide a contrast to ideas, prevalent in later, classical times, that are used routinely as sources for discussions in business ethics.

After offering methodological comments on the use of Hesiod and Homer as historical sources, I dedicate the section thereafter to Homer, and the following to Hesiod. While Homer reflects the "higher" end of the spectrum of social status by focusing on the archaic aristocracy and their values, Hesiod aims "lower" by issuing advice to the small, independent farmer. There are thus contrasts between Homer and Hesiod with regard to the nature and acquisition of wealth and the role and status of commerce. I question the common view that Hesiod and Homer hold commerce in low repute. Although there are elements of a critique of commerce in both poets, Greek prejudice against commerce does not manifest itself fully until the classical period, with authors such as Plato, Xenophon, and Aristotle, whose views I compare to Hesiod's and Homer's.

HISTORICIZING HESIOD AND HOMER: METHODOLOGICAL REMARKS

Hesiod's and Homer's works contain much "pure fiction"—for example, the gods on Olympus and superstitious tips on farming. That the poets and their audiences might have believed such "fictions" does not bring us any closer to the "real" history of the societies the works reflect. Nevertheless, classical scholars attempt to reconstruct a "world" of Hesiod or Homer by emphasizing textual, archaeological, and comparative resources.[1] Scholars abstract from aspects that are obviously fictional or elements that have been deliberately "archaized," such as the use of bronze (rather than iron) weapons in Homeric battle, and focus instead on the background values and institutions of the works without which the texts make little sense. One example is the institution of gift giving, mentioned by Hesiod but revealed in greater depth by Homer. That neither Hesiod nor Homer explains gift giving in detail implies knowledge of the practice among the poets' audiences, a knowledge that presumably came from the societies in which they lived or from a recent past.[2] The nature, use, and acquisition of wealth likewise form part of the background to Hesiod and Homer that reveals something about the societies the poets describe.

A further methodological point regarding the use of Hesiod and Homer as historical sources comes from the study of oral poetry. Oral poetry is usually passed down over generations, yet a bard who recites poetry infuses that recitation with references to the society in which he or she lives. Oral poetry is not static. Consequently, one bard will recite a saga or epic differently from one who recited the "same" tale generations previously;[3] in fact, the same bard tailors a performance to a particular audience. If the foregoing holds true of the poems of Hesiod and Homer, then their work will shed light on the epoch in which they were transcribed or on a small number of generations prior to transcription. In the case of Homer, the latter part of the eighth century is a common estimate of the epics' transcription (with some passages being added later and the *Iliad* preceding the *Odyssey*, perhaps by a generation);[4] Hesiod is later, just after the turn of the seventh century, a date that a few scholars see as more likely for Homer.[5] If they tell us anything at all about history, then, Hesiod and Homer inform us about these centuries of the early archaic period.

WEALTH AND COMMERCE IN HOMER'S EPICS

Odysseus's swineherd enumerates his master's wealth (*aphenos*) as follows: "Twelve herds of cattle on the mainland. As many sheepflocks. As many troops of pigs and again as many wide goatflocks."[6] He thereby reveals the agricultural basis of Homeric wealth. The number of slaves belonging to the household (*oikos*) would also constitute wealth, as Odysseus divulges when, disguised as a beggar, he boasts that he once "had serving men by thousands."[7] Apart from livestock (and the land on which they are kept) and slaves, wealth in Homer consists of precious objects that often circulate among the elite as gifts, prizes, or compensation. Examples include robes, weapons, and utensils made of gold and silver. These items have not only intrinsic value but also a "biography"; rather than describe the appearance or qualities of Agamemnon's scepter, for example, Homer writes:

> Powerful Agamemnon stood up holding the sceptre Hephaistos had wrought him carefully. Hephaistos gave it to Zeus the king, the son of Kronos, and Zeus in turn gave it to the courier Argeïphontes, and lord Hermes gave it to Pelops, driver of horses, and Pelops again gave it to Atreus, the shepherd of the people. Atreus dying left it to Thyestes of the rich flocks, and Thyestes left it in turn to Agamemnon.[8]

Although Homer sometimes describes only the material properties of valuable items,[9] their history confers as much value as their material properties; the status of those who previously owned or wrought such items increases their value. The passage quoted also gives us insight into the movement of wealth, a subject that I bifurcate into *internal* (within a community) and *external* movement (between different communities).

Wealth: Internal Movement

A community (*dēmos*) occupies a region in which a number of *oikoi* (aristocratic households/estates) are situated, each *oikos* headed by a "king" (*basileus*). Of these kings, one is the leader, not only of an *oikos*, but of the community. The community's leader is often dubbed a *primus inter pares*, the *pares* being the other "kings," each of whom heads an *oikos*.[10] The Phaiakians, for example, are ruled by thirteen kings, of whom their leader, Alkinoös, is foremost.[11] Odysseus's community is larger than the Phaiakians' to judge from the 108 suitors, all from noble families, who woo his wife.[12] What makes a particular household's king the leader of the community is his superior skills in speaking or fighting, and his superior wealth, as Homer's description of Alkinoös's and Odysseus's magnificent houses (*dōmata*) makes clear.[13] A leader is expected to lead prudently, to ensure the security and prosperity of his community, and to manifest heroism in war.[14] Wealth moves to the leader of the community for various reasons, and his household's wealth will swell as a result of being leader.[15] The community, for instance, can grant the leader a plot of land (*temenos*).[16]

The movement of wealth within a community takes many forms and is related to the community's political system, to which I attend forthwith. The leader hosts communal religious feasts that involve the consumption and distribution of sacrificial meat.[17] There is also a system of tribute payment whereby the leader recoups costs he has borne at the expense of the public (dēmothen).[18] This system falls short of regular taxation, for the payments cover extraordinary, not routine, expenses, such as the costs of war and of providing hospitality to strangers or to guest-friends (xeniē).[19] Wealth can be allocated by the leader to subordinates in return for acts of supererogatory service or heroism on the battlefield, though these, too, are extraordinary payments.[20] There are also more humdrum acts of service that members of a community provide. Each king, for instance, sits in his community's assembly, an informal political gathering in which opinions are exchanged and policies agreed upon. Whether, though, the kings are rewarded (and how) is not clear.[21]

The leader's rule is not absolute, and his opinion can be overridden by the assembly.[22] The leader's authority is closely linked to the distribution of wealth over which he presides. Subordinates withhold obedience when their leader is perceived to take more than his fair share: Agamemnon, commander of the Greek forces at Troy, faces revolt because he is deemed to be less heroic than others in battle but claims the greatest spoils of war.[23] The source of wealth to be redistributed within a community is war or raiding (about which see the next section); it is the leader's responsibility to acquire wealth through these means, and because this acquisition is a communal effort, subordinates expect a share of the booty. The relationship between the leader and his people approximates to "balanced reciprocity,"[24] whereby the leader "give[s] as good as he gets,"[25] and each party expects a roughly equivalent service of the other, although reciprocation does not have to be immediate, as in Marshall Sahlins's ideal type of balanced reciprocity.

As this analysis suggests, the internal movement of wealth is effected via redistribution rather than commerce, or market exchange. Indeed, Moses Finley claims that market exchange is not attested between members of the same community.[26] The only exception is suggested by the pig iron that Achilles offers as a prize in the shot-put competition in the athletic contests of the Iliad.[27] When announcing the prize, Achilles says that neither the shepherd nor the plowman of the winner will, "for want of iron, have to go into the city for it." This suggests that slaves (plowmen or shepherds) acquire articles like iron from the city (polis) at their masters' behest, presumably by bartering the produce of the oikos.[28] This oblique mention of commerce within a community gives us little with which to infer relationships between "town" and "country," and the exception rather proves the rule that Finley suggests: there is no intracommunity commerce in Homer; in contrast to long-distance trade (emporia), there is no word in Homer to describe intracommunity commerce. To pursue the role of commerce in the epics, then, we must turn to the external movement of wealth between different communities and peoples.

Wealth: External Movement

There are three means through which wealth is transferred between communities in Homeric society: gift exchange, plunder/raiding/war (henceforth, raiding), and commerce. Gift exchange occurs among Homer's aristocratic elite and involves splendid, often elaborately wrought "prestige" articles. It can involve exchange between gods and mortals, though it is usually carried on between mortals as a means of creating peaceful relationships between individuals in different communities.[29] An example is that of the Trojan ally, Glaukos, and the Greek Diomedes, who meet on the battlefield at Troy and ascertain that their grandfathers had been guest-friends of one another. The relationship of guest-friendship is bequeathed to future generations, and so the two warriors exchange armor as a token of friendship.[30] Gifts sometimes remain stored until occasion arises for giving them once again, but they often become objects of use with important consequences for the narrative.[31]

The transfer of wealth through gift exchange raises the question of whether gifts between two parties are expected to be of equal value or whether gifts are the subject of unequal exchange. Answering this question is not facilitated by the fact that parties to Homeric gifts do not normally exchange their gifts simultaneously. In favor of rough equivalence of gifts' value is the exchange in which Diomedes gives his bronze armor to Glaukos and receives gold armor in return; Homer adverts to the "bad deal" that Glaukos gets by noting that Zeus stole his wits, for he relinquished armor worth one hundred oxen for that worth nine.[32] The exchange between Glaukos and Diomedes suggests that a great disparity in the value of gifts is not the norm, but there are examples of gift exchange in which equivalents are not exchanged. The gifts the Phaiakians bestow on Odysseus, for instance, have little prospect of being reciprocated because the Phaiakians "live far apart" and have little intercourse with other peoples.[33] Menelaos's suggestion that his gift to Telemachus be "esteemed at the highest value" of all those in his possession implies that Telemachus, if he reciprocates the gift at all, will not be able to do so with an item of equal value.[34] Menelaos's statement points to a motivation on the part of the giver, namely, that in "outgiving" his counterpart, his gift (and its splendor) will bestow prestige on its giver. Gift exchange, then, might approximate a system of "generalized reciprocity" in which the giving of a return gift is often delayed indefinitely, and the return gift is not necessarily of equal value to the one given.[35]

Let us now turn to a different way in which Homeric heroes acquire wealth, namely, through force (raiding). Raiding has a mixed reception among scholars. Some see it as a "low-prestige" activity because it is often associated with trade;[36] other scholars take a neutral line and see raiding as a fact of Homeric life—the "principal means" of acquiring wealth;[37] others still deem raiding "honorable."[38] In favor of the latter characterization is not only the commonness of raiding, but also the fact that Homer's nobles recount raiding escapades without bashfulness (sometimes boastfully);[39] this does not bespeak an activity of low prestige or reprehensibility. Raiding is also, as noted above, the source of wealth that is redistributed within the community, thereby cementing the leader's rule and holding the community together; it therefore plays an integral role in the life of a Homeric community, and, within the community, a leader's successful raiding exploits promote obedience and solidarity.[40]

The third method of acquiring wealth from outside one's community is commerce, or long-distance trade (*emporia*). In Homeric epic, commerce is associated particularly with the (non-Greek) Phoenicians, of whom, it is widely held, Homer's opinion is low. Whether he casts commerce negatively because the Phoenicians are its main purveyors, or whether the Phoenicians are scorned because they pursue commerce (the latter's reprehensibility having an independent source) is less easy to ascertain. Nevertheless, many scholars share the view that Homer characterizes the Phoenicians' reputation as "totally" and "thoroughly negative,"[41] the reason for this opprobrium being related to their commercial activities. Indeed, some aspects of Phoenician commerce call its moral status into question, for Phoenicians seem to mix commerce with the kidnapping of innocent people to sell them into slavery.[42] Attempts to identify characteristics of Phoenician commerce that explain its poor repute are, however, beset by the problem that few, if any, Phoenician exploits (including commerce) are not shared by other groups depicted in the epics. Whereas Homer allegedly casts the Phoenicians in a poor light, others are spared invective when they engage in similar pursuits. Kidnapping, for instance, is practiced by the Taphians, who, like the Phoenicians, are involved in the slave trade, yet the Taphian leader, Mentes, is a guest-friend of Odysseus and pursues commerce without apparently detracting from his noble reputation.[43] Other scholars seek characteristics of Phoenician commerce itself (and not of their other pursuits) to explain their disrepute. One such characteristic is that Phoenician trade is "professional" as opposed to "occasional." Through this distinction we learn much about the nature of trade and of money in Homeric society.

"Professional" trade is marked by the production or acquisition of goods for the purpose of selling them. "Occasional" trade, by contrast, consists in opportunistic selling of something of which one happens to possess a surplus but not producing or buying goods with a view to selling whatever one possesses. Occasional trade is pursued by Achilles, who sells Trojan prisoners of war, and by Euneos, who sells wine to the Greek army at Troy in a "one-time" (not a regular) market.[44] Trade is conducted by barter, with the Greeks exchanging bronze, iron, skins, oxen, and slaves for Euneos's wine. Neither this nor any other instance of Homeric commerce is characterized by the use of a single medium of exchange. This typifies the state of the Homeric monetary economy, in which, of all the functions of money (medium of exchange, means of payment, store of value, and unit of account), only one—that of unit of account—is performed exclusively by one item, namely, oxen. Oxen, and only they, are used to value various items in the epics. The list of such valuations encompasses the following: the aegis of Zeus (100 oxen); the armor of Diomedes and Glaukos (Diomedes's 9 oxen, Glaukos's 100); Lykaon, a Trojan prisoner of war whom Achilles sells into slavery (100 oxen); Evrycleia, a maidservant bought by Odysseus's father, Laertes (20 oxen); and three prizes offered by Achilles in the athletic contests held in honour of Patroklus (a slave woman at 4 oxen, a tripod at 12, and a cauldron at 1 ox).[45] Even for the cases in which the "goods" are valued in the context of market exchange (Eurycleia and Lykaon), we should not be led by the bovine valuations to conclude that cattle actually changed hands in these transactions. Achilles received a silver mixing bowl worth 100 oxen in return for Lykaon, and the word with which he describes Eurycleia's price (*eeikosaboia*) indicates that whatever was given in exchange for the maidservant was worth 20 oxen but not 20 oxen themselves.[46] We should also note the rudimentary nature of Homer's valuations: they give a value for one item only rather than for an agglomeration of heterogeneous items. These are far from the mental accounting exercises that we, today, perform routinely and in which items as diverse as trucks, pieces of land, works of art, and restaurant meals can be grouped together and given a unitary value in a particular currency.

Money in Homeric society is, then, not the "all-purpose" sort whereby one medium, such as coin, gold, banknotes, or cattle, performs the four standard functions of money listed in the previous paragraph and performs some or all exclusively.[47]

Having examined money in Homeric society, let us return to trade and ask whether Phoenician commerce answers plausibly to the name of "professional trade." Homer's Phoenicians sell slaves and jewelry while they probably buy staples (wine, meat, and grain).[48] This depiction corresponds partly to what we know about the "historical" Phoenicians, namely, that they sold luxuries (textiles and objects made of ivory and precious metals) and acquired staples, although Homer makes no mention of the raw materials (particularly metals) that the historical Phoenicians sought in trade.[49] Homer's Phoenicians do seem to produce or acquire items for the purpose of commerce, something that makes their commerce "professional." But whether this suffices to explain Homer's antipathy toward Phoenicians is doubtful, for the fact that the items they sell have been produced for sale does not deter Homer from praising with great effusion the skill and workmanship of Phoenician craftspeople.[50] An alternative explanation for what is reprehensible about the Phoenicians is that they are motivated by profit. In this, once again, they are not alone: the disguised

Odysseus tells his wife that the real Odysseus delayed his return from Troy because he thought it "profitable" (*kerdion*) to amass wealth abroad.[51] Menelaos, too, amasses enormous wealth on his return from Troy, and, although neither his nor Odysseus's means of acquisition is revealed, trade is a probable source.[52]

The strongest evidence in Homer for a negative attitude to commerce comes when Odysseus declines the invitation of his Phaiakian hosts to participate in athletic contests. A Phaiakian noble, Euryalos, responds to Odysseus's reluctance to participate by asserting that Odysseus resembles not an athlete but rather "one who plies his ways in his many-locked vessel, master over mariners who also are men of business, a man who, careful of his cargo and grasping for profits, goes carefully on his way."[53] Odysseus, in turn, responds indignantly and demonstrates his athleticism by hurling a discus farther than any Phaiakian throw.[54] From his reaction, scholars usually infer that Odysseus feels insulted by Euryalos's likeness, and, to assert his nobility, demonstrates his athletic prowess, thus removing the suspicion that he is a profit-seeking trader. Euryalos certainly intends his comment to disparage: for the Phaiakians, being a (common) trader and being a (noble) athlete exclude one another. Yet from Odysseus's perspective, nobility does not exclude trading. From the black-and-white perspective of the Phaiakians, Odysseus's athletic prowess excludes the possibility that he is a trader and hence, once Odysseus has established his noble credentials, he is beyond suspicion in Phaiakian eyes. He is then able to exploit Phaiakian naïveté (and curiosity) by recounting yarns of his travels from Troy, and, in return, he receives the unspeakably valuable treasures (in the form of gifts) that the Phaiakians bestow on him. One might see in this nothing more than typical Homeric gift-giving rituals whereby the Phaiakians make the first act of giving, but, as I noted above, Odysseus can be assured that a future occasion to reciprocate will not come around. Odysseus's actions come close to profiteering through trading stories of his travels in return for the magnificent wealth the Phaiakians bestow upon him.[55] His strategy exemplifies the wiliness and cunning Homer ascribes to him again and again, and through which he profits handsomely without, thereby, earning a poor reputation.

Although a great deal more can be said about Homer's attitude to commerce, it is not clear whether the Phoenicians' commerce and its attendant characteristics are unique and therefore subject to particular disapproval. This has led some scholars to attribute Homer's low opinion of the Phoenicians to ethnic prejudice (they are non-Greek). But one may also argue that Homer's attitude to commerce and to the Phoenicians is not terribly disparaging. Nowhere in the *Iliad* does Homer censure the Phoenicians, and only two passages in the *Odyssey* indicate disapproval, but these are to be counterposed to other passages that cast a neutral or positive light on the Phoenicians.[56]

To close this discussion of wealth and commerce in Homer, let us, in preparation for our discussion of Hesiod, consider the "lower" end of the social hierarchy, in particular, the status of laborers who acquire their means of living by hiring themselves to Homer's elite. Trades such as medicine, prophecy, poetry/music, carpentry, and smithery are mentioned; their practitioners are not disparaged by Homer.[57] Such skilled laborers, unlike slaves, who tend to be household servants (if women) or involved in husbandry (if men), are not formally attached to an *oikos,* but they might find peripatetic employment in one or more *oikoi* for periods of time. To what extent they are free to "come and go" is not clear. Less respected (if respected at all) are unskilled or manual laborers who are not slaves to a household; the god Poseidon recalls how he and Apollo worked for a year as hired servants to the Trojan king, Laomedon, Poseidon building the city's walls, Apollo herding Trojan cattle. At the end of their contract, Laomedon refused to pay them and threatened to enslave them.[58] This demonstrates laborers' vulnerability and lowly status, a further indication of which is revealed in the underworld, where the ghost of Achilles tells Odysseus that he would rather be a hireling to a landless man than ruler over the dead in Hades.[59] Achilles's comparandum makes sense only if the status of laborers is low; only the status of beggars seems lower.[60] Labour, qua working activity, though, is not something contemptible, for Odysseus has skill in husbandry and carpentry. Indeed, he prides himself on his prowess in war and skill in husbandry in one and the same passage, which indicates that he values these skills equally.[61] Manual labor is not even beneath the gods, for one of their number—Hephaistos—is a smith, though his deformity might indicate that his smithery makes him somewhat "less equal" to his immortal peers. With regard to labor, then, the status of the laborer—one who is in the hire of another—but not the laboring activity marks the laborer as inferior. If there are glimpses of a negative attitude to laborers in Homer, it is an attitude that outlived the archaic period and is manifest in classical Greece, as I shall argue in the conclusion.

WEALTH AND COMMERCE IN HESIOD'S *WORKS AND DAYS*

Lines 383–707 of *Works and Days* have been described as a "farmer's almanac";[62] they contain advice to farmers who pursue *economics*, in the term's original sense, that is, running an *oikos* located on a plot of land (*klēros*). The ideal Hesiodic *oikos* consists of a small family (preferably with one son), one or two slaves of each sex and the same number of seasonal wage-laborers, who, strictly speaking, do not belong to the *oikos*; the designation "laborer" (*thēs*) is the substantive relation of *thēteuō,* the verb "to work as a laborer" that Homer uses in two passages (cited in notes 59 and 60). In his depiction of laborers, Hesiod does not advert to the miserable existence and low status of a *thēs*. Augmenting Hesiod's household personnel are a couple of oxen, a dog, and some sheep and goats.[63] Hesiod's advice for organizing the *oikos* is directed to one Perses, the narrator's (and thus, presumably, Hesiod's own) brother, with whom he has shared their father's inheritance. Either Perses has cheated Hesiod out of an equal share or the estate has been divided, but Perses is litigating post hoc to gain a larger share at Hesiod's expense.[64] What is clear is that Perses has fallen on hard times, and Hesiod admonishes him to engage in hard, honest work and piety; only once he has acquired enough livelihood (*bios*) does Hesiod countenance the idea of Perses pursuing litigation (31–35).

Hesiod's world is one in which the small to middling landowner can acquire sufficient livelihood if he and the members of his *oikos* toil in accord with the seasons' rhythms. Wealth is understood more or less as the means necessary to live.[65] Although Hesiod mentions gifts, as we shall see in the following paragraph, Hesiodic wealth does not have the splendor of its Homeric counterpart. Consequently, Hesiod has little cause to mention (or censure) excessive wealth.

Hesiod advises the farmer to acquire livelihood through hard work in order to avoid want. He sets no limit to the wealth one may acquire, probably on the assumption that a typical farmer, however industrious, will not acquire extravagant wealth. Hesiod's preference is for producing one's wealth, as far possible, through one's own labors or those of members of one's *oikos*. The principle of self-sufficiency is thus to be followed and only to be relaxed under the force of necessity. Hesiod's notion of self-sufficiency extends beyond the production of agricultural produce and includes making one's own boat (809), farming tools (422–29), and clothing (537–44) and building one's house (746).

Wealth in Hesiod has significance beyond being a means to live, for possessing wealth is a sign of its owner's excellence (*aretē*) and glory (*kudos*) (314). The means of acquiring wealth—namely, hard work—is thus of normative import, and idleness is frowned upon by both men and gods: "It is from works that men are many-sheeped and rich, and the man who works is much dearer to the deathless ones" (309–10). Wealth is also a means of making one's neighbors envious (thus spurring them to industry) (312–13). This is one of many remarks Hesiod makes on neighboring villagers. Neighboring families are largely independent of one another, even though they take a close (and envious) interest in each other's wealth. Apart from the communal feast, Hesiod mentions no communal activities among villagers. At a feast, Hesiod tells the farmer not to be surly (722–23), though, in the context of Hesiod's other comments on neighbors, complaisance at a feast might well be little more than a calculated means to acquire a good reputation with one's neighbors, who will then more likely come to one's aid in difficult times, for in difficult times, a farmer might have to borrow from a neighbor. There appear to be no obligations on the part of neighbors to help, and Hesiod's advice to farmers seems designed to obviate the need to beg or borrow; the industrious farmer will have sufficient sustenance without neighborly support (408–9). Neighbors' willingness to help is limited, and any sense of obligation to mutual help among neighbors wears thin after one solicits help more than two or three times (400–401). In light of this, Hesiod advises that one earn the goodwill of a neighbor, by paying back to a neighbor more than one owes (348–51), for instance, and he urges the farmer not to give to those who themselves do not give (354–55). Relations among neighbors, then, like those among members of a Homeric community, have a strong element of "balanced" reciprocity, for unrequited favors are not tolerated, although immediate reciprocation, a characteristic of Sahlins's "generalized" rather than "balanced" reciprocity, is not a feature of neighborly relations, and hence debt relations between people can persist.[66]

One type of economic interaction between neighbors absent from *Works and Days* is "commerce" in the sense of market exchange. In this respect, Hesiod's world mirrors that of Homer, in which intracommunity commerce is, at most, marginal. One instance of the transference of wealth within Hesiod's village (though not via commerce) concerns the acquisition of another farmer's *klēros* (336–41). Hesiod enjoins Perses to offer libations and make sacrifices to the gods "so that you may acquire the *klēros* of other men, not another man yours" (340–41). The verb *ōneomai*, translated as "acquire," also means "buy" or "barter." Hesiod therefore envisages piety as a means to gaining wealth that can enable a farmer to buy the *klēros* of others who can no longer sustain theirs. Land is thus alienable in Hesiod's world, but only when its owner is sufficiently impoverished;[67] this falls short of "commerce" if, under that term, one imagines a free market in land, for land in Hesiod is not ordinarily subject to purchase and sale. A further manner of acquiring land is available to "immigrants" such as Hesiod's father, who migrated to Ascra and acquired the *klēros* over which his sons are squabbling (635–41). Scholars usually hold that Hesiod's father acquired previously unoccupied land; it is unlikely that he purchased it, for he was impoverished (hence his motivation to migrate), but there is no indication in Hesiod of the means of allocating land to newcomers.[68] Hesiod also mentions seizing wealth "by force"; any attempt dishonestly to acquire possessions is punished by the gods, and Hesiod attributes such behavior to people being deceived by the desire to make a profit (*kerdos*) (321–27). This is not to say that profit *sans phrase* is reprehensible, but only that bad men can be led astray by the desire for "evil profits" (*kaka kerdea*) (352).

None of the examples of acquiring wealth mentioned in the previous paragraph answers to the name of "commerce" in the sense of straightforward buying and selling. What does answer to that name is discussed under the term "sailing." Sailing takes a farmer to a place beyond his own community, to some sort of market or trading post. The aim of the farmer who sails is to seek profit (632, 644). This activity attracts no criticism from Hesiod, who tells Perses that the greater his cargo, the greater his profits will be (642–44). Hesiod's penchant for self-sufficiency comes to the fore here, for he envisages that farmers build, own, and man their own boat.[69] His account of sailing corresponds to what Alfonso Mele terms "commercio ἔργον," commerce pursued through one's own work.[70] Well before his advice on sailing, Hesiod notes that Zeus grants prosperity to those who are just: just people therefore "do not board ships [to trade]," because they can sustain themselves (235–36). David Tandy and Walter Neale see a "strong distaste for the sea" in this remark,[71] but this is not necessarily distaste of commerce as such, however closely Hesiod associates sailing with commerce; rather Hesiod might simply be expressing the causal connection between the need to sail and the state of one's livelihood: one does not sail unless forced by necessity. An aversion to sailing on Hesiod's part is largely explained by its attendant perils, to which I turn presently. On the other hand, one could read a moral critique of sailing into Hesiod: those who have no need to sail possess much livelihood and do so because they are just; they therefore stand in Zeus's favor. Is the implication that *only* those who are unjust (and hence are not allowed by Zeus to prosper) need to sail? Hesiod's remarks here are insufficiently clear to speak in favor of one interpretation or the other. Let us, then, turn to Hesiod's advice on sailing (618–94), which he issues as one who has sailed only once and not for the purpose of commerce (649–51).

Hesiod counsels against sailing in winter when winds are fierce (618–29). Summer sailing is preferable, during the period which begins fifty days after the summer solstice (663).[72] He encourages the use of a big ship rather than a small one, for the former will make one's mission more profitable (642–44). An alternative sailing time is spring (late April/early May), though Hesiod cautions against this because of its risks (678, 682–84). People who sail in spring do so from lack of thought (*aidreiēsi*) (685). In an apparent attempt to explain the imprudent decision to sail in spring, Hesiod adds: "for wealth (*chrēmata*) is the life breath to wretched mortals" (686). One glimpses a possible critique of wealth, here, which M. L. West's commentary reinforces: of those who sail in spring, West writes that "their concern for property takes the place of their concern for life."[73] If this is so, then those who sail in spring wrongly identify what is good in life; their desire to sail leads them astray. This interpretation is problematic because it is not clear what leads such mortals astray. The pursuit of profit is one possibility, but, as stated above, Hesiod does not disapprove of profit when pursued in the right way. Robin Osborne argues that the "wretched mortals" for whom "goods are life" (his translation of line 686, just quoted) are those who do not trade occasionally as an adjunct to their farming activities when they happen to have a surplus of which to dispose in local markets; rather they are those whose main or sole means of livelihood is trade.[74] According to this interpretation, Hesiod reveals an awareness of professional traders and an aversion to them that, as we saw above, some scholars attribute to Homer. Whether this indicates distaste for such trading is unclear, for Hesiod immediately issues what seems to be prudential advice against sailing in spring but not moral condemnation thereof (690–93); he brings the profits to be had from sailing into opposition with the risks. Hesiod's warnings about spring sailing apply also to summer sailing, and he also issues prudential advice to the summer mariner, who is urged not to stay away too long, for the seas become rough as winter approaches (673–77). Although he sees summer as a safer time to sail than spring, there is no moral criticism of spring sailing and professional trade. I thus submit that Hesiod, like Homer, was less critical of commerce than many scholars have argued.

FROM ARCHAIC TO CLASSICAL GREECE: PLATO, ARISTOTLE, XENOPHON

To conclude, I compare Homer's and Hesiod's views on labor, commerce, and wealth to those of three of the best-known classical authors, Aristotle, Plato, and Xenophon. My remarks illustrate the "aristocratic" viewpoint taken by the three authors and should not be held to be representative of classical Athenian thought generally. A thorough treatment of the influence I address would require detailed attention to classical orators and to epigraphic evidence.

With regard to labor, Homer does not censure the activity of laboring; nevertheless, the status of a laborer who is hired by an *oikos* is a lowly one. For Hesiod, hard work by the (nearly) self-sufficient farmer is something of a virtue. Aristotle, Plato, and Xenophon take a harsher attitude toward labor. If a *polis* admits artisans (*banausoi*) or laborers (*thētes*) to the citizenry, they will, Aristotle holds, be inferior citizens on account of being "necessary people" who "minister to the wants of the community" and who are therefore not properly "free"; "for no man can practise excellence who is living the life of a mechanic or labourer."[75] For Aristotle, the activity of labor is the cause of a person's degradation (rather than a person's degradation being the cause of his suitability for labor), for he writes that manual occupations and paid employment generally "absorb and degrade the mind."[76] Aristotle qualifies this statement when he relates activities to the ends that they serve: when done in pursuit of excellence, an activity is not "illiberal," that is, unworthy of a freeman, but when done in the service of others, the same activity is servile.[77] This is arguably reminiscent of Homer, for whom the status of the person conducting laboring activities was of central concern, although Aristotle brings the end that the activity serves to the fore. Xenophon, like Aristotle, posits a causal relation between the activity of labor and the detrimental influence on laborers: the manual professions ruin the bodies and minds of those who practice them, and the pursuit of these professions leaves laborers insufficient leisure to dedicate to the concerns of friends and the city; they do not make good citizens.[78] Plato, too, although he includes manual workers among citizens of the ideal polis, classes them as inferior to those who rule, and he leaves no doubt that practicing a manual occupation deforms people mentally and physically.[79] The causal relation between work and character found in all three classical authors marks a departure from Homer and Hesiod for whom labor is not held to be degrading or deforming.

Turning to wealth, let us recall the centrality of agricultural wealth (livestock, the means of subsistence, and slaves) in Homer; wealth also consists of elaborately wrought items, often of precious metal, which circulate among the Homeric elite. Hesiodic wealth is more prosaic and less prodigious, but neither poet suggests that wealth has limits; the more of it one has, the better. Consequently, possession of wealth does not call one's status into question; on the contrary, heroes like Menelaos boast of their wealth in a way suggesting that wealth and (high) status are close bedfellows. When it comes to the manner in which wealth is acquired, Homer does not appear to take exception to the violent appropriation of wealth in war or through plundering. For Hesiod, seizing wealth "by force" is shameful, as is, for Homer, taking more than one's share of intracommunal wealth.[80] In such cases, as David Schaps remarks, "it is the injustice that is bad, not the wealth."[81] Later in the archaic period, the Athenian legislator Solon, who was appointed in 594 BCE, allows us to glimpse a more critical attitude to wealth. Solon, like Hesiod, censures the unjust acquisition of wealth, for unjustly acquired wealth is valued "out of *hubris*" and is punished by the gods.[82] But though Solon holds that men who value wealth hubristically are "persuaded by unjust deeds," elsewhere he also lays the blame at the door of wealth itself, for, "persuaded by wealth," men perform vain deeds that ruin their city.[83] Solon also thematizes limits to wealth explicitly: "To men there is no end clearly laid down for wealth."[84] Solon's remarks must be seen in the context of the civil strife at Athens that preceded his rule and that Solon was expected to address through legislation. Prior to Solon, Athens' citizens became polarized into those who became wealthy often at the expense of those who were impoverished, indebted, and enslaved when they could not pay off their debts. This divisiveness of inequality is not reflected in Homer, and obliquely (if at all) in Hesiod.[85] A memory of the discord of the early sixth century, however, lasted into the classical period and might have had an influence on Plato's, Xenophon's, and Aristotle's thoughts on wealth.

Plato's aversion to inequality can be held to bear on the influence of the stratification of the seventh and early sixth centuries expressed by Solon.[86] Plato also asserts that wealth and goodness are antithetical: "When one rises, the other must fall." Wealth corrupts the soul and produces "luxury and idleness." Wealth might be of value to those of a good nature, but the goodness of the person is a necessary condition for the value of wealth.[87] Xenophon, too, has Socrates's interlocutor, Critobulus, define wealth as that which is "beneficial to its owner." The implication of this definition is that the same items "can be wealth for the person who knows how to use each of them, but not wealth for one who does not know," because to those who do not know, an item will prove to be harmful and so, ipso facto, not wealth.[88] A horse is not wealth to one who does not know how to ride. An article cannot, then, be wealth per se but only relative to our knowledge. Aristotle, too, makes wealth relative, not to knowledge, but to the natural needs of the person. Wealth, for Aristotle, is a good that is instrumental to the higher end of happiness.[89] Because of its (mere) usefulness, wealth is not the end of the most choiceworthy life; indeed, some people are destroyed by their wealth.[90] The misapprehension that wealth is an end in itself rather than a means to living well is the focus of Aristotle's censure. If one follows West's interpretation of *Works and Days*,[91] one might see a common ground between Hesiod and Aristotle, for Hesiod, as argued by West, censures those who sail in spring (686); they are preoccupied with wealth and lose sight of the proper ends of life. One might argue that Hesiod anticipates Aristotle here by holding that wealth is an instrument of the good life, not its final end. I have already raised doubt about West's interpretation of Hesiod's spring mariners, but even if one agrees with West, any commonality between Hesiod and Aristotle is tempered by the novel way in which Aristotle approaches wealth.[92] Aristotle distinguishes two types of acquiring wealth, one natural, because it is limited by the needs of people, the other unnatural, because it imposes no bounds on wealth. People's needs and desires are limited, and those who pursue wealth without limit have excessive, and therefore unnatural, desires.[93] The classical themes that question the acquisition of wealth—that wealth is bad for those who lack wisdom or goodness, and that wealth is good only when acquired to fulfill natural human needs—are absent from archaic sources.

CONCLUDING REMARKS

Homeric commerce consists in long-distance trade (*emporia*), while market exchange within one community is scarcely, if at all, mentioned. Internal commerce is likewise absent from Hesiod, and though he mentions *emporia* once (646), he usually adverts to (external) trade in the context of "sailing." For classical authors, internal commerce (*kapēleia*, a word not found in Homer or Hesiod) is far more significant. "Retail traders" (*kapēloi*), as Plato calls them, should be those "least fit physically, and unsuitable for other work," a judgment he does not extend to overseas traders (*emporoi*) who provide the polis with imported goods.[94] In the *Laws*, Plato mentions the "insatiable profiteering" of *emporoi* and uses the term *emporos*, not *kapēloi*, as a term of abuse.[95] *Kapēloi* are not, however, spared criticism, for the class of retail traders is to be kept small and entrusted to those whose corruption (through trade) will damage the state least.[96] Xenophon associates *emporoi* with buying cheap and selling dear, a remark not designed to shine a favorable light on traders; he locates the activity of *emporoi* in the marketplace (*agora*), which would, contrary to the usual use of the term *emporos*, imply internal commerce rather than long-distance trade.[97] Aristotle's remarks on retail trade follow from those he makes on wealth: through retail trade, one can acquire wealth in the form of coin; if one believes that coin is wealth, one will acquire it without limit and mistake the accumulation of wealth with the proper end of living well.[98] By the fourth century BCE, in which Aristotle wrote, coin was widespread at Athens and in many other Greek poleis. That it was used to store wealth is demonstrated by Lysias's inventory of items stolen from him, which included coins, silver bullion, and wrought items of silver.[99] That coin was a highly liquid form of wealth is suggested by the example of Pericles, who, already in the fifth century, sold the entire produce of his estate and "bought from the market anything he needed to get on with living."[100] Plutarch, our source for this adage, does not reveal the form in which Pericles held his wealth, yet coin is the most likely candidate in light of the rapid development of coin in fifth-century Athens and its regular use in exchange and payment. The drachma also became the unit of account in classical Athens. Thus, in both the theory and the practice of wealth and commerce, the three or so centuries that separate Homer and Hesiod from our classical trinity mark some very far-reaching changes. These divergences must be taken into account in any appeal to Greek perspectives on wealth, commerce, and the value of labor.

ACKNOWLEDGMENTS

I would like to thank Eugene Heath and Byron Kaldis for their perseverance and patience in commenting on various drafts of this essay, without which the results would have been far poorer.

NOTES

1. Moses Finley, *The World of Odysseus* (Middlesex: Penguin, 1978); Paul Millett, "Hesiod and His World," *Proceedings of the Cambridge Philological Society* 210 (1984), 84–115; Kurt A. Raaflaub, "Homeric Society," in *A New Companion to Homer*, ed. Ian Morris and Barry Powell (Leiden: Brill, 1997), 624–48.

2. Kurt Raaflaub, "Homer to Solon: The Rise of the *Polis*," in *The Ancient Greek City-State*, ed. Mogens Hansen (Copenhagen: Kongelige Danske Videnskabernes Selskab, 1993), 42–59.

3. Ian Morris, "The Use and Abuse of Homer," *Classical Antiquity* 5 (1986): §2; Albert Lord, *The Singer of Tales* (Cambridge, MA: Harvard University Press, 1960).

4. Richard Seaford, *Reciprocity and Ritual: Homer and Tragedy in the Developing City-State* (Oxford: Oxford University Press, 1994), chap. 5.

5. Robin Osborne, "Homer's Society," in *The Cambridge Companion to Homer*, ed. Robert Fowler (Cambridge: Cambridge University Press, 2004), 218.

6. *The Odyssey of Homer,* trans. Richmond Lattimore (New York: HarperPerennial, 1991), XIV.100–102. When referring to Homer's epics, I cite book (Roman numeral) and line number(s) (Arabic numeral); I use Lattimore's translations throughout.

7. *Od.* XI.78.

8. *The Iliad of Homer,* trans. Richmond Lattimore (Chicago: University of Chicago Press, 1951), II.100–107.

9. *Il.* XI.631–34.

10. Raaflaub, "Homer to Solon," 50.

11. *Od.* VIII.390–91.

12. *Od.* XVI.247–51.

13. *Od.* VI.299–302, XVII.264–65.

14. *Od.* XIX.111–14; *Il.* IV.341–44, XII.310–21.

15. *Od.* I.390–93.

16. *Il.* VII.320–22, XII.310–14.

17. *Od.* III.4–8; Walter Donlan, "Reciprocities in Homer," *Classical World* 75 (1982): 165–66.

18. *Od.* XIII.14–15, XIX.197–98.

19. Walter Donlan, "The Homeric Economy," in Morris and Powell, *A New Companion to Homer*, 665–66.

20. *Il.* VII.314–22, X.303–12; *Od.* XI.505–35.

21. Bernhard Laum's contention that subordinate kings were "paid" for such service with portions of sacrificial meat is not clearly supported in Homer's epics. See Laum, *Heiliges Geld: Eine historische Untersuchung über den sakralen Ursprung des Geldes* (Tübingen: Mohr, 1924), 49.

22. *Il.* XVIII.721.

23. *Il.* I.163–68, II.226–28.

24. Marshall Sahlins, *Stone Age Economics* (Chicago: Aldine-Atherton, 1972), 194–95.

25. Donlan, "Reciprocities in Homer," 167.

26. Moses Finley, *Economy and Society in Ancient Greece* (1953; New York: Viking Press, 1982), 235. In this essay, I use the term "commerce" rather than "trade" to reflect the title of the volume of which this essay is a part. However, classicists often prefer "trade," and some distinguish the more respectable "trade" from a reprehensible "commerce" (e.g., David Schaps, *The Invention of Coinage and the Monetization of Ancient Greece* [Ann Arbor: University of Michigan Press, 2004], 74–75).

27. *Il.* XXIII.826–49.

28. Laum, *Heiliges Geld*, 12.

29. Gifts are also given as compensation for a wrong or in marriage, as bride-price or dowry (Finley, *Economy and Society*, 240–41).

30. *Il.* VI.215–36.

31. *Od.* IX.195–205, X.19–22, XXI.5–41. That gifts often become objects of use contradict Finley's claim that gifts are stored until they are given again (Finley, *World of Odysseus*, 61). Although Homer's word for "treasure" (*keimēlion*) means "that which can be stored away," it is misleading to hold that such gifts were usually stored rather than used.

32. *Il.* VI.234–36.

33. *Od.* VI.204; Carol Dougherty, *The Raft of Odysseus: The Ethnographic Imagination of Homer's "Odyssey"* (Oxford: Oxford University Press, 2001), 117.

34. *Od.* IV.614.

35. Sahlins, *Stone Age Economics*, 193–94.

36. Raaflaub, "Homeric Society," 636–37; see also Dougherty, *Raft of Odysseus*, 46.

37. Donlan, "Reciprocities in Homer," 142.

38. Fridolf Kudlien, "Der archaisch-griechische Seehändler," *Münsterische Beiträge zur antiken Handelsgeschichte* 18 (1999): 66.

39. *Il.* XI.673–80; *Od.* IX.39–43.

40. *Il.* XI.686–87, 695–706; *Od.* IX.42–43.

41. Finley, *World of Odysseus*, 102; Donlan, "Homeric Economy," 653.

42. *Od.* XV.415–84.

43. *Od.* XV.425–29, XIV.449–52, I.180–89.

44. Michel Austin and Pierre Vidal-Naquet, *Economic and Social History of Ancient Greece* (Berkeley: University of California Press, 1977), 43; Hans van Wees, *Status Warriors: War, Violence, and Society in Homer and History* (Amsterdam: J.C. Gieben, 1992), 238; *Il.* VII.470–75, XXI.40–41. Cf. Donlan, "Homeric Economy," 652–53; David Tandy, *Warriors into Traders: The Power of the Market in Early Greece* (Berkeley: University of California Press, 1997), 72–73.

45. *Il.* II.448–49; VI.236; XXI.79; XXIII.703–5, 885–86; *Od.* I.431, XXII.54–59. See Mark Peacock, *Introducing Money* (London: Routledge, 2013), 71–81.

46. *Od.* I.431; cf. Schaps, *Invention of Coinage*, 70 n. 34.

47. George Dalton, "Economic Theory and Primitive Society," *American Anthropologist* 63 (1961): 12–13.

48. *Od.* XV.405–6, 459–63; XIV.285–97.

49. Hans Georg Niemeyer, "The Phoenicians and the Birth of a Multinational Mediterranean Society," in *Commerce and Monetary Systems in the Ancient World*, ed. Robert Rollinger and Christoph Ulf (Wiesbaden: Franz Steiner, 2004), 249.

50. *Il.* VI.289–95, XXIII.741–45.

51. *Od.* XIX.283–84.

52. *Od.* III.301. Cf. Dougherty, *Raft of Odysseus*, 48; Sarah Morris, "Homer and the Near East," in Morris and Powell, *A New Companion to Homer*, 613; Mark Peacock, "Rehabilitating Homer's Phoenicians," *Ancient Society* 41 (2011): §V.

53. *Od.* VIII.161–64.

54. *Od.* VIII.186–98.

55. Cf. Dougherty, *Raft of Odysseus*, 55.

56. Peacock, "Rehabilitating Homer's Phoenicians," 1–29; van Wees, *Status Warriors*, 242.

57. *Od.* XVII.340–41, 382–85; XVIII.328.

58. *Il.* XXI.441–54.

59. *Od.* XI.489–91.

60. *Od.* XVIII.357–64.

61. *Od.* XVIII.366–80, XXIII.188–204.

62. David Tandy and Walter Neale, *Hesiod's Works and Days: A Translation and Commentary for the Social Sciences* (Berkeley: University of California Press, 1996), 37. When referring to Hesiod's *Works and Days*, I cite line numbers parenthetically in the text.

63. Tandy, *Warriors into Traders*, 210–11.

64. Michael Gagarin, "Hesiod's Dispute with Perses," *Transactions of the American Philological Association* 104 (1974): 103–11.

65. Apostolos Athanassakis, "Cattle and Honour in Homer and Hesiod," *Ramus* 21 (1992): 169.

66. For differing interpretations of the reciprocity involved, cf. Anthony Edwards, *Hesiod's Ascra* (Berkeley: University of California Press, 2004), 95–97; Thomas Gallant,

"Agricultural Systems, Land Tenure, and the Reforms of Solon," *Annual of the British School at Athens* 77 (1982): 112.

67. Aristotle cites a law of the Locrians (of southern Italy) that forbids a man to sell his land unless "he can prove unmistakably that some misfortune has befallen him" (Aristotle, *The Politics and the Constitution of Athens,* trans. Benjamin Jowett [Cambridge: Cambridge University Press, 1996], 1266b19–21). I use Jowett's translation of Aristotle's *Politics* throughout.

68. Gallant, "Agricultural Systems," 113.

69. M. L. West, *Hesiod: Works and Days* (Oxford: Clarendon Press, 1978), 313.

70. Alfonso Mele, *Il commercio greco arcaico: Prexis ed emporie* (Naples: Institut Français de Naples, 1979), chap. 7. I disagree with Mele's thesis that, in addition to "commercio ἔργον," Hesiod invokes a different kind of commerce, pursued by a "professional trader" (*nautēs prēktēres*), of whom Hesiod disapproves. Homer puts the bracketed term into the mouth of Euryalos (*Od.* VIII.164), but there is little evidence that Hesiod distinguishes the lone farmer-merchant from a professional trader. For a critique of Mele, see Edwards, *Hesiod's Ascra*, 45–48.

71. Tandy and Neale, *Hesiod's Works and Days*, 76 n. 64.

72. G. Snider, "Hesiod's Sailing Season," *American Journal of Ancient History* 3 (1978): 129–30.

73. West, *Hesiod*, 325.

74. Robin Osborne, "Pots, Trade, and the Archaic Greek Economy," *Antiquity* 70 (1996): 41.

75. Arist., *Pol.* 1278a8–12, 20–21; cf. 1328b39–40.

76. Arist., *Pol.* 1337b8–12.

77. Arist., *Pol.* 1337b16–21.

78. Xenophon, *Oeconomicus: A Social and Economic History,* trans. Sarah Pomeroy (Oxford: Oxford University Press, 1995), IV.2–3. I use Pomeroy's translation throughout.

79. Plato, *The Republic,* trans. Desmond Lee (London: Penguin, 1987), 405d-e, 590c.

80. *Il.* I.122; *Od.* IX.229; Tandy and Neale, *Works and Days*, 321–27.

81. David Schaps, "Socrates and the Socratics: When Wealth Became a Problem," *Classical World* 96 (2003): 135.

82. Solon, frag. 13.7–13, in Ron Owens, *Solon of Athens: Poet, Philosopher, Soldier, Statesman* (Brighton: Suxxex Academic Press, 2010).

83. Solon, frag. 4.5–11, in Owens, *Solon of Athens*.

84. Solon, frag. 13.71, in Owens, *Solon of Athens*. On the ambiguous status of wealth in Solon's writings, see John Lewis, *Solon the Thinker: Political Thought in Archaic Athens* (London: Duckworth, 2006), chap. 6.

85. However, for a contrary opinion on Hesiod, see Édouard Will, "Aux origines du régime foncier grec," *Revue des Études Anciennes* 59 (1957), 5–50. For a critique of Will, see Millett, "Hesiod and His World," 104–6.

86. Pl., *Rep.* 421e–422a.

87. Pl., *Rep.* 550e, 422a, 331a, 591a-d.

88. Xen., *Oec.* I.7–10.

89. Aristotle, *Nicomachean Ethics,* trans. Terence Irwin (Indianapolis: Hackett, 1985), 1099a31–1099b2.

90. Arist., *NE* 1094b16–19.

91. West, *Hesiod,* 325 (West's interpretation is also cited in the final paragraph of the previous section).

92. Aristotle cites Hesiod and even does so in book I (*Pol.* 1252b11), in which he also discusses wealth. But the remarks on wealth seem uninfluenced by Hesiod's passage on spring sailing and "wretched mortals."

93. Arist., *Pol.* 1257a3–5, 19; 1257b24; 1258b2, 6.

94. Pl., *Rep.* 370e–371c. See Joshua Weinstein, "The Market in Plato's *Republic*," *Classical Philology* 104 (2009): 454, for a plausible interpretation of this remark as having no critical intent.

95. Plato, *The Laws*, trans. Trevor Saunders (London: Penguin, 1970), 918d, 831e.

96. Pl., *Laws* 919c.

97. Xenophon, *Memorabilia*, trans. Amy Bonnette (Ithaca, NY: Cornell University Press, 2001), III.7.6.

98. Arist., *Pol.* 1257a1–1258a18.

99. Lysias, "Against Eratosthenes," in *Lysias*, trans. W. R. M. Lamb (Cambridge, MA: Harvard University Press, 1930), lines 11–12.

100. "Pericles," in *Plutarch: Greek Lives*, trans. Robin Waterfield (Oxford: Oxford University Press, 1998), §16.

CHAPTER 2

Aristotle and Business: Friend or Foe?

Fred D. Miller Jr.

A much revered figure in the history of philosophy, Aristotle (384–322 BCE) is still frequently invoked even in works of applied philosophy. In the field of business ethics, however, Aristotle is an ambiguous authority, as can be seen in two contrasting perspectives. The following statement encapsulates one approach:

> I am firmly convinced that if we are prepared to philosophize in all the right ways about the crucial challenge of corporate spirit, and equally prepared to do something with what we learn, we can attain and sustain that level of corporate and individual excellence we all want, as well as that depth of personal satisfaction we all need. We then can make our mark in this world in the most positive way possible. If Aristotle ran General Motors, I think this is what he would do. Why indeed should we settle for anything less?[1]

This "neo-Aristotelian" vision of business is shared by prominent theorists of business ethics such as Robert Solomon and Edwin Hartman.[2]

A stark alternative, however, is presented by Alasdair MacIntyre, a critic of capitalism who contends that "the [Aristotelian] tradition of the virtues is at variance with central features of the modern economic order, [namely,] . . . individualism, . . . acquisitiveness and its elevation of the values of the market to a central social place."[3] Likewise, Antony Flew, himself a defender of capitalism, takes note of Aristotle's sweeping critique of commerce:

> Aristotle's contention was that any [gainful] exchange, any trade, is essentially exploitative. For he believed that the acquisitions of any trader, must necessarily be at the expense of that trader's trading partner. . . .

Aristotle's was the same thesis and the same misconception, as can be found in John Ruskin's *Unto This Last*. It was that fiercely anti-capitalist work that greatly influenced Mahatma Gandhi and many of the founding fathers of the British Labour Party. In it Ruskin insisted that "Whenever material gain follows exchange, for every plus there is a precisely equal minus."[4]

Which, then, is the more faithful portrait of Aristotle: sage of business or critic of capitalism? It would not be surprising if there were a grain of truth in each interpretation. But more important is the question of where Aristotle stands in terms of fundamental principle: can his critique of business be disassociated from his own theory of virtue ethics, or would any attempt to do so inevitably distort and misrepresent his views? This essay will accordingly identify the general principles on which Aristotle relied in criticizing common business practices and will consider whether he applied these principles in a convincing way. On the basis of this discussion it will be possible to take up the questions of whether the conduct of business is consistent with Aristotelian virtue and, if so, whether a theory of virtue such as Aristotle's could provide guidance for modern businesspeople.

THE BUSINESS WORLD IN ARISTOTLE'S DAY

Before examining Aristotle's arguments, we should consider how business was in fact conducted and how businesspeople were generally regarded in Greece in the fourth century BCE. The ancient Greek economy looks quite primitive by comparison to the capitalist economies of today, with their large multinational corporations, financial institutions, labor unions, and far-flung stock and bond markets.[5] Still, to the extent that ancient Greek business practices can be viewed as fundamentally similar to our own, we can better appreciate the possible relevance of Aristotle's pronouncements to modern business practice.[6]

The ancient Greek world was divided into hundreds of comparatively small and sparsely populated city-states located around the Mediterranean Sea, which Plato likened to "frogs around a pond" (*Phaedo* 109a-b). The largest of these was Athens, a political, religious, and cultural center as well as a commercial hub. It was here that Aristotle spent much of his life, first as a student of Plato's Academy and later as head of his own school in the Lyceum. Although the Greeks prized self-sufficiency, the city-states had limited natural resources, so that they were more or less reliant on imports. Athens in particular depended on imported goods (such as metals, timber, stone, and wine) and on slaves. Although farmers in the countryside produced olives, grapes, cereals, and food, Athens had to import large quantities of grain to sustain a population in excess of 300,000.

Agriculture was, however, the dominant industry. Most citizens were farmers; indeed, only citizens were permitted to own land. The social and political elite were large landowners, but most citizens had only small plots of land, and about a quarter of them were landless and obliged to work as craftsmen and laborers. Many were self-employed as carpenters, stonecutters, blacksmiths, shoemakers, potters, jewelers, bakers, butchers, fishermen and fishmongers, doctors, and so forth. Affluent businessmen owned workshops and small factories producing furniture, weapons, jewelry, pottery, and the like. Mine operators entered into leases with the state to work the publicly owned silver mines. Others, including architects and shipbuilders, contracted with the government to construct public buildings and temples, as on the Acropolis, and to build warships, and they subcontracted in turn with carpenters, stonemasons, sculptors, shipwrights, and so forth. All of these enterprises relied heavily on the labor of slaves, who were affordable and readily available in slave markets and who comprised over a third of the population. Poor free men also toiled alongside slaves on farms and in workshops, shipyards, mines, and building projects, and they were stigmatized by association.[7]

Business was conducted in the marketplace (*agora*) located below the Acropolis. There was also an import-export market (*emporion*) in the nearby seaport of Piraeus. Self-employed craftsmen typically sold their wares in the marketplace, some out of their own workshops but many from stalls or tables in designated locations. Farmers also brought their produce to market. But much of the dealing was by tradesmen (*kapēloi*) who bought goods from farmers, craftsmen, manufacturers, or importers and resold them at retail. Foreign commerce was carried out by merchants (*emporoi*) who generally rented cargo space from shipowners, though in some cases the shipowners also operated as merchants.[8]

Individuals borrowed money from other individuals. In addition to independently wealthy individuals, money changers and pawnbrokers drew on their profits to make loans for interest. Another important source of loans was the banker, with whom individuals deposited their money to keep it safe or conceal it (for example, from tax collectors). Bankers paid interest to depositors and in turn lent money to borrowers for interest. Although many borrowers needed the money for consumption, using their land as collateral, merchants also sought loans for ventures such as large grain shipments. Maritime loans included features of insurance and investment: for if the cargo was lost at sea the merchant did not have to repay the loan, but if it reached its destination he owed substantial interest—for example, 30 percent of the principal.[9]

Government played a comparatively limited role in the ancient Greek economy. Commerce was regulated by public officials (*agoranomoi*), who settled disagreements, collected fees from sellers, inspected weights and measures, and kept a lookout for adulterated or fraudulent products and for counterfeit coins. More serious disputes concerning inheritances, property rights, and fraud were adjudicated in courts of law; surviving orations composed by Demosthenes and others provide valuable details about how business was conducted.

An apparently simple transaction, such as buying a jar of olive oil in the marketplace, could thus rest upon a complex network of economic transactions. For example, a farmer grows olives on his trees and rents a press to make oil; he sells the oil to a local retailer who transports it to the port market for resale to a merchant. The merchant borrows money from a banker and rents space from a shipowner in order to convey the oil and other goods to another city-state. Upon arriving in the foreign port he sells oil in bulk to a middleman (*palinemporos*) who resells it to a local retailer who finally sells the jar of oil to a consumer in the local marketplace.

Without a science of economics the ancient Greeks had little appreciation of the vital role that businesspeople played in their society. According to surviving written accounts, someone involved in a productive craft was denigrated as "vulgar" (*banausos*). Manufacturers, merchants, and bankers were often foreigners, former slaves, or citizens of doubtful descent. Businesspeople were frequently the butt of humor in ancient comedies, as reported by Kenneth Dover:

> Since a buyer wishes to pay less than a seller demands, contempt for the seller as economically dependent can be coupled with hostility towards him as avaricious and unreasonable; hence Attic comedy's consistently unfriendly attitude to fish-mongers ("all murderers," Amphis fr. 30.5ff), slave-traders ("insatiable," Aristophanes *Wealth* 521), landladies (a subject of broad humour in Aristophanes *Frogs* 549–78), bread-sellers (cf. Aristophanes *Wasps* 1388–1414) and moneylenders (Demosthenes 37.52).[10]

The Athenians had no appreciation of modern "bourgeois virtues," as Dover further remarks:

> People who acquired wealth do not seem to have been admired by the Greeks for commercial acumen, inventiveness, flair for the exploitation of opportunities, or the single-minded pursuit of profit which causes the self-made millionaire to be an object of admiration in some modern societies. In comedy, some use is made of the assumption that dishonest men become rich and honest men remain poor; this is the theme of Aristophanes' *Wealth* and cf. Menander *Colax* 43, "No one gets rich quickly by being honest."[11]

Not surprisingly, then, successful businessmen tended to be viewed with envy and resentment and were condemned when they or their families indulged in conspicuous consumption; and they were expected instead to make substantial public contributions in support of wars, such as for the building of triremes (warships), and to finance festivals and choruses.

An unfavorable view of business is also expressed in Plato's dialogue *The Laws*, in which the spokesman, known only as "the Athenian Stranger," describes a constitution for a fictional colony to be established in Crete. The Stranger remarks that "every kind of retail trade, and wholesale trade, and innkeeping has come to be discredited and held in shameful blame." This is because the general run of men, when in want, "want without measure, and when it's possible for them to gain measured amounts, they choose to gain insatiably" (*Laws* XI.918d).[12] Because profit seeking is morally corrupting, the Stranger would prohibit citizens from partaking in commerce and trades and confine those activities to foreign residents (V.736e–741e, VIII.846d–847b, XI.918a–920c). The Stranger is especially critical of the import-export business, calling the sea "a briny and bitter neighbor": "It infects a place with commerce and the money-making that comes with retail trade, and engenders shifty and untrustworthy dispositions in souls; it thereby takes away the trust and friendship a city feels for itself and the rest of humanity" (IV.705a).[13]

Aristotle expresses similar views in his *Politics*: "It is impossible to engage in virtuous pursuits while living the life of a vulgar craftsman or a hired laborer" (III.5.1278a20–21; cf. I.13.1260a38–b1).[14] These sorts of pursuits are considered "vulgar" because they "render the body or mind of free people useless for these practices and activities of virtue," for "they debase the mind and deprive it of leisure" (VIII.2.1337a11–15). Aristotle's point seems to be that instead of striving to lead virtuous lives craftsmen aim at the production of "external goods" such as physical possessions and money, which are necessary for sustaining life or making it enjoyable. Consequently, he thinks, a vulgar craftsman is in a way even worse off than a slave who has a master to teach him a modicum of virtue: "For a slave shares his master's life, whereas a vulgar craftsman is at a greater remove, and virtue pertains to him to just the extent that slavery does; for a vulgar craftsman has a kind of delimited slavery" (*Pol.* I.13.1260a39–b1; cf. *Rhet.* I.9.1367a31–32).[15] Consequently, when Aristotle outlines his own ideal constitution in which all the citizens are virtuous, he consigns the craftsmen to a separate class without political rights: "The citizens should not live the life of a vulgar craftsman or tradesman. For these sorts are ignoble and inimical to virtue" (*Pol.* VII.9.1328b39–1329a2; cf. III.4.1277b3–7, VIII.2.1337b5–15). Moreover, when Aristotle considers the political systems of his own day—mainly either democracies (literally, "rule by the people," but in effect rule by the poor, who were in the majority) or oligarchies (literally, "rule by the few," but in fact rule by the wealthy and well-born)—he condemns democracies, which include "the multitude of vulgar craftsmen, tradesmen, and laborers" as citizens (VI.4.1319a26–28), and, conversely, praises oligarchies which exclude the nouveau riche recently engaged in trade (VI.7.1321a28–29, III.5.1278a25–26). If Aristotle seems disdainful of vulgar craftsmen, he is even more contemptuous of commerce, which he says is "justly disparaged," and especially of lending money for interest, which he regards as the "most unnatural" way of seeking wealth (I.10.1258b1–8).

Aristotle does not make altogether explicit his reasons for denigrating craftsmen, but they seem to rest on a distinction, in the *Nicomachean Ethics* (I.1 and VI.4), between production and action. An example of production (*poiēsis*) is building a house: it is the bringing into existence of a product that would not otherwise exist. Productive labor (e.g., house building) has merely instrumental value, deriving from the value of its product (e.g., a house). In contrast, an action (*praxis*) is performed for its own sake; it has intrinsic value independent of any result it may have. For example, on Aristotle's view philosophical activity is intrinsically valuable regardless of whether it results, for example, in the publication of a book or article. Likewise, a virtuous action (e.g., courageously defending one's city) is noble and performed for its own sake even when it also benefits others. Because productive labor is valuable only as a means and never as an end in itself, Aristotle regards it as toilsome and ignoble, and he disparages the productive crafts as vulgar and ignoble, and treats their practitioners (especially those devoted to moneymaking) as moral outcasts.[16]

ARISTOTLE'S VIRTUE ETHICS

In fairness to Aristotle it should be emphasized that his condemnation of business dealings was based not on mere prejudice but on philosophical arguments, which must be carefully analyzed and evaluated. These arguments presuppose his moral theory, a form of virtue ethics. It is accordingly necessary to distinguish between two different questions: What conclusions does Aristotle himself draw from his theory of virtue? And are his conclusions justified on the basis of that theory? Before examining his critique of business, therefore, it is necessary to set forth the general outline of his theory of virtue, which may be summed up in four main principles.

The first principle is that happiness (*eudaimonia*) is the highest good for human beings. Human action has an ultimate end: "There is some end of the things which we do, which we desire for its own sake (everything else being desired for the sake of this)" (*NE* I.2.1094a18–22).[17] Aristotle holds that happiness is the only thing fitting this description: "This we choose always for itself and never for the sake of something else, but honor, pleasure, reason, and every excellence we choose indeed for themselves . . . but we choose them also for the sake of happiness, judging that through them we shall be happy. Happiness, on the other hand, no one chooses for the sake of these, nor, in general for anything other than itself" (I.7.1097a34–b6).

Aristotle's second principle is that happiness consists in virtuous activity.

Fred D. Miller Jr.

Happiness is not a passive condition like pleasure or a subjective state such as the satisfaction of whatever desires we happen to have. (To emphasize this active dimension some translators render Aristotle's term *eudaimonia* as "flourishing" rather than "happiness.") Instead happiness consists in doing well as a human being, which Aristotle explains by analogy with the activity of an artist such as a lyre player or sculptor. Just as we say that flute players do well when they succeed in performing their characteristic or defining function (*ergon*), which is to play music, we should say the same of human beings if they perform their function well. Aristotle argues that this function involves the unique faculty of human beings, their rational soul. Hence, happiness (or flourishing) consists of an activity of the soul in accordance with reason. Furthermore, human beings are virtuous when reason rules over their souls and keeps their desires and passions in check. Therefore, "the human good turns out to be the activity of the soul in conformity with virtue . . . in a complete life" (*NE* I.7.1097b22–1098a20).

Aristotle's third principle is that virtue involves choosing a mean between extremes. Human beings perpetually confront alternatives, which typically involve a choice between more or less of something. For example, when we eat a meal we choose how much food to consume. We can eat too much, not enough, or the right amount for us, which Aristotle calls "the mean." We find this mean by using our rational faculty. In moral situations virtue enables us to choose the mean, while vice leads to the extremes. For example, when people are in perilous situations, cowards tend to be overly fearful and to lack confidence, and foolhardy persons tend to be overly confident and fearless to a fault, whereas courageous people experience these feelings to the right degree and act accordingly. The same sort of analysis applies to the actions that are the expressions of such passions and desires—for example, whether a soldier retreats under fire, attacks needlessly, or takes a stand and fights when the commander orders. In general, then, "virtue is a state concerned with choice, lying in a mean relative to us, this being determined by reason" (*NE* II.6.1106b36–1107a1).

Aristotle's fourth principle is that justice is one of the virtues and is thus analyzable in terms of the mean. This is clear in the case of distributive justice: when some common asset is distributed to individuals, the distribution is just provided that each party receives an amount that is intermediate in the sense that neither gets too much or too little. Each must receive a share that is fair or equal (*ison*),[18] but this does not mean that each gets exactly the same amount. For example, suppose that two farmers are dividing a harvest that they planted, tilled, reaped, and sold at market together. But suppose that one of them worked twice as hard as the other. It would seem hardly fair for the less productive farmer to insist that their earnings be split fifty-fifty (assuming he made no other contribution). The harder-working farmer clearly deserves a greater share. Aristotle analyzes this in terms of what he calls a "geometrical proportion," or equality of ratios. That is, the ratio between two individuals A and B in terms of their desert or merit should be equal to the ratio between their shares C and D. That is, $A/B = C/D$. In the example above, if the diligent farmer is twice as deserving as his lazy partner, it is only just that his share be twice as much (see *NE* I.3.1131a29–b16).

Now let us see why Aristotle thinks these principles entail a condemnation of ordinary business transactions.

ARISTOTLE'S CRITIQUE OF BUSINESS

Just Exchange

Aristotle's analysis of justice in exchange is similar to his analysis of distributive justice. Both types of justice involve proportionate equality, but they raise different complications. In the case of distributive justice the problem involves "equalizing" the recipients of the distribution in terms of their desert. In the case of justice in exchange the problem involves equalizing the commodities exchanged in terms of their value, as Aristotle shows in this example of bartering:

> Let A be a builder, B a shoemaker, C a house, D a shoe. The builder, then, must get from the shoemaker the latter's product, and must himself give him in return his own. . . . They must therefore be equated. . . . The number of shoes exchanged for a house must therefore correspond to the ratio of builder to shoemaker. For if this be not so, there will be no exchange and no interaction. And this proportion will not be effected unless the goods are somehow equal. (*NE* V.3.1133a7–14)

How is this equalization supposed to take place? Let one hundred pairs of shoes equal one house. For this to be so, there must be some unit of measurement such that one pair of shoes equals N units and one house equals one hundred times N units. But what might this unit be? It cannot be a coin, because the monetary price may not reflect a commodity's true value. But Aristotle offers a solution:

> Now this unit is in truth need (*chreia*), which holds all things together (for if men did not need one another's goods at all, or did not need them equally, there would be either no exchange or not the same exchange); but money has become by convention a sort of representative of need. (1133a26–29)

Aristotle's solution is, to put it mildly, opaque.[19] For he does not explain how we can assign units of need to a pair of shoes and units of need to a house in order to establish an equality. It is correct that in a monetary system a certain quantity of shoes will be regarded as equal in price to a house, but it is unclear how money can become a "representative of need" in the sense that a certain amount of money is equivalent to a certain unit of need. It is noteworthy that Aristotle assumes that if there is a just exchange there is an objective equality between the goods exchanged. This has a further implication, made explicit by medieval Aristotelian Scholastic theorists, namely, that this equality can be measured in monetary terms as the *just price* of a shoe or a house.[20] If the shoemaker manages to obtain more than the just price for his shoes, the builder must receive less than the just price for his house, so that the exchange is unjust. This just price defines the mean that virtuous agents must observe when they exchange goods with each other and that could be imposed on businessmen through laws and regulations.

Commerce

Aristotle argues that a possession such as a shoe has both a proper and an improper use:

> Every piece of property has two uses. Both of these are uses of it as such, but they are not the same uses of it as such: one is proper to the thing and the other is not. Take the wearing of a shoe, for example, and its use in exchange. Both are uses to which shoes can be put. For someone who exchanges a shoe, for money or food, with someone else who needs a shoe, is using the shoe as a shoe. But this is not the proper use because it does not come to exist for the sake of exchange. (*Pol.* I.9.1257a6–13)

When used improperly the shoe becomes a commodity, an item to be used in exchange.[21] Nonetheless, Aristotle allows that barter is consistent with moral virtue because "it first arises out of the natural circumstance of some having more than enough and others less" (1257a15–17). For example, the shoemaker and the farmer exchange shoes and food until each of them has all he needs of shoes and food. As long as individuals are accumulating what they require to maintain their households, Aristotle regards this as an honorable and natural activity. Things change dramatically, however, after the discovery of coinage. For it makes commercial exchange possible. "Commerce," Aristotle says, "has to do with the production of goods, not in the full sense, but through their exchange. It is held to be concerned with money, on the grounds that money is the unit and limit [i.e., goal] of exchange" (1257b20–23). For example, a merchant can buy shoes from the shoemaker for money and resell the goods to somebody else for more money and thereby make profits; through repeated transactions he can amass money without limit.

Aristotle contends that such profits are inimical to virtue: "Commerce is justly disparaged, since it is not natural but is [a mode of acquisition in which people take] from one another" (*Pol.* I.10.1258b1–2). To understand this claim, it is necessary to consider what Aristotle means here by "not natural." Nature (*phusis*) is a technical notion for Aristotle. In its primary meaning, "nature" refers to a principle or cause of motion or rest intrinsic to a thing (*Physics* II.1.192b12–23). For example, an acorn has a nature because it has an innate impulse to grow into an oak tree. However, "nature" has a secondary meaning for Aristotle, the determinate end or goal at which a thing ends. In this sense the acorn realizes its nature when it has become an oak tree. Thus, the term "nature" may refer to the *natural origin* of a thing or to its *natural end*. Aristotle also speaks of things as "natural" in different, though analogous, senses. In the first sense, as we have just seen, a thing is called "natural" because it has a natural origin. For instance, an oak tree is a natural entity because it grew out of an acorn that had an innate impulse to do so. In contrast, a bed is an artificial rather than a natural entity. For it did not come into existence because its materials contained an innate impulse to become a bed, but because they were assembled by an external cause, the craftsman. Hence Aristotle says that a bed exists by craft and not by nature. In the second sense, a thing is called "natural" when it fulfills or promotes a thing's natural end, and "unnatural" when it prevents or interferes with the natural ends of a thing.

For example, it is natural for a human to have the sense of sight, and blindness is an unnatural condition. Likewise, a practice is natural if it promotes our natural ends, and unnatural if it frustrates or subverts them. In this way Aristotle speaks of "natural property acquisition" (*chrēmatistikē*), which includes agriculture, animal husbandry, hunting, and even the capture of natural slaves. This natural art acquires the "natural wealth" required for the self-sufficiency and well-being of the household and city-state (see *Pol.* I.8–10).[22] In contrast, he regards commerce as "unnatural" in both the senses distinguished above. First, commerce does not have a natural origin. Unlike natural property acquisition, which emerges along with the household out of natural instincts for self-preservation and reproduction, commerce "is not natural, but comes from a sort of experience and craft" (9.1257a4–5). Second, when Aristotle says that commerce is "not natural" but is a mode of acquisition in which people take "from one another" (10.1258b1–2), he implies that the merchant is taking advantage of others by taking from them the things they need to pursue their natural ends. Aristotle assumes here that if either party to an exchange makes a profit or gain (*kerdos*), he must be doing so unjustly. This seems to follow directly from Aristotle's analysis of just exchange. If a merchant buys shoes from a shoemaker and resells them at a profit to a farmer, he can accomplish this only by paying the shoemaker *less* than the just price of the shoes or by charging the farmer *more* than their just price (or by doing both). Either way the merchant has deviated from the virtuous mean between two vicious extremes.[23]

Banking

Among the various forms of retail exchange, according to Aristotle, "the most hated sort, and with the greatest reason, is usury" (*Pol.* I.10.1258b2–3). He has two objections against usury or lending money at interest.[24] The first is that usury "makes a gain out of money itself, and not from the natural object of it. For money was intended to be used in exchange, but not to increase at interest." This assumes that money like other goods has two uses: its proper use is to facilitate exchange between ordinary commodities, but using it to collect interest is an improper use. Aristotle's second objection is related to the fact that *tokos*, the Greek term for "interest," literally means "offspring." He adds: "That is how it gets its name; for offspring resemble their parents, and interest is money that comes from money. Hence of all the kinds of wealth acquisition this one is the most unnatural" (1258b2–8). This assumes Aristotle's earlier point that the value of money is merely conventional and not natural. His reasoning here seems to be as follows: if a farmer grows wheat, he has acquired wealth in a natural way, since—as we have seen above regarding the meaning of "natural" as both natural origin and natural end—the seed is a natural entity that grows into wheat by a natural process; but if a banker uses money to produce interest, he cannot have acquired wealth in a natural way, because money is created by convention and cannot reproduce itself by nature like a plant. (Later Scholastic commentators referred to coins as "sterile metal.") To collect interest is to take a value in return for a non-value, so that it is even more unjust than other forms of retail exchange.[25]

Commodity Speculation

Aristotle gives a report of commodity speculation in his day involving Thales of Miletus, the first philosopher:

> People were reproaching Thales for being poor, claiming that it showed his philosophy was useless. The story goes that he realized through his knowledge of the stars that a good olive harvest was coming. So, while it was still winter, he raised a little money and put a deposit on all the olive presses in Miletus and Chios for future lease. He hired these at a low rate, because no one was bidding against him. When the olive season came and many people suddenly sought olive presses at the same time, he hired them out at whatever rate he chose. He collected a lot of money, showing that philosophers could easily become wealthy if they wished, but that this is not their concern. Thales is said to have demonstrated his own wisdom in this way. But . . . his scheme involves a generally applicable principle of wealth acquisition: to secure a monopoly if one can. Hence some city-states also adopt this scheme when they are in need of money: they secure a monopoly in goods for sale. (*Pol.* I.11.1259a9–23)

By cornering the market on olive presses, Aristotle implies, Thales was able to charge more for them than their just price—to engage in what is now called "price gouging."

A CRITIQUE OF ARISTOTLE'S CRITIQUE OF BUSINESS

The preceding arguments of Aristotle seem to support the view of him as a foe of business. However, are Aristotle's criticisms of business a correct application of his own theory of moral virtue? An important theme throughout is that in economic transactions the virtuous mean is defined in terms of an *equal* value that each party gives and receives. But recall that Aristotle describes virtue as "lying in a mean *relative to us*, this being determined by reason." He distinguishes "a mean relative to us" from "a mean in the object" in the following passage:

> By the intermediate *in the object* I mean that which is equidistant from each of the extremes, which is one and the same for all men; by the intermediate *relatively to us* that which is neither too much nor too little—and this is not one, nor the same for all. For instance, if ten is many and two is few, six is intermediate, taken in terms of the object; for it exceeds and is exceeded by an equal amount; this is intermediate according to arithmetical proportion. But the intermediate *relatively to us* is not to be taken so; if ten pounds are too much for a particular person to eat and two too little, it does not follow that the trainer will order six pounds; for this also is perhaps too much for the person who is to take it, or too little—too little for Milo, too much for the beginner in athletic exercises. . . . Thus a master of any art avoids excess and defect, but seeks the intermediate and chooses this—the intermediate *not in the object but relatively to us*. (NE II.6.1106a26–b5, emphasis added)

Aristotle's analogy to Milo the Olympic athlete sheds valuable light on his theory of the virtuous mean. Aristotle does not realize, however, what additional light this analogy can shed on whether gainful market transactions must violate the virtuous mean.

Commerce

Suppose that the mean relative to Milo is eight pounds of food, while the mean relative to Micro (an amateur athlete) is four pounds. However, each has six pounds of food, which is too much for Micro but not enough for Milo. Suppose also that Milo has collected twenty-four logs of firewood, which is more than he needs to cook his food, but Micro has no wood at all. If Milo offers to exchange eight logs with Micro for two pounds of food and Micro agrees, they will both be better off and enjoy what economists call "mutual gains from trade." The result of their exchange is that in effect new value has been created where none existed before.[26] Not only that, but each will wind up with the mean relative to him, since Milo will have eight pounds of food and sixteen logs, and Micro will have four pounds of food and eight logs. It is not necessary to find a unit of measurement whereby a pound of food is equal to four logs. Seeking such an equal unit might have a point if the mean were "in the object," but as Aristotle himself explains the mean must be "relative to us and not the same for all." Finally, this analysis provides a way of understanding Aristotle's insight that exchanges are based on mutual need without accepting his inference that need serves as a unit by which commodities can be equalized.

Now suppose that Milo and Micro live in separate towns and are unaware of each other's existence, but a certain merchant Emporos learns of their willingness to trade. Suppose further that Emporos knows that food costs twice as much in Micro's town (for example, two drachmas per pound as opposed to one in Milo's town) and that there are no logs for sale in Micro's town. Emporos spends two drachmas to buy two pounds of food in Milo's town and trades them with Milo for eight logs. He then takes the eight logs to Micro and trades them for two pounds of food, which he resells for four drachmas in Micro's town. Although Emporos has netted two drachmas, neither Milo nor Micro is worse off. On the contrary Emporos has enabled both of them to attain the mean relative to themselves, since Milo and Micro each end up with the amount (according to Aristotle) of food they need and the wood with which to cook it. If Aristotle were to allege that Emporos made his profit by "taking it from" Milo and Micro, Emporos could reply that both Milo and Micro are both better off because of his services and he deserves his profit as a just return for his entrepreneurial contribution. In effect, Emporos has created an increase in value for both Milo and Micro, for which he deserves compensation. His entrepreneurial service is, arguably, an exercise of intellectual virtue by which he discovers potential value for each trading party and finds a way to make these potential values actual.

Banking

Aristotle's virtue theory also has a dimension relevant to moneylending and interest. For he describes how a mean can be intermediate between extremes in several respects:

> Moral virtue . . . is concerned with passions and actions, and in these there is excess, defect, and the intermediate. For instance, both fear and confidence and appetite and anger and pity and in general pleasure and pain may be felt both too much and too little, and in both cases not well; but to feel them *at*

the right times, with reference to the right objects, towards the right people, with the right aim, and in the right way, is what is both intermediate and best, and this is characteristic of excellence. Similarly with regard to actions also there is excess, defect, and the intermediate. (*NE* II.6.1106b16–24, emphasis added)

It is noteworthy that the first respect Aristotle mentions is "at the right times." Economists observe that agents prefer to have beneficial outcomes sooner (i.e., closer to the time of action) than later.[27] This seems reasonable. For example, it is better, other things being equal, for Phormio the banker to have 100 drachmas at his disposal now than to have them a year hence. Phormio might, however, prefer having 110 drachmas a year from now to having 100 drachmas now. On the other hand, in order to carry out a current project Aiteon might value having the 100 drachmas now over 110 drachmas a year from now. In this case, if Phormio lends the 100 drachmas to Aiteon, who agrees to repay him 110 drachmas a year from now, this is consistent with the payment and receipt of these amounts being the mean relatively to each of them when time preference is taken into consideration. If so, Phormio is not in the least compromising his virtue of justice by lending his money to Aiteon for interest. Indeed this may put the money to the best use for both of them. Once again this shows how a fair financial exchange can be based on mutual need (Aristotle's insight) and thus be compatible with moral virtue even though one party collects interest from the other.[28]

Commodity Speculation

In his anecdote about Thales and the olive presses, Aristotle alleges that Thales secured a monopoly so that he was able to charge "at whatever rate he chose." This involves two questionable claims. The first is that Thales established a monopoly. Though literally true because the Greek word *monopōlia* means "only one seller," it is misleading for Aristotle to identify Thales's scheme with that of city-states. For a state is able to establish a monopoly by legally permitting only one seller and erecting barriers to any competitors. Although Thales succeeded in becoming the only one subletting the presses, he was not in a position to prohibit competitors from entering the market. Hence, his advantageous position would be relatively short-lived, since others could make new olive presses and offer them for sale over time, which would tend to drive down the price. The second questionable claim is that Thales was able to charge "at whatever rate he chose." In fact, olive growers would not rent the presses for a higher amount than they expected they could earn from selling their oil. Hence, if Thales continued to increase the rate, more growers would be unwilling to rent, until beyond a certain price there would be no renters. Thales's optimal strategy would be to seek the rate at which he could maximize his earnings.[29]

Even granting these two points, however, Aristotle might still argue that through successful speculation about future prices Thales was able to reap "windfall" profits by charging more for the olive presses than their just price. In defense of Thales, however, it can be argued that he made a valuable contribution. Why did the olive-press owners not keep their presses until harvesttime and lend them out themselves? The answer, presumably, is that they did not know that the rate would go up; and, being disinclined to run the risk of a poor olive harvest, they were willing to pass the risk on to Thales. It can be argued that Thales's profits were the result of assuming this risk.[30] Aristotle also points out that Thales possessed knowledge that put him in an advantageous position. But knowledge is not a free good. It is costly to acquire, though it can yield benefits in a scenario such as that of Thales and the olive presses, in which case there is an incentive for others to gain access to this sort of knowledge.[31] Even if others lack Thales's prescience, if he were to make a successful career of commodity speculation, he would serve as an "early warning signal" of future gluts or shortages. Hence a case could be made that a speculator such as Thales is playing a valuable social role and is not a mere exploiter. For, again, it could be argued that he is using his knowledge to produce a value for others for which he has a just claim to compensation.

In conclusion, Aristotle's criticisms of practices such as commerce, banking, and speculation are not supported by his own virtue theory. It would seem that people could engage in these sorts of practices with their virtue intact. So far, however, what has been established, at most, is that these business practices are not necessarily unjust. It remains to be seen whether the actions of a businessperson could be the *expression* of moral virtue as Aristotle understands it.

THE GOOD PERSON AND THE GOOD BUSINESSPERSON

In order to consider in a more positive way the relationship between business practice and moral virtue it is helpful to distinguish between a good businessperson and a good person. Aristotle makes a similar distinction in diagnosing a sophistical joke perpetrated by Euthydemus of Chios: "Can a good person who is a shoemaker be bad? Yes, because the good person may also be a bad shoemaker, so that the good shoemaker will be bad!" (*Sophistical Refutations* 20.177b13–15). As Aristotle explains, this reasoning is fallacious because it trades on the ambiguity of the terms "good" and "bad." It is one thing to say that someone is a bad shoemaker and altogether another to say that someone is bad without qualification. This difference is implicit in the discussion of Aristotle's ethical principles discussed above. To be a bad shoemaker is to perform the function of a shoemaker poorly, while to be bad without qualification is to perform the function of a human being poorly, that is, to act irrationally and viciously. Since it is possible to perform the one function without performing the other, a bad shoemaker is not necessarily a bad human being: the same person could turn out inferior footwear and still act courageously or generously. Likewise a good shoemaker could be a bad human being: turning out fine footwear by day and committing heinous crimes like burglary or murder by night. Analogously, even if it were conceded that somebody could be a "good" businessperson in the sense of being good at business, a good (i.e., successful) businessperson could turn out to be a bad (i.e., vicious) human being.

Unfortunately, Aristotle goes further than this when he argues that commerce is an inherently "unnatural" and "justly disparaged" mode of seeking wealth, in contrast to the "necessary and commendable" way of acquiring wealth that belongs to the art of household management (*Pol.* I.9.1257b19–22, 10.1258a38–b8). According to Aristotle the household arises naturally out of the natural desire for self-preservation and reproduction and exists in order to satisfy the everyday needs of its members (I.2.1252a26–35, b12–14). It is the job of the household manager to acquire sufficient property necessary to meet these needs—for example, food, clothing, chattel, and implements. Hence, household management includes as a "natural part" the art of property acquisition the function of which is to obtain and preserve this necessary property (I.8.1256b26–39). In contrast, according to Aristotle, the aim of commerce is to exchange goods in order to increase the money in one's possession. He argues that this implies that commerce leads to the unlimited accumulation of money:

"For medicine aims at unlimited health, and each of the crafts acts to achieve its end in an unlimited way, since each tries to achieve it as fully as possible. (But none of the things that promote the end is unlimited, since the end itself constitutes a limit for all crafts)" (*Pol.* I.9.1257b23–28). Commerce is unnatural in Aristotle's view because it takes wealth, which should be a means to the highest human good (*eudaimonia*), and transforms it into an end in itself. Aristotle goes on to argue that people's baser desires attract them to this occupation: "They are preoccupied with living, not with living well. And since their appetite for life is unlimited, they also want an unlimited amount of what sustains it. And those who do aim at living well seek what promotes physical gratification. So, since this too seems to depend on having property, they spend their time acquiring wealth." Commerce arose because of this.[32] "For since their gratification lies in excess, they seek the craft that produces the excess needed for gratification" (1257b40–1258a8).

This argument assumes along with Aristotle's ethical theory that the best life consists in rational, morally virtuous activity. Happiness does not consist in mere physical gratification and the indulgence of whatever desires and appetites one happens to have. Material possessions are merely means to achieving the good life, and the same goes for the money needed to buy these things. Therefore, it would be "unnatural" (i.e., not in accord with the human natural end of the good life) for human beings to treat the accumulation of money as their ultimate end.

Even granting all of this, there are problems with Aristotle's argument, which could be understood in different ways. First, he might mean that commerce is objectionable because it has as its end the unlimited accumulation of wealth, which is in fact only a means to the good life. The problem with this argument is that commerce seems analogous to medicine. For medicine aims at health, which is also a means to the good life and not an end in itself. Even if Aristotle is correct that "medicine aims at unlimited health," it does not follow (nor would Aristotle suggest) that medicine is an unnatural art (that is, "unnatural" in the sense of frustrating human natural ends). We might agree that anyone who (happened to be a physician) made unlimited health care his summum bonum, the ultimate aim of all of his endeavors, would be acting unnaturally and irrationally (though some might see modern social democracies heading in this direction). But the highest end of an art can be subordinated to the end of another, higher art—for example, the art of living well. The same goes for business: even if business has as its sole end making profits, it does not follow that its end cannot be subordinate to a higher end such as living well (see *NE* I.1–2).[33] Alternatively, Aristotle might mean that commerce is unlike respectable arts like medicine because commerce sets no limits to the means to its goal. Unlike the doctor who limits a dose of a drug in order to cure a particular patient, the merchant strives for money without limit.[34] But this is unconvincing. For, as indicated in the example of Thales and the olive presses, Thales can make a profit only if he limits the price he charges a particular customer. If he tries to raise the price without limit, he will have no customers. Finally, Aristotle suggests that anyone engaged in business has unlimited self-gratification as a personal goal. Now it is true that some people enter business because they want to amass as much wealth as possible in order to indulge as many desires as possible. But other businesspeople have other motives that do not involve wealth maximization as a goal. They may simply want to become well-off enough to support their families, to raise money for a church or favorite charity, to support a nonlucrative avocation, and so forth.[35]

Despite the problems with Aristotle's argument, it does offer a valuable insight. Business occupations, including medicine, shoemaking, and other "walks of life," have specific aims that should not be confused with our highest ends as human beings. Human happiness or flourishing consists in the full actualization of our highest potentialities. "We must strain every nerve to live in accordance with the best thing in us" (*NE* X.7.1177b33–34). The best thing in us according to Aristotle is our rational capacity, which we should devote as far as possible to the pursuit of knowledge. Nonetheless, he further remarks that because we are human beings with bodies as well as souls who must live in society with other human beings, our happiness also involves practical wisdom and moral virtue (8.1178b5–6). And in order to perform these virtuous actions we require what Aristotle calls "external goods," including bodily health and strength, family and friends, education, material possessions, and, yes, money. The provision and preserving of these external goods constitute the function of a wide range of arts and crafts. Even if we disagree with Aristotle and recognize commerce and banking as legitimate occupations, we can still agree with him that the function of such endeavors is to provide the external goods required for human flourishing and moral virtue. Insofar as businesspeople are virtuous moral agents, they should practice business in a manner conducive to these higher ends. That is, they should promote, and not undermine, the happiness (or flourishing) and moral character of themselves and of their customers and associates.[36]

Aristotle's argument has recently been restated by Alasdair MacIntyre, who contends that the myopic preoccupation of modern businesspeople with the bottom line is inimical to virtue. Businesspeople aim only to heap up external goods like physical possessions and money. But these are external goods of which there is only a limited supply. The inevitable result is dog-eat-dog competition, like a zero-sum game in which there can be gainers only if there are losers. In contrast, virtue is manifested in what MacIntyre calls "practices," that is, socially established cooperative activities that involve internal goods. An internal good consists in successfully satisfying the standards of excellence appropriate to the practice: in other words, doing a job well.[37] Virtue so understood, according to MacIntyre, is inevitably crowded out by an obsession with profits. He contrasts the pride of workmanship found in traditional crafts such as carpentry, husbandry, fishing, and so forth.[38] Against MacIntyre's view, John Dobson argues persuasively that businesspeople can strive for personal excellence in the same way as other practitioners. He argues further that profit seeking is consistent with adopting a virtuous corporate mission and strategy, namely, of producing something of value worthy of exchange for value.[39]

CONCLUDING REMARKS

The foregoing discussion hopefully sheds light on our initial puzzle: why Aristotle is viewed as both friend and foe of business. Aristotle's own criticisms of commerce, banking, speculation, and profit seeking have been echoed by opponents of business down through the centuries. Nonetheless, as I have argued here, one could accept the principles of Aristotle's virtue ethics but reject the manner in which he applies them when he unqualifiedly condemns business practices. But even if "virtuous businessperson" is not an oxymoron, we should still grant that being good at business is not the same thing as being virtuous. This is where Aristotle may still have something to offer. A neo-Aristotelian virtue ethics—that is, a theory of virtue based on Aristotle's principles but freed from his erroneous applications—may after all provide a framework for modern business ethics.

ACKNOWLEDGMENTS

Ben Bryan, Lawrence Jost, David Keyt, Alexander Rosenberg, and the editors of this volume made valuable comments on earlier drafts. I also received helpful feedback during presentations at the Center for the Philosophy of Freedom at the University of Arizona, George Mason University, Georgetown University, the University of Kansas, the Catholic University of Leuven, the University of Vienna, Loyola University New Orleans, and California State University, San Bernardino.

NOTES

1. Tom Morris, *If Aristotle Ran General Motors: The New Soul of Business* (New York: Henry Holt, 1997), 213–14.

2. See Robert C. Solomon, "Corporate Roles, Personal Virtues: An Aristotelian Approach to Business Ethics," *Business Ethics Quarterly* 2 (1992): 317–39; Solomon, "Aristotle, Ethics, and Business Organizations," *Organization Studies* 25 (2004): 1021–43; and Solomon, *Ethics and Excellence: Cooperation and Integrity in Business* (Oxford: Oxford University Press, 1993). Several essays by Edwin M. Hartman are collected in *Virtue in Business: Conversations with Aristotle* (Cambridge: Cambridge University Press, 2013).

3. Alasdair MacIntyre, *After Virtue: A Study in Moral Theory* (Notre Dame, IN: University of Notre Dame Press, 1984), 254.

4. Antony Flew, *Social Life and Moral Judgment* (New Brunswick, NJ: Transaction, 2003), 120.

5. Scholars disagree over whether the ancient Greek economy was essentially modern or primitive. Michael Rostovtzeff, in *The Social and Economic History of the Hellenistic World* (Oxford: Oxford University Press, 1941), defends the view that the Hellenistic Greeks had a fully functioning market economy. Against this, Johannes Hasebroek, *Trade and Politics in Ancient Greece* (London: G. Bell, 1933; repr., Chicago: Ares, 1978), and M. I. Finley, *Economy and Society in Ancient Greece* (New York: Viking, 1982), argue that ancient Greek economic relations were "embedded" in other social institutions and thus not subject to impersonal forces of supply and demand as in modern economies. The controversy hinges, in part, on how a "market economy" is defined, and it is also often obscured by ideological presuppositions.

6. A useful overview by Darel Tai Engen, "The Economy of Ancient Greece," *Economic History Services*, February 1, 2010, http://eh.net/encyclopedia/article/engen.greece, is the

source of some of the information in this section. For in-depth discussion, see *The Cambridge Economic History of the Greco-Roman World*, ed. Walter Scheidel, Ian Morris, and Richard P. Saller (Cambridge: Cambridge University Press, 2007) , chaps. 12–14, on the economy of classical Greece.

7. William T. Loomis argues that wage levels were influenced by market forces and responded to inflation and deflation; Loomis, *Wages, Welfare Costs, and Inflation in Classical Athens* (Ann Arbor: University of Michigan Press, 1998).

8. See H. Knorringa, *Emporos: Data on Trade and Trader in Greek Literature from Homer to Aristotle* (Amsterdam: H. J. Paris, 1926; repr., Chicago: Ares, 1987).

9. P. Millett contends that the Greek economy was precapitalist: lending and borrowing were mainly for the sake of consumption, and bankers played no significant role in making loans; Millett, *Lending and Borrowing in Ancient Athens* (Cambridge: Cambridge University Press, 1991). Against this, Edward E. Cohen argues that fourth-century Athenian bankers engaged in sophisticated commercial transactions including maritime loans; Cohen, *Athenian Economy and Society: A Banking Perspective* (Princeton, NJ: Princeton University Press, 1992). Cohen provides evidence that banking activities were largely unregulated except for the enforcement of contracts. There is, however, no evidence of fractional reserve banking.

10. K. J. Dover, *Greek Popular Morality in the Time of Plato and Aristotle* (Indianapolis: Hackett, 1994), 40–41.

11. Ibid., 172–73. For an opposing modern view that virtue ethics is consistent with business practice, see Deirdre N. McCloskey, *The Bourgeois Virtues: Ethics for an Age of Commerce* (Chicago: University of Chicago Press, 2006).

12. Translations of Plato's *Laws* are from Thomas L. Pangle, *The Laws of Plato* (Chicago: University of Chicago Press, 1980).

13. See Mark S. Peacock's essay in this volume for further discussion of Plato and his predecessors.

14. Translations from Aristotle's *Politics* (abbreviated *Pol.*) are from Aristotle, *Politics*, trans. C. D. C. Reeve (Indianapolis: Hackett, 1998).

15. For a recent interpretation and critical examination, see David Keyt, "Aristotle and the Joy of Working" in *Nature and Justice: Studies in the Ethical and Political Philosophy of Plato and Aristotle* (Louvain-la-Neuve: Peeters, 2016), 223–39.

16. This argument assumes Aristotle's theory that some human beings are suited by nature to be slaves (see *Pol.* I.3–7). For modern commentary on one of Aristotle's most objectionable doctrines, see Malcolm Schofield, "Ideology and Philosophy in Aristotle's Theory of Slavery," in *Aristotle's Politics: Critical Essays*, ed. Richard Kraut and Steven Skultety (Lanham, MD: Rowman and Littlefield, 2005), 91–119; and Nicholas D. Smith, "Aristotle's Theory of Natural Slavery," in *A Companion to Aristotle's "Politics,"* ed. David Keyt and Fred D. Miller, Jr. (Oxford: Blackwell, 1991), 142–55.

17. Translations from Aristotle's *Nicomachean Ethics* (abbreviated *NE*) are by W. D. Ross (revised by J. O. Urmson), from Jonathan Barnes, ed., *The Complete Works of Aristotle: The Revised Oxford Translation* (Princeton, NJ: Princeton University Press, 1984).

18. Aristotle's term *ison* can mean either "equal" or "fair" and is equivalent to *dikaion*, "just," in this context. See *NE* V.1.1129a31–b1.

19. On this and other issues in Aristotle's economic theory, see the excellent collection of reprinted articles edited by Mark Blaug: *Aristotle (383–211 BC)* (Brookfield, VT: Elgar, 1991). This volume includes M. I. Finley's influential and highly critical essay "Aristotle and Economic Analysis" (1970). Scott Meikle offers a sympathetic interpretation in *Aristotle's Economic Thought* (Oxford: Clarendon Press, 1995). Meikle also argues that Aristotle was an important influence on Karl Marx's theory of value in *Capital*. For a critical review of Meikle, see Fred D. Miller, Jr., "Was Aristotle the First Economist?," *Apeiron* 31, no. 4 (1998): 387–98.

20. See Raymond de Roover, "The Concept of the Just Price: Theory and Economic Policy," *Journal of Economic History* 18 (1958): 418–34; and John W. Baldwin, "The Medieval

Theories of the Just Price: Romanists, Canonists, and Theologians in the Twelfth and Thirteenth Centuries," *Transactions of the American Philosophical Society* 49, no. 4 (1959): 5–90. See also Martin Schlag's essay on Thomas Aquinas in this volume.

21. See Todd S. Mei, "The Preeminence of Use: Reevaluating the Relation between Use and Exchange in Aristotle's Economic Thought," *Journal of the History of Philosophy* 47, no. 4 (2009): 523–48.

22. Peter Hadreas discusses the relationship of virtue to wealth in "Aristotle on the Vices and Virtue of Wealth," *Journal of Business Ethics* 39 (2002): 361–76.

23. For further discussion, see Scott Meikle, "Aristotle on Business," *Classical Quarterly*, n.s., 46 (1996): 138–51; and Denis Collins, "Aristotle and Business," *Journal of Business Ethics* 6 (1987): 567–72.

24. "Usury" translates *obolostatikē*, literally, "the art of weighing coins" (an obol was an Athenian coin). For the ancient Greeks the related term *obolostatēs*, "coin weigher," had a connotation like "loan shark." Today "usury" commonly means "charging exorbitant interest," but it formerly referred to any charging of interest on a loan.

25. See Odd Langholm, *The Aristotelian Analysis of Usury* (Bergen: Universitetsforlaget, 1984).

26. This discussion follows the analysis offered by A. R. J. Turgot in an essay written in 1769 and republished as "Value and Money," in *The Economics of A. R. J. Turgot*, ed. and trans. P. D. Groenewegen (Hague: Martinus Nijhoff, 1977), 133–48. Turgot observes: "The introduction of exchange between our two men increases the wealth of both of them, that is, it gives them both a greater quantity of satisfaction in return for the same resources" (144). The example used here is adapted from Turgot to relate to Aristotle's virtue theory.

27. See Murray N. Rothbard, "Time Preference," in *The New Palgrave: A Dictionary of Economics*, ed. John Eatwell, Murray White, and Peter Newman (London: Macmillan, 1987), 4:644–46.

28. Turgot explains originary interest in terms of time preference in a paper written in 1770 and republished in condensed form as "Extracts from 'Paper on Lending at Interest,'" in Groenewegen, *The Economics of A. R. J. Turgot*, 149–63. Turgot rejects the view that exchange should be judged as just or unjust based on the "intrinsic value" or "metaphysical equality" of the commodities exchanged.

29. This strategy may have been followed by a Sicilian (mentioned by Aristotle) who managed to triple his investment in iron ore without charging an exorbitant amount (*Pol.* I.12.1259a23–28).

30. Modern economists distinguish between risk (where an outcome has an objective probability) and uncertainty. Perhaps the olive-press owners were acting under uncertainty (regarding how the weather would affect the future harvest and hence the demand for olive presses) and made a rational decision to lease them to Thales, who was also acting rationally based on his scientific expertise. See Frank H. Knight, *Risk, Uncertainty, and Profit* (Boston: Houghton Mifflin, 1921). On the role of speculation in the modern economy, see also Gregory J. Millman, "Futures and Options Markets," in *The Concise Encyclopedia of Economics*, ed. David R. Henderson, 2nd ed. (Indianapolis: Liberty Fund, 2007), 207–11.

31. Thomas Sowell remarks that "knowledge can be enormously costly": a basic problem of society is how to communicate and coordinate the knowledge scattered throughout the population; Sowell, *Knowledge and Decisions* (New York: Basic Books, 1980), 26. See also Friedrich A. Hayek, "The Use of Knowledge in Society," *American Economic Review* 35, no. 4 (1945): 519–30; reprinted in Hayek, *Individualism and Economic Order* (Chicago: University of Chicago Press, 1972), 77–91. See Karen I. Vaughn's essay on Hayek in this volume.

32. At 1258a5–6 he says: "The other kind of wealth acquisition arose because of this"; and at 1257b20 he identifies commerce with this other kind of wealth acquisition.

33. The economist Milton Friedman sparked a debate by contending that "the social responsibility of business is to increase its profits" (*New York Times Magazine* September 13,

1970). A neo-Aristotelian might argue that this contention turns on how "social responsibility" is defined. If it means the function of a businessperson *as* businessperson, Friedman's claim is correct. But if we mean by it the function of a businessperson as a virtuous human being, he is incorrect.

34. See Hadreas, "Aristotle on the Vices and Virtue of Wealth," 370, for this interpretation.

35. This may be the point of the parenthetical remark that "the end itself constitutes a limit for all crafts" (1257b27–28). Compare Hadreas, "Aristotle on the Vices and Virtue of Wealth," 371.

36. Edwin M. Hartman argues that business firms competing in the market can generate social capital, "a set of connections that encourage collective action that is mutually beneficial in that it leads to win-win situations and preservation of the commons"; Hartman, "Virtue, Profit, and the Separation Thesis: An Aristotelian View," *Journal of Business Ethics* 99 (2011): 15 n. 18.

37. MacIntyre, *After Virtue*, 187.

38. Alasdair MacIntyre, "Why Are the Problems of Business Ethics Insoluble?," in *Moral Responsibility and the Professions*, ed. Bernard Baumrin and Benjamin Freedman (New York: Haven Publishing, 1982), 227–50; and MacIntyre, "A Partial Response to My Critics," in *After MacIntyre: Critical Perspectives on the Work of Alasdair MacIntyre*, ed. J. Horton and S. Mendus (Notre Dame, IN: University of Notre Dame Press, 1994).

39. John Dobson, "Alasdair MacIntyre's Aristotelian Business Ethics: A Critique," *Journal of Business Ethics* 86 (2009): 43–50. In support, Dobson cites John Roberts, who maintains that "firms are institutions created to serve human needs [and] to provide meaningful experiences"; Roberts, *The Modern Firm: Organizational Design for Performance and Growth* (Oxford: Oxford University Press, 2004), 18.

CHAPTER 3

Confucian Business Ethics: Possibilities and Challenges

David Elstein and Qing Tian

Confucianism was, at least in name, the dominant political ideology in China for much of the imperial period (roughly the tenth to twentieth century),[1] but it was also extremely significant in shaping moral and political theories in premodern Korea and Japan. Its legacy today remains contested. Max Weber, famously, held Confucianism responsible for obstructing the development of capitalism in East Asia.[2] More recently some scholars credit Confucianism for the current economic rise of East Asia, whereas others see it as either irrelevant, or even an obstruction.[3] The negative portrayal may be motivated by the fact that Confucian philosophy historically has not handled nonideal situations well (i.e., what to do when moral persuasion fails); in fact, the proper employment of laws and other coercive measures remains a contested issue among Confucians. However, the contribution of Confucianism to business and economic ethics is particularly relevant because of the recent resurgence of interest in Confucian thought and practices in China.[4] In this essay we explore what a Confucian business ethics would look like, with some attention to the problems that attend the all-too-easy conflation of "Chinese culture" with "Confucianism" and the common lack of attention to actual Confucian sources. Confucian thought may be able to provide some ground for a practical ethics for business, but this requires creative extrapolation from original sources. Contrary to some claims,[5] Confucianism is less a closed ethical system than an evolving tradition that historically focused on practical morals rather than theory construction. Because of this, there is potential to derive some general and practical conclusions about business ethics from what is found in the texts. This is one of the aims of this essay.

Ethics is at the heart of Confucian philosophy. Classical Confucian philosophers were particularly concerned about the effects of unchecked selfishness and greed. This has led some scholars to claim its precepts and principles can be applied to businesses. Yet often these discussions equate Confucianism with East Asian culture, asserting a strong Confucian influence in modern East Asia without specifying what that is and often without connecting its alleged influence to ideas in specific Confucian texts.[6] The difficulty of generating practical recommendations for the conduct of business from Confucian thought is not always appreciated. At times, whether or not Confucian ideas are true is assumed without argument or simply brushed aside.[7] Other times, Confucianism is held responsible for flawed business practices in China, without careful consideration of whether such practices are in fact justified by Confucian thought, or whether they derive from other sources.[8] Our goal here is to move beyond simplistic accounts of Confucian ethics by attending closely to classical Confucian texts and how their philosophy might apply to business, while also noting where Confucian ethics may be vague or unable to address certain business problems.

An additional difficulty is defining "Confucianism." Frequently "Confucianism" is employed as a metonym for Chineseness or Chinese culture in general, but this usage neglects the diversity of Chinese culture and the variations within Confucianism itself. The move to identify "Chinese" with "Confucian" probably dates from the criticisms of Chinese tradition that became particularly heated during the early twentieth century. Proponents of modernization in China were very critical of virtually all traditional practices and ways of thinking, and latched onto Confucianism as a convenient catchall for what they wanted to eliminate. This sparked a conservative reaction that agreed that Confucianism is the essence of being Chinese but argued that casting Confucianism aside meant giving up on Chinese culture.[9] Shades of this continue today: some scholars blame Confucianism for *everything* that is wrong in China, while others see Confucianism as the *only* possible source of salvation. Both sides tend to a monolithic and essentialized understanding of Confucianism at odds with historical sources. Often scholars attribute values or practices to Confucianism without tracing them to specific texts, rendering it questionable whether these are part of Confucian philosophy or parts of Chinese culture unrelated to Confucian thought.

Relations among individuals and between individuals and institutions are major areas of concern in Confucian thought. Many discussions of business ethics address the role of the individual in ethical decision-making, as well as the responsibilities of organizations. In this essay, we provide a description and analysis of how Confucian philosophy can influence the ethical decision-making of both individuals and firms, taking into account the relation between persons and organizations. In this respect, Confucianism does have implications for business ethics. The frequent criticisms leveled against Confucian thought have little to do with Confucian philosophy as articulated in the foundational texts. At the same time, Confucianism does have weak points, particularly in developing institutions and regulations, and it is hardly a solution to all potential ethical problems in commerce.[10]

The immediate difficulty faced when trying to write about Confucian business ethics is that there are few clear statements in the texts: early Confucian philosophers had much to say about ethics and politics but fairly little on the ethics of exchange and commerce. Economic matters are most often addressed at the political level, and exchange between individuals or nonpolitical actors is not a common topic. So it must be recognized at the outset that when we speak about "Confucian business ethics," we mean mainly what can be reasonably extrapolated from Confucian philosophy, not what is expressed explicitly. There will naturally be some controversy about the core tenets of Confucian philosophy and, especially, about what counts as a reasonable extrapolation from them. Such potential controversy is fruitful: extrapolation is one way Confucianism continues to evolve as a tradition.

It is naturally impossible to review every significant Confucian text of the past two thousand and more years, so we focus on the two most historically significant thinkers, Kongzi (Confucius) and Mengzi (Mencius), and how they are represented in the classical texts associated with them. Given that virtually every Confucian up to the present day sees them as having established the basic doctrines of Confucianism, if an idea cannot be found in their works, or is not consistent with what they said, it does not have much claim on being part of Confucian thought.

Since classical Confucian philosophers did not directly address business ethics, the method here will be to consider Confucian thought in general and politics in particular and then apply these principles to particular questions in business ethics. When considered this way, both Confucian conceptions of the person and the relation between the state and the people are relevant to developing Confucian business ethics. We will look at Confucian ideas of virtue and the communal nature of the person as well as the Confucian conception of government and leadership. We first outline Confucian ethics and then set forth the basis on which a business ethics might, in principle, be developed from such a perspective. We then consider some specific applications to issues in business, and conclude with a description of the Confucian idea of the harmonious society and its implications for business conduct.

CONFUCIAN VIRTUES

Both Kongzi and Mengzi talk about cultivating states of character more than adhering to principles or utilizing a decision procedure for determining ethical action. Exactly how to categorize Confucian ethics is a matter of debate in the contemporary literature.[11] A virtue ethics interpretation is common among Anglophone scholars, while a number of Sinophone scholars maintain instead that Confucianism is a form of deontology.[12] Both have textual support: Kongzi and Mengzi did talk frequently about states of character, but on occasion there are appeals to rules and to the importance of intentions. It is somewhat anachronistic to insist that Confucian philosophy must be one or the other, when a strict separation between them did not exist at the time: rules or virtues might be emphasized in different contexts. For application to business ethics we recognize that character dispositions prove significant even as we sidestep the question of the ultimate source or grounding of the virtues.

There is greater consensus among contemporary Confucians on what the virtues are than about how to categorize Confucian ethics. Mengzi lists four main virtues: benevolence (*ren*), righteousness (*yi*), ritual propriety (*li*), and wisdom (*zhi*). Of these, he talks about benevolence and righteousness the most. These are both prominent in Kongzi's thought as well ("benevolence" is more general for Kongzi and is sometimes translated simply as "Goodness"), along with trustworthiness (*xin*), dutifulness (*zhong*), filial piety (*xiao*), and understanding (*shu*, also translated as "empathy" or "reciprocity").

There is no attempt at defining these virtues systematically in Kongzi; even in Mengzi it is not always clear how to understand them, and there are different accounts in various commentaries. Confucians do not provide necessary and sufficient conditions for them. Let us start with the less controversial virtues.

Trustworthiness means being true to one's word, and often is associated with considering one's words carefully before speaking. Dutifulness is serving conscientiously, usually directed toward someone higher in status.[13] Filial piety is serving one's parents with respect. Though it is often associated with obedience, early Confucians make clear it does not mean blind obedience to parental wishes and commands, a point relevant for Confucian leadership.[14] Propriety is both knowing and following ritual standards appropriately, but also knowing how and when to bend them. Wisdom means knowing what is right and what is wrong.[15]

Understanding (reciprocity) is akin to the Golden Rule. Kongzi described it as "not impos[ing] upon others what you yourself do not desire."[16] Understanding includes elements of altruism and empathy. People should not impose on others what they themselves do not want and, more positively, should realize that advancing the self requires advancing others. Understanding is the act of considering and to some extent identifying with the interests of others. Such a virtue emphasizes the dialectical unity of self-interest and altruism and affirms people's responsibility to others and the community.

This leaves the more difficult-to-define qualities of benevolence and righteousness, but here we find greater discrepancies between Kongzi and Mengzi. As mentioned above, "benevolence" or "goodness" is used as a general term for "virtue" for Kongzi, but in Mengzi it is used more narrowly to mean an attitude of sincere interest in others' well-being. In Kongzi, goodness results from an individual's self-cultivation.[17] Confucian goodness represents an attitude toward others and helps shape behavior for proper social interaction. Kongzi said, "Desiring to take his stand, one who is Good helps others to take their stand; wanting to realize himself, he helps others realize themselves."[18] One is obligated to help others to develop morally in the process of developing one's moral self. Moral development and flourishing occurs not in isolation but in close connection with others. Mengzi used the parent-child relationship as the paradigm of benevolence: a benevolent person cares for others as children care for their parents, which Kongzi pointed out is based on children initially receiving care from their parents.[19] Extended to politics, Mengzi encouraged rulers to practice benevolent government, implying that those holding power should demonstrate sincere concern for their subjects' well-being.[20] This model of benevolent leadership will be examined below in connection with corporations and business ethics.

Kongzi regarded righteousness in terms of a conscious adherence to the norms and moral standards of society. Righteousness in Mengzi is something like according respect appropriate to another's social role, though it is also connected with a sense of shame more generally.[21] The connection with shame is apparent in Kongzi's thought. There righteousness is linked to not having excessive concern for profit,[22] a point we return to subsequently. Mengzi's more explicit definitions of benevolence and righteousness were dominant in most of the Confucian tradition. Both Kongzi and Mengzi describe a person who has all of the above virtues and knows how to balance them as an ethical exemplar—a "superior man," a "gentleman," or the more exalted "sage." The opposite of the superior is the petty man. A focus on exemplary role models is characteristic of Confucian ethical education.

Having outlined the core ideas of each virtue, we turn briefly to a salient element of moral education, the social context, and then consider how a Confucian business ethics may build upon an analogy between politics and corporations. The social environment has a tremendous effect on the development of virtue according to Confucians. An emphasis on family relations is in large part due to the fact that the family is the first site for learning moral values. However, it is not the only one. Community more generally has substantial influence. The practice of the Confucian virtues is also primarily social. Most virtues require a community for their realization; moreover, to put the virtues into practice requires understanding social norms and the roles of the people involved. Some scholars go so far as to say that the person is defined entirely in terms of social relations in Confucian thought.[23] Although that is textually and philosophically controversial, the details of the debate need not concern us. The importance of the proper social environment is sufficient for our purposes.

We suggest that Confucian conceptions of government and society and their proper relation provide one useful model for understanding the role of business. Obviously corporations did not exist in ancient China, and trade was probably a fairly marginal part of the economy. If we are to derive anything approaching guidelines for corporations, then we must look to other, analogous aspects of Confucian thought. Confucian views on politics are one route, since Confucians have a great deal to say about political leadership. Classical Confucians were especially concerned about government, probably because it was the institution with the greatest power to influence people. They assumed significant individual mobility and that people would move to states with superior government, much as people can choose to patronize the businesses that they prefer. In contemporary developed economies, corporate influence can have substantial effect on both public policy and individuals' lives; therefore, extrapolation from Confucian political thought offers a fruitful way of developing Confucian conceptions of the role of the corporation and of the responsibilities of leadership in business.[24]

Based on Confucian political and economic thought, we can speculate on general principles that would inform Confucian business ethics. Here we summarize these general principles; subsequent sections will develop the applications to contemporary business ethics. Confucian philosophers did not oppose pursuing wealth, but did insist it be done in an ethical manner. The purpose of trade is to distribute goods where they are needed. Mengzi said, "When the ancients had markets, they were for exchanging what they had for what they lacked."[25] Although merchants had a poor reputation in traditional China, Confucian philosophers did recognize that trade is valuable.[26] They opposed excessive accumulations of wealth by rulers, and the unequal distribution of wealth in general was a concern. Mengzi encouraged rulers to share their wealth with the people rather than hoard it themselves, since the people's interests are more important. When there is a conflict between what is profitable and what is right, the choice should always be what is right. With these general views in mind, we will consider how they apply to particular questions in management and business ethics.

SPECIFIC APPLICATIONS TO BUSINESS ETHICS

Confucian Leadership

In Confucian political thought, the government's primary duty is conceived in terms of providing for the people's economic and ethical fulfillment. Economic needs take priority, but the government must also take an active role in providing ethical education; without this, as Mengzi said, people "come close to being animals."[27] Education should encourage development of the Confucian virtues, such as filial piety; in addition, rulers should conduct

David Elstein and Qing Tian

themselves so as to be moral exemplars. Economically, good rulership meant refraining from excessive taxation and other policies that would unduly burden the people, but rulers are also enjoined to share their wealth with the people (classical Chinese philosophers did not distinguish state wealth from the ruler's personal property). Confucian government can be usefully understood as a kind of trusteeship: the ruler is given power to make decisions that will benefit the people, but this power is conditional on exercising it properly. Rulers who disregard the public's welfare can be removed.[28] Confucian government is more activist than classical liberalism: the government should do more than prevent people from interfering with each other; it should promote particular virtues and provide for people's economic needs, both by ensuring the conditions for people to pursue reasonable livelihoods and by direct economic assistance when necessary.

By considering the government's obligations to the people and looking at the few discussions of ethical issues surrounding wealth accumulation in the early sources, we can derive some basic principles for Confucian business ethics. In Kongzi and Mengzi's time, China was divided into numerous small states that competed among each other for territory and power, analogous to the way modern corporations compete for market share. This again suggests that understanding how Confucians looked at political competition may provide insight regarding economic competition.

Foremost, the role of the government is to serve the people's real interests (which may diverge from their felt preferences). As Mengzi said, the people are the most important part of the state; the ruler is last. The government is to enrich the people, not accumulate wealth itself.[29] Although rulers may have particular obligations to their own people, they are not to fulfill these at the expense of their neighbors (such as by invading them).[30] Applied to corporations, this may discourage efforts to put competitors out of business solely for the sake of market share, but would encourage competition to best serve consumers. Mengzi set fairly restrictive conditions for the justifiable invasion of another state and imposed strict limits as to who could lead such an incursion. It would have to be in the best interest of the people of the occupied state and could not be motivated simply by gain for territory and power.[31] On the other hand, attracting people to one's state by providing better conditions was praised. Kongzi spoke out against obtaining wealth by improper means and further enriching the wealthy.[32] This suggests that Confucians would see the purpose of corporations as producing wealth for society at large, not enriching the already wealthy. In terms of business practice, these principles suggest ethical limits (and legal restrictions when necessary) on practices that may benefit a business but not the larger public, such as attempting to secure a monopoly or lobbying for government favors (rent seeking).

Economic practices should benefit all classes of society, not just those in power. As Confucians were mainly addressing rulers, they focused on how those in power could economically oppress the less-advantaged. Confucians did not insist on a strictly equal distribution of wealth but were concerned with the least well-off. Kongzi said, "Those who possess a state or noble house are not [directly] concerned about . . . poverty, but rather concerned that what wealth they have is fairly distributed. If wealth is fairly distributed, there should be no poverty."[33] However, what fair distribution means is not spelled out, and it is unclear what this means for wealth distribution in society. A general Confucian principle is that the closer the relationship, the greater the obligation to care for the needs of the other party, so family takes priority over neighbors, who in turn take priority over strangers.[34] Mengzi presumes that rulers will be concerned for the welfare of their people more than those of neighboring states. Applied to businesses, this might mean that corporations have greater obligations to their shareholders and employees—those with a closer relationship to the corporation—but these would not justify courses of action that could harm others. Although there are greater obligations to those with whom one has closer relationships, some level of benevolence should be extended to everyone. Mengzi, for example, talks about caring for all within the four seas (i.e., the entire world),[35] though he does not mean treating everyone identically. One weakness in Confucian thought is balancing particular obligations with more impartial demands. For example, how businesses should balance employee interests and overall consumer good would be a difficult problem for Confucian business ethics.

Confucian concepts of benevolence and virtue manifest in the superior person, and may find application in moral leadership and governance. Confucian leadership is often mistakenly identified with paternalism. However, paternalism is not unique to China but prevalent in other non-Western regions, such as the Asia-Pacific, Middle East, and Latin America.[36] Some scholars claim paternalistic leadership, at least in Chinese culture, is influenced by Confucianism.[37] To be sure, there are paternalistic elements in Confucian theories of government: rulers are referred to as "father and mother to the people," and the public is given virtually no decision-making power.[38] Whether Confucian leadership *is* paternalistic is debatable, but it is surely weaker than paternalistic leadership that uses law or regulation. A good Confucian leader should lead by the power of example, not by coercion.[39] A leader who has to use threats to compel obedience has failed. In business as well, leaders should themselves model the kind of conduct they want in their employees; the manager whose conduct exemplifies dedication, honesty, and fair treatment will inspire employees to act accordingly. Confucians never thought obedience should be unconditional: people are expected to make moral judgments on their own. As already mentioned, a bad ruler can be removed. Kongzi and Mengzi expect people to leave the service or territory of a poor ruler to find a better one.[40] Analogously, business leaders have an obligation to model virtuous behavior at least within the context of the business; moreover, competition is necessary: both employees and consumers need to be able to leave one enterprise for another to induce firms to address their interests.

Nonetheless, leader-centered businesses, especially those with structures of institutionalized paternalism, could be a breeding ground for cronyism, favoritism, or nepotism when the leader's power is used illegitimately. Cronyism is likely to occur in organizations when the stress on the relationship between leaders and subordinates is so great that it transforms into strong in-group bias or when loyalty becomes unconditional.[41] For instance, cronyism is involved if private enterprises obtain illegal access to credit through a personal relationship with the executives of Chinese banks.[42] By way of further illustration, consider the leader who uses his power to help a friend's child secure a job in his firm. It is doubtful whether Confucianism actually justifies such favoritism, but it is true that historically Confucians struggled with actual or potential conflicts between family loyalty and upholding impartial morality and law.[43]

Confucianism does not support nepotism and cronyism, but in practice it may not provide sufficient safeguards against them, especially given its preference for relying on individual moral decisions. Historically Confucians have been suspicious of relying on laws and institutions to reform behavior, and even some contemporary Confucians seem to think penal law is ideally unnecessary.[44] In fact, Confucianism does not reject law and punishment but is only against the *replacement* of the rule of virtue or benevolence by the rule of law. This emphasis on the power of virtue has sometimes led to underestimating the limits of ethical models or the influence of virtue and disregarding the role of law and other coercive measures. While the texts themselves do not spell this out precisely, the ideal situation is one in which most people are transformed by exemplary models to the extent that they behave virtuously to a significant degree, even if they are not strictly speaking virtuous. This sort of ideal situation, not always attainable of course, is the end state at which Confucian morality and politics aims.

In politics, the Confucian ideal situation includes two crucial assumptions: rulers must be virtuous (*shengjun xianxiang*, "sagely rulers and worthy ministers"), and virtuous rulers will influence citizens to transform themselves of their own accord, rendering coercive measures largely unnecessary. As Joseph Chan notes, this ideal may not be realistic for a variety of reasons, and even when attained, it cannot be guaranteed. What to do when these circumstances do not obtain was never a significant topic in classical Confucianism. Contemporary Confucians will probably have to give more attention to nonideal situations than they have historically.[45] The necessity to give more attention to nonideal circumstances likely extends to regulating commerce. A more approachable aim is reducing the need for punishment through ethical cultivation, rather than hoping to eliminate punishments completely.[46]

Recognizing the limits of ethical appeals provides the basis on which we can expect virtuous leadership and the legal system to complement each other.[47] In practice, without an ethical culture and climate, autocratic or authoritarian leadership and punishment alone can neither effectively build trust and understanding between leaders and employees or regulate employees' work behavior. Confucian ideals or virtues, when applied, may lead to the moral improvement of people engaged in business and help them acquire the attitudes and behavior that organizations require. Yet legal measures may still be necessary in cases where socialization is inadequate or the temptations of gain too strong.

Organizational Citizenship Behavior

There may be a motivational similarity between Confucian virtue and what is commonly referred to as "organizational citizenship behavior." The essential element in this notion is the importance of behaviors "that lubricate the social machinery of the organization but that do not directly inhere in the usual notion of task performance."[48] Whether as act or omission, organizational citizenship behavior refers to conduct beneficial to the goals of the firm and helpful to colleagues, even as the conduct is not specified by contractual requirements, receives no formal compensation, nor is sanctioned by any penalty. Such voluntary behavior is closely related to the Confucian virtues of benevolence (*ren*) and understanding (*shu*). The phrase ("organizational citizenship behavior") does not appear in ancient Confucian texts, but similar ideas are evident, including obligations to one's community and the virtue of empathy or reciprocity. Empathy may be understood as "an other-oriented response involving some vicariously induced emotion (e.g., concern)."[49] Although it is not affect-based, the Confucian analogue of empathy, understanding or reciprocity (*shu*), requires one to consider and to respect the interests of others, even as one acknowledges one's own interests. Empathy correlates significantly with organizational citizenship behavior and helpfulness.[50]

Confucian reciprocity could also motivate organizational citizenship behavior. The ethic of reciprocity, as in the Golden Rule, is widely accepted as a moral tenet. In reciprocal interaction, "the recipient feels indebted to the favor or benefit giver until [that person] repays,"[51] and the giver who provides favors will trust that the obligation will be repaid.[52] Although this form of egoistic motivation is not strictly moral, Confucians recognize two levels of motivation. At the higher level one experiences joy in virtue for its own sake,[53] but Confucians also appeal to the lower motivation of self-interest by pointing out the benefits of virtuous action, recognizing that some persons may not appreciate the intrinsic value of virtue.

The Confucian virtue of understanding can also enhance positive workplace behavior. As described above, it includes a disposition to help others, but it also requires that one not do to others what one does not desire done to oneself. In business literature, organizational citizenship behavior is regarded as an outcome of exchange and reciprocity.[54] When employees feel well treated by their managers or the organization they serve, they will generally be motivated to reciprocate that favorable treatment and contribute to the organization beyond their in-role duties.[55] How much voluntary behavior an employee exhibits is related to how much help he or she has received from coworkers and the organization. Employees will demonstrate more helping behavior (one type of organizational citizenship behavior) to coworkers because they try to follow their leader's model and help coworkers achieve their goals. An employee's perceived support from the organization (or supervisor) and coworkers is an underlying causal explanation for citizenship behavior and helping behavior.[56] All things equal, such an employee outperforms those who do not exhibit organizational citizenship behavior. Confucians can recognize these practical benefits to encouraging better employer-employee relationships, while still justifying them on moral grounds.

Is organizational citizenship behavior in Confucian cultures the same as in Western cultures? Some dimensions of organizational behavior in China have not been reported in the Western literature, while others are more prevalent in Western countries. For example, preserving interpersonal and departmental harmony is reported prevalent among employees in Chinese organizations.[57] Meanwhile, specific qualities of "taking charge" and "advocacy participation" appear in Western countries but not in mainland China.[58] When managers want to encourage voluntary work behavior, they should be particularly concerned about establishing a reciprocal and empathetic relationship with employees. To encourage the behavior of "taking charge" and "advocacy participation," managers should be aware of the negative influence of employees' power distance orientation[59] in organizational culture, because people with a high power distance orientation are assumed to believe that hierarchical structures of organizations are appropriate, status differences accepted, and that individuals in positions of power should be able to make decisions unilaterally.[60]

Ethical Decision-Making

Confucian values can influence an individual's moral outlook, thereby affecting decisions in business. Some scholars contend that Confucianism actually influenced merchants in Chinese history, but the causal connection is open to question.[61] We instead focus on *potential* influences. Drawing from Confucian views regarding the proper balance between righteousness and profit, we will illustrate their influences in deciding conflicts of interests and optimizing mutual benefits in business. We discuss several principles extracted from Confucian views on conflicts between righteousness and profit seeking, and whether these can be reconciled.

Confucian ethics does not condemn wealth and profit seeking, but unethical methods should not be employed to gain advantage. According to Kongzi, profit seeking is permissible, provided it is done in the proper way: if what is right conflicts with what is profitable, the choice should be to do what is right.[62] For Confucians, the principle of "when seeing gain, [focus] on what is right"[63] should be applied. The possibility of significant corporate or personal benefit can be a strong temptation to violate moral standards, and the cultivation of a commitment to what is right—personal moral integrity—is the Confucian method of resisting temptation.[64] For those without such a commitment, the general principle of putting right ahead of gain can serve as a guideline for choosing the appropriate ways of pursuing profit.

Based on the principle of putting right ahead of profit, organizations should seek to pursue profit in ways compatible with the demands of ethics, thereby incorporating both objectives into the organization's strategy. Doing so is indeed difficult for many profit-focused business managers, but Confucian managers should regulate their behavior by prioritizing adherence to the virtues of benevolence, righteousness and propriety above business profitability.

In Kongzi's thought, pursuing one's own interest is not necessarily bad, but one would be a better, righteous person by following a path that leads to the greater good. The exclusive pursuit of personal interests generates disorder.[65] The interrelationship between righteousness and profit seeking can also be applied to harmonize conflicts of interests between employer and employees. Businesses should respect employees and provide them with appropriate support to promote job satisfaction, commitment, and job performance so as to reach the organizational goal. As a Confucian political leader should care for the people's interests, so should a Confucian business leader care for employees. Historically, moral education was part of the government's responsibility in Confucian thought, and many contemporary Confucians still see the government as having a role in encouraging moral development.[66] Drawing from our original analogy between government and corporation, and given the more limited purpose of a corporate firm, Confucians may wish to see businesses limit their scope of concern to employees' economic interests and moral behavior as these relate to the work environment of the firm.

THE HARMONIOUS SOCIETY

The Confucian social ideal is the harmonious society, the result of (at least in part) unselfish cooperation rather than a spontaneous consequence of individuals' pursuit of their own interests. Confucians believe a harmonious society *requires* other-regarding interests. An important source for this ideal is "The Motions of Ritual (*Li yun*)," a chapter of the Confucian classic *Record of Rites*. The ideal of the "Grand Union" is described thusly:

> When the great Way was practiced, a public spirit ruled the world. [Those in power] employed men of virtue and ability. Their words were sincere, and they cultivated harmony. And so people did not love their parents only, nor treat as children only their own sons. The elderly were provided for, the able-bodied had employment, and the young were nurtured. . . . The people accumulated goods, disliking that they should be thrown away, but not wishing to keep them for themselves. They labored with their strength, disliking that it should not be exerted, but not exerting it only for themselves. . . . This was called the Grand Union.[67]

This picture of a harmonious society continues to be influential today, illustrating the focus on cooperation over competition in Confucian thought. Competition is not necessarily bad if it serves the greater goals of society, but pursuit of profit for its own sake is never valued.

For Confucians, a virtuous person understands that one's good is not in conflict with others. The realization of one's good requires helping others realize theirs.[68] When most or all people understand this, the result is a harmonious society. This society is not entirely free of dispute, nor does it entail repressing criticism. Kongzi also said, "A gentleman harmonizes, but does not merely agree. The petty person agrees, but does not harmonize."[69] Kongzi favored seeking harmony in diversity and difference, and difference is in fact necessary for harmony.[70] How much diversity can be tolerated is not clearly specified in early Confucian texts. The common metaphors used for harmony, music and cooking, suggest there are limits on what can blend together harmoniously.[71] However, early Confucian texts do not define the limits explicitly. The view of "harmony in diversity" can also guide people in resolving contradictions in interpersonal relationships and business communication. Both classical and contemporary Confucians often conceive of society as similar to a large-scale version of a family. This analogy is not necessarily understood literally but is a metaphor to illustrate how people should relate: members of society should have sincere concern for each other, help each other realize their interests at least some of the time, and ideally resolve conflicts through a process of accommodation that is not a zero-sum game.[72]

The idea of harmony is sometimes extended to nature through the Confucian view of heaven. According to some Confucian scholars, human beings have an important role in the unity of humanity and nature. Since at least the Han dynasty (206 BCE–8 CE), Confucians used a triadic formula of heaven, earth, and humanity.[73] Neo-Confucians in particular regarded heaven as the basis of moral objectivity and universality and attempted to awaken a conscious moral awareness and promote feelings of awe and veneration toward heaven. Many contemporary Confucians as well refer to a moral order immanent in the universe as the source of human morality.[74] Though we can see that Kongzi sought harmonious human-society relationships rather than human-nature relationships, some scholars claim that heaven also refers to living nature independent of human will.[75] Yet "heaven" as used by Confucian philosophers does not mean "nature" in the contemporary sense. The move from "heaven" to "nature" is suspect for the following reasons.

In Confucian texts, "heaven" usually refers to either a directed or a spontaneous order that human beings can understand and respond to but cannot affect positively or negatively.[76] The early Confucian Xunzi is the best exponent of the view that human beings should not concern themselves with heaven. He said, "That which is accomplished without your doing it and which is obtained without your seeking it is called the work of Heaven."[77] Although there are differing views on heaven in early Confucian texts (as well as later ones), the term is almost never used to mean the natural world, at least as subject to significant human interference. Confucian philosophers do express the need to manage resources and not slaughter animals indiscriminately, but mainly to conserve them for future generations or as an aspect of virtuous behavior generally.[78] Such actions need not be understood as part of respecting or understanding heaven. In this regard, a Confucian environmental ethic is closer to an anthropocentric ethic, since environmental concern is justified on the basis of human needs and goods.

Confucianism can absolutely endorse husbanding resources and limiting pollution for the welfare of current and future generations, and this is sufficient to oppose current business practices in China, which frequently disregard the effects of pollution or the overconsumption of resources in pursuit of profit. Since such practices neglect an important aspect of harmony, the manager who intentionally engages in these would lack virtue. In the case of the environment, legal restrictions alone have proven ineffective because of lax enforcement or corruption, demonstrating how relying on laws without changing people's values is insufficient. As we mentioned above the ideal situation of relying entirely on virtue is not likely to be entirely successful either. Employing both approaches, where law provides an additional way of regulating those who are not yet sufficiently morally motivated, is likely to work better.

Even if law and other institutional measures are necessary in some instances, the Confucian ideal is to be motivated by intrinsically valuing the Way.[79] For those with this motivation, Confucian ideas of harmony can pro-

David Elstein and Qing Tian

vide loose guidelines to understand and correctly handle relationships among persons, between individuals and society, and between people and nature. Harmony is more a matter of practical wisdom than a specific set of rules. At the individual level, a moral person cannot stop at cultivating himself but must extend concern to others, as required by the virtue of benevolence and exemplified in the superior person.[80] The mark of a superior person is skill in navigating and balancing among and between potentially conflicting goods. The sagacious manager, for example, may need to balance an increase in employee pay without so raising prices that customers are driven away. At the organizational level, the goal of a harmonious society leads to emphasis on harmonious relationships within and outside the firm. The virtue-oriented nature of Confucian ethics precludes hard and fast rules about how to handle such situations, emphasizing instead the ability to make wise choices. Businesses that have strong commitments to ethical behavior may influence consumers' perception of the corporation and increase product loyalty. Similarly, such businesses may improve employee retention and increase employee satisfaction. Emphasizing the benefits of such commitments may be a good strategy for corporate leaders focused on market success, much as classical Confucians appealed to the practical benefits of their political ideas when talking with rulers who were not intrinsically morally motivated.[81] Well-managed businesses should focus on balancing the different interests of those affected by them, although the nature of the Confucian conception of harmony precludes specifying exactly how to do so.

CONCLUDING REMARKS

Once left for dead, Confucianism has been undergoing a revival in China in recent years. The political and cultural stakes make an objective assessment of the strengths and weaknesses of Confucian ethics difficult. The identification of Confucianism with Chinese culture has led some Confucian revivalists to latch onto it as the sole way of preserving Chinese culture and resisting Westernization.[82] Others see Confucian values as obstructions to modernization and inducements to corruption and other negative social effects.[83] These polarized positions are not conducive to a sober examination of how Confucian philosophy can contribute to improving moral life and where this perspective may require modification. More forward-looking Confucian philosophers understand that there will need to be transformation of certain Confucian moral values so as to make them relevant and applicable to modern society.[84] For the case of business ethics, we have suggested that Confucian political ideas are a good place from which to extrapolate to questions of business and commerce, which are discussed very little in the classical texts. Business and politics are after all not identical, and so the analogy has limits, but it provides a starting point to consider the form of Confucian business ethics.

In this respect, Confucianism may have certain implications for business leadership and organizational behavior. It recognizes legitimate desires for wealth but insists that the pursuit of wealth and profit be limited by moral considerations. The goal of harmony also provides some orientation for developing good social relationships and relationships with nature. Yet weak points remain. Confucian virtues are not always clearly defined or lexically ordered, so how to apply them and what to do in case of conflicts remain vague. Confucians recognize a need for a kind of practical wisdom, but this means clear guidelines are absent. Confucians have maintained faith in moral solutions, but these give insufficient attention to the limits of moral suasion and the need for political and legal institutions.

If Confucian ethics and certain political ideas (as indicated above) can be applied or extended to business practices, Confucianism can be seen to contribute to ethical business decision-making and corporate governance. What is distinctive about Confucian ethics is the importance it gives to moral transformation, to a degree beyond what contemporary liberals usually admit. Confucians recognize coercive measures alone are not enough. Many contemporary Confucians have also described the limits of relying on personal virtue, even within the sphere of business. Emphasizing personal virtue may abate but not eliminate corporate misconduct. The impartial rule of law, consistent and fair enforcement of existing laws, increased government transparency, and a freer press would also prove helpful, probably essential. Increased attention only to Confucian morals (or virtue ethics) in business may well be beneficial but is not in itself a substitute for institutional measures.

NOTES

1. "Imperial" China generally refers to the period from the establishment of the Qin dynasty, 221 BCE, to the abdication of the last emperor in 1911. Imperial ideologies shifted, however, until the tenth century CE when Confucianism became established as the ruling ideology.

2. Max Weber, *The Religion of China*, trans. Hans Gerth (New York: Free Press, 1951), 237–49.

3. Some positive assessments are Seok-Choon Lew, *The Korean Economic Developmental Path: Confucian Tradition, Affective Network* (New York: Palgrave Macmillan, 2013); Wei-ming Tu, ed., *Confucian Traditions in Modern East Asia: Moral Education and Economic Culture in Japan and the Four Mini-Dragons* (Cambridge, MA, and London: Harvard University Press, 1996). For more ambivalent or negative assessments, see Po-Keung Ip, "Is Confucianism Good for Business Ethics in China?," *Journal of Business Ethics* 88, no. 3 (September 2009):

463–76; Kui-Wai Li, *Capitalist Development and Economism in East Asia: The Rise of Hong Kong, Singapore, Taiwan, and South Korea* (London and New York: Routledge, 2002).

4. Sébastien Billioud, "Carrying the Confucian Torch to the Masses: The Challenge of Structuring the Confucian Revival in the People's Republic of China," *Oriens Extremus* 49 (2010): 201–24; John Makeham, *Lost Soul: "Confucianism" in Contemporary Academic Discourse* (Cambridge, MA: Harvard University East Asia Center, 2008).

5. E.g., Edward J. Romar, "Confucian Virtues and Business Ethics," in *Handbook of the Philosophical Foundations of Business Ethics*, ed. Christoph Luetge (Dordrecht: Springer Netherlands, 2013), 983. He refers to Confucianism as an "ethical system." For arguments against the notion that the *Analects* are systematic, see Bryan W. Van Norden, "Unweaving the 'One Thread' of *Analects* 4:15," in *Confucius and the Analects: New Essays*, ed. Bryan W. Van Norden (Oxford and New York: Oxford University Press, 2002), 216–36.

6. Gary Kok Yew Chan, "The Relevance and Value of Confucianism in Contemporary Business Ethics," *Journal of Business Ethics* 77, no. 3 (2008): 347–60; Wenzhong Zhu and Yucheng Yao, "On the Value of Traditional Confucian Culture and the Value of Modern Corporate Social Responsibility," *International Journal of Business and Management* 3, no. 2 (2008): 58–62.

7. E.g., Chung-ying Cheng, "On Yijing as Basis of Chinese Business Ethics and Management," in Luetge, *Handbook of the Philosophical Foundations of Business Ethics*, 1027–48. Cheng writes that "we come to know we [human beings] are created from the creative force of the cosmos" (1030). The meaning of this is opaque, and Cheng gives no consideration as to whether this belief of classical Confucianism is true.

8. Po-Keung Ip, "Corporate Social Responsibility and Crony Capitalism in Taiwan," *Journal of Business Ethics* 79, nos. 1–2 (April 2008): 167–77; Ip, "Is Confucianism Good for Business Ethics in China?"

9. Hao Chang, "New Confucianism and the Intellectual Crisis of Contemporary China," in *The Limits of Change: Essays on Conservative Alternatives in Republican China*, ed. Charlotte Furth (Cambridge, MA, and London: Harvard University Press, 1976), 276–304; Yü-sheng Lin, *The Crisis of Chinese Consciousness: Radical Antitraditionalism in the May Fourth Era* (Madison: University of Wisconsin Press, 1979); Vera Schwarcz, *The Chinese Enlightenment: Intellectuals and the Legacy of the May Fourth Movement of 1919* (Berkeley and Los Angeles: University of California Press, 1986).

10. Edward J. Romar, "Virtue Is Good Business: Confucianism as a Practical Business Ethic," *Journal of Business Ethics* 38, nos. 1–2 (June 2002): 119, claims Confucianism is more suited to business ethics than any other moral code. This assertion seems questionable.

11. For additional discussion, see Stephen C. Angle, "The *Analects* and Moral Theory," in *Dao Companion to the "Analects,"* ed. Amy Olberding, Dao Companions to Chinese Philosophy 4 (Dordrecht: Springer, 2014), 225–57; David Elstein, "Contemporary Confucianism," in *Routledge Companion to Virtue Ethics*, ed. Lorraine Besser-Jones and Michael Slote (New York: Routledge, 2015), 237–51.

12. Representatives of the virtue ethics position include Philip J. Ivanhoe, *Ethics in the Confucian Tradition: The Thought of Mengzi and Wang Yangming*, 2nd ed. (Indianapolis: Hackett, 2002); Bryan W. Van Norden, *Virtue Ethics and Consequentialism in Early Chinese Philosophy* (New York: Cambridge University Press, 2007). The deontological interpretation is not widely represented in Anglophone scholarship. One source is Ming-huei Lee, "Confucianism, Kant, and Virtue Ethics," in *Virtue Ethics and Confucianism*, ed. Stephen C. Angle and Michael Slote (New York: Routledge, 2013), 47–55. For discussion of Lee's position, see Angle, "The *Analects* and Moral Theory"; David Elstein, *Democracy in Contemporary Confucian Philosophy* (New York: Routledge, 2014), chap. 5.

13. Philip J. Ivanhoe, "Reweaving the 'One Thread' of the *Analects*," *Philosophy East and West* 40, no. 1 (January 1990): 17–33.

14. David Elstein, "The Authority of the Master in the *Analects*," *Philosophy East and*

West 59, no. 2 (2009): 148–50; Sor-hoon Tan, "Authoritative Master Kong (Confucius) in an Authoritarian Age," *Dao: A Journal of Comparative Philosophy* 9, no. 2 (June 2010): 143–45.

15. *Mengzi*, trans. Bryan W. Van Norden (Indianapolis: Hackett, 2008), 2A6, 4A27. On changing rituals, see *Mengzi* 4A17; and *Analects*, trans. Edward Slingerland (Indianapolis: Hackett, 2003), 9.3.

16. *Analects* 15.24.

17. *Analects* 7.30.

18. *Analects* 6.30.

19. *Mengzi* 4A27, 7A15; *Analects* 17.21.

20. *Mengzi* 1A7, 2A3.

21. *Mengzi* 2A6. See also Bryan W. Van Norden, "The Emotion of Shame and the Virtue of Righteousness in Mencius," *Dao: A Journal of Comparative Philosophy* 2, no. 1 (December 2002): 45–77.

22. *Analects* 4.16, 7.16.

23. Roger Ames, *Confucian Role Ethics: A Vocabulary* (Honolulu: University of Hawaii Press, 2011), 75–125; Henry Rosemont, "Human Rights: A Bill of Worries," in *Confucianism and Human Rights*, ed. Wm Theodore de Bary and Wei-ming Tu (New York: Columbia University Press, 1998), 54–66.

24. Romar, "Virtue Is Good Business," 129–30 n. 1.

25. *Mengzi* 2B10; see also 3B4.

26. *Mengzi* 2A5, 3A4.

27. *Mengzi* 3A4. In *Analects* 13.9 one finds a similar emphasis on ensuring basic material conditions prior to delivering moral instruction.

28. *Mengzi* 1B8.

29. *Mengzi* 7B14, 1B5.

30. The extent to which Confucian governments should prioritize their own citizens' interests is controversial. Confucian critics of democracy often point to the fact that democracies neglect the interests of noncitizens as a reason for preferring meritocratic government. See Tongdong Bai, "A Confucian Version of Hybrid Regime: How Does It Work, and Why Is It Superior?," in *The East Asian Challenge for Democracy: Political Meritocracy in Comparative Perspective*, ed. Daniel A. Bell and Chenyang Li (New York: Cambridge University Press, 2013), 55–87; Qing Jiang, *A Confucian Constitutional Order*, ed. Daniel Bell and Ruiping Fan (Princeton, NJ: Princeton University Press, 2012).

31. See Justin Tiwald, "A Right of Rebellion in the Mengzi?," *Dao: A Journal of Comparative Philosophy* 7, no. 3 (Fall 2008): 269–82, for more details.

32. *Analects* 6.4, 11.17.

33. *Analects* 16.1.

34. This principle is implicit in early Confucian texts. See *Mengzi* 4B29, 6A4, and 6A5 for illustrations.

35. *Mengzi* 2A6.

36. Zeynep Aycan et al., "Impact of Culture on Human Resource Management Practices: A 10-Country Comparison," *Applied Psychology* 49, no. 1 (2000): 192–221; Patricia G. Martínez, "Paternalism as a Positive Form of Leader-Subordinate Exchange: Evidence from Mexico," *Management Research: The Journal of the Iberoamerican Academy of Management* 1, no. 3 (2003): 227–42.

37. Kwang-kuo Hwang, "Confucian and Legalist Basis of Leadership and Business Ethics," in Luetge, *Handbook of the Philosophical Foundations of Business Ethics*, 1005; Hao-Yi Chen et al., "The Effects of Chinese Paternalistic Leadership on Multinational Subordinates' Psychological Health: A Study of Chinese Expatiate Managers," *Research in Applied Psychology* 36 (Winter 2007): 223–44 [in Chinese]; Robert Westwood, "Harmony and Patriarchy: The Cultural Basis for 'Paternalistic Headship' among the Overseas Chinese," *Organization Studies* 18, no. 3 (May 1, 1997): 445–80.

38. David Elstein, "Why Early Confucianism Cannot Generate Democracy," *Dao: A Journal of Comparative Philosophy* 9, no. 4 (2010): 427–43.

39. *Analects* 13.6.

40. *Analects* 13.16, 16.1; *Mengzi* 2A5, 5A9.

41. Naresh Khatri and Eric W. K. Tsang, "Antecedents and Consequences of Cronyism in Organizations," *Journal of Business Ethics* 43, no. 4 (April 2003): 289–303.

42. An example noted in Khatri and Tsang, "Antecedents and Consequences," 289.

43. For some classical examples, see *Analects* 13.18; *Mengzi* 5A3, 7A35.

44. Elstein, *Democracy in Contemporary Confucian Philosophy*, chaps. 3–4.

45. Joseph Chan, *Confucian Perfectionism: A Political Philosophy for Modern Times* (Princeton, NJ: Princeton University Press, 2013), 1–23.

46. Chenyang Li, *The Confucian Philosophy of Harmony* (London and New York: Routledge, 2014), 119; Romar, "Virtue Is Good Business," 986.

47. *Mengzi* 4A1. Contemporary views about how to balance virtue and legal regulation can be found in Stephen C. Angle, *Contemporary Confucian Political Philosophy* (Cambridge: Polity Press, 2012); and in Chan, *Confucian Perfectionism*.

48. Thomas S. Bateman and Dennis W. Organ, "Job Satisfaction and the Good Soldier: The Relationship between Affect and Employee 'Citizenship,'" *Academy of Management Journal* 26, no. 4 (1983): 587.

49. Nancy Eisenberg and Richard A. Fabes, "Empathy: Conceptualization, Measurement, and Relation to Prosocial Behavior," *Motivation and Emotion* 14, no. 2 (June 1990): 132.

50. Louis A. Penner , Alison R. Midili, and Jill Kegelmeyer, "Beyond Job Attitudes: A Personality and Social Psychology Perspective on the Causes of Organizational Citizenship Behavior," *Human Performance* 10, no. 2 (1997): 111–31; Richard P. Bagozzi and David J. Moore, "Public Service Advertisements: Emotions and Empathy Guide Prosocial Behavior," *Journal of Marketing* 58, no. 1 (January 1994): 56–70.

51. Ya-Ru Chen, Xiao-Ping Chen, and Rebecca Portnoy, "To Whom Do Positive Norm and Negative Norm of Reciprocity Apply? Effects of Inequitable Offer, Relationship, and Relational-Self Orientation," *Journal of Experimental Social Psychology* 45, no. 1 (January 2009): 24.

52. John R. Deckop, Carol C. Cirke, and Lynne M. Andersson, "Doing unto Others: The Reciprocity of Helping Behavior in Organizations," *Journal of Business Ethics* 47, no. 2 (October 2003): 103.

53. *Analects* 6.19. The point is also set forth by the classical Confucian Xunzi. See Philip J. Ivanhoe and Bryan W. Van Norden, eds., "Xunzi," in *Readings in Classical Chinese Philosophy*, trans. Eric L. Hutton, 2nd ed. (Indianapolis and Cambridge: Hackett, 2001), 260–61.

54. Deckop, Cirke, and Andersson, "Doing unto Others"; Dennis W. Organ, "The Motivational Basis of Organizational Citizenship Behavior," in *Research in Organizational Behavior*, ed. Barry M. Staw and L. L. Cummings, vol. 12 (Greenwich, CT: JAI Press, 1990), 12:43–72.

55. Linn Van Dyne, Dishan Kamdar, and Jeffrey Joireman, "In-Role Perceptions Buffer the Negative Impact of Low LMX on Helping and Enhance the Positive Impact of High LMX on Voice," *Journal of Applied Psychology* 93, no. 6 (2008): 1195–1207.

56. Robert Eisenberger et al., "Reciprocation of Perceived Organizational Support," *Journal of Applied Psychology* 86, no. 1 (February 2001): 42–51; Suzanne S. Masterson et al., "Integrating Justice and Social Exchange: The Differing Effects of Fair Procedures and Treatment on Work Relationships," *Academy of Management Journal* 43, no. 4 (August 1, 2000): 738–48.

57. Jiing-Lih Farh, Chen-Bo Zhong, and Dennis W. Organ, "Organizational Citizenship Behavior in the People's Republic of China," *Organization Science* 15, no. 2 (April 2004): 241–53.

58. Yong Han and Yochanan Altman, "Confucian Moral Roots of Citizenship Behaviour in China," *Asia-Pacific Journal of Business Administration* 2, no. 1 (2010): 37. "Taking charge" refers to elective and discretionary behavior to effect positive change in the organization. See

Elizabeth Wolfe Morrison and Corey C. Phelps, "Taking Charge at Work: Extrarole Efforts to Initiate Workplace Change," *Academy of Management Journal* 42, no. 4 (August 1999): 403–19. "Advocacy participation" refers to behavior that challenges others in the organization and serves to advocate for improvement. On this notion, see Linn Van Dyne, Jill W. Graham, and Richard M. Dienesch, "Organizational Citizenship Behavior: Construct Redefinition, Measurement, and Validation," *Academy of Management Journal* 37, no. 4 (August 1994): 780–83.

59. Developed by Geert Hofstede, power distance, one of five dimensions to measure cross-cultural differences, refers to the degree of inequality that exists—and is accepted—among people with and without power. See Hofstede, *Culture's Consequences: Comparing Values, Behaviors, Institutions, and Organizations across Nations* (Thousand Oaks, CA: Sage, 2001).

60. M. Clugston, J. P. Howell, and P. W. Dorfman, "Does Cultural Socialization Predict Multiple Bases and Foci of Commitment?," *Journal of Management* 26, no. 1 (January–February 2000): 5–30.

61. Joanna Kit-Chun Lam, "Confucian Business Ethics and the Economy," *Journal of Business Ethics* 43, nos. 1–2 (March 2003): 153–62; Dennis P. McCann, "Business Ethics in the Perspectives of Christian Social Teaching and Confucian Moral Philosophy: Two Ships Passing in the Night," *Journal of International Business Ethics* 3, no. 2 (2010): 16–28.

62. In addition to *Analects* 4.16, 7.16, 16.10, and 19.1, see the discussions in Lam, "Confucian Business Ethics and the Economy," 154; Romar, "Virtue Is Good Business," 124.

63. *Analects* 16.10.

64. *Mengzi* 6A10.

65. *Mengzi* 1A1.

66. For examples, see Elstein, *Democracy in Contemporary Confucian Philosophy*, chaps. 3, 7; Ruiping Fan, *Reconstructionist Confucianism: Rethinking Morality after the West* (Dordrecht: Springer, 2010), esp. 90–95 and 243–48.

67. "Li Yun," *Chinese Text Project*, http://ctext.org/liji/li-yun; translation modified.

68. *Analects* 6.30.

69. *Analects* 13.23; translation slightly modified.

70. Li, *Confucian Philosophy of Harmony*, 143–47.

71. Ibid., chap. 2.

72. Lam, "Confucian Business Ethics and the Economy," 158.

73. This originated in the *Classic of Changes* (*Yijing*) and was developed by the Han dynasty Confucian Dong Zhongshu. See Li, *Confucian Philosophy of Harmony*, 160–62.

74. For some discussion, see Elstein, *Democracy in Contemporary Confucian Philosophy*, chap. 9.

75. Xianlin Ji, *Discussion on Chinese Ancient Civilization*, in *Collected Works of Ji Xianlin* (Beijing: Huayi Publishing House, 2008); Tianchen Li, "Confucian Ethics and the Environment," *Culture Mandala: The Bulletin of the Centre for East-West Cultural and Economic Studies* 6, no. 1 (2003): 1–6.

76. For some discussion of the different views, see Philip J. Ivanhoe, "Heaven as a Source for Ethical Warrant in Early Confucianism," *Dao: A Journal of Comparative Philosophy* 6, no. 3 (Fall 2007): 211–20.

77. Ivanhoe and Van Norden, "Xunzi," 270.

78. *Analects* 7.27; *Mengzi* 1A3.

79. "The Way" for Confucians refers to the way a person should live as well as the way society should be ordered. As a general term for what the aim of human activity should be, it functions much like "the good" in other philosophies.

80. *Mengzi* 1A7, 2A6.

81. E.g., *Mengzi* 1A3, 1A5, 1A7.

82. The best-known of these is Jiang Qing. English accounts of his thought can be found in Ruiping Fan, ed., *The Renaissance of Confucianism in Contemporary China* (Dordrecht: Springer, 2011); Jiang, *Confucian Constitutional Order*.

83. Yusheng Huang, "The Starting Point of Universal Ethics: Free Individual or Relational Character?," *Contemporary Chinese Thought* 39, no. 1 (Fall 2007): 35–45; Ip, "Corporate Social Responsibility and Crony Capitalism in Taiwan"; Qingping Liu, "Confucianism and Corruption: An Analysis of Shun's Two Actions Described by Mencius," *Dao: A Journal of Comparative Philosophy* 6, no. 1 (March 2007): 1–19. Similar criticisms date back to early twentieth-century figures such as Chen Duxiu and Hu Shi. See Lin, *Crisis of Chinese Consciousness*.

84. One such example is Ming-huei Lee. See Elstein, *Democracy in Contemporary Confucian Philosophy*, chap. 5.

CHAPTER 4

The Earthly City and the Ethics of Exchange: Spiritual, Social, and Material Economy in Augustine's Theological Anthropology

Todd Breyfogle

Augustine's understanding of the ethics of material exchange is firmly rooted in his conception of the social and spiritual nature of the human person. The material economy is inseparable, in Augustine's view, from the social and spiritual economies. This essay aims to sketch the complexity of the inter-relationship of these three economies in Augustine's thought and to illumi-nate the criteria by which Augustine thinks responsible human beings make their decisions in the market and under the rule of law. The first two sections look at the social value of wealth in the classical tradition, which Augustine adopts and adapts to a late antique Christian emphasis on the dignity of the human person. The third section explicates the created value of the human person and other creations as a criterion for Augustine's evaluation of market price and the enjoyment, use, and abuse of property. These considerations are placed, in the fourth section, in the context of Augustine's famous dis-tinction between the earthly and heavenly cities and the loves that form them. The final two sections clarify Augustine's articulation of wealth and its increase in terms of social and spiritual unity in which individually held property is put in service of a common, spiritual good whose benefits are expressed in the increase of material and social goods. There emerges, then, no abstract economic theory; Augustine had no theory of "the economy" apart from the texture of concrete human exchanges in an earthly city con-ditioned by original sin.[1] Consequently, this essay strives to bring to life the historical and practical conditions under which Augustine lived, wrote, and formulated his understanding of the ethics of exchange.

A year or so before he died, Augustine wrote a letter to his old friend Aly-pius expressing concern, bordering on desperation, about a plague of slave trading affecting the North African coast. Augustine laments the breakdown in civil order, which allows marauding bands to raid rural villages, kidnapping their inhabitants and selling them, including women and children, to the ever-growing number of slave merchants.[2] "But if there were no slave merchants," Augustine continues, "those things would not happen."[3] Market demand has created "a wicked traffic out of an amazing blindness due to greed" that has taken on the character of an infectious disease. A woman has been found in Hippo who—under the pretext of buying wood—traps, imprisons, and sells other women into slavery. Even a well-off member of Augustine's own church has sold off his wife, "driven only by the heat of this plague."[4]

Augustine's letter illustrates some of the more extreme if still not uncommon aspects of everyday life against which he formulated his philosophical and theological reflections on wealth and the ethics of exchange. As a bishop, Augustine was not just a thinker but a man making decisions for an organization (his church) and a de facto authority in civic affairs. He understood the complex workings of a market that both responds to and creates demand. He recognized also the need for a stable legal order as a precondition for commerce. Indeed, one purpose of his letter is to prompt his old friend to lobby the emperor to enforce existing laws against the slave trade. Very few of those kidnapped in the slave trade "have been sold by their parents . . . , as the laws of Rome allow, for work lasting twenty-five years."[5] Some but not all slave trading is permitted; the law must be respected, and it must be enforced. At the same time, Augustine urges the mitigation of the prescribed punishment for slave trading—the use of a leaden-tipped whip could cause death. Augustine thinks and acts in strict deference to the existing laws, especially the Roman law of property, even when those laws offend his more humane sensibilities.

That said, Augustine cannot separate the structures of economic exchange and the rule of law from their practical impact on human beings. The material economy and its supports are not abstractions, but the necessary conditions of living and of living together. Law and economics exist to serve the human person, not the other way around. The material economy is undergirded and superseded by a spiritual economy.

Augustine's letter to Alypius brings home the full practical and theoretical dimensions of his reflections on the ethics of exchange. What is the value of a human person? What are the legal dimensions of property? What are the moral dimensions of ownership and use? Why do human beings value what they do, and what are the consequences of that valuation? What specifically Christian responsibilities should inform the practices of economic exchange under secular Roman law? What do we mean by wealth? These are not simply economic questions; they are human questions. Correspondingly, our account will weave together the human as well as the theoretical dimensions of Augustine's reflections on the ethics of exchange. For Augustine, ultimately, the ethics of exchange are an expression of what—and who—we love.

THE SOCIAL VALUE OF WEALTH: THE CLASSICAL HERITAGE

Augustine was born in Thagaste, North Africa, in 354 CE, into a family of *honesti,* or modest gentry—his father was a member of the town council, owned an estate, and had slaves. Augustine himself never endured the necessities of manual labor or trade. Looking down the social pyramid, Augustine's family was wealthy, though still not in the inner circle of Thagaste; looking up, and looking across to the Italian mainland, Augustine's provincial family was far from senatorial aristocracy. Augustine rose through the system of patronage to become a speechwriter for the emperor in Milan. Had he followed the standard career path, he would have eventually retired from his imperial service, returning to his hometown, lauded and admitted to the inner circle of local rulers.[6]

Augustine's own history provides an important part of the picture of wealth and the ethics of exchange in the late antique empire. Augustine's world was not one of economic class distinction; "it was," in the words of Peter Brown, "a world of patrons and friends." At a certain level, society "was not divided primarily between rich and poor; it was divided between those who could get ahead and those who could not. . . . What you owned was less important than who you knew."[7] In this world of aristocratic values, wealth was a means to a social end, not an end in itself. Wealth could be exchanged for opportunity, opportunity for patronage, and patronage for reputation. With wealth came responsibilities—not only the responsibility of managing one's property, but the obligation of using one's wealth to advance one's friends and for the greater good.

Using wealth for the common good was part of the long shadow cast forward to the fourth and fifth centuries by the virtues Cicero celebrated in his *De officiis.* Cicero criticizes what he calls the unjust acquisition of wealth, but celebrates the use of wealth for the provision of basic needs, for pleasure, and with an eye to power, influence, and the bestowing of favors.[8] That is, wealth was properly not an end in itself but rather a means to larger social (as distinct from private) ends; the use of wealth was to be directed outward, toward others, in communal enjoyment rather than individual consumption. At the same time, Cicero warns his readers not to have an undue ambition for wealth, "for there is nothing so characteristic of narrowness and littleness of soul as the love of riches; and there is nothing more honourable and noble than to be indifferent to money, if one does not possess it, and to devote it to beneficence and liberality, if one does possess it."[9] More precious than any wealth is a reputation for virtue and worthy deeds.[10]

Augustine knew and followed Cicero in celebrating those who put their wealth at the disposition of the *res publica* they served—acts of public generosity, whether in the construction of civic buildings, the sponsorship of public festivals, or in supporting oneself (or one's friends) in pursuit of positions of civic leadership. In the *City of God*, Augustine praises those Romans who lived in poverty in their houses while the republic was "richly endowed with all resources."[11] He holds out to monks in his own community the example of Scipio Africanus as one among many Roman republicans who "placed a shared commitment to the interests of the entire people of their city above their own private interests."[12] Private wealth was private, but it was properly directed toward the public good. Wealth was not to be accumulated but used; spending rather than accumulating wealth put one in service not only of the material economy but of the economy of social exchange manifest in acts of public generosity. Scipio, in his public liberality (to return to Augustine's example), could not raise a dowry for his daughters, but he is not poor—he is certainly not subject to the necessities of working the land for food. He is "unwealthy" in the sense that he has put his property (we might call it capital) to use rather than simply letting it accumulate.[13]

Against this Ciceronian celebration of "unwealth" there emerged, in the early fourth century, a new and different sparkle. "From Constantine onward, the Roman state flooded the economy with gold" in an effort to secure the loyalty of its forces and bureaucracy.[14] Instead of demanding a fraction of the harvest, the empire insisted on receiving as much tax revenue as possible in gold. Gold coinage began to change the nature of the wealthy elites; gold became an object of accumulation rather than a medium of exchange, sparking a desire for more that, as John Locke would later put it, "altered the intrinsic value of things." A common tie of all to the land was gradually replaced by a separation between those who had gold and those who did not, irrespective of their standing in the traditional, agrarian social order.[15] The introduction and spread of the gold solidus created a new, monetary scarcity whose ripples were still felt more than a hundred years later, creating stronger incentives to seek a currency increasingly divorced from either the land or a social good. The lure of gold and the necessity of meeting imperial demands frequently resulted in excessive, oppressive taxation. In another letter to Alypius, Augustine laments the shortage of clergy, because clergy, as de facto local public officials, were required by law "to be involved in civic duties at their own expense" as a source of imperial revenue.[16] Heavy taxation, he continues, not only created significant disincentives for traditional public service but eroded traditional class distinctions, impoverishing all and reducing voluntary public-spiritedness to a necessary burden.[17]

The attitudes of "unwealth" are being replaced by a coarsening of attitudes even among the Christian well-to-do, whom Augustine sees as less concerned with human suffering. For example, Augustine rebukes a convert, Romulus, for collecting a second tax after his tenant farmers had already mistakenly paid tax collectors presumed to be representing Romulus himself.[18] Augustine's response to Romulus's actions suggests the different frame that Christianity brought to the dimensions of wealth in the late empire. Romulus should acknowledge his own error, Augustine says, reverse his decision, and attend to the needs of the poor. But in so urging, Augustine not only defends the well-being of the tenant farmers, but also petitions Romulus to attend to the state of his own soul: "Make peace with yourself in order that he whom you ask may be at peace with you."[19] Cicero and his followers had sought to limit the material economy with the social economy of noble thought and action; Augustine, like other Christians before him, sought to reframe the pursuit of wealth in terms of a new, spiritual economy.

THE SPIRITUAL DIMENSIONS OF WEALTH: THE CHRISTIAN CRITIQUE

The upwardly mobile Augustine arrived at the Western imperial court at Milan in late 384 carrying the endorsement of the prominent pagan Roman senator Symmachus, whose patronage had secured Augustine's employment with the emperor. Augustine carried with him a religious commitment to Manichaeanism, a dualistic, syncretic Christian sect of Persian origin. Augustine was also accompanied by his unnamed concubine. Augustine's family wealth had bought opportunity, but it was not so great as to burden him with aristocratic responsibility. Talent had merited patronage of increasingly higher profile, irrespective of his idiosyncratic religious affiliation and irregular marital status.[20]

Ambrose, bishop of Milan, would likely have looked askance at the younger Augustine, talented, but so evidently compromised in politics, religion, and society. Symmachus was Ambrose's pagan rival; Manichaeanism was viewed dimly by the orthodox Catholic establishment; Ambrose's aristocratic and Christian propriety would have made him think twice about Augustine's evident lack of continence. If Augustine reflects the status of modest wealth in the provincial empire, Ambrose, by contrast, embodies that new Christian figure—the Roman aristocrat who had forsaken the gods of Symmachus and put his family's goods in service to Christianity. The son of a Gallic praetorian prefect, Ambrose was well educated, well connected, and was a perfect fit for the position of consul of Milan. When Ambrose was installed as the new bishop by popular will, among his first acts was to divest himself of his considerable family wealth, distributing some to the poor and placing the rest in trust for others to manage.[21] In Ambrose, Augustine would have seen a man who had taken the Ciceronian ideal of service to the *res publica* one step further—Ambrose not only saw to it that his wealth was used for the common good, whether through provisions for the church or assistance to the poor, but he divested himself entirely from the management of his wealth, devoting himself to service to the public good through the institution of the church.

Ambrose preached what he practiced. Augustine may well have heard sermons that Ambrose later collected as *De Nabuthe Jezraelita*, inveighing against the luxurious avarice of the rich and their treatment of the poor. "The earth was made in common for all. . . . Nature, which begets all poor, does not know the rich. . . . Naked it brings people into the light, wanting food, clothing and drink. . . . Nature, therefore, knows not how to discriminate when we are born, it knows not how we die."[22] Echoing the Stoics, Ambrose insists: "It is a law of nature that we seek only what suffices for living."[23] Ambrose is keen to stress the misplaced attention of the rich and the collateral human suffering. The poor man seeks his daily bread while the horses of the rich champ on golden bits. "The jewel in your ring could preserve the lives of the whole people."[24]

Ambrose does not assert an explicit causal connection between the possessions of the rich and the destitution of the poor. What concerns him is the responsibility of the rich, who are in positions of trust in possessing something that is properly common to all: "For what has been given as common for the use of all, you appropriate to yourself alone." Ambrose does not seem to argue that the rich are rich at the expense of the poor, but that to the extent that the poor suffer it is from a failure of the rich to live up to their responsibility to care for the poor. Caring for the poor is the payment of a debt of stewardship—stewardship of the material goods with which one has been entrusted, and stewardship of the social responsibility one owes toward one's dependents.[25] Failing to exercise this duty of stewardship inverts the natural relationship between human beings and wealth; the greedy man has become a slave to his possessions rather than a master of them: "You who bury gold in the earth are the custodian, not the master of your wealth; surely you are its servant and not its lord. But: 'Where thy treasure is, there is thy heart also.' Hence with that gold you have buried your heart in the earth."[26] In Ambrose, Stoic Roman aristocratic responsibility is bathed in the waters of Christian baptism. The language of nature is wrapped in the cloak of Christian creation and conformity to divine providence. By stressing the natural equality of all human beings, regardless of class, Ambrose sought to reinforce the notion that the church was home to rich and poor alike.[27] Unlike clergy, the rich could possess their property without opprobrium, so long as they were attentive to their responsibilities to use it well. Here, the social, the material, and the spiritual economies converge—the wealthy have a social responsibility; greed, in forsaking stewardship, is a form of slavery to material things; social and material stewardship properly manifest themselves in a spiritual unity that does not differentiate between rich and poor.

As a Manichaean, Augustine subscribed to a starker dualism that rejected the possession of material things; baptized Manichaeans were not to own fields or houses or to possess money.[28] Among more mainstream Christians, the renunciation of wealth in the form of common ownership can be traced from the time of the New Testament forward, quite distinct from the sensibilities of the aristocratic nobility—even the poor were to share goods with one another in a spirit of brotherly love. In Augustine's day, Christian asceticism was at full boil, even among orthodox Catholic ascetics. Later, Augustine's doctrinal opponent, Pelagius, insisted that Christian purity required the renunciation of wealth altogether.[29] Within a short time, Augustine would be persuaded to Ambrose's more moderate position on wealth, distinguishing further between monastic renunciation, proper use, and the abuse or unjust use of wealth.

In part because of Ambrose's sermons, Augustine withdrew from Milan to the countryside in 387 with an eye to being baptized a Catholic and resigning his imperial appointment. While on retreat he and his companions explored and then abandoned the possibility of founding a philosophical commune. But Augustine was also aware of the expectation that he return to civic life and the management of his now-deceased father's estates in Thagaste. As a Christian and a Roman, how was he to think about his responsibilities in regard to wealth?

NATURAL VALUE AND MARKET PRICE: ENJOYMENT, USE, AND ABUSE

After resigning his imperial position and returning to North Africa, Augustine sold his family property and distributed the proceeds to the poor. He then gathered some friends in monastic community—first in Thagaste and, later, in Hippo—a community characterized by common possession of material goods. As Augustine would indicate in his influential outline of monastic living (*Praeceptum*), the chief motivation for sharing life together "is to live harmoniously in the [one] house and to have one heart and one soul seeking God. . . . Do not call anything your own. Possess everything in common."[30]

Augustine's injunction to common ownership in a monastic setting is a specifically Christian, clerical aspiration, not a normative plan for Christians or others in a secular society. For Augustine, a Christian life may be manifest in a plurality of conventional social forms, consistent with the duties of one's existing responsibilities. For those who are called to an ascetic, monastic life, the purpose of such a community was twofold: to provide the circumstances under which those so inclined could pursue spiritual re-formation, and to be a beacon to those outside the community that the principles of material exchange could be informed by relationships of spiritual dignity. The exemplary nature of monastic community underscores a crucial element in Augustine's thinking—Christians in different forms of community will have differentiated relationships with respect to material wealth. Each properly shares the goal of relationships of spiritual dignity through, nevertheless, variegated social forms.

The world of variegated social forms in which we live is, for Augustine, a world conditioned—deformed—by original sin. In his accounts of Genesis, Augustine distinguishes four moments that define the origins, ends, and conduct of our common human life: our created nature, our fallen condition, our fallen condition under grace in time, and our perfected nature in eternity. This fourfold lens provides a framework of analysis that allows Augustine to be both descriptive and normative about the ethics of exchange. In our created nature, we are made for grateful communion. God is our creator; the proper response of his creatures is worshipful thanksgiving.[31] God is "the fountain of our happiness" and so "is the end of all our desires." "Being attached to Him, or rather let me say, re-attached—for we had detached ourselves and lost hold of Him . . . we tend towards him by love, that we may rest in Him, and find our blessedness by attaining that end."[32] We are born to love God and his creation. Our happiness comes in submitting to that love, and in this, Augustine says, we achieve what the ancient philosophers took to be the highest human aim. Human life in its fallen condition is thus a journey of reattachment to the ground of our being. That reattachment is made possible by the grace of Christ reforming our habits, our loves, in anticipation of a renewed nature in eternity.[33]

Our origins and ends as defined by communion with God and his creation are the normative position by which Augustine judges all individual action and social-economic-political arrangements. In describing the practical human predicament in time, Augustine embraces the tension between our fallen condition and our fallen condition under grace. In our fallen condition, we are detached from God, our neighbor, and the rest of creation. We mistake material things as ends rather than means, forming disordered attachments to things; we are drawn by the beauty of creation to settle our attention on material things in reference to ourselves alone.[34] In our fallen condition under grace, our gaze goes beyond the thing to apprehend and give thanks to its Creator, a gratitude that resolves itself in friendship with God himself and is manifest in friendship toward others.[35]

The journey of human life, for Augustine, is properly one of reattachment or re-formation in which we are increasingly (but never, in this life, perfectly) restored to the wholeness for which we were originally created. Our souls are formed by God, deformed by sin, and reformed—for good or for ill—by the objects of our love.[36] These loves go to the heart of what we value. This capacity to assess the value of things is a powerful force, which extends (in ignorance of the interrelated wholeness of creation) even to the annihilation of beings deemed to have no value at all. "Who, for example, would not rather have bread in his house than mice, or gold than fleas? But there is little to wonder at in this. For even in the estimation of men themselves (whose nature is certainly of the highest dignity), more is often given for a horse than for a slave, for a jewel than for a maid."[37]

Augustine is not arguing that the market price of a thing should be based on some normative natural value (what could be the just price of a human being?). Instead, he is arguing for two distinct scales of value: one where a thing's market price derives from its contingent utility or exchange value; the other where a thing's value derives from its created nature and its place in the hierarchy of being. Augustine respects market value; he does not argue for a correlative "natural value" expressed in price. Created value is a recognition of a thing's or person's end, and while created or natural value cannot determine a market value or just price, it does provide a basis for judgment in material exchange. In our fallen condition, we place greater value on bread than on mice; this is simply a fact. But under grace, we should see that the natural value of a living being is greater than that of an inanimate object.

How we value a thing will depend upon whether we consider it materially, according to its market utility, or spiritually, according to its natural value. Goods can be aggregated with respect to market price, but human beings cannot be so aggregated. "So far as freedom of judgment is concerned, then, the reason of the thoughtful man is far different from the necessity of one who is in need, or the desire of the pleasure-seeker. For reason considers what value a thing in itself has in the order of created nature, while necessity considers how to obtain what will meet its need. Reason looks for what is true according to the light of the mind, while pleasure looks for what will gratify the body's senses."[38] Created nature participates in the order of enjoyment not of use; as such, it is not properly subject to possessive desire or necessity, but rests on the liberty of a love that expands beyond desire.

Augustine has refined the lens of value further. Reason stands between necessity and pleasure seeking in its valuation of a thing. Necessity and pleasure seeking value an object according to opposite but nonetheless self-regarding utilities. Reason, by contrast, considers the value of the object according to its created nature in reference to its maker and the whole of creation. Reason looks to embrace the other; necessity and pleasure look to possess and consume it. When Augustine set up his monastic community on principles of common ownership he was prioritizing the rational valuation of human nature over the judgment of necessity on the one hand and pleasure on the other. The life of common possession was freely chosen, not a matter of necessity, and its material status aimed at comfortable sufficiency not destitution. The spiritual economy is not one of deprivation, but of moderation. Augustine sees necessity and pleasure seeking as two sides of the same coin; both are distortions of one's spiritual loves.

Whether in wealth or in poverty, human beings may enjoy, use, or abuse things. Augustine outlines this core of his moral theory as follows: "There are some things which are to be enjoyed (*frui*), others which are to be used (*uti*), others which are enjoyed and used. Those things which are objects of enjoyment make us happy. Those things which are objects of use assist us, and (so to speak) support us in our efforts after happiness, so that we can attain the things that make us happy and rest in them." Wealth, for example, is only to be used as a means to an end, as in the generosity that fosters friendship; friendship, for example, may be either a means (a business acquaintance) or an end (true friendship). The use of something is licit only if the end to which it is directed is also licit, as determined by the order of created nature. Material possessions are properly means to an end not ends in themselves, and as such, when pursued as ends yield neither happiness nor peace of mind. Only when put in service of spiritual—and the concomitant social—ends does wealth assist in our being happy. Distinguishing between things that are to be enjoyed rather than used is made difficult by the fact that we ourselves are "placed among both kinds of objects." That is, we can mistake ourselves as objects of use or enjoyment; an undue attachment to self entangles us in a love that interferes with "the pursuit of the real and proper objects of enjoyment."[39]

To enjoy something means "to cling to it with affection for its own sake," that is, in accordance with its place in created nature. To use something "is to employ what we have received for our use to obtain what we want, provided that it is right for us to want it." If it is not right for us to want it, it is an "unlawfully applied use," which is properly called "abuse." "If we wish to return to our native country where we can be happy," he concludes, "we must use this world and not enjoy it."[40]

The distinction between market price and natural value helps Augustine make a further threefold distinction: monastic common use of property is a Christian clerical ideal; the right use and enjoyment of property is a permissible good to which Christians and non-Christians alike may aspire; the abuse of property—using or enjoying it wrongly (that which undermines the harmony of the social unit or of the individual soul, as we shall see)—is unjust. The ethics of exchange must be viewed from the vantage point not only of the created nature from which we originate, but of the true end in which we find our happiness. Common ownership is neither poverty defined as necessity nor an embrace of luxury; rather, it is a rational division of material goods in support of a spiritual journey.[41] Monastic community is not a life to which everyone can commit, but it illuminates the texture of human relations that we might aspire to outside of the monastery, putting the valuation of people and things in their proper order. Each form of *societas* has an order appropriate to it.[42] The rules governing a monastic community would be inappropriate in a family, where different customs of hierarchy and the division of property are in play; similarly, business arrangements or other enterprise associations have their own purposes and principles of just division. A city, too, is a particular form of *societas* whose valuations depend upon the order of their loves. According to the order of created nature, the valuation of the human person is the same; according to the contingent, conventional social order, those valuations are necessarily expressed in social forms that will differ within and across cultures.

TWO LOVES, TWO CITIES

If we are wanderers in a foreign land looking for our way home, how are we to think of our responsibilities while we undertake our journey on earth? Augustine had already been exploring the contours of this question when the aftermath of the sack of Rome in 410 CE prompted him to write the *City of God*. Augustine began this monumental work in 413 but finished it in 427, only two years before the likely date of the letter to Alypius with which we began. Whereas in his letter Augustine is building up from the experience of individual human beings, in the *City of God* he develops a broader theoretical and historical framework for viewing wealth and the ethics of exchange.

Augustine writes: "Accordingly, two cities have been formed by two loves: the earthly city by the love of self, extending even to the contempt of God; the heavenly city by the love of God, extending to the contempt of self. . . . In the earthly city, princes are as much mastered by the lust for mastery as the nations they subdue are by them; in the heavenly city, all serve one another in love, rulers by their counsel and subjects by their obedience."[43] The pride of the earthly city manifests itself in mastery—the lust for domination (*libido dominandi*)—and so in turn is mastered by its own lusts, including the desire to accumulate wealth. "You are full, yet you crave for more. That is not wealth; it is a disease."[44] The lust for domination in the material economy turns upon itself—the avaricious are mastered by their own endlessly multiplying desires and master each other in turn, just as bigger fish devour smaller ones.[45]

The two cities are an eschatological shorthand for the moral allegiances of two very different kinds of citizenship and are not to be, strictly speaking, identified with historical Rome and the historical church.[46] Citizens of the earthly city, Augustine says, seek an earthly peace, manifest in "the well-ordered concord of civic obedience and rule," which aims at "the combination of men's wills to attain the things which are helpful to this life." The heavenly city "makes use of the earthly peace only because it must, until this mortal condition which necessitates it shall pass away."[47] Citizens of the heavenly city live as strangers—pilgrims in, but not of, the world—and as such obey the laws of the earthly city, which aim at the peaceful coordination of divergent wills. "Use money as the traveler at an inn uses a table, cup, pitcher, and couch, with the purpose of not remaining, but of leaving them behind."[48] The lesson for political economy might be summarized as "Invest, don't accumulate"; as a matter of imagining our place in time, Augustine might say, "Travel lightly." Here we see the principles of *uti* and *frui* writ large on the political and historical stage. Keeping a steady eye on the spiritual goods whose enjoyment brings true happiness allows us to make good use of those things that are properly not ends in themselves.

Cicero described people's peaceful coordination of divergent wills as "an assemblage associated by a common acknowledgement of right (*ius*) and by a community of interest."[49] Augustine offers this reformulation: "A people is an assemblage of reasonable beings bound together by a common agreement as to the objects of their love." In so doing, he shifts the criterion of value from utility to love and subjects all republics to the judgment of the hierarchy of natural value. Augustine continues: "In order to discover the character of any people, we have only to observe what they love."[50] A republic both reflects and reinforces the character of the people from whose aggregated loves it is formed. Citizens of the heavenly city respect and make use of the agreements of others concerning a more general peace as a means to a higher end—namely, the love of neighbor; citizens of the earthly city love peace and its material fruits as the highest ends, thereby subjecting themselves to anxiety, fear, and discontent.[51]

It is not hard to pass judgment on slave traders and those who exact double taxation, but for Augustine, those who put wealth before human well-being differ from these extremes not in kind but only in degree. For this reason as well, Augustine's critique of exchange as practiced according to the loves of the earthly city has a double echo: not only does self-love injure others; it injures the self whose loves are disordered.

UNITY AND PROPERTY

The loves of the heavenly city are perhaps equally subject to disorder insofar as all human beings in this life are subject to the sin of pride, or self-love. Such is the case of one of Augustine's correspondents, a Christian woman,

Ecdicia, who in spiritually motivated selfishness has embraced chastity without her husband's consent (in marriage, according to Augustine, neither husband nor wife can embrace marital celibacy without the other's agreement) and has, again without her husband's consent, given away most of their possessions to two wandering monks for distribution to the poor. These, Augustine tells her, are spiritual acts wrongly undertaken. She has deprived her husband of his lawful possessions without his consent, robbed their son of his rightful patrimony, and risked her husband's spiritual well-being by creating conditions for his adultery and excluding him from the spiritual benefits of voluntarily electing to participate in distributing his property to the poor. It is true, Augustine remonstrates, that "bread shared with a poor person has great weight in heaven," but how much more weight ought we give to someone's spiritual well-being?[52]

In Christian renunciation, material exchange—even emotional and physical exchange—is subject to the strictest of spiritual standards of concern for the people to whom one is closest: "The relation of strangers is not the same as that of persons bound together in a society."[53] Ecdicia's responsibilities to her husband and son take precedence over her desire to assist wandering monks in service to the poor. Her commitment is to her family's physical, emotional, and spiritual well-being altogether, including deference to established familial property rights and doctrines of consent, regardless of whether she thinks their wealth can be used for more edifying spiritual purposes. In the end, Augustine prizes the unity of the social unit— the husband's unity of heart, Ecdicia's own rightly ordered loves, and the well-being of their son. "Your son needs oneness of heart between you and your husband."[54]

The priority of the harmony and unity of the family extends to society as a whole. Where Ambrose emphasized the equality of social classes before God and each other, Augustine emphasizes the unity of social bonds even within conditions of social and economic inequality. Consider the dual injunction to poor and rich from one of Augustine's sermons. To the poor he says: "You have a common universe with the rich. You may not have a common house with them, but you do have a common sky, a common light. Seek sufficiency, seek what is enough, and more do not seek." To the rich: "Have you brought along anything into this world? No, not even you rich people have brought anything. You have found everything here. With the poor, you were born naked."[55] The poor who envy the rich and their riches are as spiritually compromised as the rich who neglect the poor. Both suffer from pride.[56] The rich who neglect the poor have deprived themselves of the true spiritual wealth and unity that comes when gifts are given and received.[57] Rich and poor stand in mutual material and spiritual dependence.[58] Both rich and poor are involved in the creation of wealth, which is a by-product of the care of one's material property. The creation of material wealth, for Augustine, is not a zero-sum game. But wealth itself is not the ultimate measure; the true value of material wealth rests in the extent to which it creates spiritual and social unity. The care of another human being's material needs is simultaneously a means to the end and a reflection of that unity.

Augustine's conception of the unity of the social order—the common agreement as to objects of love—depends upon a robust regime of law and virtuous administrators, that is, property rights and public-spirited leaders. Like John Locke, Augustine holds that God, as Creator, is the sole owner and supreme governor of all the earth and its produce; God gives the earth equally to human beings for their proper use and enjoyment.[59] In the state of created nature, human beings would use and share the earth in accordance with rightly ordered loves, both in respect to individual consumption and in sharing with others. In the absence of sin, human beings would have cultivated the land freely, not out of the necessity introduced by our fallen condition. This necessity gives rise to possessive self-love, which in turn gives rise to scarcity.[60] Logically and theologically, there is no problem of scarcity in Eden before the fall.

Property rights, and their legitimate transfer through commerce, inheritance, and gift, are a function of our fallen condition and are derived from human law rather than divine law. "For by divine law, the earth and its fullness are the Lord's; the poor and the rich God has made from one mud, and the poor and the rich he sustains on one earth. Nevertheless, by human law, one says, 'This estate is mine, this house is mine, this servant is mine.' "[61] Property is conventional, not natural; human beings are one by nature and by divine law, holding as stewards under human law that which by right belongs only to God. The land should be made to be fruitful and to multiply, not for prideful accumulation but in efficient obedience to God's command. The appropriation of goods is natural, but the legal regimes of property ownership are conventional, yielding a dual responsibility. On the one hand, Augustine affirms the responsibility to use property according to the principles of created nature; on the other, he also insists on respect for existing property regimes as a form of love of neighbor, even if owners use property wrongly.

Responsible use and enjoyment, for rich and poor alike, require a prudent valuation of what is really necessary. "But we possess many superfluous things, unless we keep only what is necessary. For if we seek useless things, nothing suffices." Augustine sees clearly the infinite expansion of desire for greater consumption. The only antidote is an adjustment of one's loves. Implicit in Augustine's position is an ethic of voluntary individual, corporate, and political social responsibility rooted in an abhorrence of waste. "The superfluous things of the wealthy are the necessities of the poor. When superfluous things are possessed, other's property is possessed."[62] Augustine is not arguing that goods have been wrongly taken from the poor, but that superfluous use withholds goods from the poor—both the material goods and the human potential of the poor are wasted. Ownership of superfluities does not entail the involuntary redistribution of property on ethical grounds. One can legally possess property under human law despite being of an illicit moral disposition, and redistribution curbs neither the illicit loves of the rich nor the greed of the poor. How much does one person really need? How much does a family really need? To what extent does the pursuit of superfluities impede the richness of social and spiritual relationships to which our created nature calls us? Possessions, for Augustine, are properly directed to social and spiritual unity; we are called to balance our personal, legal rights with our moral responsibilities toward the social whole of which we are a part.

Service to the common good does not require public ownership; individual ownership may be directed toward a public good—property may be individually held and yet not solely enjoyed in reference to oneself. Whereas Adam Smith saw that the pursuit of one's own material good produces an unintended public benefit, Augustine maintains that the pursuit of the common good bears ancillary individual spiritual fruits. In inverting what was to be the Smithian position, Augustine's ethics firmly distinguish ends from means and ancillary benefits. An Augustinian ethic of environmental sustainability, for example, might see reducing habits of consumption as a means to and consequence of better-ordered loves. An Augustinian ethic of philanthropy might see material relief of the poor as both a means to and a benefit of greater social and spiritual solidarity. An Augustinian ethic of corporate social responsibility would improve employee working conditions as a form of the love of neighbor, with higher productivity and an enhanced brand as attendant benefits. Intentions matter for Augustine: they reflect the order of our loves.

Augustine's understanding of the relationship between the moral injunction to the proper use of wealth and the legal protection of property rights comes out clearly in a letter discussing a law concerning the repayment of interest on a loan.[63] Although he opposes the effects of usury, Augustine states clearly that the law requiring the repayment of interest must be honored, though with concern for the poor within the bounds of the law. If someone uses property wrongly, he possesses it wrongly, and thus unjustly. In this case, "you can see then how many people ought in fact to return property that isn't theirs, and how few can be found who ought to have property returned to them! Wherever such people exist, the more justly they own property, the more they despise it."[64] In preaching to his congregation, Augustine finds lending at interest permissible, but urges moneylenders to collect the principal only, counting the rest as kindness and, above all, not oppressing those who cannot pay.[65] The judgment of the moral or divine law is that very few people have loves worthy of the property they own.

According to the civil law, however, "there is toleration for the injustice of those in wrongful possession." Civil laws "are not intended to make [owners] use possessions rightly, but rather to make them less oppressive in misusing them." Earthly laws and customs must prevail, even when they conform poorly to divine law, though Augustine concludes by enjoining officials to be conciliatory toward those who are bad. "This isn't to keep them happy or help them remain bad, but because those who become good come from among them."[66] The virtuous administrator upholds the rule of law, defends the poor as much as the law allows, and pursues reconciliation with evildoers, all in support of social unity. The moral order informs the legal order through the dispositions of public-spirited administrators and through legitimate legislation. The loves of the earthly and heavenly cities coexist in tension, but with the patient deference of the citizens of the heavenly city toward the unity and fragile peace of the earthly city.

THE ETHICS OF EXCHANGE: FROM PRIVATE RIGHT TO COMMON GOOD

Human beings, for Augustine, were placed in paradise to cultivate and to care for all of creation—to make it productive and to exercise an inner discipline in which the care for creation engenders the proper care of one's self.[67] God formed human beings for justice, and our work in time is intended to reflect growth and learning in response to God's own cultivation of and care for his creations. We do this by using and enjoying things and each other wisely and justly.[68] Material productivity is itself an occasion for learning to refine our loves and to cultivate our souls. To the extent that the cultivation and use of wealth turn us in on ourselves in selfishness, they are evil; to the extent that they draw us out of ourselves to love of neighbor and of God in the proper cultivation of our own souls and the common good, the cultivation and use of wealth are good. In this, corporate social responsibility or social entrepreneurship that aims significantly at social unity may prepare the way for an increase in spiritual wealth. It is not wealth itself but the degree of our attachment to it that determines its moral valence; it is impossible for the proverbial rich man to enter the kingdom of heaven not because he is rich, but only to the extent that his love of money has distorted and deformed his spirit.[69]

The improper love of wealth is a material expression of a more general spiritual malady. Augustine defines avarice as "the attitude by which a person desires more than what is due by reason of his excellence, and a certain love of one's own interest, his private interest . . . turning from the pursuit of the common good to one's own individual good out of a destructive self-love."[70]

The private prefers the part to the whole. The antidote to this disease, Augustine says, is *caritas* (charity, love), that love that embraces the other according to its created nature. "There are, then, two loves, of which one is holy, the other unclean; one turned towards the neighbor, the other centered on self." These two loves have marked the limits of "the two cities established among men under the sublime and wonderful providence of God, who administers and orders all that He creates; and one city is the city of the just, and the other city is the city of the wicked. With these two cities intermingled to a certain extent in time, the world [*saeculum*] moves on until they will be separated at the last judgment."[71]

In this life, the material and spiritual economies remain mixed. Our decisions are formed by our loves, which are also mixed. In his exposition of the Sermon on the Mount, Augustine reminds us that our hearts follow our treasure. We cannot serve two masters; one either serves God or is mastered by wealth (*mammon*).[72] Most of us, Augustine insists elsewhere, are storing up treasure without knowing for whom, or why.[73] Riches are good, but they cannot make us good. In using our wealth well—that is, in support of social and spiritual unity—we change for the better and grow in solidarity with those for whom we show acts of care.[74] We praise the trader who exchanges one thing for profit; so, too, we should praise those exchanges by which material goods are transformed into occasions for an increase in spiritual wealth.[75] To give our material goods is to give something of ourselves, but to use material goods to create circumstances in which giver and recipient grow together in love is to realize the potential of our created natures. In simple economic transactions, one might recognize others as persons, as beings rather than appendages to the machine or abstract objects in the naked cash nexus. Corporations and philanthropies might donate employee time as well as money so that bonds of human love are formed. Social entrepreneurship—those efforts to bring market innovations to specifically social problems—might aim at building spiritual as well as social capital. Augustine is less concerned about the substance of the material exchange than its form; the same material goods may be exchanged in a business or social entrepreneurship transaction, but material exchange, whether economic or philanthropic, without the bonds of human love is ultimately partial unless it includes a spiritual dimension. Only in the bonds of love are rich and poor brought into greater social and spiritual unity among themselves and between each other. Only in the bonds of love are material goods expanded and transformed into spiritual wealth.

CONCLUDING REMARKS

Augustine offers us no formulation for a specifically Christian business ethics. Rather than suggesting a route, he offers a constellation of reckoning points in the hope that we will better navigate the moral landscape in which material exchange takes place. Augustine weaves the classical tradition of unwealth in service of the public good with a Christian insistence on spiritual unity to illustrate not an ethical system but a pattern of considerations that shape the texture of human relationships. Is our attachment to the material economy rightly situated with respect to our social and spiritual loves? Have we seen things and people according to the order of their created natures and not simply in the order of market exchange? Our pilgrim journey is one of learning to increase material productivity in service of a spiritual wealth that has no price, no scarcity, and no propriety, because its sum is increased to the extent that it is enjoyed in common. The material and social economies grow when we each see ourselves, each other, and material things in the light of the order of created nature. True wealth—the treasure in heaven—is valued by the expansion of the heart in love.

NOTES

1. As an important terminological matter, Timothy Mitchell, *Rule of Experts: Egypt, Techno-Politics, Modernity* (Berkeley: University of California, 2002), 80–83, argues that it is only in the late 1930s that the substantive conception of "the economy" (with the definite article) replaces the adjectival use of "economy," which refers more broadly to the concrete material and cultural human practices of the thrifty use of resources. The closest word to "economy" in Augustine's Latin vocabulary is "frugality" (*frugalitas*).

2. *Letters,* trans. Roland J. Teske, in *The Works of Saint Augustine*, ed. B. Ramsey (Hyde Park, NY: New City Press, 2005), 10*.2, p. 263.

3. *Letter 10*.3, pp. 263–64.

4. *Letter 10*.6, p. 265.

5. *Letter 10*.2, 4, pp. 263–64.

6. Peter Brown, *Through the Eye of a Needle: Wealth, the Fall of Rome, and the Making of Christianity in the West, 350–550 AD* (Princeton, NJ: Princeton University Press, 2012), 148–60. The bibliography on Augustine is vast. Allan D. Fitzgerald's *Augustine through the Ages: An Encyclopedia* (Grand Rapids, MI: Eerdmans, 1999) remains a fundamental starting point, with bibliography, especially for nonspecialists. Augustine's reflections on the material economy and wealth are scattered throughout his systematic writings and his occasional letters and sermons. Peter Brown's *The Ransom of the Soul: Afterlife and Wealth in Early Western Christianity* (Cambridge, MA: Harvard University Press, 2015) and Robin Lane Fox's *Augustine: Conversions to Confessions* (New York: Basic Books, 2015) appeared too late to be considered in this essay.

7. Brown, *Through the Eye of a Needle,* 154–55.

8. *De officiis,* trans. Walter Miller, Loeb Classical Library (Cambridge, MA: Harvard University Press, 1913), 1.8.25.

9. Cic., *De officiis* 1.20.67.

10. Cic., *De officiis* 1.33.121.

11. *City of God* 5.18, quoted in Brown, *Through the Eye of a Needle,* 179.

12. *De opere monachorum,* 25.32, quoted in Brown, *Through the Eye of a Needle,* 179.

13. Brown, *Through the Eye of a Needle*, 179.

14. Ibid., 14.

15. See Brown, *Through the Eye of a Needle*, 3–30; John Locke, *Second Treatise of Government*, chap. 5, "Of Property," sec. 37.

16. *Letter 22*.1*, p. 314.

17. *Letter 22*.2*, p. 315.

18. *Letter 247*, pp. 177–79.

19. *Letter 247.2*, p. 178.

20. We know much of Augustine's personal life through his *Confessions*. See Brown, *Through the Eye of a Needle*, 150–52. The biographies by Peter Brown, *Augustine of Hippo: A Biography* (Berkeley: University of California Press, 2000), and James J. O'Donnell, *Augustine: A New Biography* (New York: Ecco Press, 2005), are most useful.

21. See Neil B. McLynn, *Ambrose of Milan: Church and Court in a Christian Capital* (Berkeley: University of California Press, 1994); see also Charles Avila, *Ownership: Early Christian Teaching* (Maryknoll, NY: Orbis Books, 1983), 59–80.

22. *De Nabuthe Jezraelita* 1, quoted in Avila, *Ownership*, 62.

23. *Hexameron* 5.26, quoted in Avila, *Ownership*, 64.

24. *De Nab.* 11, quoted in Avila, *Ownership*, 65.

25. *De Nab.* 11, quoted in Avila, *Ownership*, 66.

26. *De Nab.* 14, quoted in Avila, *Ownership*, 67; see further *De Nab.* 15.

27. See Brown, *Through the Eye of a Needle*, 120–47.

28. *De moribus ecclesiae*, ed. Roy J. Deferrari, The Fathers of the Church, vol. 56 (Washington, DC: The Catholic University Press of America, 1966), 1.34.75–1.35.77.

29. Brown, *Through the Eye of a Needle*, 308–21. See also J. L. González, *Faith and Wealth: A History of Early Christian Ideas on the Origin, Significance, and Use of Money* (San Francisco: Harper & Row, 1990).

30. *Praeceptum* 2, quoted in Brown, *Through the Eye of a Needle*, 172.

31. *City of God* 10.1. (Unless there is a direct quotation, references to the *City of God* will not cite a particular edition.)

32. *City of God* 10.3, trans. Marcus Dods (New York: Random House, 2000), 306–7.

33. *City of God* 10.20–25, and 22 passim.

34. *Confessions* 10.6.9–10; *City of God* 11.2.

35. *City of God* 11.4.

36. *Literal Meaning of Genesis*, trans. and ed. John Hammond Taylor, Ancient Christian Writers Series, vol. 41 (New York: Newman Press, 1982), 1.5.10.

37. *City of God* 11.16, adapted from Dods, 360, and from *Augustine: The City of God against the Pagans*, trans. R. W. Dyson (Cambridge: Cambridge University Press, 1998), 470.

38. *City of God* 11.16, adapted from Dods, 360, and Dyson, 470.

39. *On Christian Doctrine* 1.3, trans. J. F. Shaw (New York: Dover, 2009).

40. *On Christian Doctrine* 1.4, trans. Shaw.

41. *Letter* 157.23; *Sermons*, trans. Edmund Hill, The Works of Saint Augustine (Hyde Park, NY: New City Press), 50.

42. *City of God* 19.13.

43. *City of God* 14.28, adapted from Dods, 477, and Dyson, 632.

44. *Sermon* 61.3, in Augustine, *Commentary on the Lord's Sermon on the Mount with Seventeen Related Sermons*, trans. Denis J. Kavanagh, The Fathers of the Church, vol. 11 (New York: Fathers of the Church, 1951), 277.

45. *Ennarationes in Psalmos*, ed. Johannes Quasten and Joseph C. Plumpe, Ancient Christian Writers (Westminster, MD: Newman, 1946–), 64.9.

46. See F. E. Cranz, "*De Civitate Dei* XV, 2 and Augustine's Idea of the Christian Society," in *Augustine: A Collection of Critical Essays*, ed. R. A. Markus (Garden City, NY: Doubleday, 1972), 404–21.

47. *City of God* 19.17, trans. Dods, 695.

48. *Tractates on the Gospel of John* 40.10; quoted in Herbert Andrew Deane, *The Political and Social Ideas of St. Augustine* (New York: Columbia University Press, 1963), 44; cf. *Sermon* 7.229.

49. *City of God* 2.21, trans. mine, adapted from Dods, 56.

50. *City of God* 19.24, trans. Dods, 706.

51. *City of God* 19.26, 4.3; *Sermon* 60.4.

52. *Letter* 262.6, p. 206.

53. *Letter* 262.7, p. 206.

54. *Letter* 262.11, p. 208.

55. *Sermon* 85.5, 6, quoted in Avila, *Ownership,* 113.

56. *Sermon* 85, quoted in Avila, *Ownership,* 113.

57. See Allan Fitzgerald, "Diuitiae," *Augustinus-Lexikon,* 2:526–32.

58. *Sermon* 85; 44; 46.

59. *Ennarationes in Psalmos* 49.17; on property, see D. J. MacQueen, "Saint Augustine's Concept of Property Ownership," *Recherches Augustiniennes* 8 (1972): 187–229; and Richard Dougherty, "Catholicism and the Economy: Augustine and Aquinas on Property Ownership," *Journal of Markets and Morality* 6, no. 2 (Fall 2003): 479–95. On self-love, see O. M. T. O'Donovan, *Common Objects of Love: Moral Reflection and the Shaping of Community* (Grand Rapids, MI: Eerdmans, 2002). On sociability, see Todd Breyfogle, "Toward a Contemporary Augustinian Understanding of Politics," in *Augustine and Politics,* ed. John Doody et al. (Lanham, MD: Lexington Books, 2005), 217–36.

60. *Literal Meaning of Genesis* 8.15–16, 18.

61. *Tractates on the Gospel of John* 6.25, quoted in Avila, *Ownership,* 111.

62. *Ennarationes in Psalmos* 147.12.

63. *Letter* 153.25–26.

64. *Letter* 153.26, in *Augustine: Political Writings,* trans. E. M. Atkins and R. J. Dodaro (Cambridge: Cambridge University Press, 2001), 87.

65. *Sermon* 239.4.

66. *Letter* 153.26, trans. Atkins and Dodaro, 87.

67. *Literal Meaning of Genesis* 8.10.19–20.

68. *Literal Meaning of Genesis* 8.10.23; Alfred Schindler, "Auaritia," *Augustinus-Lexikon,* 1:493–98.

69. *Ennarationes in Psalmos* 51.14.

70. *Literal Meaning of Genesis* 11.15.19, p. 146.

71. *Literal Meaning of Genesis* 11.15.19–20, p. 147.

72. *Commentary on the Lord's Sermon on the Mount,* trans. Kavanagh, 44, 46, 47.

73. *Sermon* 60.

74. *Sermon* 60.11.

75. *Sermon* 61.4.

CHAPTER 5

Thomas Aquinas: The Economy at the Service of Justice and the Common Good

Martin Schlag

The son of an Italian nobleman, Thomas Aquinas was born in 1225 or 1226 in the Kingdom of Naples, then governed by the Roman emperor Frederick II. A member of the Dominicans, a mendicant order, Thomas dedicated his life to prayer, study, and teaching. On his death in 1274, he left an enormous and priceless collection of writings. The enduring importance of Thomas becomes apparent when his thinking is translated not only into modern language but also into modern concepts. He combines faith and reason, happiness and duty, body and soul, virtues and norms, into a single vision. At the same time, Thomas's system is not rigid, like a legal code or a closed system. His arguments are based on reasoning, not authority, except in matters pertaining exclusively to faith. Even in understanding matters of faith, however, he seeks to employ reason.

Thomas lived in a time of great economic and social expansion, an era that has been called the "Commercial Revolution."[1] This period of exponential economic growth in Catholic Europe during the twelfth and thirteenth centuries was brought about by stable demographic growth, the tilling of more arable land, technical innovations, an influx of silver and gold, and commercial expansion abroad. Thomas could therefore not ignore economic questions, even though he hardly ever turned to economics or commerce as a deliberately chosen subject. Thomas never authored a specific treatise on economics, the only exception being a short letter on deferment of payment.[2] In his era, economics was not an independent science but a branch of ethics. He dealt with the economy and social phenomena in general with a view to their role in God's great plan for the world and human beings. His economic teachings are thus scattered throughout his many works and are woven into his reflections on virtues, in particular justice, and vices.[3]

In this essay I will deal with Thomas's reflections on wealth and poverty, private property, commerce, justice in exchange, and the just price, as well as with money and its abuses, issues that fall under the twin moral considerations central to Thomas's thought: justice and the common good. I will also point to the relevance of his thought for contemporary business ethics.

WEALTH AND POVERTY

The essence, the measure, and the ultimate reason for ethics according to Thomas is the pursuit of happiness.[4] In line with the Aristotelian analysis of *eudaimonia*, Thomas distinguishes happiness from sensual pleasures, riches, and honors.[5] Unlike classical utilitarians, he does not identify happiness with pleasure, or unhappiness with pain. Happiness on earth consists in a virtuous life,[6] because the virtues constitute the fullest flourishing and development of the individual person's human nature.

External riches alone or as an aim in themselves cannot procure happiness, but since the human body depends upon material things, material wealth is, to a certain extent, necessary as an instrument: wealth can be put both to good and to bad use. According to Thomas, the same is true of poverty understood as detachment from possessions. This is an extraordinary thing for a member of a mendicant order devoted to poverty to say. However, poverty, like wealth, is only an instrument for a virtuous, contemplative, and religious life. If involuntary, it may prove to be a great distraction for those living in such a condition because they worry about what they lack.[7] Of course, misery and indigence can never be considered as conducive to human flourishing.

We do and should desire and strive for the material goods and the wealth we lack in order to lead a happy and virtuous life. When, however, is this desire no longer virtuous? Thomas draws a double line. The first line is subjective, dependent upon a person's intention. Aspiring to greater wealth becomes evil when it develops into the ultimate aim of one's life instead of being a means to something nobler. The second line is objective: a desire for more becomes evil when one desires superfluous things. This is called greed or avarice, an excessive desire for money and other material goods for oneself.[8] As such, it is a capital sin, because from it stem other sins such as violence and hard-heartedness. Contrariwise, Thomas considered the desire for money to be used for moral and noble purposes as virtuous. However, in the static society he lived in, social roles were defined. An average person was not able to amass great wealth in order to be beneficent. Beneficence was the task of the nobility and the church. Avarice played a central role in Christian ethics, giving rise to the highly controversial issue of what was necessary and what was superfluous, or in other words, "How much is enough?" Some authors limited the list of necessary items strictly to what was needed for survival or sustenance. According to these teachers, anything beyond what was necessary for survival was to be given to the poor as alms.[9] Thomas resolved the question in a more moderate manner, characteristic of his ethics. Avarice consisted in striving for material goods beyond what was needed to live in dignity and comfort according to one's social condition, and to care for one's family.[10] This constitutes the second, objective line: desiring the material means for maintaining the inherited social condition of one's family and avoiding social descent is not avarice. As Thomas lived in a static society, however, he did not allow for the wish to ascend the social ladder. This possibility simply did not exist in his time, and thus he would have considered it to be illicit.

Thomas did not enter the subtle discussion on the intricate balance between consumption and production, and the unintended consequences of their reduction. Such an analysis was simply beyond him and his times. Nonetheless, his understanding of production and consumption remains pivotal for all other aspects of his teachings on economic activities. Production of material goods and their exchange are to serve the human person, the family, and society as a whole, and to help people to acquire the amount of material well-being necessary to live in peace and harmony and to exercise the virtues. Every element of the economy, including wealth, money, and commerce, has a serving and ministerial character.

PRIVATE PROPERTY: NATURAL LAW, JUSTICE, AND THE COMMON GOOD

External riches may also be discussed in terms of private property. For Thomas, the rational arguments brought forward in favor of private property are economic arguments formulated in terms of natural law. However, even though Thomas defends private property, he does not dedicate a specific work or chapter to this topic. He deals with private property in order to establish when a claim is just, and to set up the rules for individual ethical behavior (e.g., the prohibition of theft presupposes the existence of property), approaching these through the general theory of natural law.

Thomas employs the notion of "natural law," in one of its senses, to define the set of rules that conform to social necessity or expedience.[11] In the case of various social and economic institutions, natural law could be changed through addition for the benefit of human life. Alternatively, natural law could be altered by subtraction, as, for example, in the rare and exceptional cases in which special causes hindered the observance of the precepts of natural law (even though these precepts remain always valid and unchanged). An example of subtraction is the legitimate exception from the duty to return things entrusted to one's care in rare cases of adverse social or political consequences (for example, you need not return a sword to a madman).

An example of the addition to natural law that concerns us especially is private property. Something is in accordance with natural law when nature has not provided for the contrary (e.g., a human being is naturally brought into the world naked because nature does not provide for the contrary condition, i.e., clothes). We have this in common with irrational animals. What is naturally just, Thomas writes, is adequate to, or commensurate with, a real being. This can be so in an absolute sense, such as the adequacy of man and woman for the generation of children. In this case, natural law is what nature imposes on all creatures, rational as well as irrational. Something can, however, be naturally adequate not in an absolute sense but according to the consequences that derive from it, such as a field. In itself and absolutely speaking, there is nothing in the nature of a field as a piece of land by which it would belong more to one person than to another. But if we consider its cultivation and its peaceful use, then there is a natural cause (or reason) for ascribing the field to one person rather than to another. Such ascription(s) are established by human reason, which considers the consequences of an institution.[12]

As can be glimpsed from what has been said so far, in determining the correct functioning of human institutions such as property, Thomas and the thirteenth-century Scholastics rely on a notion of final causality (a notion incompatible with that of modern natural science, which is based on mechanics).[13] Contrary to this modern conception, for Thomas and the teleological view, all creatures, animate or inanimate, are brought into being not only *by* an efficient cause but also *for* a final cause (in line with the Aristotelian legacy of teleology in Thomas's thought). All creatures are directed toward an aim in which their perfection consists. From this explicitly teleological perspective, nature possesses finality and meaning. Laws are derived from this finality.

Given the centrality of teleological reasoning in Thomas and other medieval theologians, and, in contrast, its absence in the modern understanding of scientific knowledge, it follows that the nature of modern social scientific knowledge is similarly affected. Modern economics is meant to function as an empirical, value-free science: it seeks to *describe* how economic mechanisms work. In doing so it formulates self-interest as the central, factually existing driving force of economic activity. Contrary to this modern approach, Scholastics were interested in *prescribing* how businesspeople should act in order to become virtuous persons. Their concern was not so much with how things worked as a matter of fact but with the consequences the social virtue of justice ideally generated. In order to draw all the conclusions from this virtue, the Scholastic teachers and Thomas with them, had to apply it to existing practices. They therefore studied them, and discovered a series of economic laws—for instance, the formation of market prices through demand and supply. However, in their system this employment of economic "laws" has a different meaning from our modern comprehension. For instance, in the above case, Thomas saw in the market price a tentative guideline that helped to discover the "*just* price" and thus avoid exploitation and ensure *just* behavior. By contrast, in late Scholastic thinkers, and then fully in neoclassical economics, the market would take on an impersonal character and would soon become an anonymous entity governed by aggregate market forces. An analytical depersonalization took place in economics.[14]

Before this was the case, however, Thomas, following Aristotle, applied his natural law method to private property. Albert the Great and Thomas overcame the somewhat negative attitude toward private property predominant in the tradition that preceded them, founding a positive justification of private property on natural reason. From Aristotle's arguments for property,[15] they developed (1) the argument from efficiency, (2) the argument from order, and (3) the argument from peace. First, people tend to take better care of what is their own. Holding goods in common is inefficient, because people leave the work to others. Second, without a division of property, there is confusion. If everybody knows exactly what things are in their care, things are treated better. Third, with private property, everybody has their own and can be content with it. Undivided communal goods among sinful men lead to frequent quarrels.[16]

In connection with justice, the preeminently social virtue central to economic life, Thomas's thought focuses on another chief consideration or end—the common good. Following Aristotle, Thomas grants a logical priority to the common over the individual good: the very concept of the individual good requires some notion of the common good, and the realization of that good, in practice, demands the presence of a common whole, society. These ideas apply to the institution of private property, so Thomas's arguments for property aim at the better functioning of the whole: if private people own things individually, then they will use them more efficiently, and that is better for us all.

The idea of the common good central to Thomas's ethical system appears in his definition of the law[17] as an ordering of reason toward the common good. It is furthermore reflected in his conception of how an individual belongs to his or her community: "All who are included in a community stand in relation to that community as parts to a whole";[18] "Every individual person is compared to the whole community as part to whole."[19] How is this whole, this community, to be understood? Although the notion of a "whole" may be comprehended as a substantial unity, whereby a whole is understood as one in substance, the reverse holds here: the relevant idea for society is a "unity of composition and order";[20] in other words, "the many men are one people" or become one under a particular aspect or reason (in our case socially or legally composed into one whole), while severally they are many different human beings or distinct substances. Thomas illustrates this idea through the example of an army in which each soldier engages in his own actions independently of the movements of the whole (e.g., he writes letters to his family, buys food for himself, etc.) even as the army, as such, acts in order to achieve the aims for which it exists: it moves, attacks, and hopefully wins against an enemy.[21] Similarly, a society has its naturally given aims even as individuals within that society may act independently of these or have their own chosen relations to one another. A social whole, as a unity of composition and order, will have a proper ordering of its elements or parts (individuals and institutions) among and between each other. This is the intrinsic common good (or form) of the whole. But the whole will also have its common end (an extrinsic common good).[22] It is this combination of intrinsic and extrinsic ends that Thomas regards as the common good of society, for by it the community is perfected and for for it society exists. And natural law directs our reason, as properly oriented, toward this end.

According to Thomas the common good of a community is not reducible to the particular goods of its members. "The common good of the city and the particular good of the individual differ not only in respect of the many and the few, but also under a formal aspect."[23] This means not only that there is a quantitative difference between who enjoys the good (individual or society), but that the two goods differ in their essential substance or content. This difference has important consequences. The common good is not a sum of the particular goods of its members, but a good of its own kind. "What is fundamentally good about the common good of a community is that the common good is perfective of the community as a whole, precisely in connection with the kind of unity and being that the community has."[24]

Nor is the individual good the same as the common good. The parts are not good simply by virtue of the goodness of the whole, even though the realization of the good of the parts depends on the realization of the goodness of the whole. Individual actions aim at particular matters, and these refer to the common good as to the final cause or teleological end (and not simply as individuals to a common genus). And this common good or end is what the law aims at.[25]

The common good is essentially shareable. An individual good cannot be shared, and consuming it excludes others from doing the same. With the common good the contrary is true: it exists only when shared. I cannot swallow the same bite of food that my partner has just put into his or her mouth, but we can both enjoy the same meal and the conversation during it "without division or subtraction."[26]

Under the aspect of the particular and the common good, the same action can be judged differently. A judge that correctly condemns a criminal can consider his or her judgment to be good; whereas the wife or the children of the criminal can consider the same judgment to be bad. Both judgments are good in their order: one seen from the perspective of the common good, the other from that of the particular good of the family.[27]

With these distinctions in hand, one can discern how the individual should orient to the common good. "For Aquinas, a good citizen is one who is willing to subordinate his or her willing of particular goods to his or her willing of the political community's common good."[28] Thomas links this with the virtue of *love*. Thomas affirms that we naturally love the common good more than our own particular good.[29] Seeing the amount of egotism and selfishness that exists in real life, we might consider this to be slightly too optimistic, but Thomas does not have romantic love in mind. He explains that the virtue of love for the common good is a naturally and rationally good tendency in human beings. When somebody effectively becomes a member of a community, by virtue of partaking in the common good, it becomes connatural for him or her to love the common good and to work for it. Loving the common good means conserving and defending it and placing it above one's personal interests. As the hand is sacrificed to protect the whole body from a blow, so the individual, who affectively and effectively unites with others, has the tendency to offer himself up for them. A tyrant, to the contrary, also "loves" the commonwealth but in order to possess it: he loves himself more than the community.[30]

Given this account of the idea of a common good for society, there remains the substantive question, What is the common good? Thomas does not explicitly and in detail define the content of the common good. However, he refers to justice, virtues, and peace as the great aims of human society that require the protection of law. More precisely, just human laws should prohibit actions that harm others, not thoughts, opinions, or ideas that remain in the interior mental sphere, and are thus ordered by God's law.[31] We can therefore define Thomas's substantive notion of the common good as justice and peace in society.

Scholastic analysis justified economic institutions or individual economic "rights," to use modern terminology, to the extent that these contributed to the common good. The modern position, represented paradigmatically by John Locke, chose the inverse path of justification. Man acquires property through labor. Property is thus an original natural right that goes before the formation of the commonwealth and is not justified by the common good. On the contrary, human beings later form states and create public authority in order to ensure the protection of their property rights.[32]

So Thomas justified several economic phenomena, among them private property, not by means of the innate natural rights of the individual but through his understanding of natural law and the common good. Because and insofar as certain institutions are, on the whole, advantageous to the common good, they thereby also benefit individual persons: private property, commerce and trade, and free bargaining are justified on these grounds. In the same vein, Thomas was aware of the social benefits of morally forbidden usury, or rather, he was aware of the disadvantages that would arise from a prohibition of usury by civil law. Civil law must not prohibit every morally wrong action—for example, all usury: "Some derive great advantages from the money they borrow even if they have to pay usury (interest) for it,"[33] and without it business as a whole would not work. Other important ideas are contained in the distinction between positive law and morality: not everything that is wrong in a moral sense need be prohibited by law, and, as a consequence, not every social problem can be solved by statutory regulation. Morality, particularly in a society that heeds it, can relieve the legislator of the onerous task of flooding society with an excessive number of laws.

As part and parcel of his derivation of private property from the common good, Thomas maintained that those who owned goods were obliged to share them with others in time of need. This goes so far that someone in immediate and extreme need may take what is another's in order to sustain his or her life (e.g., taking bread to survive from starvation, or a horse to flee from assassins).[34] Jean Porter has rendered Thomas's argument as follows: the right to private property serves the common good. "Ordinarily, the institution of private property serves this intention by providing a structure for distributing material resources. But when it fails to do so, the claims to which this institution gives rise are superseded by the more fundamental claim to make use of material goods to sustain one's life."[35] This limitation on private property mitigates the tension inherent in the institution of private property with the ideal of solidarity. Thomas provides for material solidarity by condoning or allowing the forceful impounding of material things in times of grave and urgent need or imminent danger disregarding the divisions into, and appropriations of, private property. Thus no natural law as such is violated, as would have been in a theft, since the case of grave need or imminent danger is a radically different situation. Thomas taught that the help given to the poor by the rich should always be voluntary, except in the case of extreme need, that is, situations of life and death: the dying have no time to ask.[36]

COMMERCE

Thomas understood commerce as the set of activities connected to trade. It included traveling abroad to purchase goods and transporting, storing, and—perhaps—improving them. The aim of commerce was to sell goods for profit. Thomas distinguished this activity from household management and from the administration of the public needs of the political community. Procuring the necessary means is good and natural, Thomas insists; however, that activity pertains to the *oeconomici* who manage the household and to the politicians who run the city rather than to the merchants (*negotiatores*).[37] These latter tend to exchange goods not out of necessity but for profit, and the greed of profit knows no bounds.

However, there is no condemnation of merchants in Thomas but rather a careful justification based upon a distinction. If the profit is modest, serving to maintain the merchant and his family as well as to provide alms for the poor, then this profit can be considered as "wages for labor," a just retribution for the merchants' service to the common good.[38] He writes, however, that clerics should in any case refrain from commerce, because they must avoid not only what *is* evil but also what *seems* to be evil, because of the vices frequently connected with commerce.[39]

In the range of the different moral judgments of commerce that were pronounced by medieval moralists, Thomas thus occupied a middle position. Diana Wood has described this as an evolution from condemnation to justification to exaltation.[40]

On the one extreme, feudalism had condemned commerce, and had influenced church teaching in a negative way. An important canonical and theological source of the twelfth century, the Decretum Gratiani, had declared commerce an illicit profession for Christians. On the other extreme, we find teachers like Duns Scotus, who exalted merchants as the builders of public happiness, whose work was so important for public well-being that government would have to employ people to fulfill their task if they did not exist. In this line of development, Thomas is to be placed in the middle: he justified commerce and merchants but remained skeptical as to their moral qualities. On this point he had Saint Augustine as ally: commerce in itself was not evil; only the vices of some merchants were such. Cheating, fraud, and lying were not qualities of trade as such but deplorable vices of some individuals. If one were to confuse these contingencies with the essence and nature of trade, one would also have to condemn farming. There were enough farmers who cheated, committed fraud, lied, and had other vices.[41]

In view of Thomas's multilayered and developing position on commerce it is pertinent to distinguish examples of his views. Thomas gives us an example of his skeptical attitude (or middle position) toward commerce as well as of his macroeconomic analysis in *De regimine principum*, II, 3.[42] In this short but influential *speculum principis*, a literary genre consisting of a collection of ethical rules for princes, Thomas dedicates a chapter to the material autarchy of a kingdom. Starting from the general principle that everything that is self-sufficient is superior to those that are not—"the more excellent something is, the more self-sufficient it is"—Thomas deduces, in this particular case regarding economics, that a materially self-sufficient polity is superior to one that is not. Economic self-sufficiency could be ensured in two ways, either by the fertility of the region to ensure material abundance or by trade. However, for Thomas the former is preferable to the latter on many counts, both economic and moral. The perfect city will make only a moderate use of merchants inasmuch as they are necessary for supplying those goods that are lacking, but will tend to rely more heavily on its own privately owned arable land to produce the necessary aliments. Trade can be interrupted, for example, in times of war, thus leaving the city exposed to starvation; commerce with other nations, not among the private owners of land, opens one to foreign customs and laws and hence to vice, affirms Thomas; in addition, each merchant works for his own profit, despising the public good, and thus the cultivation of virtue fails, since honor will then be bestowed on riches. Therefore, civic life necessarily will be corrupt if the citizens devote themselves to trade. However, there is nothing in Thomas that explains how labor for profit is distinct from labor for wages, and why the former turns one from the public good and the latter not. This shows that profit remained suspicious for Thomas.

Contrary to his analysis in *De regimine principum,* in other passages Thomas does show that he has understood the fundamentally positive role of exchange, and thus also of trade. Following Aristotle, Thomas wrote that societies form because people need to barter and exchange goods, and this is decisively facilitated by money.[43] In his analysis of commerce, Thomas is not yet able to apply his own vision of exchange of goods in friendship as a principle that forms societies[44] to trade in general. He is still too concentrated upon his rejection of greed to accept the inner logic and positive consequences of international commerce based on profit. Subsequent Scholastic authors were to make such a connection.[45] However, Thomas's skepticism finds an interesting parallel in the modern critique of contemporary exaggerations in the other direction. Michael J. Sandel, for instance, as others before him, argues that we have drifted from *having* a market economy to *being* a market society. Market reasoning does not pass judgment on the preferences satisfied, and this nonjudgmental stance is part of its appeal. Market logic has crowded out morals.[46] In this sense, Thomas's teaching on central economic topics, such as exchange, value, price, and so forth, and their intrinsic nexus with the ethical sphere could make a valuable contribution to contemporary debates critical of the logic of markets and their invasion of all areas of social life. Bringing ethics into business does not imply negating modernity's process of emancipation and secularization but realizing that there is an inner link between economic action and the human person endowed with dignity. Human dignity excludes certain practices from business not as an "intrusion" of external ethical criteria but as an integral and constitutive element of what the economy is: a service to humanity. Criminal forms of wealth creation (e.g., drug dealing), corruption, exploitation, disregard for human needs, parasitic ways of creating artificial financial profit through mechanisms of the financial markets, and so forth are not only unethical but would not deserve the name "economic." In Thomas's understanding, economic activity is seen and analyzed as human agency, and therefore as essentially ethical or unethical behavior.

JUSTICE IN EXCHANGE AND THE JUST PRICE

Thomas's economic thought was essentially a part of his ethical theory. As economic relations are fundamentally interactions among persons about things, his analysis is primarily a *theory of justice* in regard to exchange. The Scholastic ideal was justice between buyer and seller. Thomas too was of this opinion and deduced the justification for economic exchange from the *common good*. Here we have another instance of the notion of the common good: economic exchange is necessary to satisfy the needs and wants of people. Exchange is established for the common advantage of both buyer and seller, he writes, and should therefore not hurt or damage one more than the other, or, put in positive terms, be of mutual advantage. Understood in terms of justice, exchange requires equality. Thus, a sale is just when the price equals the value (just price) of the thing being sold.[47] Justice pervades all aspects of Thomas's reflections on economic topics, especially the question of price and value. Money functions as a measure of value according to human law. Money is thus *medium iustitiae*,[48] serving the conservation or creation of *aequalitas*.

Therefore, the endeavor to ensure equality in exchange is identical with the calculation of the just price. The idea of *iustum pretium* evolved in Roman law in connection with the legal device of *laesio enormis*: anybody could buy and sell at a freely negotiated price. However, if this price was more than 150 percent of the "just price," the contract was invalid. Originally applied to real estate sales, *laesio enormis* in postclassical Roman law was extended to all kinds of sales contracts. In the Scholastic tradition, the just price was the competitive market price, along with some important specifications. The first is that the legally possible price was not the same as the morally licit price. In the liberal Roman juridical tradition, a thing was worth as much as could be had for it. This meant that according to medieval civil law, a seller was allowed to try to obtain the highest possible price as long as it was within the 150 percent range of the "just price." The Scholastics, and Thomas with them, warned that the moral law was stricter: a thing was not to be sold intentionally for more than it was worth. Thomas explained that civil law could not prescribe ideal behavior, because it was made for a multitude of people who lacked many virtues. Thus, civil law tolerated the selling of goods above their value within the limits of *laesio enormis*, as long as no fraud or lies were implied. However, according to the divine moral law, the "equality of justice" had to be observed.[49]

The second specification refers to the medieval understanding of the market. This market, for the medieval scholar or citizen, was not an abstract social institution of anonymous aggregate forces, but a geographically identifiable place where salespeople at a certain time set up their wares for sale. In this situation, a certain price would result from multiple transactions. This price, that at which the good sold was valued according to the estimation of the market, was the "just price." This is to be understood as an ethical principle, as a standard of justice, in order to protect the buyer from overpricing out of need or inferiority of bargaining power.[50]

Thomas was aware of the fact that the estimation of the price of a good by the market can be seriously off the mark. He therefore developed a calculus that was influential throughout the Scholastic period. Odd Langholm refers to it as the "double rule of just pricing."[51] If the seller incurs a serious loss by selling something (for example, because his production costs have been unexpectedly high, and he must sell, as a farmer his crops, in order to survive), then the seller may seek indemnity from the buyer. He may justly charge a higher price in order to cover his loss. On the other hand, if the seller suffers no special loss from the sale, but the buyer draws great advantage from the purchase, then the seller is not morally allowed to raise the price. The utility of the buyer does not come from the seller, and, says Thomas, nobody may sell something (in this case a thing's utility that stems from purely subjective factors on the buyer's side), which does not belong to him. The buyer can, however, as a show of honesty, voluntarily pay more to thank the seller.[52] Thomas's notion of trade suggests that not only does the seller have obligations but so might the customer. That a customer may have some duties of fairness to a seller underscores Thomas's conception of trade as a mutual relationship between persons.

Thomas's principles for fair pricing are of startling contemporary relevance.[53] Although prices are generally characterized as the result of an agreement following supply and demand under competitive conditions, the ideal conditions of market equilibrium, in which marginal costs equal marginal revenue, are rarely achieved. Problems of fairness arise today, as they did in Thomas's time, when the bargaining power of the contracting parties is greatly unbalanced. Thus, excessive pricing, on the one hand, and predatory pricing, on the other, are at present ethically, and to some extent also legally, forbidden.[54]

From a modern perspective, what is missing in Thomas is what we would call "social justice." Thomas does not criticize social structures as such. The society he lived in was stationary, and people remained in the social group into which they had been born. His ethical analysis therefore concentrated upon the rights and the duties people possessed in the existing social framework, which he did not strive to change. However, he did criticize evil behavior and analyze social structures, as demonstrated in his commendation of a mixed polity, a combination of monarchy, aristocracy and democracy, as the best form of organization.[55]

MONEY (AND ITS ABUSES): BUSINESS VIRTUES AND VICES

Despite the monetary expansion and the development of different kinds of financial instruments during his time,[56] Thomas's conception of money was physical—namely, that of substantial silver coins. The concept of money in terms of bank accounts, bank transfers, or bills of exchange is thus lacking.

Thomas did not stigmatize money as evil. In accordance with the Aristotelian tradition, he cherished money as (1) a measure of value, (2) a means of exchange, and (3) a store of value. Without money, commercial exchange would not be possible, and societies based upon a division of labor and service would be incapable of forming. He was aware that money fluctuated in value, and thus was concerned that states maintain the value of coins and avoid the devaluation of currencies.[57] For our contemporary situation it might be useful to let ourselves be reminded by Thomas that there is an ethical dimension to money, and it rests on its nature as a repository of value and as an instrument of a voluntary and fair exchange. Money too is a social institution, and, as something created by man's free will, possesses a moral nature. It is not a purely or merely technical or mechanical means.

Money concerns several virtues and vices. First and foremost, money is a "measure of justice" in the context of exchange. Justice is directed toward securing right relations for the community as a whole and between individuals. Justice strengthens our will to give to others what has been objectively established by reason as due to them by law or by contract. However, money is also the object of the virtue of generosity, *liberalitas*, which, in Thomas's system, does not direct and strengthen the will alone but also our passions of desire. While the virtue of justice creates equality in *exterior* acts, its aim is not to moderate our *interior* passions. This is rather the aim of *liberalitas*, which is the virtue of spending and giving money well and with joy where it is due or convenient, and of not spending it when it is not due or inconvenient. Generally speaking, for Thomas, money is meant to be spent and used, not hoarded. Excessive attachment to money would prevent our being just, decent, and friendly persons. Generosity overcomes an excessive attachment to money (greed) and ensures its good use. By nature, we are inclined to spend money on our own interests. Therefore, it is proper to the virtue of generosity to spend money on others.[58]

On the other hand, the virtue of *liberalitas* preserves us from being profligate or prodigal. Just as a good soldier must not only draw his sword but also sharpen it and preserve it in its sheath, Thomas analogizes, the truly generous person not only uses money but earns it and saves it for future convenient use.[59]

Another virtue relevant to business is *magnificentia*, which we would best translate as the courage to allocate great resources in order to achieve great aims, or in other words, the courage to take risks.[60] With "great aims" Thomas does not mean "magnificence" as a type of pomp; he means true greatness in quantity, value, or dignity. He would certainly agree with the idea that greatness requires a high level of modern values like leadership and entrepreneurship, of love of truth, of discipline, and of technical means.[61]

The positive connotations and the encouragement to use money contrast with Thomas's analysis of the vices, such as the aforementioned prodigality and greed. Specifically within the context of money, Thomas highlighted three abuses: *obolostatica*, the gleaning of disproportional profit from mint through the abuse of the king's power to create coins as currency;[62] *campsoria*, money changing; and *usura*, usury, or interest on loans. These concepts stem from the Latin translation of Aristotle's *Politics*. Of these, *obolostatica* became particularly important in the fourteenth century, when kings frequently tried to solve financial crises by devaluing their currencies, by reducing either the amount of precious metal in the coins or the coins' weight. Thomas condemns these practices, because they are forms of greed and unjust in the face of the kings' subjects.[63] The relevance of these ideas today becomes evident when applied to inflation. Inflation is a hidden form of taxation, a reduction of individual wealth stored in money. When intentionally used by governments to reduce their own public debt it becomes a moral problem: the willed confiscation of private property by the state.

Finally, the Scholastic doctrine on usury is the element of medieval economic thought that has attracted the greatest contemporary critique for its reputation of being irrational and contrary to economic logic.[64] For our purposes, a brief summary should suffice.[65] The Scholastics taught that charging interest on a loan of fungible goods (e.g., money) was always unjust, independent of the rate of interest. Even the hidden intention of receiving anything above the given sum was sinful. Thomas inherited the condemnation of usury from a tradition that by the thirteenth century was already several hundred years old. Teaching and reflecting in a theological atmosphere, however, he did not simply accept this rejection as a "dogma" but was sincerely convinced that any form of interest was contrary to human reason and therefore a breach of natural law. In the relevant question of his book *De malo*, he lists twenty-one arguments against interest. Twenty of these arguments are not necessarily the points Thomas himself would make, but rather refutations of arguments brought forward in favor of interest by others. In his refutations Thomas does repeat the general Scholastic doctrine on usury but consistently refers to his own argument of "consumptibility" (explained below).

The arguments contrived by other teachers and also present in Thomas were inspired by the nature of the Roman contract law of *mutuum* (loan), which did not grant interest and transferred the property of the lent money.[66] The money given as a loan became the property of the borrower. Anything he gained with this loan was fruit of his own efforts. Thus the moneylender, if he charged interest, gained profit from what was legally not his own. From this transfer of property stemmed a second argument that referred to risk. A loan became the property of the borrower who consequently bore all risk, especially the risk of loss, whereas the creditor had no risk. The creditor had the right to receive the sum, in spite of the borrower's loss. Why should the creditor therefore receive more than the sum lent to the debtor? Of course, from a modern point of view, the Scholastics forgot the risk of insolvency borne by the creditor. A third argument criticized how the usurer did not work but idly waited for his money to grow, exploiting the labor of the debtor. What the usurer thus sold was time, but time belonged to God, so usury was a theft of God's property. A fourth argument, also shared by Thomas, suggested usury was not given voluntarily but only conditionally: the debtor was in need and thus he consented to usury conditionally. Thomas never adopted the idea of the *physical* sterility of money (originally forwarded by Aristotle), but he did develop an argument of his own from "consumptibility,"[67] which was very influential throughout Scholasticism (except in Duns Scotus and his school). Thomas points to his argument as the justification underlying all the rest. Money is sterile in a *moral* sense: money cannot produce money but is meant to be a means of exchange for a useful good. Money had no other value than when exchanged. Therefore, counting substance and use separately is sinful and usurious.[68] The use and ownership of money in this argument are indistinguishable. The essence of money, according to Thomas, is its consumption (hence the argument from consumptibility). It does not have any other use. Thus, having to pay back more than what one has received, merely for having used this money, means paying twice. From a modern point of view, we can understand that the notion Thomas obviously lacks is that of the opportunity costs of liquid funds. Interest compensates the creditor for these costs.

Thomas, however, somehow does intuit our contemporary notion of the opportunity costs of liquid funds, albeit not clearly. In the medieval commercial practice, instruments had to be found not to circumvent the prohibition of usury but to grant indemnity to creditors who had suffered unjust loss through the blameworthy conduct of the debtor. To achieve this aim, three so-called extrinsic titles to interest were developed: *poena morae, damnum emergens*, and *lucrum cessans*. *Poena morae* was punishment for delay: a debtor who did not pay back his debt punctually had to indemnify his creditor by paying interest, not from the beginning of the debt but solely from the moment of delay. Thomas granted this kind of compensation only if there had really been damages.[69] In other words, he included this case in another extrinsic title, called *damnum emergens*: a debtor shall reimburse the creditor for the damages the debtor incurs, because the creditor has granted an otherwise gratuitous loan. The third extrinsic title, rejected by Thomas Aquinas, *lucrum cessans*, meant gains that could not be realized. A creditor who gives away his money as a loan cannot use this money for his own business. He therefore loses profitable opportunities. However, as these gains were speculative, Thomas did not accept them as a title to interest.[70]

CONCLUDING REMARKS

As has become clear in this essay, Thomas Aquinas certainly lacks an understanding of certain important aspects of modern economics. This is especially true of the condemnation of all forms of interest as usury, independently of the rate of interest. On the other hand, in the course of his ethical analysis, he penetrates and understands some of the more fundamental social mechanisms that govern economic life: supply and demand, the use value of goods, risk management, and so forth. Moreover, some of his insights are worth rediscovering.

The prohibition of usury was aimed at avoiding the exploitation of the poor, and thus expresses a value of unabated actuality. The distinction between usury and interest and the establishment of so-called extrinsic titles to interest paved the way for the modern system of regulated interest rates in legal financial markets. Moreover, the many rational arguments put forward against nongratuitous loans do pose questions regarding modern business ethics that are worth considering: exorbitant interest rates were and are a severe problem; unwise indebtedness, then as now a deplorable phenomenon, becomes apparent in pure consumer credits, and most of all, in the immense public debt that has accumulated in recent decades. Thomas's summons to greater sobriety, to voluntary simplicity, and to the avoidance of greed would be well worth heeding. Thomas raised his voice against the unproductive hoarding of wealth locked up in a chest, instead of being put to the service of society through investment. Then and now, the underlying ideal of fraternity to be spread among men was and is important: there are always the poor who need help.

The economic thought of Thomas was characterized by an approach to economic questions that, first, placed the personal relationship between the buyer and the seller at the center, and, second, evaluated economic phenomena as part of a greater whole, the ethical perfection of the persons involved in economic exchange. This is why the virtue of justice and the equality of the value of the goods exchanged were of central importance to his thought. This holistic approach ensures lasting interest in the economic thought of Thomas Aquinas.

In the context of Scholasticism's struggle for an economy based on just exchanges, Thomas offered the "double rule of just pricing," which can still be of use, not as a legal rule but as a moral orientation. It is an invitation to the seller to be generous in order not to abuse a special need or interest of the buyer, and at the same time demands of the buyer to be generous when the production costs of the seller have been extraordinarily high. This introduces a flexible system of balances and mutual consideration into the market that requires personal knowledge and relationship among the economic agents.

The other crucial aspect, along with that of justice, is the importance attributed to the common good. As has been shown, this goes so far as to legitimize the various institutions, rights, and duties of economic life through their contribution to the common good. The common good is prior to all individual goods.[71] Modernity has chosen the inverse approach: individual natural rights come first; the commonwealth needs to be reintegrated. Without wishing to return to past models, the Scholastic teachings can serve as a measure: institutions and actions of private advantage should also serve others and the common good. Freedom and the free economy need a culture of common good to develop. Freedom and responsibility go together.

With this conviction society could also curb greed and reconduct individuals to the appropriate limits of self-interest. Self-interest is a powerful motor for the creation of wealth and of economic development. However, it must not be confused with greed. Self-interest is not egoism, if it is guided, structured, and ordered by a greater love—the love for the common good, as Thomas Aquinas has beautifully described it—and by the love of God that makes us citizens of the eternal city while leading our lives on earth. In the midst of hardships and the struggles of material survival and progress, we can already experience a first taste of the joy and the harmony that we will have everlastingly in the love of God and of one another. Actually this, and nothing less, is the aim of Thomas's economic ethics: to experience God's presence, and to taste eternal life also in the economy and in daily work.

NOTES

1. See Robert S. Lopez, *The Commercial Revolution of the Middle Ages, 950–1350* (1971; repr., Cambridge: Cambridge University Press, 1976).

2. Thomas Aquinas, *De emptione et venditione ad tempus*, in *Opera omnia*, vol. 42 (Rome: Commissio Leonina, 1979), 393–94.

3. See Odd Langholm, *Economics in the Medieval Schools: Wealth, Exchange, Value, Money, and Usury according to the Paris Theological Tradition, 1200–1350* (Leiden: E.J. Brill, 1992), 206–7.

4. Thomas Aquinas, *Summa theologiae*, 3rd ed. (Cinisello Balsamo: San Paolo, 1999), I-II, qq. 2–5. I cite the *Summa theologiae* as follows: I-II means "first half of the second part"; II-II, "second half of the second part"; q(q). is "question(s)," and a(a).,"article(s)."

5. *Summa*, I-II, q. 2, aa. 1–6; Thomas had developed this position from his earlier work *Summa contra gentiles*, in *Opera omnia*, vol. 14 (Rome: Commissio Leonina, 1926), 3.27–33.

6. *Summa*, I-II, q. 5, a. 5.

7. *Summa*, II-II, q. 186, a. 3, ad 2.

8. Thomas Aquinas, *De malo*, in *Opera omnia*, vol. 23 (Rome: Commissio Leonina, 1982), q. 13, a. 1; *Summa*, II-II, q. 118, a. 1.

9. See Langholm, *Economics in the Medieval Schools*, 42.

10. *Summa*, II-II, q. 32, aa. 5–6; q. 118, a. 1; *In orationem dominicam expositio*, ed. Raimondo Spiazzi (Turin and Rome: Marietti, 1954), Petitio 4.

11. See *Summa*, I-II, q. 94, a. 5; II-II, q. 57, a. 3 c.

12. See *Summa*, II-II, q. 57, a. 3.

13. See Odd Langholm, *The Legacy of Scholasticism in Economic Thought: Antecedents of Choice and Power* (Cambridge: Cambridge University Press, 1998), 160.

14. See Langholm, *Legacy of Scholasticism*, 162–63 and 185.

15. See Aristotle, *Politics*, ed. and trans. Harris Rackham, Loeb Classical Library (Cambridge, MA: Harvard University Press, 1990), II.2.1263a1–40, 85–89.

16. Thus, Thomas renders two of Aristotle's arguments, adding one of his own (on order): *Summa*, II-II, q. 66, a. 2; *In libros Politicorum Aristotelis expositio*, ed. Raimondo Spiazzi (Rome: Marietti, 1966), book 4, lectio 4; see also Langholm, *Economics in the Medieval Schools*, 171–73 (Albert) and 210–16 (Thomas).

17. See *Summa*, I-II, q. 90, a. 4 c: *quaedam rationis ordinatio ad bonum commune, ab eo qui curam communitatis habet, promulgata*.

18. *Summa*, II-II, q. 58, a. 5.

19. *Summa*, II-II, q. 64, a. 2. The analogy goes as follows: since generally the imperfect is directed to the perfect, and every part is directed to the whole as imperfect to perfect, i.e., every part is naturally for the sake of the whole, therefore every individual person is compared to the community as part to whole.

20. *Summa*, I-II q. 17, a. 4 (*unitas compositionis aut ordinis*).

21. See Thomas Aquinas, *Sententia libri Ethicorum*, in *Opera omnia*, vol. 47/1 (Rome: Commissio Leonina, 1969), I.1, p. 4.

22. In this distinction and in the following explanation of the concept of the common good in Thomas, I follow Michael Baur, "Law and Natural Law," in *The Oxford Handbook of Aquinas*, ed. Brian Davies and Eleonore Stump (Oxford: Oxford University Press, 2012), 238–54.

23. *Summa*, II-II, q. 58, a. 7, ad 2; see Baur, "Law and Natural Law," 241.

24. Baur, "Law and Natural Law," 241.

25. See *Summa*, I-II, q. 90, a. 2, ad 1 and 2.

26. Baur, "Law and Natural Law," 241.

27. See *Summa*, I-II, q. 19, a. 10.

28. Baur, "Law and Natural Law," 243.

29. See *Summa*, II-II, q. 26, a. 3; I, q. 60, a. 5; Thomas Aquinas, *De caritate*, in *Quaestiones disputatae*, ed. P. Bazzi, M. Calcaterra, T. S. Centi, E. Odetto, and P. M. Pession (Turin and Rome: Marietti, 1953), 2.

30. See *De caritate*, 2. The example of the hand and the blow is from *Summa*, I, q. 60, a. 5.

31. See *Summa*, I-II, q. 95, a. 1; q. 100, a. 2. This is true also of the jarring topic of Thomas's treatment of heresy. He justifies the persecution of heresy because, on his view, heretics

harm others, not because it harms the individual heretic himself, whose interior act of faith cannot be touched by human laws (cf. *Summa*, II-II, q. 11, a. 3).

32. For a comparison between the Scholastic and the modern justification of private property as well as its treatment in the Christian tradition, see Thomas Aquinas, *Recht und Gerechtigkeit*, with commentary by Arthur F. Utz, Die Deutsche Thomas-Ausgabe, vol. 18, ed. Heinrich M. Christmann (Heidelberg: Kerle/Pustet, 1953), 491–527.

33. *De malo*, q. 13, a. 4, ad 6.

34. *Summa*, II-II, q. 66, a. 7.

35. Jean Porter, "The Virtue of Justice (IIa IIae, qq. 58–122)," in *The Ethics of Thomas*, ed. Stephen J. Pope (Washington, DC: Georgetown University Press, 2002), 281–82.

36. See *Summa*, II-II, q. 66, a. 7: "in extreme need all things are common" (*in necessitate sunt omnia communia*).

37. *Summa*, II-II, q. 77, a. 4 c.

38. *Summa*, II-II, q. 77, a. 4 c: *quasi stipendium laboris*.

39. See *Summa*, II-II, q. 77, a. 4, ad 3; also q. 187, a. 2. In his Rule of monastic life, Benedict allows the monks to sell goods for their own livelihood but at a price below the market average, in order to give all glory to God. See *The Rule of Benedict: A Guide to Christian Living*, trans. Monks of Glenstal Abbey (Dublin: Four Courts Press, 1994), chap. 57, p. 258.

40. See Diana Wood, *Medieval Economic Thought* (Cambridge: Cambridge University Press, 2002), 110–20; Martin Schlag, "The Encyclical *Caritas in Veritate*, Christian Tradition, and the Modern World," in *Free Markets and the Culture of Common Good*, ed. Martin Schlag and Juan Andrés Mercado (Heidelberg: Springer, 2012), 93–109.

41. Thus Augustine, *Ennarationes in Psalmos*, in *Corpus Christianorum, Series Latina*, vol. 39 (Turnholt: Brepols, 1956), Ps. 70, 17, p. 954; quoted in *Summa*, II-II, q. 77, a. 4 *sed contra*.

42. *De regimine principum et De regimine Judaeorum politica opuscula duo*, 2nd rev. ed. (Turin and Rome: Marietti, 1948). Thomas never completed this book.

43. See Thomas Aquinas, *Sententia libri Ethicorum*, in *Opera omnia*, vol. 47/2 (Rome: Commissio Leonina, 1969), V.9, p. 296.

44. See *Summa*, II-II, q. 114. In *Summa*, II-II, q. 157, a. 3, ad 3, he beautifully writes: *homo naturaliter est omni homini amicus.*

45. One of whom, Richard of Middleton (see Langholm, *Economics in the Medieval Schools*, 327–41), led, along with other Franciscans, the movement in exalting merchants as builders of the common good. See Giacomo Todeschini, *Ricchezza francescana: Dalla povertà volontaria alla società di mercato* (Bologna: Il Mulino, 2004).

46. Michael J. Sandel, *What Money Can't Buy: The Moral Limits of Markets* (New York: Farrar, Straus and Giroux, 2012).

47. *Summa*, II-II, q. 77, a. 1 c; Thomas Aquinas, *Quodlibet*, II, q. 5, a. 2, [10], in *Quaestiones quodlibetales*, ed. Raymundo Spiazzi (Turin: Marietti, 1956), 32.

48. Thomas states this explicitly in *Sententia libri Ethicorum*, in *Opera omnia*, vol. 47/2, V.9, p. 294.

49. *Summa*, II-II, q. 77, a. 1, ad 1.

50. Odd Langholm, *The Merchant in the Confessional: Trade and Price in the Pre-Reformation Penitential Handbooks* (Leiden: Brill, 2003), 244–46.

51. Langholm, *Economics in the Medieval Schools*, 233.

52. *Summa*, II-II, q. 77, a. 1 c; this solution is also accepted by other Scholastic authors; see Langholm, *Merchant in the Confessional*, 121; Martin Schlag, "Economic and Business Ethics in Select Italian Scholastics (ca. 1200–1450)," in *Handbook of the Philosophical Foundations of Business Ethics*, ed. Christoph Luetge (Heidelberg: Springer, 2012), 179–205.

53. See Albino Barrera, "Exchange-Value Determination: Scholastic *Just Price*, Economic Theory, and Modern Catholic Social Thought," *History of Political Economy* 29 (1997): 83–116.

54. See Andrew Crane and Dirk Matten, *Business Ethics*, 3rd ed. (Oxford: Oxford University Press, 2010), 355–59.

55. See *Summa*, I-II, q. 105, a. 1.

56. For further information, consult Raymond de Roover, *Business, Banking, and Economic Thought in Late Medieval and Early Modern Europe,* ed. Julius Kirshner (Chicago: University of Chicago Press, 1974); Wood, *Medieval Economic Thought,* 197–201; Fabian Wittreck, *Geld als Instrument der Gerechtigkeit: Die Geldlehre des Hl. Thomas von Aquin in ihrem interkulturellen Kontext* (Paderborn: Schöningh, 2002), 147–51.

57. See *Sententia libri Ethicorum,* in *Opera omnia,* vol. 47/2, V.9, p. 296; Wittreck, *Geld als Instrument der Gerechtigkeit,* 322–35.

58. *Summa,* II-II, q. 117, aa. 3–4; *Sententia libri Ethicorum,* in *Opera omnia,* vol. 47/2, 4.2, p. 206.

59. *Summa,* II-II, q. 117, a. 3, ad 2.

60. Thomas himself defines *magnificentia* as the virtue of using big financial means in order to achieve great and noble ends. It differs from courage insofar as courage is defined by the danger for life and limb a person takes upon herself to achieve a good end. *Magnificentia* refers only to financial risks. As is apparent throughout this essay, Thomas's concepts must be translated in their context and according to their real meaning. It would be wide of the mark to render *liberalitas* as "liberality" and *magnificentia* as "magnificence," just as it would be misleading to understand *oeconomia* as "business."

61. Cf. the well-known analysis in Jim Collins, *Good to Great: Why Some Companies Make the Leap and Others Don't* (New York: Harper Business, 2001).

62. Coin clipping by individuals was downright theft and fraud and thus not considered *obolostatica.*

63. See *In libros Politicorum Aristotelis expositio,* I.8; Wittreck, *Geld als Instrument der Gerechtigkeit,* 345–46. The passage in question is not clear, and its interpretation is contested. However, the interpretation that I propose is in accordance with the Latin translation of Aristotle by William of Moerbeke. For examples of *obolostatica,* see Wood, *Medieval Economic Thought,* 100–109.

64. Even Raymond de Roover accuses Scholasticism of having fallen into a "quagmire of contradictions" on this topic; see his "Scholastic Economics: Survival and Lasting Influence from the Sixteenth Century to Adam Smith," in *Business, Banking, and Economic Thought in Late Medieval and Early Modern Europe,* 318.

65. On the development of the Scholastic evaluation of usury, see John T. Noonan, Jr., *The Scholastic Analysis of Usury* (Cambridge, MA: Harvard University Press, 1957); Gabriel Le Bras, "Usure," *Dictionnaire de théologie catholique* 15/2 (1950): 2316–72.

66. In Roman law, interest was allowed, but it had to be stipulated in additional contracts to the loan.

67. *De malo,* q. 13, a. 4; *Summa,* II-II, q. 78.

68. *De malo,* q. 13, a. 4 c; see Langholm, *Economics in the Medieval Schools,* 243.

69. See *Summa,* II-II, q. 62, a. 4

70. See *Summa,* II-II, q. 78, a. 2, ad 1.

71. "Now the good of the whole universe is that which is apprehended by God, who is the Maker and Governor of all things: hence whatever he wills, he wills it under the aspect of the common good; this is his own goodness, which is the good of the whole universe" (*Summa,* I-II, q. 19, a. 10).

CHAPTER 6

The Ethics of Commerce in Islam: Ibn Khaldun's *Muqaddimah* Revisited

Munir Quddus and Salim Rashid

The rich and varied contributions of classical Islamic scholars to philosophy, ethics, and the social sciences are virtually unknown outside specialized circles in the West. This unfortunate situation extends to ideas on the morality and ethics of market exchange and commerce. Ibn Khaldun (1332–1406), one of the most influential scholars of classical Islam, set forth a vision of history and society that is increasingly recognized by scholars as a remarkable precursor to concepts and ideas found in a range of modern disciplines.[1] He may be the only Muslim thinker to have influenced a contemporary American president, a conservative no less, on a core policy issue.[2] This essay focuses on Ibn Khaldun's varied and original contributions to business and commercial ethics as these appear in his monumental work, the *Muqaddimah*.[3]

In the *Muqaddimah*, this profound fourteenth-century thinker from the Maghreb expounds on topics that today we would classify as historiography, sociology, philosophy, political theory, commerce, and economics. His observations form part of an extensive analysis of the rise and fall of civilizations. This analysis assigns a significant role to productive commerce, even though Ibn Khaldun expresses concerns regarding certain practices of traders. He believes a civilization that is strong militarily and politically is built upon the foundations of robust commerce. The court (effectively, governing authorities and their relations) is presented as the key to robust commerce, both for sustaining the basic legal foundation for business and as the major source of spending on goods, especially crafts and luxuries. For Ibn Khaldun, history is cyclical: a civilization that has reached its peak is ripe for a decline. The decline of a civilization that has reached its zenith is intimately linked to the society's moral and spiritual collapse, starting with the court's excessive attachment to sedentary living and luxury, borrowing, and wasteful spending.

In his various discussions of commerce, Ibn Khaldun draws important distinctions that we examine below. Commercial activities may be understood as "natural" if they contribute to the overall welfare of society. The natural or productive forms of commerce include everyday buying and selling, as well as investments with an eye to future profits.[4] Ibn Khaldun often points out that productive commercial exchange may involve practices not considered ethically proper, even if permissible. These include trading strategies such as the use of "cunning" to outwit competition.

The employment of strategy and sharp-eyed gamesmanship in business may be regarded as dubious in some spheres of life. In Ibn Khaldun's accounts of such tactics, one is reminded of the concerns of another modern, more widely acclaimed advocate of commerce, the eighteenth-century Scottish philosopher and political economist Adam Smith. In *The Wealth of Nations*, Smith worries less about speculative traders (or about their self-interested behavior) than about the propensity of merchants to gain monopoly power through collusive behavior at the expense of the ordinary citizen.[5] Although both thinkers are acutely aware that traders and merchants behave in their own best interests, both advocate competitive commerce because this leads to growing prosperity. Both oppose acts or policies that might restrain competition, create pockets of power, or, more generally, reduce the welfare of the larger citizenry.

Their unique and lasting insight is that self-interested behavior (or private vices) of traders and market participants leads generally to greater welfare (a public good) for society. Nevertheless, like Smith, Ibn Khaldun proposes judicious regulations to protect citizens from corrupt traders and merchants. Specifically, he supports the appointment of a powerful market regulator (*muhtasib*) to ensure that markets serve the interests of the general public. Unlike Smith, he is not as concerned with monopoly and big business, but argues passionately for justice and the rule of law, essential preconditions for trade and commerce to flourish. The safety and protection of rightfully acquired income and assets (property rights) is emphasized in several places in the *Muqaddimah*. Ibn Khaldun's insightful treatment of markets and the movement of prices, his analysis of the role of labor in creating value, his appeal for the protection of private property, and his examination of how onerous taxes weaken both the economy and society remain profoundly relevant to modern times.

In contemporary policy circles, Ibn Khaldun is perhaps most celebrated for his analysis of taxes and their impact on society. He believes that good governance is exemplified when the ruler facilitates commerce, protects the citizenry from fraud and exploitation, and safeguards the property of all citizens, including the rich. The following passages neatly capture his ideas on the significance of commerce and the ethical dilemmas involved in market exchange:

> Civilization and its well-being as well as business prosperity depend on productivity and people's efforts in all directions in their own interest and profit. When people no longer do business in order to make a living, and when they cease all gainful activity, the business of civilization slumps, and everything decays. (238)

> Commerce is a natural way of making profit. However, most of its practices and methods are tricky and designed to obtain the (profit) margin between purchase prices and sale prices. This surplus makes it possible to earn a profit. Therefore, the law permits cunning in commerce, since (commerce) contains an element of gambling. It does not, however, mean taking away the property of others without giving anything in return. Therefore, it is legal. (300)[6]

The first passage neatly encapsulates Ibn Khaldun's view that the welfare of society is linked directly to robust commerce. On the sources of prosperity, Adam Smith could not have said it better: the individual's self-interested pursuit of profits leads to society's prosperity. The second passage establishes that the commercial arena provides an appropriate (natural) setting for earning a livelihood. Nevertheless, since risk and uncertainty are inherent in market exchange, a degree of trickery and cunning is normal, even essential to commerce. As will be discussed more fully below, the term "natural," which Ibn Khaldun employs extensively, implies a normatively sanctioned legal and productive course of action that enhances the welfare of society. To be clear, theft, forceful expropriation, and injustice are considered harmful to both business and society.

In the first section of this essay, we present an introduction to Ibn Khaldun, his intellectual inheritance, and his most famous work, the *Muqaddimah*. In the subsequent section we explore Ibn Khaldun's cyclical theory of civilizational change, a theory based on the idea that advanced societies, having achieved a level of prosperity, inevitably suffer decline as they grow increasingly sedentary, addicted to luxury, and bereft of enterprise. The notion of "group cohesion," or *Asabiyah*, plays an essential role in this cyclical theory, and throughout the *Muqaddimah*. In the third section we present the traditional Islamic view of commerce and explore three related concepts relevant to an ethical assessment of commerce: that of productive activity, the notion of "natural," and the idea that commerce may sometimes involve strategic practices that exist in tension with the highest standards of ethics. The final section focuses on policy and governance.

IBN KHALDUN AND THE *MUQADDIMAH*

Ibn Khaldun was born in Tunis in 1332 into an upper-class family.[7] Several family members had held high administrative offices in Andalusia (Muslim Spain) and migrated to Tunisia after the fall of Seville to Fernando III in the middle of the thirteenth century. Benefiting from his family's aristocratic status, Ibn Khaldun studied with the most renowned scholars in North Africa, receiving an education above and beyond the traditional Islamic schooling of his time. He memorized the Qur'an and studied Arabic linguistics, *hadith* (collected sayings of the Prophet Muhammad), *sharia* (law), and *fiqh* (jurisprudence), as well as mathematics, logic, and philosophy.[8] Tragically, at an early age, he lost his parents and many teachers and mentors to the Great Plague (Black Death) of 1348–50.

He started his career as a twenty-year-old public servant in Tunis in 1352, but soon entered the service of the sultan of Morocco at Fez, where he completed his studies under the tutelage of several eminent scholars. A brilliant, ambitious, and erudite young man, Ibn Khaldun also possessed refined political and diplomatic skills. With these talents, his reputation grew, and his services were in high demand. Over the next three decades, in the course of a rich political career, he traveled extensively, raised an army, fought in battles, suffered imprisonment, and in the process was deeply influenced by many cultures and thinkers. He served various rulers occupying high political, administrative, diplomatic, and judicial positions.

These rich and varied experiences prepared him for the monumental task of writing the *Muqaddimah,* which means "Introduction." He had planned to complete the initial work in 1377 as an introduction to a larger, more ambitious project, *History of the World (Kitab al-Ibar).* However, it took him another four years to complete the *Muqaddimah.* In 1384 he was appointed a professor of the Qamhiya Madrasah, and the grand qadi of the Maliki school of *fiqh,* a position in which he served with great distinction improving the administration of justice in Egypt. The same year a profound personal misfortune befell him when the ship carrying his family was lost in a storm. In 1399, he was appointed to the most prestigious academic post of the day in Egypt, the Malikite judgeship in Cairo. Two years later, in January 1401, during the historic siege of Damascus by the Tartar army, he had the rare and dangerous opportunity to meet the terrifying Mongol conqueror Tamerlane face-to-face. Fortunately, he lived and was able to leave the world with a firsthand account of his historic meeting with one of history's most enigmatic figures.[9] The last five years of his life were spent in Cairo where he wrote his autobiography and completed the manuscript on the history of the world. He died March 17, 1406, and was buried in a Sufi cemetery outside Cairo.

Ibn Khaldun's great treatise, the *Muqaddimah,* widely recognized as one of the most profound works of scholarship produced by Islamic civilization, has influenced thinkers beyond the Islamic world and has made foundational contributions to the development of the modern social sciences. N. J. Dawood regards the *Muqaddimah* "as the earliest attempt by any historian to discover a pattern in the changes that occur in man's political and social organization."[10] The historian Arnold Toynbee observed that the treatise was "undoubtedly the greatest work of its kind that has ever yet been created by any mind in any time or place."[11] Ibn Khaldun's book continues to influence modern scholars across many disciplines.[12]

Virtually everyone who has read Ibn Khaldun is impressed with his methodology—and his vision of what a historian of civilizations must do, even if, as in the case of any thinker, his thoughts and writings reflect the context of his era.[13] Moreover, Ibn Khaldun's contributions to economics have been the subject of much research and admiration.[14] He has an excellent appreciation of concepts considered fundamental in modern economics— the legal framework and market forces of supply and demand. What is more, the *Muqaddimah* recognizes the importance of human capital in economics, a strikingly modern concept now posited as an important factor in economic development. Ibn Khaldun also explains how demand is essential for value, and how labor is the basis of economic value. He precedes Adam Smith, by nearly four centuries, in presenting an analysis of how specialization enhances productivity, and how individual behavior based on self-interest leads to the prosperity of society.[15]

THE CYCLICAL THEORY OF CIVILIZATION AND MORAL DECLINE: WEALTH, LUXURY, AND *ASABIYAH*

The corrupting influence of wealth and luxury has been a matter of deep concern in the scriptures of many faith traditions, including the Abrahamic. Although Islam encourages economic progress, Islamic teachings emphasize modest living, and at times seem to celebrate poverty. A centuries-old Islamic mystical tradition, *Sufism,* encourages an ascetic lifestyle inspired by what the Sufis believe to be a practice of the Prophet himself, who shunned luxury and the trappings of power. For Ibn Khaldun, the inclination to luxury is a flawed human trait that plays a significant role in the moral decline of individuals and groups. An attachment to luxury leads to a significant increase in corruption, a precursor to the downfall of a civilization: "Luxury corrupts the character. . . . People lose the good qualities. . . . They adopt the contrary bad qualities. This points toward retrogression and ruin" (135). Because of this focus on luxury, Ibn Khaldun understands how commercial productivity and the ethics of acquisition, wealth, and spending prove crucial to the rise and fall of a civilization.

Ibn Khaldun describes several stages in a dynasty's rise and fall, with the first involving victory over the enemy (141–42). Given the strong *Asabiyah* ("social cohesion," as discussed below)[16] that enables the ruler to gain power and authority, he remains benevolent toward his subjects during the first stage of rule. In the second stage, however, the ruler claims all authority for himself and his family. In the third stage, leisure and tranquillity set in as the court enjoys the fruits of success. The fourth stage is one of "contentment and peacefulness": the ruler becomes satisfied with his accomplishments and expends no effort to sustain the conditions of a prosperous society. The last stage is one of "waste and squandering." The ruler indulges in pleasures and excessive amusements and surrounds himself with incompetent "low-class followers" (142).

The process of decline begins once a civilization has reached the heights of wealth and prosperity. Few thinkers have presented a more detailed analysis of how at the zenith of prosperity an inexorable decline sets in that influences both the ethics of individuals and the larger society and the production and distribution of wealth.[17] This historical rise and fall proves inexorable and unstoppable. Customs dictate behavior, and as wealth increases, moderate behavior evolves into extravagant behavior. The enemy of spiritual peace and moral development is worldly success.[18] The corrupting influence of extravagant spending and lack of discipline leads to high levels of indebtedness and loss of moral values for many who were previously wealthy. As demand for luxury by the ruling class (and their retainers) increases, so does the tax burden on ordinary citizens. The intemperate spending of the ruling class leads to a decline in military and administrative capabilities. The rot that starts at the highest levels of society ultimately spreads to the youth and the ordinary citizens. For Ibn Khaldun, the decline in material well-being begins with the loss of character as cherished ethical values are abandoned, resulting in the breakdown of the moral scaffolding of the entire society. In fact, economic decline *follows* moral decline. As virtues yield to vices, there is a loss of economic dynamism. The escalating public and private indebtedness weakens the state and the family unit, accelerating the decay of society.

What leads to corruption and declining morality in business and society? The title of chapter 4, section 18, of the *Muqaddimah* reveals an inherent conflict: "Sedentary culture is the goal[19] of civilization: It means the end of its life span and brings about its corruption" (285). According to the Khaldunian perspective, man's ambition and desire for progress lead him to seek a life of comfort and pleasure as an end. "When luxury and prosperity come to civilized people, it naturally causes them to follow the ways of sedentary culture and adopt its customs" (285). Unfortunately, the path leads to a state of "subservience to desires," an addiction to excess. "From all of these customs, the human soul receives a multiple stamp that undermines its religion and worldly well-being" (285). Thus the very progress that was the goal and desire of the citizens contains the seeds of eventual decline. The habits and customs of high living, once acquired, cannot be discarded. They trigger a moral and spiritual collapse of the society, spiraling inflation, extravagant and unsustainable spending, mounting debts, the eventual decline of the commercial economy, and the collapse of the civilization:[20]

> Corruption of the individual inhabitants is the result of painful and trying efforts to satisfy the needs caused by their (luxury) customs; (the result) of bad qualities they have acquired in the process of satisfying (those needs); and the damage the soul suffers after it has obtained them. Immorality, wrongdoing, insincerity, and trickery, for the purpose of making a living in a proper or an improper manner, increase among them. . . . People are now devoted to lying, gambling, cheating, fraud, theft, perjury, and usury. . . . The city, then, teems with low people of blameworthy character. (286–87)

The Khaldunian view of the perils of luxury is consistent with the teachings of Islam that caution against excessive attachment to wealth. Such fixation leads to greed and materialism (luxury) and away from the spiritual path; the recommended alternative is a prosperous life but one balanced toward the spiritual. The greater the wealth, the greater would be the soul's accountability after death. Sharing one's wealth with the poor and needy, and simple living, are celebrated as great virtues. Caliph Ali is reported to have stressed that God has made it obligatory for the rich to take care of the poor.[21]

The royal court proves to be a major contributor to economic prosperity as well as to eventual decline:

> It is the ruling dynasty that demands crafts and their improvement. It causes the demand for them and makes them desirable. . . . *The dynasty is the biggest market.*[22]

Although this passage refers specifically to the market for crafts, the broader context is that the spending of the court has an outsize influence on the entire economy.[23] Ibn Khaldun describes how royalty and government officials are among the first to become addicted to opulence, wasting large sums of public monies on frivolous events such as banquets and weddings. The irresponsible spending by the court (royalty) leads to a weakening of the military and the imposition of higher taxes. However, higher taxes fail to generate additional revenues, since they undermine commercial incentives. Thus the economy, the military, and society are all weakened.

Do regulations, including punitive penalties, prevent fraud and corruption? Ibn Khaldun doubts the effectiveness of financial penalties used in isolation, especially when potential gains from fraud and corruption substantially exceed the fines.[24] However, he supports the role of regulators in ensuring that unethical traders do not take advantage of the consumer. Although a strong supporter of unhindered commerce, he understands that there are corrupt individuals, and hence the necessity for regulators to police the markets. His concern focuses on traders and merchants who employ fraudulent means to exploit the citizenry, not on petty traders who use sharp-elbowed strategies to gain an edge over fellow traders—he regards these latter tactics as largely innocuous.

Asabiyah: Ethics and Leadership

A seminal concept Ibn Khaldun employed to analyze the rise and fall of civilizations refers to the internal cohesion or solidarity of a group—*Asabiyah*.[25] The term can be roughly translated as "nationhood" or "patriotism," but in his era it would have referred principally to tribal solidarity. Ernest Gellner, for example, refers to *Asabiyah* as "social cohesion."[26] Allen Fromherz maintains that by holding *Asabiyah* to be the "primal social glue" that forms the basis of a rising civilization, Ibn Khaldun agrees implicitly with the dictum that man is a social animal.[27] Not only does Ibn Khaldun employ numerous illustrations of sociality; he also contends that a strong sense of group identity provides social cohesiveness, essential for a people to rise to greatness as a civilization. On the other hand, with the dissipation of *Asabiyah*, decline inevitably ensues for a people.

How is the concept of *Asabiyah* related to commercial ethics? *Asabiyah* reflects qualities of sharing and sacrifice abundantly found among tribes and communities in the countryside. People with a strong sense of community are not only more willing to share their incomes and wealth with their neighbors but more eager to sacrifice individual interests for the greater good of the community. These communal traits lead to an ethical and moral community, which is not only caring and humane but also united and militarily strong.[28] Ibn Khaldun argues that the territorial integrity of a people as well as internal social order depends on the strength of the community's *Asabiyah*. "Group feeling produces the ability to defend oneself, to offer opposition, to protect oneself, and to press one's claims. Whoever loses it is too weak to do any of these things" (111). In this way, a nation with a strong *Asabiyah* is expected to be militarily strong, and thus is able to press its commercial and territorial claims against other nations and people. Given that *Asabiyah* is a form of national "social capital," its abundance can translate into not only military prowess but also what is sometimes called "soft power." Similarly, the loss of *Asabiyah* would be detrimental to a nation. Ibn Khaldun writes, "When group feeling is destroyed, the tribe is no longer able to protect itself, let alone press any claims. It will be swallowed up by other nations" (109).

Asabiyah captures the complex societal dynamics necessary to coordinate large groups of people to attain progress and prosperity.[29] In the first place, Ibn Khaldun's ideas on the division of labor connect to *Asabiyah*. He believes greater social cohesion enables more complex forms of the division of labor, which, in turn, create conditions suitable for rapid economic progress. Along with specialization, other social conditions prove propitious for steady advance, including population growth, the development of human capital, and technological improvements.

There is a second sense in which *Asabiyah* relates to social coordination. *Asabiyah* provides the critical "gel" that modern writers, such as Francis Fukuyama, refer to as "social capital" and "trust."[30] Fukuyama (among other social capital theorists) has argued that culture in some societies includes a "high degree of generalized social trust" contributing to a "propensity for spontaneous sociability" that leads to "important economic consequences."[31] Even though modern social theorists do not use the term *Asabiyah,* the common underlying spirit of these two concepts is undeniable. When there is greater collaboration and less hostility, an important outcome is more efficient, ethical, and transparent commerce.[32]

Ibn Khaldun links *Asabiyah* to ethics and virtue (goodness) in the following enumeration of desirable qualities:

> Whenever we observe people who possess group feeling and who have gained control over many lands and nations, we find in them an eager desire for goodness and good qualities, such as generosity, the forgiveness of error, tolerance toward the weak, hospitality toward guests, the support of dependents, maintenance of the indigent, patience in adverse circumstances, faithful fulfillment of obligations, . . . fairness to and care for those who are too weak to take care of themselves, humility toward the poor, attentiveness to the complaints of supplicants, fulfilment of the duties of the religious law and divine worship in all details, avoidance of fraud, cunning, deceit, and shirking of obligations, and similar things. (112)

The passage presents a comprehensive "code of conduct" for citizens who aspire to a strong sense of nationhood and greatness. Although a significant force by itself, *Asabiyah,* in the absence of other enabling forces, such as good leadership, cannot produce a great and lasting civilization. Ethical leadership (possessing "praiseworthy" qualities) is identified as the handmaiden of *Asabiyah* in shaping a strong community.[33]

ETHICAL COMPLEXITIES IN COMMERCE

Throughout the *Muqaddimah,* Ibn Khaldun quotes from the Qur'an and *hadith*, the primary sources of faith and ethical guidance for Muslims. He holds that religion provides the best shield against the corrupting influences of society and moral decline. He argues, "Evil is the quality that is closest to man when he fails to improve his customs and when religion is not used as the model to improve him" (97). The all-too-human attraction to evil is a common theme in the traditional Islamic worldview. Indeed all major Abrahamic faith traditions emphasize the constant struggle between good and evil and the necessity for constant vigilance against one's inner demons (the "greater jihad" in Islam). Ibn Khaldun bemoans that many citizens fail to benefit from the moral code taught by the faith traditions:

> The great mass of mankind is in that condition, with the exception of those to whom God gives success. Evil qualities in man are injustice and mutual aggression. He who casts his eye upon the property of his brother will lay his hands upon it to take it, unless there is a restraining influence to hold him back. (97)

As a deterrent to moral turpitude and decline, society must reinforce the internal religious beliefs of its citizens as well as impose external constraints via law and the threat of punishment. The best strategy for ensuring ethical outcomes in society is to reinforce the citizens' inner moral compass, rather than to take punitive measures.

It is notable that mainstream Islamic thought, although highly critical of excesses such as greed and profiteering, has generally been friendly to commerce and the private economy, even praising trade and commerce as respectable ways to earn one's livelihood. The Prophet Muhammad and his first wife, Khadijah, were merchants engaged in transborder commerce. Islamic teachings do not condemn markets, trade, commerce, profits, or wealth as such; they urge, however, that the pursuit of worldly success be balanced with spiritual pursuits, and an avoidance of greed, luxury, exploitation, and injustice. Business activities should be conducted in accordance with the laws of the land and be subservient to the goal of seeking the pleasure of God. For example, labor should be compensated fairly, and workers should not be exploited; usurious interest on loans that exploit the poor or the vulnerable is condemned as sinful, if not otherwise illegal; similarly, fraud and cheating in market exchange are sinful acts in the eyes of God and, typically, punishable under the law.

Ibn Khaldun is not critical of profits, even high profits. He does not consider profits as resulting from exploitation. There is no clarion call for policy-driven redistribution of income and wealth. The Khaldunian view is that profits are a natural part of commerce and represent honest income: "Commerce means the attempt to make a profit by increasing capital, through buying goods at a low price and selling them at a high price, whether these goods consist of slaves, grain, animals, weapons, or clothing material. The accrued (amount) is called profit" (309–10). Commerce is market exchange motivated by profit: "Buy cheap and sell dear. There is commerce for you" (310).

In addition, Ibn Khaldun elevates labor to a high plane, for labor is an essential factor behind profits, capital accumulation, and indeed all commerce. "Everything comes from God. But human labour is necessary for every profit and capital accumulation" (298). Although in some instances profits may be obtained without individual effort (e.g., rain makes fields productive, thereby generating profits for the farmer), these are exceptions to the rule. "However, these things are only contributory. His [the farmer's] own efforts must be combined with them." Ibn Khaldun explains further, "(The part of the income) that is obtained by a person through his own effort and strength is called 'profit'" (297).

It is not surprising, therefore, that throughout the *Muqaddimah*, Ibn Khaldun admonishes rulers to protect the rightfully acquired wealth and private property of merchants, to minimize the state's direct involvement in commerce (so that private commerce may flourish), to keep taxes low, and to avoid injustice and preserve incentives. In short, he celebrates commerce and its participants for their role in underpinning a prosperous civilization.

This positive stance toward wealth and commerce in general is supplemented by an interesting analysis in which Ibn Khaldun describes several classifications relevant to assessing the ethics of markets. He distinguishes *productive* from *unproductive* activities, the *natural* from the *unnatural*, and the *cunning* from the *unethical*. We address these in turn.

Productive endeavor may include several varieties of activity, all of which serve to provide a livelihood. For example, a first source of sustenance is identified with nature—hunting, fishing, and farming. "Agriculture" includes raising domesticated animals, cultivating silkworms, nurturing bees for honey, and selling fruits and grains. In terms of origins and legitimacy, he ranks agriculture above all other activities, for Adam, the father of mankind, practiced it: "Agriculture is prior to all the other (ways of making a living) by its very nature, since it is something simple and innately natural" (299). A second productive approach to earning a livelihood involves "human labor as applied to specific materials." Lumped together as "crafts," these activities include writing, carpentry, tailoring, weaving, and horsemanship, as well as architecture, midwifery, book production, singing, and medicine (318–19). When labor is applied to offer "services," then we have "all the other professions and activities."[34] Crafts are "composite and scientific": their value increases with the application of "thinking and speculation" (300). The prosperity of artisans who practice crafts depends largely on the demand emanating from the cities. Since it is the city dwellers and sedentary people who desire crafts, when a city or civilization declines, so do crafts (317). A third productive way to earn a living is commerce, or dealing (trading) in manufactured products (merchandise). Merchants can earn a profit by traveling to other lands to buy and sell goods, or by hoarding grain to take advantage of price fluctuations to earn a profit (299). Commerce is thus classified as a *productive* and, as discussed below, a *natural* way of earning an honest living: "Commerce means the attempt to make a profit by increasing capital, through buying goods at low price and selling them at high price. . . . The accrued amount is called 'profit'" (309–10). Buying cheap and selling dear is the essence of commerce. Although commerce includes trading that thrives on the use of cunning and strategy, it is nevertheless a legitimate sphere of human endeavor, contributing to the prosperity of a civilization.[35]

A second category in the taxonomy of commerce is that of the "natural," a term used abundantly throughout the *Muqaddimah*. Ibn Khaldun uses the term "natural" in two main ways: in a descriptive or factual sense and in a normative sense. He often employs "natural" (or a cognate) to describe, for example, an essence, a biological process, an expected or typical phenomenon, or even common sense. It is the second (normative) usage that is more relevant to this essay. In this sense, a natural activity is one that contributes toward an *appropriate* goal or set of purposes. Such a conception draws, of course, from Aristotle, for whom natural activity contributes to an end appropriate to the agent's nature (i.e., the one who carries out the activity), both as an individual human being and as a member of society.[36] Throughout the *Muqaddimah*, one finds a number of references to Aristotle and other Greek thinkers.

The notion of the "natural" is broader in scope than the "productive," referring as well to legal and ethical activities that foster or augment the welfare of society (as opposed, say, to policies that redistribute existing incomes and wealth, or worse, cause harm to the society). An illustration of such a broader conception of naturalness is manifest when Ibn Khaldun describes the strength of the royal authority as a natural end of society: if the ruler is weak, the administration will be ineffective, leading to instability and eventual decline in the economy and society. A second illustration points out how robust commerce contributes to strengthening the state in many ways, including supporting farming and various crafts. Commerce is "natural" in this sense in that it produces a livelihood: "Commerce is a *natural* way of making profits" (300).

What about the "unnatural"? Which activities illustrate that which is not natural? First, highly speculative activities such as searching for buried treasures are deemed "devious" on the grounds that they manifest the attempt to shirk or avoid steady exertion and, ultimately, prove unproductive and wasteful. These activities are *un*natural (and morally undesirable). The use of the word "devious" may at first seem puzzling, since the word "wasteful" or "unproductive" would have better captured the idea. However, the term expresses the idea of a wily attempt to avoid labor, an activity, as noted above, that Ibn Khaldun holds in high esteem. Ibn Khaldun is clear in his negative evaluation of specific instances of devious (and unnatural) acts: "In addition to a *weak mind*, a motive that leads people to hunt for treasure is their inability to make a living in one of the *natural* ways that earn a profit, such as commerce, agriculture, or the crafts. Therefore, they try to make a living in *devious* ways such as treasure hunting and the like . . . they trust they can gain their sustenance without effort or trouble" (302, emphasis added). Another illustration of an unnatural activity offered by Ibn Khaldun is the employment of private servants by the rich for (minor) personal needs. It is unbecoming (i.e., not natural) of the rich to be dependent on servants for minor personal needs. The employment of servants for minor personal matters—activities that one could do on one's own, without any sacrifice of other endeavors—is viewed as an indulgence and is, therefore, considered unnatural and not praiseworthy.[37]

A third category emerges once one asks whether there are any activities that fall in the realm of natural and yet are not fully ethical? The answer is yes. For example, Ibn Khaldun discusses the use of cunning (stratagems) in business. He writes, "The religious law legalizes the use of cunning in trading, but forbids depriving people of their property illegally" (242). Here he is making the case that given the nature of market exchange, a degree of cunning, cleverness, and subterfuge is unavoidable in commercial transactions. However, since neither commerce nor the greater society is undermined by these practices, commerce is natural and good.

When discussing commerce, Ibn Khaldun describes a myriad of productive economic activities besides trading—farming, manufacturing, crafts—from which people derive an honest living. These activities do not simply complement trading but are, in essence, the building blocks of commerce. However, to highlight questionable strategies or activities in business, Ibn Khaldun sets forth a section entitled "The kind of people who should practice commerce, and those who should not" (see *Muqaddimah*, chapter 5, section 13, p. 312). He argues that trading generally involves cunning and conflict (because of competition and risk); hence he recommends trading as a profession only to those who are naturally inclined to cunning and willing to engage in conflicts inherent in market exchange:

> Now, honest traders are few. It is unavoidable [in trading] that there should be cheating, tampering with the merchandise which may ruin it, and delay in payment which may ruin the profit, since (such delay) while it lasts prevents any activity that could bring profit. There will also be non-acknowledgement or denial of obligations, which may prove destructive of one's capital. (312)

The passage suggests that honest and meek traders find it difficult to prosper. Nevertheless, "honest" traders do exist. To be successful in business the honest trader must be willing to engage in conflict and stay alert to clever strategies pursued by fellow traders. The terms employed to describe merchants' behavior—"cunning," "clever," "skillful"—form a continuum of strategies and tactical practices available in the toolbox of traders. The word "cleverness" captures best the skills employed by successful traders. For example, to succeed in a competitive bazaar, the trader must be smart and strategic in his moves, whether buying or selling. However, a cunning trader seeks to disguise his real motives from competitors. In this way, the words that might describe the cunning or clever trader would include terms such as "sharp," "aggressive," and "quick to see advantage," all of which refer to skills and behavior that provide a "competitive advantage" and that also suggest an ethically neutral adaptation to circumstances.

The unsavory practices in everyday trading are not considered criminal or pernicious. Although these practices are not praiseworthy, Ibn Khaldun seems unconcerned that they might harm commerce or the larger society. Since these stratagems are more nuisance than threat, they should be tolerated. However, pernicious activities such as outright deception (lying, fraudulent sales, and so on) must be penalized. Nevertheless, society should consider the trader's private vices including greed, a desire for greater profits, and cunning as normal aspects of business that result in the society's overall prosperity. In this sense, one might say, private vices are a source of public benefits.

This view of commerce anticipates the sentiments popularized three centuries later by the Dutch-English author Bernard Mandeville (1670–1733), who argues that markets enhance society's welfare, even though the practices of the participants are not just self-serving but often less than ethical. Mandeville's satirical poem, *The Grumbling Hive: or, Knaves Turn'd Honest*, first published in 1705, and reappearing, in 1714, in a volume called *The Fable of the Bees: or, Private Vices, Publick Benefits,* raised the paradox of vicious motivation leading to societal benefits.[38] Using the parable of a thriving colony of bees, Mandeville argued that the commercial prosperity (public benefit) of a community depends on passions and appetites such as selfishness and greed (private vices), which, somewhat ironically and hypocritically, are looked down upon by society.

PRINCIPLES OF GOOD GOVERNANCE: THE ROLE OF THE STATE, PROPERTY, AND TAXATION

Part of Ibn Khaldun's contemporary fame rests on his policy prescriptions relating to the economy and administration, many of which remain surprisingly fresh and relevant to modern times.[39] Ibn Khaldun does not recommend a significant role for the state in the economy. He is forceful in his recommendation that the state (ruler) should avoid any direct engagement in commerce, as this will drain resources from private businesses. Profit-seeking activities by the ruler are harmful to private businesses and therefore ruinous for tax revenues. Since the ruler (and the court as a whole) has significant advantages that the average business lacks, the power imbalance will lead to unfair competition, a decline in private commerce, and eventually reduced tax revenues (233). Ibn Khaldun builds a compelling case that the state should avoid direct involvement in commerce.

What then is the role of the state in the economy? The state should focus primarily on protecting individual property rights—ensuring that individual and business properties remain safe from expropriation, including predatory acts initiated by corrupt officials. This is an important prerequisite to the rule of law and the preservation of justice. When incomes and assets are insecure, commerce will cease to flourish, and the civilization will decline. Prosperity through commerce cannot be sustained without the maintenance of economic justice and the rule of law. Unfortunately, this important lesson is often lost on modern governments, whose attempts to attain economic growth and alleviate poverty frequently fail because the existing policies, laws, and regulations undermine trust and the rule of law, thereby creating uncertainties for private businesses and potential investors regarding returns on their investments.

Ibn Khaldun teaches that injustice is the enemy of prosperity: "Injustice brings about the ruin of civilization" (240). The unjust actions that undermine commerce include not just confiscation of property without cause or compensation, but any coercive act that threatens or does harm. For example, if someone forcibly acquires property or employs forced labor or presses a false claim, an injustice is committed. Officials who impose burdensome taxes also commit an injustice. Those who deny people their rights commit an injustice (240). All citizens, including those who have prospered, deserve protection under the law.

Ibn Khaldun is best known in contemporary policy circles for his original and incisive commentary on the role of taxation in the economy and society. In a section entitled "Taxation and the reason for low and high tax revenues" (230), he makes the case for low taxes on both "efficiency" and "equity" considerations. Low taxes entail a positive sum strategy because they bring higher revenues and serve as incentives to invest, produce, and work: "When tax assessments and imposts upon the subjects are low, the latter have the energy and desire to do things. Cultural [commercial] enterprises grow and increase, because the low taxes bring satisfaction. . . . In consequence, the tax revenue, which is the sum total of (the individual assessments), increases" (230). On the other hand, high taxes ("beyond the limits of equity") create a disincentive for commerce: "When they [subjects] compare expenditures and taxes with their income and gain and see the little profit they make, they lose all hope. Therefore, many of them refrain from all cultural [commercial] activity. The result is that the total tax revenue goes down, as individual assessments go down. . . . Finally, civilization is destroyed, because the incentive for cultural [commercial] activity is gone" (231).

Ibn Khaldun supports the office of a powerful market supervisor (*muhtasib*) with discretionary authority to prevent fraud and protect citizens from unscrupulous businesses. Interestingly, he makes the case that regulations should serve the public good, not private or individual interests. "He [the market supervisor] investigates abuses and applies the appropriate punishments and corrective measures. He sees to it that the people act in accord with the public interest in the town" (178). Extending beyond the prevention of fraud, the supervisor's responsibilities ensure an atmosphere in which commerce would prosper. Although, written six centuries ago, these guidelines compare well in spirit with the intent of modern consumer protection laws designed to protect the public interest.

CONCLUDING REMARKS

Islamic civilization has produced a number of outstanding thinkers whose writings have enriched our understanding of history, economy, and society. It is unfortunate that much of this learning is lost to the Western reader.[40]

Islam is supportive of business and yet hostile to excesses in market exchange fueled by greed and power. In this respect Islam shares a common heritage with other faith traditions.[41] It has been said that the Bible sends a strong message regarding justice and yet accepts commerce as a legitimate activity in God's eyes. In the *Muqaddimah* we learn that the market economy, commerce, and the profit motive are accepted in Islam as both *natural* and *productive*. These institutions and practices serve society as a whole and are, thereby, natural; they also generate wealth and prosperity and are, thereby, productive. Nonetheless, the interactions that occur in markets may feature elements of cunning and devious stratagems that seem less than praiseworthy. But so long as markets and trade are framed within the rule of law and justice, the cunning methods of aggressive traders need not detract from the positive benefits of commerce. After all, although judicious regulation may be necessary, a spiritually developed citizenry is more important than punitive regulations in preventing corruption and fraud.

In many remarkable ways Ibn Khaldun anticipates future developments in a range of social sciences including the idea of social capital. He employs the concept of *Asabiyah* or group solidarity to explain how societies that enjoy a high degree of mutual trust and internal cohesion are sufficiently empowered, and often rise to greatness under strong ethical leadership. These societies also tend to be more humane and caring. If its leadership is moral and ethical, a civilization will enjoy a more sustained period of prosperity and success than in the absence of such leadership. However, human progress is seldom linear, and in every civilizational ascent, there are seeds of decline. As the force of *Asabiyah* dissipates over time, the desire for sedentary living and luxury takes over. The result is escalating indebtedness and a deterioration of public and private morality, a harbinger of a decline in commercial ethics and, ultimately, the demise of the civilization. We learn from Ibn Khaldun that commerce and commercial ethics play a central role in the rise and fall of civilizations.

ACKNOWLEDGMENTS

We are grateful to Omar Farooq, Anisuzzaman Chowdhury, Allen Fromherz, William Vetter, Reginald Bell, Mark Tschaepe, S. M. Ghazanfar, and especially the editors of this volume for their detailed feedback, which has helped us improve this essay. The usual disclaimer applies.

NOTES

1. See Joseph J. Spengler, "Economic Thought of Islam: Ibn Khaldun," *Comparative Studies in Society and History* 6 (April 1964): 268–306; and S. M. Ghazanfar, *Medieval Islamic Economic Thought: Filling the Great Gap in European Economics* (London: Routledge, 2003).

2. Drawing inspiration from Ibn Khaldun's analysis of tax policy and his advocacy of low taxes, President Ronald Reagan said, "A principle that goes back at least, I know, as far as the fourteenth century, when a Moslem philosopher named Ibn Khaldun said, 'In the beginning of the dynasty, great tax revenues were gained from small assessments. At the end of the dynasty, small tax revenues were gained from large assessments.'" "Administration of Ronald Reagan," in *Public Papers of the Presidents of the United States, Ronald Reagan: January 20 to December 31, 1981* (Washington, DC: U.S. Government Printing Office, 1981), 871 (October 1, 1981). The full passage from which this quotation is drawn can be found in Ibn Khaldun, *The Muqaddimah: An Introduction to History*, trans. Franz Rosenthal, abr. and ed. N. J. Dawood (Princeton, NJ: Princeton University Press, 1989), 230. For a more elaborate treatment of this subject, see Ibrahim M. Oweiss, "Ibn Khaldun, the Father of Economics," in *Arab Civilization: Challenges and Responses*, ed. George N. Atiyeh and Oweiss (Albany: State University of New York Press, 1988), 112–27.

3. Several translations of the *Muqaddimah* have made Ibn Khaldun familiar to the Western reader. The best-known is Franz Rosenthal's splendid three-volume translation (Princeton, NJ: Princeton University Press, 1958), which has achieved canonical status. An abridged and edited version of Rosenthal's translation by N. J. Dawood has made Ibn Khaldun's work more accessible in the West. Unless otherwise noted, all quotations from the *Muqaddimah*

are from Dawood's abridged version (Princeton, NJ: Princeton University Press, 1989), with the relevant page references cited parenthetically in the text. It is worth noting that although Rosenthal's translation is excellent, occasionally he employs words that do not sound correct in modern usage. For example, he uses the term "cultural" when he presumably means "economic" or "commercial" activity.

4. Aristotle calls "natural" those activities that contribute to some appropriate end. Ibn Khaldun follows this practice. For example, he takes the strength of the ruling courts as symptomatic of a flourishing society, and a robust commerce contributes to this end. See Aristotle, *Politics*, trans. C. D. C. Reeve (Indianapolis: Hackett, 1998), 1252b28–1253a40.

5. "People of the same trade seldom meet together, even for merriment and diversion, but the conversation ends in a conspiracy against the publick, or in some contrivance to raise prices." Adam Smith, *An Inquiry into the Nature and Causes of the Wealth of Nations*, ed. R. H. Campbell, A. S. Skinner, and W. B. Todd (Indianapolis: Liberty Fund, 1981), I.x.c.27, p. 145.

6. The use of parentheses within a quotation, original to Rosenthal's translation and retained in Dawood's abridgment, indicates where the translator has either added a term (when there is no equivalent word in the original Arabic text) or otherwise sought to clarify the text.

7. This brief biography is based on several sources, including Allen J. Fromherz, *Ibn Khaldun: Life and Times* (Edinburgh: Edinburgh University Press, 2011), and Bruce B. Lawrence, introduction to *The Muqaddimah: An Introduction to History*, trans. Rosenthal, ed. Dawood, vii–xxv; see also Alfred Gierer, "Ibn Khaldun on Solidarity ('Asabiyah')—Modern Science on Cooperativeness and Empathy: A Comparison," *Philosophia Naturalis* 38, no. 1 (2001): 93.

8. Ibn Khaldun's body of work reveals familiarity with the works of Aristotle and other Greek philosophers. For example, in the *Muqaddimah*, he refers to Aristotle's *Politics* (as on p. 41) and his *Organon* (p. 39).

9. For a firsthand description of this famous rendezvous, see Ibn Khaldun's memoirs (in Arabic), *Al-Ta'rif bi-Ibn Khaldun wa-rihlatuhu gharban wa-sharqan*, ed. Muhammad Ibn-Tawit al-Tanji (Cairo, 1951), 366–77. Fromherz, *Ibn Khaldun,* presents a dramatic account of this surreal but historic meeting (1).

10. "Rational in its approach, analytical in its method, encyclopedic in detail, it represents an almost complete departure from traditional historiography, discarding conventional concepts and clichés and seeking, beyond the mere chronicle of events, an explanation—and hence a philosophy—of history." Dawood, introduction to *The Muqaddimah* (1989), ix.

11. Arnold J. Toynbee, *A Study of History*, 2nd ed. (London: Oxford University Press, 1935), 322.

12. Fromherz writes, "Ibn Khaldun's theories have caught fire among intellectuals of both East and West far outside the medievalist and orientalist community. Ernest Gellner, one of the most influential intellectuals and anthropologists of the twentieth century, used Ibn Khaldun's ideas as one of his primary inspirations." Fromherz, *Ibn Khaldun,* 4.

13. Fromherz explains how despite being of a scientific bent ("I am a man of science," Khaldun informs Tamerlane), Ibn Khaldun's analyses and predictions are sometimes based more on the "divination of saints or mystics" than logical and scientific considerations. Fromherz, *Ibn Khaldun,* 4 and 5, respectively.

14. For example, see Spengler, "Economic Thought of Islam"; Oweiss, "Ibn Khaldun"; Adil H. Mouhammed, "On Ibn Khaldun's Critique of the Market Economy with Some Lessons to the Arab World," *Journal of Third World Studies* 25, no. 2 (2008): 207–26; and Ghazanfar, *Medieval Islamic Economic Thought.*

15. For a discussion of how self-interested behavior leads to general welfare, see Ibn Khaldun, *The Muqaddimah* (1989), 238; on the significance of labor (human capital), 274.

16. Since there is no consistent spelling of the word *Asabiyah* in the literature, we adopt the spelling in Lawrence, introduction to *The Muqaddimah* (2005), xiv.

17. For a detailed description of the process of decline, see L. Haddad, "A Fourteenth-Century Theory of Economic Growth," *Kyklos* 30, no. 2 (1977): 203.

18. According to Ibn Khaldun, "[A civilization] has a physical life, just as any individual has a physical life . . . because there is a limit that cannot be overstepped. When luxury and prosperity come to civilized people, it naturally causes them to follow the ways of sedentary culture and adopt its customs" (285).

19. The translation employs the term "goal," although another term such as "end" or "limit" would have worked better: "The goal of civilization is sedentary culture and luxury. When civilization reaches that goal, it turns towards corruption and starts being senile, as happens in the natural life of living beings. Indeed, we may say that the qualities of character resulting from sedentary culture and luxury are identical with corruption" (288).

20. Spengler, "Economic Thought of Islam," 269.

21. Umar Chapra quotes Ali, the fourth caliph of Islam and a major Islamic thinker: "God has made it obligatory on the rich to provide the poor with what is adequate for them; if the poor are hungry or naked or troubled, it is because the rich have deprived them [of their right], and it will be proper for God to hold them responsible for this deprivation and to punish them." Chapra, "The Islamic Welfare State and Its Role in the Economy," in *Studies in Islamic Economics,* ed. Khurshid Ahmad (Markfield, Leicestershire, UK: Islamic Foundation, 1981), 157.

22. Ibn Khaldun, *Muqaddimah* (1958), 2:352, emphasis added.

23. In contrast, in the *Wealth of Nations*, Adam Smith distinguishes between cities built on commerce from those built largely on patronage. See Smith, *Wealth of Nations*, II.iii, "Of the accumulation of Capital . . ."

24. Referring to the practice of the Bedouins, Ibn Khaldun writes, "They often punish crimes by fines on property, in their desire to increase the tax revenues and to obtain some (pecuniary) advantage. That is no deterrent" (121).

25. The standard dictionary meaning of *Asabiyah* suggests zealous partisanship, bigotry, fanaticism, party or team spirit, esprit de corps, tribal solidarity, and nationalism; for the related word *usab,* possible meanings include "union," "league," "federation," "association"; "group," "troop," "band," "gang," "clique"; for *asaba,* "paternal relations," "relationships." See J. M. Cowan, ed., *Arabic-English Dictionary: The Hans Wehr Dictionary of Modern Written Arabic* (Ithaca, NY: Snowball, 2011), 615–16.

26. Ernest Gellner, *Muslim Society* (Cambridge: Cambridge University Press, 1981) 41. Johann P. Arnason and Georg Stauth maintain that *Asabiyah* is "a capacity for collective will-formation and commitment to sustained action, rather than simply a high degree of social cohesion"; Arnason and Stauth, "Civilization and State Formation in the Islamic Context: Re-reading Ibn Khaldun," *Thesis Eleven* 76, no. 1 (2004): 34. See also Gierer, "Ibn Khaldun on Solidarity," for a discussion of what generates and strengthens *Asabiyah*—common descent versus common socialization. Gierer argues that the concept is more sociological than biological.

27. Fromherz (*Ibn Khaldun,* 128) makes the case that Ibn Khaldun was influenced by Aristotle, though he notes differences in their views. For example, unlike Aristotle, Ibn Khaldun did not believe human civilization develops in a linear fashion, but that progress is cyclical.

28. Fromherz, *Ibn Khaldun,* 128.

29. Ibid., 33 n. 5.

30. Francis Fukuyama argues that the benefits to the society from higher levels of trust are both economic and noneconomic, including easier adaptation of business organizations to changes in markets and technology, a more flexible workplace where workers are given higher levels of responsibilities, and greater decentralization of power within organizations.

Fukuyama, *Trust: The Social Virtues and the Creation of Prosperity* (New York: Free Press, 1996), 30–32.

31. Fukuyama, *Trust*, 29.

32. Hence the emphasis by some capital theorists on "moral education" that will strengthen a society's existing competitive advantage. On the ethical advantages that may accrue to some societies over others, see Thomas Donaldson, "The Ethical Wealth of Nations," *Journal of Business Ethics* 31, no. 1 (2001): 25–36.

33. Ibn Khaldun's attempt to equate power and virtue gives rise to some inconsistencies in his narrative. For example, if one examines the lives of history's great conquerors such as Genghis Khan or Tamerlane, one is hard pressed to discern an abundance of goodness in their characters.

34. Interestingly, although he discusses professions such as serving as an attendant (servant), he does not address "service" as a separate category of productive activity.

35. The view that hoarding grain, although risky for the trader, is actually productive (a view later propagated by Adam Smith) is yet another example of Ibn Khaldun's insight into the workings of markets and the economy. According to modern economics, all trading involves decisions made with incomplete information and are, therefore, speculative. Ibn Khaldun also notes that "intelligent and experienced people in the cities know that it is inauspicious to hoard grain" (311), since the food stocks may be lost to spoilage. Even though hoarding food is risky for the merchant, Ibn Khaldun does not regard the activity as unproductive.

36. For example, Arist., *Pol.* 1252b28–1253a40. Fromherz contends that Ibn Khaldun was "an indirect student of Aristotle" (*Ibn Khaldun,* 122) and "steeped . . . in the traditions of rational philosophy and systematic theology" (123).

37. As is the profession of servitude: "*Being a servant is not a natural way of making a living*" (300).

38. Bernard Mandeville, *The Fable of the Bees: or, Private Vices, Publick Benefits,* ed. F. B. Kaye (Indianapolis: Liberty Fund, 1988). See also Eugene Heath's essay on Bernard Mandeville in this volume.

39. Ralph Benko, "Ronald Reagan, Ibn Khaldun, Mahathir Mohamad: Back to Capitalist Basics," *Forbes*, March 5, 2012, http://www.forbes.com/sites/ralphbenko/2012/03/05/ronald-reagan-ibn-khaldun-mahathir-mohamad-back-to-capitalist-basics/.

40. Jonathan Lyons, *The House of Wisdom: How the Arabs Transformed Western Civilization* (New York: Bloomsbury Press, 2009), describes how starting around the twelfth century, European scholars such as Adelard of Bath discovered and benefited from the vast reservoirs of knowledge ("buried for six centuries"), including that of the Greeks, that the Arabs had preserved and substantially enhanced over the previous centuries.

41. See G. Rice, "Islamic Ethics and the Implications for Business," *Journal of Business Ethics* 18, no. 4 (1999): 345–58; and Munir Quddus, Henri Bailey, and Larry R. White, "Business Ethics: Perspectives from Judaic, Christian, and Islamic Scriptures," *Journal of Management, Spirituality, and Religion* 6, no. 4 (2009): 323–34.

CHAPTER 7

Hobbes's Idea of Moral Conduct in a Society of Free Individuals

Timothy Fuller

The aim of this essay is to consider what light Thomas Hobbes's *Leviathan*, a masterpiece of the modern moral imagination,[1] might shed on the issues raised in the study of business ethics today. What most people know or have heard about Hobbes is his dark comment on the life of man as "solitary, poore, nasty, brutish, and short" (XIII, 76) or perhaps his observation of a "general inclination of all mankind, a perpetual and restless desire for power after power, that ceaseth only in death" (XI, 58). The first of these remarks in context refers to a "mere condition of nature" where there is no government, where all are on their own to fend for themselves. The second observes that we must continually seek the means to gain the satisfactions we wish for, an activity coterminous with life. These and other such remarks prepare for Hobbes's larger argument, which actually offers a hopeful project.

Hobbes describes human beings who can establish relationships of reliable civility, under a rule of law, protecting thereby both the fruits of their industry and the opportunity for creative and reflective thought, and accepting an order compatible with thinking of themselves as free individuals. Hobbes not only sets forth the precepts of rational conduct for such a society, but shows how these precepts, accessible to the reason that all individual human beings share, can advance civilized life. Reason is common to all even though our interests vary and may conflict.

The study of business ethics today, including the incorporation of required courses on business ethics in schools of business, recognizes the need for careful thought on the morality of commerce, on facilitating commercial transactions through the rational pursuit of one's interests in an atmosphere of mutually understood precepts of conduct, where the manner of interaction, and the necessity of trust, are crucial considerations in the pursuit of success.[2] Although the case study method dominates in the teaching of business ethics, a substantial body of opinion holds that awareness of the larger context of the tradition of moral philosophy is an important complement to case studies. Hobbes is especially relevant to this approach.

In this context, Hobbes's *Leviathan* is particularly significant for at least two reasons. First, he is a major theorist of the modern state, which is the political form that has become dominant in the Western world, superseding the Greek city, the Roman Empire, and the Catholic Church as models of human organization. Second, Hobbes was aware of the growth of commerce as an essential aspect of civic life; the *Leviathan* is a substantial investigation of the relation between the emergent political form and expanding civil society. In short, Hobbes offers a comprehensive political theory that presents the compatibility of economics and ethics, advancing both a realist appraisal of the springs of human conduct and an account of ethics that does not ignore or evade real life conduct. He anticipates the issues of today. For example, the business ethicist R. Edward Freeman writes, "One cannot assess the worth of capitalism outside of some framework for the just distribution of goods and services, rights and duties in society. Likewise, philosophical theories of justice are uninteresting absent real discussions about the features of various economic systems. The separation of economics from politics, sociality, and philosophy leads to arid pseudoscience or an unworkable political ideology."[3]

Of course, Hobbes did not write about "business ethics" as such. But he did elaborate a conception of human conduct fit for a society increasingly characterized by commercial transactions, providing a philosophic account of the assumptions operative in such a society.[4] Hobbes's intention is to show how "diffidence"—in his parlance "lack of confidence or faith" in others— can be overcome to establish conditions conducive to trust (XIII, 75). He offers a comprehensive account of rational conduct that anticipates much of what studies of business ethics emphasize. In developing a carefully worked-out idea of the rule of law in protection of voluntary transactions, Hobbes tied together his awareness of a growing commercial life with a concept of justice. Hobbes thus illuminates a larger historic context of assumptions with which to approach particular practical moral issues in modern commercial life.

Hobbes discusses the laws of nature or, more exactly, maxims or precepts of rational conduct, which are accessible to all human beings if they but reflect on the experience of their interaction with others. This aspect of Hobbes's thought needs emphasis, for in it we discern Hobbes's concept of the modern moral imagination as it crystallized in a growing civil society emphasizing commercial activity.[5] Hobbes observes that the instinct to self-preservation is accompanied by reason's capacity to promote self-restraint. We can mediate the tension between self-advancement and self-restraint so as to make the tension manageable and productive in the form of enlightened self-interest. The pursuit of one's wished-for satisfactions thus implies careful consideration with regard to maintaining continuing success, not merely immediate gratification. This describes a basic feature of a free market economy, essential to what Adam Smith called the system of natural liberty. Here is Smith a century after Hobbes:

> A man has almost constant occasion for the help of his brethren, and it is in vain for him to expect it from their benevolence only. He will be more likely to prevail if he can interest their self-love in his favour, and show them that it is for their own advantage to do what he requires of them. Whoever offers to another a bargain of any kind, proposes to do this. . . . As it is by treaty, by barter, and by purchase, that we obtain from one another the greater part of those mutual good offices which we stand in need of.[6]

Smith sees that a person who claims to be individual and free does not want to be dependent on the charity of others: "Nobody but a beggar chooses to depend chiefly upon the benevolence of his fellow citizens. Even a beggar does not depend upon it entirely."[7] It is perfectly possible to exercise benevolence or charity out of compassion, but in the emerging moral imagination, it is not desirable to be in need of such benevolence—interdependency is one thing, dependency is another. Hobbes already formulated a version of this thought. A contemporary version of this is suggested when John Hendry describes us as living in a "bimoral society": "Very few people would argue with the fact that the traditional morality of obligation is not merely socially legitimate, but absolutely essential. . . . At the same time . . . few people today would deny that individual self-interest is also quite normal and acceptable."[8] Hendry goes on to suggest that we need to harmonize these tendencies. He describes what Hobbes already had begun to analyze.

However, as Hobbes argues, the continuing reality of this tension spurs the dynamism of a modern, productive society. The idea of resolving or transcending the tension appeals abstractly but would mean the end of social life as we know it. Hendry seems to recognize this in the end: "We have no need to curtail business and blunt the forces of enterprise by disciplinary forms of governance. But we do need to trust businesses to be open and honest about their interests and activities, and we do need them to engage in constructive dialogue around the relationship between those interests and the interests of society at large."[9]

While human beings possess reason in common, Hobbes analyzes this capacity in the context of his observation of the economic, political, and religious transformation of European, and especially English, society. Hobbes is attentive to the changing character of the world in which he lives and how people are responding to it, how they are coming to understand themselves as selves in the presence of other selves, how their moral imagination is developing. Let us look in more detail at the character of this moral imagination, then turning, in the second section, to a consideration of liberty and authority and the idea of civic virtue. In the third section we take up the nature of law, both natural and civil, along with the idea of contract. In the fourth section we consider how the idea of representative government is appropriate for free persons who need to live together in peace The concluding section restates the idea that moral insight arises from self-reflection and imagination, so both the practices of commerce and the ethics of business more generally require no expertise, revelation, or particular insight.

THE MORAL IMAGINATION

By "moral imagination" I mean how, through interaction over time, people visualize their associations in terms of what they can expect of each other in seeking accommodation, in relying on agreed-upon procedures under normal circumstances, in the assumptions they reasonably believe they share and count on to be recognized in how they go about things, in a common understanding of what is generally acceptable conduct, what is questionable, and so on. Here are some of Hobbes's ways of expressing this concept:

> And the science of them [the laws of nature] is the true and only moral philosophy. For moral philosophy is nothing else but the science of what is *good* and *evil* in the conversation and society of mankind. (XV, 100)

In his "Introduction" to *Leviathan*, Hobbes observes:

> But there is another saying not of late understood, by which [human beings] might learn truly to read one another . . . and that is *nosce teipsum, read thy self:* . . . to teach us that for the similitude of the thoughts and passions of one man to the thoughts and passions of another, whosoever looketh into himself and considereth what he doth, when he does *think, opine, reason, hope, &c,* and upon what grounds, he shall thereby read and know, what are the thoughts and passions of all other men upon the like occasions. . . . He that is to govern a whole nation must read in himself, not this or that particular man, but mankind, which though it be hard to do, harder than to learn any language or science, yet when I shall have set down my own reading orderly and perspicuously, the pains left another will be only to consider if he also find not the same in himself. (Introduction, 4–5)

And the following:

> By *manners* I mean not here decency of behaviour, as how one man should salute another, or how a man should wash his mouth or pick his teeth before company, and such other points of the *small morals*, but those qualities of mankind that concern their living together in peace and unity (XI, 57).

What is Hobbes saying to us? (1) Reason and the passions are basically similar from one person to the next; (2) by introspection of one's own experience one can imagine the basic pattern of reasoning and passion that is common, and thus infer how others are likely to respond in similar circumstances; (3) at the level of governing a nation this knowledge is essential because the task of governing extends far beyond our personal relations—indeed, governing requires a kind of impersonal or depersonalized relationship through law to all subjects of a commonwealth; (4) at the same time, since there is no fundamental difference in these patterns between rulers and subjects, there is (5) a common capacity of insight among human beings regardless of station; (6) what distinguishes one human being from another is the relative ability accurately to grasp the basic structure of human conduct by bracketing one's idiosyncrasies, foibles, and particular goals; the office or station in life one occupies does not change the primary task; (7) the *Leviathan* presents in detail what the basic similitude is, and the test of the argument is for the reader, through self-examination, to consider whether Hobbes has expounded the fundamental character of human relations "scientifically," that is, in detachment from merely personal preferences, interests, and goals.

Hobbes does not treat the growth of material wealth as an end in itself. Such a goal may only reveal the triumph of passion over reason. Hobbes recognizes that there are those whose ambition far exceeds what their security requires, and they can force others who are by disposition more modest to respond in kind (XIII, 75). Rather, his foremost concern is to understand how rational conduct is possible among those who think of themselves as free individuals, and for whom the preservation of their capacity to do for themselves is primary.

Hobbes presents the idea of a moral imagination that emphasizes not mere self-interestedness—that oft-discussed aspect of Hobbes's thought, and of modern commercial society—but also the capacity to enter into the views of others by inference from the universal features of human conduct; it is necessary (even for those who think it a "necessary evil") for us to be interested in others. We grasp, implicitly or explicitly, enlightened or rational self-interest, the conscious and disciplined pursuit of one's interests through which we accept our inevitable implication in the lives of others who are similarly self-interested and capable of disciplining their pursuits in the same way. Reflection on experience shows us that our desire to set ourselves apart from, or above, others will be frustrated if we do not learn how to conduct ourselves morally, that is, with self-restraint. The moral way is the disciplined way of enlightened self-interest gained in reflecting on our experience, through which we learn to practice self-regulation.

Hobbes sets the stage for further development of the modern moral imagination. Later writers such as Adam Smith emphasize the instinct for sympathy, the capacity for fellow feeling that can incite compassion or pity at the sight of others' pain, alongside the instinctive pursuit of self-interest.[10] The moral imagination gives us an idea of the thinking of others even though we are and must be individuals who are "for ourselves." We can visualize the experience of a more or less spontaneous form of association comprising innumerable voluntary transactions, governed by laws laid down and enforced by a sovereign, permitting both the growth of wealth and also freedom for undistracted thought and reflection and the cultivation of philosophy and the arts. Hobbes could imagine such an order because the experience of it was already expanding in his time. By the time of Adam Smith it was possible to theorize its character in a powerfully systematic way, and to assess the advantages of commercial societies against societies resistant to it.

Hobbes's realism about the possibilities and limitations of the human condition is prerequisite to his outline of a basic science of human conduct that will make it possible to conceive reforms in political institutions stimulated by the changes in the moral imagination. Locke, Kant, and Hegel, in theorizing the modern state, did precisely this. These thinkers elaborated the basis for confidence that a more or less spontaneous commercial order, supported by constitutionally limited government and the rule of law, need not depend only on coercive power. What is promised is a more enduring stability than coercion alone could ever provide, based on accepting the necessity of sovereign power but leaving open the question of its extent or scope in considering the increasing disposition to insist on individual liberty. In this vision, the moral capacities of individuals are as important as those of the occupants of the offices of authority.

Granting that we enjoy considerable stability through a shared moral imagination, how do students of business ethics come to understand more fully what they, as members of society, already in varying degrees understand implicitly? Must they not put specific case studies, and a few reasonably obvious ethical maxims, into a larger reflective context? What they need is "cultural or civic literacy and ethical literacy, or the ability to use moral language effectively. . . . Literacy stimulates imagination and gives us a new way of seeing. . . . We can develop moral imagination in our students."[11] This is a goal served by the study of Hobbes's *Leviathan*. In fact, his ideas of authority and representation shed light on his concept of the moral imagination.

LIBERTY AND AUTHORITY

In the Introduction, and in Chapter XVI ("Of Persons, Authors, and Things personated"), Hobbes distinguishes between a "natural" and an "artificial" person. The "artificial man," a human creation imitating God's creation of natural man, allows us, within broad limits, to think of ourselves as self-making beings, that is, that we are the "matter" to be made over. Human artifice cannot replace the natural man, since the availability of the "matter" depends on God's having created it or us in the first place. Rather, it means that we can fashion ourselves in ways that nature neither produces nor precludes. Reason allows us to think of ourselves as a work in progress. The basis in nature of all that we do does not prevent us from adding to nature (imposing on ourselves) artifices that derive from the creative imagination. In more familiar terms, this means we have to choose our conduct for ourselves in the presence of other selves.

We can imagine ourselves in various ways, and we can take measures to conform ourselves to what we imagine it is desirable for us to be. Nature, God's artifice, provides the matter, but the human matter must also provide for itself. We are both a resource for ourselves and the artificers of ourselves as resource: "Nature (the art whereby God hath made and governs the world) is by the *art* of man, as in many other things, so in this also imitated, that it can make an artificial animal" (Introduction, 3).

For Hobbes, freedom (in addition to meaning the absence of external impediments to our actions) may be understood as making ourselves over in accordance with our ideas of what is advantageous and disadvantageous for us. "And because *going*, *speaking*, and the like voluntary motions depend always upon a precedent thought of *whither*, *which way*, and *what*, it is evident that the imagination is the first internal beginning of all voluntary motion" (VI, 27).

As a consequence, we will inevitably ask ourselves what the right or best use of this freedom may be, while lacking initial agreement and without independent guidance, since imagination's exercise is in each individual:

> And therefore, as when there is a controversy in an account, the parties must by their own accord set up for right reason the reason of some arbitrator or judge to whose sentence they will both stand, or their controversy must come to blows or be undecided, for want of a right reason constituted by nature, so is it also in all debates of what kind soever. And when men that think themselves wiser than all others clamour and demand right reason for judge, yet seek no more but that things should be determined by no other men's reason but their own, it is as intolerable in the society of men as it is in play, after trump is turned, to use for trump on every occasion that suit whereof they have most in their hand. (V, 23)

We have the concept of "right reason" without consensus on what the right use of reason is. This is both an advantage and a disadvantage: without the sense of the right use of natural liberty there might be no motive for creatively ordering ourselves, or seeking a peaceful state; at the same time, the natural individuality of opinion makes the motive for peace also a source of conflict. In the condition of mere nature, human beings respond to their natural instinct to survive and prosper on their own terms. Yet through reason they also reflect on their experience of the unavoidable presence of others, stimulating them to formulate the maxims of conduct, the observance of which would mitigate the hostile and potentially warlike conditions they otherwise encounter in the pursuit of their wished-for satisfactions.

Common to all human beings, reasoning is both a source of our predicament, because we differentiate ourselves from each other, and the remedy for it, because we can conceive of what the remedy would be. The capacity to reflect is as much part of us as is the pursuit of our passionate desires; the internal contest of motives must be resolved. We learn in Chapter XIV that the "Right of Nature," the liberty we have to do anything according to our own judgment that we are not prevented from doing by external impediments, has a corresponding "Law of Nature" "found out by reason," which tells us not to engage in self-destruction (XIV, 79). Individuals must mediate the conflict between passion and reason; we have a duty to ourselves alongside the passion to fulfill our desires. We define that duty for ourselves, and, in the absence of a system of laws, we interpret its demands for ourselves, judging others' responses from our own perspective. Moral duty as an individual may conceive it is not yet a legal obligation, which can only derive from a rule of law instituted by agreeing, through covenant with each other, to submit to an authority to make laws for us, which implies willingness to subscribe to rules thus made. The capacity to imagine the erection of a rule of law as a way out of mutual self-destruction leads to this conclusion, and encourages the will to achieve it.

Human beings are passionate creatures, and while they may differ in the desires they pursue, they also have reason in common. Despite having reason in common, Hobbes asserts that there is no *summum bonum* as was spoken of by the old moral philosophers, while there is a *summum malum*— namely, violent death (XI, 57) Mortality is not a matter of opinion; we are equally and evidently mortal. Whether one believes in a highest good or not, we must reckon with the lack of agreement on what it is, since there is no avoiding the necessity of individuals to interpret the meaning of their experiences for themselves. To achieve peaceful order in this situation, laws must be made by an authority we acknowledge to be entrusted to make laws, and to make the laws such that they are compatible with the full range of individuals, who, knowing themselves to be by nature free, can acknowledge an obligatory rule that is in each of their interests to accept because civil peace requires it. Such laws in principle favor no one or any special interests in particular in order to serve all who are subject to them.

We are equal in the decisive respect that we are all mortal, but there are those with intense desires for wealth, command, or sensual delight, or the desire to stand alone or be first, all of which can make us forgetful of our mortality (XI, 58). Hobbes exalts none of these motives. Whatever the highest good may be, whether or not there is a highest good, we cannot rely on how the old moral philosophers conceived it. The *summum malum* forces itself upon us, while the quest for the *summum bonum* promotes argument, debate, violence, when we really need conversation and caution about reaching decisive conclusions. Death does not wait upon our agreement to it. But to pursue the good demands sobriety and skepticism about those who claim to have discovered it, including ourselves. The worst situation is self-deception or pridefulness, the remedy for which is self-discipline. We may have strong convictions, but we cannot expect agreement or acquiescence from others.

The "laws of nature"—which are not laws properly so called (XV, 100), but maxims or precepts accessible to, and individually interpreted by, each human being—show that in exercising our freedom we cannot avoid wondering how this freedom is to be used. We must face the issue of the right use of our natural liberty. A sense of moral duty (to ourselves to begin with) is natural. Hobbes is, to say the least, skeptical about how this freedom has in fact been exercised, given the history of human relations both past and present. Invoking a biblical image, he remarks that when Adam and Eve disobeyed the divine command they took upon themselves the authority to judge of good and evil without having first acquired the wisdom necessary to judge rightly (XX, 134). It is as if God then left us on our own recognizance to find our way out of the predicament we created for ourselves.

If there is a way out of this predicament, or a way to moderate its consequences, then humans will have to think through the right use of their freedom more carefully. Because this is the common predicament of mankind altogether, we need an understanding that is in principle accessible to any human being who will take the trouble to learn it. Hobbes believes all can learn it. The new order will be transparent in the sense that everyone can see it is in their interest to accept it, and can rationally subject themselves to it because it is in their interest to do so:

> The final cause, end, or design of men (who naturally love liberty and dominion over others) in the introduction of that restraint upon themselves in which we see them live in commonwealths is the foresight of their own preservation, and of a more contented life thereby. (XVII, 106)

In turn the holders of the office of sovereignty, even if sovereignty is "absolute," are limited by the common understanding of what form the laws properly so called should take. They know also that the purpose of sovereigns is not to extend infinitely the scope of their power, but to do what is necessary to maintain civil peace for a set of human beings who naturally love liberty. The "final cause" of those who naturally love liberty—a cause or goal that all can recognize—is civil peace; to claim the wisdom to go beyond that, except in private reflection or conversation, is to perpetuate the threats to the secure and fruitful exercise of liberty.

Authority derives from holding an office of authority "by right" because the officeholder is recognized by those who, although natural lovers of liberty who understand themselves to be by nature individual and free, have good reasons to subject themselves to that exercise of authority in order to rescue themselves from the war of all against all in the pursuit of their desired satisfactions. The distinction between a man as subject and a man as ruler is not a distinction between different kinds of men, but between different offices or stations.

The formal order of a polity (for Hobbes, its form could be democratic, aristocratic, or monarchic) does not eliminate the inherent natural freedom of human beings. Human beings interpret the world from the standpoint of their own experiences, and thus, in principle, a common understanding ultimately depends on individuals fashioning an outlook and a vocabulary to share. Hobbes's attention to making the terms of political discourse more precise recognizes this.

Achieving such unity requires a well-made, well-understood artifice. Of course, those with great power at their disposal may impose an apparent uniformity of belief, but this is only apparent and will disintegrate as and when that power falters:

> For though a man may covenant thus *unless I do so, or so, kill me*, he cannot covenant thus *unless I do, or so, I will not resist when you come to kill me*. For man by nature chooseth the lesser evil, which is danger of death in resisting, rather than the greater, which is certain and present death in not resisting. (XIV, 87)

It is true that Hobbes famously remarks that covenants without the sword are but words, that the fear of punishment is indispensable. But he understood that a peaceful civil order cannot rest merely on the enforcement power of a sovereign. There must be "authority" that is other than the mere exercise of force and that stems from acknowledgment by subjects who recognize its value in maintaining order beyond what force alone can achieve. To authorize, by acknowledging, a sovereign is not merely negative; such acknowledgment facilitates our capacity for private transactions. There must, in short, be an idea of civic virtue, itself distinct from adherence to the legal framework, which allows us to foresee the possibility of protecting our self-chosen pursuits while recognizing that others enjoy the same possibility. This implies the will to sustain a civic character against our self-assertive natural humanity, even when the power of the sovereign to threaten us is not immediately present. The latter is possible insofar as the imagining of the civic relationship arises through our reflection, not through prior imposition upon us.

Hobbes has a strong notion of the necessity of legal rules to facilitate transactions within the commonwealth. Indeed, although liberty reigns "where the sovereign has prescribed no rule" (XXI, 143), the law's silence is no license for reigniting the war of all against all, since the commonwealth mitigates the conditions conducive to hostility. The maxims of the right use of liberty are natural to us and observable in a commonwealth that constrains the condition of war, even though individuals, while adopting the civil character, remain natural beings. The purpose of the commonwealth is not to supersede our natural freedom but to provide the conditions under which its right or rational use may be maximized.

Indeed, if the first law of nature is to seek peace, then to live in a civil order increases the chance to live in peace, and to enjoy the fruits thereby available, which is an incentive to act in accord with what the maxims of peace tell us. A lasting order will require broad understanding of civic requirements such that individuals learn to be self-governing. We are not only self-assertive; there is also in us an inclination to law-abidingness, which, whether the motive for it is noble or fearful, promotes the desired result. One of these "helps" or motives for submitting—a sense of honor and pride in one's self-restraint—is admirable, but too rare to be counted on so as to preclude the necessity to rely on fear of consequences, which includes rational pursuit of one's interests (XIV, 87). Both the higher and the lower motives conduce to the end that is sought but the lower—fear of consequences—is more dependable. We cannot see into each other's hearts; subjects who are equally law-abiding in their observable conduct are, whatever interior nobility or gallantry they may or may not possess, satisfactory. Nobility now lies not in pretension and display, but in a kind of aristocratic disdain for public glory manifested in self-contained self-respect. Self-sufficiency is the noble attitude for one whose self-respect does not require external reinforcement or flattery.

How is all this to be accomplished? First, we must identify the basic precepts of a stable and peaceful civil order while acknowledging the natural individuality of man. We require an order, artificial in the strict sense that it is a work of art envisioned through the creative imagination of human beings responding to their common natural condition. We, the matter to be formed, must make ourselves subjects, as it is in our interest to do so.

Through a covenant with each other (which might emerge as an evolving set of expectations over time according to how our moral imagination develops) we express commitment to the civil life through an act of will to constrain our natural humanity. Commerce is an experiential source of coming to recognize the necessity of accommodation, which makes practical the maxims of peaceful conduct. The constraint must be self-imposed in order for it to be functional on a more than occasional basis. The rules must emanate from an acknowledged authority, and have the proper character of rules: (1) No natural man without office has authority to impose rules on another; (2) none of us can choose our own obligations; and (3) every obligation arises from our consent to be obliged. There is no authority by nature, no natural hierarchy of persons, and no authority by divine right.

It is significant that Hobbes titles Chapter XIV *"Of the First and Second* Natural Laws *and of* Contracts." The natural laws and contractual relations are intimately tied. We implement these natural laws typically in contracts, and we make contracts in the light of the laws of nature; each is to be understood in the context of the other. Hobbes is considering the moral imagination as it informs a society of persons who regularly engage each other in voluntary transactions. Contracts involve the mutual transferring of right, and

> In contracts the right passeth, not only where the words are of the time present or past, but also where they are of the future, because all contract is mutual translation, or change of right; and therefore he that promiseth only (because he hath already received the benefit for which he promiseth) is to be understood as if he intended the right should pass; for unless he had been content to have his words so understood, the other would not have performed his part first. And for that cause, in buying and selling, and other acts of contract, a promise is equivalent to a covenant, and therefore obligatory. (XIV, 83)

For Hobbes, a promise translates the moral duty implied in the maxims of rational conduct into an obligation. In the commonwealth there is an enforcement power to assure contractual promises are kept. But before that is the disposition to relate to others contractually that instantiates the emerging modern moral imagination, and that legitimates the use of enforcement power as a practical reinforcement of this moral imagination. The sovereign does not create the moral imagination; the sovereign is a logical consequence of the moral imagination, indispensable to reinforcing it.

The concept of the sovereign implies responsibility on the part of both governors and the governed. Hobbes makes it clear from the start that he is speaking of the idea of sovereignty (see the Dedicatory Epistle), not of a particular person or persons. The idea of sovereignty and its purpose is accessible to all individuals who reflect on their situation. Responsibility for maintaining order, establishing trust, and facilitating productive transactions is dispersed throughout. Here is one modern expression of this, specific to the business context:

> Consider that ethical transgressions can occur on countless levels. . . . Consider how your ethical miscues can affect people—employees, colleagues and superiors, suppliers, customers, internal regulators (lawyers, auditors, the board of directors), external regulators (government, interest groups, and the like), shareholders, or the public at large in your community. . . . With so many opportunities and audiences with which to cross the ethical line, attempting to define or legislate proper behavior is impossible. Some legal absolutes can be defined. But real ethical behavior and understanding can only result when the right norms and examples are shared and internalized by an organization's leaders.[12]

Hobbes does not claim to be inventing the moral imagination as here described; rather, he is theorizing what he finds to be present already in experience. As he says in the Introduction to *Leviathan*, he intends to provide guidance for the introspection each of us may undertake. He hopes to make explicit what he believes to be implicit in our experience.

LAW: NATURAL AND CIVIL AND THE MEANING OF CONTRACT

What are these universally comprehensible maxims of conduct that inform the making of laws, laws that make a rule of reason operative as an obligatory law of the land and facilitate relationships through contracts?

The first law or maxim is to seek peace as the means to make one's natural liberty meaningful and productive. The second is

> *to lay down this right to all things, and be contented with so much liberty against other men, as he would allow other men against himself.* (XIV, 80)

Hobbes took the "Golden Rule" to be a naturally accessible, universally knowable rule of reason. So long as it remains a precept of "duty" it is not yet a "law" in the full sense. When a sovereign is acknowledged through a covenant among the individuals seeking escape from a condition of mere nature, the understanding of moral duty in practice can be shared by all.

The task of creating a system of laws properly so called will be informed by these background considerations. It is not the specific content of the laws a sovereign sets forth that counts so much as whether those laws conform to the maxims that define the character that laws need to have.[13] For Hobbes, the civil law is the natural law put into practice: "The law of nature and the civil law contain each other, and are of equal extent" (XXVI, 174). The laws of the land properly drawn are the natural laws put into practice. The civil law pertains to all members of the commonwealth alike, stemming only from the commonwealth (that is, neither from a divine source nor from particular interests within the commonwealth). The rules may be drawn in different ways—but there are standards by which to judge their conformity or approximation to the maxims of peace that guide the making of the laws. Even if the sovereign is not technically under the laws (for the sovereign is "absolute"), the character of law is rationally knowable; the sovereign did not create the character of law but only makes particular laws that make "law" operative. Nor does the "absoluteness" of the sovereign suggest or require extensive, minute regulation through law. Rather, the laws are to achieve the civil peace that the individual subjects, each in his or her own rational self-interest, require.

The other "laws of nature" or precepts may be summarized as follows. We must perform the covenants we have made, a law that, Hobbes says, is "the fountain and original of JUSTICE" (XV, 89). Hobbes goes on to describe the laws that follow from the first laws: gratitude, complaisance (willingness to accommodate others), the capacity to pardon, to restrain the urge to revenge, to avoid expressing hatred or contempt, to acknowledge others to be equal to oneself by overcoming pride, to avoid arrogance, to adjudicate disputes impartially, to acknowledge equal access to what is common, to observe as far as possible equal distribution recognizing the right of first possession, to safeguard those whose duty it is to mediate disputes, to accept the decisions of arbitrators, not to demand to be judge in one's own case, but to ask that judges be impartial, and thus to seek competent, disinterested witnesses in determining facts. All of this he summarizes for those who need a simple formula: *"Do not that to another, which thou wouldst not have done to thyself"* (XV, 99). And

> the laws of nature are immutable and eternal; for injustice, ingratitude, arrogance, pride, iniquity, acception of persons, and the rest, can never be made lawful. For it can never be that war shall preserve life, and peace destroy it. (XV, 100)

Hobbes here lays a foundation for the *concept* of the rule of law that importantly does not depend on the technical knowledge of lawyers:

> By Civil Laws I understand the laws that men are therefore bound to observe because they are members, not of this or that commonwealth in particular, but of a commonwealth. For the knowledge of particular laws belongeth to them that profess the study of the laws of their several countries; but the knowledge of civil law in general to any man. (XXVI, 172–73)

Hobbes offers an independent standard for assessing the actual laws we have by reference to the idea of law and its purpose, while insisting on respect for the lawmaking authority to provide the laws that instantiate the concept of law in a manner appropriate to the local circumstances. The effectiveness of authority is constituted in the reciprocity of understanding among rulers and ruled. The reason to acknowledge authority is equally knowable to those who exercise authority and to those who submit to the exercise of authority.

Even if we doubt such an order could have actually arisen historically (as we say, through a "social contract") in the way Hobbes describes it, we can see how all existing orders might be judged and over time reformed to conform to an order of the sort Hobbes envisions as if the order actually had been founded in an original covenant. Even if, as Machiavelli argued (for instance in chapter 6 of *The Prince*), all political orders arose historically through force or fraud, Hobbes's argument gains strength in its forward-looking character, rather than as a historical explanation of origins. Hobbes is skeptical in order to be optimistic about the revolutionary potential of his vision.

Because we are self-making beings, we make ourselves into subjects of the commonwealth without ceasing to be selves. We do not relinquish the motive to direct ourselves as we think best within the limits we have accepted as necessary to our security. To direct ourselves means deciding for ourselves, within the framework of a shared moral imagination, how to interact with others; in this way, we can develop and maintain relations with others not designed by the sovereign or any central office. Within the background constraints there is expanded room for spontaneous, not centrally directed, transactions. The maxims of rational conduct, accessible to every mind, set forth the basic requirements for productive interactions, and the covenant assigns to the sovereign the duty through civil law to make practical our capacity to act in accord with the maxims. The basic structure of security, which enables us to employ our energies in ways of our own choosing, with all the risks that may involve, is far more important than specific policies. Hobbes takes the basic structure of what we know as the modern state to be a permanent insight. He knows, of course, that we can fail to manage the tension between self- advancement and self-restraint; the power to punish cannot be dispensed with. But the combination of fear of the war of all against all and the positive advantages of commerce in civil society intends to diminish reliance on punishment.

We should direct our attention to maintaining and exploiting the possibilities the covenant, and its system of laws, afford us. Allegiance to the covenant is the signal to each other of our capacity for rational understanding of how, in submitting to the sovereign's authority, we gain advantages for self-development we otherwise could not enjoy. Though we are self-interested individuals, reason nevertheless is our common possession. We can grasp not merely particular laws or rules, but the idea of obligation itself, and thus we can resolve the tension between the common interest and our particular interests. In embracing this distinction we bring the ethical dimension into our transactions with each other.

Hobbes's argument articulates the foundation for rational conduct of selves, who understand themselves as selves among other selves in the same predicament. The sovereign does not supplant the interactions that ensue by our choice; it encourages them. The function and value of the sovereign, then, lies not in guaranteeing to any particular individuals or groups the success of their undertakings. The covenant is suspect if the sovereign, qua sovereign, is partial in advance to any particular interests. Sovereign authority provides the background conditions to make lawful risk-taking reasonable, but leaves us susceptible to failure. Blaming the sovereign for failure to enforce the law on which our transactions depend is one thing; blaming the sovereign for the failure of our self-chosen enterprises is another matter. The entrepreneurial spirit, rationally constrained in pursuit of self-interest, may flourish in Hobbes's commonwealth. Hobbes knew that human beings differ in the degree of their ambition and willingness to take risks. Many may be happy with a sufficiency. As long as those of great ambition subscribe to the covenant and the laws, those of greater and those of lesser ambition may coexist peacefully and productively. The law of the commonwealth as such neither caters to nor suppresses either disposition.

ACTORS, AUTHORS, AND REPRESENTATIVE GOVERNMENT

The great invention of modern politics is the idea of representative government. Representative government is the appropriate form of political order for a world of people who understand themselves to be by nature free while needing to get along with each other, a many seeking workable unity. Hobbes is a major contributor to this invention, as he is to the modern concept of authority.

In *Leviathan* XVI, Hobbes discusses what a "Person" is. "Person" refers to one's outward appearance or mask, how human beings present themselves to others. Human beings try to disclose their inner dispositions as they want others to see them. A person is like an actor on a stage. There may be tension between what I am thinking and what I am presenting to the world, but living with this tension is necessary in order to balance our self-assertion with our desire to remain at peace with others. Self-assertion must be balanced by self-control. The actor on the stage speaks the lines composed by a playwright; he is not the "author" of the speech. The actor acts according to—in effect, acknowledges—the "authority" of the author. The actor is entrusted by the author with the right to do or say something. The actor is "authorized" to play his part. In interpreting his role, the actor subscribes to, interprets, and appropriates, the author's direction. The actor cannot simply, as a human being, be identified with the thoughts and actions he has been authorized to perform; he may or may not inwardly subscribe to them. But as a whole composition the play depends on the actor's willingness to act in accord with the requirements of the author—to acknowledge the author's authority. The composition depends on the actor acknowledging the authority of the playwright. Individuals, qua individuals, both write their scripts and enact them. As subjects in a commonwealth, we are actors in the play composed by the sovereign. The private thoughts of the subjects are unregulated as their public words and actions are not. The covenanters are the author of the sovereign, as the sovereign then becomes the author of the laws. Just as the playwright can write the script, but the actors must perform it, figuring out how to bring alive the words on the page, so the subjects must enact the laws in practice; the sovereign cannot perform the innumerable interactions of subjects on their behalf, or follow the law merely abstractly.

When actors play their part, they bind the author as well, since we know the author to be responsible for what is on display, but we also know that we are responsible for the sovereign exercising authority. Both the author and the actor are subject to appraisal and criticism. We are spectators of each other and of the sovereign, and the sovereign is the spectator of us all. As spectators we know the author of the play is responsible for the story, but we also know that we are responsible for the author.

Divided or contested authority threatens or destroys the wholeness of the composition. When individuals or groups resist they may be appealing to rival authorities or to no clear authority. This happens because an actor or actors believe that the sovereign wants them to act in betrayal of the laws of nature, to which they can, of course, always appeal if they so choose, or because they think the authority has undermined the covenant, the original purpose of which was to eliminate violence and to facilitate our capacity to enjoy the fruits of our industry. The actor is then claiming personal authority against the very authority he has authorized, or is appealing to some other authority as an alternative to the sovereign's authority. Hobbes calls this a logical absurdity, but knows that does not prevent it from happening. There is potential conflict between the obligation to maintain the covenant and rival interpretations of what the covenant intended the sovereign to do. Hobbes says:

> He that maketh a covenant with the actor, or representer, not knowing the authority he hath, doth it at his own peril. For no man is obliged by a covenant whereof he is not the author, nor consequently by a covenant made against or beside the authority he gave. (XVI, 102)

Who has authority? When the answer to this is unclear or contested, the seeds of disorder germinate. Since the subjects are the source of the authority of the sovereign, that sovereign's task is to provide for their unity in a way that works for all or most of them. The sovereign power, as the source of laws, is "absolute" for Hobbes because, as the source of the laws, the sovereign is above the laws. But the scope of the exercise of power is in principle limited by what can attain general assent from the subjects, or most of them. The capacity to overawe the subjects is necessary but not sufficient. Obligation presupposes recognition, not mere imposition; recognition requires us to admit our limitations, although under no circumstances is one obliged except by consent:

> It is not therefore the victory that giveth the right of dominion over the vanquished, but his own covenant. Nor is he obliged because he is conquered (that is to say, beaten, and taken or put to flight), but because he cometh in, and submitteth to the victor. . . . And then only is his life in security, and his service due, when the victor hath trusted him with his corporal liberty. . . . In sum, the rights and consequences of both *paternal* and *despotical* dominion are the very same with those of a sovereign by institution, and for the same reasons. (XX, 131)

Rulers need in the end to trust subjects with corporal liberty. The artificial unity does not end the natural diversity of the individual subjects; that unity depends on the subjects' continually willing that the artificial unity should be maintained. There is no natural unity, no ideal order, that can perfect the artificial unity. The foundation of civil order lies in the wills of the individual subjects, not in the construction of a collective identity:

> For it is the *unity* of the representer, not the *unity* of the represented, that maketh the person *one*. And it is the representer that beareth the person, and but one person, and *unity* cannot otherwise be understood in multitude. (XVI, 104)

When institutions come to be dissolved

> not by external violence but intestine disorder, the fault is not in men as they are the *matter*, but as they are the *makers* and orderers of them. (XXIX, 210)

The faults in the makers, which are lurking threats to good order, are inadequate power in the sovereign, the public assertion of private judgments on law and policy, the belief that one's conscience trumps the law, the belief that one possesses a supernatural revelation, ambitious cultivation of popular followings, the belief that the sovereign is subject to the laws, that the sovereign has no right to taxes in support of government functions, the division of sovereign power among competing claimants to authority, appealing to the orders of other nations against one's own, and the belief that the ancient orders of Greece and Rome are more appropriate than the modern understanding of order Hobbes is presenting (XXIX).

Unity must be of a multitude. Hobbes thus both defends absolute sovereignty and demythologizes and depersonalizes it. The task of the subjects is not to give up their private thoughts and beliefs, but to chasten their hopes that those thoughts and beliefs can gain universal ascendancy, consoled by the thought that this is also denied to others. Hobbes argues in Parts III and IV of *Leviathan* to the effect that private religious convictions so far as they remain private are not a threat. Hobbes does not intend that the sovereign should invade the private thoughts of subjects so long as they remain private. Hobbes is skeptical of higher truths except for the "laws of nature"—the rational maxims conducive to peace—which are accessible, but not teleological in character; the maxims provide guidelines for interaction but do not prescribe where such interactions ought to lead beyond the civil order itself. Hobbes's commonwealth admits maximum freedom of thought but not unlimited public expression. There is no precise answer to the question of how to draw the line between the public and the private. This is a matter for deliberation and judgment in the search for unity in the midst of multiplicity, and the sovereign must determine this.

The private life is thus protected, while the public life is, for the subject, in the background. The drama of life arises in the interior lives of individuals and is outwardly disclosed in the pursuit of their individual self-chosen satisfactions. The noblest individuals are those who mind their own business, concerning themselves with what others think and believe insofar as they are in search of mutually advantageous relations. Hobbes is a political skeptic. The need for a strong sovereign need not entail the need for an expansive sovereign exercising minute control. The more expansive the sovereign's commitments, the more occasions there will be for the temptation to resist authority to arise, including efforts to protect particular interests by attaining privileged relations with the sovereign. Hobbes is both skeptical and yet optimistic about the human capacity to exercise self-regulation in pursuing our desired satisfactions within commonwealths adequately protected from worms in the body politic. He offers a basis for deep reflection on human conduct, of which the ethics of conduct in business is no small part.

CONCLUDING REMARKS

As set forth in this essay, the various strands of Hobbes's thought furnish a rich foundational ground for a different kind of business ethics. This is a business ethics that commences with a moral imagination whose first step is introspection or self-consciousness. Through this activity each person recognizes the universal nature of humankind, at the heart of which lies the tension between self-interest and self-restraint. The capacity of reason to promote self-restraint mediates the tension between self-advancement and self-restraint so as to make the tension manageable and productive in the form of that enlightened self-interest that fuels business life. The mediation of reason also expands to the political association and yields the contractual relations that inform social and commercial conduct. But the stability of social association and commercial exchange is secured not simply by means of the sanctions of the sovereign but through both civic virtue and a disposition, as much rational as passionate, to relate to others.

In Hobbes's account one arrives at a business ethics that is not anchored exclusively within moral thought but rests on a wider plain that links philosophy, ethics, moral psychology, and politics and relates these to conduct, including the prominent case, discerned by Hobbes, of commercial conduct.

Thus, Hobbes begins *Leviathan* with the stipulation that rational conduct requires us not to "read" (understand) only ourselves but "mankind." Through introspection we can distinguish our idiosyncratic, personal predilections from the springs of conduct that are universal, and recognize that the human predicament is common even though we know our own individual experiences of it first and immediately. To judge from our own point of view is an unavoidable starting point but not an insuperable limit to our self-understanding. Hobbes offers extended investigation into the norms of self-consciousness. The study of ethics, and of business ethics, should encourage expanded self-consciousness, which inevitably means expanded awareness and understanding of others.

The English version of *Leviathan* was intended for any intelligent reader. Hobbes wanted it taught in universities and preached from pulpits. Moreover, Hobbes tells us that the proof of his argument depends on each of us considering the analysis *Leviathan* lays out and deciding for ourselves if we see what he sees (there is, he says, no other way to demonstrate it). There is thus a method for expanding self-consciousness as important as the specific conclusions produced by the method. The method is intense introspection. Hobbes does not depend on moral virtuosos, the philosophic few who see what the rest of us cannot see. All the basic insights required can be gained by persistent introspection coupled with observation of what we see around us. Each of us is both an individual and an instance of mankind. Hobbes's book is not offered as a substitute for self-reflection, but as an aide to its advance. Hobbes's argument is directed to rulers and subjects, governors and the governed, managers and their employees, leaders and followers—to all of us.

With regard to maxims of moral conduct there is no secret knowledge, no precepts that are knowable only to a few, and no special training in law or theology is required. Hobbes looks for the emergence of a common agreement on the precepts of conduct that will facilitate how we conduct ourselves with each other—the "modern moral imagination." These precepts, clarified by experience, are relevant to all our interactions and applicable to our economic transactions as well as to other forms. Hobbes's "commonwealth," or what we call the modern state, reinforces the emergent moral imagination.

Individuals define satisfactory lives for themselves according to their own wished-for satisfactions. Commerce is a means of connecting such people to each other in their pursuits without preventing the continual exploration of new possibilities—it provides for an orderly pursuit of what is not already ordered or invented. The requirements of moral conduct are not antithetical to the pursuit of one's self-interest. There is, to be sure, tension between self-interest and regard for others, but, as Hobbes sees it, the considerations required to make the tension manageable are well within the range of human self-understanding on a broad scale. The strong, external organization of the polity is compatible with individuals capable of considerable self-regulation. Business ethics is a particular instance of the general maxims of conduct knowable to us without need of esoteric insight or revelation. Moral philosophy facilitates our recognition of what is already implicit in us, and it is nothing but the conversation about good and evil in human society.

NOTES

1. Thomas Hobbes, *Leviathan* (1651), ed. Edwin Curley (Indianapolis: Hackett, 1994). All references are to this edition and cited parenthetically in the text by chapter and page number. All italics are original.

2. See Francis Fukuyama, *Trust: The Social Virtues and the Creation of Prosperity* (New York: Free Press, 1996).

3. R. Edward Freeman, introduction to *Business Ethics: The State of the Art*, ed. Freeman (New York: Oxford University Press, 1991), 5.

4. The answers to questions of business ethics "cannot be discovered by managerial or business ethics alone. These questions require the more fundamental disciplines of ethics and political philosophy. The standard for proper managerial conduct cannot be derived independently of those ethical principles that determine how human beings ought to live their lives and those political principles that determine the ethical principles by which human beings must live their lives, that is, be a matter of law." Douglas B. Rasmussen, "Managerial Ethics," in *Commerce and Morality*, ed. Tibor Machan (Totowa, NJ: Rowman & Littlefield, 1988), 25–26.

5. "Western Europe, from the twelfth century on, had experienced a gradual penetration of its economic structure by the commercial institutions and relationships that accompanied the emergence of urban populations, urban institutions, and urban producers whose economic roles were vitally dependent upon commerce." Nathan Rosenberg and L. E. Birdzell, Jr., *How the West Grew Rich: The Economic Transformation of the Industrial World* (New York: Basic Books, 1986), 79. The "English political system . . . guaranteed peace through the control of feuding, taxes were light and justice was uniform and firmly administered from the thirteenth to the eighteenth centuries. This offered the framework within which there developed that competitive individualism whose later history I have tried to analyse elsewhere." Alan MacFarlane, *The Culture of Capitalism* (Oxford: Basil Blackwell, 1987), 189. See also MacFarlane, *The Origins of English Individualism* (Oxford: Wiley-Blackwell, 1991).

6. Adam Smith, *An Inquiry into the Nature and Causes of the Wealth of Nations*, ed. R. H. Campbell and A. S. Skinner (Indianapolis: Liberty Fund, 1981), I.ii, pp. 26–27.

7. Ibid., I.ii, p. 27.

8. John Hendry, *Between Enterprise and Ethics: Business and Management in a Bimoral Society* (Oxford: Oxford University Press, 2004), 231.

9. Ibid., 260. The term "bimoral" is problematic: it might suggest two separate realms of moral thinking rather than a tension between two dimensions of the same moral outlook.

10. Adam Smith, *The Theory of Moral Sentiments* (1759), ed. D. D. Raphael and A. L. Macfie (Indianapolis: Liberty Fund, 1982).

11. Joanne B. Ciulla, "Business Ethics as Moral Imagination," in *Business Ethics: The State of the Art*, ed. R. Edward Freeman (New York: Oxford University Press, 1991), 212. I am happy to see Ciulla use the term "moral imagination." She goes on to say: "Business students have a basic understanding of right and wrong. . . . They possess the right moral concepts or linguistic tools but have not mastered them in the environment of business and the culture of particular organizations. . . . It makes perfect sense to say that experience can enrich our concept of, say, 'honesty,' while the concept itself remains the same" (214).

12. Noel M. Tichy and Andrew R. McGill, introduction to *The Ethical Challenge: How to Lead with Unyielding Integrity*, ed. Tichy and McGill (San Francisco: Jossey-Bass/Wiley, 2003), 3, and quoting Warren Buffett: "In looking for people to hire, you look for three qualities: integrity, intelligence and energy. And if they don't have the first, the other two will kill you. You think about it; it's true. If you hire somebody without the first, you really want them to be dumb and lazy. . . . Contemplating any business act, an employee should ask himself whether he would be willing to see it immediately described by an informed and critical reporter on the front page of his local paper, there to be read by his spouse, children, and friends . . . we simply want no part of any activities that pass legal tests, but that we, as citizens, would find offensive. . . . It takes 20 years to build a reputation, and five minutes to ruin it. If you think about that, you'll do things differently" (9). This is the moral imagination at work.

13. "Ethics can be thought of in business as the 'implicit contracts' that represent who you are and what you stand for. These are the things your constituents expect to rely on, even if they aren't explicitly stated in a written contract. Implicit contracts reflect your ethical core. The dividing line between law and ethics is a constantly moving one. . . . Economists see being ethical as nothing more than honoring implicit contracts with investors, creditors, employees, senior executives, and other constituents. And it makes good business sense—not necessarily in the short term but always in the long run—to honor these implicit contracts." Anjan Thakor, "Competence without Credibility Won't Win in the Long Run," in Tichy and McGill, *Ethical Challenge*, 127. This is part of what Hobbes means in saying that the natural and civil law contain each other in practice.

CHAPTER 8

John Locke's Defense of Commercial Society: Individual Rights, Voluntary Cooperation, and Mutual Gain

Eric Mack

John Locke's enormous contribution to social and political theory and to human well-being consists substantially in his being the founding father of liberal individualism and a key philosophical defender of modern liberal commercial society. Indeed, his articulation of individualistic liberalism and his support of commercial society are deeply connected.[1] Central to Locke's liberal individualism is his endorsement of each individual's pursuit of both temporal and eternal happiness, and the moral rights that immunize individuals from interference in their pursuit of happiness—especially the moral rights of property and contract—and his radical limitation of governmental authority to the promulgation and enforcement of "laws of liberty" that "secure protection and incouragement to the honest industry of Mankind" (*ST* §42). These central features of Locke's liberal individualism underwrite his support of commercial society, to be understood as a social-economic order many members of which engage in extensive marketplace economic interaction on the basis of their acquisition and exercise of private property and contractual rights. The moral rights and the protective legal framework affirmed by Lockean liberalism provide the moral and institutional framework for commercial society. The main Lockean line of argument that will concern us runs from the endorsement of liberal individualism to the endorsement of commercial society.

However, there are also Lockean arguments that connect the fundamental norms of liberal individualism, the institutions of commercial society, and religious toleration. The basic norms of liberal individualism that underwrite commercial society *also* provide the key justification for religious toleration. Moreover, the central institutions of commercial society—private property rights and contract—provide the institutional structure for actual regimes of religious toleration. If religious toleration is to be justified and practiced, the norms that underlie commercial society and its central institutions must be affirmed and respected. Indeed, in his first defense of toleration, "An Essay on Toleration," Locke maintains that the principle that all individuals are to be protected against invasion and injury in their "private civil concernments" and their "prosecution of their private interests" *is* the principle of "perfect toleration."[2]

In this essay I will provide a critical—albeit sympathetic—account of Locke's liberal individualism, trace the connections between Locke's liberalism and his endorsement of commercial society, and describe the connections between Locke's support for commercial society and his advocacy of religious freedom. However, at the outset I need to clarify what I mean and do not mean when I describe Locke as a philosophical defender of commercial society.

First, by "commercial society" I do *not* mean a society in which for everyone (or nearly everyone) the most important dimension of life is market-oriented economic efforts and endeavors. In a commercial society, *a* salient feature of *many* people's lives will be marketplace economic activities and relationships. Yet this is compatible with there being a multiplicity of other salient dimensions to people's lives and with the commercial dimension playing little or no role in *some* people's lives. Still, within a commercial society, the moral space for the noncommercial facets of people's lives is defined and secured by their property and contractual rights. For instance, familial autonomy is morally and legally protected by the property and contractual rights of family members, and the autonomy of churches is morally and legally protected by the property rights they have acquired in their voluntary interactions with their congregants. In addition, in a commercial society the marketplace economic endeavors of some agents provide the lion's share of the material resources employed even in the noncommercial dimensions of people's lives. Spheres of protected freedom endowed with resources engendered by commerce allow individuals, families, churches, and other civil associations to pursue their own chosen noncommercial ends in their own chosen ways.

Second, Locke's liberalism does not *require* individuals to exercise or even to acquire the sorts of property and contract rights the deployment of which characterize a commercial social order. Individuals are morally at liberty individually or jointly to eschew or waive these rights and to retreat into their chosen noncommercial enclaves. Still, Locke thinks that there are moral reasons for welcoming people's exercise of their rights to enter into and participate in commercial activities. One reason is that participation in the increasingly elaborate forms of production and trade that characterize commercial society enhances the material prosperity of all (or nearly all) of the participants and, thus, increases their prospects for self-preservation and worldly happiness. Another reason for individuals' participation in commercial society is that commercial society calls upon and rewards two character traits that Locke takes to be core virtues—namely, prudence and self-responsibility. Individuals (or households) ought to identify and industriously promote their own happiness, and each agent should have a sense that the attainment of his (worldly and extraworldly) good is primarily his own responsibility. Of course, Locke's commendation of economic prudence and self-responsibility is not a call for life as an atomistic Robinson Crusoe but a call for voluntary cooperative industrious interaction with one's fellow rights-bearers.

Third, in describing Locke as a defender of commercial society, I am not asserting that his writings were primarily directed to *that* end. Probably Locke's primary self-conscious purpose in defending robust private property rights was to limit radically the scope of monarchical authority. That authority was to be fenced in by the independent moral rights—including property rights—of those over whom the monarch claimed authority. However, in the course of defending property rights, Locke develops a powerful argument for the advantages of commercial society, that is, the sort of society to which respect for those rights gives rise. Nor am I asserting that Locke fully recognized the implications of his defense of *liberal* commercial society. For Locke seems never to have explicitly condemned state-sanctioned economic monopolies and kindred restraints on trade that were a prominent feature of the commercial world of seventeenth-century England—even though *we* can see that the enforcement of these monopolies and restraints infringed upon the moral rights that stand at the center of Locke's liberalism.[3]

In the following four sections, I will provide an account of Locke's liberal individualist principles, explicate Locke's doctrine of private property rights and his crucial claim that as commercial society develops, the moral proviso that each be left with "enough, and as good" is not violated, recount Locke's views on the relationship of just price and market price and on assistance to the impoverished, and explore the relationships between Locke's endorsement of commercial society and his advocacy of religious toleration.

FUNDAMENTAL MORAL AND POLITICAL PRINCIPLES

Throughout his philosophical writings Locke advances two distinct and seemingly incompatible programs for identifying the fundamental moral norms that govern human interaction. One program is a species of the divine command theory. God's pronouncements determine what is obligatory, permissible, and impermissible. For, Locke says, all law must proceed from the will of a legislator; and the relevant legislator for fundamental, extrapositive law must be God. So, for example, in his *Essays on the Law of Nature*,

Locke declares that "there is no law without a lawmaker, and the law has no purpose without punishment" (113).[4] I shall refer to this as the "divine command program."

However, Locke also holds there are crucial and accessible facts about human nature, that is, our inborn constitution, and a thoughtful appreciation of these facts supports belief in certain fundamental moral principles. Although our existence as beings with the constitution that we have may be due to God's will, this inborn constitution underwrites the most basic norms that apply to our interactions. Locke explains, "Since man has been made such as he is, equipped with reason and his other faculties and destined for this mode of life, there necessarily results from his inborn constitution some definite duties for him, which cannot be other than they are" (*ELN* 125). In the same vein, Locke tells us that the law of nature is a "permanent rule of morals" because it is "firmly rooted in the soil of human nature" (125). Since man's natural law duties "follow from his very nature," Locke asserts that "natural law stands and falls together with the nature of man as it is at present" (126). I shall refer to this as the "inborn constitution program."

We cannot here discuss whether there can be any significant reconciliation of the divine command and the inborn constitution programs. Nevertheless, two facts justify concentration on Locke's inborn constitution program.[5] First, to carry out the divine command program one must have a grasp of God's will and intentions, which—especially in his later writings—Locke himself denies that we can have.[6] Second, when, at the beginning of the *Second Treatise of Government*, he sets out to explain why the state of nature has a law of nature to govern it, Locke pursues the inborn constitution program.

By the time Locke was writing and revising the *Second Treatise*, he had come to hold that one deep fact about our inborn constitution is that we each pursue happiness *and* it is rational and proper for each of us to pursue his or her own happiness. In a fragment written in the late 1670s, Locke maintains that

> Morality is the rule of man's actions for the attaining of happiness. . . . For the end and aim of all men being happiness alone, nothing could be a rule or a law to them whose observation did not lead to happiness and whose breach did [not] draw misery after it.[7]

In another fragment composed shortly before the publication of the *Second Treatise*, Locke wrote:

> 'Tis a man's proper business to seek happiness and avoid misery. . . . I will therefore make it my business to seek satisfaction and delight and avoid un-

easiness and disquiet and to have as much of the one and as little of the other as may be. But here I must have a care I mistake not, for if I prefer a short pleasure to a lasting one, 'tis plain I cross my own happiness.[8]

In his discussion of happiness in *An Essay Concerning Human Understanding*[9]—published in the same year as the *Two Treatises of Government*—Locke asserts that although all happiness is "the proper object of desire in general," not every instance of happiness moves every particular agent. Rather, each agent is moved only by those portions of happiness at large "which make a necessary part of his happiness."

> All other good, however great in reality or appearance, excites not a man's desires who looks not on it to make a part of that happiness wherewith he, in his present thoughts, can satisfy himself. Happiness, under this view, everyone constantly pursues, and desires what makes any part of it: other things, acknowledged to be good, he can look upon without desire, pass by, and be content without. (*ECHU*, vol. 1, bk. II, 341)

Since the crucial precondition of happiness is self-preservation, and the desire for and rationality of self-preservation are the standard starting points within seventeenth-century state-of-nature theorizing, when Locke turns to political philosophy his focus shifts from the drive for and the rationality of pursuing individual happiness to the drive for and the rationality of pursuing self-preservation. Nevertheless, Locke reminds us of the connection between happiness and self-preservation by explicating the right of self-preservation as the "equal Right" of all the descendants of Adam to pursue "the *comfortable* preservation of their Beings" (*FT* §88, emphasis added).

Indeed, there is a further shift in the immediate focus of Locke's political argument from self-preservation and the rationality of its pursuit to freedom and the rationality of one's pursuit of freedom. There are two overlapping reasons for this further shift. The first and explicit reason is that the primary danger to anyone's (comfortable) self-preservation is that person's subordination to the will of another. Such subordination will (almost always) diminish one's prospects for material well-being; and anyone who seeks to take one's freedom may very well go on to take one's life. "To be free from such force is the only security of my Preservation; and reason bids me look on him, as an Enemy to my Preservation, who would take away that *Freedom* which is the Fence to it" (*ST* §17). The second and implicit reason for focusing on freedom is that human beings are, by and large, quite capable of dealing with extrapersonal reality; the real threat to people's worldly success comes from other people. By and large, if human beings take pains, if they are rational and industrious, they can transform the "waste"[10] that is nature in ways that are conducive to their self-preservation and happiness—*unless* they are prevented from doing so or are deprived of the fruits of their efforts by other persons.

So the first deep fact about human nature relevant to political theorizing is that all rational human beings seek freedom from interference by others. The second deep fact about our inborn constitution is our underlying moral equality. Since we are all "Creatures of the same species and rank promiscuously born to all the same advantages of Nature, and the use of the same faculties," and there is no manifest sign that God has conferred special authority upon certain individuals, we can presume that we are all "equal one amongst another without Subordination or Subjection" (*ST* §4). These two deep facts about our inborn constitution work together to imply a natural symmetry of moral authority or jurisdiction (§4).

Locke tells us that, because of our natural moral equality, "there cannot be supposed any such *Subordination* among us, that may Authorize us to destroy one another as if we were made for one anothers uses" (*ST* §6). Locke's claim is not merely that the subordinating party has no positive authority to subordinate the other party, but the much stronger claim that the subordinating party *wrongs* the subordinated party. Why, according to Locke, is such subordination *wrong*? It is wrong precisely because persons are rationally directed to their own distinct ends—their own temporal (and eternal) happiness; each person exists for—indeed, Locke would say is made for—his or her own purposes. Subordinating another to one's own ends falsely presumes that he is not rationally oriented to his own distinct ends. Such subordinating action is a practical contravention of the fact that the subordinated party has his own happiness (and comfortable self-preservation) as his sanctified end.

Furthermore, because of the rationality of promoting one's happiness and the necessity of self-preservation to happiness and of freedom to self-preservation, each individual is rational to claim for himself a right against all others not to be deprived of freedom. However, since we are morally equal beings, all others must possess the same fundamental original rights. Hence, if one rationally claims for oneself a right against all others not to be deprived of freedom, it is also rationally incumbent upon one to acknowledge like rights possessed by all others (*ST* §5).

One takes cognizance of the fact that each other person is like oneself in having his own happiness and comfortable preservation as his ultimate ends not by expanding one's ends to include each other person's happiness and comfortable preservation but, instead, by not subverting others' pursuit of their distinct ends. The natural duty to preserve the rest of mankind is not a positive duty to promote their happiness or self-preservation. It is a duty not to "take away, or impair the life, or what tends to the Preservation of the Life, the Liberty, Health, Limb, or Goods of another" (*ST* §6).[11] Correlative to the negative duty not to preclude others from advancing their ends in their own chosen ways is the basic moral claim of all persons to freedom from interference with their respective pursuit of happiness and (comfortable) self-preservation.

It is often said that, according to Locke, the one fundamental moral claim or right is the right of self-ownership.[12] It would, however, be more accurate to say that for Locke this right is *part of* the sensible articulation of a more basic moral claim to freedom. Indeed, Locke does not speak of self-ownership within the *Second Treatise*'s early chapter "Of the State of Nature" where he lays out the case for the state of nature having a law of nature to govern it. He indicates that part of this law of nature is the natural right possessed by each individual that others abide by the promises and bargains that they have made with him (*ST* §14). Self-ownership as part of the articulation of this primal moral claim does not appear until Locke turns to the justification of individual property rights in the chapter "Of Property."

For Locke, a further part of the articulation of each person's primal claim to freedom is a natural right of property.[13] This is a right not to be precluded from using or acquiring property (in extrapersonal objects) and from exercising discretionary control over that property. This right exists because the use or acquisition and the ongoing discretionary control over extrapersonal objects are normally essential to the attainment by individuals of their happiness and self-preservation. Since individuals have rights to pursue their happiness and self-preservation free from the interference of others, they possess this right to make portions of nature their own and to exercise discretionary control over their own possessions. Locke distinguishes between this natural (hence, *nonacquired*) right to use natural material or to make and treat things as one's own and specific *acquired* rights to particular items of property (*FT* §§86–88)

PROPERTY RIGHTS AND MUTUAL GAIN

In the *Second Treatise*'s chapter "Of Property," Locke offers his well-known account of initial *acquired* private property rights. Since each individual possesses a moral self-proprietorship, each individual has rights over his own labor—understood broadly as industrious activity. When an individual transforms some bit of raw nature for the sake of some anticipated end, that individual "mixes" his labor with that raw material. He invests his rightfully held industrious capacity and effort in the transformed object. Because of this investment, the transformed object cannot be taken from this individual without his consent without depriving him of that invested labor without his consent. Since any such taking will violate the investor's rights, the labor investor has a right over the transformed object (*ST* §27).

Moreover, Locke presumes that when rightfully held objects—including an agent's labor—are voluntarily exchanged, the rights over those objects are transferred in accordance with that voluntary contract. Thus, Locke endorses what Robert Nozick more recently called an "historical entitlement" conception of justice in holdings.[14] Each individual has entitlements over those objects (and only those objects) that he (1) has created through the transformation of some portion of unowned nature or (2) has acquired through voluntary exchange with (or donation by) a rightful holder or (3), to add the final component of the entitlement view, has acquired as a matter of just restitution from an agent who has deprived him of some rightfully held object.

Nevertheless, Locke holds that there are at least theoretical limits on how much an individual may rightfully acquire even by entirely peaceful means (*ST* §§31, 33). According to one limit—the spoilage proviso—an individual will not have a right to the perishables that he has acquired through labor investment or voluntary exchange (or just restitution) if those perishables will spoil in his possession. However, this proviso has almost no practical significance because (1) in a world in which money has not yet been created individuals will have no incentive to produce or trade for more perishables than they can consume or barter, and (2) in a world in which money exists (in the form of nonperishable coins) individuals will have a strong incentive to exchange whatever will spoil in their possession for nonperishable money. And, according to Locke, there is no limit to the amount of *nonperishable* goods one can rightfully acquire.

According to the other and more interesting limit on private acquisition, one has a right to what one has joined one's labor to "at least where there is enough, and as good left in common for others" (*ST* §27). The "enough and as good" proviso is explicitly cast in terms of enough and as good natural material being left in the commons for individuals to use or convert into their own private property.[15] Imagine that other persons acquire so much from nature that some individual is left without as much natural material to use or acquire as would have been available were these other persons not engaged in transforming natural materials into their property. According to the enough and as good proviso, these acquirers will not be entitled to those of their acquisitions that make less available for that individual's use or acquisition than would have been available to him were the others not transforming natural material into property.[16] In contrast, if five people each scoop a gourd full of water from a bountiful stream and respectively make those gourds of water their own, this will not run afoul of the proviso because there will still be as much water available for a sixth individual's use (or acquisition) as would have been available to him had the other five not been acquirers. Note that the enough and as good proviso does *not* require that equal amounts of resources be left for others. It merely requires that others' acquisition does not leave one worse off in one's capacity to use natural materials than one would have been if all that material had remained in the commons.[17]

In discussing why, according to Locke, the enough and as good proviso will (almost always) be satisfied if acquisition takes place in accordance with his principles of just initial acquisition and just transfer we again have to consider the world before and after the appearance of money. For Locke the transition from the earth being unowned, that is, from its being an open commons, to the earth being substantially converted into private holdings corresponds with the transition from the hunter-gatherer stage of human existence to the agricultural stage. Locke envisions agriculture beginning with hunter-gatherer households settling down and turning to cultivation in ways that make the cultivated land their rightful private property. Why according to Locke does this process of privatizing land—which precedes the appearance of money—*not* run afoul of the enough and as good proviso?

The basis of Locke's answer is twofold: (1) before the creation of money individuals (or households) will put under cultivation only as much land as will yield crops that they themselves can consume or can barter locally for consumables produced by other households; *and* (2) the amount of land a household will need to yield those consumable crops through private ownership and cultivation will be vastly less than the amount of land that household would need to attain a comparable level—or, indeed, a lower level—of comfortable preservation as hunter-gatherers. Suppose that initially there are 100 hunter-gatherer households wandering throughout a 50,000-acre commons. In effect and on average, each household uses 500 acres. When the first household settles down as cultivators it makes, say, 20 acres its own. In doing so, this household increases the land available to the remaining 99 hunter-gatherer households. In effect and on average, each of the 99 households now has use of nearly 505 acres. As more households settle down and make 20 acres of land their own, more acres of open commons land become available to the remaining hunter-gatherers (*ST* §37).[18] Thus, before the introduction of money the enough and as good proviso is readily satisfied.

It is crucial to see why, according to Locke, the household that makes 20 acres its own and cultivates that land does better than it did as a hunter-gatherer unit. It does better because cultivation (and the increased invention and use of productive devices associated with cultivation) channels and magnifies the household's industrious efforts. It is not so much that this household does more labor but, rather, that it labors more effectively, more productively. Were the land itself the fundamental source of its material well-being, this household would be radically worse off by confining its efforts to those 20 acres, and the only way it could really raise its material well-being over the hunter-gatherer status quo would be to kill or drive off some of the other households who have also been wandering through those 50,000 acres. As Locke repeatedly emphasizes, it is precisely because wealth derives almost entirely from labor (*ST* §§42–44), that is, from the industrious application of human capital, that one economic agent's gain does not require other agents' losses. This is why the key to a regime characterized by mutual gains in material prosperity is the recognition and enforcement of norms that encourage individuals to develop and deploy their human capital.

Nevertheless, things become much more complicated after money comes on the scene. Money—silver and gold coins—is both a store of value and a great facilitator of trade. The appearance of money greatly increases people's incentives to produce more and more varied goods and services for exchange. For the production and sale of those more extensive and varied goods and services enables producers and traders to acquire for themselves some of the more extensive and varied goods and services that others are producing and trading for the sake of acquiring more of the more extensive and varied goods and services that these producers and traders are creating and exchanging. In this mutually reinforcing cycle, the introduction of money is a crucial event in the rise of commercial society. It radically increases both the intensity of the market and its geographical extension.

Quite understandably, the introduction of money greatly increases people's incentives to make larger portions of the earth—cultivatable land, mineral deposits, flows of water, and so on—their own (*ST* §49). One result of people acting on these motives will be an increase in economic inequality. Although "different degrees of industry" among individuals itself engenders inequality of wealth, these differences will be enlarged after money comes on the scene (§48). Another result will be that less natural material will be left for some to acquire or, perhaps, even to use than would have been available were all land to have remained unowned. Thus, it seems that after money comes on the scene, the enough and as good proviso will be violated. Yet Locke denies this. On what basis can Locke maintain that this proviso is not violated in advanced commercial society?

At one level, Locke's denial is based upon his claim that the money comes into existence "only from the consent of Men" (*ST* §50). For Locke maintains that if one consents to some practice or institution, and some outcome is an obvious consequence of that practice or institution, one also consents to that consequence. Since greater economic inequality and less natural material being left for some are obvious consequences of the introduction of money, people have consented to these consequences in the course of consenting to money. On this line of argument, within more advanced commercial society the enough and as good proviso is not so much satisfied as it is (by consent) set aside. However, this argument is unsatisfactory for many reasons. Two of them are that money does not really arise through anything that deserves to be called consent, and that even if it did arise through consent, it would not arise through everyone's consent.

What is important though is not consent but, rather, the *reason* that Locke gives for why every rational person would consent to money. That reason is that every rational person would expect on net to gain *in overall material opportunities* through the introduction of money. Every rational agent would *not* expect to gain with respect to the availability of unowned natural resources. Nevertheless, every rational agent (or *nearly* everyone—see below) would expect to gain with respect to opportunities to bring his industrious capacities to bear in pursuit of his self-preservation and happiness. For every rational person would see that the introduction of money will vastly increase the incentives for individuals to develop and deploy their human capital for the sake of ever more elaborate and varied productive engagements and exchanges; and these more elaborate and varied productive engagements and exchanges will yield greater material opportunities for all (or nearly all) than would exist in the absence of money.

Of course, were all opportunity a matter of access to raw material, the dynamic activity engendered by money would have to lessen some people's stock of opportunity. But Locke's emphasis on the relative unimportance of raw material compared to the development and application of human capital allows him to break away from the presumption that all (or nearly all) opportunity is a matter of access to raw material. Locke's crucial insight about the possibility of expanding human industrious powers leads to his further insight that developed commercial society offers opportunity that is *created* for individuals at large by the vastly enhanced and ongoing productive activity that the norms and rewards of such a society call forth. Property-based, market-ordered, commercial societies provide all (or nearly all) individuals with an economic environment that is at least as receptive to their industrious efforts—by way of employment opportunities and opportunities to rent or purchase the fruits of increasingly productive human labor—as the premonetary and open commons environment.[19] It is because of the rise of increasingly complex forms of commerce that the day laborer in England is better fed, clothed, and lodged than the king of a large domain bereft of commerce (*ST* §41).[20]

The ultimate concern of Locke with respect to his second proviso is that no individual be "straitened" (*ST* §36) in his use of his own human capital in pursuit of his ends by the economic activity of others. If we limit our understanding of opportunity to the use (or acquisition) of raw natural material, then the requirement that one not straiten others will amount to the requirement that enough and as good raw natural material be left for others. One should, however, drop this narrow understanding of opportunity if one acknowledges Locke's claims that intelligently transformed material has vastly more value than "waste" material and that this additional value is entirely due to labor. If one appropriately broadens one's understanding of opportunity, Locke's concern about straitening amounts to a concern about whether individuals enjoy less economic opportunity to bring their human capital to bear for their own purposes in a property-based, market-oriented, commercial society than they would in a world bereft of property or in a property-based, market-oriented, but premonetary world. Locke's assertion that the enough and as good proviso is satisfied in the monetary commercial world rests on his claim that, in the appropriately broadened sense of opportunity, the development of this world increases economic opportunity for all.

Absolutely central to Locke's case for commercial society is his rejection of a zero-sum view of economic activity. When Locke, still a cloistered academic, delivered his 1663–64 lectures on the law of nature, he declared that

> when any man snatches for himself as much as he can, he takes away from another man's heap the amount he adds to his own, and it is impossible for anyone to grow rich except at the expense of someone else . . . because surely no gain falls to you which does not involve somebody else's loss. (*ELN* 131)

Locke breaks radically with this zero-sum view in his mature thinking through his focus on the fruitfulness of labor. Value is *created* by labor, which, I have suggested, should be understood broadly as the purposive exercise of human capital. Hence, gains need not be achieved through *snatching*.[21] One can add to one's own heap without taking away from anyone else's heap.

Furthermore, the creation of value by some people strongly tends to enhance other people's opportunities for engaging—to their benefit—in value creating labor. The recognition and enforcement of people's individual rights—most conspicuously their rights of property and contract—encourage the development and deployment of people's value-creating powers, and discourage the pursuit of wealth through snatching.

When the "laws of liberty" (*ST* §42) are in place, the presence of other people who are seeking their own gain enhances, rather than diminishes, one's opportunities. Thus, Locke holds that the crucial ingredient for the production of wealth and economic opportunity is not "largenesse of dominions" but "numbers of men" (§42). As Julian Simon put it, people are the ultimate resource.[22] Since, according to Locke, "'Tis the number of people that make the riches of any country,"[23] he opposed barriers to immigration into Britain. If immigrants cannot expect to be maintained in idleness, "they must depend only on what they bring with them, either their estates or industry, both which are equally profitable to the kingdom" (*GN* 324). Such immigrants do not *intend* to add to the wealth of the nation; but they will do so if the laws of liberty are in place.[24]

Locke's championing of the rights of property and exchange and his insistence on the broadly bestowed benefits of a dynamic market order naturally lead one to expect that he would break decisively with traditional notions of "just price," according to which some standard external to the market itself identifies the price at which justice requires particular items to be exchanged. After all, if both parties are fully owners of whatever they bring to the market, it would seem that each party may decline to accept any terms of exchange offered by the other. There are no terms of exchange upon which both parties can be required to converge in the name of justice. Hence, it would seem that the justice of any given terms of exchange must itself arise from the parties actually freely converging upon those terms rather than from those parties obeying some external determination of just price.

In a fragment entitled "Vendito" from 1695,[25] Locke seems at first to endorse this equation of just price with actually emerging market price. He asks at what price one must sell "to keep within the bounds of equity and justice." And his answer is "the market price at the place where he sells" (*V* 340). Moreover, markets are individuated by time as well as place. The fact that wheat sold for 5*s* per bushel last year in Somerset does not make 5*s* the market price (and, hence, the just price) this year in Somerset. The market price and just price of wheat, Locke tells us, "lies in the proportion of quantity of wheat to the proportion of money in that place and the need of one and the other" (340).

Suppose that the market price for wheat at Somerset has risen to 10*s* per bushel, and a poor person wants to buy that bushel. Is it just for me to insist upon the 10*s* market price? Locke has an interesting, if not totally persuasive, argument that it is not unjust to sell to the poor person at the market price: "If it be unjust to sell it to a poor man at 10*s* per bushel it is also unjust to sell it to the rich at 10*s* a bushel, for justice has but one measure for all men." Since it is not unjust to sell to the rich at the current market price, it cannot be unjust to sell to the poor at that price.[26] Moreover, Locke argues, it is implausible to think that justice requires that one sell to *both* the poor and the rich at below market price, because if one does, one's rich customer may well simply turn around and resell the bushel at the market price and thereby realize for herself the gain that one has forgone (*V* 340).

Nevertheless, Locke seems to revert to a type of just price theory by holding that the price for an item that is established in some markets determines the just price for that item in other markets. Individual P has a horse that he is unwilling to sell for £20, which is the price it would bring at the local fair. But Q is quite eager to purchase that horse. He comes to P's house and presses P to name his price. P honestly reveals that he would sell the horse to Q for £40; but Q is not that eager and he passes on that offer. Locke goes out of his way to say that P would have done no injustice to Q had Q accepted P's offer to sell at £40. Locke insists that the reason that the price at the local fair is not the measure of the just price for the exchange between P and Q is that there are two different markets—one at the fair, the other at P's home. The next day, R shows up at P's home. He is even more eager to purchase the horse than Q was—because the survival of R's business depends upon his acquisition of this horse. Sensing his need, P insists upon and receives from R a payment of £50 for the horse. According to Locke, the additional £10 that P receives from R *is* unjust; in bargaining for that extra £10, P oppresses R, extorts from R, and robs R (*V* 341). The price that the horse would bring at the fair is not a just measure of the price for Q's purchase of the horse; but the price that the horse would bring were P to sell the horse to Q is, according to Locke, the just measure of the price for R's purchase of the horse from P.

Why doesn't Locke say that the negotiation between P and R is a different market from the negotiation between P and Q—just as the negotiation between P and Q is a different market from the negotiation that would ensue were P to bring his horse to the local fair? If Locke recognized this threefold differentiation, he could say that there are three distinct market prices, and none is the measure for justice in any of the other two market interactions. Locke does not say this because, within his discussion of the sale of the horse, he has insisted that markets must be differentiated by place, and there is no place differentiation between the P-Q negotiation and the P-R negotiation.[27] Hence, if the horse is sold at P's house, there is one market price that determines the just price for the horse, and that price is what Q would have paid had he accepted P's offer.

It is difficult to say *exactly* why Locke has gone wrong here. Let us note just a few internal problems with his position.[28] First, the fact that P would have sold the horse to Q for £40 hardly shows that it would have been unjust for him to have sold it *to* Q for, say, £50—had Q been willing to pay £50 (as R is). (After all, we cannot infer from the supposition that P would have sold the horse to Q for £38 that a sale to Q at £40 would have been unjust.) And, if it would not have been unjust to sell the horse to Q for £50, it could hardly be unjust for P to sell it to R for £50. For, as Locke says, "justice has but one measure for all men" (*V* 340).

Suppose that, on the basis of more extended negotiation, P and Q would have settled on a £38 payment for the horse. Presumably, both parties would gain from that trade. What if that deal then falls apart, and, instead, on the next day P and R settle on a £50 payment for the horse? Presumably P gains more than he would have had the previous deal gone through. Nevertheless, given the high value of the horse *for* R, R may well gain as much or more than Q would have gained. So where is the injustice in the second transaction?

Suppose, that Q accepts P's £40 offer. Then along comes R. Would it be unjust for Q to *resell* the horse to R for £50? (Does it depend upon the *location* of that resale, e.g., whether R meets Q right by P's house or a mile or two down the road?) Would Q be oppressing, extorting, or robbing R if he (Q) were to engage in this transaction? Does justice require that both parties abstain from this mutually advantageous exchange? Presumably Locke would want to answer all of these questions in the negative. If, however, there would be no injustice in Q selling the horse to R for £50, then by Locke's own principle that there is "but one measure for all men," there would be no injustice in *P* selling the horse to R for £50 (assuming he had not yet sold it to Q). If P has an inkling that R may be coming along, would justice require that he not charge Q more than £40 even though P knows that Q may resell to R?

I suspect that the ultimate lesson here is that although Locke has a profound theory about how the *prospect* of trade benefits everyone by vastly multiplying industrious activity, he does not have an understanding of why *acts* of trade in themselves are mutually beneficial. He lacks that understanding because he has not anticipated the "subjectivist" revolution in economics of the 1870s. That revolution turned on the recognition that the value of the horse *for* P may be much less than the value of the £50 *for* P, while, at the same time, the value of the horse *for* R may be much greater than the value of the £50 *for* R. *Each* party, therefore, can exchange what is of lesser value *for* him or her for what is of greater value *for* him or her.

Let us turn to Locke's treatment of the poor in the commercial society of his time—a time at which the extraordinary enhancement in the general standard of life in commercial society was just beginning. We have seen that a duly broadened enough and as good proviso requires that the rise of private property not render anyone a net loser of economic opportunity. In some respects Locke's late work "An Essay on the Poor Law" (1697) can be read as an application of this proviso.[29] Individuals who find themselves deprived of opportunity to bring their labor to bear for the preservation and enhancement of their lives *must* be offered employment opportunities so as not to be net losers in the process.

In other words, Locke's *Essay on the Poor Law* traces out the *workfare* implications if individuals actually are straitened by the development of private property and commercial society.[30] Some of these work opportunities are to be provided by private employers. "For it is not to be supposed that anyone should be refused to be employed by his neighbors"—albeit that employment can be at somewhat less than the market wage (*PL* 188). Straitened individuals are as much as possible to be inducted into commercial society rather than being made wards of the state. However, there are also strongly antiliberal and mercantilist strands within Locke's essay. Locke proposes that indigents be *forced* to accept the various employment opportunities offered.

Vagabonds are not to be allowed to ramble at liberty (185). And vagrants found in maritime counties are to be impressed into the navy.[31] Locke's worries about "the relaxation of discipline and the corruption of manners" (184) are at work here, as well as a policy concern for maximizing the employment of labor for the sake of national wealth (189). The unemployed poor are to be forced to labor because otherwise "their labour is wholly lost: which is much loss to the public" (189). The poor must be maintained; but the nation cannot maintain the poor unless they contribute as much as possible to their own relief (189).

COMMERCIAL SOCIETY AND TOLERATION

In seventeenth-century England, political and religious authority were tightly aligned. The monarch was the head of the Church of England and sustained the church's highly privileged position. In turn, the church provided crucial ideological and institutional support for monarchical authority. Religious dissent, therefore, meant opposition to the existing political authority. The intellectual defenders of religious dissenters often called for (more or less) general freedom of religious belief, practice, and association, that is, for radical limits on the authority of the state in religious matters. The demand for limits on the authority of the state in religious matters readily generalized to a demand for radical limits on state authority across all matters of individual choice. Individuals ought to be responsible for their own salvation and, hence, ought to be free to choose their own religious paths. "The Care . . . of every man's Soul belongs unto himself, and is to be left unto himself" (*LCT* 35). If so, surely persons ought also to be responsible for their own commercial (and familial and health care) endeavors and, hence, ought to be free to choose their own commercial (and familial and health care) paths.

Since another individual's choice of a mistaken path to salvation or commercial success (or familial bliss or health) does not itself do injury to others, no one else can have the moral or political authority to block that path: "One Man does not violate the Right of another, by his Erroneous Opinions, and undue manner of Worship, nor is his Perdition any prejudice to another Mans Affairs" (*LCT* 47). No other individual or official has the moral or political authority to suppress one's noninjurious actions on the basis of their judgment that one is disposing of one's person or possessions in a misguided way. No one possesses any natural authority to impose his own judgments on other peaceful individuals; and no rational individual would through consent confer such authority upon any political superior. To confer such an authority would be to surrender one's self-responsibility and would require one to presume falsely that the authorized agent both cares more about one's success and has clearer perception of the paths that will bring one success than one does oneself. "I cannot safely take him for my Guide, who may probably be as ignorant of the way as my self, and who certainly is less concerned for my Salvation than I my self am" (37).

Thus, Locke's overall vindication of individual liberty and radical limits on state authority and, hence, the freedoms at the core of commercial society can readily be seen as generalizations and inferences from his arguments for religious freedom and toleration. (Recall that Locke's first clear break with authoritarian modes of thinking is his 1667 "An Essay on Toleration.") Nevertheless, Lockean lines of argument also run in the opposition direction—from his general profreedom and antiauthoritarian political doctrine to religious toleration and from his more specific endorsement of property rights and commercial freedom to religious toleration. All of these relationships of mutual intellectual support are nicely tied up by Locke's contention that religious liberty itself is a matter of respect for the very rights of property and contract that are essential to the existence of commercial society.

In *A Letter Concerning Toleration* Locke also moves *from* his general and highly restrictive view of the proper scope of temporal law *to* the denial of the sovereign's religious authority:

> Laws provide, as much as is possible, that the Goods and Health of Subjects be not injured by the Fraud and Violence of others; they do not guard them from the Negligence of Ill-husbandry of the Possessors themselves. No man can be forced to be Rich or Healthful, whether he will or no. Nay, God himself will not save men against their wills. (*LCT* 35)

Men enter into political society so that "by mutual Assistance, and joint Force, they may secure unto each other their Proprieties in the things that contribute to the Comfort and Happiness of this Life." This process leaves to each man "the care of his own Eternal Happiness" (47). Directing his subjects to what he takes to be their eternal happiness is simply "not within the Verge of the Magistrate's Authority" (48).

Both in his early "An Essay on Toleration" and in *A Letter Concerning Toleration* Locke also argues *from* the economic freedoms embedded in commercial society *to* religious freedom. Religious freedom is simply a natural extension of the obviously proper freedoms of commercial society. It is incongruous to recognize commercial freedom—as, of course, any reasonable person does—and not also religious freedom:

> In private domestick Affairs, in the management of Estates, in the conservation of Bodily Health, every man may consider what suits his own conveniency, and follow what course he likes best. No man complains of the ill management of his Neighbor's Affairs. No man is angry with another for an

Error committed in sowing his Land, or in marrying his Daughter. No body corrects a Spendthrift for consuming his Substance in Taverns. Let any man pull down, or build, or make whatsoever Expences he please, no body murmurs, no body controls him; he has his Liberty. But if any man do not frequent the Church, if he do not there conform his Behaviour exactly to the accustomed Ceremonies, or if he brings not his Children to be initiated in the Sacred Mysteries of this or the other Congregation; this immediately causes an Uproar. The Neighborhood is filled with Noise and Clamour. Every one is ready to be the Avenger of so great a Crime. (*LCT* 34)

One man's religious errors no more violate the rights of another than do one man's errors in managing his own property. Since the magistrate's judgment that an individual is mismanaging his commercial affairs *clearly* does not justify the magistrate's interference in those commercial affairs, neither does any magistrate's judgment that an individual is mismanaging his spiritual affairs. The underlying maxim of commercial society is that everyone should be allowed to mind his own business, and, hence, everyone *must* allow others to mind their own business (*LCT* 34). Religious toleration, therefore, is simply the extension to religious belief and practice of the fundamental norm of commercial society.

In addition, the key institutions of commercial society—private property rights and voluntary contract—are the necessary institutional ingredients of a regime of religious toleration. Within a regime of Lockean freedom, affiliation for religious purposes—like the affiliations of "Philosophers for Learning" and of "Merchants for Commerce" (*LCT* 28)—must be a matter of individual voluntary consent: "No Man by nature is bound unto any particular Church or Sect" (28). And every religious society must have the right to exclude those who will not abide by the terms set by its members for inclusion in that society. Otherwise the members of that church will be deprived of their right of voluntary association.

Yet how can we determine whether an excluded individual who wishes to participate in a certain church's ceremonies is wronged by his exclusion? The answer depends on an identification of the relevant property rights. The excluded party is wronged if and only if the bread and wine consumed in that church's ceremonies are bought with *that* party's money rather than the money of the nonexcluded participants (*LCT* 31). More generally, the legitimate scope of operation of any church, as with any business, must be ascertained through an inquiry about the property and contractual rights that this church has justly acquired.

Suppose that members of one church believe it pleasing to God for them to sacrifice a calf; yet members of other churches are equally certain that the sacrifice of the calf will offend God. Locke asks how it is to be determined whether the sacrifice is to be allowed. Locke's answer is that one has to determine only "whose Calf it is" (*LCT* 42). Each individual or religious association may dispose of its rightful holdings for religious purposes in any way that would be permissible for nonreligious purposes. If the members of a drinking association may gather in the building that they own to sing beer-drinking tunes, the members of a congregation may gather in the building they own to sing their chosen psalms. Conversely, if some sort of action is impermissible "in the ordinary course of life" (42)—as the killing of infants is—then acts of that sort may not be performed no matter how intense their religious purpose.[32]

The absolutely crucial point is that private property rights are a device for decentralizing (and depoliticizing) decision making. Otherwise intractable disputes about what is the religiously (or commercially, matrimonially, or medically) best use of some extrapersonal resource are circumvented by recognizing particular individuals (or associations) as the respective rightful owners of those resources and, hence, as uniquely having authority to determine their particular use. Property rights call upon each to recognize the rightful discretionary domains of others without having to approve of the actions that others choose to perform within those domains. Respect for private property is the essence of toleration; and it is the security of those rights—through the promulgation and enforcement of the "laws of liberty"—that enables all (or nearly all) individuals to participate in commercial society to their mutual advantage.

CONCLUDING REMARKS

I have focused on three main and related elements in Locke's defense of commercial society. The first element is his affirmation of each person's moral rights to life, liberty, estate, and the fulfillment of contracts. Respect for such rights enables individuals to engage in the peaceful pursuit of their material and spiritual ends; those rights provide the moral framework for a regime of voluntary economic, vocational, and religious interactions and associations. The second element is Locke's account of why persons' peaceful pursuit of their economic ends under the "laws of liberty" at least strongly tends to be mutually advantageous; participation in the commercial world is a positive-sum game. For Locke, this is primarily because the moral and legal framework of the commercial world calls forth the development and exercise of human capital, and gains to oneself through one's industrious activities do not come at the expense of others. Indeed, persons' increased economic success strongly tends to increase others' opportunities for success. The third element is the multileveled connection between Locke's case for private property and market-based economic interaction and religious toleration. In one respect religious toleration is simply an application of the fundamental maxim of commercial society—namely, mind your own business. In another respect, the economic freedoms of commercial society are simply applications of an ethic of self-responsibility the most salient instance of which is everyone's responsibility for his or her own salvation. In both the economic and the religious arenas, the key institutional condition for individuals and associations to pursue their peaceful ends in their own chosen ways is respect for private property and voluntary contract.

NOTES

1. Locke's core doctrine is presented in his *Second Treatise of Government*, published in 1689 as Book II of *Two Treatises of Government*; see Peter Laslett's edition of the latter (Cambridge: Cambridge University Press, 1960). The *First Treatise* is cited as *FT* in the text, and the *Second Treatise* as *ST*. Locke's second most important work in political theory, also published in 1689, is *A Letter Concerning Toleration* (Indianapolis: Hackett, 1983), cited in the text as *LCT*.

2. John Locke, "An Essay on Toleration" (1667), in *Locke: Political Essays*, ed. Mark Goldie (Cambridge: Cambridge University Press, 1997), 138.

3. See D. Acemoglu and J. Robinson, *Why Nations Fail* (New York: Crown Publishing, 2012), 187–202, for the prominence and gradual decline of state-sanctioned economic monopolies in seventeenth-century England. The authors cite a nice example of a restraint on economic choice that, although not quite a monopoly, contravenes Lockean principles—namely, sumptuary laws that forbade people to wear (or be buried in) nonwoolen garb and, thus, provided privileged economic protection to the wool industry.

4. Versions of these essays were delivered as lectures in 1663–64. They were first published in 1954. See Goldie, *Locke: Political Essays*, 81–133. The essays are cited in the text as *ELN*.

5. See Eric Mack, *John Locke* (London: Continuum Publishing, 2009), 28–35, on why these programs cannot be reconciled. Many commentators on Locke insist on the centrality of Locke's theological commitments to his moral and political philosophy. See, e.g., John Dunn, *The Political Thought of John Locke* (Cambridge: Cambridge University Press, 1965); and Jeremy Waldron, *God, Locke, and Equality* (Cambridge: Cambridge University Press, 2002).

6. See Locke's second and third letters on toleration in vol. 6 of *The Collected Works of John Locke* (London: printed for Thomas Tegg et. al., 1823).

7. "Morality," in Goldie, *Locke: Political Essays*, 267.

8. "Thus I Think," in Goldie, *Locke: Political Essays*, 296.

9. John Locke, *An Essay Concerning Human Understanding*, ed. A. C. Fraser (New York: Dover, 1959); cited in the text as *ECHU*.

10. Land (including any potentially useful natural material) that is waste in the sense of being unused is also, for Locke, land that is waste in the sense of being (nearly) valueless and also waste in the sense of wasted opportunity. Unused land is (nearly) valueless because economic value derives (almost) entirely from the application of human labor, and it is wasted opportunity because morality calls upon us to put that waste to productive use. See,

e.g., *ST* §42: "Even amongst us, Land that is left wholly to Nature, that hath no improvement of Pasturage, Tillage, or Planting, is called, as indeed it is, *waste*; and we shall find the benefit of it amount to little more than nothing."

11. See the similarly negative parsing of the duty to preserve mankind in §7. The "Law of Nature" that wills the "Preservation of all Mankind" requires that "all Men may be restrained from invading others Rights, and from doing hurt to one another."

12. Friends *and* foes of Locke often take him to hold that self-ownership is *the* fundamental right. Among friends, see Murray Rothbard, *The Ethics of Liberty* (Atlantic Highlands, NJ: Humanities Press, 1982). And among foes, see G. A. Cohen, *Self-Ownership, Freedom, and Equality* (Cambridge: Cambridge University Press, 1995).

13. Eric Mack, "The Natural Right of Property," *Social Philosophy and Policy* 27, no. 1 (Winter 2010): 53–79.

14. See Robert Nozick, *Anarchy, State, and Utopia* (New York: Basic Books, 1974), 150–60.

15. My discussion follows Nozick's *Anarchy, State, and Utopia,* 174–82; and Mack, "The Self-Ownership Proviso: A New and Improved Lockean Proviso," *Social Philosophy and Policy* 12, no. 1 (Winter 1995): 186–218.

16. It cannot be a matter of less natural material *by weight* or *by volume*. It has got to be something like less natural material in terms of the *opportunities* it provides for the individual to bring his powers to bear to advance his self-preservation and happiness.

17. Many commentators mistakenly advance this egalitarian reading of the "enough and as good" proviso. For instance, in his *An Essay on Rights* (Oxford: Blackwell Publishers, 1994) Hillel Steiner equates Locke's "enough and as good" proviso with a natural right "to equal bundles of [natural] things" (235).

18. Indeed, the cultivators will produce a surplus for trade with the remaining hunter-gatherers to both parties' advantage. An increase in households *in the premonetary phase* would counteract the tendency for the proviso to be satisfied.

19. Compare the level of opportunity for millions of current inhabitants of Hong Kong with the level of opportunity that radically fewer people would enjoy were that territory still an open commons.

20. This is a stronger claim than Locke needs. That each member of a commercial society is better off than *that person* would be in a preproperty or premonetary world would suffice for Locke's purposes.

21. Locke's emphasis on the *value-creating* power of labor should *not* be understood as a subscription to a proto-Marxian labor theory of economic value.

22. Julian Simon, *The Ultimate Resource 2* (Princeton, NJ: Princeton University Press, 1998).

23. "For a General Naturalisation," in Goldie, *Locke: Political Essays,* 322; cited in the text as *GN.*

24. For an account of Locke's economic thought, see Karen Vaughn, *John Locke: Economist and Social Scientist* (Chicago: University of Chicago Press, 1980).

25. In Goldie, *Locke: Political Essays,* 339–43; cited in the text as *V.*

26. It may, however, be uncharitable not to sell to the poor at a less than market price. But Locke generally holds that the claims of charity are *not* properly subject to legal enforcement. See *LCT* 44: "Covetousness, Uncharitableness, Idleness, and many other things are sins, by the consent of all men, which yet no man ever said were to be punished by the Magistrate."

27. Locke precludes time differentiation—which was allowed to play a role in the wheat story—by having R show up the very next day after Q's inquiries.

28. A fuller analysis would consider Locke's interesting discussion of ships at sea bargaining over scarce anchors. See *V* 341–43.

29. In Goldie, *Locke: Political Essays,* 182–98; cited in the text as *PL.*

30. To grant the straitened individual an *unconditional* claim to sustenance would be to grant a claim "to the benefit of another's Pains, which he had no right to" (*ST* §34).

31. In contrast, see the passage from *LCT* cited in note 26, in which Locke includes *idleness* among the sins that the magistrate may not punish.

32. Locke denies toleration to Catholics and to atheists on the grounds, respectively, of their political and moral unreliability, not on the basis of the content of their beliefs.

CHAPTER 9

As Free for Acorns as for Honesty: Mandevillean Maxims for the Ethics of Commerce

Eugene Heath

Bernard Mandeville may appear an unlikely authority on the ethics of business. The author of *The Fable of the Bees: or, Private Vices, Public Benefits*, Mandeville was regarded in his era as an advocate of egoism and an enemy of morals. In his satiric poem *The Grumbling Hive: Or, Knaves turn'd Honest*, first published in 1705, then incorporated into *The Fable* in 1714, he portrays a bustling hive of bees whose self-interested interactions generate a large, prosperous commercial society: "Thus every Part was full of Vice, / Yet the whole Mass a Paradise" (I, 24).[1] The bees so complain about the prevalence of vice that the god Jove grows weary and cleanses the hive of vice. With virtue comes contentment, along with the decline of commerce and the loss of prosperity. Mandeville contends that his poetic tale is not a defense of vice but a delineation of the distinct consequences of two moral alternatives: "If I have shewn the way to worldly Greatness, I have always without Hesitation preferr'd the Road that leads to Virtue" (I, 231).[2]

If vice leads to prosperity and greatness and virtue to contentment and poverty, then it might appear that any embrace of commerce would require either an endorsement of vice or a life of utter hypocrisy. Certainly, Mandeville delights in charging the "Beau Monde" (II, 11) with hypocrisy, for they enjoy the products and pleasures of commercial society even as they condemn the vicious appetites that make it possible. Nonetheless, if there is an essential link between vice and commercial prosperity, then it might appear that the only conclusion the ethicist could draw is to follow virtue and live contentedly in a small, noncommercial society. Perhaps this construal of Mandeville's *Fable* explains why few business ethicists pay heed to his work.[3]

Taking into account his varied works,[4] one might conclude that Mandeville offers no account as to how to conduct oneself in business. Yet his overall outlook offers a perspective from which one may glean heuristic maxims relevant to business ethics as a theoretical discipline. The contemporary business ethicist may, therefore, follow the lead of eighteenth-century thinkers who recognized the significance of Mandeville's "framework of ideas" even as they rejected what they took to be his errors.[5] Some three hundred years after the publication of the first of two volumes of *The Fable*, Mandeville's works remain a vital examination of commerce as well as the implications of social interaction more generally. Mandeville's thought provides a perspective worth revisiting.

It is fitting to begin with a summary of salient themes in Mandeville's works (emphasizing *The Fable*) and to situate these within their historical context. Following this discussion is an overview of Mandeville's understanding of commerce, taking into account his defenses of luxury and of pluralism, as well as his overall view of commerce. In the final section, the focus turns to three maxims gleaned from Mandeville's thought and relevant to any inquiry into the ethics of business. The first maxim distinguishes between individual intention and social outcome, the second attends to the power of practical knowledge or know-how, and the third delineates the importance of the compatibility between ideals and empirical realities.

THE POEM AND ITS CONTEXT

When the poem *The Grumbling Hive* appeared in 1705, it garnered scant attention. Yet its themes enliven much of Mandeville's later works, including the first volume of *The Fable* (1714), which commenced with the poem, followed by an essay, *An Enquiry into the Origin of Moral Virtue*, as well as a set of "Remarks" on various notions invoked in the poem. Later editions would include further developments of the "Remarks," as well as two additional essays, *An Essay on Charity and Charity-Schools*, and *A Search into the Nature of Society*. A second volume, composed of six dialogues, would appear in 1728.[6]

In the poem, a large, powerful, and prosperous hive symbolizes the commercial England of the day. Although the "private vices" of the bees yield "publick benefits," the bees so grumble and grouse about fraud and dishonesty that Jove rids the hive of vice. As the bees gain in virtue, their appetites and desires diminish: "All Arts and Crafts neglected lie; Content, the Bane of Industry" (I, 34). The virtuous bees, poorer and fewer in numbers, had little to do, so "They flew into a hollow Tree, / Blest with Content and Honesty" (I, 35). To his poem Mandeville appends a "Moral," which includes these lines:

> So Vice is beneficial found,
> When it's by Justice lopt and bound;
> . . . .

Bare Virtue can't make Nations live
In Splendor; they, that would revive
A Golden Age, must be as free,
For Acorns, as for Honesty. (I, 37)

The indulgence of appetite Mandeville regards as "vice," and it may be contrasted to genuine virtue—the denial of appetite in order to benefit others as motivated by a "Rational Ambition of being good."[7] Human beings are actuated primarily by passions or appetites, which are based in self-love (or self-preservation) or self-liking (an affection for and overvaluation of self).[8] Any action born of appetite is, therefore, vicious, regardless of whether the act may be characterized as commercial or not. Nonetheless, Mandeville draws linkages between vice and the benefits of commercial trade. If the law prohibits certain vices (presumably those that interfere with or unduly affect the lives of others) and otherwise provides conditions for commerce, then the cultivation of appetite and continual interaction and exchange generate public benefits. However, if persons adhere to genuine virtue, then the result will be self-constraint, contentment, and relative poverty. In providing this account of motivation and social consequence, Mandeville contends that he is not arguing *for* vice so much as he is analyzing the distinct consequences of one set of traits over another. In this sense, Mandeville's analysis implies that the human being has a moral choice as to which ends to pursue.

Not only does Mandeville set forth this decision for his readers, but he employs his wit to indict those who hypocritically enjoy prosperity while condemning its motivational foundations. Mandeville's tactics reflect some of the moral ambivalence of his epoch. By the middle of the seventeenth century, commercial enterprise had penetrated into large sectors of English society. By the turn of the century, about a third of the population was engaged in "industry, building and commerce"—a proportion higher than the European average.[9] A rising class of farmers, craftsmen, merchants, and professionals aspired to acquire goods ("luxuries") previously unavailable to them, including teas, coffees, linens, and pictures, among others.[10] Goods such as these now featured in the ambitions of ordinary citizens, for whom frugal living and simple desires had long been counseled.[11] In 1726, when Voltaire arrived in London, he observed that commerce had rendered the English not only wealthy and powerful but free and proud: after all, he remarked, English merchants were not, as in France, regarded "disparagingly."[12]

The emergence of an economy of trade and exchange disturbed many who worried that good governance and strong morals would be weakened by a rising tide of self-interest. Drawing inspiration from classical and Christian sources, groups emerged (such as the Society for the Reformation of Manners) dedicated to the improvement of morals and the cultivation of public spirit over baser motives of private trade and enrichment. The indulgence of appetite might also weaken the willingness to work, or occasion drinking, gambling, and luxurious indulgence.[13] In the advocacy of civic virtue (or what has come to be regarded as civic humanism or republicanism), frugality and constraint were deemed essential to the good society, not indulgence of appetite or ambition for status or money.[14] An illustration of this general concern finds expression in a sermon, "Reformation of Manners the True Way of Honouring God," preached by the bishop of Worcester, Edward Stillingfleet:

> Who can deny that luxury and debauchery, and all sorts of intemperance, not only sink the reputation of a people, but effeminates and softens them, and makes them careless and idle, regardless of any thing but what makes for their own ease and voluptuousness?[15]

The outlook set forth by the Society for the Reformation of Manners, of which Bishop Stillingfleet was a supporter,[16] found notable defense in Richard Steele's journal, the *Tatler,* appearing in 1709. This journal spawned a number of imitations, including the *Female Tatler,* in which Mandeville would write under the personages of two ladies, Lucinda and Artesia. One target of Mandeville's wit would be the character of Isaac Bickerstaff, the "Censor of Great Britain," who appeared in *The Tatler* as a member of the reforming societies and an advocate of the public, not private, good.[17]

Some ideas appearing in later editions of *The Fable* emerge first in the *Female Tatler.* There Mandeville challenges the exhortation that one *must* act from a virtuous desire to serve the public interest. He delights in revealing how most persons do not, in fact, act from genuine virtue but from a lesser standard of sociability whose real motive rests in some form of self-love (or self-liking). In his account of this lesser form of conduct he includes an acute and significant social theory: via a desire for the approval of others, self-liking is redirected in such a way that norms of sociable cooperation are cultivated and sustained. To appreciate more fully Mandeville's analysis on this subject (and others), it is essential to consider his conception of commerce. In so doing we shall see how his defense of luxury and his articulation of a version of pluralism serve to articulate a perspective in opposition to the defenders of public virtue.

MANDEVILLE'S CONCEPTION OF COMMERCE

Mandeville offers little exploration of the elements or operations of economic production or exchange, but he comprehends the essential problem of economics: how to get individuals to interact in voluntary, mutually beneficial, and cooperative ways. Mandeville offers characterizations of such interaction in the sixth dialogue of volume II of *The Fable*. The character Cleomenes, who often speaks for Mandeville, asserts that money is essential to the "very Existence" of society, which itself is based upon our "Wants":

> So the whole Superstructure is made up of the reciprocal Services, which Men do to each other. How to get these Services perform'd by others, when we have Occasion for them, is the grand and almost constant Sollicitude in Life of every individual Person. To expect, that others should serve us for nothing, is unreasonable; therefore all Commerce, that Men can have together, must be a continual bartering of one thing for another. The Seller, who transfers the Property of a Thing, has his own Interest as much at Heart as the Buyer, who purchases that Property; and, if you want or like a thing, the Owner of it, whatever Stock or Provision he may have of the same, or how greatly soever you may stand in need of it, will never part with it, but for a Consideration, which he likes better, than he does the thing you want. (II, 349)

This passage, which anticipates Adam Smith's ruminations on the basis of exchange,[18] points out that we cannot rely on others simply to "serve us for nothing"; reciprocal exchange offers a method of cooperation and thus a means for sustained interaction among human beings.

An excerpt such as the above might easily lead one to conclude that Mandeville was an advocate of laissez-faire. However, it seems more plausible to regard him as maneuvering within some of the operating notions of mercantilism even as his insights moved him toward broader and less interventionist views of the economy.[19] Indeed, if one measure of mercantilism is the extent to which the nation as a whole is treated as a single "joint-stock company,"[20] then Mandeville's reiterated appeals to diverse and incommensurable ends—encapsulated in the final phrase of *The Grumbling Hive*, "they, that would revive / A Golden Age, must be as free, / For Acorns, as for Honesty" (I, 37)—suggest that he was pulling away from consistent mercantilism.

Another of Mandeville's economic insights is his defense of luxury goods. The growth of luxury vexed an aristocracy unused to the spectacle of ordinary citizens enjoying goods once the province of a small minority. Devoting one of his "Remarks" to such apparent indulgence, Mandeville defines "luxury" in terms of whatever "is not immediately necessary to make Man subsist as he is a living Creature" (I, 107). In this sense, anything beyond physical subsistence is, effectively, luxurious. The implication, of course, is that the very notion of luxury is more fluid and relative than typically admitted (I, 108).[21] Luxury is not, in fact, destructive of society, nor frugality necessary. The notion that the Dutch achieved wealth through frugality is assailed by Mandeville (I, 187–91). The prevailing assumption that luxury weakens the will and diminishes vigor also proves dubious, for the animating appetites of human beings remain regardless of the *means* by which they are satisfied (I, 118–19). Nor does Mandeville think that luxury will affect the fighting spirit, especially since there are always "loose, idle, extravagant Fellows enough to spare for an Army" (I, 120).

Even if Mandeville provides no unified theoretical portrait of a market economy, he advocates nonetheless that the activity of commercial endeavor is a worthwhile end. In the *Female Tatler,* in response to the protestations of moral reformers exemplified in the persona of Isaac Bickerstaff, Mandeville defends a pluralist view of ends, among which he includes commerce. The character of Artesia is first to voice the view of moral reformers who maintain that the improvement of mankind has been wrought through the efforts of persons acting with an eye to the public good. In this she follows the counsel of Bickerstaff, for whom only those persons "are to be counted Alive" who have turned away from "all private Interest and Personal Pleasure."[22] An "Oxford Gentleman" then enters the conversation and responds, contrarily, that the great "Benefactors to Human Society" are those who "take no other Care than to please themselves" and who seek, thereby, to create and gratify new appetites (*FT* 99). By his account, those who "make Money Circulate" prove to be the "real Encouragers of every useful Art and Science" (105). In a later issue of the *Female Tatler,* Mandeville introduces a wealthy old man aptly named Laborio whose main activity is the making of money. Laborio immerses himself in his work and rises early to engage in business: "to People that take Pleasure in getting Money, looking after their Business is a Diversion" (225).[23]

Although business may be a diversion, in the sense of a pleasurable activity, neither the Oxford Gentleman nor Laborio asserts that the pursuit of money should be the aim of every individual. In fact, the Gentleman suggests that society need not be conceived as if it were a single enterprise oriented or organized to the same end: "the Fabrick of Society must not be the same in all its Parts," for the "jarring Discord of Contraries makes the Harmony of the whole" (*FT* 105). The Oxford Gentleman quotes from Virgil ("Each is drawn by his own pleasure"; *Eclogues*; *FT* 105) to suggest that divergent pleasures point to distinct conceptions of good. Indeed, the Gentleman remarks that the merchant who relishes the activity of business may lead a good life without even knowing Latin (*FT* 110)![24] In a subsequent issue of the *Female Tatler* appearing the following year, Mandeville makes clear that the goods that individuals seek may be either specific *things* to be enjoyed or *activities* to be undertaken (224).

Distinct values arise from individual appetite or desire. One may infer, therefore, that Mandeville espouses a Hobbesian view of value, not simply because Thomas Hobbes rejects a notion of a *summum bonum* but because the author of *Leviathan* regards goodness as a function of desire.[25] For Mandeville, pluralism rests on the notion that the ends of desires—whether understood as pleasures or goods, or as things or activities—are essentially in-commensurable across persons. On these ends, there is no disputing, and so individuals should be "as free, / For Acorns, as for Honesty" (I, 37). Mandeville's portrayal of Laborio's "Diligence and Industry in getting a penny" (*FT* 223) offers an endorsement of one particular pursuit ("getting Money"), but this approval is set within a pluralist outlook in which the pleasures of disparate individuals cannot be judged equitably ("we are all very unequitable Judges of one anothers Pleasure"; 223). This view of plural values—which incorporates ends commercial and noncommercial—is developed again in volume I of *The Fable*. In the essay *A Search into the Nature of Society*, in a critique of the views of the third Earl of Shaftesbury, Mandeville challenges the notion that there are "permanent Realities that must ever be the same in all Countries and all Ages" (I, 324). Just as customs may differ, so may morality: "the hunting after this [Shaftesbury's] *Pulchrum & Honestum* is not much better than a Wild-Good-Chace" (I, 331).

If commerce is a legitimate pursuit, one among others, then how does Mandeville comprehend it? Even without a theory or summary portrait of commerce, Mandeville characterizes its effects and its institutional conditions. One of his insights is that trade is a mutually beneficial act, a positive-sum transaction: "Parties directly opposite, / Assist each other, as 'twere for Spight" (I, 25). Trade not only benefits the participants but yields a more general consequence: public benefits. These comprise those goods, or luxuries, now available to innumerable citizens who enjoy "Pleasures, Comforts, Ease" (I, 26), but they also include more general benefits: employment (I, 197) in a "Variety of Manufactures" (I, 184), as well as the encouragement of traits of industry that allow for the maintenance of families and the payment of taxes (I, 85). Moreover, commerce provides conditions conducive to seeking and realizing improvements (I, 130). The net result is a society that is more prosperous, powerful, and populated than could otherwise be achieved through virtuous motives alone.

These benefits emerge as individuals follow what Mandeville regards as vicious motivations. So motivated, these individuals interact within a framework of law that defines property and allows for voluntary interaction among and between individuals. Even though Mandeville often thinks of commercial society in terms of exchange, he recognizes, albeit in summary fashion, the importance of institutions: property must be secure, justice enforced, and laws prudently wrought and consistently executed (I, 116; and see 184–85). The law, having "lopt and bound" appetites inimical to the pursuit of a plurality of aims, provides spheres of liberty in which individuals may act on their passions or desires. Devising these laws is not a purely rational enterprise but requires experience, both individual and collective (II, 321–23). The legal framework and the motivation of appetite, along with an innate desire to improve one's circumstances, will also generate a division of labor: individuals find it beneficial to specialize in specific activities coordinated by commerce to produce and distribute specific products and services. As Mandeville explains, "What a Bustle is there to be made in several Parts of the World, before a fine Scarlet or crimson Cloth can be produced, what Multiplicity of Trades and Artificers must be employ'd!" (I, 356).

Mandeville offers distinct portraits of commercial interaction. In *The Grumbling Hive*, the bees are motivated by appetites marked with designs of cheating and deceit: "All Trades and Places knew some Cheat, / No Calling was without Deceit" (I, 20). For example, physicians strive for "Fame and Wealth" not by improving their medical skills or by attending to the patient's health but by appearing "Grave" and "pensive" (I, 20). The Priests are no better, if not worse, for they attempt to "hide / Their Sloth, Lust, Avarice and Pride" (I, 21), all cardinal sins. The ministers of the king grow rich by cheating the government (I, 22), and justice so loses its impartiality that "the Sword she bore / Check'd but the Desp'rate and the Poor" (I, 23).

Within *The Grumbling Hive*, tension emerges between Mandeville's sardonic illustrations and the "Moral" that closes his poem. His concluding recommendation is that vice must not be freewheeling license but should be "lopt and bound." Yet his acerbic portraits show that our interactions are motivated not only by traditional vices (avarice, pride, and that form of gluttony called "luxury"), but by fraud and deceit, qualities that render an action unjust. Presumably, therefore, laws should prohibit these and relevantly similar excrescences of vice even as other forms of avarice, pride, lust, and gluttony would continue to motivate industry and commerce. Even so, Mandeville's characterizations are meant to drive two points: that a bustling and prosperous society rests on the activation, not the minimization, of appetites, *and* that these passions go awry unless bounded by law.[26] The appetites that remain in play—all presumably vicious by Mandeville's criterion—reflect a plural set of valuations whose overall pursuit and realization establish a general prosperity. It is in this sense that Mandeville may conclude in the moral to his poetic tale:

> T' enjoy the World's Conveniencies,
> Be fam'd in War, yet live in Ease,
> Without great Vices, is a vain
> Eutopia seated in the Brain. (I, 36)

Once one moves beyond the poem, Mandeville offers characterizations of exchange that do not feature fraud or deceit. These examples, in which commerce still operates out of vicious appetites, illuminate further Mandeville's vantage point on business.[27] In "Remark B," in *The Fable*, Mandeville contends that there are "innumerable Artifices" (I, 61) by which traders seek to outwit one another, perhaps by exaggerating the qualities of a good, or by failing to relate its defects. To illustrate, Mandeville describes a man, Decio, who wishes to buy sugar, and a West India sugar merchant, Alcander. Decio wishes to buy cheaply, Alcander to sell dear. After setting a price higher than Decio wishes to pay, Alcander learns that a larger-than-expected supply of sugar is en route to England. The increased supply will result in lower prices. So Alcander decides to sell at Decio's price *before* the news of the sugar supply becomes public. So as not to appear too eager to sell at a lower price, Alcander invites Decio into his home. On the following day, while on a walk, Decio learns from an acquaintance that the fleet sailing from the Indies was destroyed by a storm. Expecting the loss of the fleet and its load of sugar to diminish the overall supply and drive up the price at least 25 percent, Decio returns hurriedly to Alcander's house and agrees to buy the sugar at Alcander's original offer price! With this outcome Alcander receives his preferred selling price; by the next day, however, Decio is able to resell the sugar to a profit of some 500 pounds. This interaction, says Mandeville, is "fair dealing," but he then admits, "I am sure neither of them [Alcander or Decio] would have desired to be done by, as they did to each other" (I, 63).

In this illustration, each party is driven by appetite to secure for himself the best price. Mandeville records how such commercial dealings may not accord with one version of the Golden Rule (Do not do unto others as one would not have done to oneself). However, in contradistinction to Mandeville's accounts of trade in *The Grumbling Hive*, neither Alcander or Decio makes any positive attempts to deceive or to defraud the other, and in this sense each is following the Golden Rule, at least if that rule is construed to refer to acts of commission![28] In this sense, Alcander and Decio are engaged in reciprocating acts, neither of which violates a minimum of fair dealing, at least if commercial transactions may allow the permissibility of nondisclosure of facts *relevant* to the trade. Such facts should not concern qualities or characteristics of the product itself, but may involve circumstances within the context of the trade, including, for example, the expectation that prices will fall in the near future.[29] Taking into account that voluntary transactions presume, in general, that the agents are rational, have knowledge of the product, and enter the trade in noncompulsory ways, then the sale of the sugar is clearly noncompulsory, and each party has knowledge of the nature and quality of the product. One question that arises is whether one can make a fully rational decision on a purchase without knowing the various possibilities regarding its price. However, Mandeville's story illustrates how buyers and sellers make these decisions all the time. Second, knowledge of relative (or future) prices, if available, is sometimes a matter of one's own effort and is not, for that reason, a cost-free good. Even so, Decio's knowledge comes as a result of fortune rather than effort. Yet it is hard to conclude that the nondisclosure of one's beliefs about future prices would violate rationality, especially since many trades are executed precisely because the two participants have differing expectations about prices. Drawing from Mandeville, one might conclude that failure to disclose, in cases analogous to that of Alcander and Decio, is not the same as an intention to mislead.

Portrayals such as these provide some sense of Mandeville's comprehension of commerce, in both its foundations and effects and its everyday encounters. But are there further Mandevillean insights relevant to contemporary inquiries into the ethics of business and the morals of commerce? To consider this question, we turn to Mandeville's descriptive analysis of society, gleaning from it three maxims relevant to contemporary considerations of commercial conduct.

MANDEVILLEAN MAXIMS FOR BUSINESS ETHICS

Mandeville professes to be engaged not in prescription but description (e.g., I, 407), an endeavor he often characterizes in terms of an *anatomization* of human nature (I, 145; II, 93). He declares that he shall examine what is either "overlook'd, or else . . . inconsiderable to Vulgar Eyes" (I, 3), pointing out that such an examination may yield surprising results (I, 4). An anatomization pulls back the surface appearances to reveal the "invisible Part of Man" (I, 145), the underlying springs and motives of actions, the universal elements of human nature that individuals either omit to see, or desire not to see. Commencing with observation (II, 128), anatomization yields a causal analysis of human action and interaction.[30] Mandeville's appeal to anatomization and his theoretical account of human nature yield valuable judgments about the nature of social interaction, the fundamental importance of skilled knowledge (or "know-how"), and the tension between moral ideals and empirical realities. These insights, which undergird Mandeville's overall perspective, prove worthwhile not because they determine any particular conclusion about business conduct, or the morals of markets more generally, but because they illuminate relevant features of social and commercial interaction that often remain ignored or overlooked. Distilled from Mandeville's overall perspective, these insights may be understood as maxims, heuristic guides, relevant to scholarly inquiry into the ethics of business.

Beneficial Social Order May Emerge in Unintended Ways

The subtitle of *The Fable of the Bees* has long been associated with the idea that social outcomes may be both unintended and beneficial, at least when the initial conditions out of which the consequences emerge have a certain character. In the *Female Tatler*, the character of Artesia entertains the contrary notion that humanity is indebted to those who act *for* the public good (*FT* 98).[31] The same point surfaces in the second volume of *The Fable*: "ought not all private Advantage to give way to this general Interest . . . and ought it not to be every one's Endeavour . . . to render himself a serviceable and useful Member of that whole Body which he belongs to" (II, 46; see also 49). Mandeville forwards these perspectives in order to counter them: he seeks, in other words, to challenge the idea that the only way to generate benefits in society is for these to be intended by well-meaning agents. For example, he sometimes points out how the acts of discrete individuals may unintentionally yield beneficial consequences, but he also analyzes, more interestingly, how the systematic accumulation or aggregation of acts may, over time, yield beneficial outcomes.

In the first instance, Mandeville points out how vicious intentions may lead to beneficial outcomes: "Pride and Vanity have built more Hospitals than all the Virtues together" (I, 261). Self-liking, the desire for applause and approval, may be redirected, in specific situations, by praise and flattery: the prospect of garnering applause orients individuals to benefit others rather than to serve only the self. For Mandeville, the appetitive pursuits of various individuals will prove more beneficial than if all were to act for some end designated as a public good.

Turning to the more systematic accounts, one of Mandeville's great insights is how orders, patterns, norms, and institutions may emerge over a period of time in an unintended fashion. Such a theory of society may be considered an example of a natural or conjectural history as also found in later thinkers, including Jean-Jacques Rousseau, David Hume, Adam Ferguson, and Adam Smith, among others. For example, one finds in volume II of *The Fable* a conjectural history of normativity, as well as the structural lines of an evolutionary theory of language. In his explanation of the origin of norms, Mandeville indicates a clear mechanism (flattery) for the systematic coordination of normative standards of conduct. Spectators employ praise and flattery to coax from others the sort of cooperative conduct (politeness, manners, and other-regarding actions) that would otherwise not be forthcoming; as praise is replicated across a variety of circumstances so do expectations emerge as to what is acceptable and what is not. In this way, praise and flattery aggregate and coordinate out of discrete acts a standard of judgment and conduct regarding other-regarding conduct. The emergent standards appear qualitatively different from the originating causes, specifically, an agent's "vicious" desire for praise and a spectator's (similarly) "vicious" desire to secure from the agent a more cooperative mode of behavior. The conduct that conforms to the resultant standard may not equate to genuine (self-denying) virtue, but it constitutes, nonetheless, a form of civil and cooperative interaction.[32] In this manner, it could be said, "a most beautiful Superstructure may be rais'd upon a rotten and despicable Foundation" (II,

64). This sort of evolutionary explanation suggests that Mandeville holds to the view that norms of various sorts may emerge endogenously to society without being imposed by divine or political authority.

For the business ethicist, this sort of social theory provides an illuminating perspective. If norms of conduct may emerge via social interaction, then commercial trade may come to acquire its own normative expectations and standards. That buying and selling could be supplemented, even improved, through extralegal norms of sociability and civility is illustrated in one of Mandeville's extended examples. In his portrait of a "Mercer and a young Lady" (I, 349), a man seeks to sell silk at what he "proposes to be a reasonable" price, but a young Lady seeks to buy more cheaply. The young Lady conducts herself in a sweet and kind manner and "endeavours to render her self as Amiable as Virtue and the Rules of Decency allow" (I, 350). The Mercer appears willing to entertain her every wish so that the young Lady "has always before her a cheerful Countenance, where Joy and Respect seem to be blended with Good-humour" (I, 351). As the young Lady makes her decision, the Mercer proceeds cautiously, but the moment she decides, then "he immediately becomes positive," adding that "the more he looks upon it, the more he wonders he should not before have discovered the preeminence of it over any thing he has in his Shop" (I, 351). The Mercer uses such flattery to extol the sagacity of the young Lady so as to extract from her the highest price possible. But the result of this mutual interplay of politeness and flattery is that "she has bought her Silk exactly at the same Price as any body else might have done" (I, 352). Out of this redirection of self-centered desires, norms of sociability emerge.

In business ethics, questions often arise as to what to do in instances in which businesspersons do not exhibit responsible or decent behavior. In such cases one may appeal to individual self-regulation, or to an external intervention of the government, via law or regulation. However, Mandeville's account suggests that there is another avenue to consider, complementary to self-regulation: could a norm of conduct (sufficient to resolve the problem) emerge on its own, internal to the market, or perhaps requiring but an alteration of the basic regulatory and legal framework? Any investigation of this possibility would require an inquiry into the conditions that frame interaction, for the underlying circumstances may affect the possibility that ongoing interaction will yield norms to resolve the original problem. Given the importance of the conditions that structure interaction ("So Vice is beneficial found, / When it's by Justice lopt and bound"), the juridical and regulatory framework that shapes exchange is an important ethical focus, distinct from moral analysis of a specific event or kind of event, and divergent from considerations of business codes, theories of social responsibility, or stakeholding. The implication for business ethicists is that it is just as important to take into account the underlying conditions of interaction (and the incentives they provide for conduct) as to examine actual conduct and its consequences. An ethical problem may be relieved by addressing the conditions that motivate instead of instituting an additional law, regulation, or policy prescription.

Moral Conduct Contains a Nonreflective Quality (the Significance of Know-How)

Mandeville may not be alone in thinking that commercial societies rely on self-interested motivations. Many business ethicists seem to hold a received view that untutored commerce tends to the unethical.[33] Therefore, they reason, to sustain business as a moral endeavor, if not to reform it altogether, it is essential to inculcate a business ethic in managers, executives, and board members. Whether or not this general assessment of business bears truth, and regardless of whether Mandeville's thesis of egoism (in the form of vicious appetites) is either true or sincerely held, the notion that conduct may be reformed through counsel, education, or arguments runs counter to another Mandevillean thesis, one independent of any appeal to egoism. The thesis suggests that knowledge is anchored in practical activity, know-how. If this is the case, then theoretical counsel or education, not to mention ethical argument, may prove less effective than generally thought.

For Mandeville, knowledge is, broadly speaking, empirical. He downplays the possibility of a priori knowledge and offers no evidence that it is even a possibility for humans (as in II, 261, 186). Of greater relevance is a distinction between two kinds of knowledge, propositional (knowing that) and practical (knowing how). In volume II of *The Fable*, in recalling a book by the Chevalier Reneau on sailing, Mandeville points out that mathematical explications of the mechanisms and movements of sailing ships were not known by those who first invented or later improved such ships, and neither are they known by sailors who now guide, maneuver, and steer sailing vessels (II, 143). Mathematical propositions may explain the relation of rudder position to the direction of the boat, but the knowledge of these propositions is not necessary for a sailor to know how to steer a vessel.[34] Knowing *how* to steer is independent of the knowledge of those propositions that describe successful steering.[35]

Mandeville applies his distinction not only to technical skills but to everyday conduct, including the manner in which individuals redirect their appetites so as to develop or conform to sociable standards of behavior. In describing how individuals come to behave in sociable ways, he proclaims, "it is incredible, how many useful Cautions, Shifts, and Stratagems, they will learn to practice by Experience and Imitation, from conversing together;

without being aware of the natural Causes that oblige them to act as they do, *viz.* The Passions within, that, unknown to themselves, govern their Will and direct their Behaviour" (II, 139; and see 141). In this way, normative conduct may rest less on knowledge *that* some principle is right or wrong than in knowing *how* to behave.

If know-how is a form of knowledge that is nonpropositional, then conduct is often neither motivated nor informed by propositions. The articulation of propositions may come along, after the fact, to describe and summarize conduct, either for the individual or for society, but the proposition itself need not be the chief or only motivating element. Mandeville's supposition that human action contains this primary element of know-how suggests that conduct is, in significant ways, nonreflective. To the extent that articulated principles affect conduct, they do so, presumably, by attaching themselves to appetites and drawing from an agent's practical know-how. Such principles, as with the rules of sailing, must emerge out of activity; they do not motivate action or otherwise inform conduct on their own (II, 140–44). For example, as one is moved to act in specific circumstances one draws from prior skills, practices, habits; given some comprehension of particular circumstances, one either acts in conformity to one's habit or makes alterations, changes, and refinements—incremental adaptations applied through a process of trial and error in specific circumstances, perhaps as responses to the prospects of praise and flattery, as Mandeville suggests. As acts replicate across society and generate expectations, then so do they come to acquire an articulated formulation (*FT* 100; II, 144, 186–87, 267, 318–19).

Know-how raises two parallel problems for any discipline that aspires to practical influence. One challenge confronts business ethics education, whether occurring in the corporation or at the university. The appeal of such education is obvious, but it is less clear how *theoretical* instruction relates to business practice. Of course, Mandeville's own solution, described above, would suggest that the problem of moral education may disappear as norms of sociability emerge through the activity of buying and selling: via an unintended process of socialization, norms of cooperative interaction emerge and constrain our self-liking. However, this solution may prove too optimistic for many. Thus, education of a different sort may be required to supplement or encourage ethical conduct. If such education assumes a theoretical cast, whether through the exploration of theories, the consideration of case studies, or the contemplation of problems, then Mandeville's appeal to the foundational character of know-how poses a challenge. Given the significance of know-how, then unless the businessperson already possesses moral experience, it is not clear how a university class (or executive workshop) devoted to emblematic concepts, propositions, theories, or case studies will provide the sort of habituated experience essential to ethical conduct, especially if these classes do not relate to motivating passions.[36] A theoretical education would seem, on its own, incapable of altering conduct. Indeed, the possibility that such an education will prove effective, in a practical sense, seems to require the very experience that it purports to inculcate.

A similar problem arises regarding codes of conduct devised by businesses and corporations to guide and inspire the decisions and actions of employees, managers, and executives. Such codes are typically general, if not vague (perhaps purposefully so); they often reflect, as is natural, the moral ethos of the surrounding society. To be effective these codes require a practical knowledge by which a person would not only recognize that a situation calls for moral action (or the omission of certain acts) but know how to apply a specific part of the code. Without such practical knowledge the principles of these codes would prove less than useful. In this sense the codes presume the sort of conduct they prescribe. An even more difficult challenge confronts the global or international corporation: if its code reflects the norms of the home country, then that code may prove less than relevant to individuals of other cultures who come to the corporation with differing forms of practical knowledge. If codes are to retain relevance, they must reflect and articulate ideals embedded in the ethical know-how of employees.

Not All Moral Ideals Are Mutually Compatible—or Compatible with Empirical Reality

A final yet signal maxim returns us to Mandeville's overall project. Mandeville claimed that he was not advocating vicious action (I, 95), only demonstrating the conditions for a bustling commercial society as opposed to a small and virtuous one.[37] His point is not simply to decry the hypocrisy of those who excoriate vice while nonetheless enjoying the power and riches it creates (II, 102), but to illuminate how moral ideals may not conform to empirical reality, a point made clear in his "Vindication" (esp. I, 405–7) and in his preface to his poem *The Grumbling Hive*: "For the main Design of the Fable . . . is to shew the Impossibility of enjoying all the most elegant Comforts of Life that are to be met with in an industrious, wealthy and powerful Nation, and at the same time be bless'd with all the Virtue and Innocence that can be wish'd for in a Golden Age" (I, 6–7). Whether or not Mandeville is sincere in his statement that he prefers genuine virtue to vice, his deeper point calls on individuals to scrutinize aspirations that otherwise seem compatible. In particular, moral ideals (a conception of virtue) may not be compatible with empirical reality (the nature of human beings and the conditions of prosperity). To put an ideal, such as a rigoristic notion of virtue, into practical effect may preclude the realization of other goods, such as prosperity, that are just as much desired but whose realization depends on a set of empirical circumstances effectively precluded by the other aspiration.

Extrapolating from Mandeville, one could infer that political and moral theorists must take into account something other than the meaning and logic of concepts; they must consider as well how these concepts fit together or apply to a specific set of empirical and historical circumstances. The business ethicist must, therefore, employ care (know-how) in determining whether a principle, concept, or norm could apply to some set of circumstances, practices, or institutions and at what cost. How might this task relate to a major theme of business ethics? Within the field of business ethics the consensus is that corporations should act in socially responsible ways (or, alternatively, with any eye to stakeholders rather than shareholders alone). Here we have a moral ideal (social responsibility) married to an empirical reality (the nature of business). However, even if the appeal to social responsibility has its own justification, it is not clearly compatible with the practice of business as a for-profit enterprise.[38] The theory of social responsibility suggests (a) that there are societal goals worth pursuing and (b) that those in business (or at least in corporations) should endeavor to meet these goals. In fact, one might add, social responsibility should be pursued precisely because (c) the business organization seeks to earn a profit.[39] Therefore, the socially responsible business manager is to attend to business and take care that her engagement in the enterprise contributes to certain social outcomes. In sum, the socially responsible manager of a for-profit organization must attend to something other than for-profit exchange.

Is there an incompatibility here of the sort that Mandeville noted? The manager is to pursue profit but also to seek ends that are socially responsible. Surely it is possible for both pursuits to be undertaken by the same manager! Of course, but the pursuit of social responsibility is distinct from the pursuit of profit: the incompatibility arises precisely because the business ethicist regards the former as an ethical requirement of the latter.[40] Yet the pursuit of social responsibility has nothing to do with the aims of a for-profit enterprise. If ethical business is identified with socially responsible business, then business becomes ethical *only* insofar as the manager engages in something *other* than business. It is as if the business ethicist were to assert that the person engaged in a for-profit enterprise is morally required to seek aims contrary to the pursuit of profit. If an appeal to social responsibility is outfitted as a general thesis about the ethics of business, then one must explain how socially responsible endeavors, which are not in themselves profit-making activities, lend ethical justification to business production or business exchange. (Perhaps there is a utilitarian justification for this recommendation. However, it is not obvious that advocates of social responsibility rest their counsels on utilitarianism, nor is it clear that calculations of utilitarian good would come down on the side of socially responsible activities rather than the exclusive pursuit of profit.)

Another possible incompatibility emerges if one endorses both social responsibility and pluralism about ends. Does the demand for socially responsible endeavors exist in tension with pluralism? Not only does Mandeville reject a monistic view of social aims; he also rejects the assumption that any pursuit of the private, without regard to the public, is mistaken (e.g., II, 46). Of course, if one rejects this sort of pluralism, then there is no issue of concern. However, if a society embraces a pluralism about individual and organizational ends, then why must *some* organizations or individuals pursue specific social goals? Some of the earliest advocates of social responsibility issued their calls in terms of "the objectives and values of our society" or its "needs and goals"; others demanded that "society's economic and human resources . . . [be] utilized for broad social ends."[41] Later advocates offer various and seemingly sophisticated appeals and suggest that the idea of "corporate responsibility is not unitary."[42] Nonetheless, the idea of social responsibility still involves "a balance between the firm's operations and the society's aspirations."[43] The pluralism argument possesses particular power against notions of social responsibility whose content extends beyond a call to observe everyday moral duties or to avoid rights violations in the conduct of business. A firm may engage in socially responsible endeavors or not, just as a person may engage in business or in nonprofit activities. To maintain that the business firm *must* (always) be socially responsible suggests that there is, apart from compliance with one's ethical and legal duties, a set of socially approved ends for the corporation. To regard social responsibility as a normative obligation, a *constant* task for business, when it is but one aim among others, seems scarcely compatible with a pluralist perspective.[44]

CONCLUDING REMARKS

The maxims gleaned above do not exhaust the power of the Mandevillean vantage point, but they indicate how this neglected thinker has something to say about the scope of social processes, the necessity of individual choice, the power of moral practice, and the compatibility of seemingly ethical demands (social responsibility) with the nature of the business firm and the value of pluralism. Such maxims need not determine any particular conclusion in business ethics, but they do provide parameters of consideration essential to an inquiry into the morals of commerce and the possibilities of ethical business practice.

In the case of Mandeville's particular claims, his notion of vice (as passion or appetite) is presented in terms of self-liking and overvaluation. Such a characterization allows him to infer paradoxical claims and to challenge hypocrisy. His account of individuals and their desires need not be understood as definitive even though market societies require individuals who are active, productive, and aspirational. Mandeville's perspective affords something important and valuable—an illuminating view of modern society and how the continual interactions of individuals yield consequences both beneficial and unintended. This is an insight worthy of some consideration, and the business ethicist would do well to reflect on how the rule of law and the dynamic of social and commercial interaction not only generate and sustain prosperity but ensure a modicum of cooperative and decent conduct.

ACKNOWLEDGMENTS

I thank Reva Wolf and Byron Kaldis for their insightful and helpful comments on earlier versions of this essay.

NOTES

1. *The Fable of the Bees: or, Private Vices, Publick Benefits,* ed. F. B. Kaye, 2 vols. (Indianapolis: Liberty Fund, 1988). Parenthetical citations of *The Fable* in the text refer to volume and page number in the Kaye edition.

2. Mandeville often iterates the distinct consequences that accrue to living by virtue as opposed to vice; for example, "whoever reckons a general Temperance, Frugality, and Disinterestedness among the national Blessings, and at the same time sollicites Heaven for Ease and Plenty, and the Encrease of Trade, seems to me, little to understand what he is about" (II, 335). Mandeville conceives of virtue as exacting: genuine virtue incorporates both the denial of passion (appetite) and a rational orientation to good.

3. Within the literature of business ethics the mentions of Mandeville are, typically, brief asides that highlight his appeal to self-interest or his link between private intention and public good. The notable exception to this pattern is the essay by George Bragues, "Business Is One Thing, Ethics Is Another: Revisiting Bernard Mandeville's *Fable of the Bees,*" *Business Ethics Quarterly* 15, no. 2 (April 2005): 179–203. Bragues contends that Mandeville adheres to a rigoristic notion of individual virtue while embracing a standard of utility for public policy.

4. Along with *The Fable*, these include (among others) *The Virgin Unmasked: Or Female Dialogues Betwixt an Elderly Maiden Lady and her Niece* (London, 1709), *A Treatise of the Hypochondriack and Hysterick Passions,* 2nd ed. (1711; London: Tonson, 1730), *An Enquiry into the Origin of Honour and the Usefulness of Christianity in War* (London, 1732), as well as essays in the *Female Tatler* (1709–10), noted below.

5. Irwin Primer recounts how Adam Smith and other "serious thinkers" were left with an "indelible impression of the Mandevillean framework of ideas." See Primer's introduction to *Mandeville Studies: New Explorations in the Art and Thought of Dr. Bernard Mandeville (1670–1733),* ed. Primer (The Hague: Martinus Nijhoff, 1975), x.

6. Mikko Tolonen contends that the content and publishing history of this second volume provide reasons to think that "volume II" was, in fact, not a continuation of the first but a distinct work. See Tolonen, *Mandeville and Hume: Anatomists of Civil Society* (Oxford: Voltaire Foundation, 2013), esp. chap. 2.

7. In *An Enquiry into the Origin of Moral Virtue* (appearing in the 1714 edition of *The Fable*) Mandeville suggests that one may "give the Name of VIRTUE to every Performance,

by which Man, contrary to the impulse of Nature, should endeavour the Benefit of others, or the Conquest of his own Passions out of a Rational Ambition of being good" (I, 48–49). Mandeville's notion of virtue, combining asceticism and rationalism, is referred to by Kaye as "rigoristic" (Kaye, introduction to *The Fable of the Bees*, xlviii). Such a notion owes much to French moralists (such as Pierre Bayle, La Rochefoucauld, and Pierre Nicole), as well as to Calvinist doctrines with which Mandeville was surely familiar, as he grew to maturity in the Netherlands. On his relation to French thinkers, see Kaye, introduction to *The Fable of the Bees*, lxxvii–xciv; E. J. Hundert, *The Enlightenment's Fable: Bernard Mandeville and the Discovery of Society* (Cambridge: Cambridge University Press, 1994), 30–37; and, in particular, Laurence Dickey, "Pride, Hypocrisy, and Civility in Mandeville's Social and Historical Theory," *Critical Review* 4, no. 3 (Summer 1990): 387–431.

8. Mandeville's notions of self-love and self-liking undergo transition from the first to the second volume of *The Fable*. In the first, he employs "self-love" to refer to an affection for self, but in the second volume he distinguishes "self-love," as a form of self-preservation, from "self-liking," an affection for self that generates pride, overvaluation, and continual attempts to prove oneself to others and gain their approval.

9. John Rule, "Manufacturing and Commerce," in *A Companion to Eighteenth-Century Britain*, ed. H. T. Dickinson (Oxford: Blackwell, 2002), 127.

10. See Joel Mokyr, *The Enlightened Economy: An Economic History of Britain, 1700–1850* (New Haven, CT: Yale University Press, 2009), 15; Joyce Appleby, "Consumption in Early Modern Social Thought," in *Consumption and the World of Goods*, ed. John Brewer and Roy Porter (London: Routledge, 1993), 167.

11. Neil McKendrick, introduction to McKendrick, John Brewer, and J. H. Plumb, *The Birth of a Consumer Society: The Commercialization of Eighteenth-Century England* (Bloomington: Indiana University Press, 1982), 1.

12. Voltaire adds, in words redolent of Mandeville, "Yet I wonder which is more the useful to a nation, a well-powdered nobleman who knows exactly at what minute the King gets up and goes to bed . . . or a business man who enriches his country." Voltaire, "On Commerce," in *Letters on England*, trans. Leonard Tancock (Harmondsworth, UK: Penguin, 1980), 52.

13. Maurice Goldsmith, *Private Vices, Public Benefits: Bernard Mandeville's Social and Political Thought* (Cambridge: Cambridge University Press, 1985), 27–29. See also Thomas A. Horne, *The Social Thought of Bernard Mandeville: Virtue and Commerce in Early Eighteenth-Century England* (New York: Columbia University Press, 1978), chap. 1.

14. In a strict sense, the ends of one's appetites need not necessarily be of a material sort (such as luxury goods, even high social status), though this seems to be assumed in the rhetoric of those advocating public spirit over private appetite. On the appeals to civic virtue, see, in particular, Hundert, *Enlightenment's Fable*, 8–13, 177–80; and Appleby, "Consumption in Early Modern Social Thought," esp. 165–67.

15. The sermon may be dated around 1700. This excerpt is taken from W. A. Speck, "Mandeville and the Eutopia Seated in the Brain," in Primer, *Mandeville Studies,* 69.

16. Speck, "Mandeville and the Eutopia Seated in the Brain," 69.

17. See Maurice Goldsmith's introduction to *By a Society of Ladies: Essays in the "Female Tatler"* (Bristol: Thoemmes Press, 1999), esp. 33–41.

18. "Whoever offers to another a bargain of any kind, proposes to do this. Give me that which I want, and you shall have this which you want. . . . It is not from the benevolence of the butcher, the brewer, or the baker, that we expect our dinner, but from their regard to their own interest. We address ourselves, not to their humanity but to their self-love, and never talk to them of our own necessities but of their advantages." Adam Smith, *An Inquiry into the Nature and Causes of the Wealth of Nations*, ed. R. H. Campbell, R. S. Skinner, and W. B. Todd (Indianapolis: Liberty Fund, 1981), I.ii.2, pp. 26–27.

19. Mandeville's appeals to national greatness and to the political management of trade

reflect mercantilist notions. However, Nathan Rosenberg's judgment remains sound: Mandeville proves an economic interventionist in foreign trade, but in the domestic scene he advocates a rule of law and an evolutionary approach to reform. See Rosenberg, "Mandeville and Laissez-Faire," *Journal of the History of Ideas* 24 (April–June 1963): 183–96. F. B. Kaye had suggested that Mandeville was an explicit advocate of laissez-faire (see his introduction to *The Fable of the Bees*, cxxxix). However, Horne regards Mandeville as, in general, a mercantilist (see Horne, *Social Thought of Bernard Mandeville*, esp. 51–75). More recently, see Benjamin Dew, "'Damn'd to Sythes and Spades': Labour and Wealth Creation in the Writing of Bernard Mandeville," *Intellectual History Review* 23, no. 2 (2013): 187–205, for the argument that Mandeville merged an Augustinian and Epicurean perspective with elements of mercantilism.

20. Joyce Appelby, *Liberalism and Republicanism in the Historical Imagination* (Cambridge, MA: Harvard University Press, 1992), 37.

21. See Christopher J. Berry, *The Idea of Luxury: A Conceptual and Historical Investigation* (Cambridge: Cambridge University Press, 1994), esp. 126–34 (his discussion of Mandeville). In his essay in this volume Berry discusses Hume's defense of luxury.

22. *By a Society of Ladies: Essays in the "Female Tatler,"* 98 (further citations of the *Female Tatler* refer to page numbers in this edition and appear in this format: *FT* 98). Note that Artesia has linked "private interest" and "personal pleasure," a connection that allows a contrast to a public good that is not, apparently, individually pleasurable. However, within Mandeville's developed thought, a self-loving individual may reap pleasure from acting for the public, at least so long as the publicly oriented action generates a positive and pleasurable reception from others.

23. A pluralist view is defended subsequently by Artesia herself: "For whether a Man loves to get or to spend Money, a great hurry of Business or a quiet Country Life, he that always seems to be pleased, and shews himself easy in his Station, is certainly the Man that is Happy" (*FT* 232). On pluralism in the work of Rawls, see Matt Zwolinski's essay in this volume; on pluralism and Milton Friedman, see the essay by Alexei Marcoux.

24. One is reminded of Molière's "bourgeois gentleman," Monsieur Jourdain, who in his first encounter with the "Philosopher" affirms, "Above all I want knowledge." When the philosopher quotes a Latin phrase and adds, "You know Latin, of course," M. Jourdain responds, "Of course, but let's just pretend I don't." *The Bourgeois Gentleman* (1670), translated and adapted by Bernard Sahlins (Chicago: Ivan R. Dee, 2000), 26.

25. On the *summum bonum*, see *Leviathan*, ed. Edwin Curley (Indianapolis: Hackett, 1994), chap. XI; on desire and value, see VI, 7.

26. Hundert suggests that Mandeville came to realize that the polemics of the first volume, including those in the poem *The Grumbling Hive*, required editing if his more significant points were not to be lost. See Hundert, *Enlightenment's Fable*, 189.

27. Goldsmith contends that Mandeville's portraits of commerce, especially in the *Female Tatler*, suggest an early view of the "spirit of capitalism" (*Private Vices, Public Benefits*, 120). For a criticism of this view, see Dario Castiglione, "Excess, Frugality, and the Spirit of Capitalism: Readings of Mandeville on Commercial Society," in *Culture in History: Production, Consumption, and Values in Historical Perspective*, ed. Joseph Melling and Jonathan Berry (Exeter: University of Exeter Press, 1992), esp. 167–70.

28. Neither engages in the commission of a lie, even though each omits to tell the *whole* truth. I assume that the nondisclosure of the *whole* truth does not, in this instance, equate to deception or lying. In other cases, commercial or not, nondisclosure may be deceptive.

29. Despite Goldsmith's judgment, this scenario does not exemplify the traditional doctrine of *caveat emptor*, at least if that principle refers to the product and not the more general conditions of the sale (*Private Vices, Public Benefits*, 140).

30. The allusion to "anatomization," which reflects Mandeville's medical training as well as his rejection of a priori theorizing (I, 170–71), calls attention to the difficulty of

recognizing and examining one's assumptions. The obvious parts of one's anatomy—"hard Bones, strong Muscles and Nerves" (I,3)—may not be the elements that motivate action: the "small trifling Films and little Pipes" that are "either over-look'd, or else seem inconsiderable" (I, 3).

31. As Artesia exclaims, "I can never forbear thinking, how infinitely we are indebted to all those that ever invented any thing for the Public Good: It is they that actually have meliorated their kind" (*FT* 98).

32. On conjectural history, see H. M. Höpfl, "From Savage to Scotsman: Conjectural History in the Scottish Enlightenment," *Journal of British Studies* 17, no. 2 (1978): 19–40; see, more recently, Frank Palmeri, *State of Nature, Stages of Society: Enlightenment Conjectural History and Modern Social Discourse* (New York: Columbia University Press, 2016). On Mandeville's evolutionary theory of norms, see Hundert, *Enlightenment's Fable,* 62–86; and Eugene Heath, "Mandeville's Bewitching Engine of Praise," *History of Philosophy Quarterly* 15, no 2 (April 1998): 205–26. A reconstruction of Mandeville's account of language may be found in Heath, "'Carrying Matters too Far'? Mandeville and the Eighteenth-Century Scots on the Evolution of Morals," *Journal of Scottish Philosophy* 12, no. 1 (2014): 95–118. Mandeville's conjectural account of society may be understood either in terms of the actions of politicians, interpreted literally (as in volume I), or as an evolutionary process that reflects, as often pointed out in volume II of *The Fable*, the "joynt Labour of several ages" (II, 322).

33. Such a view might be labeled a "negative folk model" according to which the market is understood as an amoral or otherwise egoistic sphere in which greedy participants not only cheat but act in ways that thwart the achievement of any ends other than the material. Consider the following statements, drawn from contemporary business ethics scholarship. "But for people who enter the life of business, the pronouncement that their ambition is to make money is considered par for the course; it is what is expected and what is demanded of that life itself" (Robert Solomon, *Above the Bottom Line* [Fort Worth, TX: Harcourt Brace Jovanovich, 1994], 35). A feature of "business activity" is "the seeming unremitting need to be doing others down" (Jennifer Jackson, *An Introduction to Business Ethics* [Oxford: Basil Blackwell, 1996], 80). Joanne B. Ciulla, who otherwise refers, in the same essay, to the general vagaries of human nature, offers a more nuanced perspective, even as she adds, "Business has always had the ability to bring out the worst in people" (Ciulla, "Is Business Ethics Getting Better? A Historical Perspective," *Business Ethics Quarterly* 21, no. 2 [April 2011]: 338).

34. A similar distinction is iterated in another passage: "There is a great Difference between knowing a Violin when you see it, and knowing how to play upon it" (II, 171). This statement suggests a third kind of knowledge—knowledge by acquaintance.

35. The essential treatment of the distinction is Gilbert Ryle's chapter "Knowing How and Knowing That," in *The Concept of Mind* (Chicago: University of Chicago Press, 1949). For contemporary treatments, see John Bengson and Marc A. Moffett, eds., *Knowing How: Essays on Knowledge, Mind, and Action* (Oxford: Oxford University Press, 2012).

36. "Preach and Demonstrate to a Coward the unreasonableness of his Fears and you'll not make him Valiant, more than you can make him Taller by bidding him to be Ten Foot high" (I, 333).

37. "Frugality is like Honesty, a mean starving Virtue, that is only fit for small Societies of good peaceable Men, who are contented to be poor so they may be easy; but in a large stirring Nation you may have soon enough of it. 'Tis an idle dreaming Virtue that employs no Hands, and therefore very useless in a trading Country, where there are vast Numbers that one way or other must be all set to Work" (I, 104–5; see also 124).

38. A similar phenomenon holds for the theory of stakeholding insofar as it stipulates that managers of corporations have a duty to serve the interests of all stakeholders. See Eugene Heath, "The Qualities of Virtue and Its Rivals: Business, Entrepreneurship, and Business Ethics," in *Virtues in Entrepreneurship*, ed. Nils Karlson, Mikolaj Norek, and Karl Wennberg (Stockholm: Ratio, 2015), 58–80.

39. The reasoning for clause c pivots on the fact that numerous endeavors not conceived as profit seeking—the work of artists or the activities of nonprofit organizations—are regarded typically as exempt from appeals to social responsibility.

40. Some of the difficulties of pursuing both profit and ends distinct from profit are explored in Michael C. Jensen, "Value, Maximisation, Stakeholder Theory, and the Corporate Objective Function," *European Financial Management* 7, no. 3 (2001): 297–317.

41. The phrases are from Howard R. Bowen, *Social Responsibilities of the Businessman* (New York: Harper & Row, 1953), 6; Richard Eels and Clarence Walton, *Conceptual Foundations of Business,* 3rd ed. (Homewood, IL: Richard D. Irwin, 1974), 247; and William C. Frederick, "The Growing Concern over Business Responsibility," *California Management Review* 2 (1960): 60; all are quoted in Archie B. Carroll's essay "A History of Corporate Social Responsibility: Concepts and Practices," in *The Oxford Handbook of Corporate Social Responsibility*, ed. Andrew Crane et al. (Oxford: Oxford University Press, 2008), 25, 30, 27, respectively.

42. Archie B. Carroll et al., *Corporate Responsibility: The American Experience,* ed. Kenneth E. Goodpaster (New York: Cambridge University Press, 2012), 6.

43. William C. Frederick, "Corporate Social Responsibility: Deep Roots, Flourishing Growth, Promising Future," in Crane et al., *Oxford Handbook of Corporate Social Responsibility,* 523.

44. One might argue that "social responsibility" represents no single, unified end but multiple, varied, and changing ends. But this conception is itself an appeal to pluralism about social responsibilities. Why this sort of pluralism should *not* be extended more broadly is a question for its advocates.

CHAPTER 10

"Commerce Cures Destructive Prejudices": Montesquieu and the Spirit of Commercial Society

Henry C. Clark

Charles-Louis de Secondat, Baron of La Brède and of Montesquieu (1689–1755), is normally thought of in constitutional rather than business ethics terms. But the man quoted more frequently than anyone else during the American founding period,[1] and whose concepts of the separation of powers and checks-and-balances have become canonical in the modern practice of limited government throughout the world, was also an enormously influential commentator on commerce and finance in his own time. By one count, fully one-sixth of the content of his 1748 classic *The Spirit of the Laws* concerns the study of wealth in its many dimensions.[2] Writing after the growth of trade had become a priority in European statecraft, but just before the crystallization of the first real "school" of political economy (the Physiocrats under François Quesnay in the late 1750s), Montesquieu did much to shape the public discussion of economic and financial policy in his time and beyond.

One of the things that made his own time a transitional period was that Montesquieu still approached the subject of business life from within a classical literary and philosophical tradition that included, among many other features, a prominent place for the virtues—for analyzing both individual conduct and social mores. From its fairly systemic neglect in the twentieth century in all but the more isolated redoubts of philosophical Thomism, virtue ethics has enjoyed a revival in recent decades. Philosophers like Alasdair MacIntyre and economists like Deirdre McCloskey have succeeded in making the language of the virtues among the viable options for understanding both our own experience and that of past generations.[3] A broadly eclectic version of this virtue ethics turns out to be a useful, indeed necessary prism through which to view Montesquieu's thinking about business life.

In taking the measure of this thinking, it is useful to begin with a lexical distinction. If business ethics, as it has come to be understood since the 1970s, is an essentially normative framework for professionals in a world dominated by impersonal corporations, we will require some other term to capture the broader comparative and historical category of analysis that is more descriptive of Montesquieu's own enterprise. For one thing, unlike the medieval Scholastics or the early modern casuists, the Baron of La Brède never offered a sustained discussion of the moral or religious implications of specific business practices such as usury. For another, he of course wrote before the rise of the modern corporation. Montesquieu himself sometimes refers to the "spirit of commerce"; an alternative term I propose for this essay is "commercial morality."

In the pages that follow, I will sketch the contours of this commercial morality. First I will explore the resolutely historical approach to the moral effects and implications of commerce that one finds in the writings of Montesquieu. Much of his thinking occurred through an investigation of the *moeurs* or mores of different peoples in different times, articulated in a language of the virtues. I will examine the significance of his version of a stadial theory of historical development, as well as pairs of categories essential to his thought, such as ancient vs. modern and commerce vs. conquest. Then I will situate Montesquieu's commercial morality in the historical context furnished by the contemporary celebrity of Bernard Mandeville's scandalous and epoch-making work *The Fable of the Bees* (1723). What will emerge from this analysis is that although Montesquieu offered a strikingly original variation on Mandeville's famous formula "Private Vices, Publick Benefits," he ultimately subscribed to a view of commercial morality resting crucially upon two intimately related virtues—namely, humanity and justice. This essay will conclude by pointing to some of the implications for business ethics of this virtue ethics approach.

COMMERCIAL MORALITY IN HISTORICAL PERSPECTIVE

Montesquieu's approach to commercial morality, like his approach to virtually everything else, is best regarded as a work continually in progress. Our understanding of it can thus be grasped only approximately and piecemeal, by trying to identify and sort out the multiplicity of conceptual devices that he deployed in his writings. Most of these devices are historical in nature. For contemporaries, one of his great achievements in *The Spirit of the Laws* was to put the rational and comprehensive but rather static analysis of laws—part of the university curriculum and the general intellectual life of Europe since the great works of Hugo Grotius and Samuel Pufendorf in the seventeenth century—in historical motion. The laws now became a specific part of a broader context, which included manners, mores, terrain, climate, religion, and anything else that might contribute to what Montesquieu called the "general spirit" of a particular people. Thus, when he referred to the "spirit of commerce," he meant trade as an activity in dynamic relation to these other dimensions of human existence. It was largely the vitality, openness, and sensitivity of this method that John Millar had in mind when, in describing the newly ascendant history of "civil society," he opined that Montesquieu was the "Bacon" of that novel science of man, and Adam Smith (Millar's own teacher) the "Newton."[4]

Montesquieu's different types of historical treatment may be divided into three categories of comparison. The first concerns his conception of periodization. Though it is sometimes forgotten, it seems to have been Montesquieu who first outlined the kind of stadial theory that Anne-Robert-Jacques Turgot and Adam Smith would pick up and articulate only a few years later as the famous four-stages theory (1750 in Turgot's case, 1753 in Smith's).[5] "There is bound to be a more extensive code of laws," Montesquieu writes, "for a people attached to commerce and the sea than for a people satisfied to cultivate their lands. There is bound to be a greater one for the latter than for a people who live by their herds. There is bound to be a greater one for these last than for a people who live by hunting."[6]

He does not elaborate on this notion of the four modes of subsistence, but it seems he has in mind a more evolutionary conception of their mutual relationship than the synchronic inventory found, for example, in the first book of Aristotle's *Politics*.[7] One thing, in any event, is clear: we can expect a thicker web of legal arrangements in commercial societies than in precommercial ones, if for no other reason than that property relations are more complex in such societies—though the moral significance of this point will appear in greater relief below.

A second historical framework Montesquieu sometimes resorts to concerns the contrast between ancient and modern. He was becoming a member of the cultural elite at just the time when the famous literary quarrel of ancients vs. moderns was raging, and his intellectual diary contains numerous reflections on that debate.[8] Commerce, it turns out, is central to his own understanding of the differences between those two epochs. Montesquieu was of course aware that commerce had existed in antiquity, and had in fact been quite extensive. But he disagreed with those defenders of modern commercial society who wanted to appropriate Rome for their cause by claiming it as a commercial civilization.[9] For him, Rome was marked by an assemblage of virtue, religion, patriotism, and a ferocious culture of conquest that eventually swamped local morals, customs, and trade routes, and replaced them with a cult of *Romanitas*, whose sheer steamrolling uniformity he mostly lamented.

In the course of his *Considerations on the Romans* (1734), Montesquieu offers an extended contrast between ancient and modern statecraft that is of some interest for our purposes. "Great military initiatives," he writes, "seem to be more difficult to conduct with us than they were with the ancients."[10] The reason, he explains, is that modern communications—especially the invention of the printing press, engraving (important for mapmaking), newspapers, and the postal service—have meant that "the public has all private secrets in its power."

For Montesquieu, as for other eighteenth-century commentators, commerce and communications are intimately linked, sometimes nearly synonymous. On one occasion, for example, he asserts that "the history of commerce is that of communication among peoples."[11] Thus, in the same discussion of ancient vs. modern statecraft, he writes, "Great military initiatives cannot be accomplished without money, and merchants have been in control of money since the invention of letters of exchange. For this reason, the affairs of merchants are frequently bound up with the secrets of states, and these men neglect nothing to discover them." As we shall see, the specific device whose late medieval invention he cites here, the letters of exchange, has an honored place in Montesquieu's explanation of the moral revaluation of commerce in modern society. For the present, the general point is obvious enough: when it comes to statecraft at least, the contrast between ancient and modern is overlaid with a sharp contrast in the role of commerce, communications, and merchants in those two eras.

But our theme comes more sharply into focus if we move to still a third Montesquieuan comparison, one that cuts across each of the preceding two. That comparison is defined by two dominant activities—conquest and commerce—which seem to bring whole modes of civilization in their respective trains. In Montesquieu's hands, this comparison becomes the vehicle for suggestive and wide-ranging observations on moral life—not only on the key virtues of humanity and justice, but on historically contextualized vices such as pride, ambition, honor, vanity, arrogance, gravity, and laziness, all of which the author treats in genuinely original ways.

The conquest-commerce trope may in general be regarded as a modern variation on the soldier vs. statesman comparison from antiquity.[12] It had assumed prominence in the seventeenth century because of the surprising emergence of the small, resource-deprived Dutch states, which were somehow able to rise out of nowhere to rival in global power the proud absolute monarchies of Habsburg Spain and Bourbon France. Some patriotic Dutch writers, such as the commercial republican brothers Johan and Pieter De la Court, had argued that Dutch security and even expansion were best achieved peacefully through freedom of trade.[13]

The English Whigs also made a stark distinction between conquest and commerce as modes of national advancement, priding themselves on the English preference for the second against the French king Louis XIV's predilection for the first.[14] Even in France, especially after the latter's death in

1715, there was a growing tendency to adopt this Anglo-Dutch paradigm as a feature of the modern world, rather than a peculiarity of certain regimes. The popular Jansenist historian Charles Rollin expressly declared the "spirit of conquest" and the "spirit of commerce" to be "mutually exclusive within the same nation," since one brings "tumult, disorder, desolation and trouble" and the other "only peace and tranquility."[15]

Montesquieu's own thinking about conquest vs. commerce has a groping, experimental character, taking several forms over time. In each iteration, however, his abiding assumption is that commerce, but not conquest, is a characteristic imperative of the modern world. In an unpublished note, he put the contrasting "spirits" of the two activities this way: "Each age has its particular character: a spirit of disorderly independence was created in Europe with Gothic government; the monastic spirit infected the times of Charlemagne's successors; then reigned that of chivalry; that of conquest appeared with orderly troops; and it's the spirit of commerce that dominates today."[16] Here, it appears that the historical periodization with which Montesquieu is experimenting contains three medieval phases—one in what we would call the early Middle Ages and two in the High Middle Ages—and that "conquest" is a function of state growth under the Renaissance monarchies and seventeenth-century absolutism. "Commerce" would then serve as a synecdoche for a postabsolutist, eighteenth-century modernity.

In another diary entry, this one on the hero, the Baron of La Brède explored the possibility that there might be different historical stages of heroism: from the beneficent (Hercules and Theseus) to the courageous (Achilles) to the conquering (Philip and Alexander) to the love-making (modern romance novels). Here, conquest would be an ancient phase of heroism, and would not be tied to the emergence of the modern state with its standing armies. But he closes this entry by confessing, "At present, I don't know what they [i.e., heroes] are." And in any case, he contrasts all these forms of heroism with "cash," again evoking commercial modernity.[17]

One important metaphor that Montesquieu evidently found useful for expressing this contrast between conquest and commerce was that of the single continental or even global nation or state. It is here that the distinctive modernity of commerce appears most vividly. The groping quality of his enterprise is highlighted by the fact that the metaphorical entity he describes is sometimes called a "nation," sometimes a "state"—the former usually meaning the collective moral, social, and economic resources of the people, the latter referring to the government itself. Complicating the picture further is that Montesquieu departed from contemporary dictionary usage in defining even the "state" (*état*) in a broader way, as when he cites the Roman-law expert Giovanni Gravina's remark that "the union of all individual powers forms what is called the *political state*."[18] It will be useful to keep such nuances in mind in what follows.

Montesquieu reverts on numerous occasions to this image of a single community as a way of describing the modern world as a whole, in passages that seem to look backward to Stoic cosmopolitanism as well as forward to our theorists of "globalization." His first use of the image appears in the manuscript of an essay on Spanish wealth that he probably wrote in the 1720s. There the emphasis is on communication, though as something of a synonym for commerce, as discussed above: "Nowadays, communication is such that the world is virtually composed of one nation. Each people communicates its advantages to each other, offers its superfluous merchandise, and receives that of other peoples, and since a people is rich only to the extent that it has any, each people can receive only to the extent that it has the wherewithal to give." When he revised the same manuscript a little later, he shifted the emphasis subtly to knowledge rather than communication, while continuing the emphasis on global economic rather than political ties: "Now that the world is virtually composed of one nation, and each people knows what it has in surplus and what it is lacking, and seeks to provide itself with the means to receive the latter, gold and silver are drawn from everywhere on earth; those metals are transported everywhere, each people communicates them to each other, and there isn't a single nation whose capital in gold and silver is not growing every year (albeit more promptly and more abundantly in some than in others)."[19] His point in this work is to expose the systemic fallacy in Spain's policy of bullionism—that is, the assumption that national wealth consists in the accumulation of precious metals.

In his "Reflections on Universal Monarchy in Europe," written in 1734, Montesquieu uses the same one-nation metaphor, but to different effect. Here, the topic is not bullionism but trade as a general instrument of national rivalry, and the subject is Europe rather than the world. "Europe," he now writes, "is no longer anything other than one nation composed of many. France and England need the opulence of Poland and Muscovy, just like one of their Provinces needs the others. The State that thinks it can increase its power by ruining a State that concerns it will ordinarily weaken itself as well."[20] The contrast in this case—which originated as a one state–many provinces metaphor in *Pensée* 318—is not exactly between commerce and conquest; instead, what Montesquieu suggests is that the moral logic of international trade is that of positive-sum interdependence, and that treating it as a weapon in zero-sum rivalries over status or power is a distortion. Along those lines, this passage also contains a subtle but unmistakable contrast between the one "nation" formed by international trade and the two or more "states" locked in mercantilistic battle, suggesting a difference between governments (states) and their peoples (nations). His intent here is thus to appeal against the "jealousy of trade" argument that loomed so large in eighteenth-century strategic thinking.[21] The same theme is sounded in a more global and categorical fashion in *Pensée* 1694, where

Montesquieu adapts the Stoic emperor Marcus Aurelius's remark that "what is not useful to the swarm is not useful to the bee" to argue that "all nations hold together in a chain."[22]

In *The Spirit of the Laws*, finally, the single-state metaphor appears in the context of a distinction between landed property and movable property. The land is part of each individual nation, but of mobile property, he writes this: "Moveable effects, such as silver, notes, letters of exchange, shares in companies, ships, and all commodities, belong to the whole world, which in this regard comprises but a single state of which all societies are members."[23] Here, another truly global metaphor seems to apply only to the financial sector of modern economies, although that sector has such a close relationship to states that its relevance for a contrast between commerce and conquest is still strong. So it matters for both states and individuals that, whereas gold had dried up daily in Europe under the less commercially centered regime of the Roman Empire, the world now contains a permanent supply that is continually traded from one country to another, replenishing trade wherever it goes.[24] A key reason, then, that commerce has come to overtake conquest as a paradigm of the modern world concerns its irrepressible mobility, as Montesquieu makes clear at one point in almost elegiac terms: "Commerce, sometimes destroyed by conquerors, sometimes hampered by monarchs, wanders across the earth, flees from where it is oppressed, and remains where it is left to breathe."[25]

One way Montesquieu sharpens the contrast between commerce and conquest is by reworking a traditional distinction between what he calls a "commerce of luxury" and a "commerce of economy."[26] Aristotle and the Scholastics had made a similar distinction, but for them, household retail trade for subsistence was really the only proper "commerce of economy" (or of "necessity," as they would have put it). Montesquieu, on the other hand, expands the definition to embrace the realities of a modern interconnected world. Often throughout history, he writes, "violence and harassment have brought forth economic commerce among men who are constrained to hide in marshes, on islands, on the shoals, and even among dangerous reefs. . . . They had to live; they drew their living from the whole world."[27] More surprisingly, economic commerce seems also to apply to the world of high finance, including notably the role of the Jews in medieval Europe. Thus, Montesquieu attacks the governments and theologians of that time for attempting to prohibit moneylending, based on their distorted reading of Aristotle's view of usury. Because of this misinterpretation, "commerce, which had been only the profession of low-status people, also became that of dishonest people." The lesson is clear: "Whenever one prohibits something that is naturally permitted or necessary, one only makes the people who engage in it dishonest."[28]

But ultimately, the effort failed. When the Jews, who had for centuries been plundered and persecuted by European rulers for engaging in these "naturally permitted or necessary" activities, ultimately responded by "invent[ing] letters of exchange," they put substantial wealth out of the reach of government. And herein lies a crucial moment in the historical rise of commercial society. Not unlike Adam Smith, whose better-known theory of medieval baubles and trinkets supposedly seduced the feudal lords into replacing personal bonds with monetary ones and thus set the stage for modernity,[29] Montesquieu has his own version of the moral irony of commercialization, and it occurs in two parts. "Theologians," he first notes, "were obliged to curb their principles, and commerce, which had been violently linked to insincerity and bad faith, returned, so to speak, to the bosom of integrity." But this moral revaluation of commerce was mainly possible because of a prior political revaluation in the relationship between the interests of church and state, as the late medieval emergence of sovereign territorial states limited papal jurisdiction. In this regard, he sees a double irony: "To the speculations of the schoolmen we owe all the misfortunes that accompanied the destruction of commerce; to the avarice of princes we owe the establishment of a device that puts commerce, in a way, out of their [i.e., the princes'] power."[30] Montesquieu is here reversing a standard relationship: philosophy was often seen as a remedy for the passions; but in this case, the passion of avarice undoes the damage wrought by the (misguided) philosophizing of the Scholastics. The commerce of necessity ends up being a morally charged activity even on those occasions when it involves complex finance and long-distance moneylending that might seem merely pragmatic in nature.

MANDEVILLE AND THE MACULATE CONCEPTION OF COMMERCIAL SOCIETY

If we turn now from a historical and comparative perspective to one more overtly normative, we find that the best way of approaching Montesquieu's treatment of commercial morality is to situate him within the most heated debate on the subject in his lifetime—namely, the polemic surrounding Bernard Mandeville's *Fable of the Bees: or, Private Vices, Publick Benefits*. As the subtitle foretells, Mandeville revolutionized moral debate by suggesting that the acceptance, indeed encouragement, of vice was necessary in a modern commercial society to promote the public interest. Adopting a generally Hobbesian psychology of universal passions and self-interests, Mandeville seemed to be claiming both that a community of virtue was not possible, and that society would be gravely harmed if it were. Modern societies in particular, committed as they are to becoming opulent and powerful states, require the channeling of these passions and interests for the achievement of public ends.

Montesquieu had read Mandeville, and his view of the latter's challenge was complex and nuanced.[31] On the one hand, his concessions to this scandalous new theory were numerous and multilayered. The Anglo-Dutchman's robust embrace of modernity overlapped considerably with Montesquieu's own sense of the advantages of modern over ancient, of commerce over conquest. But on the other hand, the Baron of La Brède was less ready to heap satirical scorn on the traditional moral categories of his own society. And as we shall see, he believed there were such things as virtues and vices, and that they both had a place in the analysis of past and present. Part of our task will consist in identifying the relationship between these two perspectives.

Already in *The Persian Letters* (1721), the main character, Usbek, utters a paradoxical line eminently worthy of Mandeville: "For a prince to be powerful, his subjects must live in luxury." The paradox here is that by the contemporary royal ideology of *majestas*, it is the princes who ought to live in luxury, the better to project their glory. And this paradox is immediately followed by a converse one: "Self-interest is the greatest monarch on earth," extending its dominion equally to all, monarchs and artisans alike.[32] Later on, in his intellectual diary, he was more explicit in his endorsement of Mandeville's system: "I will gladly conform to the ideas of the man who wrote the *Fable of the Bees*, and I will ask to be shown grave citizens, in any country, who do as much good there as their dandies do for certain commercial nations."[33] Elsewhere in that collection, he had sketched a preface to the *Histoire véritable* (*True History*, published posthumously) elaborating on his praise of this unpromising social group: "I am stating here the true reason why I have all my life had a particular esteem for our young court dandies. . . . Although they promote the main branches of our trade, . . . they perform a service to their Country without demanding the least gratitude." It is true that their heads are "a bit harebrained," but this does not diminish the share of credit they deserve for French national charm, sociability, vivacity, even loyal service to throne and nation.[34] Through the medium of luxury consumption, their vanity leads to social and economic benefits for the *patrie*; Mandeville could scarcely have put it better.

Once again, Montesquieu's thinking seems to have evolved concerning the precise varieties of self-regard and their role in shaping a commercial morality. His *Pensées*, for example, show him experimenting with a contrast between *orgueil* and *arrogance*. The latter, a cognate, is an unambiguous evil, but the former, best translated here as "pride," is a generic human frailty—one of the seven deadly sins—that in Montesquieu's view can be either positive or negative for society as a whole. Arrogance always divides people; pride, paradoxically enough, can sometimes unite them. It does this when it takes the form of vanity, and the dandies are again the essential social alchemists for this transmutation. For it is they who, "instead of that arrogance that appears . . . among some peoples, change our pride into a pleasing impertinence produced in a thousand ways." It is the dandies, with their ever-present vanity, who in typical Mandevillean fashion "bring about a happy harmony between persons whom the old mores would have made incompatible."[35] The claims of birth and the claims of wealth, so often locked in mortal combat under the rules of these "old mores," are harmonized under the tacit commercial morality of the fashionable elite, a morality that allows and even encourages others to give vent to their vanity even as we give vent to our own.

By the time Montesquieu wrote his magnum opus, *The Spirit of the Laws*, he had apparently modified his thinking: the arrogance-pride pairing now appears as a more extended distinction between vanity (*vanité*) and pride (*orgueil*). After evoking Mandeville explicitly on the positive connection between frivolous fashions and trade,[36] he moves to a chapter-length contrast between these two vices. The context is a discussion of national character. Pride, he argues, is part of a whole complex of dispositions—including gravity and laziness—that leads some peoples, notably the Spanish, to opt for the conquest or even destruction of other peoples rather than for work. On the other hand, he cites "the innumerable benefits resulting from vanity: luxury, industry, the arts, fashions, politeness, and taste." He sharpens the contrast by observing, "The pride of a Spaniard will incline him not to work; the vanity of a Frenchman will incline him to try to work better than other people."[37] This time, then, *orgueil* for Montesquieu is no longer a generic category but a specific and deeply divisive vice. It seems virtually synonymous with *arrogance* in *Pensée* 1439.

Typically, he ends the chapter by cautioning against overinterpretation of his framework and by reminding the reader of the inescapable role of circumstance and comparison in all human history: "It goes without saying that moral qualities have different effects according to the other qualities united with them; thus pride joined to a vast ambition, to the greatness of ideas, etc. produced among the Romans the effects which are known to all."[38] Nonetheless, despite his distinction here between the ancient Romans and the modern Spaniards, his overarching conception is consistent with Mandeville's view that at least some private vices can lead to public benefits through the exchange of goods and services. Conversely, there is the hint of a commerce vs. conquest duality at work here, inasmuch as pride but not vanity leads to conquest, whereas vanity instead leads to trade.

Montesquieu's treatment of vanity forms part of a larger pattern in his thought. One of his most controversial doctrines concerned a redefinition of "honor" in the typology of political constitutions. Honor had been regarded as the equivalent of "virtue" by many contemporaries, and as central to the function of the nobility in contemporary society, but the Baron of La Brède scandalized some readers with his argument that the "spirit of monarchy" is not self-renouncing virtue, but the laws, in conjunction with "honor" conceived of as personal status and recognition.[39] Since monarchy hinges by his definition on a manifest hierarchy of ranks and orders, it is useful rather than harmful for noblemen and would-be noblemen to spend their lives scrambling for what they see as their proper place in this visible hierarchy. The resulting competition for honor animates monarchy in much the way that vanity animates trade: by tapping into people's individual interests and their irrepressible desire to be admired by others. Unlike republican ambition, this monarchical honor is "not dangerous because it can constantly be repressed."[40]

It is striking that Montesquieu regards pride but not the "prejudice" of honor as "dangerous." Forty years later, many French revolutionaries would strongly disagree, as the National Assembly proceeded to abolish first feudalism (August 11, 1789) and then hereditary noble titles altogether (June 19, 1790).[41] One explanation would seem to be that in addition to being repressible, honor, like vanity, is interactive; it engages the individuals affected by it to enter at least somewhat sympathetically into the plans and desires of others if they want acknowledgment and validation for their own self-regarding purposes. Pride, on the other hand, is on this later account not interactive; it looks down at others with dismissive contempt and lofty disengagement. Just as Adam Smith would have his readers look for their dinner not to the "benevolence" or "humanity" of the butcher or baker but to their "self-love,"[42] so too does our Frenchman see the dynamic interactions of self-regarding people as paradoxically conducive to civilized social life.

Montesquieu's method of explaining this principle of interactivity is drawn directly from modern physics. "You could say," he writes, "that it is like the system of the universe, where there is a force constantly repelling all bodies from the center and a force of gravitation attracting them to it. Honor makes all the parts of the body politic move; its very action binds them, and each person works for the common good, while believing that he is working for his individual interests."[43] The process by which honor makes monarchy work is similar to the process by which the "slightly harebrained" dandies stimulate harmonious social action through the brisk trade and sociable exchanges called forth by their vanity. And both of these Mandevillean phenomena bear a family resemblance to Adam Smith's "invisible hand," by which the public economy is assured through the self-regarding actions of private people.[44]

TOWARD A VIRTUE ETHICS FOR COMMERCIAL SOCIETY: HUMANITY AND JUSTICE

Having said these things, one must nonetheless conclude that at bottom, Montesquieu's view of commercial morality was not really a Mandevillean one. His acceptance of the paradox that private prejudices and interests (honor and vanity) can contribute to the public good was never paired with a full-scale attack on the moral epistemology of prevailing Christian culture, as Mandeville's was. Instead, Montesquieu seems to have consistently harbored some version of the Stoic cosmopolitan view that the virtues are real, and that the social virtues bind human beings to each other in ever-expanding concentric circles of relationships. They begin with one's ties to friends and family (the moral virtues), move through one's attachments to the polity (the political virtues), and eventuate in one's affinity for all mankind (the virtues of humanity).

The very preface of his magnum opus shines a spotlight on the importance of the cosmopolitan virtues. He explains his authorial intention by writing, "By seeking to instruct men, one can practice the general virtue that includes love of all."[45] And in a later edition of the same work, he inserted a new section on what he dubbed "political virtue," primarily to rescue his work from the mistaken view that the unorthodox doctrine of honor surveyed above was meant to deny the possibility of virtue in monarchies. He defines political virtue as love of country and of the public good, and although he continues to maintain that such a disposition is unlikely in court-based societies, he parts company with Mandeville in attributing to this virtue a genuine "renunciation of self" in those places where it does exist.[46]

Underlying both the political and cosmopolitan virtues, and more important for our purposes, are the individual moral virtues. Their portrait is vividly rendered in the story of the Troglodytes. This tale, set forth early in *The Persian Letters*, tells of a people who have risen to prosperity and power by dint of two specific moral virtues planted in all of us by nature—namely, humanity and justice. Their Shaftesburian natural virtue, taught them at first by two Noah-like founder-figures, triumphs over a previously dominant Hobbesian egoism that had led them to the brink of extinction.[47] But having achieved this wealth and power, the people now want to elect a king. The elderly gentleman they choose—in terms redolent of the Israelites' demand for a king in 1 Samuel 8—warns them of the tragic mistake they would be making. Whereas in the Old Testament story, the error had been in rejecting the Lord (1 Samuel 8:7), the Troglodytes' miscalculation is in rejecting the life of natural virtue that they had been living. "Your virtue is beginning to burden you," he complains to them through bitter tears.[48]

As to the anatomy of this "virtue," Montesquieu is remarkably clear that it consists in the realization of two natural human dispositions: toward humanity and justice. In letter XI, for example, a physician who had cured the Troglodytes of their physical illnesses only to have them renege on their promises of payment accuses them of having "no humanity, no sense of the rules of justice." Then, in letter XII, after the Troglodyte community has been destroyed by its mutual egoism and just when its two Noah-like restorers are introduced to us, we are told these men are "humane, just, and lovers of virtue."[49]

Humanity and justice can thus be seen to emerge as key concepts for understanding both Montesquieu's tacit "virtue ethic" in general and the contours of his commercial morality in particular. Although they are natural dispositions, they form a distinctly modern pattern for Montesquieu. In his Roman history of a decade or so later he would write, "Since the Romans were accustomed to making sport of human nature in the person of their children and their slaves, they could scarcely know the virtue we call humanity."[50] Justice was prevalent in antiquity, but humanity was not; the latter, in fact, is presumed to be mostly a recent phenomenon. A major reason for this, it turns out, is that commerce is far more paradigmatic of the modern world than it was of antiquity.

COMMERCE AS SCHOOL OF HUMANITY AND JUSTICE

We are now in a better position to understand the most important statements that Montesquieu made about what I have called "commercial morality" and what he might have labeled the "spirit of commerce." They amplify and illuminate the author's long-standing pairing of humanity and justice, and they appear in the first of three books on commerce and money in *The Spirit of the Laws* (bks. 20–22). In the first chapter, the author makes a comment destined for a long future. "Commerce cures destructive prejudices," he writes, "and it is an almost general rule that wherever there are mild mores, there is commerce, and wherever there is commerce, there are mild mores."[51] The French phrase *le doux commerce* (mild commerce) has virtually passed into English usage since the 1970s.[52] Important in light of the foregoing is the interactive origin of these mild mores, as the author immediately adds, "Commerce has spread knowledge of the mores of all nations everywhere; they have been compared to each other, and good things have resulted from this."[53] Although the "mild mores" associated with commercial life are not expressly defined as identical to the key modern virtue of "humanity," they are clearly the soil in which that virtue naturally grows—even if much of the fertilizer had been supplied by the socially productive vice of vanity.

Also noteworthy here is that whereas humanity had earlier appeared as a natural and spontaneous disposition, it now seems that humanity is a function of knowledge bred by repeated cultural interaction, and of the reflection that arises out of such interaction. Humanity has thus moved from being a natural tendency to being a mature and ripened virtue that one should expect to be produced by an extended commercial order.[54] It is this riper virtue that Montesquieu no doubt had in mind when he remarked upon the absence of "the virtue we call humanity" among the Romans.

Such a favorable view of the moral dimension of trade is historically of the first importance; its novel character has been properly underscored by numerous commentators. But our humanity-justice spectrum helps put this treatment of commerce in its proper context. It turns out that these two important virtues do not automatically form a harmonious relationship in commercial society. Indeed, we find a double qualification to Montesquieu's "commerce equals mild mores" formula. The first is that although commerce "polishes and softens barbarous mores," it also "corrupts pure mores."[55] Here, Montesquieu evokes without resolving the fundamental issue that Rousseau would highlight for the later Enlightenment: the moral character of natural man. Although his contrasts between ancient and modern and between commerce and conquest make it unlikely that he would go as far as Rousseau in asserting the moral superiority of the "pure mores" of simple peoples, his story of the Troglodytes—where virtue seems to be corrupted partly at least by wealth and power—along with his comment here about the corruption of "pure mores" by commerce, remind us that for Montesquieu, civilization was not a one-dimensional process; there was loss as well as gain in the spread of commercial exchange.

A second qualification of the *doux commerce* theory lies in a distinction Montesquieu draws between the effects of commerce on state relations and on interpersonal ones. "The natural effect of commerce," he writes, "is to lead to peace."[56] This may be seen as his ultimate formulation of the commerce vs. conquest trope prevalent for nearly a century. But the pacifying effect applies only to relations between states. Trade does not necessarily have the same effect on the moral lives of individuals. He puts this qualification as follows: "In countries where one is affected *only* by the spirit of commerce, there is traffic in all human activities and all moral virtues; the smallest things, [even] those *required by humanity*, are done or given for money."[57] In the next sentence, he makes the same point in a somewhat different way: "The spirit of commerce produces in men a certain feeling for exact justice, opposed on the one hand to banditry and on the other to those moral virtues that make it so that one does not always discuss one's own interests alone and that one can neglect them for others' interests."[58]

The tepid quality of this endorsement of commercial morality is somewhat reminiscent of Adam Smith's famous discussion of the virtue of prudence, which, he asserts, "commands a certain cold esteem, but seems not entitled to any very ardent love or admiration."[59] And Smith, too, had a conception of "justice" far removed from the lofty heights of the Socratic dialogues, defining it as mainly a "negative virtue" that "does no real positive good" but instead "only hinders us from hurting our neighbor."[60] For Montesquieu, then, it appears that justice thusly conceived is an essential virtue but one that can become distorted if its sole function is to serve in the unbridled pursuit of one's own material interests. Better if it is somehow balanced with "humanity" or other "moral virtues."

His description of countries where *only* the spirit of commerce reigns contains a one-word footnote reading simply, "Holland." In a memoir of his travels to the Dutch republic in the late 1720s (published posthumously), he had complained that "nothing said about Dutch greed, fraud, and knavery is made up; it is all the pure truth. . . . The common people will ask for your whole wallet just for carrying your suitcase."[61] Government policy is partly to blame for these grasping habits. The Dutch face "ridiculous" and "crushing" taxes wherever they turn, and since many of these taxes had to be paid in cash on the spot, it was necessary to carry money around for the occasion. But whatever its cause, Montesquieu clearly believed—not unlike Adam Smith, of course—that an exclusively commercial spirit could put the virtues of justice and humanity out of balance.

Montesquieu never explicitly theorizes the relationship between the self-regarding passions of honor and vanity, on the one hand, and the moral virtues of justice and humanity, on the other. But even in his criticism of the grasping Dutch, the implication is strong that the mild mores associated with the rise of commercial society *ought* to make the virtues of both justice and humanity more rather than less prevalent. In fact, one can go further. The French verb in his famous sentence "Commerce cures destructive prejudices" is *guérit*, the same used for remedying a disease. That remedy itself, it seems clear, is the most important prerequisite for the flourishing of the modern tandem of virtues. Although both Montesquieu and Smith would adopt elements of Mandeville's moral revolution—in the Frenchman's case, by affirming the positive role of vanity and honor in certain economic and political circumstances—both thinkers nonetheless went beyond Mandeville in reconciling real moral character with the pragmatic requirements of modern commercial society, and in ways that are surprisingly similar.

CONCLUDING REMARKS: FROM COMMERCIAL MORALITY TO BUSINESS ETHICS?

It is clear, then, that virtue ethics is a helpful way to understand Montesquieu's distinctive approach to commercial morality in general and to business ethics in particular. He no doubt believed, with Mandeville, that vices were inescapable features of any human society. He further agreed that certain hitherto crudely reviled vices turned out to be indispensable in fueling the thriving commercial society of the age. Indeed, he applied this broadly Mandevillean perspective to his discussion of both vanity in commerce and honor in monarchical government.

On the other hand, Montesquieu gives a much narrower berth to "vices" than does his Anglo-Dutch predecessor. He takes much greater pains in distinguishing between what a behavioral scientist today might call "pro-social" and "anti-social" vices. Pro-social vices such as vanity and honor are not only acceptable but necessary because they serve the public interest, whether an extended trading network or the maintenance of a sociolegal hierarchy. Anti-social vices such as pride and arrogance are condemned because they divide men from each other and put the public interest at risk.

A commercial society must ultimately be judged not by the vices that it validates and channels, but by its effects on the virtues, and especially on the two essential virtues in Montesquieu's lexicon—namely, justice and humanity. When commerce cures destructive prejudices, its softening of mores becomes markedly conducive to the virtue of humanity, and it entails a thickening in the web of property relations that itself refines the natural disposition toward justice. Business ethics unfolds under the canopy provided by these two general virtues. It would consist in all the subsidiary virtues necessary to bring the broader virtues of humanity and justice to fruition. Montesquieu gives us some indication of what this would involve. He states summarily at one point, without elaborating, that "the spirit of commerce brings with it the spirit of frugality, economy, moderation, work, prudence, tranquility, order, and regularity."[62] This catalogue is a fair snapshot of the array of virtues that Montesquieu sees as sustaining the day-to-day routine of a commercial society. As long as they are active, moreover, the Frenchman believed they enable such a society to avoid the sort of systemic corruption that gross inequality of wealth brought to the great republics of antiquity, contributing so much to their downfall. A successful commercial society, then, would be one in which businesspeople conduct their affairs consistent with the requirements of the virtues of humanity and justice, and promote the subsidiary virtues just mentioned, while at the same time minimizing the distortive capacities of the "spirit of commerce" that defines the modern age.

NOTES

1. See Donald S. Lutz, "The Relative Importance of European Writers in Late Eighteenth-Century American Political Thought," *American Political Science Review* 189 (1984): 189–97.

2. See Claude Morilhat, *Montesquieu: Politique et richesses* (Paris: Presses universitaires de France, 1996), 6; see also Henry C. Clark, *Compass of Society: Commerce and Absolutism in Old-Regime France* (Lanham, MD: Lexington Books, 2007), 114.

3. Alasdair MacIntyre, *After Virtue: A Study in Moral Theory* (Notre Dame, IN: University of Notre Dame Press, 1981); and Deirdre McCloskey, *The Bourgeois Virtues: Ethics for an Age of Commerce* (Chicago: University of Chicago Press, 2006).

4. John Millar, *An Historical View of the English Government* (London: Mawman, 1803), 2:429–30n.

5. See Ronald Meek, "Smith, Turgot, and the 'Four-Stages' Theory," *History of Political Economy* 3, no. 1 (Spring 1971): 9–27. See also Henry C. Clark, "Montesquieu in Smith's Method of 'Theory and History,'" *Adam Smith Review* 4 (2008): 132–57. Istvan Hont, *Jealousy of Trade: International Competition and the Nation-State in Historical Perspective* (Cambridge, MA: Harvard University Press, 2005), 102, suggests that Montesquieu may in turn have gotten the idea from his fellow Bordelais Jean-François Melon's 1734 work *Essai politique sur le commerce*.

6. Montesquieu, *The Spirit of the Laws*, ed. and trans. Anne Cohler, Basia Miller, and Harold Stone (Cambridge: Cambridge University Press, 1989), 18.8, p. 289. Here and throughout, I cite the most readily available English-language editions of Montesquieu's works for convenience of reference, though I sometimes modify the translation itself.

7. See Aristotle, *Politics* I.8.1256a.31–1256b.8.

8. See, for example, Montesquieu, *My Thoughts*, ed. and trans. Henry C. Clark (Indianapolis: Liberty Fund, 2012), *Pensée*s 111, 118–22, 894–95, 1315, 1424, 2181. On this theme, see also Dan Edelstein, *The Enlightenment: A Genealogy* (Chicago: University of Chicago Press, 2010), esp. chap. 5.

9. For one example, see Abbé Gabriel-François Coyer, *La noblesse commerçante* (London: Duchesne, 1756), excerpted in Henry C. Clark, ed., *Commerce, Culture, and Liberty: Readings on Capitalism before Adam Smith* (Indianapolis: Liberty Fund, 2003), 418–23. For Montesquieu's explicit criticism of this view, see *The Spirit of the Laws*, 21.14.

10. The full title is *Considerations on the Causes of the Greatness of the Romans and Their Decline*, ed. and trans. David Lowenthal (New York: The Free Press, 1965; repr., Indianapolis: Hackett, 1999), XXI, 198.

11. Montesquieu, *The Spirit of the Laws*, 21.5, p. 357.

12. See Cicero's contrast of the naval hero Themistocles and the lawgiver Solon in *De officiis* I.22 for a typical example.

13. See Arthur Weststeijn, *Commercial Republicanism in the Dutch Golden Age: The Political Thought of Johan and Pieter De la Court* (Leiden: Brill, 2012), esp. 219–25.

14. For conquest vs. commerce as goals of modern states, see John Trenchard and Thomas Gordon, *Cato's Letters: Or, Essays on Liberty, Civil and Religious, And other Important Subjects*, ed. Ronald Hamowy, 4 vols. in 2 (Indianapolis: Liberty Fund, 1995), nos. 74, 87, 93, and 103, in 2:544–50, 626–31, 661–69, and 727–33. See also Steve Pincus, *1688: The First Modern Revolution* (New Haven, CT: Yale University Press, 2009), 347, 354, and passim.

15. Charles Rollin, *Histoire ancienne* (Paris: Estienne, 1740), 5:557; see Clark, *Compass of Society*, 106 n. 69.

16. Montesquieu, *My Thoughts, Pensée* 810, p. 236.

17. Ibid., *Pensée* 1602.

18. Montesquieu, *The Spirit of the Laws*, 1.3, p. 8.

19. "Richesses de l'Espagne," in Montesquieu, *Oeuvres complètes*, ed. André Masson (Paris: Nagel, 1950–55), 3:142–43 and 143 note a. This edition is cited as Montesquieu, *Oeuvres complètes*, below.

20. "Réflexions sur la monarchie universelle en Europe," XVIII, in Montesquieu, *Oeuvres complètes*, 3:378.

21. See Hont, introduction to *Jealousy of Trade*, 1–156.

22. Interestingly enough, he titles this diary entry "THAT IN ESSENCE, EVERYTHING IS EXCHANGE." See *My Thoughts, Pensée* 1694. The passage cited comes from Marcus Aurelius, *Meditations* VI.49.

23. Montesquieu, *The Spirit of the Laws*, 20.23, p. 352. The French word for "societies" (*sociétés*) can also mean "companies," as in commercial or financial enterprises.

24. See "Richesses de l'Espagne," in *Oeuvres complètes*, 3:142–43. But see his remarks on Poland in *The Spirit of the Laws*, 20.23, p. 352.

25. Montesquieu, *The Spirit of the Laws*, 21.5, p. 356. Similar personification had been found earlier in, for example, *Cato's Letters*, no. 64, 1:448: "Sometimes, indeed, trade, like a phantom, has made a faint appearance at an arbitrary court, but disappeared again at the first approach of the morning light: She is the portion of free states, is married to liberty, and ever flies the foul and polluted embraces of a tyrant." Here, however, commerce is distinctive of the English; for Montesquieu, on the other hand, it is distinctive of the modern world.

26. On this distinction, see Clark, *Compass of Society*, 117–19. See also Aristotle, *Politics* I.8–9; and Thomas Aquinas, *Summa theologiae*, II-II, q. 77, a. 4, obj. 3.

27. Montesquieu, *The Spirit of the Laws*, 20.5, p. 341.

28. Ibid., 21.20, p. 388.

29. Adam Smith, *An Inquiry into the Nature and Causes of the Wealth of Nations*, ed. R. H. Campbell, A. S. Skinner, and W. B. Todd (Indianapolis: Liberty Fund, 1981), III.iv.10–11, pp. 418–19.

30. Montesquieu, *The Spirit of the Laws*, 21.20, p. 389.

31. The fullest argument for a Mandevillean interpretation of Montesquieu is Céline Spector, *Montesquieu et l'émergence de l'économie politique* (Paris: Champion, 2006).

32. Montesquieu, *The Persian Letters*, ed. and trans. George Healy (1964; Indianapolis: Hackett, 1999), CVI, pp. 178–79.

33. Montesquieu, *My Thoughts, Pensée* 1553.

34. Ibid., *Pensée* 1439.

35. Ibid.

36. Montesquieu, *The Spirit of the Laws*, 19.8, p. 312. This is one of two explicit citations of Mandeville in the work; the other one appears at 7.1, p. 97, in a book on luxury.

37. Montesquieu, *The Spirit of the Laws*, 19.9, p. 312.

38. Ibid.

39. Ibid., 3.5–3.7.

40. Ibid., 3.7, p. 27.

41. On this theme, see Johnson Kent Wright, "A Rhetoric of Aristocratic Reaction? Nobility in *De l'esprit des lois*," in *The French Nobility in the Eighteenth Century*, ed. Jay Smith (University Park: Pennsylvania State University Press, 2006), 227–51.

42. Smith, *Wealth of Nations*, I.ii.2, pp. 26–27.

43. Montesquieu, *The Spirit of the Laws*, 3.7, p. 27.

44. See Smith, *Wealth of Nations*, IV.ii.9, p. 456; and Smith, *The Theory of Moral Sentiments*, ed. D. D. Raphael and A. L. Macfie (Indianapolis: Liberty Fund, 1982), IV.i.10, pp. 184–85, for this justly influential image.

45. Montesquieu, *The Spirit of the Laws*, Preface, xliv.

46. Ibid., 4.5, p. 35.

47. See the theory of the "moral sense" in Anthony Ashley Cooper (1671–1713), third Earl of Shaftesbury, *Characteristicks of Men, Manners, Opinions, Times* (1711), 3 vols. (Indianapolis: Liberty Fund, 2001), which answered Hobbes's egoism in *Leviathan* (1651), ed. Edwin Curley (Indianapolis: Hackett, 1994).

48. Montesquieu, *The Persian Letters*, XIV, p. 30.

49. Ibid., XI, XII, p. 25.

50. Montesquieu, *Considerations on the Romans*, XV, p. 136.

51. Montesquieu, *The Spirit of the Laws*, 20.1, p. 338.

52. For one indication, see the Google Ngram for *doux commerce* in English books from 1970 to the present: http://books.google.com/ngrams/graph?content=doux+commerce&year_start=1970&year_end=2012&corpus=0&smoothing=3. Albert Hirschman's *The Passions and the Interests: Political Arguments for Capitalism before Its Triumph* (Princeton, NJ: Princeton University Press, 1977), esp. 56–63, did much to revive this terminology. It is worth noting

that Montesquieu was adapting a term already widespread as a description of interpersonal relationships, especially between the two sexes.

53. Montesquieu, *The Spirit of the Laws*, 20.1, p. 338.

54. Relatedly, in a diary entry entitled "HISTORY OF COMMERCE," he wrote, "All peoples are so bound together [now] that the history of one always illuminates that of the others." See Montesquieu, *My Thoughts*, *Pensée* 1887.

55. Montesquieu, *The Spirit of the Laws*, 20.1, p. 338. The examples Montesquieu cites, such as the ancient Gauls, make clear that he is engaging in the familiar Tacitean move of pitting unspoiled tribal peoples against luxury-corrupted civilized ones.

56. Montesquieu, *The Spirit of the Laws*, 20.2, p. 338.

57. Ibid., 20.2, pp. 338–39, emphasis added.

58. Ibid., 20.2, p. 339.

59. See Smith, *Theory of Moral Sentiments*, VI.i.14, p. 216.

60. See Smith, *Theory of Moral Sentiments*, II.ii.i.9, p. 82.

61. Montesquieu, "Voyage en Hollande," in *Oeuvres complètes*, 2:1290.

62. Montesquieu, *The Spirit of the Laws*, 5.6, p. 48; see also Hirschman, *Passions and the Interests*, 71.

CHAPTER 11

Hume on Commerce, Society, and Ethics

Christopher J. Berry

In his lifetime (1711–76) David Hume was predominantly recognized as a (provocative) historian and as an essayist. Although *A Treatise of Human Nature* (1739–40) and its partial reworking in the *Enquiry concerning Human Understanding* (1748) and *Enquiry concerning the Principles of Morals* (1751) have now established him as a philosopher of world-historical importance and the focus of a library of academic commentary, some recent scholarship has revisited the publications for which he was contemporaneously known. In this essay I participate in that enterprise. My aim is to illustrate how Hume's combative defense of the emerging economic order required him, negatively, to overturn some long-established assumptions about the good life and economic activity and, positively, to fashion (albeit indicatively) a new ethical basis for the pursuit of commerce.[1]

In my execution of that aim I start with a cursory outline of the historical antipathy to commerce, and Hume's relation to some broad developments that questioned that disapprobation. The bulk of this essay traces how Hume set about overturning the prejudice against commerce. I argue that he undermines the critique of luxury, which was a key dimension of the case against commerce, while constructively he establishes that a modern commercial society is ethically superior, embodying as it does liberty for all under law, a materially better standard of living, and civilized personal relations.

THE CLASSICAL HERITAGE

Hume opens the first essay in his 1752 *Political Discourses*, the most immediately influential of his works, by making some justificatory methodological

observations. He states that it is his aim to develop some general propositions that will go beyond the particulars with which coffeehouse conversation concerns itself. This ability to "regard the general course of things"
he identifies as the "chief business of philosophers," who are able to take
an "enlarged" view and encompass the "infinite number of individuals" in
"universal propositions."[2] These observations set the scene for the volume
as a whole, as Hume tackles mistaken views about money and the rate of interest, develops arguments about taxation, population, and credit, and defends commerce and luxury. It is an aspect of that defense with which I am
here concerned.

In his essays "Of Commerce" and "Of Refinement in the Arts" (originally "Of Luxury" and retitled in 1760) Hume defends what his friend Adam
Smith calls a "commercial society." In summary, what he defends is not
only a society that is prosperous but also one in which prosperity is diffused;
all participants in the market, even the relatively poor, are better off absolutely than in any other period. The common good in a commercial society
is judged in terms of what promotes the material well-being of the many
not the few, something sumptuary laws were designed to preclude. Once
"triggered," modern prosperity develops in a mutually supportive fashion
alongside the rule of law and the strict administration of justice, with this
institutionalization of equity again being contrary to the legally enforced
hierarchy of sumptuary law and slavery. It is only through the operation
of a secure and equitable system of law, with its embedment of constancy
and predictability, that the confidence required for future-oriented market
behavior is enabled.

Life in a commercial society inherently involves interacting with large
numbers of people. The majority of these interactions would be indirect
and anonymous, and even when direct the majority of those would be with
strangers, so that in a commercial society the mode of interaction is predominantly impersonal and discretely functional rather than personal and
engaged in for its own sake. Living in a society where the rule of law is oper-
ant gives a particular modern form to liberty: the freedom to pursue one's
own interests in one's own way. A society that underwrites those diverse
pursuits will be pluralistic. Whether or not these pursuits are commercial
they will be undertaken within a peaceful environment or at least one in
which lawlessness is not endemic.[3]

The Humean defense was necessary because of a still-present social and
ethical prejudice against "trade" and merchants and what they stood for. As
a sweeping generalization, they represented private interests, which unless
contained were liable to undermine the public interest. The liability rested
on the inherent unlimited desire for those goods, typically supplied by trade
(unlike the local, principally agricultural produce), that provide pleasure,

Christopher J. Berry

especially of a corporeal or somatic sort. This unbridled desire constituted a threat because the distinction between the public/political and the private/economic was loaded. The former was understood to encompass intrinsically worthwhile activity exercised in the *agora* or *forum*, which was qualitatively distinct from the instrumental private tasks undertaken in the *oikos* or *familia*. The generic structure of this threat is that this instrumental role becomes perversely an end in itself, when, that is, particular private interests subvert the general public good.

This set of assumptions and prejudices was encapsulated in a negative view of luxury. A crucially influential expression was provided by Livy, who in the strategically placed preface to his history of Rome (*Ab urbe condita*) declared:

> No republic was ever greater, none purer (*sanctior*) or richer in good examples, none into which luxury and avarice entered so late or where poverty and parsimony were so honoured. It is true that the less wealth there was so there was less desire (*cupiditatis*). More recently riches have imported avarice and excessive pleasures (*voluptates*) with a craving for luxury and licence (*desiderium per luxum atque libidinem*) to the ruination of ourselves and all things.[4]

Livy was not alone. Sallust, who was, as we shall see, an explicit target of Hume's critique of this heritage, declared that public morals had been corrupted by the evils of luxury and avarice, the effects of which rendered men effeminate. Like Livy, he contrasted this corrupted condition with an earlier period in Rome's history when its citizens were frugal, just, and brave.[5] And as a final example we can cite Cicero, perhaps the most influential of all the Roman thinkers among eighteenth-century moralists, who proclaimed in *De officiis* that it was dishonorable (*turpe*) to sink into luxury and to live a soft life, but, in contrast, honorable (*honestum*) to live frugally, simply, soberly, and with self-restraint.[6]

Before proceeding to examine how Hume systematically dismantles these positions, we need to consider why this negative assessment of luxury resonated in the seventeenth and, especially, the eighteenth centuries. Once again we are forced into brazen generalization. The increasing pace of commercialization, evident in the availability of consumable goods like glass, chinaware, and silver tableware to an increasing percentage of the population (especially in England),[7] produced a raft of anxieties that commerce was destabilizing the social order. These Latin texts, which were educational staples,[8] served as a ready-made resource for critical responses. One of the most egregious responses was John Brown's enormously popular *Estimate* (1758). Brown exclaimed characteristically that once commerce has developed beyond the provision of conveniencies it "brings in superfluity and vast Wealth, [and] begets Avarice, gross Luxury or effeminate Refinement."[9]

THE CONTEXT OF HUME'S RESPONSE

It is a central part of Hume's entire project, as originally announced in the Introduction to the *Treatise*, to put philosophy on a "new footing" and, in so doing, reject this set of prejudices.[10] Of course he is not alone, and of course he is not a pioneer. We can identify (again sweepingly) two developments to which he is the heir. The first is a broad movement in early modern thought to displace the Aristotelian teleological framework. While Galilean physics was a decisive development, this was accompanied by a fundamental reevaluation of epistemology and ethics. Reason's motivating force is rejected in favor of that role being played by passions or desires. Hume accepts broadly John Locke's empirical version of this reevaluation, in that he rejects, on the one hand, the Cartesian strand of modern rationalism, and, on the other, departs from the egocentric individualistic implications of the work of Thomas Hobbes. That departure, however, does not contest Hobbes's basic proposition that humans are motivated by the passions (their appetites and aversions) so that reason's role is subordinately instrumental. Hence one of Hume's most famous/notorious declarations: "Reason is and ought only to be the slave of the passions, and can never pretend to any other office than to serve and obey them."[11]

The second development, and of more moment for this essay, was a defense of commerce. This had begun in the seventeenth century in pamphlets defending "trade." These writings were typically *pièces d'occasion* (defending, for instance, the private operations of East India Company) but employed the rhetoric of the national or public interest. The rhetoric betrayed a defensiveness. This can be detected, for example, in Thomas Mun's *England's Treasure by Forraign Trade* (published in 1664 but probably written earlier). Therein Mun defends what he calls the "noble profession" of the merchant, whose private endeavors will, when properly conducted, accompany the public good. However, in his text Mun still feels he has to criticize "Piping, Potting, Feasting, Fashion," which "hath made us effeminate . . . declined in our Valour." That is to say, he rehearses the stock ingredients of the Livian legacy.[12] The legacy began to weaken, for example, in 1690, Nicholas Barbon, while sidestepping the still-opprobrious term "luxury," produces a defense of "fashion" and "wants of the mind." By the latter he means anything that satisfies desire, such as those goods that "can gratifie his Senses, adorn his Body and promote the Ease, pleasure and Pomp of Life."[13] It is this gradual shift that Bernard Mandeville notoriously represents in the increasingly elaborate iterations of *The Fable of the Bees* (1721–32), with its more open defense of luxury.

HUME'S DEFENSE

I commence my analysis of Hume's vindication of commerce by selecting some elements of his defense of luxury.[14] His ostensible strategy in "Of Refinement of Arts" is to correct the extreme positions of those who, on the one hand, decry and those who, on the other, praise luxury tout court. In practice, the former, whom he calls "severe moralists" (Sallust is named as an example), more than the latter (represented, though he is unnamed, by Mandeville) are Hume's main target. While admitting that "luxury" is a word of "uncertain signification," Hume proceeds to define it as "great refinement in the gratification of senses."[15] This is far from an endorsement of the "severe" position, because he proceeds to observe that "ages of refinement" are "both the happiest and most virtuous."[16] There are two dimensions to that linkage. Luxury goods represent a source of pleasure or enjoyment that is intrinsically valuable in its own right.[17] In addition, instrumental benefits flow from the production of luxuries as consumption goods, since their participation in a system of commerce redounds to the general advantage or public good.

In a commercial society individuals are "happy and prosperous."[18] Hume analyzes happiness by identifying three interrelated components—repose, pleasure, and action.[19] Of these, the latter two are the most significant. The first of these is agreeable only as a necessary recuperative interlude, but if prolonged it subsides into lethargy and, in fact, "destroys all enjoyment." More telling is that Hume associates pleasure, the second component, with the corporeal enjoyment of commodities so far as "they gratify the senses and appetite."[20] In line with his definition, these commodities will be luxuries that "serve to the ornament and pleasure of life."[21] As such they are objects of desire, and given Hume's modernist psychology, humans are motivated to attain them; more exactly and significantly, it is the "desire for a more splendid way of life than what their ancestors enjoyed" that "rouses men from indolence."[22] This now leads to the third source of happiness. Hume thinks pleasure is attained as much from the activity itself as from its outcomes. There is, he affirms, "no craving or demand of the human mind more constant and insatiable than that for exercise and employment"; this "desire" seems, as a result, to be the "foundation of most of our passions and pursuits."[23]

There is a clear departure here from the classical disparagement of a commercial life. Instead of the good life where reason disciplined unruly desires, especially those for bodily satisfactions that are embodied in luxury goods, desires are the source of motivation. Hume's philosophical distance from this view of the good life is captured in his observation that the effective human motivations are "avarice and industry, art and luxury."[24]

Avarice was uniformly condemned by the classical moralists and standardly reiterated by their modern heirs. Hence, for example, Francis Hutcheson (whose opinion of the *Treatise* the young Hume sought), while a post-Lockean in his epistemology, judges avarice the "most deformed and most uneasy of vices."[25] When set against this backdrop, Hume's noncensorious invocation of avarice is notable. The statement from "Of Commerce" quoted above is not an isolated occurrence. Elsewhere avarice is depicted as one of the "chief governing principles" (alongside ambition and emulation);[26] indeed it is universal, operating "at all times on all persons."[27] There are scattered references in the *Second Enquiry* (where again it is often linked with ambition),[28] and Hume wrote a short essay explicitly on the topic for his first collection of *Essays* (1741), but it was one of those he later withdrew (1770). This essay does not contest the judgment that avarice is a vice, and acknowledges that it has always been criticized by moralists, but, observing that is also irreclaimable, Hume states his approval of those who treat it with "wit and humour" rather than in a more serious vein.[29] This "literary" theme is what pervades this exercise (the original title of the collection of essays described them as moral, political, and literary), and I do not regard this conceit as a serious counterweight to his other references.

What for our purposes is more significant is how avarice as a universal passion connects with Hume's science of man project. At the center of that project is his commitment to the uniformity of nature, which necessarily includes human nature. Human behavior, and thence human institutions, are fathomable because of "the constant and universal principles of human nature." On their basis the "moral philosopher," in exactly the same manner as "the natural philosopher," can fix "the principles of his science." These "principles" comprise the "regular springs" of human behavior. These "springs" are human passions, and in the *First Enquiry* Hume lists seven. One of these is avarice (ambition is another), but Hume's list also includes straightforwardly (in contrast to Hobbes's convolutions) friendship, generosity, and public spirit. These operate regardless of particular social context.[30] Hume supposes that a traveler's report that described a society of humans without avarice or ambition would immediately be detected as false, and the traveler a liar, just as it would be if the presence of centaurs and dragons were reported.[31]

Given that avarice is a fixed component of human nature then, like all such components, it cannot be moralistically wished away. Hume makes this point strongly. A regime (he has Sparta in mind) where everyone has a "passion for the public good" is contrary to the "natural bent of the mind."[32] Indeed to govern men along Spartan lines would require a "miraculous transformation of mankind."[33] Scientists of man do not deal in miracles but with what can be gleaned from experience, "from a cautious observation of human life . . . in the common course of the world."[34] On that basis, the effective human, all-too-human, motivations are "avarice" and "industry, art and luxury." These go "with the grain of human nature." To go against the "natural bent" is destructive on two fronts.

First, to go against the grain is "violent," as when a laborer is forced to toil to raise more from the land than what he needs for his family. If, rather, the laborer is furnished with "manufactures and commodities," then in line with human nature, he will of his own volition raise a surplus.[35] Hume makes a further point. Because it is in accord with "the most natural course of things" that "industry and arts and trade encrease the power of the sovereign as well as the happiness of the subjects,"[36] then policies that work with the grain make the nation stronger. From this it follows that an appropriate "economic policy" (such as free trade, property rights) is a key to the greater power enjoyed by modern states. Second, to work against the grain is counterproductive. Accordingly, if luxury were to be banished, then, in a point to be developed shortly, given it is "the spur of industry,"[37] incentives would disappear, and indolence would appear.[38] That is, by curing one supposed vice, another (and worse) is stimulated. Ethical questions in commerce or business are balancing acts more than they are pure prescriptions. Moreover, what tips the scales is which policy promotes the happiness (the material well-being) of individuals. On those grounds the sumptuary legislation enjoined by the severe moralists (past and present) is unwarranted and fruitless. Hume judged restrictions on consumption, as purposed by such laws, as not only ineffectual but also detrimental to human happiness, the enjoyment of material things.[39]

Hume's argument is that avarice should not be condemned root and branch in the manner of the severe moralists. They emphasize its deleterious societal consequences (the pursuit of luxuries); Hume, however, gives avarice a consequentially positive role. I want to develop this by picking up on the reference to "industry" as stimulated by avarice. Industry is an important notion in Hume. In the sense of "industriousness" (for which "business" is almost in all cases a synonym) it constitutes the major mode of expression for "action," a key component, as we have seen, in human happiness. Part of the significance of it taking this mode is negative. Action in the form of industry is to be distinguished from Cicero's *negotiis publicis*, the involvement in public or political affairs. Humean industry is a private endeavor. This has a further implication. The Ciceronian view reflects a particular Livian (civic) republican strain of liberty, which Cicero himself judges superior to another classical view of liberty, one that is manifest in those (such as Epictetus) who withdraw from the *forum* and in their "leisure" (*otium*) look for a literally apathetic (tranquil, contemplative) life.[40]

Hume typically, though not exclusively, associates industry with frugality.[41] This association reflects a shift. In the classical (and neoclassical) tradition *frugalitas* meant living simply, in accordance with the requirements of natural needs.[42] Frugality, along with austerity and poverty, was a component of Hume's "severe" morality.[43] This family of ideas characterized both strands of ancient liberty (each with their representatives in post-Renaissance thought). Cicero captured the common or shared core by explicitly associating *frugalitas* with *sōphrosunē*, the virtue of self-command, as crucially exhibited by control of (bodily) appetites and desires (*libidini*).[44] Those who exercise that control cannot experience poverty; it is only those who are governed by desire who judge they are poor when they cannot attain what they want. By the same token those who are rich are never rich enough; the seeker of the pleasures of luxury can never be satisfied.[45] As Livy declared, Rome's decline was caused by the falling away from frugality and falling into the embrace of luxury, occasioned by imports from the "East." This moral story still had a powerful hold; the Fall of Rome, according to eighteenth-century moralists, held a profound lesson for their own time.

Hume's account of frugality constitutes an implicit rejection of this family of ideas. He employs the term against the background of his account of the emergence of commerce out of the collapse of feudalism (see below). Where there is nothing but "a landed interest" there will be "little frugality" because landlords are "prodigal."[46] But with the development of commerce there is an increase in industry. This he declares "encreases frugality" because it gives rise to merchants. In sharp contrast to the "classical" prejudice, Hume describes merchants as "one of the most useful races of men," whose passion, he identifies without censure, is love of gain. Merchants are not inclined to dissipate this on selfish pleasure. Indeed in a reversal of that classical association their activities redound to the benefit of all. The explanation for this is that merchants "beget industry" as they distribute resources throughout society. This sets in train a process whereby competition among traders reduces profits, which causes a willing acceptance of low interest rates, which makes commodities cheaper, thus encouraging consumption and thereby "heightening the industry."[47] This marks a clear advance on an agricultural, as well as *oikos*-based, "economy."

One measure of this is improvement in the condition of the poor. Hume's modernist rejection of Aristotelian teleology enables him to displace the ethic of poverty, which made it matter of choice or will or reason, with a notion of impoverishment or necessitousness, that is, having no choice. In a commercial society the "poor" possess not merely the necessaries but also "many of the conveniencies" of life.[48] This is a resolutely positive development. Hume asseverates that "refinement on the pleasures and conveniencies of life has no natural tendency to beget venality and corruption."[49] This is a fairly obvious allusion to Sallust, for whom this tendency was the gravamen of his indictment of Catiline, who used his wealth corruptly to conspire against the integrity of the republic. For Hume the denial of the tendency means that any argument that "the poor" should not be allowed to enjoy refinement is misplaced. Hence, too, any justification for sumptuary legislation is invalid. There is still a further dimension to Hume's argument because it also enables him to distance his position from Mandeville, who advocated in a typically artful fashion that the poor should be "well-managed," so that while they should not starve, yet they "should receive nothing worth saving." Hume pointedly declares that even if the high price of labor has some disadvantage for foreign trade, nevertheless this consideration is insignificant in the face of the "happiness of many millions."[50] Appropriately, in ages of refinement "many" can now rightly "enjoy" the "finer arts"; such pleasures are not the prerogative of the (few) rich. This enjoyment, he affirms, adds more to the happiness of the poor than it diminishes that of the rich. Hume is no egalitarian, but he is clear that the poor enjoy the goods of life on the same materially sensory basis as anyone else.[51]

In the light of the moralized discourse he is overturning it is important that Hume rebuts the claim that a commercial society—one where, as Adam Smith said, "Everyman is . . . in some measure a merchant,"[52] that is, a society geared to the production of private wealth—is a militarily weak one. Hume has two strings to his bow. He first appeals to the evidence (a ploy also adopted by Mandeville).[53] The supposed causal link between a soft emasculating life of luxury and military weakness fails the test of constant conjunction, as manifest in the cases of France and England, that is, the two most powerful *and* most polished and commercial societies.[54] This latter causal link relies, as we noted above, on another, where the effect of "industry and arts and trade" is to enhance the power of the sovereign without at the same time impoverishing the people.[55]

The second string provides an explanation for this causality. The combination of strength and industry is made possible by the very "superfluity" that industry in the pursuit of luxury has created. In times of peace this superfluity goes to the maintenance of manufactures and the "improvers of liberal arts" (hallmarks of civilization), but should an army be needed the sovereign levies a tax, the effect of which is to reduce expenditure on luxuries. This frees up, for the military service, those who were previously employed in luxury-good production; they constitute a sort of "storehouse" of labor.[56] Nor does it follow that these will be inferior troops. The reverse is the case. Hume's explanation for this is that industry is one link in an "indissoluble chain" with knowledge and humanity.[57] While warfare is now conducted more humanely (better treatment of prisoners and so on),[58] the link to knowledge signals both the superior military hardware and the overall higher level of intellectual competence enjoyed by commercial societies. All that the "ignorant and unskilful" soldiers of rude nations can achieve are "sudden and violent conquests."[59] Behind this lies a more general point. If a society where luxury is enjoyed has not weakened military capacity, then the societal salience of martial virtues, such as courage, is diminished. Moreover, this for Hume is a positive development. He pointedly observes in the *Second Enquiry* that courage is the "predominant excellence" in "uncultivated nations," which lack comparatively "beneficence, justice, and the social virtues."[60] It is better to live in a beneficent and just society than in one where war is endemic. And once courage and other masculine virtues are downgraded, then the accusations of effeminacy and commitment to their own private good (rather than that of the public) leveled at merchants can be dismissed as irrelevant. In a well-established linkage, commerce is conducive to peace; if anything is central to the ethics of doing business it is that force is proscribed.[61]

REFINEMENT

We noted earlier that one expression of human desire was for a "more splendid way of life" than that experienced by the previous generations, and that this was a key incentive. The sought-for splendor is the essence of "refinement," which we can identify as the recognition of qualitative differences. The "severe" view treats all departures from functionality as redundant. More than that it is a moral failing, as exemplified by Seneca, who pointed out that since the "end" of food is to assuage hunger (and fuel the body), then stale bread is as functional as fresh, so that to desire fresh bread in preference is to succumb to the allurements of luxury.[62] To develop refinement, as manifest both in the presence of qualitatively differentiated goods and in the ability to appreciate both the skill and the beauty of a fine meal or splendid apparel, is not to indulge in excess. Excess, as exhibited by the uncultivated "gluttonous Tartars,"[63] is mere quantitative increase beyond some fixed sum, but, as such, it is conceptually distinct from qualitative refinement.

This recognition of the value of refinement, what Hume also calls "delicacy," is thus intrinsic to the advantages conveyed by industry. In an apt coupling, Hume refers to an "industrious and civilized" nation. Such a society is characterized by its inhabitants possessing the "desire to have every commodity in the utmost perfection."[64] There is an implicit dynamism here. Hume recognizes, as did Melon and Mandeville before him,[65] that onetime luxuries become necessities. This implies that the relation between them is relative. There is not some fixed intrinsic natural/rational criterion (such as "need") to distinguish them, as implied by classical and neoclassical Stoics alike.[66] In the absence of some immutable or given norm, in terms of which appropriate limits can be established, the "value" humans attach to "any particular pleasure depends on comparison and experience."[67]

A commercial society, galvanized by the pursuit of consumables to gratify human desires, promotes employment, industry, and population, together with all-around national strength and relative opulence, which improves the conditions of the poor, is thus in sum a superior form of life to that enjoined by Aristotle and his many heirs. Before turning to an additional positive factor, we can note that Hume's argument enables him to allow that luxury can be "vicious" as well as innocent (virtuous). What he means by vicious is non-beneficial or without advantage to the public.[68] This permits him to dismiss Mandeville's position as casuistry—he sees no need to deny (using Sallustian imagery) that pernicious luxury is poisonous.[69] In effect, "vicious luxury" for Hume describes an individual who, by seeking to gratify only his own desires, is unable to execute those "acts of duty and generosity" that his station and fortune require. Even here the thrust is that the effect of the virtue of relieving the poor is to disperse gratifications more widely to public advantage. This is a utilitarian calculation, a trade-off. Without the spur to industry that luxury supplies, individuals (and thence their society) will fall into sloth and idleness and become impoverished. The social and individual cost of such outcomes outweighs any benefits that might conceivably accrue from proscribing luxury—a circumstance the historical record bears out.[70]

JUSTICE, LAW, AND LIBERTY

One of the key advantages of a commercial society is that "the progress of arts" that it exemplifies is "favourable to liberty."[71] This is both a historical and a conceptual argument. The former, merely sketched in his *Essays*, is spelled out at length in his *History of England*. He refers to a "secret revolution [of government]," the crux of which is the institution of the rule of law, or, as he terms it, the emergence of "general and regular execution of laws."[72] This arose causally from a two-stage process.[73] First, the cause was the loss by the barons of their localized power bases, which thus removed the key obstacle to central authority.[74] In the feudal era, these barons expended their surplus on "ancient hospitality" and maintained many dependent retainers. However, "by degrees" the nobility acquired a "taste for elegant luxury" in housing and apparel. Their surplus was now expended on the attainment of these goods for their personal gratification, which caused them to release their now-useless retainers and thus eroded their power. The second stage has itself two phases. Initially, in the wake of the decline of the barons, the sovereign took advantage to assume an "authority almost absolute," but, then, in England this discretionary power too began to be curtailed by "regular execution of laws." The cause of this subsequent curtailment was the rise of the Commons, composed of the middle rank, who comprised the now-independent former retainers. As the wealth of this rank increased, pari passu with the growth of commerce (and cities) that had been initially fueled by the provision of luxury goods, so they accreted financial power. These tradesmen and merchants "covet equal laws" and, in so doing, they constitute the "best and firmest basis of public liberty," because their business requires the security that comes from the consistent and predictable (regular) operation of law and without which "markets" will not function.[75]

This "modernization process," as Carl Wennerlind calls it,[76] now introduces the conceptual argument that links the emergence of commerce, industry, including merchants, and liberty in its definitive modern form (the "new plan of liberty")[77] of those "equal laws." A manufacturer will only specialize in producing a particular product on the expectation that others will want it, and that belief about their desire is itself premised on the belief that others are producing different products. For markets to function the participants have to act now in expectation of future return. Hume captures this:

> The poorest artificer, who labours alone, *expects* at least the protection of the magistrate, to ensure him the enjoyment of the fruits of his labour. He also *expects* that when he carries his goods to market and offers them at a reasonable price, he shall find purchasers and shall be able, by the money he acquires, to engage others to supply him with those commodities which are requisite for his subsistence. In proportion as men extend their dealings and render their intercourse with others more complicated, they always comprehend in their schemes of life a greater variety of voluntary actions which they *expect*, from the proper motives, to co-operate with their own. In all these conclusions they take their measures from past experience.[78]

Although Hume prefaces this observation with the declaration that "the mutual dependence of men is so great in all societies," it is clear that he is here presuming a commercial context. What is required to underwrite this interdependency is predictability or confidence. This relies on social stability and security, the source of which is the "protection of the magistrate" together with the administration of government, which "must act by general laws that are previously known to all the members."[79] When that obtains, then the state is free. Where rule is capricious or fickle (the hallmarks of absolute rule) not only is liberty imperiled but the consequence will be that the actions of others are not predictable, whereupon it is better (more prudent) to be independent and self-sufficient.[80] Of course, since this is generalizable, then there is effectively no market and hence, as Smith was to spell out, for all intents and purposes no division of labor, and thus miserable poverty.[81] It is this set of conceptual linkages that provides a key explanation for the central role that justice plays in Hume's political philosophy; without the "inflexible" operation of justice, he proclaims, "society must immediately dissolve."[82]

Hume's analysis of justice is the most examined (and criticized) aspect of his entire social and political philosophy, and all I can aim to do is intimate where it might bear most obviously on "business ethics." Justice is constituted by rules, and these must operate inflexibly, otherwise the background certainty required for specialization will not occur. The central subject matter of justice is property. The first of Hume's three rules of justice serves to stabilize possession so that it becomes "property" (the second governs transfer of property by consent, and the third deals with promising or contracts).[83] The polemical dimension to this "narrow" construction of justice I cannot here pursue,[84] but this particular emphasis on justice is the closest Hume gets to a sense of "business ethics." Business, in the sense of economic transactions, is governed by strict observance of justice. This can be inferred from Hume's discussion of the miser, who justly receives a great fortune. He neither deserves this bounty (he did nothing to obtain it) nor does he need it because ex hypothesi his antipathy to profligacy means he has the resources to meet whatever self-limited needs he has. Others in greater need or in some regard more deserving could make better use of this bounty. The miser did, however, receive his money justly, and to "interfere" is to compromise his property rights. Hume admits this "single act" of justice may be "in itself prejudicial to society," but what matters is the "whole plan or scheme."[85] If that "plan" loses its integrity, if justice is made flexible, and thus the security of property rights compromised, then the expectations, necessarily accreted by experience, as Hume famously outlines in the *Treatise* in his discussion of the emergence of conventions, will be damaged and undermine the whole basis upon which social order is built.[86]

This theory thus distinguishes justice from other virtues. In line with jurisprudential conventions one criterion of that distinction is that questions of justice are enforceable, while the obligations attending (say) benevolence or mercy are less exacting. One consequence of this is that any wider notion of "corporate responsibility" cannot be made compulsory; by contrast, infringements of justice, such as breaking contracts, fraudulent practices, are justiciable. It is not that Hume has no room for benevolence or other social virtues, which, unlike the artifice of justice, are natural, but they are prone to flexibility and unable to sustain society, given the confined generosity of humankind in a situation of relative scarcity.[87] To think a society, especially perhaps but not exclusively a commercial one, could operate as if benevolence were the dominant motive is once again to go against the grain of human nature; as Hume puts it in the *Treatise*, "Being thus acquainted with the nature of man we expect not any impossibilities from him."[88] Hume immediately glosses that point to counsel that when making moral judgments we should "confine our view to that narrow circle" in which a person moves. We in our turn can gloss that to signal that economic actors, individual and corporate, should be assessed within the operational context of their "business." As would be the case if the imperfect duty of charity were to be imposed, so to impose a duty of "social responsibility" could be judged from a Humean perspective to be "violent."

Hume's argument here reverts back to his view of liberty. He supports positive action to remove hindrances to the exercise of economic liberty. For him government has "no other object or purpose but the distribution of justice."[89] Deviations from that "purpose" are thus properly subject to criticism. Hence he calls "absurd" the limitations on industry imposed by city corporations or companies of merchant adventurers, the seven-year apprenticeship in the cloth industry, and the fixing of wages by statute. In a similar vein he judges usury laws "unreasonable and iniquitous" and regards as "pernicious" the consequences of granting patent monopolies.[90] In addition to advocating the removal of hindrances, Hume argues for consistent, non-arbitrary taxation[91] and free trade, arguing forcefully against the "narrow and malignant" policies of prohibition.[92]

CONCLUDING REMARKS

Hume's philosophical contribution to the ethical foundations of wealth and commerce is both positive and negative. In the latter register he supplies one of the most powerful "de-moralizations" of luxury.[93] This is a significant contribution in two respects. First, he helped to undermine the authority of the long-standing condemnation of luxury as a source, and as an expression, of individual and societal corruption, as it gave deleterious rein to the limitlessness of desires and what pandered to them. Second, because this tradition still carried authority in the intense debate in the eighteenth century (re)generated by the emergence of a new form of economy, based on commerce and industry rather than land, then this excavation was not of merely antiquarian interest but helped shape that debate in favor of the emergent commercial order.

His positive contribution was to sketch out the conceptual and ethical underpinnings of that order. The solidity of a commercial society lies in the security of opinion (on which all authority ultimately rests), in that subjects (many) have to believe in the rightfulness (of the few) to govern.[94] That security in turn reposes proximately on the consistent operation of the rule of law (the inflexible administration of justice), and that operation itself reposes ultimately on the regularity of human behavior. As Hume says in the *Treatise*, in "politics, war, commerce, oeconomy,"[95] there is an evidential basis for that regularity, which, thus, can be scientifically investigated. The outcome of this investigation will (he is confident) put all knowledge on a "new footing." The science of man also in this way encompasses morality. Hume is clear that a modern society is normatively superior to those supported by Aristotle, Epictetus, Aquinas, or Machiavelli and their various modern followers. This superiority is evident in the greater extent of material satisfactions as more people legitimately enjoy better food, housing, and apparel. They also experience more "civilized" relations, as they aptly engage civilly and urbanely with each other in the cities and towns to which they now flock.[96] Perhaps above all those who live in a commercial society enjoy a degree of freedom, of personal liberty, that is not found in earlier societies. Of course, Hume is not blind to disadvantages such as the dangerous growth of public debt, but in his eyes we are now happier and freer than heretofore and on those grounds the morals of commerce are to be commended.

NOTES

1. In this discussion I refer primarily to "commerce." In Hume's time "business" generally conveyed the meaning of "busy-ness" rather than a particular trade or occupation, let alone a sphere of "society." There are occasional references that seemingly prefigure later usage; see, for example, "Of Commerce" in David Hume, *Essays: Moral, Political, and Literary*, ed. Eugene Miller (Indianapolis: Liberty Fund, 1985), 254; or consider Hume's reference to war as the "business of soldiers" in "Of Refinement in the Arts," in *Essays*, 275.

2. Hume, "Of Commerce," in *Essays*, 253–54.

3. For a full account, see Christopher J. Berry, *The Idea of Commercial Society in the Scottish Enlightenment* (Edinburgh: Edinburgh University Press, 2013). I borrow this summary characterization from chapter 7 of that work.

4. Livy, *From the Founding of the City*, Loeb Classical Library (London: Heinemann, 1919), I.11–12; translation modified.

5. Sallust, *The War with Catiline*, Loeb Classical Library (London: Heinemann, 1921), paras. 5, 9.

6. Cicero, *The Offices*, Loeb Classical Library (London: Heinemann, 1913), I.30.

7. See, for example, M. Berg, *Luxury and Pleasure in Eighteenth-Century Britain* (Oxford: Oxford University Press, 2005); N. McKendrick, J. Brewer, and J. H. Plumb, eds., *The Birth of a Consumer Society* (London: Hutchinson, 1983).

8. Hume, "Of Refinement in the Arts," 275, refers to "all the Latin classics whom we peruse in our infancy."

9. John Brown, *An Estimate of the Manners and Principles of the Times*, 7th ed. (London, 1758), 1:153. Brown also captured in a telling image the fear of destabilization, caused by the advancement of commerce, when he judged "a chain of Self-Interest is indeed no better than a Rope of Sand: There is no Cement nor Cohesion between the Parts" (1:111).

10. Hume, *A Treatise of Human Nature*, ed. L. A. Selby-Bigge, 2nd ed., rev. P. H. Nidditch (Oxford: Clarendon Press, 1978), xvi.

11. Hume, *Treatise*, 415.

12. Thomas Mun, *England's Treasure by Forraign Trade*, in *Early English Tracts on Commerce*, ed. J. McCulloch (Cambridge: Economic History Society, 1952), 122, 193.

13. Nicholas Barbon, *A Discourse of Trade*, ed. J. Hollander (Baltimore: Johns Hopkins University Press, 1905), 14.

14. For fuller versions, see Christopher J. Berry, *The Idea of Luxury* (Cambridge: Cambridge University Press, 1994); and Berry, "Hume and Superfluous Value (or What's Wrong with Epictetus' Slippers)," in *David Hume's Political Economy*, ed. Carl Wennerlind and Margaret Schabas (London: Routledge, 2008), 49–64. I draw on some of this material in what follows.

15. Hume, "Of Refinement in the Arts," 268.

16. Ibid., 269.

17. Hume, "Of Commerce," 264.

18. Hume, "Of Refinement in the Arts," 272.

19. Ibid., 269–70.

20. Hume, "Of Commerce," 263.

21. Hume, "Of Refinement in the Arts," 272.

22. Hume, "Of Commerce," 264.

23. Hume, "Of Interest," in *Essays*, 300.

24. Hume, "Of Commerce," 263.

25. Francis Hutcheson, *A Short Introduction to Moral Philosophy* (1747), ed. Luigi Turco (Indianapolis: Liberty Fund, 2007), 92.

26. Hume, "Of Some Remarkable Customs," in *Essays*, 371.

27. Hume, "Of the Rise of the Arts and Sciences," in *Essays*, 113.

28. Hume, *Enquiries Concerning Human Understanding and Concerning the Principles of Morals*, ed. L. A. Selby-Bigge, 3rd ed., rev. P. H. Nidditch (Oxford: Clarendon Press, 1975), 189, 271, 282.

29. Hume, "Of Avarice," in *Essays*, 571.

30. I have elsewhere labeled this a "non-contextualist" theory; Christopher J. Berry, *Hume, Hegel, and Human Nature* (The Hague: Nihoff, 1982).

31. Hume, *Enquiries*, 84.

32. Hume, "Of Commerce," 262–63. Compare James Moore, "Hume's Political Science and the Classical Republican Tradition," *Canadian Journal of Political Science* 10 (1977): 809–39.

33. Hume, "Of Refinement in the Arts," 280. Sparta was a standard "model" for an uncorrupt society, in contrast to the degeneracy, as it was seen, in contemporary Britain. See Peter N. Miller, *Defining the Common Good* (Cambridge: Cambridge University Press, 1994), 113–20.

34. Hume, *Treatise*, xix.

35. Hume, "Of Commerce," 262.

36. Ibid., 260.

37. Hume, "Of Civil Liberty," in *Essays*, 93.

38. Hume, "Of Refinement in the Arts," 280.

39. Hume, *History of England* (London: George Routledge, 1894), 1:535; 2:231, 602. There is an extensive literature on sumptuary legislation as enacted across Europe. For a recent survey, see Maria Giuseppina Muzzarelli, "Reconciling the Privilege of the Few with the Common Good: Sumptuary Laws in Medieval and Early Modern Europe," *Journal of Medieval and Early Modern Studies* 39 (2009): 587–617. Although this legislation petered out earlier in England than elsewhere, it still had advocates in the eighteenth century, as exemplified by George Berkeley in his "Essay toward preventing the ruin of Great Britain" (1727), in *The Works of George Berkeley, Bishop of Cloyne*, ed. A. A. Luce and T. E. Jessop (Edinburgh: Nelson, 1953), VI, 77.

40. Cicero, *Offices*, I.20–21.

41. Hume, *Enquiries*, 242, 277, 313.

42. For Seneca, for example, poverty is experienced only by those who exceed natural limits (*De consolatione ad Helviam*, in his *Moral Essays*, Loeb Classical Library [London: Heinemann, 1932], 11. 3), while Sir George Mackenzie, in 1691, enjoined "us [to] embrace ancient Frugality, under whose empire Vice was of old curbed with great success and which by freeing us from Poverty, secures us against all Snares which it occasions" (*Moral History of Frugality* [London, 1711], 292). Similarly the civic republican Algernon Sidney declared in 1698 that poverty is "the mother and nurse of . . . virtue" (*Discourses concerning Government* [1698], ed. Thomas G. West [Indianapolis: Liberty Press, 1990], 254). Supporters of frugality also typically enjoined sumptuary legislation. See, for example, Charles Davenant, "Foreign Trade Beneficial" and "Essays on Peace and War," both in *The Political and Commercial Works of Charles Davenant* (London, 1771), 1:390–92, 4:424.

43. Hume, "Of Refinement in the Arts," 269. See Cicero quoted above in the text.

44. Cicero, *Tusculan Disputations,* Loeb Classical Library (London: Heinemann, 1927), 3.8.

45. See Epictetus, *The Manual and Discourse,* Loeb Classical Library (London: Heinemann, 1928), I, 483.

46. Hume, "Of Interest," 298–99.

47. Ibid., 302–3.

48. Hume, "Of Commerce," 266.

49. Hume, "Of Refinement in the Arts," 276.

50. Bernard Mandeville, *The Fable of the Bees* (1732), ed. F. B. Kaye (Indianapolis: Liberty Fund, 1988), I, 193; Hume "Of Commerce," 265.

51. E. G. Hundert identifies in Hume a commitment to a "psychological egalitarianism"; Hundert, "The Achievement Motive in Hume's Political Economy," *Journal of the History of Ideas* 35 (1974): 139–43.

52. Adam Smith, *An Inquiry into the Nature and Causes of the Wealth of Nations*, ed. R. H. Campbell, A. S. Skinner, and W. B. Todd (Indianapolis: Liberty Fund, 1982), I.iv.1, p. 37.

53. Mandeville, *Fable*, I, 122–23.

54. Hume, "Of Refinement in the Arts," 275; *History of England,* II, 598–99.

55. Hume, "Of Commerce," 260.

56. Ibid., 261–62; "Of Refinement in the Arts," 272.

57. Hume, "Of Refinement in the Arts," 271.

58. In his *History of England* (I, 498) Hume implicitly connects the development of artillery with humanity when he observes that, though "contrived for the destruction of mankind," it has "rendered battles less bloody and has given greater stability to civil societies."

59. Hume, "Of Commerce" 261; *History of England,* I, 627.

60. Hume, *Enquiries*, 255. Compare *History of England,* I, 115; II, 81.

61. The doctrine of *doux commerce* was most influentially propounded by Montesquieu; see Montesquieu, *De l'esprit des lois* (1748) (Paris: Garnier, 1989), 20.2.

62. Seneca, *Moral Letters,* Loeb Classical Library (London: Heinemann, 1917), no. 119.

63. Hume, "Of Refinement in the Arts," 272.

64. Hume, "Of the Jealousy of Trade," in *Essays,* 329.

65. J-F. Melon, *Essai politique sur le commerce* (Amsterdam, 1735), 123; Mandeville, *Fable*, I, 169–72.

66. Fénelon, the most influential critic of luxury in early eighteenth-century France, contrasted *les arts superflus* to *les vrais besoins,* which were imposed by nature; see François Fénelon, *Les aventures de Télémaque* (1699), ed. J. Goré (Florence: Sansoni, 1962), 454. For discussion of Fénelon, see P. Bonolas, "Fénelon et le luxe dans le Télémaque," *Voltaire Studies* 249 (1987): 81–90; and for his impact, Istvan Hont, "The Early Enlightenment Debate on Commerce and Luxury," in *The Cambridge History of Eighteenth-Century Political Thought,* ed. M. Goldie and R. Wokler (Cambridge: Cambridge University Press, 2006), 371–418. Hume's rapidly translated *Discourses* made a notable contribution to the French debate; see L. Charles,

"French 'New Politics' and the Dissemination of David Hume's *Political Discourses* on the Continent," in Wennerlind and Schabas, *David Hume's Political Economy*, 181–202.

67. Hume, "Of Refinement in the Arts," 276; *Treatise*, 290.

68. Hume, "Of Refinement in the Arts," 269, 278.

69. Ibid., 279. See Sallust, *Catiline,* para. 11.

70. See his account of England under Elizabeth, when the "nobility were by degrees acquiring a taste for elegant luxury"; although this led to the decay of "glorious hospitality," yet it is "more reasonable to think that this new turn of expense promoted arts and industry, while the ancient hospitality was the source of vice, disorder, sedition and idleness" (*History of England,* II, 601).

71. Hume, "Of Refinement in the Arts," 277.

72. Hume, *History of England,* II, 603.

73. This is famously described by Smith, but he acknowledges Hume's account in the *Essays*; see Smith, *Wealth of Nations*, III.iv.4, p. 412.

74. Hume, *History of England,* II, 602–3.

75. Hume, "Of Refinement in the Arts," 277–78.

76. Carl Wennerlind, "David Hume"s Political Philosophy: A Theory of Commercial Modernization," *Hume Studies* 28 (2002): 247–70. See also John Danford, *David Hume and the Problem of Reason* (New Haven, CT: Yale University Press, 1990), chap. 7.

77. Hume, *History of England,* II, 602.

78. Hume, *Enquiries,* 89, emphasis added.

79. Hume, "Of the Origin of Government," in *Essays*, 41.

80. Hume, "Of Civil Liberty," 92.

81. Smith, *Wealth of Nations*, Introduction.4, p. 10. Hume himself claims ("Of Commerce," 265) that "the poverty of the common people is a natural, if not an infallible effect of absolute monarchy."

82. Hume, *Treatise,* 494, 532; compare *Enquiries,* 199.

83. Hume, *Treatise,* 526.

84. For perhaps the most painstaking treatment, see Jonathan Harrison, *Hume's Theory of Justice* (Oxford: Clarendon Press, 1981). I have given an explanation for that putative narrowness in Christopher J. Berry, *David Hume* (New York: Continuum, 2009) and a wider contextual account in Berry, *Idea of Commercial Society*, chap. 5.

85. Hume, *Treatise,* 497, 579.

86. Ibid., 490. Hume's account lends itself to analytical treatments: see Russell Hardin, *Hume's Moral and Political Theory* (Oxford: Oxford University Press, 2007), chap. 6, for a robust nontechnical account; see also William Charron, "Convention, Games of Strategy, and Hume's Philosophy of Law and Government," *American Philosophical Quarterly* 17 (1980): 327–34; and P. Vanderschraaf, "Hume's Game Theoretic Business Ethics," *Business Ethics Quarterly* 9 (1999): 47–67.

87. Hume, *Treatise,* 484–85.

88. Ibid., 602.

89. Hume, "Of the Origin of Government," 37.

90. Hume, *History of England,* II, 56–57, 323, 231, 573, 595; III, 83–84n.

91. Hume, "Of Taxation," in *Essays,* 345.

92. Hume, "Of the Jealousy of Trade," 328; and see also "Of the Balance of Trade," in *Essays*. The case for Hume as a "liberal" is well made in John B. Stewart, *Opinion and Reform in Hume's Political Philosophy* (Princeton, NJ: Princeton University Press, 1992) and in Neil McArthur, *David Hume's Political Theory: Law, Commerce, and the Constitution of Government* (Toronto: University of Toronto Press, 2007). These works counter the reading of Hume as a "conservative"; I discuss this question, and the literature it has generated, in Christopher J. Berry, "Science and Superstition: Hume and Conservatism," *European Journal of Political Theory* 10 (2011): 141–55.

93. I coined this term in Berry, *Idea of Luxury,* pt. 3, to summarize the shift from the classical/Christian moralized perspective to that developed in early modern thinking. It has become a common referent in the literature.

94. Hume, "Of First Principles of Government," in *Essays,* 322–23. See also "Of the Origin of Government," 40; and *History of England,* III, 395.

95. Hume, *Treatise,* 405.

96. Hume, "Of Refinement of the Arts," 271.

CHAPTER 12

The Fortune of Others: Adam Smith and the Beauty of Commerce

Douglas J. Den Uyl

I know of a professor of economics who used to tell his students that if they could find any positive statements about businessmen in Adam Smith's *Wealth of Nations* he would give them a thousand dollars. The challenge is no doubt risky, but the point it makes is worth notice. It is Adam Smith who is commonly regarded as an apologist for business interests and for the system that allows those very interests to predominate. It is also Adam Smith who has historically been considered by some scholars to have effectively abandoned ethical concerns when it came to writing the *Wealth of Nations*, despite the fact that he has a long and subtle treatise on ethics entitled *A Theory of Moral Sentiments*.[1] In this respect, both of these views of Smith have the common dimension of being significantly misleading or mistaken. It shall be part of our mission in what follows to alter these impressions.

Because the question of commerce generally is so central to interpreting Smith's social theory as a whole, dealing with it adequately would require a comprehensive interpretation of his entire corpus. Obviously such an effort cannot be accomplished here.[2] Instead, we shall try to limit ourselves to the chief characteristics of the commercial actor and the norms that might govern her conduct. In doing so we shall begin by clearing away a few misconceptions about Smith and then continue by using Smith's *Theory of Moral Sentiments* as a base for understanding the parameters of appropriate commercial action. One of the main misconceptions was just mentioned—namely, that Smith was a mere apologist for business and the free market. Smith, as my economist friend suggested, did not have an overly rosy, or often even favorable, view of persons engaged in trade, at least when they turn their focus to public matters. The following well-known passage is representative rather than unique in the *Wealth of Nations*:

> People of the same trade seldom meet together, even for merriment and diversion, but the conversation ends in a conspiracy against the publick, or in some contrivance to raise prices. (*WN* I.x.c.27)[3]

Of course, that Smith may have had some harsh things to say about business-people does not show that he is a critic of a system that encourages commercial conduct. Indeed, critical comments like the foregoing address a subset of the class of commercial actors, not commercial *action* per se. In modern society, virtually every ordinary citizen is a commercial actor, indicating that these sorts of criticisms concern abuses of commercial conduct, not a description of their essence.

Does this last point imply that Smith is an advocate of laissez-faire and an apologist for business interests? Such conclusions are themselves miscontruals of Smith's thought. In recent years a cadre of scholars known as "left Smitheans" has emerged who see Smith as a precursor to contemporary left-leaning social sympathies and ideological outlooks. In large part this reading is fueled by Smith's evident concern for relieving the plight of the lower classes,[4] his allowances for interventions by the state,[5] and his comments about businessmen identified above.[6]

By contrast, "right Smitheans" like to point to Smith's general approval of commercial culture, his advocacy of a "system of natural liberty,"[7] his view that public benefits can arrise unintentionally through private action (*WN* IV.i.1.10), and his rather parsimonious employment of state interventions in the economy (V.i.f.16). However, it shall not be, and cannot be, our purpose here to adjudicate between the alternative ideological readings of Smith. Our purpose instead is to identify the salient features of commercial action[8] and to derive certain principles of wise and appropriate conduct as Smith might see it. Our focus is thus not limited to certain subgroups of commercial actors such as managers, laborers, or employers, but to commercial actors generally, since Smith clearly measures—as we shall see—the conduct of individuals or groups against general social norms of appropriateness. In exploring appropriateness, we shall be offering an "aesthetic" reading of Smith. We shall, in other words, be arguing that an important dimension of commercial conduct is the "vision" of the actors, both as they see themselves fitting into society and as they envision the various elements of their own lives. By "vision" we mean an act of the imagination whereby diverse elements are regarded by the agent as fitting together in such a way that their interrelationship becomes both attractive in itself and normative for determining what is and is not appropriate. That fittingness is the basis for what is called "beauty" in what follows. Our overall thesis then is that commerce for Smith has more to do with beauty than utility at both the individual and social levels. Furthermore, the beauty of commerce is the basis for establishing norms of appropriateness for the governance of commerce.

The first section concentrates on the qualities Smith expects will and should characterize the actor in a commercial order. Here we learn, through an examination of certain qualities of character, especially prudence, that the priority of beauty over utility is found at the individual level. The following section situates the individual more directly within a social setting—namely, one that is itself appropriate to our nature and that is characterized by a certain sort of fittingness that defines beauty in a commercial context. In the third section, then, we consider the sort of actions an individual must take to realize that fittingness by exploring the distinction between cleverness and practical wisdom. Finally, the final section discusses how we might employ a Smithean understanding of appropriate commercial action in our own global corporate environment, and takes up some of the main issues we face in doing so.

THE COMMERCIAL ACTOR—THE PRUDENT MAN

The title and theme of this essay come from the opening sentence of Smith's *Theory of Moral Sentiments*:

> How selfish soever man may be supposed, there are evidently some principles in his nature, which interest him in *the fortune of others*, and render their happiness necessary to him, though he derives nothing from it except the pleasure of seeing it. (*TMS* I.i.1, emphasis added)

If, as this passage suggests, it is the case that human beings have a natural interest in the "fortune of others," we open our inquiry with a kind of paradox: it would seem that commercial action is quintessentially *not* about taking an interest in the fortune of others, but about taking an interest in one's own fortune. Or to put the point more accurately, our interest in the fortunes of others, insofar as we are commercial actors, is predicated entirely upon how those others contribute to our *own* fortune, their value resting solely upon the degree to which they do so. Smith's passage suggests something different, however—namely, that irrespective of what they do for us, we have an interest in the fortunes of others. The passage also suggests both that we would have other-oriented concerns in commercial relations and that an important constituent of acting properly and successfully in such contexts is to have such concerns.

To help us understand the nature of the commercial actor, the first and obvious place to look would be Smith's discussion of the prudent man in *A Theory of Moral Sentiments* (VI), since, if for no other reason, ordinary discourse makes prudence the central virtue of commerce. We shall see, however, that prudence evolves from a narrowly self-focused disposition to one governed by notions of fittingness as just described above.

Smith does not actually link the prudent man directly to commerce in section VI of *A Theory of Moral Sentiments*, since he speaks of the characteristics of the prudent man in general terms. However, he does reference the prudent man's frugality and industry, and it is clear that the actor described is someone living and acting in a commercial society.[9] The general point of the section is to discuss how one's character can affect one's own happiness. One quality of character necessary for that end is prudence, which Smith defines as follows:

> The care of the health, of the fortune, of the rank and reputation of the individual, the objects upon which his comfort and happiness in this life are supposed principally to depend, is considered as the proper business of that virtue which is commonly called prudence. (*TMS* VI.i.5)

Despite the fact that prudence is a virtue oriented toward one's own happiness, it does not follow that such an orientation means a lack of consideration for others. Indeed, Smith makes explicit this very point:

> The desire of becoming the proper object of this respect, of deserving and obtaining this credit and rank among our equals, is, perhaps, the strongest of all our desires, and our anxiety to obtain the advantages of fortune is accordingly much more excited and irritated by this desire, than by that of supplying all the necessities and conveniencies of the body, which are always very easily supplied. (VI.i.3)

Our own happiness is thus inextricably oriented toward others. Indeed, one would expect that our "anxiety" over obtaining such respect would no doubt influence the very ways we choose to effect our *own* fortunes. In any case, this desire for respect is also a central feature of the constraints upon our conduct and a significant source of the norms that come to guide that conduct:

> A man of rank and fortune is by his station the distinguished member of a great society, who attend to every part of his conduct, and who thereby oblige him to attend to every part of it himself. His authority and consideration depend very much upon the respect which this society bears to him. (*WN* V.i.g.12)

In thus coming to understand in what prudence consists, we learn that the first and principal object of prudential conduct for Smith is security (*TMS* VI.i.6). Although security initially means minimizing, or not exposing ourselves to, risks that will adversely affect our health, fortune, or social standing, it also has a positive side—namely, the development of "real knowledge and skill in our trade or profession, assiduity and industry in the exercise of it, frugality, and even some degree of parsimony, in all our expenses" (VI.i.6). Hence the prudent man does not simply avoid risk but seeks *improvement* of his condition through knowledge and skill development. The outcome of the possession of these qualities is that "the prudent man is always both supported and rewarded by the entire approbation of the impartial spectator" (VI.i.11).

The idea that security incorporates a particular kind of drive toward improvement implies that we cannot take security to mean simply the realization of a state of well-being. Smith's notion of security also refers to qualities of mind useful for initiating and guiding acts of improvement:

> The qualities most useful to ourselves are, first of all, superior reason and understanding, by which we are capable of discerning the remote consequences of all our actions, and of foreseeing the advantage or detriment which is likely to result from them: and secondly, self-command, by which we are enabled to abstain from present pleasure or to endure present pain, in order to obtain a greater pleasure or to avoid a greater pain in some future time. In the union of those two qualities consists the virtue of prudence, of all the virtues that which is most useful to the individual. (*TMS* IV.2.6)[10]

The cultivation of a "superior reason and understanding" thus marks the essential intellectual quality of the prudent individual. If one were to rely on this passage alone, one would be tempted to read "superior reason and understanding" in pragmatic consequentialist terms. It is not, however, because the consequences are so beneficial to the individual that superior reason and understanding are approved. Rather it is almost the reverse: because superior reason and understanding are regarded as attractive and valuable in themselves, the consequences of their cultivation are given such approval (IV.2.7). In this regard, then, it is the effort to make reason practical, rather than the inherent practicality of certain forms of reasoning, that marks the Smithean prudent individual.[11]

Smith's extension of the notion of practical wisdom beyond the pragmatic is coupled, as we saw in the passage above, with the quality of self-command. In this context, self-command makes possible the "frugality, and even some degree of parsimony" we are to exercise with the resources in our charge. Yet one of the interesting features of self-command in this context is that it is predicated upon the impartial spectator being *un*able to distinguish between present and future desires: "The spectator does not feel the solicitations of our present appetites. To him the pleasure which we are to enjoy a week hence, or a year hence, is just as interesting as that which we are to enjoy this moment" (*TMS* IV.2.8).[12] Indeed, when we actually do sacrifice a present pleasure for a future one "our conduct appears to [the spectator] absurd and . . . he cannot enter into the principles which influence it" (IV.2.8).

Yet rather than offering a reason for undermining respect for self-command, Smith argues for the opposite. Since there seems to be no reason to forgo a present pleasure for a later one, the spectator is surprised by those capable of doing so, as the spectator realizes that most actors would find this trade-off too difficult to execute. From the ability to do so, however, "arises the eminent esteem with which all men naturally regard a steady perseverance in the practice of frugality, industry, and application, though directed to no other purpose than the acquisition of fortune. The resolute firmness of the person who acts in this manner . . . necessarily commands our approbation" (*TMS* IV.2.8). It is not the quantity of benefits that impresses the spectator, but the quality of character. Indeed, because we approve such conduct, "it is the consciousness of this merited approbation and esteem which is alone capable of supporting the agent in this tenour of conduct" (IV.2.8). The security we seek from prudent conduct is, in the end, less a security of body and comfort than of social acceptance in the form of "merited approbation." This last point marks an interesting conclusion: if the foregoing suggestion that commerce is a function of prudence is correct, then commerce would depend more on qualities of character than on expected utility. The following paragraphs of this section should further establish the correctness of that suggestion and its implication about the priority of beauty over utility.

The different forces acting upon the prudent individual—especially the desire to benefit oneself and the desire to obtain the approval and respect of others—represent rather different, though potentially complementary, taskmasters. These two forces are jointly operative in an endeavor to make one fit for society, with the second being given as much (if not more) attention as the first (*TMS* III.2.6). The individual therefore pleases herself by pleasing others. Yet the process is not haphazard or passive. We actively seek such affirmations and moderate our own interest accordingly (II.ii.2.1). The desire to benefit oneself and the desire to gain the respect of others are essentially natural dispositions. Although both propensities factor into the nature of prudence, prudence is finally realized only upon the presence of a third consideration—the approval of the impartial spectator. This third "taskmaster" appears, as we have noted, to have little interest in benefits. The impartial spectator seems moved by qualities of character alone.

We thus moderate our own desires and interests to achieve what Smith calls a "correspondence of sentiments" between ourselves and others (*TMS* I.i.3.3). Fitting ourselves into society is thus "in our interest," though Smith is quite clear it is not "selfish" (VII.iii.1.4). The endeavor thus to adapt ourselves to others (and them to us) is refined by the introduction of the "impartial spectator," who helps monitor our fittingness:

Nature, accordingly, has endowed him, not only with a desire of being approved of, but with a desire of being what ought to be approved of; or of being what he himself approves of in other men. The first desire could only have made him wish to appear to be fit for society. The second was necessary in order to render him anxious to be really fit. (III.2.7)

So we seek not only approval, but approval for the right reasons. Impartial spectating is more about "right reasons" than expressions of sentiment such as approval, benevolence, or sympathy, though the fittingness for society implied by the notion of "right reasons" does, of course, incorporate all of these sentiments.[13]

Understanding prudence in this way helps us to reconcile the conflicting tendencies evident in a famous illustration of Smith's, that of the "poor boy," found in *A Theory of Moral Sentiments* IV.I.8–10. In this example, a poor boy, "whom heaven in its anger has visited with ambition," is obsessed with obtaining the sorts of goods possessed by the rich. Smith's description of the extended toil and unhappiness the poor boy undergoes in his pursuit of wealth might seem contrary to what one would expect from the reputed defender of commercial life, for Smith's portrayal of the pursuit of wealth is certainly not an attractive one. The poor boy is seduced by an image of the life of the rich that "strike[s] the imagination as something grand and beautiful and noble, of which the attainment is well worth all the toil and anxiety which we are so apt to bestow upon it" (IV.I.9). The reality is rather different from the image, however, for neither the poor boy nor the rich actually achieve the degree of happiness that the image would suggest. Nevertheless, we are all to some degree seduced by images of this sort.

Smith's point in this section of *A Theory of Moral Sentiments* is to show that the sort of "beauty" mentioned in the passage cited just above has superiority over utility in motivating even commercial action.[14] In other words, we are moved more by our vision of the life we envision ourselves leading than by the realities that attend the actual living of it. It is this expectation that is important for the incentive toward commerce:

And it is well that nature imposes upon us in this manner. It is this deception which rouses and keeps in continual motion the industry of mankind. It is this which first prompted them to cultivate the ground, to build houses, to found cities and commonwealths, and to invent and improve all the sciences and arts, which ennoble and embellish human life. (IV.1.10)[15]

It has long been noticed that if commerce is founded upon a lie, as this passage seems to suggest, it would appear that commerce is indefensible as a thoroughly moral endeavor. However, though there may be some deception involved in the imagined life being more appealing than the real one, there is not necessarily a lie.

Although the poor boy apparently achieves the wealth he seeks, Smith's narration offers no words of admiration for the boy's prudence, which we have every reason to suppose helped to gain him his wealth. The issue of prudence does not arise in this context, only the distance between the life imagined and the degree of actual pleasure and tranquillity gained in its pursuit. Yet whether the poor boy actually experiences his desired state of tranquillity and pleasure is essentially irrelevant to the spectator because, as we saw earlier, the spectator is indifferent between current and future pleasures and judges character rather than utility.[16] Perhaps because utility is so particularized, what the poor boy experiences is largely beside the point for the spectator.[17] The poor boy may be deceived about what degree of happiness his life will actually possess, but provided he adheres to the judgments of the impartial spectator along the way, his "fitness for society" ends up serving society itself. Commerce thus does not lie to anyone. It promises only fittingness and progress, not personal happiness.[18] In this way Smith can reasonably claim that one can have unfavorable attitudes toward many of the actors within a commercial setting while still being favorably disposed toward commerce generally.[19]

The poor boy like the rest of us—though perhaps with more ambition—desires to improve his condition and benefit himself. With his vision of a certain form of life, however, particular transactions will be directed toward an end in the pursuit of which the poor boy endeavors to put the particulars together in accordance with his envisioned pattern. The imagined pattern creates a form of "fittingness" that renders the particular utility of the transactions at any given moment of secondary concern. It is not just that one is willing to forgo a current pleasure to receive a greater one later—a perspective too bound up with expected utility to explain the poor boy's sacrifice. One needs instead a bigger vision, one that certainly holds the promise of greater utility, but that draws us in by its own attractiveness without having to be a function of a calculation of that utility, or even when it will arrive. Moreover, the vision needs to be one that holds up whether things are going well or badly at any given moment.[20] Ironically, perhaps, the successful, that is, prudent, commercial actor is one not only proficient at conserving resources, but also moved by a "beautiful" vision—a *conception* of fittingness.

One is perhaps tempted to see the "poor boy" as the quintessential commercial actor, always deceived by a false vision of the good life, as are the rich he emulates. Our point here, however, is quite the opposite. Instead of holding the poor boy up as the core commercial actor, our position is that commercial life is so suited to our nature that even deceptions are reconciled to our benefit. The poor boy is one extreme end of a continuum where one's aspirational vision of life is distinct from the actual utility received, but without some type of vision there would be no motivation for improvement, whatever the level of utility finally received. Commercial orders are hospitable to developing in us a sense of what is fitting with respect to both what is needed to coordinate the elements of our own lives, and what is required to coordinate with others, all of which in turn can be a more powerful draw upon our actions than expected utility. The commercial order, one that follows the rules of justice but otherwise leaves people free to pursue their own ends, is for that reason inclined toward rewarding harmonizing forces with respect to both individuals as they formulate their own plans and society generally.[21] Indeed, Smith's "system of natural liberty"—his term for the commercial order—is natural in just this sense—namely, that it encourages endeavors to create unity from diversity through adaptation, mutual influence, and ordered plans of action. This understanding of "natural" differs from one in which the "natural" is seen in terms of a simple empirical accounting of what is usual or for the most part.[22] How most societies or individuals often actually behave is less the issue than how they would behave were they fitted together properly.

THE BEAUTY OF THE BEAST

The preceding discussion of the prudent individual within a commercial culture offers a picture of a "natural" state of normal human living—that is, a condition we were "meant" to enjoy should we succeed at reconciling the diverse propensities of our nature within our likely circumstances. Above we have described or mentioned the desire for merited social esteem, care in the use of resources, the desire to improve our condition, the propensity to exchange, and growth in our knowledge as either natural or developed propensities that secure this "natural" state. Perhaps we need only mention in addition Smith's view that "man was made for action" (*TMS* II.iii.3) to suggest that our active management and integration of these various propensities and dispositions are the basic business of life. In this regard, then, our "natural" state is characterized by what might be called "extended prudence." Differing from both a narrower form of physical comfort and security and what Smith himself calls a "superior" form, extended prudence incorporates various forms of self-command:

> Temperance, decency, modesty, and moderation, are always amiable, and can seldom be directed to any bad end. It is from the unremitting steadiness of those gentler exertions of self-command, and the amiable virtue of chastity, that the respectable virtues of industry and frugality, derive all that sober lustre which attends them. The conduct of all those who are contented to walk in the humble paths of private and peaceable life, derives from the same

principle the greater part of the beauty and grace which belong to it; a beauty and grace, which, though much less dazzling, is not always less pleasing than those which accompany the more splendid actions of the hero, the statesman, or the legislator. (VI.iii.13)

From the narrower forms of prudence, concerned mainly with industry and frugality, to the "gentler exertions of self-command," which lead to the "beauty and grace" characteristic of a life of extended prudence, Smith depicts the core of "normal" life for those not thrown into the circumstances of having to be a hero, statesman, or legislator. Notice that the appeal of this life is once again understood in terms of the "pull " that "beauty and grace" exert upon us rather than in terms of benefits and accomplishments, though certainly these latter accompany it. All that is missing from the foregoing description are the qualities of character that affect the happiness of other people, such as family, friends, and countrymen, which Smith treats prior to this passage and which concern one of his other major virtues besides prudence—namely, benevolence (justice being the third major virtue).

It is my contention that the foregoing passage describes the ideal of a prudential actor within a commercial society. The reading is somewhat at odds with a Rousseauian approach, which sees the commercial order as fundamentally defective and in need of correction by the various virtues.[23] On this other reading, the virtues serve as palliatives for the dehumanizing forces of commercial life. By contrast, I am arguing that commerce is inherently civil and that the problems of commercial actors are, in Smith's estimate, deviations from this "natural" state, which represents the general tendency of interaction in a commercial world.

As the passage above suggests, the life depicted is in fact a pleasing one and is consequently in accord with the endorsement of the spectator who "is most disposed to sympathize with" sensations "more or less agreeable to the person principally concerned" (*TMS* VI.iii.14). If indeed the spectator is our standard for assessing appropriate patterns of living, one need not pause long to realize how much more attracted we are to the life described above than to the descriptions of the poor boy mentioned earlier. There is something inharmonious about the relationship between the poor boy's image of his life and his actual experience of it. We find none of that in the foregoing passage. Moreover, it is not simply that the foregoing passage pleases us more than reading about the poor boy. We actually believe that the persons depicted in the passage are more *suited* for society than the poor boy. Even though the poor boy is never completely devoid of sociability, his limited dimensionality disturbs us.

There is little doubt that the "push" to many of our actions is expected utility, but the pull is what I am calling "beauty." Beauty here means a form of fitness whose elements are coordinated in our imagination in a way we feel they are supposed to be related. And as Smith puts it, "that this fitness, . . . should be more valued, than the very end for which it [a given conveniency] was intended; and that the exact adjustment of the means for attaining any conveniency or pleasure, should frequently be more regarded, than that very conveniency or pleasure" (*TMS* IV.1.3) turns out to make the pull often more powerful than the push of utility. Smith illustrates this point just prior to the poor boy example with an example of someone walking into his room where the furniture has been misarranged. Because of his conception of how the room *should be* arranged to achieve the most "conveniency," he is moved to put in order the furniture even though "to attain this conveniency he voluntarily puts himself to more trouble than all he could have suffered from the want of it; since nothing was more easy, than to have set himself down upon one of them, which is probably what he does when his labour is over" (IV.1.4). Like the poor boy, this person in pursuit of his vision of order may have, on balance, expended more effort than he gained back in pleasure.

We have seen from our foregoing discussion that there is more than just a suggestion here that prosperity may depend on beauty in the sense of actors being motivated by a vision of how various dimensions of their lives can and should be fitted together.[24] Commercial activity understood simply as trade misses this dimension, because exchange needs to be undertaken to some purpose to turn mere benefit into progress. The more expanded and integrated the vision, with respect to both one's own projects and also how those projects coordinate with other social processes, the more likely our actions are suited to prosperity. Beauty in this sense is a form of efficiency: a well-integrated vision insures that actions are not wasted because they are measured in terms of how those actions conform to, or express, the vision that defines their fittingness.

Smith does contrast narrower forms of prudence with a "superior prudence": "Wise and judicious conduct, when directed to greater and nobler purposes than the care of the health, the fortune, the rank and reputation of the individual, is frequently and very properly called prudence" (*TMS* VI.i.15). Yet by the time Smith gets to these lines, he has moved well beyond what has any general applicability. Extended prudence, while certainly a version of superior prudence, is the sort of prudence most suited to the ordinary person's living and acting in a commercial order.[25]

It is clear that extended prudence involves some sort of Aristotelian mean between excesses of various sorts. The mean seems to be a balanced state where dispersed, and often opposing, forces are harmonized in some way according to some conception of their mutual fittingness; as envisioned together these forces constitute a form of beauty. Excesses are deviations from this state. The commercial society may not permit "men of system" to indulge their vision of social order by using individuals as mere pieces in a fashioning of that order (*TMS* VI.ii.17). But the commercial society allows *individuals* to pursue their respective visions within constraints offered by their need for recognition, acceptance, and propriety. Indeed, by emphasizing individual responsibility, the commercial society thereby encourages the development of such visions, since one's role in society must be created as opposed to defined, as would be the case in societies where an individual's station in life is fixed.

What has thus emerged clearly from our discussion is that success in the commercial order is not necessarily equivalent to what is standardly thought of as commercial success. They are not opposed. Indeed, they are "meant" to be reconciled, but the standard Smith uses to measure success is more a function of the happiness of the individual and the agreeability of the impartial spectator than a matter of utility or accumulation. The reason, as we have seen, is precisely because beauty is more compelling than utility. We are drawn more to those with a sense of how their life fits together than to those who merely accumulate. Yet if "commercial success" can be distinguished from "success in a commercial society," what is their connection, and how are they finally to be integrated? To that issue we now turn.

THE PROBLEM OF PRACTICAL WISDOM

In a world where the norms exhibited in action are not supplied by authority and hierarchy, but result from mutual interaction and adaptation and are thus largely a function of social context, it is nonetheless possible to employ a distinction, first made by Aristotle, between practical wisdom and cleverness. Cleverness is the ability to "do things that tend towards the mark we have set for ourselves, and to hit it."[26] Practical wisdom depends upon this ability to achieve one's ends—without it, one's actions would be ineffective, and there would be virtually no practice. But the ability to achieve one's ends says nothing about their value or appropriateness, or that one is doing anything more than satisfying one's desires. Aristotle's "person of practical wisdom," by contrast, organizes his desires according to his insight into the nature of the good, thereby knowing what is appropriate. Although reliance upon the impartial spectator, rather than insight into the nature of the good, is the basis for a Smithean conception of practical reason, the person of practical character would nonetheless be concerned that his desires accord with appropriateness. The mere ability to achieve one's ends is quite distinct from achieving them appropriately.

This distinction between cleverness and practical wisdom is rather important for our overall point here, because in the realm of commerce it is easy to conflate the two. From popular literature to public opinion the ability to get what one wants has been thought to be the mark of commercial success, the essence of commercial conduct. But Smith, for example, speaks unfavorably of the "natural selfishness and rapacity" of the rich, who "mean only their own conveniency" and "the gratification of their own vain and insatiable desires" (*TMS* IV.I.10). That one might be adept at satisfying those desires would not mollify Smith's judgment. He distinguishes clearly between the ability to satisfy one's desires and the ability to do so under appropriate restraints or in certain appropriate ways.[27] Success for Smith always means the achievement of ends in *appropriate* ways, never merely the achievement of ends.

Yet before being carried too far away by any quests for appropriateness, we are compelled to place a qualification upon our argument that Smith places upon his own—namely, that success matters. (In this respect, cleverness, perhaps, has something more to be said for it.) In discussing what Smith calls the "irregularity of the moral sentiments," he notes that however fitting or well intentioned our actions may be, however much they accord with the norms approved of by the spectator, if they fail to succeed they lose much of their compelling quality. Moreover, actions not so well motivated may gain respect simply on account of their success:

> Every body agrees to the general maxim, that as the event does not depend
> on the agent, it ought to have no influence upon our sentiments, with regard
> to the merit or propriety of his conduct. But when we come to the particulars,
> we find that our sentiments are scarce in any one instance exactly conform-
> able to what this equitable maxim would direct. The happy or unprosper-
> ous event of any action, is not only apt to give us a good or bad opinion of
> the prudence with which it was conducted, but almost always too animates
> our gratitude or resentment, our sense of the merit or demerit of the design.
> (*TMS* II.iii.3.1)

Thus the beauty of the design and its merit are themselves affected by success. We may forgive certain flaws in the intentions or designs behind a successful action, just as we might weaken our respect for the pure motivations behind actions that fail. Why is this the case? Smith explains as follows:

> Man was made for action. . . . The man who has performed no single ac-
> tion of importance, but whose whole conversation and deportment express
> the justest, the noblest, and most generous sentiments, can be entitled to
> demand no very high reward, even though his inutility should be owing to
> nothing but the want of an opportunity to serve. (II.iii.3.3)

If commercial activity could be described as the utilization of resources in conjunction with such utilizations by others under conditions of appropriateness, then successful commercial activity would always include some measurement in terms of outcomes. In the end, consequently, the goal for Smith seems to be one where characters can be matched with outcomes:

> The characters of men, as well as the contrivances of art, or the institutions of civil government, may be fitted either to promote or to disturb the happiness both of the individual and of the society. The prudent, the equitable, the active, resolute, and sober character promises prosperity and satisfaction, both to the person himself and to every one connected with him. The rash, the insolent, the slothful, effeminate, and voluptuous, on the contrary, forebodes ruin to the individual, and misfortune to all who have any thing to do with him. The first turn of mind has at least all the beauty which can belong to the most perfect machine that was ever invented for promoting the most agreeable purpose: and the second, all the deformity of the most awkward and clumsy contrivance. (IV.2.1)

The beauty of commerce thus does issue in prosperity through the formation of certain types of character. Its "wisdom" is Aristotelian in nature, if not exactly in structure, in that Smithean prudence also seeks to align virtue and happiness by integrating character and success.

These last remarks bring us to the final issue of this section—namely, the threats to extended prudence in what we shall call, following Smith, "the great society." The great society allows for both a deficiency of prudence and the possibility of its distorted "excess." In the former case, Smith gives the example of how the modern economy, with its vast use of the division of labor and its possibility for anonymity, can truncate one's social connectedness. This can happen in two main ways. The first is with respect to one's education, which the division of labor can make too narrow (*WN* V.i.f.50). The second concerns how the circle of one's social connections may become so limited that one's judgment becomes biased (V.i.g.12). Both pathologies are deviations from the natural condition of commerce, which is socially integrative; however, they are also deviations that the progress of a commercial order makes possible. In discussing his own solutions, Smith allows for the involvement of the state in both cases.[28] The point here, however, is that in Smith's great society, where social visibility is paramount in producing the types of character that Smith holds as valuable, there may be dangers special to that economy that are worth our reflection.[29] In sum, Smith expresses concern about these matters precisely because they mar the beauty of the commercial order and are "unnatural" to it.

Though it is somewhat incorrect to speak of an excess of prudence, since prudence is a virtue, it is not misleading to suggest that the "great society" occasions the possibility of overindulging a dimension of prudence—namely, the propensity to envision order. In this case one comes to suppose that one's own conception of overall order is to be preferred, simply because one can easily imagine it without having to consider costs or constraints (*WN* V.i.f.51). One example of this turn of mind (already mentioned) is illustrated in Smith's "man of system": a legislator treats individuals as pawns in the endeavor to remake society according to some grand vision. But commercial actors are not immune to this tendency either. The extended economy offers commercial elites numerous opportunities to indulge their own conceptions of a "better" order through special favors and privileges that come at the expense of other individuals. Because we are so prone to be moved by our own imagination of how things should fit, we are all potentially subject to being "men of system,"[30] and thus to ignoring the fact that some pieces of our picture may have a "principle of motion" of their own (*TMS* VI.I.i.17).

In general, then, as economies grow ever more extended, the sorts of pressures that limit and shape conduct and character may become either too specialized or less forceful. Though Smith in his own day was witnessing the coming into being of an extended economy, domestic and international, it is hard to know what he would say about today's global economic order.[31] What might be said in this connection concerning the beauty of commerce? To that matter we now turn.

THE NORMATIVE CHALLENGES OF A GLOBAL ENVIRONMENT

In the passage cited at the opening of this essay, Smith follows his suspicion regarding those in the same trade who gather together and conspire against the public:

> But though the law cannot hinder people of the same trade from sometimes assembling together, it ought to do nothing to facilitate such assemblies; must less to render them necessary. . . . The real and effectual discipline which is exercised over a workman, is not that of his corporation [trade], but that of his customers. (*WN* I.x.c.27, 31)

The first thing to recognize about this passage is the primacy of "liberty and justice." Without attempting here to spell out the exact nature of such terms for Smith, they are clearly meant to be structural principles of the social order that cannot be overruled for the sake of other social gains. Better to risk the chance of conspiracy, for many reasons, than generally to restrict freedom of assembly. In any social order there are, therefore, "rules of the game" within which all must act. The norms in Smith's case tend to favor strongly freedom of choice and restraint from harming one's neighbor.[32] These will be the required norms governing all commercial conduct.

Within that framework of norms, as our argument has shown, it is not utility maximization that gives the market system its strongest appeal or that captures the strongest motivations of actors within it. Rather, when considered as a whole, the constraints imposed by the commercial order upon the actions and characters of its participants through mutual adaptation help define what is fitting to that order and as a result what harmonizes it as an order. That is one reason why Smith in the passage just cited lays so much weight upon the "customers." This mutual adaptation typically has been the "invisible hand" notion attributed to Adam Smith, where the order of the market would seem to arise *as if* an invisible hand were guiding it to that order.[33] The beauty here comes from imagining the reconciliation of an immeasurably large number of particular actions into an ordered whole.[34]

Our focus above, however, has also been upon the acting agent and the meaning of the beauty of commerce with respect to her. Here beauty as fittingness has two dimensions: (1) the use of resources according to some vision of their "proper" disposition, and (2) the formation of the moral character that arises as the agent seeks to fit herself into her surrounding society. Again there is an ordered reconciliation of plurality. Both dimensions of beauty are pulls upon one's specific actions and can be significantly more powerful than utility.

Both the dimensions also depend upon the agent being subject to social controls in her interactions with others. Individually, the person is shaped by her desire for respect. Socially, her commercial activities are monitored by various social institutions and norms. Smith himself at least partially anticipates the question, as we noted above, of whether the "great society" could put some strains upon both these dimensions of the acting commercial agent's endeavors to integrate. The anonymity of mass society might loosen the constraints others place upon the agent and indeed possibly lessen the agent's ability even to recognize such constraints. This loosening of constraints may in turn weaken the need on the part of the agent for an ordered vision of the use of resources, the consequence of which might play in favor of cleverness (shortsightedness and narrowness of vision) and away from prudence. If the easing of social constraints blurs the distinction between cleverness and prudence and loosens the importance of social respect, then the mechanisms Smith relies upon to insure the beauty of commerce become problematic.[35]

The tendency toward globalization in today's business world might give one every reason to believe that the social mechanisms for monitoring the conduct of firms are absent. Recent financial crises and pronouncements of the "failures of capitalism" might suggest that globalization has indeed left firms outside of the sorts of constraining mechanisms Smith envisioned for smaller social frameworks. Such concerns may be justified. Yet before rushing to judgment, it is important to remind ourselves that most firms do indeed operate within localized environments. Large international firms may capture most of the media attention, but the bulk of commercial enterprises are still subject to many of the constraints we have identified. Even large multinational firms remain with certain checks upon their conduct aside from the ordinary market forces of supply and demand. Besides governmental regulations and laws, the forces exerted upon firms include outside investment firms, credit rating agencies, executive compensation markets, mechanisms for corporate control, consumer confidence, and prestige in an industry.

In this regard we would follow Jonathan Macy, who has written insightfully on corporate governance, in maintaining that we should avoid "a deviant subculture whose members feel free to flaunt the norms of the dominant community."[36] As Macy puts it,

> Norms are a low-cost substitute for other corporate governance mechanisms. . . . More important, from a corporate governance perspective, contracts and law simply are not possible unless a sufficient amount of social capital has been generated by informal norms. Without social capital, people will not obey laws or abide by contracts when it is not in their personal interest to do so. In the absence of sufficient levels of social capital, the trust necessary for investment will not exist.[37]

The goal, in strongly Smithean fashion, is to find managers who are reputationally sensitive and thus respond to "incentives related to social status such as the desire for prestige and the fear of being shamed [both of which] are important sources of corporate governance."[38] Macy notes that it is not always a simple matter to distinguish deviants from reputationally sensitive managers because part of the former's cleverness is to give the *appearance* of reputational sensitivity. The easiest way to disregard social norms while still appearing "respectable" is to narrow the vision by focusing upon the short term and upon particular aspects of the whole business environment. A recent example of a narrowing of focus might be the movement away from measuring corporate success in terms of a whole range of corporate values—such as product quality, treatment of employees, contributions to the community, return on investment, forward-looking corporate strategies, an integrated and clear corporate identity, and the like—and toward one particular measure, such as shareholder value. In this regard, research by John Kay has lead him to comment that

> the set of assumptions underlying the shareholder value model has brought about a management preoccupation with short-term financial performance alone, to the detriment of creating real economic value. . . . Empirical evidence shows that firms which since the mid-1990s subscribed to this model have actually destroyed shareholder value over the medium term.[39]

Of course, such a conclusion would not be surprising at all from a Smithean perspective, because the beauty of commerce lies in its outward synthetic vision, not in a narrow focus upon accumulation.

Reputational sensitivity is also a key inducement toward the sorts of character qualities we have suggested accompany extended prudence. This is because in order to be reputationally sensitive one must be looking outward toward the social environment in which one is acting in order to form effectively a conception of how to integrate within it. There is thus the suggestion in Smith that orienting oneself toward an integrated vision is an effective form of commerce in terms of resource management, personal development, and product development and integrity. As Harvard Business School professor Clayton Christensen has noted, having a vision for one's life as a whole is the path to success in a commercial order and quite consistent with narrow commercial success as well.[40]

CONCLUDING REMARKS

Our argument that Smith brings an "aesthetic perspective" to commerce has implications for individuals as well as businesses. In both cases, the beauty of commerce involves visualizing appropriate ways of integrating into society, along with the means to accomplish that end. In the case of individuals, this requires the development of character, but for businesses it might be sufficiently summed up by the term "commerce" alone, since that term connotes cooperation, mutual advantage, and a multiplicity of social connections. With both individuals and businesses the connections with others, as well as the dispositions needed to secure them, are fitted together in such a way that the well-being of both are simultaneously promoted. There is thus, as we have argued throughout, a strong sense of fittingness and appropriateness to a properly functioning commercial order. Smith regards envisioning this sort of harmonization as being both natural and appropriate, especially when the vision is bounded by the spheres of one's own competence:

> The wisdom which contrived the system of human affections, as well as that of every other part of nature, seems to have judged that the interest of the great society of mankind would be best promoted by directing the principal attention of each individual to that particular portion of it, which was most within the sphere both of his abilities and of his understanding. (*TMS* VI.ii.2.4)

The primacy of the aesthetic within the "great society" may offer endless motivations and possibilities for personal and commercial visions, yet managing one's resources well means keeping any vision within one's abilities and understanding. The wealth commerce creates can often tempt us to reach beyond our grasp in anything from ill-conceived investments to demands for subsidies. But the main beauty of commerce is that its benefits become so manifest when commercial actors, and the businesses they run, remain integrated within their "particular portion."

ACKNOWLEDGMENTS

I wish to thank Charles Griswold and Douglas Rasmussen for helpful comments on earlier drafts of this essay. I wish also to give special thanks to the organizers and participants of the "Practical Wisdom and Globalizing Practice" conference in Guangzhou, China (November 2012) for their useful remarks on a longer version of this essay. I am especially grateful to the editors of this volume for their insightful and valuable comments and corrections.

NOTES

1. References to the *Wealth of Nations* (*WN*) and *A Theory of Moral Sentiments* (*TMS*) appear below and parenthetically in the text and cite relevant section numbers followed by page numbers from the following editions: Adam Smith, *An Inquiry into the Nature and Causes of the Wealth of Nations*, ed. R. H. Campbell, A. S. Skinner, and W. B. Todd (Indianapolis: Liberty Fund, 1981); Smith, *The Theory of Moral Sentiments*, ed. D. D. Raphael and A. L. Macfie (Indianapolis: Liberty Fund, 1982).

2. Scholarship on Smith has increased exponentially in recent decades and includes these books: Charles L. Griswold, Jr., *Adam Smith and the Virtues of Enlightenment* (Cambridge: Cambridge University Press, 1999); Emma Rothschild, *Economic Sentiments: Adam Smith, Condorcet, and the Enlightenment* (Cambridge, MA: Harvard University Press, 2001); James Otteson, *Adam Smith's Marketplace of Life* (Cambridge: Cambridge University Press, 2002); Samuel Fleischacker, *On Adam Smith's "Wealth of Nations"* (Princeton, NJ: Princeton University Press, 2004); Dennis C. Rasmussen, *The Problems and Promise of Commercial Society: Adam Smith's Response to Rousseau* (University Park: Pennsylvania State University Press, 2008); Ryan Hanley, *Adam Smith and the Character of Virtue* (Cambridge: Cambridge University Press, 2009); Fonna Forman-Barzilai, *Adam Smith and the Circles of Sympathy* (Cambridge: Cambridge University Press, 2010).

3. See also *WN* I.xi.10, among other examples.

4. See *WN* I.viii.36 and I.x.c.44–47.

5. Among these "interferences" would be included education, poor relief, the imposition of customs duties, public works, and the like. Most of these are detailed in *WN* V.

6. An early challenge to the then-common reading of Smith as advocate of self-interest and laissez-faire can be found in Patricia Werhane, *Adam Smith and His Legacy for Modern Capitalism* (New York: Oxford University Press, 1991). A more recent and important challenge to the same sort of reading to which Werhane objects can be found in Fleischacker, *On Adam Smith's "Wealth of Nations"*; Fleischacker is perhaps the leading exponent of the "left Smithean" interpretation of Smith, along with Rothschild, *Economic Sentiments*.

7. See, for example, *WN* IV.ix.51: "All systems either of preference or of restraint, therefore, being thus completely taken away, the obvious and simple system of natural liberty establishes itself of its own accord. Every man, as long as he does not violate the laws of justice, is left perfectly free to pursue his own interest his own way, and to bring both his industry and capital into competition with those of any other man, or order of men."

8. By "commercial action" we refer to conduct within a commercial culture. As Smith notes, "In commercial countries . . . the authority of law is always perfectly sufficient to protect the meanest man in the state" (*TMS* VI.ii.1.13). Hence by "commercial culture" we mean a culture in which the rule of law prevails and people are left generally free to pursue their own ends. Since we have a strong propensity to "truck, barter and exchange" (*WN* I.ii.1) the likely activity of the vast majority within such a society will revolve around commerce.

9. *Prudence* is a term applied more widely than to commercial actions. That the basic characteristics of prudence remain consistent in Smith and have primarily a commercial application can be seen in his *Wealth of Nations* (e.g., II.iii.29, II.iv.2, V.i.a.14). In addition, Donald Winch likens the prudent man in *A Theory of Moral Sentiments* to the typical actor in a commercial society. See Winch, "Adam Smith: Scottish Moral Philosopher and Political Economist," in *Adam Smith: International Perspectives*, ed. Hiroshi Mizuta and Chuhei Sugiyama (New York: St. Martin Press, 1993), 98. I have noted elsewhere—Douglas J. Den Uyl, *The Virtue of Prudence* (Bern: Peter Lang, 1991), 292—that the virtue of prudence may be the central link between Smith's two main works. Interestingly, prudence has no index reference in Fleischacker's *On Adam Smith's "Wealth of Nations,"* although he does mention related ideas (see, e.g., 107) in various places. See also Griswold, *Adam Smith and the Virtues of Enlightenment*, 203–7.

10. For a useful discussion of prudence, see Otteson, *Adam Smith's Marketplace of Life*, 138–40.

11. Nonetheless, there remains some tension between the earlier rendering of prudence in part IV and the later rendering in part VI.

12. See also *TMS* VI.i.11.

13. See especially *TMS* III.3.4.

14. The reading given here differs from that offered by Ryan Hanley in his seminal work, *Adam Smith and the Character of Virtue,* esp. chap. 4. Hanley tends to read vanity as the force moving the poor boy; on the reading here, vanity is less the issue than "beauty." So for Hanley the virtue of prudence corrects the defective character of vanity. For me, vanity is a perversion of prudence, itself the primary and natural direction of commercial activity. Hanley (109) cites the same passage for his interpretation that I would cite for mine: *TMS* IV.2.1 (cited in my discussion below). Hanley, however, omits the sentence about the different "turn of mind."

15. The form of self-command we are discussing could be a more general and secularized form of the "asceticism" Max Weber claims is necessary for the the development of capitalism. See Weber, *The Protestant Ethic and the Spirit of Capitalism* (New York: Routledge, 1992), chap. 5.

16. *TMS* VI.ii.30: the "esteem and admiration" of the impartial spectator "is altogether independent of their good or bad fortune."

17. If the poor boy were to experience the process with a predominance of pleasure, the point would be the same: the spectator would remain indifferent. Smith's example, however, would have been less dramatic.

18. See, for example, Douglas Rasmussen's and my exchange with Dennis Rasmussen: "Smith on Economic Happiness: Rejoinder to Dennis C. Rasmussen," *Reason Papers* 33 (Fall 2011): 102–6 (and at http://www.reasonpapers.com/pdf/33/rp_33_7.pdf).

19. Maria Pia Paganelli, "The Adam Smith Problem in Reverse: Self-Interest in *The Wealth of Nations* and *The Theory of Moral Sentiments*," *History of Political Economy* 40, no. 2 (2008): 365–82.

20. Hanley (*Adam Smith and the Character of Virtue,* 114–15) treats this problem well, citing numerous passages from *WN* (e.g., I.xi.l.3). Despite the unfortunate choice of terms, Deirdre McCloskey criticizes what she calls the "prudence only" approach to understanding appropriate conduct in a commercial society. See McCloskey, *The Bourgeois Virtues: Ethics for an Age of Commerce* (Chicago: University of Chicago Press, 2006), chap. 6. By "prudence only" she means shortsightedness and utility maximization.

21. See *WN* IV.ix.51.

22. Smith's "simple system of natural liberty" (*WN* IV.ix.51), not much in evidence historically, serves as a standard for evaluating political orders. For a similar use of "natural" in the moral realm, see *WN* V.ii.k.64. My account here may conflict with David Levy and Sandra Peart's account of "natural" in their essay "Adam Smith and the State: Language and Reform," in *The Oxford Handbook of Adam Smith,* ed. Christopher J. Berry, Maria Pia Paganelli, and Craig Smith (Oxford: Oxford University Press, 2013), 376–77. However, given their description of our affection for "systems of the mind" in Smith (387), perhaps our views are not so opposed.

23. This seems to me to be the essence of the Hanley reading of Smith (*Adam Smith and the Character of Virtue*) and perhaps the Rasmussen one as well (*Problems and Promise of Commercial Society*). My reading may reflect more of Montesquieu than Rousseau. Charles Griswold has pointed out to me, however, that the desire for social approval is very Rousseauian. For a useful survey of connections between Montesquieu and Smith, see Henry C. Clark, "Montesquieu in Smith's Method of 'Theory and History,'" *Adam Smith Review* 4 (2008): 132–57, esp. secs. II and VI.

24. As Fonna Forman-Barzilai insightfully notes, "The *Moral Sentiments* in its entirety might profitably be read as Smith's empirical description of the very processes through which people learn actively to balance their social and unsocial passions, actively to put them into harmony." Forman-Barzilai, *Adam Smith and the Circles of Sympathy,* 48–49.

25. It may seem arbitrary that we have invented dual terms for prudence that is not yet of the superior variety, but Smith makes this type of move with his own distinction between vulgar prudence and prudence. See *TMS* VI.concl.5.

26. Aristotle, *Nicomachean Ethics,* in *The Basic Works of Aristotle,* ed. Richard McKeon (New York: Random House, 1968), 1144a26.

27. The comments about the rich, just cited, come where Smith is speaking of how it is fortuitous that even when the motives are wrong, the effects can turn out to be beneficial to society as a whole, because the market transforms such actions into social benefits. This is one of the few places where Smith uses the term "invisible hand."

28. In the case of education, see *WN* V.i.f.52. With respect to faction, see *WN* V.i.f.14–15.

29. In his discussion of character formation in the *Wealth of Nations,* Smith seems even less open to wisdom and choice than he does in *A Theory of Moral Sentiments.* Characters seem in these discussions to be simply the product of their environment. See, for example, *WN* V.i.g.10.

30. Levy and Peart, "Adam Smith and the State," regard the propensity in this regard to be natural and virtually universal; see note 22 above. The propensity described here may exemplify the motivation of "rent seeking," where some pursue benefits for themselves at the expense of others. Smith would oppose rent seeking on moral and aesthetic grounds.

31. An excellent insight into this issue may be found in Forman-Barzilai, *Adam Smith and the Circles of Sympathy.* See my review of the book and Forman-Barzilai's response in *Adam Smith Review* 7 (2013): 279–87.

32. See, for example, *TMS* II.ii.1 and 2. See also the passage cited in note 7 above.

33. Smith uses the phrase "invisible hand" only twice: in *TMS* IV.I.10 and in *WN* IV.ii.9. There have been controversies about the extent of the applicability of the idea in Smith generally (see Fleischacker, *On Adam Smith's "Wealth of Nations,"* 138–42), but we have no reason to quarrel with the received view that Smith saw the commercial order as an

undesigned order of unity out of diversity where the parts are so well suited that it seems as if the order were designed.

34. Perhaps the single best expression of both the reconciliation of diversity and its unity as an unconsciously designed plan is found in F. A. Hayek, "The Results of Human Action but Not of Human Design," in *Studies in Philosophy, Politics, and Economics* (Chicago: University of Chicago Press, 1967), 96–105.

35. One response is offered by Hanley, who suggests that virtue is intended by Smith to mitigate such problems. See especially Hanley, *Adam Smith and the Character of Virtue,* chaps. 5 and 6.

36. Jonathan R. Macy, *Corporate Governance: Promises Kept, Promises Broken* (Princeton, NJ: Princeton University Press, 2008), 42.

37. Ibid., 41. On the importance of trust and culture in a commercial order, see David C. Rose, *The Moral Foundations of Economic Behavior* (Oxford: Oxford University Press, 2011), esp. chaps. 9 and 10.

38. Macy, *Corporate Governance,* 42.

39. A comment made by John Kay at the EABIS (European Academy of Business in Society) Colloquium 2004. I thank Gilbert G. Lenssen of the EABIS for providing me with this quotation and pointing me to the related research. See also Kay's article "Decision Making, John Kay's Way," in *Financial Times*, March 20, 2010, where he concludes: "Successful decision-making is more limited in aspiration, more modest in its beliefs about its knowledge of the world, more responsive to the reactions of others, more sensitive to the complexity of the systems with which it engages. Complex goals are generally best achieved obliquely."

40. See Clayton Christensen, James Allworth, and Karen Dillon, *How Will You Measure Your Life?* (New York: HarperCollins, 2012).

CHAPTER 13

Why Kant's Insistence on Purity of the Will Does Not Preclude an Application of Kant's Ethics to For-Profit Businesses

Norman Bowie

Philosophers became active in business ethics during the 1970s. Until that decade, scholarly discussions of business ethics were typically undertaken in relation to analyses of corporate social responsibility, as found in the Social Issues in Management Division of the Academy of Management, the disciplinary body of business school faculty. Although philosophers applied traditional theories to specific issues of business ethics, it was some time before any philosophers would approach the domain of business ethics from a theoretical perspective of one of the major traditional ethical theories. This lack of an overarching theoretical framework was partly the result of the influence of the pragmatism of Richard Rorty and his follower in business ethics, R. Edward Freeman, as well as feminist theorists, all of whom were critical of grand theorizing. Those philosophers who adopted a traditional ethical theory as a framework were typically Aristotelians, with Robert Solomon as the leading figure. Among other leading business ethicists, neither Richard DeGeorge nor Patricia Werhane could be closely identified with any one specific theory. Thomas Donaldson collaborated with the legal scholar Thomas Dunfee to create what they called "Integrated Social Contracts Theory," a systematic attempt to find room both for universal standards (hypernorms) and a legitimate variety of different cultural norms (moral free space) for business.[1] All these disparate positions had one common theme—an indifference or aversion to Kantian approaches. Until the turn of the century I was the only business ethicist taking a systematic Kantian approach to problems in business ethics.

In the meantime business ethics, unlike medical, legal, or engineering ethics and other applied ethics fields, had almost no support in philosophy departments. To this day I am unaware of any major philosophy department that encourages doctoral work in business ethics. Few, if any, departments offer a graduate course in business ethics. Business ethics has no American Philosophical Association newsletter as do several of the other applied areas. To this observer it seems that the philosophical community is more than willing to let the social scientists dominate the field of business ethics.

I find a common element in the anti–business ethics stance of philosophers and the anti-Kant stance of business ethicists in the twentieth century. Both rest on fundamental misinterpretations and misunderstandings of Immanuel Kant's philosophy. The key misunderstanding was to think that Kant's ethical philosophy was exhausted by the categorical imperative and that the categorical imperative provided a system of absolute rules such as "Never tell a lie." Indeed James Rachels, in his widely used ethics textbook, *The Elements of Moral Philosophy*, titled one of his two chapters on Kant "The System of Absolute Rules."[2] The notion that Kant was something of an absolutist in ethics was reinforced by a misunderstanding of Kant's notion of the purity of the will, which required that an action had moral worth only if it were done for duty's sake—that is, from a purely moral motive. A number of business ethicists rejected Kantianism as a result of a misunderstanding of what was meant by purity of the will and duty for duty's sake.

In this essay I defend a version of Kantian capitalism, and I argue that a good or pure will is compatible with profit seeking. In order to set forth this perspective, I first consider Kant's notion of the good will. I then address some of the standard ways in which business ethicists have tried to accommodate moral principles and for-profit business, turning next to a consideration of contemporary scholarship on Kantian moral action and its reliance on a notion of pure will. In the fourth section I offer what I consider the proper Kantian approach to business ethics, by delineating how profit seeking is, in fact, compatible with the idea of the purity of will. As I then point out, a problem results if one believes, as most business ethicists do, that corporations also have moral obligations to benefit various corporate stakeholders. I resolve this challenge by appeal to the distinction between perfect and imperfect duties. In the final two sections, I explore a full notion of Kantian capitalism and point out how a corporation might respond if it appears that beneficence will affect (negatively) the pursuit of profits.

PURITY OF THE WILL

Perhaps no passage from Kant's writings has caused more problems in applying Kantian ethical theory to business than the following: "Nothing in the world—indeed nothing even beyond the world—can possibly be conceived which could be called good without qualification except a good will."[3] What makes this brief passage so problematic for business ethics? Let me illustrate the problem by discussing an example that Kant uses.[4] Kant asks us to consider a shopkeeper who will not cheat a child because the shopkeeper wants to preserve his reputation. Kant would argue that the shopkeeper had done a "good" thing because his action of not cheating the child is in accord with our duty not to cheat children. However, the shopkeeper does not deserve moral credit for his action (his action was not morally worthy) because it was not done from a moral motive (not done from the motive that the act is the right thing to do). The motive for the action determines whether the action is a moral action and is morally worthy. For Kant, a morally worthy action is not one done merely in conformity with duty but one done out of respect for duty.

Let us apply Kant's analysis to business ethics. The purpose of a publicly held corporation is to generate profits for the corporation's shareholders. A manager may do many things that are "good," such as treating employees fairly, giving to the community, paying suppliers promptly, and the like. However, so long as the manager's motivation for doing these good things is to increase profits, the manager's actions are not truly moral and are not morally worthy. The "good actions" may be good for business—thus the dictum "Good ethics is good business"—but the actions are not truly moral or morally worthy because the motivation is profitability. According to the Kantian view, to be morally worthy the actions must be motivated by duty: one must do the right thing for the sake of duty.

It is interesting to point out that the general public *regularly* takes a Kantian position on the "good" things a company does. Thus if doing something "good" is motivated by the desire to do the good thing in order to increase profit, then the public does not treat the action as deserving of moral credit. In these cases, with this type of motivation, an act of corporate responsibility or corporate charity is deemed, by the public, to lack moral worth; after all, people think, "it is done just to make money."

So long as the publicly held corporation is seen as having the purpose of making profits, and so long as people understand that for Kant doing one's duty is the only purely moral motive and that it is doing one's duty for duty's sake that makes an action truly moral, it is easy to see why there is such skepticism that Kantian ethics could really have anything important to say about business ethics or even about commerce in a capitalist world.

This essay provides a unique perspective on this issue, so that the dictum "Good ethics is good business" is shown to be consistent with a fairly rigorous interpretation of Kant's claim that the only thing good in itself is a good will. However, before developing my view it is worth pointing out and explaining briefly other ways to provide consistency between willing to do something because it is profitable and willing to do something because it is the right thing to do. Once that discussion is complete I will argue that in a publicly held corporation the managers have a contractual moral obligation to seek profit. Thus so long as the manager of a publicly held corporation is motivated to seek profit, seeking profit is perfectly consistent with Kant's insistence that an action must be motivated by duty (doing the right thing) in order to be morally worthy.

ACCOMMODATING ETHICS AND PROFITS: THE PURPOSE OF BUSINESS

A number of business ethicists have pointed out that it is not the case that the sole purpose of business is to generate profits. The largest class of such business ethicists are the stakeholder theorists who suggest that there are a number of groups besides stockholders who are necessary to the survival of the firm (the strong sense of a stakeholder) or who are affected by the firm's actions (the weak sense of stakeholder). For these stakeholder theorists there are times when the manager ought to act in the interests of a stakeholder group other than the stockholders, and in so doing the manager can do the right thing even though it is not profitable. Thus if a manager increases wages or gives money to the community on the grounds that duty requires it, and as a result profits decline, such an action would pass Kant's purity of the will criterion as popularly interpreted.

Similarly, on this view, when a manager wills something that is profitable for stockholders, and that act happens to be right (e.g., the action honors the interests of other stakeholders), the manager has done nothing moral even if he has done something good. On the other hand, when the manager wills a sacrifice in profits in order to honor, as a duty, the rights of another stakeholder group, then the manager does something truly moral in Kant's sense. (I am assuming that the motive here is to honor the legitimate rights of this other stakeholder group.) On this view, business ethics would involve spelling out those instances when the manager ought to sacrifice profits in order to honor the rights of stakeholders other than stockholders. Indeed a lot of thinking in business ethics has proceeded in just this way.

This type of thinking brings to mind an early article by William Evan and R. Edward Freeman that referred to stakeholder theory as Kantian capitalism.[5] In that article Evan and Freeman argued that management had a fiduciary obligation to balance the interests of various stakeholders.[6] They cited Kant's second formulation of the categorical imperative, "Don't treat people as a means merely," as a justification for that position. However, Freeman later came under the influence of Richard Rorty and abandoned the project of Kantian capitalism.

One problem with this strategy—that of saving a Kantian approach by limiting business ethics to cases in which profit is sacrificed in order to do the right thing—is that it is pretty much a nonstarter both in business schools and in the business community. This strategy also is unsound on philosophical grounds, as is shown below.

The strategy is a nonstarter in business schools and the business community because the underlying premise is rejected. If business academics and businesspeople take stakeholder theory seriously it is because they believe that paying attention to the interests of stakeholders in addition to stockholders makes firms more profitable. Fulfilling nonstockholder stakeholder interests is necessary for making money for stockholders. Thus both business school academics and businesspeople adopt what is called instrumental stakeholder theory. Treating all stakeholders well is good for profits. In other words these stakeholder theorists in business and in business schools believe in the "Good ethics, good business" motto. Such people believe that the task of management is to find win-win strategies that work to the interests of all stakeholders so that no stakeholder interests are sacrificed.

The best-known stakeholder theorist, R. Edward Freeman, argues explicitly for such a position: "A stakeholder approach to business is about creating as much wealth as possible for stakeholders, without resorting to tradeoffs."[7] A parallel position is taken by those business firms and businesspeople known for humane personnel relations and who, through charitable contributions, support the local community. Kenneth Dayton, a former CEO of Dayton Hudson Company (now Target) and responsible for founding the Minnesota Keystone Program, whose business members gave 5 percent of pretax profits to charity, put the case this way: "What's good for the community is good for the company."[8]

The strategy that finds room for Kant by arguing that the job of the business ethicist is to find cases where profits ought to be sacrificed in order to support the interests or rights of other stakeholders is also philosophically flawed. It rests on what Freeman calls "the separation thesis," commonly understood as the view that seeking profits is one thing and doing the right thing is another and separate undertaking.[9] Thus there is a tendency to think in terms of dichotomies that stipulate that a manager either seeks profit or does the right thing. Recall that a stakeholder theorist who accepts the traditional interpretation of Kant argues that only those actions in which the manager is motivated to sacrifice profit in order to do the right thing are morally motivated. Freeman's point is that such a stakeholder theorist sees the will to make a profit as one kind of intention and the will to do the right thing as a separate and distinct act of will. But managers should will a business decision that incorporates making a profit and doing the right thing as one act of willing. It is one of Freeman's major contributions to the field to point out that there is no separation thesis. Decisions about making profits have ethical components built in from the beginning. It is not the case that the manager can first discover what is profitable and then ask as a separate question whether this profitable thing is also ethical and then decide what to will. The rejection of the separation thesis suggests that the task of the manager is to find a "win-win" solution that provides profits for the stockholders and meets the interests of the other corporate stakeholders. It is this type of formula that should constitute the motivation for the business decision. The chief danger with the separation thesis is that ethics is seen as an add-on that subtracts from profits. As a result it is psychologically easy to ignore or devalue the ethical component of a business decision. Considerations of safety are an integral part of many business decisions. There is evidence that British Petroleum underestimated safety concerns both at a facility in Texas and at the Deepwater Horizon oil well. That oil well exploded on April 20, 2010, resulting in the loss of eleven lives and the largest oil spill in American waters in history. At one point at least a part of all the shorelines of the Gulf Coast states were affected. This event followed an earlier 2005 fatal explosion at a BP facility in Texas City, Texas. In these two cases and in others it appears that the obligation to operate the business ethically was undervalued because the ethical issues around safety got separated from questions of profitability.[10]

One feature of my approach will be to agree with Freeman that there is no separation thesis. Decisions about what is profitable involve ethical issues right from the beginning. Business ethics from a Kantian perspective is not about determining the profitable action and then secondarily asking the question as to whether this profitable action is also ethical.

UNDERSTANDING PURITY OF THE WILL

In private conversations and at academic meetings, many people either express puzzlement at or are critical of Kant's notions of the purity of the will and of doing something out of duty. One colleague, Ronald Duska, has put his puzzlement in print, claiming that he does not know what it means to "to do something simply because it is one's duty":

> I am not sure what it means to do something simply because it is the right thing to do. I do not doubt actions have moral worth. But duty is not a motive, it is an imperative. We act in accord with our duty, but that duty comes from considering what is good for ourselves and by necessity since we are social beings, what is good for others. I want to know, why it is the right thing? From my perspective, it is right if it brings about some good end.[11]

If the Kantian applies the notion of a pure will to business and argues that a for-profit corporation ought to do something because it is a requirement of duty, then Duska is similarly mystified:

Kant distinguishes between acting in accord with duty and acting from duty. For Kant, our actions do not have moral worth for us if they are acted upon from inclination, only if they come from duty. . . . Bowie objects to those who argue that we should be ethical because it will lead to more profit. This is the strategic argument: do well by doing good. . . . I presume Kant, if not Bowie, wants us to be ethical because "it is the right thing to do." . . . I find that notion a sort of abstract universal, with no concrete meaning, to which I would want to ask, why is it the right thing to do? The answer I would find intelligible is that it is the right thing to do because it leads to a desirable end.[12]

How might we resolve concerns that the dictum "Good ethics is good business" violates Kant's view that a moral action is motivated by a good will? Here precisely is the problem for Kantian business ethics as seen from the view of critics. They claim that if the only thing good in itself is a good will and if Kantian business ethicists argue that in many cases good ethics is good business, then an action we would normally call good but done because it was good business is not a truly moral action. In other words they maintain that one cannot both be a Kantian and claim that in general good ethics is good business.

There have been a number of attempts by Kant scholars to get around the problems that are presumably presented by Kant's doctrine of the purity of the will. One standard way is to point out that there can be multiple motives for an action. Let us look at the famous shopkeeper example from that perspective. In all three cases below the shopkeeper confronts two motives, the prudential motive not to harm his reputation and the moral motive to do one's duty and not cheat the child.

1. The shopkeeper would not cheat the child even if he could get away with it. Thus doing one's duty would have been a sufficient motive in this case.
2. The shopkeeper would not cheat the child only if he thought that cheating him would harm his reputation. In this case the prudent motive is necessary for the commission of the good action.
3. Neither the prudential motive nor the moral motive is sufficient for not cheating the child. Each is necessary, and they are jointly sufficient.

I think it is clear that in case 2 Kant would say that at most we have a good but not a moral act. I also think that Kant would make a similar judgment in case 3. In other words, the moral motive must be sufficient by itself if the action is judged to be truly moral. So what about case 1? Does the mere presence of the prudential motive contaminate the moral motive even though the moral motive is sufficient?

Richard Henson has argued that case 1 could be considered a genuinely moral action. For Henson all that is required is that the motive of duty be sufficient for the action if the other influences are not present. Let's apply this to business. A company could perform a socially beneficial act both because it is the right thing to do and because it is good business. So long as the company would do this act even if the good business motive were not present, the act would pass the Kantian test, it is argued, and would be done out of duty, and thus would be worthy of moral esteem.[13]

However, Henson's suggestion is not universally accepted. Barbara Herman points out that there is an ambiguity in the use of "sufficient." A motive could be sufficient if other influences were not present, or it could be sufficient even when other influences are present. Herman insists that Kant would take the latter interpretation of "sufficient." Herman argues that there are incentives for action and reasons for action. Kant would argue that the good will chooses on the basis of reasons, not incentives. So, for an action to be genuinely moral, a reason must be the sufficient motivator even if other incentives are present. Case 1 would be a genuinely moral action for Kant if morality provided the reason for doing it, even if that reason coexisted with a nonmoral incentive for doing it. Herman explains:

> When an action has moral worth, non-moral incentives may be present, but they may not be the agent's motives in acting. If the agent acts from a motive of duty, he acts because he takes the fact that the action is morally required to be the ground of choice.[14]

If we follow Herman here, most good actions by businesspeople would not have genuine moral worth. In publicly held corporations, business executives have to please Wall Street. Thus when they engage in philanthropy, for example, nearly all executives would say that they did it because it was good for business. In those instances we would have an illustration of case 2 rather than case 1. Some business executives might say that one reason they were philanthropic was because it was the right thing to do, but they would quickly add that another reason they were philanthropic was because it was good business. In other words being philanthropic because it is the right thing to do is almost never the sole reason why a business executive is philanthropic.[15] So, in almost all cases, we are back to our original dilemma.

Recent work by Allen Wood and Barbara Herman shows that the problem of multiple motives is partly a false problem created by a common misconception of Kant's doctrine of the purity of the will. If these Kant scholars are correct there may be no need to worry about multiple motives.

Allen Wood argues that there is nothing wrong with doing the right thing from a self-interested or prudential motive. The important point in moral choice is when one should go against self-interest or prudence and do the right thing. To act out of duty in those cases is when the agent deserves moral esteem.[16] Thus a businessperson who does the right thing because it is good business does something morally good but does not deserve any special moral credit for that. Wood's conclusion is exactly in accord with the public's moral intuitions. The public is happy to have business do the right thing when it is good business to do so. However, to earn special moral credit with the public the business must sacrifice profit in order to do the right thing. We have already seen how Kantian the general public is in this regard. However, it is also true that if a business is to stay in business a loss of profit cannot happen too often, so for most businesses the trick is to find the business strategy that lets the business do the right thing and be profitable. The public often does not understand that. There is nothing inconsistent with Kantianism in holding this position. However, we are still stuck with the conclusion that doing something in order to be profitable is not worthy of moral esteem even if it is good.

One could argue that the issue about the purity of the will, moral esteem, and good action is the main focus of Barbara Herman's *Moral Literacy*. Herman's strategy is to deny the sharp separation between desire and reason and then to argue that desires can respond to reason. As she says early on in the book,

> But if we are no longer restricted to a rigid oppositional model—if the system of desires is itself reason responsive—the content of desires need not remain unaffected by our developing moral and rational capacities, and the exclusion of all desire from moral action will not follow so easily.[17]

Extrapolating to business, a manager who desired to make a profit but had given doing the right thing as his reason for action would do something not only good but also morally worthy. The fact that the desire for profit was present need not detract from the moral worthiness of the act so long as doing the right thing is the reason for the action. "Good ethics is good business" could then be interpreted as the combination of "good ethics" as a reason for a manager's action with "good business" as a desideratum. Such a combination is consistent with Kant's doctrine of the purity of the will *if* one accepts Herman's account. However, such cases are extremely rare. In American capitalism seeking a profit is almost always the (or at least a) reason for corporate action. So the problem remains.

I am sympathetic to Wood's and Herman's interpretations. However, their more sophisticated interpretations of Kant's doctrine of the purity of the will do not resolve the problem. Recall that I want the pursuit of profit to count as a genuinely moral motive or, perhaps better put, as a genuinely moral reason. As Wood interprets Kant, seeking profit as a reason for action would produce a good action, but it would not be a moral motive. Since I think that seeking profit counts as a reason and not simply as a desire, Herman's willingness to let desire coexist with reason will not solve my problem. In a publicly traded firm I want to argue that seeking profit is, in fact, a reason for management action and that the reason is a moral one.

SEEKING PROFIT IS A MORAL MOTIVE

My solution to the problem is very straightforward, although it raises some complications, as we shall see. What the general public and even business ethicists do not realize is that seeking profit is a moral obligation. Indeed in Kantian terms and properly qualified, seeking profit is a perfect duty for any executive of a publicly held corporation. A classic argument that would appeal to a Kantian is found in Milton Friedman among others.

Managers have entered into a contract with the stockholders to be their agent and as agents to provide what the stockholders want. What stockholders want is a profit, and if you go as far as Milton Friedman, stockholders want to maximize profits. A contract is a type of promise.[18] Keeping one's promises is a classic example of a Kantian perfect duty. Put in a more formal way, the argument would run as follows:[19]

1. In a publicly held firm the managers (CEO and the top management team) have entered into a contract with the stockholders.[20]
2. A contract is a type of promise.
3. The terms of the contract are that the managers should attempt to seek profits for the stockholders.
4. For Kant, keeping a promise is a perfect duty.
5. Therefore managers have a moral obligation—indeed, a perfect duty—to seek profit.

Thus doing good when it leads to profit is a moral duty, all else being equal.

In a publicly held corporation, the managers of the corporation have a contractual duty to seek profits. Since that duty is a contractual duty, then managers who seek profit fulfill, thereby, a type of promise that they have with stockholders. Thus seeking profit is really a moral obligation and not in itself prudential. What makes a manager's concern with profit prudential is *not* aiming at profit per se but aiming at profit in order to increase the manager's salary, or to keep his or her job. In these latter cases, seeking profits is a means for furthering the manager's own ends. The profit seeking in these cases is not performed from a moral motive (the right reason.)

This way of looking at profits is at odds with both the way business school professors think about motivating managers and with the attitudes of the general public. Finance professors, among other business school faculty, worry about how to motivate the managers of publicly held firms to be concerned with profits. They are concerned with overcoming the agency problem, a problem created when there is no way to constantly monitor managers to make sure that they manage for the stockholders rather than their own interests. So these finance professors have proposed incentive devices like stock options to motivate managers to keep targeted on corporate profitability. This is called "aligning the interest of the manager with the interests of the stockholder." Kantians would call this prudence, and they would be correct in so doing. The executives of a corporation should seek profits because it is the right thing to do; they should be concerned with profits because it is their contractual duty. As an aside, incentive devices like stock options have not worked very well in aligning the personal interests of managers with the interests of the stockholders; indeed, large stock options can contribute to immorality.[21]

What seems counterintuitive about this analysis is the notion that profit is a good that should be sought. Some might argue there is nothing moral about seeking profits. Yes and no. There is something wrong with seeking profit at the expense of other goods, and even more importantly it is wrong to seek profits in a way that is immoral. Even Milton Friedman, who maintained that managers should maximize profits, argued that one should not maximize profits in ways that are illegal or immoral. This stipulation on profit seeking is something that Friedman did not emphasize and many of his followers (and opponents!) have ignored. But Friedman's own view is clear:

> There is one and only one social responsibility of business—to use its resources and engage in activities designed to increase its profits so long as it stays within the rules of the game, which is to say, engages in open and free competition without deception or fraud.[22]

And again:

> In a free enterprise, private-property system a corporate executive is an employee of the owners of the business. He has direct responsibility to his employers. That responsibility is to conduct the business in accordance with their desires, which generally will be to make as much money as possible while conforming to the basic rules of the society, both those embodied in law and those embodied in ethical custom.[23]

A PROBLEM FOR THE ANALYSIS

However, my solution to the purity of the will problem does create another issue. I, like many others, have argued that the managers of corporations have duties to aid society or to help solve social problems.[24] In other words, I have argued that these managers have a duty of beneficence. These are, in Kant's words, imperfect duties. Imperfect duties are real duties, but they are not duties that you must fulfill on all occasions.

However, if the duty to seek a profit is a perfect duty, and the duty to solve social problems or aid society is an imperfect duty, does that mean whenever there is a conflict between profitability and aiding society, the manager should always aim for profitability? It appears that Kant would not permit one to violate a perfect duty in order to fulfill an imperfect duty, but if that is the case, it looks like we end up in a position very much like the traditional one espoused by Milton Friedman and his followers. The manager of a publicly held corporation should be beneficent only when there is no negative effect on profit. That conclusion may seem wrong, but when it is properly understood, I think it is right.

As a preliminary, there are three possible ways to avoid this result.[25] Despite the conventional wisdom, some legal scholars have argued that the executives of a publicly held corporation are under a contractual obligation, but they point out that the contract really says that the managers are agents of the corporation itself rather than agents of the stockholders. Thus the perfect duty derived from the contract is a duty to manage for the good of the corporate entity. If this legal theory is correct, then a corporation can consistently be beneficent and fulfill its obligation to the corporate entity even if profits should suffer. Can there be such a case? Yes. What business executives must do on this account is have a business purpose for any beneficent actions. Or to put it another way, acting from an imperfect duty must be consistent with the perfect duty to the corporation. That is, the beneficent action must contribute to the good of the corporation per se, and such good must outweigh any loss in profits. Here is a hypothetical example. Suppose Walmart decides to stop selling guns. Even though profits would decline, this loss might be offset by the goodwill Walmart would receive. In other words Walmart would benefit from a normatively superior brand much the way Johnson and Johnson did for many years after the Tylenol poisonings.

A second response is to argue that managers have contracts with other stakeholders besides stockholders. This legal interpretation has been buttressed by the action of at least thirty states. Beginning with Indiana in 1987, these states permit the managers of corporations to consider the impact of their actions on corporate stakeholders. These state statutes allow the executives of corporations incorporated in the state to sacrifice profits in the interests of other stakeholders. Such statutes provide legal protection for these managers to reduce and relinquish profits in the name of achieving some other good for corporate stakeholders. Effectively, such statutes change the nature of the contract that managers have with stockholders, so that in limited circumstances honoring the interests of other corporate stakeholders would not constitute a violation of the contract. In Kantian terms, on rare occasions, to act in a way that reduced profit would not, thereby, constitute a violation of the contract and thus would not violate a perfect duty. (Most recently states have begun to enact legislation that allows for benefit or B corporations, whose purpose is the amelioration of social or environmental problems.[26] Thus the managers of a B corporation have the perfect duty to do good built into the corporate charter.)

A third response is to point out that the claim that stockholders always want their manager agents to maximize profits is false or at least false for a significant number of companies. Although I am not aware of any corporation that polled its stockholders to see how much profit they were willing to sacrifice for corporate beneficence, there is evidence that the stockholders of a large number of companies want those companies to be beneficent. Indeed there are a large number of mutual funds that invest only in companies that are socially responsible, and these mutual funds have lots of investors. Target Corporation donates 5 percent of its pretax profit to charity. Any one who invests in Target is, or should be, aware of its policy. Presumably, these investors believe the "Good ethics is good business" dictum—that these investments will have a larger payoff than investments in companies that are not socially responsible.

Although these three arguments have merit, there is a better solution to this difficulty: Kantian profit-seeking. In the remainder of this essay I will describe this alternative and show how the perfect duty to seek profit is compatible with imperfect duties, especially the duty of beneficence.

KANTIAN CAPITALISM: MORAL PROFIT-SEEKING

What counts as constraints on profit seeking from a Kantian perspective? Profit seeking is constrained by the three formulations of the categorical imperative. The norms of profit seeking should not be formally or pragmatically contradictory, they should not use corporate stakeholders as a mere means to profitability, and they should be acceptable to any rational member of that corporation.[27]

However, to leave matters here provides only a limited account of the relation of ethics to profits. What is needed is a positive account of what managers of corporations ought to do with respect to a duty to aid society—to engage what is commonly called "corporate social responsibility." With respect to the three normative criteria set forth above, none would provide a solution to the problem under discussion here, since none would provide a robust account of how to resolve conflicts between duties of beneficence and the duty to seek a profit. In this section, I shall present the remainder of a theory of Kantian capitalism. My proposal for resolving the conflict fits well with theories of capitalism and with Kant's moral philosophy, though some may think it gives too much priority to profit. If successful, this account shows both that the application of Kantian ethics to problems in business ethics is not too idealistic (fitting well with capitalism as traditionally understood) and that it possesses real moral bite, for it requires changes in how the managers of many corporations actually manage.

As a general duty, corporate executives have an imperfect duty to promote the interests of all corporate stakeholder groups—those stakeholders necessary to the survival of the firm.[28] In making this claim I am one with Kant, who claims that individuals are always bound by the duty of beneficence, although they need not act on the duty on every occasion. I also accept Kant's arguments for the existence of such a duty. In focusing on an imperfect duty to stakeholder groups, I am keeping in mind the importance of the perfect duty for managers to be concerned with profit and of the fact that a perfect duty should not be violated to conform to an imperfect duty.

Some might argue that I should be concerned with stakeholders in the broad sense—that is, with all stakeholders *affected* by the actions of a firm. However, to be concerned with all groups affected by the firm is to ask too much. Even so, I am not saying that stakeholders in the broad sense are not to be treated ethically. On the contrary, executives are still bound by the duty not to violate the categorical imperative in treating those affected by the firm. However, the corporation has no imperfect duty of beneficence to those merely affected by the firm. This analysis provides one way of limiting to whom managers have an imperfect duty of beneficence. Thus right away this account is less susceptible to the criticism that Kant's imperfect duty is too broad and thus requires too much of a moral agent.

Consider corporate philanthropy. Although many worthy organizations deserve support, a corporation's philanthropy should be strategic: it should be focused on groups or issues related to its business. Thus the executives of pharmaceutical companies should focus on working with nonprofits who would bring cheap drugs to underdeveloped countries. They should do this rather than send their money to, for example, Habitat for Humanity. After all, providing drugs rather than building houses is what their business is about. In this way acting on the imperfect duty of beneficence is consistent with the perfect duty to seek profit.[29] What I am arguing here is that morally a manager should not seek to act on the imperfect duty of beneficence when there is good reason to think that so acting would undercut the perfect duty to seek profit. Spending money on things unrelated to the business would burn into profit and would in most cases violate the perfect duty to seek profit. It should be noted that in the business context, tying beneficence to business strategy is a way to avoid a common criticism of Kant—namely, that his notion of imperfect duty is too burdensome. In the Kantian capitalism that I propose we have a powerful algorithm for determining when we are clearly not obligated to act on the imperfect duty of corporate beneficence: Do not sacrifice long-term profit for beneficence. Such an algorithm provides for significant corporate beneficence while protecting the primary purpose of business and the primary obligation of managers to seek profit.

Let us consider another example: meaningful work for employees. Kant is clear that there is an imperfect duty to develop one's talents.[30] A common way to develop one's talents is through work. One could argue that an aspect of the imperfect duty of beneficence is that corporate executives assist their employees in the development of meaningful work, that sort of work that enables the worker to develop his or her talents. Again empirical research in organizational studies and human resource management shows that enlightened policies that give the worker a sense of meaning and purpose in what he or she does contribute to profitability. As a result an imperfect duty of beneficence that is directed at providing employees an opportunity to develop their talents is consistent with the perfect duty to seek profit.

A full-blown theory of Kantian capitalism consists, therefore, of two parts. First, it provides a rich account of profit seeking as an endeavor that is not unethical but a positive good; indeed, the obligation of management to seek profit is a perfect duty. Kantian profit-seeking is, therefore, a morally constrained generator of wealth and resources—goods and services—that enhance the lives of all. Second, Kantian capitalism provides an account of imperfect duties of beneficence that are consistent with the perfect duty to seek profit. In this way the imperfect duties are suitably constrained and not overly burdensome. If we were to generalize from the two examples above, a Kantian manager should take the perspective of each of the corporate stakeholders and ask what provides value to them in their relationship to the corporation. Then the manager would seek to provide the conditions that enable these stakeholders to achieve value. I would then argue that in each case there is an imperfect duty for the managers to so act. Moreover, research from the management disciplines shows that in performing this imperfect duty, managers will likely enhance profitability rather than diminish it.[31] All of this supports my overall position that the job of a manager is to find a "win-win" resolution that aids society (or helps to solve social problems) while making a profit. Ethical management requires that ways be found to practice business so that it is both ethical and financially successful.

A RESIDUAL PROBLEM

Still there may be cases where acts of beneficence (or in management language, acts that provide value to stakeholders other than stockholders) would negatively impact profits and thus would seem to violate the perfect duty that a manager has to seek profit.

In some cases this apparent tension can be resolved. If a company like Target Corporation has a known policy of contributing 5 percent of its pretax profits to charity, then we can presume that Target's stockholders approve of that policy. It really does not matter from the perspective of the Target manager why the Target shareholders chose to invest. The fact that they did gives Target's policy implicit sanction to occasionally sacrifice profits in order to achieve greater value for other stakeholder groups.

This is especially true when one distinguishes short-run from long-run profit. Providing value to another stakeholder group that lessens profits in the short run will not violate the manager's perfect duty to be concerned with profit so long as there is a reasonable belief (known legally as the business judgment rule)[32] that providing value to another stakeholder group will contribute to profit in the long run. This move makes real sense if those legal scholars cited earlier are correct when they say the contractual duty of managers—and in Kantian language the perfect duty of managers—is to serve the good of the corporation per se.

But there still can be cases where even a focus on long-term profit would seem to require that managers avoid certain actions that would provide value to other stakeholders but would do so at the expense of long-term profit. I would argue that Kantian capitalism requires that the imperfect duty of beneficence should *not* be acted on in those cases. An imperfect duty does not have to be fulfilled on every occasion that might call for it; such a duty allows for choice and exceptions. It might appear that one of the challenges for Kantian capitalism is to specify the criteria for determining those occasions where the imperfect duty need not be enacted. However, on my account we have a minimal criterion, and that is what we need. A manager need not act on the duty of beneficence, at least in those circumstances in which doing so would undermine long-term profit. The duty of beneficence requires that a manager seek those occasions on which that duty is reasonably believed to enhance profit. And given the fact that seeking profit is a perfect duty, acting on behalf of both profit and beneficence is a morally worthy action in Kant's sense. Such actions are both good and right.

The disciplines in a business school provide, among other goods, the social science studies that tell managers which beneficent actions are most likely to be profitable. Kant could not provide much guidance here. It is the responsibility of the social sciences, when applied to business disciplines, to provide information on what beneficent management techniques will or will not contribute to long-term profitability. A firm managed by Kantian ideals and solid social science research will have many opportunities to honor both the imperfect duty of beneficence and the perfect duty to seek a profit.

CONCLUDING REMARKS

Kantian capitalism is not overly abstract or hopelessly idealistic. It accepts profit seeking, morally constrained, as a duty of managers, and it practices corporate social responsibility because the social sciences have provided tools to show how beneficence toward the corporate stakeholders (narrowly defined) can lead to profitability. In business terms, managers should try to manage so as to achieve value for all corporate stakeholders. The manager bears a perfect duty to ensure that the corporation is profitable; otherwise the corporation will not exist. By using the vast area of social science empirical research that shows how managers can provide for stakeholders while being profitable, a well-trained and morally motivated manager can meet both the perfect obligation to seek long-term profit and the imperfect obligation of beneficence. This type of management is the kind of management that would meet with Kant's approval and be morally worthy.

NOTES

1. For example, see R. Edward Freeman, Jeffrey S. Harrison, Andrew C. Wicks, Brian L. Parmar, and Simone de Colle, *Stakeholder Theory: The State of the Art* (Cambridge: Cambridge University Press, 2010); Robert C. Solomon, *Ethics and Excellence: Cooperation and Integrity in Business* (New York: Oxford University Press, 1992); Richard T. De George, *Competing with Integrity in International Business* (New York: Oxford University Press, 1993); Patricia H. Werhane, *Moral Imagination and Management Decision Making* (New York: Oxford University Press, 1999); and Thomas Donaldson and Thomas W. Dunfee, *Ties That Bind: A Social Contracts Approach to Business Ethics* (Boston: Harvard Business School Press, 1999). Donaldson and Dunfee's contractarian approach is distinct from that of John Rawls, *A Theory of Justice*, rev. ed. (Cambridge, MA: Harvard University Press, 1999).

2. James Rachels, *The Elements of Moral Philosophy*, 4th ed. (New York: McGraw-Hill, 2002).

3. Immanuel Kant, *Foundations of the Metaphysics of Morals* (1785), trans. Lewis White Beck, 2nd ed. (New York: Macmillan, 1990), 9.

4. Ibid., 13.

5. William Evan and R. Edward Freeman, "A Stakeholder Theory of the Modern Corporation: Kantian Capitalism," in *Ethical Theory and Business*, ed. Tom L. Beauchamp and Norman E. Bowie, 4th ed. (Englewood Cliffs: NJ: Prentice Hall, 1993), 97–106.

6. I assume here that any balancing would on occasion require sacrificing stockholder profits in the interests of other stakeholders.

7. Freeman et al., *Stakeholder Theory*, 28, original emphasis omitted.

8. As quoted in Archie B. Carroll et al., *Corporate Responsibility: The American Experience* (Cambridge: Cambridge University Press, 2012), 247.

9. In fact, just what the separation thesis asserts is a matter of controversy. See the following articles in the special issue of *Business Ethics Quarterly* 18, no. 4 (October 2008): 541–65, for a discussion of the thesis: Jared D. Harris and R. Edward Freeman, "The Impossibility

of the Separation Thesis," 541–48; Ben Wempe, "Understanding the Separation Thesis: Precision after the Decimal Point," 549–53; John Dienhart, "The Separation Thesis: Perhaps Nine Lives Are Enough," 555–59; and Joakim Sandberg, "The Tide Is Turning on the Separation Thesis," 561–65.

10. Sara Lyall, "In BP's Record, a History of Boldness and Costly Blunders," *New York Times*, July 12, 2010, http://www.nytimes.com/2010/07/13/business/energy-environment /13bprisk.html?pagewanted=all&_r=0.

11. Ronald Duska, "Revisiting the Egoism Question in Business," in *Kantian Business Ethics: Critical Perspectives,* ed. Denis G. Arnold and Jared Harris (Northampton, MA: Edward Elgar, 2012), 50.

12. Ibid., 52.

13. See Richard Henson, "What Kant Might Have Said: Moral Worth and the Over-Determination of Dutiful Action," *Philosophical Review* 88, no. 1 (1979): 39–54.

14. Barbara Herman, *The Practice of Moral Judgment* (Cambridge, MA: Harvard University Press, 1993), 23.

15. It is possible that a business executive in a publicly held corporation might say that he or she is doing something for reasons of profitability but not be sincere. The executive might be trying to please (fool) Wall Street while doing the good action simply because it is the right thing to do. Given the commitment to profitability in American capitalism, such a case would be rare indeed! It is also possible that a business executive could have profit as an incentive and doing the right thing as a reason. Such cases would be compatible with Herman's approach, but such cases are rare. Profitability almost always functions as a reason for action in American capitalism. I thank the editors of this volume for raising this issue.

16. Allen W. Wood, *Kantian Ethics* (Cambridge: Cambridge University Press, 2008), chap. 2.

17. Barbara Herman, *Moral Literacy* (Cambridge, MA: Harvard University Press, 2008), 13.

18. For purposes of the argument here, I take the contract to require managers to seek profit. This is a less demanding stipulation than a requirement to maximize profit, but it is more consistent with business practice and Herbert Simon's notion of satisficing with respect to profit. See Herbert A Simon, *Models of Man: Social and Rational* (New York: John Wiley and Sons, 1957).

19. This argument was briefly introduced in my book *Business Ethics: A Kantian Perspective* (Malden, MA: Blackwell, 1999), chap. 4.

20. A full specification of the parties to this contract would require an essay on its own. It seems, nonetheless, that the duty to create a profit falls on the CEO and the top management team; the board of directors has the duty to oversee the CEO and top management team to make sure that they do their duty and do not succumb to agency problems.

21. See Jared Harris and Philip Bromiley, "Incentives to Cheat: The Influence of Executive Compensation and Firm Performance on Financial Misrepresentation," *Organization Science* 18, no. 3 (2007): 350–67. For an extended and contrary view, see Robert W. Kolb, *Too Much Is Not Enough: Incentives in Executive Compensation* (New York: Oxford University Press, 2012).

22. Milton Friedman, *Capitalism and Freedom* (Chicago: University of Chicago Press, 1982), 133.

23. Milton Friedman, "The Social Responsibility of Business Is to Increase Its Profits," *New York Times Magazine*, September 13, 1970, 126.

24. In this section, I will refer to the duties of the managers of corporations and leave open the question of whether a corporation per se can have obligations.

25. See Bowie, *Business Ethics: A Kantian Perspective*, esp. chap. 4.

26. Michael R. Deskins, "Benefit Corporation Legislation Version 1:0—A Breakthrough in Stakeholder Rights," *Lewis and Clark Law Review* 15, no. 4 (2011): 1047–76, https://law .lclark.edu/live/files/10658-lcb154art7deskinspdf.

27. These constraints are explained and justified in Bowie, *Business Ethics: A Kantian Perspective.*

28. This is the standard definition of a narrow stakeholder group, as contrasted with the broad definition of stakeholder as any group affected by firm policy.

29. Of course there is no guarantee that strategic philanthropy will generate a profit. Every business decision involves the risk that it may not be successful.

30. This issue is more fully developed in Norman Bowie, "A Kantian Theory of Meaningful Work," *Journal of Business Ethics* 17 (1998): 1083–92.

31. See Jeffrey Pfeffer's studies on human relations management: *Competitive Advantage through People* (Boston: Harvard Business School Press, 1995) and *The Human Equation* (Boston: Harvard Business School Press, 1998).

32. The "business judgment rule" shields managers from legal liability when their actions lead to a loss of profitability. To benefit from the shield of the business judgment rule the managers must have acted with loyalty, candor, care, and good faith. Traditionally the Chancery Courts of Delaware have been most sympathetic to managers in determining that the manager has acted with loyalty, candor, care, and good faith. Thus it is no surprise that so many corporations are incorporated in Delaware. For a more detailed account of the "business judgment rule," see John M Holcomb, "Business Judgment Rule," in *Encyclopedia of Business Ethics and Society*, ed. Robert W Kolb (Los Angeles: Sage Publications, 2008), 1:237–39.

CHAPTER 14

Tocqueville: The Corporation as an Ethical Association

Alan S. Kahan

Alexis de Tocqueville (1805–59) is hardly the first name one thinks of in connection with business ethics. Indeed, he is not usually associated with the subject at all. Although the author of *Democracy in America* (1835 and 1840) did not discuss business ethics directly, the vocabulary he developed for analyzing democratic society is readily applicable to many of the issues central to the field of business ethics today. For example, translating debates over stockholder- or stakeholder-based theories of business ethics into Tocquevillean terms is a relatively easy process. Moreover, such a translation serves to shed light on issues that underlie the debate. Recasting questions of business ethics in Tocqueville's terms offers valuable insights as to what is at stake in the debate between stockholder and stakeholder theories of business ethics. If this translation does not resolve the question of which theory is preferable, it points out strengths and weaknesses in both.

In order to translate stockholder and stakeholder theories into Tocquevillean language, a general understanding of Tocqueville's attitude toward the role of business in democratic society is necessary. "Democracy" is a term with a special meaning in Tocqueville's writings. It describes a social rather than a political situation, one in which everyone is presumed to be equal, rather than separated at birth in classes or castes that cannot be altered. Human beings naturally, according to Tocqueville, feel a desire for material well-being, and in democratic societies everyone wants to improve their material lot, because no one feels excluded from success as a result of their unchangeable origins or status. Everyone wants to rise, and just a little higher than his neighbor. "No matter what general effort a society expends to make citizens equal and alike, pride will always impel individuals to escape the common level and somewhere establish an inequality that is to their own advantage."[1]

The widespread desire for material well-being, coupled with widespread ambition, lead to the universal pursuit of wealth.

Commerce is thus a natural pursuit for people in democratic societies, and particularly in trade and industry, because that is where one makes money quickest, rather than through agriculture (Tocqueville feels the need to point out to his French readers, accustomed to a peasantry emotionally attached to a particular plot of land, that in America, people "have turned agriculture into a form of commerce").[2] Because commerce plays such a central role in democratic societies, unlike the subordinate role it played in the aristocratic societies of the past, in Tocqueville's view the pursuit of business is central to the ethical life of democratic society.[3]

In his own time Tocqueville was disappointed that the relationship between business and ethics came in for little serious examination. He called for the development of a political economy more concerned with moral questions. As he wrote to a friend, "While all the efforts of political economy in our day seem to me to be about material issues, I would like . . . to highlight the more immaterial side of this science . . . to include in it the ideas, the feelings of morality as elements of prosperity and happiness."[4] In short, from Tocqueville's perspective, "business ethics" is not an oxymoron.

In what follows I will first describe two issues central to Tocqueville's thought and crucial to applying it to business ethics: the problem of self-interest and the role of associations in democratic societies. I will then apply Tocqueville's categories to understanding and evaluating stakeholder and stockholder theories of business ethics. I will conclude by suggesting what issues in the debate are most important from a Tocquevillean perspective.

THE CORPORATION AS A SOURCE OF DEMOCRATIC ETHICS

Tocqueville both analyzed commerce from an ethical perspective and appealed to businessmen to take an ethical perspective on their occupation. Materialism is both a necessary and a useful passion in democratic society, but it must be tempered. Individuals engaged in business, and especially in business management, have to be encouraged to behave ethically, in Tocqueville's view, through religion, a subject too vast to be considered here, or through a very broad conception of self-interest. By identifying the interest of the firm with the interests of customers—"He who serves best profits most," as the Rotary motto once went[5]—as well as with those of the broader community, management can be led to ethical behavior. Through the pursuit of an enlightened self-interest, the business success of the individual or the corporation is integrated with the success of the community as a whole, both economically and politically—and the business manager and business owner need to be aware of this.

The means by which businesses and their personnel become integrated with their community is the same means by which, according to Tocqueville, all individuals in democratic societies are encouraged to broaden their horizons: association. Tocqueville describes at length, for an audience used to French centralization, the myriad levels of government in the United States, which he calls political associations. More relevant to our concerns is his discussion of the role of civil associations, which in Tocqueville's view are far more important in America than government. America, for Tocqueville, has been built by associations, by people choosing to come together in groups to work for a common end. Americans are accustomed to associate for all kinds of purposes, whether commercial, industrial, religious, recreational, and so on. These associations are the bedrock of American freedom and prosperity for Tocqueville, the industrial and commercial ones no less than the others.[6]

In considering those social and political thinkers who are concerned about the moral state of the modern economy, we are accustomed to seeing the joint-stock corporation demonized or at best excused as a necessary or at any rate inevitable evil along the way to Pareto-optimization. This is not Tocqueville's view. Tocqueville, as even a casual reader of *Democracy in America* rapidly learns, is a great fan of association, including what he calls "industrial associations" and what we would call business corporations. He favors associations, whether in politics, business, or any other domain, not so much on the grounds of efficiency[7] as on moral grounds.

What ethical grounds does Tocqueville use to defend the business association, also known as the corporation? Corporations, as a species of association, are a powerful weapon against what Tocqueville sees as the great moral and political threat to democratic societies, "individualism." "Individualism," like "democracy," is a word to which Tocqueville gives a particular meaning. Tocqueville defines "individualism" as "a reflective and tranquil sentiment that disposes each citizen to cut himself off from the mass of his fellow men and withdraw into the circle of family and friends, so that, having created a little society for his own use, he gladly leaves the larger society to take care of itself." Individualists are not purely selfish, since they do care about some people. But they are not concerned about society as a whole. Individualism is a natural by-product of democracy (i.e., of an egalitarian society), according to Tocqueville, because in democracies everyone feels independent and equal to everyone else. This is why "individualism is democratic in origin, and it threatens to develop as conditions equalize."[8]

Why does individualism worry Tocqueville? Because the individualist cares only about himself and his family, and not about his country: "I see an innumerable host of men, all equal and alike, endlessly hastening after petty and vulgar pleasures with which they fill their souls. Each of them, withdrawn into himself, is virtually a stranger to the fate of all the others. For him, his children and personal friends comprise the entire human race."[9]

Apathy is the natural political state of the individualist.[10] Tocqueville's concern that businesses behave ethically is in the final analysis a political concern. He wants to make sure that business associations, like all forms of association, flourish, in order to make sure that the polity flourishes. In some ways businesses seem to be unlikely candidates for the role of opponents of individualism, since for Tocqueville individualism encourages, and is in turn encouraged by, the passion for material well-being. Tocqueville was no ascetic. He had nothing against material well-being in itself; rather he said, "I reproach equality not for leading men into the pursuit of forbidden pleasure but for absorbing them entirely in the search for permitted ones." America is particularly fertile soil for materialism, because of the unprecedented opportunities it offers for making money. In America, "the possibilities open to greed are endlessly breathtaking, and the human mind, constantly distracted from the pleasures of the imagination and the works of the intellect, is engaged solely by the pursuit of wealth." The universal desire for material well-being is democratic, but its strength in America is multiplied by the relatively great social mobility of American society. We may or may not agree with Tocqueville that the America he visited in the 1830s or the America of today presents unique opportunities for financial success. The point is that for Tocqueville democratic societies (and today almost all societies are democratic in Tocqueville's sense) are threatened by an individualism that promotes and is promoted by materialism, and that endangers freedom—and in the long run, economic prosperity as well.[11]

But in accord with the medieval medical doctrine that where God puts the disease, he puts the cure close by, Tocqueville finds in democratic America the remedy for the tendencies to individualism that work so powerfully in democratic societies: That remedy is association, the free coming-together of separate individuals for a common purpose. Business corporations are a form of association.[12] In *Democracy in America* Tocqueville describes at length how Americans use the technique of association, above all in politics and matters of opinion, such as the temperance movement, to construct a free society. Typically readers stop there. Tocqueville himself does not. The habit of association for political purposes, in Tocqueville's view, serves to encourage other kinds of association: "Wherever there is a new undertaking, at the head of which you would expect to see in France the government and in England some great lord, in the United States you are sure to find an association."[13] Thus by a bit of intellectual judo, Tocqueville turns the business corporation, which one might expect to find playing the usual role of armed robber, into one of the good guys in the posse of associations that rides to the rescue of democratic society. Even if created for materialistic reasons, the business association serves as a deterrent to the individualism that materialism otherwise fosters. Tocqueville titles a crucial chapter of *Democracy in*

America "How Americans Combat Individualism with Free Institutions." One of those free institutions is the business corporation.[14]

The practice of association, regardless of its purpose, serves to combat individualism by encouraging isolated individuals to join together to achieve their goals, in business just as much as in politics. Indeed the two go together for Tocqueville: "Some men have by chance a certain interest in a common affair. It concerns a commercial enterprise to direct, an industrial operation to conclude; they meet together and unite; in this way they become familiar little by little with association."[15] Thus business association teaches the practical techniques and the psychological habits necessary to make people capable of political association (and vice versa). Thus in their business practices as well as their political ones Americans used the freedom to associate, strictly limited in Europe at the time, to combat the individualism born of equality, and defeated it.[16]

Business associations, like all other associations, are thus both a tool to preserve freedom and a means of exercising one's freedom. They are both an instrument and an ethical end in themselves. The existence of the business association, the corporation, is therefore a moral weapon against individualism, both in its effects and by its very existence. Associations, whether based on politics, a love of roses, or the desire to make a profit, help people substitute for selfishness and individualism a conception of self-interest properly understood, or enlightened self-interest, which replaces selfish and illegal behavior with conduct that benefits the community and that mimics virtue well enough to be indistinguishable from it in practice. General Motors can serve the same function as the Sierra Club in this respect.[17] For Tocqueville all associations encourage their members to be concerned with people outside their own narrow circles, and incline people toward "the idea that it is man's duty as well as his interest to make himself useful to his fellow man."[18]

Association helps to enlighten self-interest, and in the idea and practice of enlightened self-interest Tocqueville sees another remedy for the threats that democracy poses to freedom. He titles a chapter of *Democracy* "How Americans Combat Individualism with the Doctrine of Self-Interest Properly Understood." But what does Tocqueville mean by "self-interest properly understood"? A proper understanding of one's interest means taking a broad, long-term view. Indeed, the more long-term the perspective, the wider the circle of interests that must be taken into account. For example, a businessman who is willing to pay higher taxes to support better schools because, in his view, this will mean better-educated and more efficient workers is displaying enlightened self-interest. Such a man may be purely self-interested at heart, but because of his long-term perspective (which Tocqueville thinks tends to be lacking in democratic societies),[19] he acts in the same way as a person with purely altruistic motives might. This enlightened view of self-interest is widespread in the United States, according to Tocqueville. Americans, he writes, like to claim they are acting from self-interest even when performing generous and disinterested actions.

Thus the business that understands its own interest properly, that pursues its self-interest in an enlightened way, will act ethically out of pure self-interest. From this habit of enlightened self-interest, real virtue, that is, actions performed for the sake of others, not oneself, may arise: "Men concern themselves with the general interest at first out of necessity and later by choice. What was calculation becomes interest, and by dint of working for the good of one's fellow citizens, one ultimately acquires the habit of serving them, along with a taste for doing so."[20]

The doctrine of enlightened self-interest is not new, according to Tocqueville. He cites the sixteenth-century French essayist Montaigne, who wrote, "When I would not follow the right road because of rectitude, I would follow it because I found by experience that in the end it is usually the happiest and most useful path."[21] But while the doctrine is not new, it attains dominance only with the rise of democratic society. For Tocqueville it does not make sense to talk about ethical questions without an understanding of their social context, most importantly an understanding of the difference between aristocratic societies, which are based on inequality, and democratic ones, which are based on equality.[22] It is only with the coming of democratic society, as seen in its purest and clearest form in America, according to Tocqueville, that the doctrine of enlightened self-interest becomes the public face of virtue. This does not mean that "men were more virtuous in aristocratic centuries than at other times, but it is certain that people then talked constantly of the beauties of virtue. Only secretly did they study the ways in which virtue might be useful." In democratic centuries, and we might add in corporate boardrooms, the natural tendency is the opposite, that is, to talk constantly about utility, and think about the beauty of virtue only in secret. Thus in democratic societies that practice enlightened self-interest "ultimately it came to seem as if man, in serving his fellow man, served himself, and as if his private interest lay in doing good." In order for democratic people to reach this level of enlightenment, the habit of association is necessary.[23]

That is why for Tocqueville "the doctrine of self-interest properly understood seems to me the most appropriate to the needs of my contemporaries." Furthermore, it is a doctrine they can understand, simple and logical and well within anyone's grasp, including that of business managers with little interest in theories of ethics or the problems that might beset a utilitarian philosophical approach. "American moralists do not hold that a man should sacrifice himself for his fellow man because it is a great thing to do; they boldly assert, rather, that such sacrifices are as necessary to the man [or business] who makes them as to the man who profits from them."[24]

Tocqueville thus implies that when we demand ethical action from business management it will be useless to demand self-sacrifice, even if we could easily determine which self is to be sacrificed (the stockholders' interests, management's, the suppliers', employees', etc.), *unless* we can justify that sacrifice in broad utilitarian terms. Any effective ethical appeal must be made in terms of enlightened self-interest, or else it is likely to have little practical impact. Tocqueville acknowledges that actions undertaken out of duty have a higher moral value than those undertaken from even an enlightened self-interest. But Tocqueville's view is not at all Kantian. He thinks that even actions undertaken primarily out of a sense of duty include an element of "personal interest, for there is a proud and private enjoyment in such points of view and hope for remuneration in a better world; but interest there is as small, as secretive and as legitimate as possible."[25] While Kant thought that we could never *know* if our actions were undertaken purely from a sense of duty, Tocqueville does not care, as long as duty is the primary element. However, Tocqueville thinks that people are far more likely to act in the ways we would like them to from enlightened self-interest than from a sense of duty.

Nevertheless, the doctrine of enlightened self-interest is not a wholly good thing in Tocqueville's eyes. Or rather, it is a good and necessary thing in a democratic society, but it is not sufficient as a foundation for business ethics or any other kind of ethics. Self-interest properly understood helps people to overcome their individualism, it discourages crime, but if it makes people better human beings, it does not lead them to become great ones. Its effects are immense and pervasive, but limited. Most fundamentally, "by itself, it cannot make a man virtuous," although it creates habits that resemble virtue. Indeed, the doctrine of self-interest properly understood has some morally deleterious effects at the margin— according to Tocqueville it makes extraordinary actions more rare. Nevertheless the best should not be allowed to be the enemy of the good: "I am not afraid to say that the doctrine of self-interest properly understood seems to me the most appropriate to the needs of our contemporaries. I see it, moreover, as the most powerful tool they have left to protect them from themselves [e.g., against the temptation to individualism]."[26]

THE PROBLEM OF COLLECTIVE INDIVIDUALISM

Up to this point, it might seem as if for Tocqueville all is for the best in the corporate world. The corporation itself, the business association, is a morally useful entity with an important role to play in educating people to work together and use their initiative for a common purpose. It thus helps to overcome individualism and combat the danger of despotism. Furthermore the practice of association inexorably reminds businesses that they are part of society and encourages them to act in enlightened ways and adopt ethical practices out of pure self-interest. Finally the corporation is itself an embodiment of the freedom to associate. It all sounds suspiciously like Adam Smith's "invisible hand." There is something of this in Tocqueville, but this is not the whole of his story.

Alongside the individualism and selfish materialism that individuals are subject to in democratic society, Tocqueville also discusses a parallel phenomenon that he calls "collective individualism," which explains why associations and their representatives/management do not necessarily display a proper understanding of their self-interest. Association can be a two-edged sword. While always preferable to individualism, there is such a thing as a bad form of association in Tocqueville's view. One job of the business ethicist, in this perspective, is to help businesses avoid the moral pitfalls of collective individualism.

The problem that Tocqueville wishes to address in his discussion of collective individualism is when the association as such acts in ways that raise ethical questions and that collide with the general interest, displaying a form of collective, corporate, selfishness. Tocqueville discusses this problem in the context of prerevolutionary France, a society in which aristocratic forms were still observed. There was no individualism in the democratic sense there, but there was a different kind: "Our ancestors lacked the word 'individualism,' which we have created for our own use, because in their era there were, in fact, no individuals who did not belong to a group and who could consider themselves absolutely alone; but each one of the thousand little groups of which society was composed thought only of itself. This was, if one can use the word thus, a kind of collective individualism." These groups acted in the same way that Tocqueville feared democratic individuals might act: "Every one of these little societies therefore lived only for itself, and was only interested in itself and in matters which directly affected it." We need only think of those thousand little groups, the guilds, castes, and so on, as so many business corporations to see that the problem of collective individualism did not disappear with the end of aristocratic society.[27]

The field of business ethics is therefore, in Tocquevillean terms, concerned with the special issue of collective individualism and how to fight it, both through institutional means, such as different structures of corporate law and governance, and through moral judgments, attitudes, and mores. In examining some of the leading theories of business ethics from a Tocquevillean perspective, a primary question is, Which theory is best placed not merely to describe accurately the ethical obligations of business management, but to help businesses properly understand their self-interest and avoid collective individualism? This instrumentalizes theories of business ethics, but it must be acknowledged that, as we have seen above, Tocqueville largely views ethical theory in an instrumental light. What ethical attitude should we encourage businesses to adopt in order to best encourage the rejection of collective individualism? What theory of business ethics, what view of the nature of the firm, will best enable business ethicists to perform this role?

Two of the leading theories of business ethics are the stockholder and stakeholder models. The stakeholder model was first developed by R. Edward Freeman, who used the term "stakeholder" to refer to anyone who "has a stake in or claim on the firm." This can be interpreted widely to include anyone at all affected by the corporation, or more narrowly to include only "those groups who are vital to the survival and success of the corporation," such as stockholders, customers, lenders, suppliers, local communities, and so on. Stakeholder theory holds that the obligation of a firm's management is not to maximize profit, which concerns only the stockholders, but to maximize the benefits to all of a firm's stakeholders, because only in this way can the survival of the firm be assured. Additionally, not merely must a firm be managed for the benefit of all stakeholders, but "the groups must participate, in some sense, in decisions that substantially affect their welfare." This is called the "principle of corporate legitimacy." The "stakeholder fiduciary principle" goes on to state that the firm's managers have fiduciary duties and hence ethical obligations toward the stakeholders. Stakeholder theory is thus both a theory of effective management, since it is presented as a means of improving the odds that the firm will survive, and an ethical theory that states the moral obligations of the firm's managers, and to a lesser extent of all the other stakeholders as well. These obligations effectively force management (and stakeholders!) to act in accord with what Tocqueville would characterize as enlightened self-interest. Acting in accord with the narrower, often short-term interests of only some stakeholders (e.g., the stockholders or upper management) would be both empirically and normatively wrong, endangering both the firm's long-term survival and its ability to enhance the good of all its stakeholders. Stakeholder theory is thus both empirical and normative. From a Tocquevillean perspective, this is an advantage.[28]

TOCQUEVILLE AND STAKEHOLDER THEORY

Stakeholder theories of business ethics possess several advantages from a Tocquevillean perspective. In some respects, they fit admirably with Tocquevillean conceptions of democratic society. Stakeholder theory is egalitarian in comparison with views such as stockholder theory, which limit management's responsibility to the relatively small group of stock owners. By broadening the universe of people to which management is and feels accountable to the much larger group of stakeholders, stakeholder theory adopts an egalitarian perspective that accords with the practices and prejudices of a democratic society. Furthermore, "according to the normative stake-holder theory, management must give equal consideration to the interests of all stakeholders." The requirement of "equal consideration" firmly aligns stakeholder theory with the moral egalitarianism central to the democratic perspective.[29]

Stakeholder theory is not only democratic; it can also appeal to the prin-ciples of association and of enlightened self-interest that are central to the Tocquevillean account of what makes business ethical. I say that it *can* rather than it *does* appeal to association and enlightened self-interest, because in his most recent formulation Freeman endorses association while rejecting any appeal to self-interest. Freeman thus argues that capitalism is "the volun-tary associations of fair, responsible, cooperating, consenting, and complex adults" but "does not include competition or self-interest as foundational assumptions."[30] For Tocqueville, by contrast, self-interest is not merely part of human nature, but is particularly important in democratic societies. It is inevitably a foundational assumption of the corporation as of any other association.

For Tocqueville the overlap between stakeholder theory as a theory of business management and stakeholder theory as a theory of business ethics is not a weakness or source of confusion, but a source of strength. Manage-ment must not further only the interests of stockholders, but those of a broad number of groups, some of which are private—employees, suppliers, and so on—but some of which are public, such as local communities. Stake-holder theory thus requires management to understand its self-interest in a very enlightened fashion, with all the positive moral consequences that entails for Tocqueville. The business is compelled to renounce any form of individualism, and the stakeholders continually remind management that the business lives in a society and cannot survive and prosper except in con-nection with that society.

A business enterprise is, from a stakeholder perspective, not merely a par-ticular association for the purpose of making a profit. It is in effect an asso-ciation of associations, with each stakeholder, be it another association (e.g., a supplier) or individuals (e.g., employees), forming part of the grand asso-ciation of stakeholders. If the goals and purposes of these various "member associations" only partly overlap (because the goals of the firm's customers, for example, differ from those of its lenders), this is all to the good from a Tocquevillean perspective, because this dissonant element forces the firm's management to take the broadest possible view of the interests for whose advancement it is responsible. Indeed, the more widely one draws the bound-aries of the circle of stakeholders, the broader the view of the firm's "self-interest" that results. In order to satisfy its stakeholders, the firm is compelled to take a broad interest in society, far broader than the maximization of its own profits, even its own long-term profits, would necessarily imply. Even if the only effect of a stakeholder view were to encourage a focus on long-term rather than short-term profit maximization, it would meet with Tocqueville's approval, because Tocqueville, as noted above, thinks people in democratic societies need encouragement to take a long-term view. A stakeholder perspective on the firm will naturally do this.

Stakeholder theory has another advantage that holds regardless of the number of stakeholders, and is perhaps stronger when the number is greater; it encourages those with a stake in the business to organize themselves so as to be able to express their views. The fact that stakeholder theory "tends to privilege those who are well-organized over those who are poorly organized" is not a bad thing from a Tocquevillean perspective.[31] It creates an incentive for organization and association, and the existence of incentives to motivate people to abandon apathy and participate in associations is all to the good.

At first glance, therefore, it would seem as if a stakeholder theory of management and of business ethics—a theory, both empirical and normative, which also explicitly relies on enlightened self-interest—would be just what Tocqueville would order. But in fact stakeholder management and ethics also present significant drawbacks from a Tocquevillean perspective. The risk of stakeholder theory is that it may impose either too few obligations on the firm's management or too many, and that it may therefore end up encouraging collective individualism, or even lead inexorably to the kind of state socialist despotism that was one of Tocqueville's nightmares.

Let us first consider the problem of how stakeholder theory may impose too few ethical obligations on management. Too broad a view of who is a stakeholder can result in the sort of reductio ad absurdum in which the firm is called upon to act in the interests of all humanity equally, or if one prefers a nonutilitarian formulation, in accordance with the categorical imperative. Freeman's own (early) Kantianism lends itself to this interpretation.[32] Tocqueville believed that human beings had difficulty rising to this level, and that attempting to persuade them to adopt the species' interests as their own was counterproductive: "Man, as God has created him (I don't know why), becomes less devoted as the object of his affections becomes larger. His heart needs the particular. . . . There are only a very small number of great souls who can inflame themselves with the love of the human species."[33] By attempting to extend the circle of stakeholders too broadly, we weaken management's sense of responsibility to the stakeholders, because there are too many of them. We further weaken the stakeholders' sense of mutual responsibility to one another, for the same reason. If multiple stakeholder relationships are accepted, there results a deafening cacophony of stakeholder claims.

A natural result, from a Tocquevillean perspective, is management apathy in the face of too many conflicting stakeholder claims, which are morally impossible to adjudicate. According to Tocqueville, when faced with a myriad of equal claims (and democratic conceptions of equality, no less than Kantian assumptions about treating all individuals as ends, require such claims to be given equal status), human beings have an unfortunate tendency to look for a despot to help them decide what to do. The most convenient despotism likely to present itself in this context is that of the stockholders, to the exclusion of all other stakeholders, and thus stakeholder theory may in practice lead to a rejection of social concerns and a retreat to collective individualism. Alternatively, those forced to make decisions in the face of cacophonous conflicting moral demands may reject all responsibility to any stakeholder whatsoever, including the stockholders, and thus management may choose to act in its own self-interest—a result that is not unheard-of in practice. Sufficiently diluting fiduciary responsibility has the practical effect of destroying it.

Conversely, stakeholder theory may lead logically to the imposition of too many moral obligations on management, such that the only possible solution is effective state ownership. The broader the circle of stakeholders in a business, the more the universe of stakeholders comes to resemble the entire nation, or even the globe. Having established the democratic principle that all stakeholders are equal, it seems logical that all stakeholders, in effect society as a whole, should direct the business. Instead of the infinite dilution of all sense of moral responsibility discussed above, an alternative reaction would be to combine all the different stakeholder claims into one, the claim of society as a whole. Management's sole real fiduciary responsibility would be to society—which in practice often means to the government. The business thus loses all its independence, and whether formal ownership is transferred to the state or not, the business becomes in effect a unit of government. This tendency is all the more natural, since among "democratic peoples, citizens often look upon such badly needed associations [Tocqueville is talking about 'industrial associations,' i.e., businesses] with secret feelings of fear and jealousy, which prevent their defending them. . . . They come close to seeing the free use that associations make of their natural faculties as a dangerous kind of privilege."[34] The result is that businesses cease to be free associations, fall under government control, and thus are no longer capable of providing the moral and political benefits that Tocqueville looks to them to provide. Stakeholder theory, particularly in its broad form, only serves to encourage this process.

To have its beneficial effect on the corporation, Tocqueville's theory of enlightened self-interest thus requires the circle of stakeholders to be limited in extent. Finding formal criteria that enable us to draw such boundaries may well be very difficult, as Alexei Marcoux suggests, but in practice it may not be an insuperable obstacle.[35] It is in any case necessary to the successful application, in both theory and practice, of stakeholder theories of the corporation.

TOCQUEVILLE AND STOCKHOLDER THEORY

From a Tocquevillean perspective there are potential advantages to stake-holder theories of business ethics, and potential disadvantages. What then of stockholder theories of business ethics? At first glance, these seem as un-congenial from Tocqueville's viewpoint as stakeholder theories seem con-genial. Is not a theory under which management's fiduciary obligations are solely to owners likely to strongly encourage collective individualism on the part of businesses? Even if those obligations are limited by a general obligation to obey the law, it is hard to see how they are likely to result in a sense of self-interest properly understood, as Tocqueville would like to see it. The further obligation stated by Milton Friedman, that the firm "engages in open and free competition, without deception or fraud," seems at least in part dubious.[36] Granted that management should not engage in deception or fraud, why is it obligated to engage in open and free competition, if by legal means it can obtain a monopoly or discourage competitors from en-tering the field? Would it not be the fiduciary obligation of management to obtain a monopoly or oligopoly position if it can, rather than encouraging "open and free competition"? Such actions would be one more instance of collective individualism on the part of the firm.

Stockholder theories of business ethics thus inevitably contain an ele-ment of collective individualism in their single-minded focus on returns on investment. They also encourage the materialism that Tocqueville thought both a natural consequence of and a danger to democratic society. If the sole social responsibility of the firm is to make a profit, an outlook strictly limited to materialism would seem to be the only one that a firm's management could ethically adopt—but that would hardly be the kind of ethics of which Tocqueville would have approved.

So prima facie it would seem that Tocqueville would find little to recom-mend in stockholder theories of business ethics. But that is not the whole of their moral content from a Tocquevillean perspective. They also possess a number of positive features. First of all, stockholder theories maintain the firm's character as a private association, whose purposes are not subject to the tyranny of the majority. Management is obliged by its sole fiduciary duty, to the stockholders, to act independently of the wishes of public opinion. The business and its management thus retain the moral freedom to act as agents who are not subject to the control of the social majority (some amorphous number of stakeholders) or the government. They are limited only by the general obligation of all individuals and associations to obey the law.

This is an extremely important point from a Tocquevillean perspec-tive. It is only the ability to associate that gives the relatively weak and iso-lated individuals of democratic society the ability to stand up to social and political pressures. Corporations attract "fear and jealousy" because they seem to be privileged aristocratic bodies not subject to the rules. Tocqueville does not wish to emancipate businesses from subjection to the law, but it is precisely because of their aristocratic character, which they share with all associations, their ability to resist and to act independently of the authority of public opinion, that Tocqueville values "industrial associations" as much as any other kind.

Stockholder theory preserves the character of the business and its management as an independent association. It offers another advantage as well. Tocqueville points out that in contrast to commercial and industrial enterprises landownership is protected against government encroachment in multiple ways. Land gives its owners independence from the government. Not so industrial property. "The industrial class," that is, those, rich and poor, who owe their livelihoods to industry, "has not become less dependent as it has become more numerous. On the contrary, it seems to carry despotism within itself, and despotism naturally spreads as the industrial class develops." The dependence Tocqueville is talking about here is dependence on the state. Since Tocqueville's time the regulations on private use of land have multiplied, but those regulations are dwarfed by the regulation of industry. Regardless of the economic and social impact of those regulations, good or bad, they have the effect of limiting the independence of business. Stakeholder theories of business ethics provide no moral grounds for resistance to such regulations, which are naturally made to defend the putative interests of stakeholders. Stockholder theories do provide moral grounds to resist state encroachment.[37]

In both these respects, that is, in favoring the independent character of the business association and in strengthening its ability to resist the social majority/government, stockholder theories paradoxically function in favor of businesses engaging with the community, not as its servants, in the manner of stakeholder theory, but as independent agents who may well, like other associations, find themselves in conflict with public opinion—and in the course of such conflict, help to shape it, just like other associations. In this process the materialism inherent in stockholder theories does not disappear, but becomes instead the kind of enlightened self-interest and community involvement (including political involvement) that Tocqueville favored. The motivation, for example, profit, does not change. Tocqueville thinks democratic societies and individuals will always be characterized by materialism. But it is now a properly understood self-interest that dominates, and that in the long run effectively encourages attention to all stakeholders as well as to the stockholders. That management properly understands its self-interest is all that can be ethically required of it under stockholder theories of business ethics—and all that needs to be required, from a Tocquevillean perspective.

Tocqueville, however, makes no prediction as to whether the stockholder-focused corporation will maintain its independence from public opinion or find that the path of least resistance is to surrender to it. Empirically, both are possible outcomes. The business ethicist, however, would under this view be obliged to encourage corporations to maintain their independent involvement in society, and by logical extension in politics. It is by no means clear that Tocqueville would have opposed the *Citizens United* decision[38] that preserved corporate access to the political process—although the possibility of anonymous political involvement raises other questions from both a Tocquevillean and a legal standpoint that are outside our scope here.

CONCLUDING REMARKS: TOCQUEVILLE ON BUSINESS ETHICS

Whether stakeholder-based or stockholder-based, business ethics when understood from a Tocquevillean perspective must address the corporation as an instrument to obtain various political and ethical goods, for its members and for society as a whole, just like any other form of association. Business ethics must simultaneously address corporations as themselves a form of ethical life, associative ends-in-themselves, that form a space in which people exercise their freedom and creativity. Neither kind of business ethics theory, stakeholder- or stockholder-based, has as yet fully answered this double-barreled challenge.

The question that naturally arises, however, is, Which kind of theory is best positioned to do so? Which kind of theory of business ethics would Tocqueville prefer, stockholder-based or stakeholder-based? In some ways this is not a fair question to ask. Tocqueville did not write about business ethics as such, and he had no particular theory of the firm. Nevertheless, by translating some contemporary debates over business ethics into Tocquevillean terms, we can see that some of the issues that most concerned Tocqueville are also at stake in debates about the corporation and business ethics. Questions about associations and about self-interest and individualism are at the heart of Tocqueville's analysis of democratic society and are also at the heart of the debate over business ethics. Stakeholder and stockholder theories are two of the most prominent contenders in the debate. Which position would Tocqueville have taken?

When two theories contend for a long time, and neither wins, it is often because both express different aspects of a larger truth. This may well be the case with stockholder and stakeholder theories. From a Tocquevillean perspective, both theories can be deployed in either harmful or beneficial ways, depending on how they fit with a larger ethical objective—maintaining freedom in democratic societies.[39] Both theories see the corporation as an association, and as far as that goes, Tocqueville would see nothing to choose between them. Where they differ is in the nature of that association, its membership, and the goals appropriate to it.

The question from a Tocquevillean perspective would be, which way of viewing the corporation is more likely to result in the enlightening, the proper understanding, of the self-interest natural to democratic societies? The task of the business ethicist, therefore, whatever approach she or he may choose to take, is to make sure that this consideration is never lost from sight.

This will not be a very satisfying task to ethicists for whom questions of interest, however well understood, are not properly ethical questions at all. Tocqueville will disappoint the Kantians among us, who may well reject a Tocquevillean perspective as a result. Tocqueville had no interest in addressing questions of universal ethical rules. His interests lay in the situational ethics of democratic society—they were, one might say, consumer driven. And in that respect they seem appropriate indeed for business ethics.

NOTES

1. Tocqueville, *Democracy in America,* trans. Arthur Goldhammer (New York: Library of America, 2004), 710; henceforth cited as *Democracy.*

2. *Democracy,* 647.

3. Ibid., 617–19, 644, 738.

4. Tocqueville to Louis de Kergorlay, September 28, 1834, in *Correspondance d'Alexis de Tocqueville et de Louis de Kergorlay,* ed. André Jardin, vol. 13 of *Oeuvres, papiers et correspondances* (Paris: Gallimard, 1977), 1:361.

5. The Rotary Club is an international service organization for business leaders and professionals, founded in the United States in 1905 and now established worldwide.

6. *Democracy,* 595–99.

7. Tocqueville thinks that the efficiency of a myriad of private associations is greater than that of a single government administration, even though the associations may be less technically competent than the government. See *Democracy,* 597.

8. *Democracy,* 585.

9. Ibid., 818.

10. Ibid., 869.

11. Ibid., 503, 516–17, 622.

12. For Tocqueville, businesses with a sole owner or a very small number of partners would have to be considered differently. They would no longer be associations, unless considered from a very strong stakeholder perspective.

13. *Democracy,* 595.

14. Of course, when Tocqueville was visiting America in 1831, the development of the joint-stock corporation, legally and practically, was still in its infancy, or at least early childhood. *Democracy,* 594.

15. *Democracy,* 604.

16. Ibid., 215, 218, 222, 590, 591, 595, 599.

17. But not the same function as the First Baptist Church, because Tocqueville sees a special role for religion that neither General Motors nor the Sierra Club can fulfill, in his view, although from a limited perspective religious associations are just like other associations, and fulfill the same functions.

18. *Democracy*, 593.

19. Ibid., 639–41

20. Ibid., 593–94; see also 610.

21. The reference to Montaigne is found in *Democracy,* 611, but I have been unable to find the original.

22. The resemblance between Tocqueville and Friedrich Nietzsche on this point is quite strong, although Nietzsche is a partisan of aristocracy and Tocqueville a partisan, albeit with reservations, of democracy. See Brigitte Krulic, *Nietzsche penseur de la hiérarchie: Pour une lecture "tocquevillienne" de Nietzsche* (Paris: l'Harmattan, 2002).

23. *Democracy*, 610.

24. Ibid., 612, 610–11.

25. This remark is taken from a passage of *Democracy* Tocqueville eliminated before publication. It can be found in the Liberty Fund edition of *Democracy in America*, ed. Eduardo Nolla, trans. James T. Schleifer (Indianapolis: Liberty Fund, 2009), 3:924 note n.

26. *Democracy*, 612.

27. Tocqueville, *The Old Regime and the Revolution*, vol. 1, ed. François Furet and Françoise Mélonio, trans. Alan S. Kahan (Chicago: University of Chicago Press, 1998), 162–63.

28. R. E. Freeman, *Strategic Management: A Stakeholder Approach* (New York: Harper-Collins, 1984); William M. Evan and R. E. Freeman, "A Stakeholder Theory of the Modern Corporation: Kantian Capitalism," in *Ethical Theory and Business,* ed. Tom L. Beauchamp and Norman E. Bowie, 4th ed. (Englewood Cliffs, NJ: Prentice-Hall, 1993), 82 n. 14; John Hasnas, "The Normative Theories of Business Ethics: A Guide for the Perplexed," *Business Ethics Quarterly* 8, no. 1 (Jan. 1998): 25–26.

29. Hasnas, "Normative Theories of Business Ethics," 26 and n. 30.

30. R. Edward Freeman, Jeffrey S. Harrison, Andrew C. Wicks, Bidhan L. Palmer, and Simone de Colle, *Stakeholder Theory: The State of the Art* (New York: Cambridge University Press, 2010), 283.

31. Joseph Heath, "Business Ethics without Stakeholders," *Business Ethics Quarterly* 16, no. 4 (Oct. 2006): 545.

32. Evan and Freeman, "Stakeholder Theory of the Modern Corporation." In later versions of his stakeholder theory, Freeman sets aside the Kantian basis.

33. Tocqueville, *The Old Regime and the Revolution,* vol. 2, ed. François Furet and Françoise Mélonio, trans. Alan S. Kahan (Chicago: University of Chicago Press, 2001), 262.

34. *Democracy*, 812.

35. Alexei Marcoux, "Who Are the Stakeholders? The Failure of the Stakeholder-as-Contractor View," *Business and Professional Ethics Journal* 17, no. 3 (Fall 1998): 79–108.

36. Milton Friedman, *Capitalism and Freedom* (Chicago: University of Chicago Press, 1962), 133.

37. *Democracy*, 809–10.

38. In *Citizens United v. Federal Election Commission*, 558 U.S. 310 (2010), the United States Supreme Court held that the American government could not limit independent political expenditures by corporations, associations, or labor unions.

39. For a discussion of Tocqueville as a thinker whose ethics are based on the idea of freedom, see Alan S. Kahan, *Alexis de Tocqueville* (London: Continuum, 2010), esp. chaps. 2 and 7.

CHAPTER 15

J. S. Mill and Business Ethics

Nicholas Capaldi

There is a tendency for philosophers who reflect on the works of philosophers in previous ages both to engage in anachronistic attribution and to see the work of predecessors as imperfect groping to their own favored position. This tendency started with Aristotle!

J. S. Mill has received the same sort of treatment.[1] Most textbooks in business ethics begin with a framework designed to help students grapple with specific issues in the contemporary business world. The framework usually includes a desultory summary of so-called ethical theories, most especially utilitarianism and deontology (sometimes adding virtue ethics and pragmatism). Utilitarianism is typically associated with J. S. Mill, whereas deontology is associated with Kant. For many students, their only acquaintance with Mill is through the so-called utilitarianism model.

This does little justice to Mill. To begin with, it puts the proverbial cart before the horse. The wrong way to read Mill is to assume that he worked out an ethical theory and then looked to apply it. This is what contemporary academic philosophers do, but it is not what Mill did. What emerges is a cardboard caricature that fails to capture a connection crucial to Mill. Mill was more than a philosopher who formulated an ethics. He famously addressed the major public policy issues of the nineteenth century. His *Principles of Political Economy*, first published in 1848, was the canonical textbook in economics and public policy for half a century. Mill's work on economics and politics (political economy) were vital expressions of his ethical views. We are more likely to understand the ethics by reading back into it his views on political economy.

Second, Mill was not what we call in contemporary parlance an ethical theorist. He thought of himself as telling us fundamental truths about ourselves (the human condition) and the norms inherent in extant institutions, as well as what he thought the future permutations of those norms should be under new historical circumstances.[2] Specifically, Mill inherited from his father, James Mill, and from Jeremy Bentham a concern with understanding the transition from feudalism to a modern industrial and commercial economy. Mill favored the economic evolution from feudalism to industrialism, but he recognized both the accompanying social disruption and the new opportunities (e.g., for the emancipation of women). Mill did not see himself as an adversary to all of modernity. As a public intellectual, Mill saw his role as Socratic. There is much about the modern world for which to be thankful.

In what follows, we shall identify Mill's understanding of ethics, specifically addressing what utilitarianism meant for him, outline his general approach to public policy issues by discussing his political economy, and conclude with the application of Mill's ideas to significant issues in business ethics.

MILL'S ETHICS (THE HUMAN CONDITION)

How then are we to understand the human condition? In the classical and medieval worlds ethics was fundamentally teleological (e.g., Aristotle). The whole universe has a telos, and every component of this whole bears its own sub-telos, which is properly attuned to contribute to the overall final telos. That is, it was assumed that human beings had a telos, that society had a telos, and that the human telos achieved fulfillment within the social telos. Modernity (in the works of René Descartes, Galileo, and Thomas Hobbes, for example) rejected Aristotelian metaphysics and therefore teleological ethics. Moderns started to talk about moral philosophy (in contradistinction to natural philosophy) instead of ethics. In addition, modern moral philosophers assumed the ontological primacy of the individual (comparable to the individual object studied by natural philosophers such as Isaac Newton). This raised two questions: (a) Who or what is the individual, and (b) how is the individual related to society?[3]

One answer was to assume that individuals had a telos (variously described) but not one that formed a seamless web with society. The relation of the individual to society was then construed as contractual (as in the work of Hobbes, John Locke, and Jeremy Bentham). A second answer rejected teleology even for individuals and asserted that human beings had free will and therefore the capacity to pursue their own self-chosen path. The relation of the individual to society is construed as one of mutual respect or recognition required by that freedom. Immanuel Kant, G. W. F. Hegel, and Mill belong here.

Nicholas Capaldi

J. S. Mill's formal expression of his ethical position is his work *Utilitarianism*.[4] But that work has to be understood in the light of the essay *On Liberty*. "I forego any advantage which could be derived to my argument from the idea of abstract right, as a thing independent of utility. I regard utility as the ultimate appeal on all ethical questions; but it must be utility in the largest sense, grounded on the permanent interests of man as a progressive being."[5] What did Mill mean by this?

Here it is necessary to distinguish between "liberty" and "freedom." For Mill, "liberty" refers to the absence of arbitrary *external* constraints. "Freedom," on the other hand, is an *internal* condition. To be free in the internal sense means (a) that human beings do not have a telos that can be discovered empirically, (b) that human desires do not form a homeostatic system about which it makes sense to talk in terms of maximizing its welfare, (c) that we can choose what kind of person we want to be, and (d) that this choice is not forced upon us either by the outside world or by our physiology—that is, the choice defies any naturalistic-scientist or reductive explanation. Individuals can be ignorant of their freedom or choose to abdicate their freedom, but the fundamental truth is that human beings have the ability to control themselves or to control their responses. The entire argument of *On Liberty* is that "liberty" is justified because it enhances the expression of human "freedom." As A. V. Dicey recognized, "Mill was so convinced of the value to be attached to individual spontaneity that he, in fact, treated the promotion of freedom as the test of utility."[6]

What does it mean to exercise this freedom responsibly? It means recognizing one's freedom, making the fundamental choice of what kind of person one wants to be, acknowledging that a free being does not and cannot act inconsistently with that freedom, specifically that one cannot abdicate responsibility or define oneself in terms of others, and accepting responsibility for the consequences of one's action. There is nothing in this concept that forbids two or more autonomous persons to be involved in a joint project as long as participation is voluntary and the autonomy of each is respected throughout the pursuit of this project, precisely what Harriet Taylor (later Harriet Taylor Mill) and Mill believed that marriage should be. It is not possible to exercise this freedom in a manner deleterious to others. Any action that requires the unwilling subordination of another human being is an act in which we define ourselves in terms of something other than ourselves. We can never be free if we are defining ourselves in terms of others, either to subordinate ourselves to them or to subordinate them to ourselves. This is Mill's incorporation of Kant's notion of the categorical imperative as an expression of the concept of autonomy. Mill incorporated as well Hegel's discussion of the master-slave relationship. To be a master is not satisfying because one's status as a master requires recognition by way of acquiescence on the part of one's inferiors. Only recognition from one's equals—equal in being responsible for themselves—gives satisfaction. Playing the role of master either domestically or in public is self-destructive. The more other people are autonomous, the more recognition my own autonomy receives. "It is only the high-minded to whom equality is really agreeable. . . . They are the only persons who are capable of strong and durable attachments to their equals."[7] Mill had read and has been influenced by thinkers who were pivotal in the romantic movement:[8] Mill speaks about "individuality," the subject of chapter 3 of *On Liberty*, and he understood it to mean self-development, what has been identified as the romantic concept of *bildung*.[9] *Bildung* requires autonomy. In sum, "individuality" for Mill connotes both freedom as autonomy and self-development.[10]

The relationship of the individual to society has to be understood within this framework. Mill rejected the Benthamite selfish hypothesis (all human action is to be explained in terms of the agent's ultimate and fundamental desire to maximize the agent's pleasure and/or to minimize his pain), which is why he rejected social philosophies based upon rights or contracts. Mill was always moved to promote concern for others. On the other hand, he rejected Comtean altruism, the view that we should be exclusively concerned about others. How can we promote the interests of others if their only interest is itself to promote the interest of others, ad infinitum? The resolution is analogous to Hegel's resolution of right and duty in ethical life. Specifically, if autonomy is our ultimate good,[11] and if the only way I can pursue my autonomy is to interact with other autonomous beings, then personal fulfillment is only possible by promoting that identical interest in others. Freedom as autonomy is not zero-sum but potentially infinite. By promoting it in others I enhance it within myself. Liberty is a means to promoting freedom as autonomy. All of Mill's public policy positions, including his positions in business ethics, are designed to enhance liberty so as to maximize freedom.

MILL'S UTILITARIANISM

Mill was formally committed to being a utilitarian, but he was engaged in a reformulation and correction of Bentham's position.[12] Mill had already distanced himself from Bentham as early as 1833 in his "Remarks on Bentham's Philosophy."[13] Here, Mill pointed out that the emphasis on expediency at the expense of virtue was incompatible with "all rational hope of good for the human species."[14] Writing after exposure to the German romantic writers, Mill argued that what was needed was a change in the inner person. In the *Autobiography* Mill defended utilitarian ethics against the unjust criticisms of Henry Sidgwick, but the defense contained "a number of opinions which constituted my views on those subjects, as distinguished from my old associates. In this I partly succeeded, though my relation to my father would have made it painful to me in any case, and impossible in a review for which he wrote, to speak out my whole mind on the subject at this time."[15] In 1852, Mill defended utility as just as compatible with traditional virtues as the a priori view of ethics, while admitting that Bentham had failed to make this clear.[16]

To be a utilitarian is to be a consequentialist, that is, someone who judges action by its consequences. The relevant consequences are those that affect human well-being or happiness. Happiness has two components, romantic *bildung* and Kantian autonomy. Happiness is thus related to freedom by way of dignity. "When Kant (as before remarked) propounds as the fundamental principle of morals, 'So act, that thy rule of conduct might be adopted as a law by all rational beings,' he virtually acknowledges that the interest of mankind collectively, or at least mankind indiscriminately, must be in the mind of the agent when conscientiously deciding on the morality of the act."[17] So when defining utilitarianism, Mill insists that what is right has to be defined in terms of what is good understood in the universalizable sense, but not in terms of what Mill regards as the Comtean altruistic sense.[18] Right is defined in terms of good, good is understood as happiness, and happiness is identified by reference to pleasure and pain. But there are, says Mill, differences between higher and lower pleasures.[19] More significantly, the good is not pleasure but happiness. Pleasure is simply a property of happiness, the empirical confirmation of its existence.

The important transition comes when Mill reconceptualizes happiness. Happiness consists of dignity:

> A being of higher faculties requires more to make him happy. . . . We may refer it to the love of liberty and personal independence . . . but *its most appropriate appellation is a sense of dignity*, which all human beings possess in one form or other, and in some, though by no means in exact, proportion to their higher faculties, and which is *so essential a part of the happiness of those in whom it is strong*, that nothing which conflicts with it could be, otherwise than momentarily, an object of desire to them. . . . It is better to be a human being dissatisfied than a pig satisfied; *better to be Socrates dissatisfied than a fool satisfied*.[20]

Finally, happiness is defined as a state in which virtue becomes constitutive of it: "The mind is not in a right state, not in a state conformable to Utility, not in the state most conducive to the general happiness, unless it does love virtue in this manner—as a thing desirable in itself. The ingredients of happiness are very various, and each of them is desirable in itself, and not merely when considered as swelling an aggregate. . . . Happiness is not an abstract idea, but a concrete whole; and these are some of its parts."[21]

What Mill characterized as the chief ingredient of happiness is dignity, and dignity as defined above is synonymous with *autonomy*. We cannot be truly happy unless we are acting with dignity, that is, autonomously. Mill made autonomy our ultimate end.[22] Traditional utilitarians such as W. S. Jevons were furious with Mill's transformation: "The view which he [Mill] professes to uphold [utilitarianism] is the direct opposite of what he really upholds."[23] In the minds of utilitarians such as Jevons, to act from a sense of duty (even to oneself) is the opposite of utilitarianism. For Mill, the most important duty we have to ourselves is to act autonomously. Mill's resolution of the problem of relating individuals to the community is not by reference to a contract or to abstract rights but (a) by making the pursuit of autonomy the universal end and (b) by making the promotion of autonomy in others part of achieving one's own autonomy. Thus, there is no ultimate conflict between one individual's autonomy and that of every other individual. With autonomy as the ultimate end, the potential conflict, with which other versions of utilitarianism are plagued, disappears.

MILL ON POLITICAL ECONOMY AND FREEDOM AS AUTONOMY

What Mill wants is a series of institutions that promote freedom as the human ideal. The most important means to freedom is liberty. But there are conflicting conceptions of "liberty." Where does Mill fit into the debate about "liberty"?

Since the seventeenth century, all public policy disputes have been formulated in terms of one of two major narratives:[24] the Lockean liberty narrative and the Rousseau/Marx equality narrative. "Lockeans" (a) endorse the technological project, the transformation of nature for human betterment; (b) argue that the project is best carried out in a free market economy that (à la Adam Smith) preserves private property; (c) maintain that the free market economy requires limited government (limited to providing the legal machinery to protect negative rights, enforce contracts, and offer dispute resolution), wherein liberty is understood as restraining government on behalf of individuals' private interests; (d) insist that limited government is achieved through the rule of law, which restrains government power by its emphasis on due process and the recognition that economic planning is incompatible with the rule of law; (e) favor a culture of personal autonomy within which individuals *pursue* happiness and are not overruled by a collectivist good. Equality for "Lockeans" means equality of opportunity and equality before the law; economic inequality is inevitable but unproblematic in a growth economy wherein "a rising tide raises all boats." Moreover, in response to criticism from advocates of the second or alternative narrative, the Lockean narrative will evolve in the works of David Hume and Adam Smith (who directly responded to Rousseau), Tocqueville and Mill (who responded to the nineteenth-century French socialists), and numerous twentieth-century writers, most notably F. A. Hayek. This is Mill's place within the debate.

The second narrative is an adversarial one formulated originally by Jean-Jacques Rousseau. The Rousseau equality narrative is a direct response to Locke. It (a) rejects the technological project (extreme environmentalists still do), but Marxists and socialists later accepted it. Both "Rousseauians" and "Marxists" (b) attribute all social problems to the market economy that accompanies the technological project. The Lockean worldview is deemed as illegitimate because it institutionalized inequality by letting everyone keep his or her original possessions in the first social contract. Hence, this is why we must start over with a new dispensation in which the original position is a radical egalitarianism. Since the rich and powerful imposed the original agreement on the weak, the present economy must be heavily regulated to promote equality of outcome, even in a global context. Limited government is to be (c) replaced by a collectivist, all-encompassing good—a "general will" to which individuals are subordinated. "Rousseauians" attribute positive rights to everyone, which means that you can have liberty only when the government provides you with the resources, through the redistribution of wealth, to achieve your goal. Instead of restraining government, the legal system (d) is the faithful servant of the general will. Finally, each citizen (e) gives up his individual identity in return for the *achievement* of happiness by serving the greater collective good. The equality of outcome is somehow compatible with inequalities of function or status and allegedly will not cause resentment. An evolution comparable to that in the Lockean chronicle takes place in the Rousseauian narrative beginning with the nineteenth-century French socialists, who were themselves criticized by Marx, through the humanistic Marxists to the American Progressives.

There is an important sense, then, in which the equality narrative sets forth a challenge to political economy with something we shall call "social economy." Poverty replaces profit as the central category of the scope and method of economic inquiry. What do "we" do with the poor? What do "we" do with the marginalized? Where is "our" social conscience? The cause of the *poverty* of a nation becomes the focus, not the cause of the *wealth* of a nation. After all, isn't there something greater than the individual? Perhaps the national good? Or the common good, class, or social good? Even the state? Shouldn't we replace the profit-seeking entrepreneur with the scientifically trained administrative expert? These are the types of questions advanced by the Rousseauian focus on social economy.

Mill's own discussion of public policy is framed in terms of this debate:

> If, therefore the choice were to be made between Communism with all
> its chances, and the present state of society with all its sufferings and

injustices; if the institution of private property necessarily carried with it as a consequence, that the produce of labour should be apportioned as we now see it, almost in an inverse ratio to the labour—the largest portions to those who have never worked at all, the next largest to those whose work is almost nominal, and so on in a descending scale, the remuneration dwindling as the work grows harder and more disagreeable, until the most fatiguing and exhausting bodily labour cannot count with certainty on being able to earn even the necessaries of life; if this or Communism were the alternative, all the difficulties, great or small, of Communism would be but as dust in the balance. But to make the comparison applicable, we must compare Communism at its best, with the régime of individual property[25], not as it is, but as it might be made. The principle of private property has never yet had a fair trial in any country; and less so, perhaps, in this country than in some others. The social arrangements of modern Europe commenced from a distribution of property which was the result, not of just partition, or acquisition by industry, but of conquest and violence: and not withstanding what industry has been doing for many centuries to modify the work of force, the system still retains many and large traces of its origin. The laws of property have never yet conformed to the principles on which the justification of private property rests[26]. They have made property of things which never ought to be property, and absolute property where only a qualified property ought to exist. They have not held the balance fairly between human beings, but have heaped impediments upon some, to give advantages to others; they have purposefully fostered inequalities, and prevented all from starting fair in the race. That all should indeed start on perfectly equal terms, is inconsistent with any law of private property[27]; but if as much pains as has been taken to aggravate the inequality of chances arising from the natural working of the principle, had been taken to temper that inequality by every means not subversive of the principle itself[28]; if the tendency of legislation had been to favor the diffusion, instead of the concentration of wealth—to encourage the subdivision of the large masses, instead of striving to keep them together; the principle of individual property would have been found to have no necessary connexion with the physical and social evils which almost all Socialist writers assume to be inseparable from it.

Private property, in every defense made of it, is supposed to mean, the guarantee to individuals of the fruits of their own labour and abstinence. The guarantee to them of the fruits of the labour and abstinence of others, transmitted to them without any merit or exertion of their own, is not of the essence of the institution, but a mere incidental consequence, which, when it reaches a certain height, does not promote, but conflicts with, the ends which render private property legitimate. To judge of the final destination of the institution of property, we must suppose everything rectified, which causes the institution to work in a manner opposed to that equitable principle, of proportion between remuneration and exertion, on which in every vindication of it that will bear the light, it is assumed to be grounded. We must also suppose two conditions realized, without which neither Communism nor any other laws or institutions could make the condition of the mass of mankind other than degraded and miserable. One of these conditions is, universal education; the other, a due limitation of the numbers of the community. With these, there could be no poverty, even under the present social institutions: and these being supposed, the question of Socialism is not, as generally stated by Socialists, a question of flying to the sole refuge against the evils which now bear down humanity; but a mere question of comparative advantages, which futurity must determine. We are too ignorant either of what individual agency in its best form, or Socialism in its best form, can accomplish, to be qualified to decide which of the two will be the ultimate form of human society.

If a conjecture may be hazarded, the decision will probably depend mainly on one consideration, viz. Which of the two systems is consistent with the greatest amount of human liberty and spontaneity.[29]

Mill endorsed all aspects of the Lockean narrative, but it was a qualified endorsement. He endorsed the technological project and economic growth. At the same time, he always recognized the dark side of industrialization, its potential for dehumanization, overdevelopment, its worship of growth for growth's sake, and the danger of social fragmentation inherent in the division of labor.[30]

Yet even though Mill endorsed the market economy, the question of his relation to socialism continues to puzzle scholars. In the *Principles of Political Economy,* Mill described himself as an "Ideal Socialist," but later wrote in the *Chapters on Socialism* a scathing critique of socialism.[31] This confusion is easily clarified.

As a boy, Mill had been introduced by his father to the economist David Ricardo. An advocate of the Lockean narrative and a defender of a market economy, Ricardo nonetheless disagreed with some aspects of Adam Smith's defense of the market economy. Smith had identified three socioeconomic classes: landlords, capitalists, and laborers. Moreover, Smith had presented a growth model in which all three classes interacted harmoniously. What Ricardo added to this analysis was a critique of landlords. Landlords were always identified with Tory aristocratic landowners who held land acquired not through labor but originally through conquest and later through inheritance. Landlords still thought in feudal terms not industrial terms, and seemed more interested in maintaining their position of social preeminence and political control than in increasing national or international wealth.

Landlords favored mercantilist policies, including monopolistic privileges and tariffs. Tariffs on the importation of grain led to a corresponding increase in the cost of subsistence, which, in turn, would lead to an increase in wages and a subsequent decrease in profits. Decreasing profits would undermine the incentive to save and form capital, and so growth would come to an end sooner. The problem was the rapacious and profligate landlords' bent on conspicuous consumption. Mill agreed with Ricardo's critique of Smith that landlords were standing in the way of economic progress.

The term "socialism" came into use around 1830 and was applied to three movements deriving respectively from Henri de Saint-Simon (1760–1825) and Charles Fourier (1772–1837) in France, and Robert Owen (1771–1858) in England. These writers were referred to as "utopian" socialists. Other French figures who influenced Mill's thinking on socialism were Pierre-Joseph Proudhon (1809–65), advocate of producers' cooperatives without centralized control, and Louis Blanc (1811–82), another advocate of worker cooperatives, initially funded by the government, but thereafter independent of government control. The utopian socialists, especially Fourier and Blanc, influenced Mill in a number of ways. First, they made Mill aware of what came to be called the "social question"—namely, (a) that the then present distribution of property was based upon historical accident, (b) that the unequal distribution of property was connected with a number of social problems, and (c) that eradicating poverty ought to be the central issue not the promotion of wealth. Nineteenth-century Britain was a world in which property was largely owned by a few individuals or families; until 1855, Parliament had proscribed all but a few limited-liability joint-stock companies.[32] Second, they proposed solutions to these problems (e.g., cooperatives) that were consistent with the preservation of the market economy. Third, they helped Mill to distance himself further from Bentham by challenging and rejecting the latter's assumption that human beings were motivated exclusively by self-interest. Hence, there need not be in a market economy a permanent (and adversarial) division in society between two classes: owners and workers.

Clearly, Mill inherited a concern regarding the transition from feudalism to a modern industrial and commercial economy, with its accompanying social disruption. But Mill did not see himself as an adversary to the emerging market economy. He also saw new and welcomed opportunities, such as the emancipation of women. Within this context, Mill faced two tasks. First, he had to address the unequal distribution of wealth as manifest in the social question. Adam Smith had defined the objective measure of the wealth of a nation as the amount of the necessities and conveniences of life divided by the number of people by whom these products were to be consumed. Smith stressed increasing production (the numerator) rather than controlling population (the denominator). Malthus's "dismal" message was that the denominator (the size of the population) will increase exponentially, even though the numerator (the size of the total production) will increase arithmetically. Mill made both the increase in production and the control of population vital aspects of his approach to political economy.

According to the Lockean liberty narrative, economic growth offers the best means to alleviate poverty. The "production of wealth" can be subject to scientific analysis, whereas the "distribution of wealth" is in part "a matter of human institution." Mill conceded to the equality narrative that the current distribution is a reflection of historical accident. If one can make the distinction between the deserving and undeserving poor—which Mill and other classical liberals do make—is it not also reasonable to make the distinction between the deserving and undeserving rich? Mill understood that deliberate changes in the distribution of wealth would impact overall productivity. Nowhere does he recommend a change that he believes will lead to an overall decrease in wealth. But improved distribution does not lead to equality of outcome. Market efficiency is inevitably accompanied by inequality of outcome. Mill accepted that in a market economy there could only be equality of opportunity and equality before the law, but never equality of starting point or equality of outcome: "That all should indeed start on perfectly equal terms, is inconsistent with any law of private property."[33]

Neither efficiency nor absolute equality can be the ultimate end. So, Mill's second task was to restate the case for individual liberty on different intellectual grounds. He abandoned natural right and the labor theory of value in order to provide a richer and deeper understanding of the Lockean narrative, one that had a much greater impact on the subsequent development of the liberty narrative. Mill's case for liberty was that it was a means to freedom in all of its forms: individual, social, economic, and political.

Mill had absorbed Alexis de Tocqueville's message from *Democracy in America* (including his warning about the *tyranny of the majority* as well as the dangers of a democratic culture). The argument in favor of individual liberty and against absolute equality is presented by Mill as an argument in favor of freedom as *autonomy* (self-rule or self-governance). Even if there were no net economic loss in an egalitarian society, there would be an end to freedom of speech and eventually freedom of thought and freedom of religion and the right to choose the government under which we live. We would see the triumph of mediocrity or a narrow public opinion imposing the same capricious and arbitrary standards on everything and everyone. These freedoms or liberties are considered good because they are instrumental to self-expression, personal autonomy, and therefore, to the pursuit of happiness. Theorists like Tocqueville and Mill argued that freedom trumps efficiency and that is why they are often, incorrectly, identified with the egalitarian narrative. The defense of liberty requires more than the case for efficiency. For Tocqueville and Mill—just as it had been implicitly for Locke, Smith, and the American founders before, and would be forthcoming from Hayek and Milton Friedman—freedom of choice trumps fraternal equality. Autonomy is an intrinsic end. Wealth is important not as an end in itself nor as a means to consumerism but because it is the means for personal accomplishment. This is the revised argument of the liberty narrative. Wealth maximization and efficiency considerations are important, but only because we need to know if such policies are maximizing opportunities for more and more people to become autonomous.

When considering the future of the laboring poor, Mill distinguished between the "theory of dependence and protection" and the theory of "self-dependence."[34] He believed that the laboring poor will come to love the taste of liberty that comes with the theory of self-dependence or self-reliance and will reject the government paternalism that comes with the theory of dependence. Mill attacked the presumption that anyone should "rivet firmly in the minds of the labouring people the persuasion that it is the business of others to take care of their condition, without any self-control on their own part; [and] that whatever is possessed by other people, more than they possess, is a wrong to them, or at least a kind of stewardship, of which an account is to be rendered to them."[35] Mill was appalled by wealthy women who engaged in charitable activity on the assumption that the poor were dysfunctional only because they lacked material resources. This merely perpetuated a bad situation.[36] There is no victimization thesis in Mill. He supported the New Poor Law of 1834 that banned "outdoor relief" and insisted that paupers could receive relief only in workhouses with less than pleasant conditions (diet, confinement, separation of men from their families) designed to incentivize the poor to seek employment and restrict the size of their families.

MILL AND BUSINESS ETHICS

The following list covers most of the main themes discussed in the business ethics literature:

1. The nature and role of a firm
2. Corporate governance
3. Role of management
4. Role of employees
5. Globalization
6. Affirmative action
7. Corporate social responsibility

If Mill presented a version of the Lockean liberty narrative and therefore was pro-market[37] in his orientation, then we should expect the following applications of these contemporary themes.

1. *Firms are a nexus of contracts designed to produce a profitable product or service.* Firms may function as privately owned entities, partnerships, or corporations (joint-stock companies). Among the first to form such companies were the English, dating back to 1553. The East India Company, where both his father and J. S. Mill were employed, was one such company. In 1844, the English passed the Joint Stock Companies Act; in 1856, such companies were allowed the privilege of limited liability. Initially, most of these companies were owned by an individual or family. Subsequently, this form of ownership became rare, so that nowadays most of these companies are "owned" by a wide and ever-changing group of people; these shareholders elect a board of directors, which in turn appoints management. Shareholders are free to sell their shares on an open market. It is often said that shareholders are the "owners" of the corporation (an analogy based on the traditional single proprietorship). It is more accurate to say that shareholders "own shares" in the company.

Mill recognized that firms may be formed for all sorts of purposes, including philanthropic ones. In the *Principles of Political Economy*, Mill focused on firms designed to produce a profitable product or service. His main concern is with autonomy. One of the obstacles to autonomy is a grinding poverty. In dealing with poverty, Mill had two main objectives: increased productivity and a more widespread distribution.[38]

The "production of wealth" could be subject to scientific analysis, whereas the "distribution of wealth" is *in part* "a matter of human institution." Mill conceded to the equality narrative that the current distribution is a reflection of historical accident. Mill was fully aware that deliberate (governmentally controlled) changes in the distribution of wealth would impact overall productivity. Nowhere did he recommend a change that he believed would lead to an overall decrease in wealth.

Market efficiency inevitably produces inequality of outcome. Improved distribution will not lead to equality of outcome, but there is no reason to believe that autonomy hinges on equality of outcome. In fact, it is just the reverse; if I define myself relative to other people's income then I am acting heteronomously, not autonomously. Mill did advocate a tax on inheritance (but not bequests) in order to undermine large feudal estates but not large productive private industrial enterprises.

Mill's solution to the distribution issue was pro-market: he advocated the extension of the joint-stock principle in the form of workers' cooperatives. The idea of a cooperative was what Mill appropriated from Fourier:

> This system does not contemplate the abolition of private property, nor
> even of inheritance; on the contrary, it avowedly takes into consideration,
> as an element in the distribution of the produce, capital as well as labour. It
> proposes that the operations of industry should be carried on by associations

of about two thousand members . . . under the guidance of chiefs selected by themselves. In the distribution, a certain minimum is first assigned for the subsistence of every member of the community. . . . The remainder of the produce is shared in certain proportions, to be determined beforehand, among the three elements, Labour, Capital, and Talent. The capital of the community may be owned in unequal shares by different members, who would in that case receive, as in any other joint-stock company, proportional dividends. The claim of each person on the share of the produce apportioned to talent, is estimated by the grade or rank which the individual occupies in the several groups of labourers to which he or she belongs; these grades being in all cases conferred by the choice of his or her companions.[39]

Here it is important to note that Mill does specify that there can be social distinctions earned through personal services and exertions. Hence, a difference in status is possible based on function and skill level. Profits were to be divided relative to earnings. The primary fiduciary responsibility is to shareholders; there is no notion here of a multifiduciary duty to stakeholders. Executive compensation is to be determined by the shareholders. While Mill stipulates that the managers cannot be paid more than the highest-paid worker, he places no limits on what the highest-paid worker can earn. Executive compensation, in short, is based on market principles: the estimate of talent and its contribution in a competitive environment.

The firm or corporation is thus a nexus of contracting individuals and not a social entity with a purpose determined by government. This was not to be the only form of ownership but something added to the existing forms of private property. Competition between associations was to be maintained for the benefit of the consumer and ultimately for associations and the "industrious classes generally," and to assure technological progress. Public ownership, where necessary, did not imply state management.[40]

Mill did not see the entire economy as a collection of cooperatives, rather such cooperatives were only one form of ownership operating within a larger market economy.[41] Nor did he stipulate that specific workers' cooperatives were to last in perpetuity. It is easy to imagine how in Mill's world, workers' cooperatives were a temporary measure. Workers were free to leave to work for other companies, including traditional ones, to form (as entrepreneurs)[42] their own companies, or to join other cooperatives. Ironically, a present-day software start-up company in Silicon Valley within which the workers are all limited partners (another form of limited liability ownership) is an analogue to Mill's workers' cooperatives. Such start-ups are the epitome of present-day capitalism, not socialism! Mill's ultimate aims are (a) to dispose of the permanent class distinctions and (b) to create a society of autonomous individuals.

2. *Corporate governance is initially shareholder-centric but ultimately management-centric.* In the case of workers' cooperatives, as opposed to traditional publicly traded corporations, the laborers collectively own the capital and work under managers elected and removable by themselves. In these cases only, shareholders and managers are the same group of people without the intervention of a board.[43] There is no notion here that managers represent stakeholders; the primary fiduciary responsibility of management is to shareholders and creditors. This appears to commit Mill to a *shareholder*-centric vision of the firm. Nevertheless, if a worker quits, the capital "remains an indivisible property."[44] If a shareholder leaves or the vast majority of shareholders are ultimately replaced, the corporation (capital) survives, so the managers' responsibility remains focused on the shareholders. Thus it is possible to foresee the survival and direction of the firm being determined by currently elected management long after the initial shareholders and managers have come and gone. This would seem to entail a *management*-centric model for the corporation. That is, a long-term managerial core might direct the company long after the initial group of workers who formed it have left.

3. *The relation of management to employees is an autonomous contractual one.* All workers are shareholders; all managers are elected by shareholders; but Mill was not advocating industrial democracy! Only shareholders vote for management. Once managers are elected and reelected, the organization becomes hierarchical. That is, workers do not vote on all policies; workers vote for or against managers who determine policy. The relation of any employee to management is a form of contractual autonomy; beyond that, management's relation to employees on a day-to-day basis is hierarchical.

What this model accomplishes for Mill is the elimination of a class distinction between owners and workers. This is exactly what has occurred in an advanced market economy such as the United States. Firms encourage profit sharing, stock options, employee pension-fund ownership of equities, and employee mobility. The terminology of "owner" and "worker" has been replaced by "employer" and "employee" understood contractually. Managers are in fact elected by stockholders, now including worker pension funds.

4. *Employees work under conditions of employment at will and the right to work.*[45] Mill wanted all workers to think of themselves as autonomous agents. As a consequence, he was opposed to trades' unionism, strikes, and collective bargaining.[46] The future lay in profit sharing.[47] This amounts to an endorsement of the right to work and employment at will.[48] "While I agree and sympathize with Socialists in this practical portion of their aims," said Mill, "I utterly dissent from the most conspicuous and vehement part of their

teaching, their declamations against competition."[49] Contract employees are replacing unions and collective bargaining. Mill would have applauded this as the "true euthanasia of trade unionism."[50] I suggest that Mill would have welcomed all of this as the contemporary analogue to his cooperatives. This is a radically pro-market conception.

Employees and shareholders may both leave without disrupting the existence of the company.[51] Within this competitive environment companies compete for employees: "Competition even in the labour market is a source not of low but of high wages, wherever the competition *for* labour exceeds the competition *of* labour, as in America."[52]

5. *Mill favored globalization (the extension of the free market globally).* It is clear from Mill's career with the East India Company and his other writings that he foresaw and favored the notion of a developing world, moving from feudalism to industrialism. Consistent with this, he favored free trade. In his essay *A Few Words on Non-Intervention*, he praises Great Britain: "This nation desire[s] no benefit to itself at the expense of other[s], it desires none in which all others do not freely participate. It makes no treaties stipulating for separate commercial advantage. . . . To command liberty of trade, whatever it demands for itself it demands for all mankind. . . . Its own ports and commerce are free. . . . all its neighbors have full liberty to resort to it. . . . Nor does it concern itself . . . and persist in the most jealous and narrow-minded exclusion of its merchants and goods."[53]

6. *Mill favored meritocracy, and equality of opportunity, not affirmative action understood as any form of equality of outcome.* In *On the Subjection of Women*, Mill argued that competition not custom should hold sway in the relationship between men and women. He also claimed that he was not asking for "protective duties and bounties in favor of women; it is only asked that the present bounties and protective duties in favor of men should be recalled."[54] Clearly what Mill was advocating was equality of opportunity and equality before the law, not equality of outcome. In his view, the family prepares individuals to be autonomous participants in civil society. Hence, the market economy cannot be expected to function independently of a reform in family life that promotes equality of opportunity and autonomy, both of which will encourage more responsible procreation as well as provide civil society with the talents of women currently excluded. Moreover, reform in family life has to be accompanied by political changes, such as allowing women to own property in their own right and to have the franchise. This is a pro-market view.[55]

7. *Mill's position on corporate social responsibility (CSR) would be pro-market.* Although he did not address this issue directly, given the infancy of corporate

development, Mill's position can be described as "neoliberal."[56] It is a reasonable presumption that Mill would have welcomed the adoption of voluntary policies by the corporation concerning a company's management of its economic, social, and environmental impacts. It is consistent with the view expressed by Friedman when he advocated that "there is one and only one social responsibility of business—to use its resources and engage in activities designed to increase its profits so long as it stays within the rules of the game, which is to say, engages in open and free competition without deception or fraud."[57]

Rather than viewing CSR as an unreasonable intrusion into and restriction on business's primary purpose, Mill would take the view that while Friedman was basically correct, the adoption of CSR policies by companies can be rational and profitable in the long run. CSR would also serve as an insurance strategy to minimize risks from negative government intervention. Mill always favored "leaving to voluntary associations all such things as they are competent to perform . . . [even] if it were certain that the work itself would be as well or better done by public officers."[58]

CONCLUDING REMARKS

As we have contended throughout this essay, Mill's ultimate objective was to achieve a society, a world, of *autonomous* individuals. This is clearly reflected in his discussion of political economy and the implications it has for specific issues in business ethics: "Eventually . . . we may, through the co-operative principle see our way to a change in society, which would combine the freedom and independence of the individual, with the moral, intellectual, and economical advantages of aggregate production; and . . . would realize, at least in the industrial department, the best aspirations of the democratic spirit, by putting an end to the division of society into the industrious and the idle, and effacing all social distinctions but those fairly earned by personal services and exertions."[59] By focusing on autonomy and not a generic conception of utility we have made Mill much more relevant to business ethics.

NOTES

1. Critiques of Mill's *Utilitarianism* have been an industry since the time of Henry Sidgwick's *Methods of Ethics* (1874) (Cambridge: University of Cambridge Press, 2011) and G. E. Moore's *Principia Ethica* (Cambridge: Cambridge University Press, 1903). "Instead of Mill's own doctrines a travesty is discussed, so that the most common criticisms of him are

simply irrelevant"; J. O. Urmson, "The Interpretation of the Moral Philosophy of J. S. Mill," in *Mill: A Collection of Critical Essays,* ed. J. B. Schneewind (Notre Dame, IN: University of Notre Dame Press, 1969), 180. Some of this egregious misrepresentation is summarized in John Skorupski, *John Stuart Mill* (London: Routledge & Kegan Paul, 1989), chap. 9. See also Fred Wilson's entry on J. S. Mill in *The Stanford Encyclopedia of Philosophy*, ed. Edward N. Zalta, http://plato.stanford.edu/archives/spr2014/entries/mill/.

2. Mill was engaged in an enterprise identified as "explication." See Nicholas Capaldi, "What Philosophy Can and Cannot Contribute to Business Ethics," *Journal of Private Enterprise* 22, no. 2 (Spring 2006): 68–86; Capaldi, "The Role of the Business Ethicist," *Ethical Perspectives: Journal of the European Ethics Network* 12, no. 3 (September 2005): 371–84.

3. "Almost all modern writing about moral conduct begins with the hypothesis of an individual human being choosing and pursuing his own directions of activity. What appeared to require explanation was not the existence of such individuals, but how they could come to have duties to others of their kind and what was the nature of those duties. . . . This is unmistakable in Hobbes. . . . Even where an individualistic conclusion was rejected, this autonomous individual remained as the starting point of ethical reflection. . . . Morality consists in the recognition of individual personality." Michael Oakeshott, "The Masses in Representative Democracy," in *Rationalism in Politics and Other Essays,* expanded ed. (Indianapolis: Liberty Fund, 1991), 367.

4. Mill began writing this work in 1854 and finished it in 1859, the same year in which he published *On Liberty*. The *Principles of Political Economy* was first published in 1848, *On Liberty* in 1859, and *Considerations on Representative Government* in 1861. *Utilitarianism* was not published until 1861, originally in *Fraser's Magazine* during October, November, and December of 1861. This chronology strengthens the contention that Mill's views on ethics reflect a lot of previous work on public policy. The public policy conclusions are not mere applications of a previously formulated ethical theory.

5. *On Liberty*, vol. XVIII of *The Collected Works of John Stuart Mill,* ed. J. M. Robson et al. (Toronto: University of Toronto Press, 1977), 224. All references to Mill are to the complete edition, the *Collected Works* (*CW*), and will be cited by the title of the work and its location in the *CW*, as follows: *On Liberty, CW*, XXVIII, 358.

6. A. V. Dicey, *Lectures on the Relation between Law and Public Opinion in England during the Nineteenth Century* (London: Macmillan, 1908), 308 n. 2.

7. *Diary*, March 29, 1854, *CW*, XXVII, 664. "All systems of morals agree in prescribing to do that, and only that, which accords with self-respect . . . [and] with the sympathy of those they respect and a just regard for the good of all." *Diary*, April 9, 1854, XXVII, 667.

8. According to R. P. Anschutz, *The Philosophy of J. S. Mill* (Oxford: Oxford University Press, 1953), 5: Mill was "thoroughly representative of his age" because "somewhere or other in his writings you can discern traces of every wind that blew in the early nineteenth century." In his introduction to *The Spirit of the Age* (Chicago: University of Chicago Press, 1942), vii, F. A. Hayek points out that Mill was "representative of his age only because his rare capacity of absorbing new ideas made him a kind of focus in which most of the significant changes of thought of his time combined."

9. What Burrow says of Humboldt applies equally to Mill: "He has an Aristotelian sense of the ways in which human beings enrich each other's lives in society, together with a quite un-Aristotelian sense that one can neither predict nor set limits to human moral and cultural experimentation. . . . [He has] a kind of informal adumbration of the status given to the greatest possible comprehensiveness of consciousness in Idealist political theory." See J. W. Burrow's introduction to William von Humboldt, *The Limits of State Action* (Indianapolis: Liberty Fund, 1993), lvii.

10. See Steven Lukes, *Individualism* (Oxford: Blackwell, 1973), for a discussion of conceptions of individualism.

11. For Mill, our ultimate good is not to achieve a specific end. Our ultimate good can be qualified negatively by avoiding a heteronymous choice—that is, we must not let something outside of us dictate our choice; the choice can be qualified positively by noting that we choose it for ourselves and in a manner that does not limit future autonomous choices (e.g., choosing slavery); this is what it means to be a progressive human being for Mill.

12. For a fuller exposition of Mill's utilitarianism, see Capaldi, *J. S. Mill*, chap. 9.

13. Mill "found that Bentham's ethics needed correction by the addition of a private morality founded on personal development." John M. Robson, *The Improvement of Mankind: The Social and Political Thought of John Stuart Mill* (London: Routledge & Kegan Paul 1968), 35.

14. "Remarks on Bentham's Philosophy," *CW*, X, 15.

15. *Autobiography, CW*, I, 209.

16. "Whewell," *CW*, X, 194.

17. *Utilitarianism, CW*, X, 249.

18. Ibid., 210, where Mill refers to Auguste Comte's *Système de politique positive*.

19. *Utilitarianism, CW*, X, chap. 2.

20. Ibid., 212, emphasis added.

21. Ibid., 235–36.

22. For a further elaboration of the notion of autonomy, see the discussion of Kant in chapter 6 of Nicholas Capaldi and Gordon Lloyd, *Liberty and Equality in Political Economy: From Locke versus Rousseau to the Present* (Northampton, MA: Edward Elgar, 2016).

23. W. S. Jevons, "John Stuart Mill's Philosophy Tested," pt. 2 of *Pure Logic and Other Minor Works* (London: Macmillan, 1890), 200–201.

24. Nicholas Capaldi and Gordon Lloyd, *Two Narratives of Political Economy* (Boston: Wiley, 2010).

25. Property owned by a voluntary cooperative in a noncentralized economy is private but not individual.

26. Mill is referring to the Lockean argument about labor, an argument accepted by Adam Smith but not by David Hume.

27. Mill makes clear he is not in favor of any kind of rectification principle.

28. Mill would be in opposition to anything like affirmative action understood in terms of quotas or to any policies whose standards or operations would conflict with the competitive system.

29. *Principles of Political Economy, CW*, II, 207–8.

30. This kind of criticism about fragmentation had been enunciated by Adam Smith, Adam Ferguson, and Benjamin Constant. See Smith, *An Inquiry into the Nature and Causes of the Wealth of Nations,* ed. R. H. Campbell, A. S. Skinner, and W. B. Todd (Indianapolis: Liberty Fund, 1976), esp. V.i.f.50; Ferguson, *An Essay on the History of Civil Society,* ed. Fania Oz-Salzberger (Cambridge: Cambridge University Press, 1995), esp. 172–79, 206–7; and Constant, *Principles of Politics Applicable to All Governments* (Indianapolis: Liberty Fund, 2003).

31. See *Chapters on Socialism, CW*, I, 625.

32. For further elaboration of why Mill was not an opponent of the market economy, see Nicholas Capaldi, "Mill and Socialism," *Tocqueville Review* 33, no. 1 (2012): 125–44; Samuel Hollander, *John Stuart Mill on Economic Theory and Method* (London: Routledge, 2000); Pedro Schwartz, *The New Political Economy of J. S. Mill* (Durham, NC: Duke University Press, 1972).

33. *Principles of Political Economy*, *CW*, II, 207.

34. Ibid., *CW*, III, Chapter VII, "On the Probable Futurity of the Labouring Classes."

35. J. S. Mill to McVey Napier, the editor of the *Edinburgh Review*, November 9, 1844, *CW*, XXII, 411. See *Principles of Political Economy, CW*, III, 643–44.

36. *The Subjection of Women, CW*, XXI, 330–31.

37. "Throw, in every instance, the burthen of making out a strong case, not on those who resist, but on those who recommend government interference. *Laisser-faire*, in short,

should be the general practice; every departure from it, unless required by some great good, is a certain evil." *Principles of Political Economy, CW*, III, 944–45.

38. *Principles of Political Economy, CW*, II, 199–214.

39. Ibid., 212.

40. Ibid., *CW*, III, 956.

41. Ibid., 793.

42. "A private capitalist, exempt from the control of a body, if he is a person of capacity, is considerably more likely than almost any association to run judicious risks, and originate costly improvement . . . [given] the competition of capable persons who in the event of failure are to have all the loss, and in case of success the greater part of the gain." *Principles of Political Economy, CW*, III, 793.

43. Nineteenth-century "rentier" capitalism has largely been replaced by entrepreneurial and finance capitalism. Entrepreneurs are not managers; it is difficult to imagine Mill rejecting entrepreneurship, the supreme expression of individualism, competition, and economic growth.

44. *Principles of Political Economy, CW*, III, 783.

45. Insider trading and whistle-blowing are understandably not issues discussed by Mill.

46. *Principles of Political Economy, CW*, III, 930.

47. "Thornton," *CW*, V, 666.

48. *Principles of Political Economy, CW*, III, 783.

49. Ibid., 794.

50. See Schwartz, *New Political Economy of J. S. Mill*, 103.

51. *Principles of Political Economy, CW*, III, 783.

52. Ibid., 795.

53. *A Few Words on Non-Intervention, CW*, XXI.

54. *Subjection of Women, CW*, XXI, Chapter I.

55. Nicholas Capaldi, "Evolving Conceptions of Women in Modern Liberal Culture: From Hegel to Mill," in *Nature, Woman, and the Art of Politics*, ed. Eduardo A. Velásquez (Lanham, MD: Rowman & Littlefield, 2000), 295–311.

56. See Theodore Roosevelt Malloch, "Corporate Social Responsibility," introduction to *Encyclopedia of Corporate Social Responsibility*, ed. Samuel O. Idowu et al. (Heidelberg: Springer, 2013).

57. Milton Friedman, "The Social Responsibility of Business Is to Increase Its Profits," in *Morality and the Market: Ethics and Virtue in the Conduct of Business*, ed. Eugene Heath (New York: McGraw-Hill, 2002), 409.

58. *Principles of Political Economy, CW*, III, 955.

59. Ibid., 793.

CHAPTER 16

Karl Marx on History, Capitalism, and . . . Business Ethics?

William H. Shaw

Karl Marx was a thinker of world-historical significance. His ideas changed the course of the twentieth century, and his deep, fecund, and multidimensional intellectual legacy had a profound impact on subsequent thinkers in a variety of fields, the importance of which it is difficult to exaggerate.[1] Marx himself thought that his two major theoretical achievements were his materialist conception of history, known as "historical materialism," and his detailed analysis of the capitalist economic system, which purports to reveal capitalism's inherent developmental tendencies and the precise nature of exploitation that occurs under that system.[2] In the first two sections of this essay, I outline these fundamental aspects of Marx's thought. Against that backdrop, I tease out his thinking about ethics in general and the ethics of commerce and business in particular, exploring its implications for normative business ethics. Although Marx poses a challenge to the whole enterprise of business ethics, he may also inspire some fresh approaches to it.

MARX'S MATERIALIST THEORY OF HISTORY

As Friedrich Engels summarizes it, the materialist conception of history that he and Marx shared

> seeks the ultimate cause and the great moving power of all important historic events in the economic development of society, in the changes in the modes of production and exchange, in the consequent division of society into distinct classes, and in the struggle of those classes against one another.[3]

Marx himself provides a more detailed, but still brief, general statement of his view of history in the Preface to his 1859 work, *A Contribution to the Critique of Political Economy*.[4] There Marx contends that the economic structure of society, constituted by its relations of production, is the real foundation of society. It is the basis "on which rises a legal and political superstructure and to which correspond definite forms of social consciousness." On the other hand, society's relations of production themselves "correspond to a definite stage of development of [society's] productive forces."

As society's productive forces develop, the Preface says, they clash with existing production relations, which now fetter their growth. "Then begins an epoch of social revolution" as this conflict divides society and as people become, in a more or less ideological form, "conscious of this conflict and fight it out." The conflict is resolved in favor of the productive forces, and new, higher relations of production emerge, relations whose material preconditions have "matured in the womb of the old society" and which better accommodate the continued expansion of society's productive capacity. The bourgeois or capitalist mode of production represents the most recent of several progressive epochs in the socioeconomic development of society, but it is the last antagonistic or class-riven form of production. With its demise, the prehistory of humanity will come to a close.[5]

A core thesis of Marx's historical materialism, then, is that the different economic systems, the different modes of production, that characterize human history arise or fall as they enable or impede the expansion of society's productive capacity. The growth of society's productive forces thus explains the broad trajectory of human history. Those productive forces are simply the powers that society has at its command in material production; they include not only the means of production (tools, machines, factories, and so on), but also labor power—the skills, knowledge, experience, and other human faculties used in work. The relations of production, which are said to correspond to society's productive level, link productive forces and human beings in the process of production. They fall into two categories, corresponding, respectively, to the material and social sides of production: on the one hand, the work relations that constitute the actual process of production; on the other hand, the relations of economic control (legally manifested as property ownership) that govern access to the forces and products of production and in which those work relations take place.[6]

The expansion of the productive forces determines the relations and mode of production that obtain because, as Marx wrote to Pavel Annenkov, "men never relinquish what they have won." In order to retain what they have acquired and not "forfeit the fruits of civilization," they will, if necessary, change their social relations of production to accommodate the acquired productive forces and facilitate their continued advance.[7] To be sure, the relations of production influence the momentum and qualitative development of the productive forces. Capitalism, in particular, is distinguished by its restless enlargement of society's productive capacity. This is in line with historical materialism, however, because Marx's thesis is that the relations of production that emerge do so precisely because they are able to promote the development of society's productive capacity. The resulting economic structure, in turn, determines the legal and political superstructure.

The nature and strength of the mechanisms hypothesized by the base-superstructure metaphor are among the most vexed and controversial questions in Marxist theory. It is clear, at least, that Marx does not view the superstructure as an epiphenomenon of the economic base, or overlook the necessity of legal and political institutions. Law, in particular, is needed to "sanction the existing order" and grant it "independence from mere accident and arbitrariness."[8] This function itself gives the legal realm some autonomy because the existing relations of production are represented and legitimated in an abstract, codified form, which in turn fosters the illusion that the law is entirely autonomous with respect to the economic structure. In addition, under capitalism the "legal fiction of a contract" between free agents obscures the real nature of production, in particular, the "invisible threads" that bind the wage laborer to capital.[9] Under feudalism, in contrast, tradition and custom perform a similar stabilizing function and may also enjoy a degree of autonomy. There, the true nature of socioeconomic relations is obscured by their entanglement with the relations of personal domination that characterize the other spheres of feudal life.[10]

Which social institutions are properly part of the superstructure is a matter of debate. Marx certainly thought that all the various spheres and realms of society reflect to some extent the dominant mode of production and that the general consciousness of an epoch is shaped by the nature of its production. Certain ideas originate or are widespread because they sanction existing social relations or promote particular class interests. The economy's determination of legal and political structures, though, will tend to be relatively direct, while its influence over other social realms, culture, and consciousness generally is more attenuated and nuanced.

Class enters the picture because in any given mode of production people stand in certain characteristic relations to the forces and products of production. The individual's economic position as understood in terms of the existing social production relations establishes certain material interests in common with others and determines class membership. Hence follow the familiar definitions of the bourgeoisie and proletariat by reference to the purchase and sale, respectively, of labor power (and the underlying ownership or nonownership of the means of production). A central thesis of Marx is that class position determines the characteristic consciousness or worldview of its members. On the basis of its socioeconomic position, each class creates "an entire superstructure of distinct and peculiarly formed sentiments, illusions, modes of thought and views of life."[11] At the same time, however, "the ideas of the ruling class are in every epoch the ruling ideas."[12]

The differing material interests of classes divide them and lead to their struggle, although the individuals involved may fail to comprehend accurately the true character of the antagonisms that rend society. The ultimate success or failure of a class is determined by its relation to the advance of the productive forces; that is, "the conditions under which definite productive forces can be applied are the conditions of the rule of a definite class of society."[13] The class that has the capacity and the incentive to introduce or preserve the relations of production required to accommodate the advance of the productive forces has its hegemony ensured. For Marx, then, the eventual success of the proletarian cause, like the earlier rise of the bourgeoisie, was guaranteed by the fundamental currents of history, whereas, for example, the slave revolts of the ancient world, however heroic, were doomed to failure.

Historical materialism views class rule, hitherto, as both inevitable and necessary to force the productivity of the direct producers beyond the subsistence level. "No antagonism, no progress," Marx writes. "This is the law that civilization has followed. . . . Till now the productive forces have been developed by virtue of this system of class antagonism."[14] The colossal productive progress brought about by capitalism, however, eliminates both the historical rationale for, and the continued viability of, class rule, thus paving the way for socialism.[15] Since the state is primarily the vehicle by which the dominant class secures its rule, it will wither away in postcapitalist society.

The idea of a progressive advance through history, spurred forward by competing forces, reflects Marx's early immersion in the thought of G. W. F. Hegel. Marx derived from Hegel the idea that history advances through stages and, more specifically, that historical processes and forces that are cruel and oppressive can have progressive consequences. Although Marx rejected Hegel's speculative and idealistic philosophy, he retained aspects of his dialectical vision—in particular, a view of social formations as organic wholes in which various conflicting forces are united but which have inherent development tendencies that ultimately lead to rupture, change, and progress. This is "the rational kernel within the mystical shell" of Hegel's dialectic. As Marx explains in *Capital*, his dialectical approach involves appreciating the fluid and transient character of existing social reality. In particular, when it comes to capitalism, as we shall see in the next section, understanding "what exists" involves "a simultaneous recognition of its negation, its inevitable destruction."[16]

MARX'S CRITIQUE OF CAPITALISM

As this restatement of Marx's materialist conception of history makes clear, in his view ideas—including moral values, ethical ideals, and normative principles—are not the deep source or motor of historical progress. Individuals and socioeconomic classes of individuals may understand themselves and their social circumstances in moral terms, and they may act on the basis of ideals, values, or principles that are moral in character. But those ideas arise and become widespread in the first place, Marx thought, only because they are the vehicle through which a socioeconomic class becomes conscious of itself, and they are historically efficacious only insofar as they are championed by an ascending class.

For this reason, Marx rejected purely[17] moral criticism of capitalism (or, indeed, of any earlier socioeconomic order) as misguided and irrelevant. This was one of the reasons that he and Engels characterized earlier socialist thinkers, in particular, Henri de Saint-Simon, Charles Fourier, and Robert Owen, as utopian theorists.[18] These thinkers believed that capitalist society was morally deficient, and designed new forms of social organization to replace it, hoping that the plausibility of their ideas or the attractiveness of their own small-scale and experimental efforts to instantiate them would attract converts and eventually lead to capitalism being supplanted by a better system. Although seeing some value in the writings of their predecessors, Marx and Engels maintained that the utopian socialists had failed to take the necessary first step of understanding the nature and true historical dynamic of capitalism before inventing systems to replace it. By contrast, Marx and Engels considered their own socialism scientific because it rested on just such an analysis of the inherent characteristics, internal contradictions, and historical trajectory of capitalism. For them, socialism was not "an accidental discovery of this or that ingenious brain," but the historically necessary outcome of the proletariat's struggle with the bourgeoisie.[19] Only by understanding the system that has produced it and by becoming conscious of itself as a historical actor can the working class throw off the yoke of capitalism. For these reasons, then, Marx devoted the bulk of his intellectual life to the economic dissection of capitalism, the mature fruit of this labor being his masterpiece, *Capital*.[20]

Capital purports to delineate the laws and tendencies of capitalism and to reveal the precise character of the exploitation that characterizes this particular form of class society. In doing so, it seeks to undercut capitalism's own self-understanding (as represented by the way that the system's beneficiaries and apologists tend to describe and defend its operation) and reveal it as tendentious and historically blind. For example, in diagnosing what he calls the "fetishism of commodities," Marx argues that the social nature of labor and the historically contingent character of capitalist production are obscured by the fact that the exchange-value of the products of human labor appears to be an objective, natural property.[21] Or, to take another example, capitalism requires certain historical preconditions—in particular, accumulations of investable wealth, on the one hand, and proletarians whose only productive asset is their labor power, on the other[22]—prerequisites that were brought about, and could only have been brought about, Marx argues, through violence. In describing this ugly history,[23] *Capital* endeavors to debunk the idea that capitalism grows naturally out of a historically innocent exchange of commodities.

Marx did not use the word *capitalism*, which seems to have been uncommon in his day. Rather, he spoke of "capitalist production" or the "capitalist mode of production" or simply "capital." What is capital? In its simplest form, the circulation of commodities follows the pattern C—M—C: one sells a commodity (C) in order to acquire a different commodity via the medium of money (M). Consumption or the satisfaction of one's wants (in Marx's terminology, "use-value") is the goal. Alongside this pattern, however, we find a different form of circulation—namely, M—C—M. Here, instead of selling in order to buy, one buys in order to sell. Rather than use-value, money or exchange-value is the goal—and not just exchange-value, but an increase in exchange-value: M—C—M´. This is the general formula for capital; it is value adding value to itself.[24]

M—C—M´ is how capital appears in the realm of circulation, but in *Capital* Marx also seeks to analyze its role in the inner workings of industrial production. The industrial capitalist purchases the inputs (raw materials, tools and machinery, labor power) that are brought together to produce new commodities. These are then sold for money—more money than the capitalist originally invested—and the process begins again. But how exactly does capital increase in value? Where does the capitalist's profit come from? Marx's answer to these questions rests on his labor theory of value, which reveals the exploitation of labor by capital that lies at the heart of the system.

According to the labor theory, the value of a commodity is determined by the average, socially necessary labor time required to produce it. This includes not only the labor involved in the immediate production of that commodity but also the labor required to acquire or manufacture the raw materials and machinery or other fixed capital used in the production process. The price of any commodity is determined by its labor-time value (although supply and demand may temporarily push its price above or below its value). Because labor power is itself a commodity, its price—the wage the laborer receives—is determined just as the price of any other commodity is—namely, by the labor cost of producing it. In the case of labor power, that reflects the cost, not only of feeding, clothing, and housing the worker, but also of educating and training labor power of a certain type and level of skill and of rearing the next generation of workers. Thus, the value of a worker's labor power is determined by the socially necessary labor time required to produce that labor power.

Suppose, for purposes of illustration, that it takes a daily average of four hours of socially necessary labor to produce (feed, clothe, train, etc.) a worker of average skill. If the worker is paid a wage equivalent to the value produced by four hours of labor time, then he has been remunerated appropriately because that is the value of the commodity (namely, his labor power) that he has brought to market. However, and this is the nub of the matter for Marx, the worker does not toil for his capitalist employer for only four hours, but, let us suppose, for ten hours. Each day, then, he produces ten hours of value although the price of his labor power is only four hours. Marx calls this discrepancy between the value of labor power (and thus a worker's daily wage) and the value created by that labor power "surplus-value." It is the source of capitalist profits. In this way, Marx thought that he had unraveled the mystery of where profit comes from and revealed wage labor to be the source of the economic surplus that is the basis of capitalist production, just as—more transparently—slavery was the source of economic surplus in the ancient world and serfdom its source under feudalism.

Marx's labor theory of value stands squarely within the conceptual framework of classical economics, and, indeed, Marx can be seen as the last of the great classical economists, with Smith and Ricardo as his acknowledged forebears. Since the marginalist revolution of the late nineteenth century, mainstream economics has left the labor theory of value and kindred classical approaches behind—precisely, some Marxists have argued, to avoid the sort of implications that Marx drew from it. But this is a charge easier to make than to sustain. In any case, the labor theory of value has few defenders today; most mainstream economists find it implausible or even conceptually incoherent.[25] And even if the model that I have sketched and that Marx elaborated and defended in *Capital*, volume 1, can survive the most common objections, it faces further problems when certain simplifying assumptions of the model are abandoned. Marx was aware of these, but never quite resolved them.[26] Marxists have, historically, clung to the labor theory of value because they want to sustain the charge that capital exploits labor. But one can challenge the idea that the labor theory of value is necessary for leveling a charge of exploitation or even that it is a suitable basis for doing so.[27] Since Marx's time, philosophers, political theorists, and others have advanced different conceptions of exploitation, and it may be possible to argue that capitalism is built on the systematic exploitation of labor without relying on the labor theory of value or, indeed, on any developed economic theory at all.[28]

In any case, although Marx prided himself on having revealed with rigor and precision the exploitation at the core of the capitalist system, he did not rest there. He wanted also to delineate its development tendencies (for example, the move from a system of manufacturing built on the division of labor to the modern factory system, the foundation of which is machinery rather than narrowly specialized human labor) and to spell out the economic contradictions that capitalism increasingly encounters, making it less and less stable and more and more crisis-ridden.

These contradictions begin with the fact, as Marx argues in *Capital*, that the system operates under two opposing tendencies: on the one hand, it seeks constantly to reduce the labor time necessary for the production of commodities; on the other hand, it attempts to appropriate the greatest quantity of surplus labor. Furthermore, the very nature of capitalist production, Marx thought, spurred on as it is by competition, necessitates that it be on an expanding scale, with an ever-increasing concentration and centralization of capital. With capital's reproduction on a progressive scale, the proletariat increases. Although demand can cause wages to rise and working conditions to ameliorate temporarily, improvements in the workers' lot can only go so far before they blunt the stimulus of gain, accumulation slackens, and the price of labor falls again to a level corresponding with the needs of capital. Thus, Marx contends, there can be no "diminution in the degree of exploitation of labour," adding: "It cannot be otherwise in a mode of production in which the worker exists to satisfy the needs of [capital], as opposed to the inverse situation, in which objective wealth is there to satisfy the worker's own need for development."[29] For Marx, this shows the futility of all attempts to reform capitalism because such efforts necessarily preserve the basic character of the capital-labor relation.

Whereas *Capital*, volume 1, focuses on the contradictions of a system that produces, at one pole, ever more wealth in fewer and fewer hands while, at the other pole, misery, degradation, and oppression grow, volumes 2 and 3 of *Capital* draw out in detail other, more purely economic contradictions only hinted at in the first volume—in particular, the tendency for the rate of profit to fall, the lack of effective demand caused by restricted consumption of the masses, imbalances between different productive sectors, and disequilibria in the circulation of capital, including the destabilizing effects of extended chains of credit.[30] Overall, the capitalist system is increasingly unable, Marx argues, to manage the productive forces that it has brought into being and that hold so much potential for humankind. Plagued as well by growing misery and inequality, it ceases to play a progressive role in history. Only socialism can do so now, and the agent of that change is the working class—called into being by capitalism, then made increasingly conscious of its collective identity and historical mission by its experiences. In pursuing its own good by struggling for socialism, it advances the overall interests of humanity.

Although Marx was harshly critical of capitalism, he emphasized the historically progressive role it has played by constantly revolutionizing not only production, but also existing ideas and social relations. Characterized by "uninterrupted disturbance of all social conditions" and by "everlasting uncertainty and agitation," capitalism sweeps away "all fixed, fast-frozen relations, with their train of ancient and venerable prejudice and opinions," and "all new-formed ones become antiquated before they can ossify."[31] Moreover, as it expands across the globe and "batters down all Chinese walls," it compels all nations, no matter how underdeveloped, to adopt— "on pain of extinction"—the capitalist mode of production. In so doing, "it creates a world after its own image."[32]

THE NORMATIVE DIMENSION OF MARX'S THOUGHT

Marx did not see himself as a moralist. He thought that his materialist conception of history and his analysis of the current socioeconomic order were objective and scientific and, in particular, that his critique of capitalism was based on its objective tendencies and contradictions rather than on any abstract principles of justice or right. Nonetheless, philosophers and others have debated whether Marx is implicitly committed to certain moral principles and whether his critique of capitalism is ultimately normative.

A focal point of this debate has been whether Marx believed that capitalism was unjust. Much has been written about this.[33] On the one hand, Marx's thundering denunciations of capitalism for producing misery, squalor, and degradation and for sacrificing the well-being of the vast bulk of the population for the benefit of a dwindling number of industrial magnates certainly suggests that he viewed the capitalist system as unjust. Indeed, the charge of exploitation seems, simply by itself, to entail injustice, especially when, as Marx thought, a more equitable, nonexploitative distribution of material goods has become possible.[34]

On the other hand, Marx never explicitly criticizes capitalism for being unjust or for failing to live up to the socialist or communist distribution standards of the future. He repeatedly emphasizes that capitalist exploitation takes place within established market norms. The laborer is not cheated but, rather, is paid the full value of his commodity. In this respect, at least, the exchange is fair and square. More generally, Marx stresses that the justice of particular transactions between economic agents depends on whether they occur as a natural consequence of that society's production relations— not on their content: "This content is just, whenever it corresponds, and is adequate, to the mode of production. It is unjust, whenever it contradicts that mode. Slavery on the basis of capitalist production is unjust; likewise fraud in the quality of commodities."[35] Similarly, Engels writes that "always this [concept of eternal] justice is but the ideologised, glorified expression of the existing economic relations."[36]

Did, then, Marx believe that capitalism was just or that it was unjust? There is ample evidence to support both sides of this exegetical divide, leading some to suggest that Marx was inconsistent or perhaps unclear or even mistaken about his own position.[37] But suppose, as seems likely, that Marx refrained, officially anyway, from charging capitalism with being unjust because he saw justice as strictly a function of a given society's relations of production. If so, the first thing to notice is that Marx is employing a juridical notion of justice, one that is conceptually linked to a legal code that reflects standards that are functionally appropriate to a given mode of production. Only with this limited conception of justice, can it make sense to say that exploitation is not unjust or that what Marx often calls "theft" and "robbery" is actually legal and fair, and even then it is difficult to believe that Marx is not being at least somewhat ironic. In any case, capitalism might be just in one sense or from one perspective while being unjust in other ways or from a broader perspective. Further, even if in Marx's view capitalism cannot properly be condemned as unjust, if *Capital*'s depiction of it is accurate, then one has ample moral grounds for rejecting it—for repudiating a system that impedes human flourishing. Doing so does not require appealing to any sophisticated or controversial normative principles.

Even if Marx were a relativist with regard to justice, this would not entail that he be a relativist in general. To be sure, by rooting a society's moral ideas in its mode of production, Marx's materialist conception of history does suggest some kind of ethical relativism. And, if relativism is true, then by definition there is no nonrelative basis from which to criticize capitalism. Proletarians who reject capitalist morality would be doing so only on the basis of norms appropriate to the socialist order they are struggling to bring about. Strictly speaking, however, Marx's emphasis on the social causation of moral ideas does not entail relativism in any variant. One could, with perfect consistency, accept Marx's materialist account of socioeconomic evolution and yet believe that there are some normative concepts and principles the valid use of which is not restricted to particular modes of production. Thus, one could believe that slavery was wrong even if earlier societies thought it was permissible and could not have been expected to have thought otherwise and even if slavery was, in some sense, a natural or unavoidable step in human social evolution. Although Marx and Engels never, it seems, explicitly described slavery as "unjust," they thought it was cruel and terrible and admired those who rebelled against it.[38] Furthermore, in everyday affairs they freely employed moral language, especially "thick" moral concepts, such as cowardice, dishonesty, hypocrisy, and so on, which are an inescapable part of commonsense morality.[39] So in advocating the overthrow of class society, socialists could, it seems, appeal simply to certain elementary and perfectly legitimate moral or humanitarian considerations.

Even if I am right about this, however, Marx certainly did not think that moral criticism of capitalism was significant or particularly effective.[40] What was important was that capitalism was not only paving the way for socialism but also creating the very force that would bring it about. However, if contrary to Marx, a contemporary Marxist believes neither that socialism is inevitable nor that there are innate economic or historical tendencies pushing us toward it, then moral criticism is likely to be essential, because if socialism is to be brought about, then people will have to be convinced that they ought to push for it. Furthermore, envisioning and constructing a postcapitalist future will require the articulation and refinement of the normative standards that are to characterize that society.

Marx said very little about socialism or the exact nature of the social order that would follow capitalism. In contrast to his utopian socialist predecessors, he was not "writing recipes . . . for the cook-shops of the future."[41] In the *Critique of the Gotha Program*, however, he states that although socialism would initially follow the principle of payment in accord with labor expended, at a higher stage of development society would move beyond "the narrow horizon of bourgeois right" and be governed by the principle "from each according to his ability, to each according to his need."[42] Where does that ideal come from, and what grounds it? Marx thought that the principle of payment in return for labor corresponds to a society emerging from capitalism, but the higher principle ("from each according to his ability . . .") is one that he predicts that unalienated and unexploited people—having moved beyond the vestiges of market morality—would choose. If the choice of this principle, not to mention the exact way in which it is to be institutionalized,[43] is not to be arbitrary, then it must rest on moral argument, and people in the socialist future would, it seems, be well situated to reason about moral matters, free from the distorting influences of class ideology. This idea gains some support from a famous passage in *Capital*, volume 3. There Marx argues that although socialism will introduce freedom into the realm of production through rational social cooperation, true freedom begins only beyond the realm of material necessity, when the working day has shrunk dramatically, and the development of human energy can blossom forth as an end in itself.[44] This suggests the possibility that in the realm of freedom, people will make moral determinations that are not relative to, or limited by, their social system but, rather, more fully human because undistorted by conditions of scarcity.[45]

IMPLICATIONS OF MARX'S THOUGHT FOR BUSINESS ETHICS

Tracing out, let alone assessing, the influence of Marx's thinking about history, society, and economics on subsequent generations of historians, economists, sociologists, and political theorists would take a multivolume tome. By contrast, his work has had little impact on the field of business ethics. Textbook presentations of Marx aside, there is little discussion of Marx in the business ethics literature or of what his thought might imply for the field.[46] Nevertheless, his ideas do have some clear implications for it.

To begin with, in *Capital* and elsewhere Marx is clear that he is critiquing an economic system, not judging capitalists as individuals. As a class, capitalists play a structurally determined role. Thus, Marx views them only as "the bearers" of certain social relations, as the personification of capital.[47] Capital itself has a basic drive to expand, he believed; by its very nature it seeks relentlessly to increase, and the capitalist is its representative.[48] In *Capital* Marx is offering a model of capitalism or studying it as an ideal type: insofar as one assumes the capitalist role, then this is how one must behave. For example, if one is a capitalist, then competition will tend to force one to produce as cheaply as possible. This is not a matter of individual choice—at least not in the same sense that it is a matter of individual choice whether to become a capitalist in the first place. So, Marx sees himself as explaining how capitalists must act; he does not blame them for being as they are. He knew, of course, that individual capitalists differ, as all people do, in their personal characteristics and attitudes. Engels, after all, was a capitalist and did the things that one must do to run a manufacturing enterprise—assiduously looking after the firm's affairs, for example, and firing unproductive workers[49]—while all the time despising the economic system of which he was part. From Marx's perspective, these individual differences are neither here nor there. Whether individual capitalists are kind, virtuous, or sympathetic to the plight of the workers they employ does not affect the analysis of the laws of motion of the capitalist system and of how capitalists must, willy-nilly, behave.

On the other hand, it is also clear that Marx thought that capitalists tend to have various less-than-admirable personality traits—for example, they are typically tightfisted, calculating, and avaricious. These characteristics reflect, he thought, the very nature of capital, which involves the relentless pursuit of profit. Capitalists also tend to understand their world in ideological, self-flattering terms and to be almost willfully blind to the deleterious effects of the system, whose prime beneficiaries they are. This, too, is something to be expected. Marx clearly wishes to debunk the insular, self-justifying worldview of the bourgeoisie, and in doing so *Capital* is full of snide comments about capitalists and their apologists. Indeed, it is difficult to find an example of Marx praising an individual capitalist for his vision, personal initiative, or entrepreneurship, although, as I have mentioned, everywhere in his writings, from the *Communist Manifesto* to *Capital*, he applauds the capitalist system as a whole for its wondrous productive achievements. As a type, however, capitalists are, in his eyes, a defective specimen of humanity. Neither admirable nor worthy of emulation, they are as deformed by the system and as alienated from their humanity as are the ignorant and oppressed proletarians.

Although one cannot criticize capitalists for being as they are and for seeing the world as they do, market society has certain norms, to which its participants must by and large adhere if the system is to function. From Marx's perspective, it is perfectly intelligible to criticize capitalists who break those norms, for example, by cheating suppliers or selling fraudulent goods because one is applying capitalism's own rules to their conduct. Here, then, there is scope for business ethics, but it is limited to criticizing market participants who violate the rules of the competitive game by resorting to deception, force, or fraud.[50] Although this sort of ethical criticism is perfectly appropriate from Marx's perspective, it was of no theoretical or political interest to him. Individual deviations from the norm or even the standing temptation for capitalists to violate the rules of their own system was unimportant. Capitalist exploitation, as we have seen, does not rest on cheating; it takes place, fairly and squarely, within the rules of the game. Insofar as business ethics is concerned with trying to ensure that market participants understand and play by the rules, it would have been seen by Marx as a historically irrelevant project.

That capitalism tends to create or reinforce motivations that lead market participants to break the rules of the game is an important insight, however, one that underscores one of the basic challenges facing business ethics. For Marx, it is probably the least important of several collective action problems facing the capitalist class, all of which essentially turn on the fact that, in pursuing their individual self-interest, capitalists often act in ways that damage their collective self-interest. The state ("a committee for managing the common affairs of the whole bourgeoisie")[51] can address some of these problems. Others—for example, the tendency for the rate of profit to decline or for effective demand to be restricted—represent basic contradictions in the capitalist system, the effects of which grow increasingly severe as capitalism matures.

Capital deals with a world of individual capitalists, but today we live in a world dominated by corporations. How does this affect Marx's analysis? Marx was aware of the growing economic importance of stock companies.[52] Along with monopolies and cartels, holding companies and stock companies expand the scale of production beyond what is possible for individual capitalists. Ownership separates from management; production ceases to be based on individually owned and directed enterprises; and the capitalist mode of production seeks to exert a kind of social control over the anarchy of production. What we would now call corporate capitalism is the "abolition of capital as private property within the boundaries of capitalist production itself."[53] It is capitalism responding in a partial and unconscious way to a historical imperative that only socialism can fulfill. There is no evidence, however, that Marx would have considered the corporate form of capital, which consolidated itself after his time, as following a different economic logic or as being less driven to maximize profits than individual capitalists are. Nor did he entertain the possibility that managers might seek goals other than, or in addition to, profit maximization. Marx was aware that a gap between ownership and managerial control was possible,[54] but he was not prescient enough to have foreseen the importance it was to come to have for contemporary capitalism—though his theory can certainly account for this development.

The gap between ownership and management holds out the promise of business ethics in a more robust sense than that of simply adhering to market norms. For if corporate managers are not simply the personifications of capital, but can be brought to see themselves as, at least in part, representing the interests of society as a whole, then the idea of corporate social responsibility would, even for a Marxist, begin to have substantive content to it. Corporate leaders do sometimes describe their job this way, but how seriously one should take this way of talking is a matter of debate, and many doubt that it has any real significance. Marx, for his part, would have thought that in any meaningful sense socially responsible corporate conduct is something that can never be achieved, or even approached, within a capitalist framework. Although the demand for it might reflect an implicit acknowledgment that production must be freed from the constraints and distortions imposed by the profit motive, it fosters the apologetic illusion that capitalism can be reformed within its own parameters. For Marx that was impossible.

Advocating corporate social responsibility and attempting to persuade business that it has moral responsibilities independent of profit are, Marx would have thought, futile, unrealistic, and utopian projects. Moreover, they are counterproductive, distracting us from the true nature of capitalism and diverting energy from the necessary task of overturning it altogether. Only if Marx is wrong about this—wrong, that is, in believing that fundamental reform of the capitalist system is impossible and that in the broad sweep of things a radical break with it is the only historically viable project—could it possibly make sense to push business to care about things other than (or in addition to) profit or to try to make itself truly and deeply socially responsible.

CONCLUDING REMARKS: MARXIST BUSINESS ETHICS—SOME POSSIBILITIES

Marx, we have seen, would have rudely dismissed the very idea of business ethics. But a Marxist today might well wonder what explains the boom in business ethics. Why have recent decades seen so much interest in it? Some Marxists have answered this question by arguing that business ethics, especially the teaching of business ethics, fulfills some important needs of contemporary capitalist society.[55] First, it serves to legitimate the existing system, especially in the eyes of those who are not its principal beneficiaries, and to assure them that they can continue to be people of integrity despite working in it. Second, it helps to restrain individual members of the bourgeoisie from pursuing their own interests at the expense of those of their class, and perhaps also helps to encourage them to consider wider social issues that, if left unattended, might destabilize the system. Whether business ethics really does serve these functions is debatable, but even if does, there is always a difficulty in arguing from the premise that X performs social function Y to the conclusion that this explains the existence of X. There needs, in addition, to be some causal story of how and why particular individuals are led to act in ways that bring X about. But, putting this point aside, even if X did come into being because it initially fulfilled some social function or satisfied some unmet need of the system, this fact would not entail that X could not change or evolve as a result of other factors. Thus, even if the above functional account of the emergence and growth of business ethics were correct, business ethics might nevertheless evolve in directions that are independent of, or even uncongenial to, the needs of the present system.

In line with this, other Marxists have sought not so much to debunk business ethics, but rather to engage it. For some of them, pursuing business ethics in a Marxist spirit involves defending various normative claims inspired by Marx's critique of capitalism, among them the following: that workers are coerced by their circumstances to sell their labor power, that they are wrongfully exploited under capitalism, that they lack important freedoms, that they are alienated in morally objectionable ways, that capitalism treats them as mere means to an end and violates various rights that they have, that private ownership of the means of production lacks moral justification, and that capitalism distributes socioeconomic burdens and benefits in an unjust way.[56] These are bold, provocative contentions. The problem is not that they are debatable. The problem is that Marx's works offer so little assistance in clarifying, let along arguing for, them. This is not to say that some or all of these propositions cannot be defended or perhaps even vindicated, but to do so one must put Marx more or less to the side and engage in normative ethics proper; that is, one must argue for these propositions, which Marx, even if he believed them, did not do or at least not with the clarity and rigor associated with contemporary analytically oriented philosophy. Marx is of far less help in this regard than is a familiarity with contemporary moral and political theory. Further, in taking this path, one quickly ends up dealing with some very abstract questions—for example, the nature of coercion, the meaning of freedom, whether exploitation is always unjust, or the relative merits of rival theories of economic justice—questions that are not easy to answer and that rapidly lead one away from the more applied concerns of business ethics.

But suppose one endeavors to treat those concerns in a Marxist spirit, that is, to do business ethics proper—and not just the critique of capitalism or left-wing social philosophy—in a way that is inspired by Marx. How might one proceed? Several related points suggest themselves. First, one would attempt to situate any ethical issue in business—for example, whistle-blowing, drug testing, CEO pay, outsourcing, business's relation to the natural environment, or the rights and responsibilities of employees—within its larger context by showing how the issue is shaped by class divisions, power imbalances, and the economic imperatives of capitalism.[57] As a teacher of business ethics, one would encourage students to look beyond the ethical dilemmas posed by a given case study to the larger social and economic forces at work.

Second, one would endeavor to free one's analysis from concepts and principles—such as that of a free contract, employee consent, or the rights of capital—that are abstract and legalistic or ideological in character. That is, one would try to analyze the moral and social conundrums of business in a way that neither reflects the capitalist worldview nor presupposes the legitimacy or necessity of the current system. In practice, this would imply looking at things from the perspective of, and siding with, those who must work for a living and, more broadly, with the socially disadvantaged.

Third, if employees, managers, or others in the world of business behave dishonestly or in socially deleterious ways, the point would be to understand what it is about their circumstances that induces them to do so. The problem from a Marxist perspective will never be one of individual malfeasance alone but, rather, the social and economic structures that conduce to that malfeasance. Someone doing business ethics in a Marxist spirit would also want to highlight the ways in which capitalism causes people to lose their moral bearings and, among other things, to participate in or go along with the undoing of others.[58]

Finally, one might point to positive examples from the world of business (such as firms with shared governance or companies that take the rights and well-being of their employees seriously) of what might be possible in the future. But the point of the analysis would be to show the intractable character of the ethical problem one is addressing and the impossibility, limited exceptions aside, of resolving it satisfactorily within the present socioeconomic order. In all these ways, then, a business ethicist with a Marxist orientation would use the philosophical analysis of various ethical issues in business as a springboard for broader social critique and, ultimately, social transformation. In other words, the point of business ethics would be not merely "to interpret the world" but "to change it."[59]

NOTES

1. For an overview of the major lines of Marxist thought after Marx, see Leszek Kolakowski, *Main Currents of Marxism*, 3 vols. (New York: Norton, 2008). To my knowledge, there is no detailed comprehensive scholarly overview of Marx's broader intellectual legacy or of the impact of specific aspects of his thought in different disciplinary areas.

2. Frederick Engels, "Karl Marx" and "Speech at the Graveside of Karl Marx," in Karl Marx and Frederick Engels, *Selected Works* (Moscow: Progress Publishers, 1969–70), 3:83–87 and 162–63.

3. Engels, *Socialism: Utopian and Scientific*, in *Selected Works*, 3:103.

4. Karl Marx, preface to *A Contribution to the Critique of Political Economy*, in *Selected Works*, 1:503–4. Although the reliability of the Preface as a guide to Marx's materialist perspective has not gone unchallenged, its authority is bolstered by the fact that he quotes key sentences from it in *Capital*. Karl Marx, *Capital: A Critique of Political Economy*, vol. 1, trans. Ben Fowkes (Harmondsworth, UK: Penguin, 1976), 175n.

5. Preface to *Contribution to the Critique*, 504. For analysis and discussion of the theory that Marx sketches here, see William H. Shaw, *Marx's Theory of History* (Stanford, CA: Stanford University Press, 1978); G. A. Cohen, *Karl Marx's Theory of History: A Defence*, expanded ed. (Princeton, NJ: Princeton University Press, 2000); Allen W. Wood, *Karl Marx*, 2nd ed. (London: Routledge, 2004); and Jon Elster, *Making Sense of Marx* (Cambridge: Cambridge University Press, 1985).

6. Shaw, *Marx's Theory of History*, 28–42; cf. Cohen, *Karl Marx's Theory of History*, 34–36.

7. Marx, "Letter to Annenkov," in *Selected Works*, 1:518–19. See also William H. Shaw, "Historical Materialism and the Development Thesis," *Philosophy of the Social Sciences* 16, no. 2 (June 1986): 197–210.

8. Karl Marx, *Capital: A Critique of Political Economy*, vol. 3, trans. Ernest Untermann (Chicago: Charles Kerr, 1909), 921.

9. *Capital*, 1:719.

10. Ibid., 170.

11. Marx, *The Eighteenth Brumaire of Louis Bonaparte,* in *Selected Works*, 1:421.

12. Marx and Engels, *The German Ideology*, in *Selected Works*, 1:47.

13. Ibid., 40.

14. Marx, *The Poverty of Philosophy* (New York: International Publishers, 1963), 61.

15. For Marx, socialism, with its rational, humane, and egalitarian ordering of production, permits humankind to harvest the full productive fruits made possible by capitalism; socialism does not relentlessly seek, as capitalism does, to maximize productivity even at the cost of the direct producers.

16. *Capital*, 1:103.

17. I say "purely" moral because, as discussed later, Marx's analysis of capitalism has a normative aspect.

18. See, in particular, Engels, *Socialism*. On Owen, see *Capital*, 1:189n and 635n.

19. Engels, *Socialism*, 132.

20. For sympathetic expositions of Marx's economic ideas, see David Harvey, *A Companion to Marx's "Capital"* (London: Verso, 2010); and Michael Heinrich, *An Introduction to the Three Volumes of Karl Marx's "Capital"* (New York: Monthly Review Press, 2012).

21. *Capital*, vol. 1, chap. 1, sec. 4.

22. Ibid., 1:873–74 and 926–27.

23. It is a history in which "conquest, enslavement, robbery, murder, in short, force, play the greatest part," a history in which capital comes into the world "dripping from head to toe, from every pore, with blood and dirt." *Capital*, 1:874 and 926.

24. See *Capital*, vol. 1, chap. 4, "The General Formula for Capital."

25. For representative criticisms, see Elster, *Making Sense of Marx*, 127–41. Unfortunately, many Marxists tend simply to ignore mainstream criticisms; see Harvey, *Companion to Marx's "Capital"*; Heinrich, *Introduction to the Three Volumes*; and Ben Fine, "Labor Theory of Value," in *The Elgar Companion to Marxist Economics*, ed. Ben Fine and Alfredo Saad-Filho (Cheltenham, UK: Edward Elgar, 2012), 194–99. In contrast, some contemporary economists have offered creative, complex mathematical reinterpretations of the labor theory of value. See, for instance, Michio Morishima, *Marx's Economics: A Dual Theory of Value and Growth* (Cambridge: Cambridge University Press, 1973), pt. 1. In the 1970s and 1980s, Piero Sraffa's slim, elegant work, *Production of Commodities by Means of Commodities* (Cambridge: Cambridge University Press, 1960), stimulated renewed interest in the labor theories of both Ricardo and Marx.

26. The key problem is that capitalists receive the average rate of profit regardless of whether they are in a labor- or capital-intensive industry. But how can this be if labor alone is the source of surplus-value, and hence profit? Marx was aware of this problem but, not wanting to further complicate the analysis of volume 1, postponed his treatment of it to volume 3, which Engels was obliged to assemble from Marx's manuscripts after his death. There Marx affirms that the profits enjoyed by an individual capitalist are not a function of how much surplus-value his particular commodities contain. Instead, he argues that the average rate of profit, which is indeed what capitalists receive, is determined by how much surplus-value the whole system produces. Whether Marx's solution works or can be made to work—that is, whether invisible values can in some intelligible way be connected to visible prices—is called the "transformation problem" and has been the subject of ongoing, albeit recondite, debate since Eugen von Böhm-Bawerk published *Karl Marx and the Close of His System* (London: Unwin, 1898). For valuable, advanced discussions, see Paul A. Samuelson, "Understanding the Marxian Notion of Exploitation: A Summary of the So-Called Transformation Problem between Marxian Values and Competitive Prices," *Journal of Economic Literature* 9, no. 2 (June 1971): 399–431; and William J. Baumol, "The Transformation of Values: What Marx 'Really' Meant (An Interpretation)," *Journal of Economic Literature* 12, no. 1 (June 1974): 51–62.

27. G. A. Cohen, *History, Labour, and Freedom: Themes from Marx* (Oxford: Oxford University Press, 1988), 208–38.

28. Ibid. See also G. A. Cohen, *Self-Ownership, Freedom, and Equality* (Cambridge: Cambridge University Press, 1995), 195–97; and John E. Roemer, *Free to Lose: An Introduction to Marxist Economic Philosophy* (Cambridge, MA: Harvard University Press, 1988), 124–47.

29. *Capital*, 1:771–72.

30. Something that was manifest, of course, in the financial meltdown of 2008.

31. Marx and Engels, "Manifesto of the Communist Party," in *Selected Works*, 1:111.

32. Ibid., 112. Although Marx foresaw globalization and discussed the role that colonialism played in the establishment and consolidation of capitalism, he said little about imperialism in its modern sense. That was left to later Marxists, and in particular to Lenin, for whom imperialism represented a stage of capitalism that developed after Marx's time (and the emergence of which helped to explain why capitalism had not yet collapsed). See Vladimir Ilyich Lenin, *Imperialism: The Highest State of Capitalism* (London: Penguin, 2010).

33. See Stephen Lukes, *Marxism and Morality* (Oxford: Oxford University Press, 1985), esp. chap. 4; Norman Geras, "The Controversy about Marx and Justice," *New Left Review* 1, no. 150 (March–April 1985), 47–85; and Hon-Lam Li, "Marx and Morality: The Clash of the Subjective and the Objective" (unpublished manuscript, Chinese University of Hong Kong, 2012).

34. What if, as Marx thought, capitalism cannot be fundamentally reformed, but yet, contrary to what he assumed, there is no feasible, economically viable, and morally preferable alternative to it? In that case, it would seem, injustice would ineliminably stain humanity's socioeconomic existence.

35. *Capital*, 3:399. See also Marx, "Critique of the Gotha Programme," in *Selected Works*, 3:16.

36. Engels, "The Housing Question," in *Selected Works*, 2:365.

37. Thus, G. A. Cohen contends that "Marx mistakenly thought that Marx did not believe that capitalism was unjust." G. A. Cohen, "Review of *Karl Marx* by Allen W. Wood," *Mind* 92, no. 367 (July 1983): 444.

38. Marx described Spartacus as one of his heroes and "the most capital fellow in the whole history of antiquity." Karl Marx and Frederick Engels, "Letter to Engels, 27 February 1861," in *Collected Works* (New York: International Publishers, 1975–2005), 41:264; "Confession," ibid., 42:567.

39. See, for example, Engels, "Housing Question," 366.

40. Thus, the *German Ideology* proclaims that "communists do not preach morality at all." Karl Marx, *Selected Writings*, ed. David McLellan (Oxford: Oxford University Press, 1977), 183.

41. *Capital*, 1:99.

42. Marx, "Critique of the Gotha Programme," 19. To be more exact, Marx contrasts here the "first phase" and the "higher phase" of *communist* society. Since Marx's time, it has become customary to refer to the first phase as socialism and the second as communism. It is an open question whether Marx thought that communism was just or that communism transcends justice.

43. One pertinent issue is whether a modern economy can function without market-derived prices, and if it cannot, how socialism or communism can accommodate this fact.

44. *Capital*, 3:954–55.

45. Here and elsewhere we see hints of the continuing importance for Marx of self-actualization and the development of our human potential—themes that loom large in his early writings, in particular, "Economic and Philosophical Manuscripts (1844)," in Karl Marx, *Early Writings*, trans. Rodney Livingstone and Gregor Benton (London: Penguin, 1992), 279–400.

46. Some exceptions are Stephen J. Massey, "Marxism and Business Ethics," *Journal of Business Ethics* 1, no. 4 (November 1982): 301–12; J. Angelo Corlett, "A Marxist Approach to Business Ethics," *Journal of Business Ethics* 17, no. 1 (January 1998): 99–103; William H. Shaw, "Marxism, Business Ethics, and Corporate Social Responsibility," *Journal of Business Ethics* 84, no. 4 (February 2009): 565–76; Corlett, "A Marxist Ethic of Business," in *Handbook of the Philosophical Foundations of Business Ethics*, ed. Christoph Luetge (Dordrecht: Springer, 2013), 463–80. See also Bill Martin, "A Marxist in the Business Ethics Classroom," in *Cutting-Edge Issues in Business Ethics: Continental Challenges to Tradition and Practice*, ed. Mollie Painter-Morland and Patricia Werhane (Dordrecht: Springer, 2008), 215–23.

47. *Capital*, 1:92 and 179.

48. Ibid., 254, 342, and 990.

49. Tristram Hunt, *Marx's General: The Revolutionary Life of Friedrich Engels* (New York: Henry Holt, 2009), 187, 189.

50. Cf. Milton Friedman, *Capitalism and Freedom* (Chicago: University of Chicago Press, 1962), 133.

51. Marx and Engels, "Manifesto of the Communist Party," 110–11.

52. *Capital*, 3:516–19.

53. Ibid., 516; see also 519; and Engels, *Socialism*, 143–45.

54. *Capital*, 1:450.

55. Massey, "Marxism and Business Ethics." Although the ideas expressed here are Massey's, I have heard others espouse similar thoughts.

56. See Corlett, "Marxist Approach to Business Ethics" and "Marxist Ethic of Business."

57. For examples from a radical, but not identifiably Marxist perspective, see Richard L. Lippke, *Radical Business Ethics* (Lanham, MD: Rowman & Littlefield, 1995).

58. Cf. Martin, "Marxist in the Business Ethics Classroom," 220 and 223. Martin remarks, "As a Marxist, I still think it is more important to teach students some Kant rather than Marx" (221).

59. Marx, "Theses on Feuerbach," in *Selected Works*, 1:15.

CHAPTER 17

Friedrich Hayek's Defense of the Market Order

Karen I. Vaughn

Friedrich Hayek (1899–1992) was a prodigious scholar whose work spanned almost seven decades and ranged over contributions to economics, scientific methodology, political philosophy, law, psychology, and social theory. Despite the impressive span of fields that he covered, the driving force for all his work emerged from his original study of economics and his belief in the overwhelming benefits of a market economy for human flourishing. He honed his distinctive contributions to economics during the 1930s and 1940s in debate with socialist economists over the technical feasibility of central economic planning—contributions that led to his being awarded the Nobel Prize in 1974. Yet, he regarded as his major life's work his writings on the broad topic of the nature of the liberal order, in particular his best-known works, *The Constitution of Liberty* and *Law, Legislation, and Liberty*, and his final work, *The Fatal Conceit*.[1] That Hayek should shift so dramatically from writing about technical economics to broader philosophical issues was no fluke: the issues that increasingly characterized his economic work led him to consider the wider context within which economic activity takes place. Unlike most economists who see exchange as a purely economic phenomenon, Hayek understood markets as embedded in a cultural and political context: what people value and the means they choose to achieve their ends are contingent upon rules and expectations of the society within which they reside. And while exchange is ubiquitous and serves as an engine of human progress, the engine can be slowed or stalled by an inhospitable culture or political regime. He saw as his task to articulate rules of political and social order that are most conducive to the growth of wealth and thus to the flourishing of civilization.

Despite the ideological motivation for Hayek's work, he was foremost an economist and as such saw himself as a scientist, not an ethicist. His brief was to focus on explaining the nature of the market order and its consequences for human beings without passing final judgment on its ultimate goodness or badness. Insofar as he had an ideological purpose, it was to discover the political and legal system that allowed human beings to achieve their own ends as they saw fit. Hayek believed that for a social scientist to pass judgment on the ultimate moral worth of human arrangements is an exercise in intellectual hubris. He believed that there was no extrahuman authority to reveal the nature of the good nor any objective means for defining the ultimate good apart from the perceptions and beliefs of individual actors. The scientist must take the values of actual human beings as his starting point for analyzing how various social structures affect the achievement of human ends. Individuals could then use the scientific appraisal of market action to assign value to the market economy for themselves. And while Hayek did not presume to argue that maximum material wealth was an ultimate value, he noted that most people desire material wealth for the simple reason that material wealth is a means to the achievement of other human values whether selfish or altruistic. Despite his adherence to a scientific agnosticism with regard to ends, he firmly believed that if people were truly to understand that extending the market order means, among other benefits, the reduction of "starvation, filth and disease,"[2] there would be few who would not choose a political environment that supported markets.

The argument of this essay proceeds as follows. The opening section delineates how Hayek's dissatisfaction with the economics profession's enthusiasm for central planning in the interwar years led to his critique of mainstream economic theory and, in particular, its conventional assumption of perfect knowledge. How to cope with the limitations of human knowledge became a central theme of his later work on social and political theory. The subsequent section, on the market order, examines Hayek's exploration of the ways in which exchange in markets permits people to benefit from each other's specialized knowledge. The mutual benefits from trade lead to reduced violence and discord in human life. The third and fourth sections of this essay take up Hayek's evolutionary account of the growth of the market economy and its reliance on social and political rules to constrain individual behavior so as to lead to growing prosperity. The last section, on social justice and prescriptive morality, sets forth how Hayek did not judge the morality of either the market itself or the actions of individuals within the market. He limited his argument to noting that societies permitting the greatest scope for market exchange constrained by rules of property, tort, and contract tended to be the wealthiest, and that wealth was widely shared among the population.

Hayek began his career as an economist, but one who early on grew increasingly out of step with his profession. In the 1930s, as a rising figure at the London School of Economics, he was viewed as John Maynard Keynes's most important rival for professional prominence.[3] While he was primarily known for his original approach to the theory of capital and money, in the middle part of the decade he became involved in an academic controversy over the feasibility of central planning that radically changed the direction of his research. During the interwar period, both the seeming achievements of the Soviet Union and the disruptions caused by the Great Depression served to fuel strong intellectual sentiment in the West for replacing the "chaotic" market with "rational economic planning," a sentiment that was shared by many mainstream economists. Hayek, on the other hand, believed that central planning was a system that would lead to declining wealth, increasing economic disruptions, and greatly reduced personal liberty, a view that led him to write a series of articles that would change the course of his life's work.

Pro-planning arguments, though socialist in sentiment, owed little to Marxist ideology. Instead, they were an exercise in determining whether or not the tools of conventional economic theory could be used to devise an efficient system of central planning that could overcome some of the perceived shortcomings of real market economies. Pro-planning economists in the 1920s and 1930s formulated schemes to achieve the goals of socialism, state ownership of the "means of production," greater rationality in capital investments (which they believed would bring about an end of business cycles), and greater income equality and security, all based on general equilibrium theory and its underlying theory of perfect competition. These economists were referred to as "market socialists" because they recognized the important role prices play in allocating resources efficiently, but wanted to find a means of bypassing genuine market exchange to arrive at "economic" prices—prices that accurately represented relative resource scarcity. With the correct set of prices, they believed, a central planning board could manage the production of goods in state-owned firms more efficiently and more equitably than was possible in the "chaos" of the market. While early attempts to devise an alternative to actual markets depended upon determining statistically generated supply and demand functions that could then be solved for equilibrium prices, an approach abandoned in recognition of the "practical" difficulties surrounding such a project, the most widely respected theory of market socialism, and the one that the economics profession agreed was a genuine alternative to actual markets, was a system of "trial and error" pricing proposed by Oscar Lange.[4]

Lange proposed that "the means of production" be organized in state firms, where managers would be told to use planned prices in their output decisions. He reasoned that since equilibrium prices are set in markets through a process of trial and error much like an auction, all the central planners had to do was to list any set of prices and then instruct managers of state-owned firms to equate price to marginal cost in order to maximize return. The central planners would then observe resulting surpluses and shortages to adjust prices accordingly to reach equilibrium, and they would use "profit" and "loss" to guide capital investment in the state firms. This way, the allocative function of price could be preserved, allowing central planners to make rational decisions about resource use. Hayek's direct response to the economics of socialism was to write several articles that criticized the details of the socialist schemes,[5] which he regarded as naïvely misinformed about the nature of market activity. More important, the debate over the economics of socialism led Hayek to publish a series of articles that presented a different view of how markets function from the one implied by general equilibrium theory.[6]

This is not the place to go into a detailed discussion of Hayek's technical reasons for criticizing Lange's scheme. As might be expected, he catalogued a myriad of difficulties that would be encountered by a central planning board, such as defining what constituted a product, what was proper firm size, how managers would be chosen and evaluated in the absence of genuine profit or loss, how often to adjust administered prices, and how to deal with changing circumstances. But at the heart of all of his objections to central planning were two methodological issues that were generally not the subject of economic inquiry: the importance of time in economic action, and the nature of the knowledge that informs decisions.[7]

In order to explain market prices, the model of perfect competition, which underlies general equilibrium theory, was essentially timeless: change was understood as comparative statics, the movement from one equilibrium position to another. Change itself was modeled as exogenous shocks that were by definition outside the parameters of the model. With such a model, it is understandable that one might think that central planners could determine a set of equilibrium prices that could guide production decisions from one period to another. But in the real world of constant change, Hayek argued, an exclusive focus on achieving equilibrium conditions diverts attention from understanding the essential nature of the market process. Central planning boards can gather statistics about past prices and quantities traded, and they might be able to gather specifications about existing production processes, but economic activity is not an exercise in endlessly repeating past patterns of behavior; it is about dealing with changing circumstances that require novel adjustments that in turn introduce more change into the system.[8] The market order that economists attempted to capture in the metaphor of general equilibrium theory could not describe this unending process of change and adjustment to change that was the central characteristic of market economies.

The timeless nature of perfect competition was further supported by the assumption that knowledge of technologies was essentially an engineering problem that could be easily shared, and that market conditions were known equally to all actors. Hayek believed that these simplifying assumptions left out the very feature of the human condition that makes markets necessary to economic order: that humans live in a world where they plan for an unknown future, and they do so in light of the unique knowledge each possesses about their own circumstances. The problem facing economic theory, according to Hayek, was to explain "how the spontaneous interaction of a number of people, each possessing only bits of knowledge, brings about a state of affairs . . . which could be brought about by deliberate direction only by somebody who possessed the combined knowledge of all those individuals."[9] What Adam Smith called the "invisible hand" of the market, Hayek was to call a "spontaneous order": an orderly process of human interaction that is planned by no single intelligence yet results in patterns of action that enable individuals mutually to achieve their ends in concert with one another.[10]

Hayek was especially disturbed by the simplifying assumption of perfect knowledge that economists took for granted. He argued that human knowledge, far from being "homogeneous" and perfectly available to all, is differentiated and personal. Knowledge is not an abstract thing to be looked up in some authoritative text. It resides in millions of human minds in fragmented form. The knowledge people possess may be technical, practical, circumstantial, or simply "techniques of thought"[11] that allow an individual to see the world differently from others. This kind of market-relevant knowledge allows individuals to form conjectures about the consequences of potential courses of action based on their own unique experiences. Most importantly, economically relevant knowledge grows in the process of people trading with each other. No one knows in advance what will be the best technology, or who will be the most skillful producer, offer the best service, or what products will most satisfy wants. That knowledge comes about only as people act upon their beliefs and bear the consequences of their actions. Further, and perhaps most important, in the process of participating in market exchanges, individuals not only revise and enhance their knowledge; they benefit from the knowledge of other market participants, knowledge embedded in the products consumed and the technologies that produced those products. When individuals trade with each other, they are trading not only goods and services, but the unique knowledge each possesses.[12] As Hayek was to later call it, a market order is a "discovery procedure,"[13] an arrangement of trading practices that permit knowledge and the fruits of knowledge to grow.

Intellectuals might focus on abstract theoretical learning as the significant achievement of human progress, but Hayek was equally impressed by practical knowledge acquired through market activity, knowledge whose application could improve lives dramatically.

Central to the advance of market knowledge is that people pursue their own interests, projects, and plans, and use their own resources to trade with others. One can consider the pursuit of one's interests as a set of problems to be solved: how to best use what I have and what I know to best achieve my goals. This, of course, is the economic problem that neoclassical economists render as "maximizing utility." What neoclassical economics and, by implication, market socialists fail to account for, however, is that "maximizing" is not an automatic process, and the solution to the maximizing problem, never obvious, must be discovered. What may be discovered can range all the way from which brand of jeans offers the best fit to a new use for an existing resource to the discovery of new resources and new ways of using them that revolutionize how we live.[14] The technological and organizational change that we have come to take for granted is a product of people pursuing their interests in the marketplace.

Human society flourishes when as much knowledge as possible that is discoverable by individual human minds is used in ways that benefit others. Like Adam Smith before him, Hayek argues that this happy result flows from allowing people to make their own economic decisions based on their own notions of their best interests: insofar as people are free to trade with each other, each has an incentive to use his own knowledge and skills as best he can to enrich himself. The consequence, as Adam Smith taught us,[15] is that by pursuing his own interests in the marketplace, each enhances the welfare of others. Or, as Hayek might put it, without addressing any notion of ultimate worth, by using his unique knowledge and skills for his own purposes, an economic actor creates value that allows others to benefit from his actions. Smith called this the "simple system of natural liberty,"[16] and invoked the metaphor of the "invisible hand"[17] to explain how the freely chosen actions of separate individuals lead to orderly patterns of trade and economic growth that seem to be the product of a planning intelligence. In Hayek's case, he offered his notion of a spontaneous order: an order that appears to be the result of a plan, but is actually the unintended result of individuals going about the business of making a living through trade constrained only by commonly followed rules of behavior.

THE MARKET ORDER OR CATALLAXY

Hayek regarded the term *economy* to be a poor description of what actually goes on in a market order. From the Greek word for the art of household management, *economy* implies a manager who chooses to maximize the welfare of a household according to his evaluation of what is best for those under his care. Yet given human differences in valuation, the metaphor of a single mind is clearly misplaced. While humans might share broad notions of what contributes to economic flourishing, they differ greatly in how that applies to their own well-being. Humans might agree that they all need food, clothing, shelter, companionship, and community, but how much of one is worth how much of another will differ from one person to the next. There is no unitary, undisputed ranking of social values by which to judge the welfare maximum of a society.[18]

A market order is better analyzed as a network of trading relationships that allow people to reshuffle things they value in such a way as to make them all come closer to satisfying their most pressing diverse interests.[19] These diverse interests cannot be aggregated into a common hierarchy of values that would satisfy all members of the group.[20] Thus, Hayek preferred to describe the phenomenon under consideration as a "catallaxy," rather than an "economy." He coined the term based on another Greek word, *katallattein*, which had a double meaning, "to trade" and also "to admit into the community" or "to change an enemy into a friend,"[21] a double meaning that Hayek found particularly significant. While the first meaning emphasizes the specific character of a market order as facilitating wealth creation through trade among diverse people, the second refers to the civilizing effects of trade. When humans see others as rivals, there is potential for conflict and violence, but where they see others as useful to their purposes, as they do in mutually beneficial acts of trade, they have an incentive to act peacefully and cooperatively. One need not think that seeing others as means to one's ends is a salutary motivation for human interaction and yet be able to appreciate the value of reducing the scope for intergroup violence in human society.[22] Hayek believed "changing a stranger into friend" was both the source of economic development and one of the foundations of civilization. There is supporting evidence for his claim.[23]

Humans evolved over the course of several million years, at first living in small bands of about fifty individuals who made a living by hunting and gathering. There is accumulating evidence that while early hominid life was surely not solitary (human ancestors, like modern-day chimps and apes, were social creatures), a case can be made that it was, indeed, poor, brutish, and short.[24] Significantly, death by violence was a common occurrence, through either unfortunate encounters with wild animals or outright warfare with rival tribes. While a person had to cooperate with others in his tribe to survive, people outside the tribe were de facto enemies, rivals for territory and resources (again like modern-day chimps and apes—and surviving hunter-gatherer tribes). In such an environment, there was precious little scope for the division of labor and the gains from trade, as evidenced by millennia of almost nonexistent technological change. The welfare of the group would be dependent on natural elements beyond anyone's control, and populations would wax and wane largely with the availability of food. Yet somewhere between 10,000 and 40,000 years ago, a major change took place. Some tribe or tribes discovered a way to trade with strangers from other tribes without killing them first, and the consequences were revolutionary. Tribes that discovered how to trade peacefully with others outside their band would necessarily expand their market, giving scope for the division of labor and all the benefits that arise therefrom.

While it is impossible to know exactly how some human groups first managed to find a way to trade with each other, Hayek points out that a group that eventually learned to suspend hostilities long enough to trade with strangers from outside of their tribe would have a great evolutionary advantage over nontrading tribes.[25] Trade would have enhanced the tribe's wealth, which would have resulted in more children surviving to adulthood and more adults dying from disease and old age rather than malnutrition and conflict. Greater wealth would have meant greater population, and as the population of traders grew, they would come to crowd out nontrading groups in the competition for resources. It is also likely that some nontrading tribes would wish to copy their wealthier rivals and themselves become traders. In either case, the resultant growth in trading populations would cause their trade-favorable practices to dominate less-advanced groups. The consequences were that within the span of a few millennia, social rules that permitted widespread trade were common throughout Europe, the Middle East, and Asia. Within a geographical blink of an eye, humans moved from a nomadic lifestyle to a settled one, then to agricultural communities, and then to large cities, which characterized ancient civilizations. And while the human condition cannot be said to have reached perfection by any means, and while it is the case that the upper echelons of political hierarchies dominated the less powerful and captured a disproportionate share of wealth created through the extension of trade, it is undeniable that populations grew, life spans increased, and an individual had a much greater chance of dying of old age or disease than from an ax to the skull. How this came about was to a large degree explained by the adoption of new rules of social order that favored trading with strangers.

THE IMPORTANCE OF RULES

If anything captures Hayek's approach to understanding social order, it is his emphasis on the importance of rules in social interaction.[26] All human action is bound by rules for the simple reason that the world is uncertain. Yet if purposeful humans are to achieve their goals they must be able to form predictions about the possible outcomes of their projects and plans. In particular, they need to have some idea about the way in which others will react to their endeavors. Thus, Hayek argues, society is possible only because humans have developed rules of behavior that govern their interactions, and not the least of these are the rules that govern the interactions of people in markets.[27] Market rules may be informal, such as the etiquette surrounding bargaining or the degree of small talk that must precede serious negotiation, or they may be formally codified into law. Fundamental to the expansion of trade were settled laws of property, tort, and contract. Without laws upholding private property, an individual's right to use resources to produce goods for sale would be at best uncertain and subject to challenge from other potential claimants. Nor would complex trades be possible without some form of assurance that contracts would be upheld in the eyes of society and wrongdoing punished. In the early stages of economic development, it is likely that rules of property and contract would have been subject to informal enforcement; as civilization grew and political authority asserted itself, significantly, informal rules would have been codified into law enforced by the power of the state.

From a Hayekian perspective, what distinguishes laws from informal rules is the method of enforcing compliance. If one fails to follow social conventions that signal a desire to enter into a negotiation, or if one does not understand the difference between goods that are acceptable objects of trade and ones that are off-limits in a culture, one very likely will lose the opportunity to profit from a trade. Egregious violations of informal rules of trade might also in the extreme lead to social ostracism. In any case, people who violate informal rules of trade can suffer short-term financial losses but ultimately can learn from their failures. Formal rules, on the other hand, are laws backed up by the power of the legal authority: they constrain behavior through the threat of force if they are not followed. While failing to follow an informal rule can hamper one's ability to profit from a potential deal, failing to follow a formal rule can mean socially sanctioned loss of wealth or freedom. This difference is crucial for understanding the forces of economic development.

Recall that Hayek saw the market as a "discovery procedure," in essence an experimental process by which people act upon their own conjectures about possible outcomes and learn from bearing the consequences of their actions. The greater the scope for experimentation, the greater will be the potential growth of knowledge that flows from entrepreneurial action, and greater knowledge leads to more wealth for the entire society. Hence, Hayek believed that societies that allow individuals the greatest degree of discretion to determine their own actions in the marketplace would be the richest societies.[28]

Just as technologies evolve as humans learn better ways of enhancing their productivity, the rules of trade also evolve with human experimentation and learning. New habits and customs surrounding trade will evolve to support new technologies and expanding markets. As long as the consequences of acting against an established social norm involve no cost greater than potentially losing money or incurring public displeasure, entrepreneurs will try out new ways of interacting in the market, and where their innovation is wealth enhancing, it will be copied by others and become established as a new norm.[29] Where norms are codified into law, however, experiments that potentially violate formal social rules will be severely limited and slow to change. This is as it should be: laws need to be predictable to allow people to plan their actions in an uncertain world. But it is also true that changing technologies that result from economic development will require changes in laws of property and contract to reflect the new economic environment.[30] If laws are too rigid or the process of adapting laws to new circumstances too inflexible, economic development will be slowed or, in extreme cases, halted entirely.[31]

THE CHARACTER OF GOOD RULES

As we have seen, for Hayek, what distinguishes a progressing nation from a stagnating one is the scope for market experimentation. In particular, this means freedom to use one's resources on the basis of one's own conjectures about the consequences of one's action. Since progress requires employing an ever-increasing stock of knowledge, much of which exists only in dispersed form, successful societies will be ones that have rules of social order that encourage individuals to deploy that knowledge to economically beneficial uses.[32] There is no certainty in life, and in a complex, evolving market order, every action contains the possibility that the consequences will differ from the actor's hopes. Each deployment of one's resources and each trade are a sort of market experiment from which one learns more than one knew before.

Learning through one's actions in the marketplace has two components. First, one must be able to risk one's own wealth in a market endeavor; traders must have clear property rights in the goods and services they wish to trade. The potential for gain or loss encourages an actor to tap into all of her market knowledge to make the best guess possible about how to profit from the action. Second, the actor must bear the consequences of the action. To be deprived of the gains from one's actions will reduce market experimentation and the deployment of knowledge that benefits society. To be insulated from losses is equally harmful. Without the discipline of losses from one's miscalculations, there is little incentive to make the best decision possible, and there is little learning from one's mistakes. In either case, society loses, a circumstance recently observed by government bailouts of businesses deemed "too big to fail."

Hayek tells us little about what specific rules fulfill these general requirements, and for good reason. The specific rules of property and contract, he argues, will be culture dependent, and they will change with changing economic circumstances. Law, he believed, was the product of an evolutionary process that allowed societies to adapt to changing conditions.[33] But, while he did not think he or anyone else was competent to design the perfect set of laws to govern economic interaction, he did describe several characteristics of such laws that would make them consistent with a progressing extended market order: they must consist of general rules that constrain certain actions, but do not command specific behaviors, and they must be impartially applied to all people.[34] Both are important for permitting individuals to use their knowledge effectively to achieve their purposes in the marketplace. To prescribe certain behavior (such as in what manner a product must be produced, or what goods one must purchase) takes away individual discretion, substituting the will of the authority for that of the actor. To enact laws that single out some for benefits or handicaps that do not apply to others violates the principle of equality before the law. Hayek believed both to be a violation of liberty, but even if one does not share his perspective, there are practical disadvantages to violating the tenets of good economic rules.

Where political authorities prescribe specific actions, or where they try to play favorites and pick winners, they are substituting their own judgment for that of market actors. This necessarily reduces the amount of knowledge employed in a decision and stifles adaptation to change, slowing and often preventing the process of entrepreneurial discovery and the growth of wealth.[35] On the other hand, a political regime that permits free employment of one's resources constrained only by impartially enforced laws of property, tort, and contract and tempered by the need to bear the consequences of actions is a political regime that encourages the sharing of knowledge that leads to economic growth and development.

THE MIRAGE OF SOCIAL JUSTICE

Even if we grant Hayek's argument that the extended market order leads to the production of the greatest amount of material wealth possible for the greatest number of people, does this constitute a moral defense of the extended market order? After all, Hayek, himself agrees that material wealth is not an ultimate value in any sense: it is merely what people desire in order to achieve their other varying purposes. These purposes can be praiseworthy, such as supporting their families or donating to charity, or they can be morally unattractive, such as wanting to wallow in sybaritic pleasures. It is not markets per se that can be judged moral or immoral; rather, it is people's actions in markets that can be so judged. In general, there are two kinds of criticisms of the extended market order that are commonly asserted. The first is that market activity may preclude the pursuit of some values that people think of as good. Perhaps the clear benefits derived from self-interested behavior in markets crowd out altruistic behavior, and perhaps the incentives to compete with others undermine actions that lead to a sense of community and solidarity.

Hayek had little patience with this argument, nor did he address it in any depth. While he might agree that people often behave in unethical ways in markets, he would likely argue that people have been known to behave badly in all social settings. If anything, the desire to prosper in market activity encourages sociability and conformity with ethical norms: success in market endeavors requires that others be willing to trade with you.[36] The great contribution of a market economy is that large areas of behavior are constrained by the need to benefit others to achieve our own purposes. Hayek finds it no accident that societies that permit greater economic freedom historically have not simply been wealthier, but more charitable as well.[37] Of course, there is no guarantee they will be so: how people use economic freedom depends upon their moral convictions. There is reason to believe, however, that markets encourage, in fact, teach, such virtues as honesty, self-reliance, and accountability because people who practice them tend to prosper. Further, Hayek pointed out, the only kinds of actions that can be given moral import are noncoerced choices, the kinds one is able to exercise within market settings. Hence, freedom in economic as well as political society permits people both to exercise virtuous behavior and to learn virtue from the responses to their actions.[38]

Hayek regarded as far more serious the second common indictment of a market order, that wealth is not distributed equally among actors. He found complaints about disparities in wealth dangerous because while fundamentally misguided, they provide ideological justification for both socialist planning and the advanced welfare state. His worry was that intolerance for wealth inequalities that follow from economic freedom, and the concomitant demands for redistribution that intolerance engenders, could seriously undermine the market order and reverse all of the benefits that modern civilization has come to take for granted. Hayek's concern is reflected in the subtitle of volume 3 of *Law, Legislation, and Liberty*: *The Mirage of Social Justice*.[39]

Calls for social justice, he argues, stem from the belief that differences in wealth that follow from market action are unjust, a claim that Hayek regarded as a misuse of the notion of justice. Justice can apply only to the acts of individuals. Unlike a society, a person is an independent mind that can choose her actions, and because the person has a choice, she can be held accountable for the consequences of her actions. If a person has no choice, no moral evaluation can be assigned to her actions. "Society" is not a single choosing entity. Rules guide individual actions within the society, but there is no single intelligence that can be held accountable for the consequences of following the rules. When actors who adhere to a common set of rules make choices among alternatives, the outcomes that emerge from their choices form recognizable patterns, but they are nevertheless unpredictable and uncontrollable.[40] Further, since no one can control the outcomes of the rule-following behavior of individuals in markets, there is really no meaning to the term "social injustice." Insofar as individuals' market transactions are consistent with the rules of property, tort, and contract that are applicable to all people, the actions are just, and the outcomes of the actions must be just.[41] The fact that people will prosper differentially in a market order is irrelevant.[42]

While one might agree with Hayek that unequal outcomes from market action cannot be avoided where there is even a modicum of economic liberty, it is also true that people often find offensive the differences in wealth that emerge from market activity. When people claim that the market is "unfair," they usually mean that market rewards do not reflect nonmarket notions of merit. Successful traders are not necessarily the strongest, the smartest, the most personally lovable, or even the most skillful in a recognized activity. And while certainly knowledge, hard work, and skill play some role in economic success, so does luck. Everyone knows someone who is honorable and hardworking but nevertheless suffers market reverses due to circumstances beyond his control. It seems unfair that a worthy person can do badly, while others, perhaps not so worthy, become wealthy because they were in the right place at the right time or guessed correctly what consumers would regard as the next "hot item." Yet, according to Hayek, the very feature that people find objectionable—that markets do not necessarily reward merit—is really one of its major strengths.[43]

If Hayek's claim[44] seems counterintuitive, consider the following: in an extended market order, personal profit accrues only to those who provide services valued by others. This central truth about market success applies to rock stars and sports heroes as well as people going about the more mundane tasks of life in a market economy. We don't choose doctors because they are kind to their families or donate to multiple charities, and we don't prefer a highly educated but incompetent plumber to one who can stop the sink from leaking. As consumers we try to deal with sellers who provide us with the greatest service for the least price regardless of their many other attributes. The income derived from market exchange, then, is an assessment of the worth of one's actions to other people. Market rewards are in essence a social judgment about the relative importance of various productive activities. Redistribution, on the other hand, substitutes some other non-agreed-upon standard for assigning rewards for productive actions, standards that can be maintained only by imposition from a political authority. Some might be quite willing to supply an alternative standard to be imposed through political means as the popularity of welfare state transfers attest, but redistribution is not a costless exercise in altruism by proxy. Further, and not incidentally, laws aimed at redistributing the wealth that actors create in market transactions will have the perverse effect of reducing the amount of wealth available in society.[45] In markets, people are motivated largely by the chance of material gain.[46] At some point, attenuating the chance of gain also chips away at the motivation to provide services for others, slowing economic growth and reducing wealth not only for the wealthy, but for all who benefit from cheaper and more plentiful goods, which are the hallmark of a vibrant market economy.[47]

CONCLUDING REMARKS

Perhaps because he was not primarily interested in formulating precepts for how people should live, Hayek was a firm believer in the importance of economic liberty. To be free to use one's own resources to shape one's own life, he believed, was both a value in itself and instrumental to the achievement of other values, not the least of which was the growth of material wealth. Material wealth, after all, is the means by which so many human purposes can be achieved. And economic growth is not simply about having more stuff: it is also about the eradication of disease, the extension of life spans, the reduction in infant mortality, and the luxury of leisure to allow the pursuit of arts and letters.

Hayek believed that twentieth-century socialist ideology with its railing against the purported shortcomings of the market order failed to appreciate the interconnectedness between economic liberty and economic growth that improved the material well-being of an entire people. For the economically advanced countries of the world, such as the United States and the countries of Western Europe, a slowing and eventual cessation of economic growth would mean a slow decline in living standards that, while unpleasant, could persist for decades. The third world would face a very different future. A slowing down or stagnation of economic growth would at best remove from the poorest of the world's population their chance to escape their poverty. At worst, Hayek dramatically argued, it would lead to even greater poverty, increasing misery, and even death through starvation and social upheaval.[48] While Hayek's argument may seem exaggerated to twenty-first-century readers, when one remembers that the examples he had in mind were the USSR and Communist China, the specter of mass starvation following the elimination of a market order is not at all far-fetched.

Hayek's answer to critics of the market order was straightforward. It may be true that in the "game of catallaxy,"[49] there will always be losers as well as winners, and some players could well find themselves worse off than they would have been under some other rules of order.[50] However, the net result of an extended market will be that the greatest number of people will have the best chance to improve their own well-being and that of their children. There is no other system of human arrangements yet discovered that has allowed as many people to better their circumstances as they see fit, or raised the standard of living of even the poorest "by assuring to all an individual liberty desirable for itself on ethical grounds."[51]

So is there a moral defense of the market order? If with Hayek, we believe that the only judge of the value of a market order is the evaluations of individual actors, then perhaps there is. As Hayek concludes his last book,

> If one considers the realities of "bourgeois" life—but not utopian demands for a life free of all conflict, pain, lack of fulfillment, and indeed, morality—one might think the pleasures and stimulations of civilisation not a bad bargain for those who do not yet enjoy them. . . . The only objective assessment of the issue is to see what people do when they are given the choice. . . . The readiness with which ordinary people of the third world—as opposed to Western-educated intellectuals—appear to embrace the opportunities offered them by the extended order, even if it means inhabiting for a time shanty towns at the periphery, complements evidence regarding the reactions of European peasants to the introduction of urban capitalism, indicating that people will usually choose civilisation if they have the choice.[52]

NOTES

1. Friedrich Hayek, *The Constitution of Liberty* (Chicago: University of Chicago Press, 1960). Hayek's *Law, Legislation, and Liberty* is a three-volume work published by the University of Chicago Press: vol. 1, *Rules and Order* (1973); vol. 2, *The Mirage of Social Justice* (1976); and vol. 3, *The Political Order of a Free People* (1979). *The Fatal Conceit: The Errors of Socialism* was also published by the University of Chicago Press, in 1988.

2. Hayek, *Constitution of Liberty*, 53.

3. For an insightful account of Hayek's career, see Bruce Caldwell, *Hayek's Challenge: An Intellectual Biography of F. A. Hayek* (Chicago: University of Chicago Press, 2004).

4. Oscar Lange and Fred M. Taylor, *On the Economic Theory of Socialism* (New York: McGraw-Hill, 1938).

5. All three articles—"Socialist Calculation I: The Nature and History of the Problem" (1935); "Socialist Calculation II: The State of the Debate" (1935); and "Socialist Calculation III: The Competitive 'Solution'" (1940)—were published in Hayek, *Individualism and Economic Order* (Chicago: University of Chicago Press, 1948), 148–208.

6. "Economics and Knowledge," 33–56, "The Use of Knowledge in Society," 77–91, and "The Meaning of Competition," 92–106, in *Individualism and Economic Order*.

7. For a comprehensive treatment of Hayek's role in what came to be known as "the economic calculation debate," see Karen I. Vaughn, *Austrian Economics in America: The Migration of a Tradition* (Cambridge: Cambridge University Press, 1994), chap. 3.

8. "The practical problem is not whether a particular method would eventually lead to a hypothetical equilibrium, but which method will secure the more rapid and complete adjustment to the daily changing conditions in different places and different industries." "Socialist Calculation III," 188.

9. "Economics and Knowledge," 51.

10. Although Hayek introduces the term "spontaneous order," in *Constitution of Liberty*, 160, a detailed development of the notion is found in *Law, Legislation, and Liberty*, vol. 1.

11. "Socialist Calculation II," 156.

12. "Economics and Knowledge," 33–56. Although learning in markets is probably most often thought of in terms of technological innovations, in fact, the simple act of shopping in a mall exposes shoppers to new products and supplies information about prices and available quantities. In turn, consumer purchasing decisions give useful information to sellers that influences what they supply in the future.

13. Hayek, "Competition as a Discovery Procedure," in *New Studies in Philosophy, Politics, Economics, and the History of Ideas* (Chicago: University of Chicago Press, 1978), 179–90.

14. One has only to think of the microprocessor to grasp the point.

15. Adam Smith, *An Inquiry into the Nature and Causes of the Wealth of Nations,* ed. R. H. Campbell, A. S. Skinner, and W. B. Todd (Indianapolis: Liberty Fund, 1981), IV.ii.10 (p. 456).

16. Ibid., IV.ix.51 (p. 687).

17. Ibid., IV.ii.9 (p. 456).

18. Obviously, Hayek is denying that there is any such thing as a social welfare function that truly reflects some aggregate, agreed-upon relative valuation of alternatives. *Law, Legislation, and Liberty,* 2:109–11.

19. As a network of relationships, a market does not have a single purpose, despite what some business ethicists might claim. The entire thrust of Hayek's work renders nonsensical the claim that "the purpose of business is to provide for the prosperity of the entire society" (Robert Solomon, *Ethics and Excellence: Cooperation and Integrity in Business* [New York: Oxford University Press, 1992], 20). Without doubt, of course, business enterprises lead to greater prosperity, so in some sense one might say that is their function, but no one *assigns* that purpose to them. Purposes are individual, and there are unintended and largely beneficial consequences to organizing production in business enterprises. Crucially, no businessman can know exactly what the "prosperity of the entire society" means. He can know only whether or not the organization is making a profit.

20. Hayek, *The Road to Serfdom* (Chicago: University of Chicago Press, 1944).

21. *Law, Legislation, and Liberty,* 2:107–11.

22. Or as Adam Smith so aptly put it, "Man has almost constant occasion for the help of his brethren, and it is vain for him to expect it from their benevolence only. He will be more likely to prevail if he can interest their self-love in his favour. . . . Give me that which I want, and you shall have this which you want [is] . . . the manner that we obtain from one another the far greater part of those good offices which we stand in need of." *Wealth of Nations,* I.ii.2 (p. 26).

23. For an account of current anthropological research that supports Hayek's evolutionary view of markets, see Matt Ridley, *The Rational Optimist: How Prosperity Evolves* (New York: Harper Collins, 2012). See also Nicholas Wade, *Before the Dawn: Recovering the Lost History of Our Ancestors* (New York: Penguin Books, 2006), for corroborating evidence from genetics.

24. We make no judgment about its ultimate nastiness.

25. *Law, Legislation, and Liberty,* 3:155.

26. Recall the subtitle of volume 1 of *Law, Legislation and Liberty: Rules and Order.* Hayek's thesis is that without rules there is no social order, and the character of the emergent order is dependent upon the nature of the rules by which it is governed. See esp. *Law, Legislation and Liberty,* 1:17–19.

27. *Constitution of Liberty,* 148–61.

28. Ibid., 156.

29. Violations might include trading with a socially unacceptable partner or offering to trade a good that was previously considered outside the scope of the market.

30. Hayek's model for a legal process that supports market innovation was English common law. Because judges apply precedent to new situations, the law would be changed gradually to accommodate economic discovery. *Law, Legislation, and Liberty,* 1:82–88.

31. Slowing or reversing the process of economic development, Hayek will argue, is not simply an inconvenience, however, or even a choice among lifestyles. It is a calamity for the society that suffers stagnation or decline. One could think of Europe after the fall of the Roman Empire or of China, which suffered close to a thousand years of economic stagnation, during which the overwhelming majority of the population lived in poverty while the politically powerful lived in relative opulence (Ridley, *Rational Optimist,* 179–84).

32. An action that is "economically beneficial" is one that benefits all those with whom one trades. In a market economy, one only benefits by providing benefits to others.

33. *Law, Legislation, and Liberty,* 1:72–91.

34. *Constitution of Liberty,* 149.

35. Hayek was not arguing against all economic regulation per se. He was merely warning that regulation that specifies certain actions comes at a high cost and should be employed sparingly if at all. See *Constitution of Liberty,* 253–396, for a detailed examination of regulatory issues.

36. Answers to the numerous critics of market values abound. See, for example, Deirdre McCloskey, *The Bourgeois Virtues: Ethics for an Age of Commerce* (Chicago: University of Chicago Press, 2006).

37. "Free societies . . . in modern times have been the source of all the great humanitarian movements aiming at active help to the weak, the ill, and the oppressed. Unfree societies . . . have as regularly developed a disrespect for the law, [and] a callous attitude toward suffering." Hayek, "The Moral Element in Free Enterprise," in *New Studies,* 230.

38. "Moral Element in Free Enterprise," 231.

39. See especially chap. 9, which is entitled "'Social' or Distributive Justice."

40. A wide body of research supports Hayek's claim by showing that economies are complex, adaptive systems (or emergent orders, as in evolutionary biology) where individual rule-following agents create orderly patterns of action that lead to emergent structures more complex than their constituent parts (e.g., bilateral trades become organized markets).).In complex, adaptive systems, specific outcomes cannot be predicted, although patterns can be perceived. See, for example, Scott E. Page, *Diversity and Complexity* (Princeton, NJ: Princeton University Press, 2011). Complexity science had its origins in the 1950s and 1960s in what was then called "systems theory," features of which Hayek incorporated into his writings on methodology and into his theory of spontaneous order. See Karen I. Vaughn, "Hayek's Theory of the Market Order as an Instance of the Theory of Complex, Adaptive Systems," *Journal des Économistes et des Études Humaines* 9, no. 2/3 (June/September 1999): 241–56.

41. Robert Nozick, *Anarchy, State, and Utopia* (New York: Basic Books, 1974), 150–53, makes a similar argument.

42. Hayek was not tone deaf to people's differences in life chances. He favored, for example, an income safety net to cushion people from devastating loss, as well as several provisions

of the modern welfare state. He simply opposed attempts to level incomes through direct intervention in market contracts or to impose massive redistribution through tax policy in the name of justice (*Constitution of Liberty*, 259).

43. *Constitution of Liberty*, 85–99.

44. "One of the great merits of a free society is that material reward is not dependent on whether the majority of our fellows like or esteem us personally. . . . So long as we keep within the accepted rules, moral pressure can be brought on us only through the esteem of those whom we ourselves respect and not through the allocation of material reward by a social authority." "Moral Element in Free Enterprise," 233–34.

45. *Law, Legislation, and Liberty*, 2:98.

46. Of course, motivations for specific actions are complex. People choose professions not simply to maximize material income: the desire for status, to do good, or just to enjoy life all play a role in how and what one does with one's working life. The argument here is simply that reducing the financial reward of any occupation will have consequences for how much of a service is provided and how well it is accomplished. Even saints need to eat.

47. *Law, Legislation, and Liberty*, 1:98.

48. *Fatal Conceit*, 134.

49. *Law, Legislation, and Liberty*, 2:115–20.

50. Sadists, for example, did very well as torturers under despotic governments, but found themselves less in demand as democracy followed expanded markets.

51. *Law, Legislation, and Liberty*, 2:71.

52. *Fatal Conceit*, 134.

CHAPTER 18

The Power and the Limits of Milton Friedman's Arguments against Corporate Social Responsibility

Alexei Marcoux

The relevance of Milton Friedman (1912–2006) to political economy can hardly be questioned. As William Ruger observes in his biography and critical appraisal, *Milton Friedman*,

> It has been years since Milton Friedman died and more than three decades since he retired. Yet he is still a relevant figure in current economic and political debates. Indeed, the shadow of his ideas has loomed large over the discussion of how to respond to the financial crisis that began in 2007 and the economic recession that followed. His relevance extends beyond this economic realm (and the discipline of economics) into broader policy debates and political battles. However, just as in life, Friedman remains a controversial, polarizing figure in death. He is missed by many . . . and inspires in terms of both his great intellectual bequest to economics and his great love of freedom. To others, Friedman is a notorious figure with noxious ideas that need burying.[1]

Four decades after being awarded the Nobel Memorial Prize in Economic Sciences (1976), Friedman's ideas remain vital in the debate over the contours of a just, humane, and prosperous political economy.

As important a figure as Friedman is acknowledged to be in past and ongoing debates over monetary policy, government regulation, military conscription, tax policy, and political economy, his significance in business ethics and the related field of corporate social responsibility (CSR) is harder to assess. On one hand, since the emergence of a self-conscious, academic business ethics field in the 1970s, Friedman's *New York Times Magazine* article, "The Social Responsibility of Business Is to Increase Its Profits," has been a staple of business ethics and CSR textbooks.[2] On the other hand, his views on the social responsibility of business are employed in business ethics pedagogy and research mainly as a foil, as if Friedman's contribution is mainly offering a clear, concise, and obvious example of what not to believe. If we take the title of the *New York Times Magazine* article to be indicative of Friedman's views,[3] then, as Thomas Carson claims,[4] in some sense almost the entire business ethics and CSR fields are reacting to him in general, even as his reasons for advancing his views usually do not receive detailed and systematic treatment. Consequently, Friedman occupies the unusual position of being both widely cited and yet little examined in the business ethics and CSR literatures.

Most academic business ethicists conceive of their field as being studied on three levels of analysis. The first is an individual or *micro* level—the level at which individual businesspeople make decisions and engage in action. The second is an organizational or *intermediate* level—the level at which firms make and execute decisions, and compete in the marketplace. The third is an economy-wide or *macro* level—the level at which the aggregate societal effects of capitalist economic institutions are felt and public policy toward business (particularly big business) is made.[5] Although in concept these levels are of coequal importance, in practice academic business ethicists are disposed to focus disproportionately on the second and third levels, particularly where these meet in the form of the large corporation whose shares are traded on public exchanges and whose interactions with the public sector and civil society provide grist for the ethicist's mill.

Given the general thrust of the academic business ethics field, it is peculiar that business ethicists don't engage Friedman more carefully. His views on CSR are concerned mainly with the macro-level, or political economy, implications of how we conceive of large corporations and the duties of their officers. These are the very questions with which academic business ethicists and CSR scholars tend to be most concerned. Friedman, by offering a perspective intentionally contrary to those prevailing in the business ethics and CSR fields, and addressing the level of discourse at which most contributions to those fields are made, should seemingly be the object of significant analysis and argument. However, deep considerations of Friedman's views, their underlying premises, and their implications are thin on the ground.[6]

Perhaps contributing to his unusual status in the business ethics and CSR literatures is the fact that Friedman expressed his views on the social responsibilities of business mostly in popular outlets—ones in which considerations of space, of addressing an audience of intelligent laymen (rather than committed scholars), and even (in one instance) of selling magazines[7] shaped the final product. Consequently, across his published statements on the topic, we find Friedman offers less a *theory of* or a *program for* the social responsibilities of business than a *view about* those responsibilities and a set of *considerations favoring* that view. It may be that those considerations can be developed in a way that makes a theory (or program) of the view Friedman advances, but Friedman himself does not undertake that project in his writings or published comments on the social responsibilities of business.[8]

In this essay, I maintain that Friedman's views are mostly formidable, especially given (what the passage of time reveals to be) the relatively limited questions of CSR he addresses. However, because his target is less CSR *as a whole* (despite rhetoric to the contrary) than *an approach to* CSR prevalent among the most vocal and visible CSR advocates of the 1960s and 1970s, Friedman's views and the considerations favoring them are of lesser force against, and are less applicable to, forms of CSR that have evolved in the four-plus decades since he wrote his famous 1970 *New York Times Magazine* article.[9]

With the benefit of hindsight, we see that Friedman offers significant considerations opposing what I will call *zero-sum* CSR. Roughly, zero-sum CSR is the view that for-profit business corporations ought to pursue socially beneficial action that is supererogatory to their legal (and perhaps ordinary moral) duties (even) at the expense of profitability. This form of CSR is zero-sum because it contemplates that what some or all nonshareholding stakeholders gain through socially responsible action, shareholders lose. What shareholders lose through socially responsible action is not to be regretted because it is their (or their company's) responsibility (read: duty) to forgo it in pursuit of societal betterment. In the zero-sum mode, CSR initiatives are intended to achieve a distributive end: taking wealth out of the hands of corporate shareholders (who, presumably, can afford it) and putting it to work for the benefit of others (who, presumably, cannot). To the extent that CSR contemplates zero-sum strategies of this kind, Friedman offers significant objections to their being undertaken by firms organized in the for-profit corporate form.

However, Friedman's objections are less forceful and less applicable to what I will call *Pareto-improving* CSR. Roughly, Pareto-improving CSR is the view that for-profit business corporations ought to pursue socially beneficial action that is supererogatory to their legal (and perhaps ordinary moral) duties both because it is socially beneficial and because it either enhances or does not undermine the performance of the firm, even in terms of profitability. This form of CSR is Pareto-improving because it contemplates that what some or all nonshareholding stakeholders gain either redounds also to the benefit of shareholders or at least does not diminish the value of their residual claims in the firm. Here, there is no shareholder loss to (avoid) regret(ting). In the Pareto-improving mode, CSR initiatives are intended to achieve a mutually beneficial end: putting wealth to work for the benefit of others without taking it out of the hands of corporate shareholders. To the extent that CSR contemplates Pareto-improving strategies of this kind, Friedman's objections to them being undertaken by firms organized in the for-profit corporate form are harder to maintain. This can be seen in the exchange between Friedman and John Mackey in the 2005 *Reason* magazine debate, "Rethinking the Social Responsibility of Business."[10]

If Friedman's (explicit or implicit) arguments are harder to maintain against Pareto-improving CSR, and CSR thinking has evolved in a more Pareto-improving direction, this underwrites the conclusion that Friedman's arguments are of lesser relevance today than when he published them. That is because in the intervening decades at least some CSR thinking has evolved (whether intentionally or not) in ways that insulate it from Friedman's criticisms. However, the emergence of *political* CSR—roughly, the view that business corporations doing business and acting politically in failed states have a social responsibility to make up for the deficiencies of those states as a condition of doing business in them—raises the prospect of reviving, in a new context, calls for the kinds of zero-sum CSR approaches Friedman's arguments address.[11] In other words, no sooner does it seem that Friedman's objections are of more historical than contemporary interest than an emerging trend in CSR scholarship appears to invest Friedman with renewed relevance.

The balance of this essay is organized as follows. First, I will explicate briefly the implicit structure and content of Friedman's views about the social responsibilities of business. Second, I will characterize Friedman's view and consequent rejection of CSR as one informed by four main concerns, the *epistemic, technocratic, fiduciary,* and *jurisdictional.* In laying out the four concerns informing his view, I will assess critically Friedman's implicit argument against CSR. I close by considering Friedman's relationship to Pareto-improving CSR and the emerging political CSR.

FRIEDMAN ON THE SOCIAL RESPONSIBILITY OF BUSINESS

Friedman's published views on CSR appear in four venues. The first is chapter 8 of *Capitalism and Freedom,* entitled "Monopoly and the Social Responsibility of Business and Labor."[12] The second is his *New York Times Magazine* article, "The Social Responsibility of Business Is to Increase Its Profits." The third is an interview appearing in the inaugural issue of *Business & Society Review.*[13] The fourth is his contribution to the *Reason* magazine debate "Rethinking the Social Responsibility of Business"—a discussion including Friedman, John Mackey, and Cypress Semiconductor CEO T. J. Rodgers.[14] From these four sources, we can construct a rough précis of Friedman's view (which will be treated in greater detail in the sections that follow).

Friedman maintains that it makes little sense to talk of the social responsibility of *business.* Individual people are the only acting agents who may properly be said to have responsibilities. Thus, the "social responsibilities of business" are really the social responsibilities of business *people.*[15] Business-people are, according to Friedman, agents of the owners of the firms employing them. In the case of the ordinary, for-profit, corporate firm, they are agents of the shareholders.[16] As agents, they are duty-bound to serve the interests of their principals and not to redirect the assets of their principals to advance interests deemed worthy by others. To spend the firm's funds on causes or projects thought to be in the public interest is to perform a public function. It is like assessing a tax on the owners of the firm, to perform a public function not of the public's choosing, and without accountability to the public.[17] Business executives perform their proper role when they either (a) undertake to make as much money as possible for their firms while staying "within the rules of the game, which is to say, [engaging] in open and free competition without deception or fraud"[18] (Friedman's "purest and most stringent" view)[19] or (b) conduct business in accordance with their principals' "desires, which generally will be to make as much money as possible while conforming to the basic rules of the society, both those embodied in law and those embodied in ethical custom"[20] (Friedman's "relaxed" view).[21]

FOUR CONCERNS INFORMING FRIEDMAN'S VIEW

Friedman's brief against what CSR advocates advertise as socially responsible business practice is informed by four distinct but related concerns: epistemic, technocratic, fiduciary, and jurisdictional. Two of these (epistemic and technocratic) are practical; they are focused on the *feasibility* of pursuing socially responsible action. These concerns suggest that businesspeople will be *unsuccessful* in their attempts to pursue socially responsible action. The other two concerns (fiduciary and jurisdictional) are normative; they are focused on whether it is *permissible* for businesspeople to pursue what is advertised as socially responsible action in their roles as business people. These concerns suggest that it is *impermissible* for businesspeople (whether or not they will be successful) to pursue what CSR advocates claim is socially responsible action. Presumably, Friedman advances both practical and normative objections because some of what CSR advocates call for is impracticable, some of what they call for is normatively impermissible, but all of it is undermined by at least one of his objections. For each concern, Friedman advances an (at least implicit) argument for why the concern cuts against practicing what CSR advocates preach. I treat each of Friedman's concerns separately, first taking up the two practical concerns and then taking up the two normative ones.

PRACTICAL CONCERNS

Epistemic. Friedman's first concern is epistemic: "If businessmen do have a social responsibility other than making maximum profits for their stockholders, how are they to *know* what it is?"[22] To engage successfully in socially responsible activity, businesspeople must know what ends are socially responsible ones. Similarly, they must have some idea what means are likely to achieve those ends, as well as the ability to employ those means. For Friedman's epistemic concern, the ends are more important.

Like the rest of us, businesspeople have no reliable knowledge about which ends are socially responsible ones. We are well supplied with views and arguments—both our own and those of concerned others—but, in the aggregate, these views and arguments conflict. There is a great deal of disagreement among people about which ends are valuable and which are not. Recent moral and political philosophers acknowledge this problem and have sought to address it under the heading of *value pluralism*.[23] People disagree over values, and even where some may share values, they disagree over the relative importance of the different values they share. Moreover, persistent disagreements of this kind are usually *reasonable* disagreements. They cannot be dissolved by appeal to evidence or argument. That is so, in part, because values are often incommensurable.[24] Because values are often in conflict and even incommensurable, Bernard Williams describes unavoidable choices between them as tragic. The fact that people experience moral regret—not out of the conviction that they ought to have acted differently but out of the conviction that there was no way to act for the best, as in the case of Agamemnon's choice—illustrates the tragedy.[25]

Recognizing the effects of value pluralism and incommensurability, liberal political orders seek to mitigate their effects, in part, by shrinking the set of decisions that must be made collectively, by political means. They expand the set of decisions made individually or through voluntary associations (like clubs or business corporations) so that people may pursue their own conceptions of the good without political society committing itself (and thus everyone within the society) to one side of contentious and irresolvable debates. Moreover, where political decision-making is unavoidable, liberal political orders usually include mechanisms precluding one faction from having its values trump all others (e.g., broad rights of political participation; majority or supermajority voting rules).

CSR advocates fail consistently to acknowledge the limits value pluralism and incommensurability place on what can be regarded as social (as opposed to merely interest-group) goals. In his *Business & Society Review* interview, Friedman adverts to this tendency:

> Let me give you an example that has often impressed me. During the 1930s, German businessmen used some corporate money to support Hitler and the Nazis. Was that a proper exercise of social responsibility? *The people who preach this hogwash talk as if everyone is always in favor of the same things,* and there is

no problem about which causes the money should be spent to further. But, of course, that's not the case.[26]

Among competing claims about what serves the social good, the business-person has no ready means by which to distinguish what is "really" socially responsible (if there is such a thing) from what is merely special pleading on behalf of an end favored by those who do the pleading.

Lest this be thought a contrived problem, consider the recent controversy surrounding the U.S. fast-food chain Chick-fil-A. In June and July 2012, the company's chief operating officer, Dan T. Cathy, made a series of statements in support of "the traditional family" and averred that those who sought to redefine marriage to include same-sex couples were "inviting God's judgment on our nation."[27] Later, it was discovered that Chick-fil-A made donations to the Family Research Council—a traditional family-promoting organization characterized by the Southern Poverty Law Center as a "hate group."[28] The subsequent fallout included both widespread boycott efforts by those who considered Cathy's statements hateful and a highly attended Chick-fil-A Appreciation Day organized by those who considered Cathy's statements morally upstanding. Are we to condemn Cathy as socially irresponsible for failing to support marriage equality? Are we instead to applaud him for taking his social responsibilities seriously in using corporate funds to save America from moral decay? More importantly, how are we to demonstrate (to Cathy or anyone else) that our judgment is correct?

The epistemic problem emerges even where the issues are less controversial and emotionally charged. Consider, for example, socially responsible investment (SRI) funds. SRI funds seek to limit their investments to the securities of firms engaged in socially responsible lines of business or doing business in a socially responsible way. However, no sooner do we encounter two SRI funds than we discover that one fund's socially responsible investment is anathema to another fund's conception of social responsibility. As Jon Entine writes,

> There are no agreed-on standards about what constitutes a "better world" or which companies are more ethical and responsible. Each individual gets to decide for herself what is a better world and which companies are deemed ethical. There are literally hundreds of funds and investment strategies with different ideological colorings and varying definitions of socially responsible and ethical corporate behavior. Social investing principles run the gamut from ultra liberal to hard conservative, from pacifist to militarist.[29]

Does social responsibility in the investment of mutual or pension funds call for embracing tobacco stocks in support of sustainable agriculture or forswearing them as "sin" stocks? More important, how are we to demonstrate (to the fund manager or anyone else) that our judgment is correct?

The CSR advocate may reply reasonably that the force of Friedman's epistemic concern depends upon the idea that, in order to satisfy their social responsibilities, business firms have to make correct judgments of what is or is not socially responsible. However, one could adopt the less exacting view that business firms ought to devote some of their resources to intentionally trying to secure some social benefit, and that they satisfy their social responsibilities whether or not their judgment of what is socially beneficial is correct.

If CSR takes that form, then Friedman's epistemic concern doesn't seem to cut against CSR. However, although that move insulates CSR from Friedman's epistemic objection, it appears also to insulate CSR from its own normative justification. Why are business firms duty-bound to pursue CSR initiatives, if not because they are duty-bound to achieve social betterment? Why is forgoing pursuit of CSR initiatives a moral failing if those initiatives will be sources of disagreement about the ends informing them? A CSR of good intentions would likely see firms doing what their managers are inclined to do anyway. Rather than expending their efforts on projects of social betterment, firms would work on crafting attractive narratives about why what they are inclined to do for other reasons is intended to benefit society. In other words, a CSR of good intentions seems to collapse into a public relations exercise—something CSR advocates are usually quick to decry rather than applaud.

Friedman's epistemic concern is a significant obstacle to establishing the case for CSR, at least in its zero-sum formulation. Unmet by a serious counterargument, it reveals CSR advocates to be an interest group—one among many—rather than the spokespersons for society they portray themselves to be.

Of course, not all calls for socially responsible action involve contested values. Presumably, there is no dispute over whether, for example, reducing infant mortality is valuable. This brings us to the second prong of Friedman's practical case against CSR.

Technocratic. Friedman's second concern is technocratic: Are businesspeople competent to do what those calling on them to act in a socially responsible manner ask them to do? To engage in socially responsible activity, businesspeople must know what ends are socially responsible ones. Similarly, they must have some idea of what means are likely to achieve those ends, as well as the ability to employ those means. For Friedman's technocratic concern, the means are more important. Even if they encounter no epistemic problem (or are able to overcome it), businesspeople must be able to identify and execute the means to achieve the socially responsible ends at which they are to aim.

The problem is that businesspeople, whether by education or experience, are competent to devise means to securing business ends, but not to formulate means to the socially responsible ends they are exhorted by CSR advocates to pursue. They are competent to devise a marketing plan with the aim of increasing sales of a product. Similarly, they are competent to design cash control procedures with the aim of facilitating more accurate accounting. However, businesspeople are typically not competent (whether by education or experience) to devise solutions to pressing social problems. At the time Friedman wrote, one such pressing social problem was price inflation. Some CSR advocates maintained that businesspeople should make product pricing decisions with an eye toward curbing inflation. About efforts to enlist businesspeople in the fight against inflation, Friedman writes:

> On the grounds of consequences, can the corporate executive in fact discharge his alleged "social responsibilities"? . . . He is told that he must contribute to fighting inflation. How is he to know what action of his will contribute to that end? He is presumably an expert in running his company—in producing a product or selling it or financing it. But nothing about his selection makes him an expert on inflation. Will his holding down the price of his product reduce inflationary pressure? Or, by leaving more spending power in the hands of his customers, simply divert it elsewhere? Or, by forcing him to produce less because of the lower price, will it simply contribute to shortages?[30]

(The notion that overcoming inflation was among the social responsibilities of businesspeople must have been especially galling to Friedman. Perhaps the twentieth century's greatest monetary economist, Friedman won a Nobel Prize for his almost single-handed revival of the quantity theory of money. This theory says, as Friedman famously put it, "inflation is always and everywhere a monetary phenomenon."[31] Consequently, the idea that businesspeople, through their pricing and purchasing decisions, influence the inflation rate—and thus have a social responsibility to make those decisions in a way that doesn't contribute to inflation—must have struck Friedman as the insult of economic illiteracy added to the injury of CSR advocates' moral hubris.)

Though closely related to the epistemic concern, the technocratic concern is distinct: although competence to address a problem involves knowledge, it is not a matter only of knowledge, but of skill. The businessperson's skills are presumably adapted to pursuing the objectives for which the firm was founded—usually making and selling a good or service and doing so in a way that brings in more revenue than it costs to produce the good or service.

Although CSR advocates no longer call for businesspeople to tackle inflation, the technocratic concern remains vital in light of calls for businesspeople to work actively to improve environmental quality, child nutrition, or marketplace offerings in less developed countries—particularly at the "bottom of the pyramid." For Friedman, it is one thing for businesspeople to do these things when they fit the firm's market niche and can be made into genuine profit opportunities. It is another when these calls are addressed to businesspeople whose skills suggest no relevant expertise.

Cast as a concern about personal expertise, Friedman's technocratic argument is less persuasive. We know of people with expertise in addressing social problems (say, in government) who then move on to successful careers in business (or vice versa). Think, for example, of Robert Rubin, who served as treasury secretary in the Clinton administration and then moved into the private sector with Citibank.[32] However, if recast as a concern about *institutional* expertise, Friedman's technocratic concern perhaps gains traction. An organization is a support structure for an activity. The most successful organizations are those whose organizational features fit best the activity they are intended to support. Thus, successful business organizations are well fitted to the activity of doing business, successful charitable organizations are well fitted to the activity of securing (or making) charitable donations, and so forth.[33] With this idea in mind, Friedman's technocratic concern applied to institutional competence comes into sharper relief: business firms are well fitted to doing business. They are ill fitted to, for example, improving environmental quality, dissipating gang violence, or conducting literacy programs.[34]

Without noting the change, Friedman recasts the technocratic concern in terms of institutional competence in his contribution to the 2005 *Reason* magazine debate on the social responsibility of business. In describing part of his disagreement with Whole Foods CEO John Mackey, Friedman writes:

> Whole Foods Market's contribution to society . . . is to enhance the pleasure of shopping for food. *Whole Foods has no special competence* in deciding how charity should be distributed. Any funds devoted to the latter would surely have contributed more to society if they had been devoted to improving still further the former.[35]

Another reason business firms may be ill fitted to solving these problems is that there may be a significant *collective action* element to the problem.[36] The time-honored example is environmental pollution: all firms in an industry pollute, unilateral action on the part of one firm will not change appreciably the environmental degradation but will place that firm at a competitive disadvantage to the others, and so no firm has the requisite incentive to diminish its pollution. Here, the problem is less expertise (as we typically understand it) and more that the firm is just *one* center of decision making in a scenario whose outcome depends upon what is decided in *many* different decision-making centers.[37] However, that fact about the firm is a disability (or lack of competence) to solve a problem whose source is (in part) polycentric decision-making.

Friedman's technocratic concern faces difficulties. First, it overstates the competence of businesspeople. Businesspeople are hardly fully competent to perform what Friedman would recognize as core business functions, such as devising marketing plans, implementing supply chain management systems, or setting up cash control systems. This we know from the existence of a thriving market for consultants, hired by business firms already staffed by businesspeople, to do these very things. If it is no abdication of the businessperson's role to hire a marketing consultant, a supply chain consultant, or a cash control consultant, what would be the *technocratic* objection to hiring, in the form of a consultant, the relevant expertise in implementing social responsibility initiatives? Second, if one doesn't wish to go to the trouble of implementing a social responsibility initiative in-house, why not make a charitable donation to a not-for-profit organization devoted to, and presumably (more) competent in pursuing, some form of philanthropic endeavor?

It seems that Friedman has available an answer to this challenge, but one that returns him to reliance on the epistemic concern, rather than establishing an independent basis for the technocratic concern. We can observe the track records of consultants in marketing or supply chain management or cash control to see how well they have delivered the sought-after marketing outcomes, supply chain outcomes, or cash control objectives. By contrast, although we can see how well a CSR consultant has delivered whatever she represents to be a social responsibility initiative (e.g., a literacy program), she can't demonstrate—for the reasons adduced under the epistemic concern—that what has been delivered is greater social responsibility.

In sum, Friedman's practical case against CSR is uneven. His epistemic concern raises a significant objection that CSR advocates tend to discount rather than address. But his technocratic concern's surface plausibility is undermined both by the existence of people who demonstrate competence in both the for-profit and not-for-profit (or public and private) sectors and by the routine practice of hiring consultants to oversee core business functions in which, on Friedman's view, businesspeople are supposed to be expert. Thus, it seems that in cases of pursuing values that are not contested and over which the relevant competence could be either hired or contributed to charitably, Friedman's practical case against CSR offers no compelling objection. It is at least to cover those cases that Friedman offers normative objections to CSR as well.

NORMATIVE CONCERNS

Fiduciary. Friedman's third concern is fiduciary: Can the directors and officers of corporations act in the way demanded by CSR advocates, consistent with their duties of loyalty and care to the shareholders of the corporation?

The business ethics and CSR literatures are laden with tedious arguments over whether or not shareholders "own" the firm and over whether or not shareholders (rather than the firm itself) are the objects of top management's fiduciary duties.[38] Friedman, however, identifies a critically important fact about corporate governance when he writes, "The whole justification for permitting the corporate executive to be selected by the stockholders is that the executive is an agent serving the interests of his principal."[39] This observation is important for two reasons—one related to the fiduciary concern under discussion here; the other related to the jurisdictional concern addressed below. The fact that equity owners elect the executives (or, more accurately, the board—which in turn selects the top management) suggests something significant about the purpose of the enterprise. The enterprise is intended to serve the equity owners *in a way that* it is not intended to serve its other constituencies. Put differently, the enterprise is "about" the equity owners in a way that it is not about the other constituencies. Why is the enterprise intended to serve the equity owners? The nexus-of-contracts theory of the firm suggests an answer.[40]

In the nexus-of-contracts theory, the firm is a point at which contracts— agreements between some people and other people—coalesce. Everyone who contracts with (or through) the firm seeks to get out of the firm what is promised to them in the agreements in which they participate. Employees seek to get the wages and benefits they contracted for, suppliers seek to get the sums promised in supply agreements, and the firm's managers seek to get the labor and the supplies they contracted for. Equity owners, however, are peculiar. They don't contract for a specific sum of money in return for use of their capital (the way employees do for the use of their labor, or suppliers do for the materials they supply to the firm, or even bondholders do for the use of their capital). Instead, they agree to provide financial capital to the firm in return for the residual claim—the claim to what is left over after all the other constituencies (employees, suppliers, etc.) receive what they are due under their contracts. This residual claim is of dubious value and likely unsalable by the firm (why would anyone pay for the privilege of taking home the leftovers without any assurance there will be any?) *unless* the purchasers of the residual claim receive a promise and a right. The promise is that the board (and the management it selects) will employ its best efforts to make the residue as large as it can be. The right is to elect the board that will be bound by this promise.

Without the idea that the firm exists to generate returns for its equity owners, this ubiquitous governance feature of investor-owned corporations is virtually impossible to explain. Why *else* would shareholders (and only shareholders) elect the board? If not for this, why would anyone pay for the privilege of collecting the firm's highly speculative and easily dissipated residue?

With the idea that the firm is duty-bound to make its best efforts to generate returns for its equity owners, calls for firms to engage in costly socially responsible activities strike a discordant note. These activities threaten to convert revenues that would otherwise be profits (going to the equity owners) into costs (going to the objects of the socially responsible activities). Put differently, the activities called for under the rubric of zero-sum CSR undermine the rationale for ordinary, for-profit business firms to operate under the governance structures that have been selected for virtually all of them—structures that make the equity owners the objects of managers' fiduciary care.

Lest it be thought that the projects called for by advocates of zero-sum CSR are part of the "ethical custom" of the society to which Friedman adverts in his relaxed formulation of the responsibilities of business executives, recall that the role of shareholders as electors of the board of directors isn't a trick foisted on the public in the dark of night. It's instead a feature built into the basic incorporation statutes of virtually all capitalist jurisdictions. Although it is a feature of the off-the-rack rules provided in each jurisdiction, organizers of for-profit corporations are free in most jurisdictions to modify those rules if they choose. That the shareholder-centric corporate form is a statutory creation suggests, at least in democratic polities, that extending fiduciary care to shareholders is—or, at least, is not inconsistent with—the ethical custom of the jurisdictions having those statutes. Moreover, the fact that so few organizers of corporations exercise their right to deviate from the off-the-rack rules—by, for example, circumscribing the role of shareholders in corporate governance or mandating CSR initiatives—is still further evidence that the ethical customs of the society are not inconsistent with extending fiduciary care to shareholders and do not mandate the projects called for by zero-sum CSR advocates.

It is unfortunate, but perhaps understandable, that Friedman uses the language of *agency* to describe the relationship between equity owners and managers. He is an economist, writing about these topics at a time when many of his contemporaries (e.g., Jensen and Meckling)[41] are developing models of the "agency problem." However, at law, although all agents are fiduciaries, not all fiduciaries are agents.[42] Agents are fiduciaries who are subject to the control of their beneficiaries (principals). Other fiduciaries, although duty-bound to serve the interests of their beneficiaries, are not subject to their control.[43] The top managers of an ordinary, for-profit business corporation are nonagent fiduciaries of the firm's equity owners. That is because although they are duty-bound to serve the interests of the equity owners, they are subject to the control of the board (not the equity owners). This confusion is compounded in the *New York Times Magazine* piece by Friedman's references to business executives serving the "desires" of the owners:

In a free-enterprise, private-property system, a corporate executive is an employee of the owners of the business. He has direct responsibility to his employers. That responsibility is to conduct the business in accordance with their desires, which generally will be to make as much money as possible while conforming to the basic rules of the society, both those embodied in law and those embodied in ethical custom.[44]

A nonagent fiduciary is duty-bound to serve the *interests* of his beneficiaries, not their desires. Where interests and desires conflict, it is the interests (not the desires) that are to be the fiduciary's guide. By casting the business executive's role in terms of agency and desire satisfaction, Friedman offers an erroneous account of the logic informing the governance structures of business firms. Although that account is erroneous, correcting its errors offers neither aid nor comfort to CSR advocates who aim to redirect the activities of the firm away from serving the interests of equity owners.

Although imperfectly expressed, Friedman's fiduciary concern is real. The projects CSR advocates call for corporate executives to pursue, at least insofar as they are contemplated to be zero-sum CSR strategies, amount to an attempt to dispossess the equity owners of firms of their holdings in contravention of the social contract between business and society, as embodied in both law and ethical custom.[45] However, it is not only concern for the contractual rights of equity owners that informs Friedman's normative case against CSR.

Jurisdictional. Friedman's fourth concern is jurisdictional: Are the matters over which businesspeople are called upon to pursue socially responsible action public or private? Friedman's jurisdictional concern connects the merits of CSR to larger questions of normative political philosophy. If the matters over which business firms and their managers are enjoined to act in a socially responsible manner are public ("social"), ought they not then to be addressed by people and institutions that are competent to do so and, more important, are accountable politically?

Earlier, I averred that Friedman identifies a critically important fact when he writes, "The whole justification for permitting the corporate executive to be selected by the stockholders is that the executive is an agent serving the interests of his principal."[46] In effect, Friedman is saying that if we accept the method by which top managers in firms are selected, we must also accept the fiduciary logic that rationalizes equity owners being the corporate constituency selecting them. Friedman's jurisdictional concern expresses the *inverse* of this proposition: if we reject the fiduciary logic that rationalizes equity owners being the corporate constituency selecting them, then we must also reject the method by which top managers in firms are selected. This is significant because, at least in its zero-sum mode, the CSR doctrine is the rejection of the fiduciary logic rationalizing the governance structure of the business firm. It reorients the firm's purpose away from generating returns for equity owners and toward serving other, "social," ends. From the sentence quoted above, Friedman continues:

> This justification disappears when the corporate executive imposes taxes
> and spends the proceeds for "social" purposes. He becomes in effect a public
> employee, a civil servant, even though he remains in name an employee of a
> private enterprise. . . . On grounds of political principle, it is intolerable that
> such civil servants—insofar as their actions in the name of social responsibility
> are real and not just window-dressing—should be selected as they are now.
> If they are to be civil servants, then they must be elected through a political
> process. If they are to impose taxes and make expenditures to foster "social"
> objectives, then political machinery must be set up to make the assessment
> of taxes and to determine through a political process the objectives to be
> served.[47]

Here, Friedman's taxation and civil servant analogies may be obscuring, rather than illustrating, his point. His point seems to be that CSR, at least in its zero-sum mode, is an attempt to renegotiate on an ad hoc, company-by-company basis the social contract between business and society. It avoids the political, publicly accountable mechanisms by which that social contract is and, in a liberal political society, ought to be formulated. In effect, Friedman says that if business firms owe more (or something different) to society than is embodied in law and in ethical custom, they should be taxed or regulated to provide more as the result of victories won in a democratic political process, not enjoined to distribute gifts or to engage in good works willy-nilly. Of course, Friedman would not *favor* this political outcome (qua political outcomes) any more than he favors CSR. However, such a political outcome would possess legitimacy as an expression of the public good that executive-led, ad hoc, company-by-company, zero-sum CSR initiatives lack.

Unlike the two components of his practical case against CSR, Friedman's fiduciary and jurisdictional concerns work together to form a picture of a well-functioning political economy. The fiduciary concern grounds a substantive case for how firms should operate. The jurisdictional concern grounds a procedural case for how best to change the prevailing politico-economic arrangement. Together, these concerns illustrate that CSR advocates favor a public, political, interest group–based approach to economic decision-making within the firm (most clearly exemplified by stakeholderism) and a private, business executive–led, piecemeal approach to changing the content of the social contract between business and society. This reverses exactly the approach favored in liberal political economy.

CONCLUDING REMARKS: WHERE DOES FRIEDMAN FIT TODAY?

I have introduced and employed a distinction between zero-sum and Pareto-improving CSR. Briefly, zero-sum CSR seeks to benefit society distributively, by diverting corporate revenues away from profit and toward costs benefiting the public; Pareto-improving CSR seeks to benefit society in ways that also improve, or do not diminish, the holdings of equity owners. Friedman's concerns are aimed at and (in varying degrees) find their target in zero-sum CSR. I have also suggested that Friedman's arguments and concerns may be less effective against Pareto-improving CSR. An illustration of this is found in Friedman's 2005 *Reason* magazine exchange with John Mackey. Mackey avers that CSR is integral to Whole Foods' business model and is a source of value creation for all of Whole Foods' constituencies, shareholders included. He writes:

> I'm a businessman and a free market libertarian, but I believe that the enlightened corporation should try to create value for *all* of its constituencies. From an investor's perspective, the purpose of the business is to maximize profits. But that's not the purpose for other stakeholders—for customers, employees, suppliers, and the community. Each of those groups will define the purpose of the business in terms of its own needs and desires, and each perspective is valid and legitimate.
>
> My argument should not be mistaken for a hostility to profit. I believe I know something about creating shareholder value. When I co-founded Whole Foods Market 27 years ago, we began with $45,000 in capital; we only had $250,000 in sales our first year. During the last 12 months we had sales of more than $4.6 billion, net profits of more than $160 million, and a market capitalization over $8 billion.
>
> But we have not achieved our tremendous increase in shareholder value by making shareholder value the primary purpose of our business.[48]

Put differently, returns to shareholders are a *benchmark* against which Mackey and Whole Foods measure their performance, but seeking returns to shareholders is not a *strategy* by which they pursue profits or any of the other benefits they seek to confer on Whole Foods' corporate constituencies. Mackey understands Whole Foods' strategy to be a version of Pareto-improving CSR: conferring benefits on nonshareholder constituencies in ways that also redound to the benefit of (or at least do not diminish) returns to shareholders. Friedman shouldn't object to *any* strategy adopted in the earnest belief that it redounds to the benefit (rather than the detriment) of shareholders *unless* it proves, after a suitable trial period, not to redound to their benefit. As John Hasnas observes, "[Friedman's] stockholder theory does not instruct managers to do anything at all to increase the profitability of the business."[49]

That is, shareholder wealth maximization is a benchmark against which the efforts of faithful managers of for-profit corporate firms are judged. It is not an action plan for pursuing profits. Thus, unlike zero-sum CSR strategies, earnestly adopted Pareto-improving CSR strategies are consistent with managers' duties of fiduciary care toward shareholders.

Strangely, rather than recognize the consistency of Mackey's Pareto-improving CSR corporate strategy with his view, Friedman undertakes to second-guess Mackey's command of his own business model, writing, "Any funds devoted to [Whole Foods' charitable endeavors] would surely have contributed more to society if they had been devoted to improving still further the [customers' enjoyment of food]."[50] In order to avoid endorsing what Mackey understands to be a form of (Pareto-improving) CSR, Friedman undertakes to transform what he heretofore has understood as the benchmark against which managers' actions should be judged into a strategy for pursuing profits. That Friedman is reduced to questioning Mackey's understanding of his own business model suggests that Friedman's case against CSR doesn't reach earnestly adopted, benchmark-tested forms of Pareto-improving CSR in a principled way. To the extent that CSR advocates promote CSR in the Pareto-improving mode, Friedman's arguments have little relevance. Moreover, Pareto-improving CSR appears to be broadly consistent with Friedman's views.

However, Mackey advances an even more fundamental challenge to Friedman when he writes:

> I believe such programs [as our 5% Days, during which Whole Foods gives five percent of its revenues to philanthropy] would be completely justifiable even if they produced no profits and no P.R. This is because I believe the entrepreneurs, not the current investors in a company's stock, have the right and responsibility to define the purpose of the company. It is the entrepreneurs who create a company, who bring all the factors of production together and coordinate it into viable business. It is the entrepreneurs who set the company strategy and who negotiate the terms of trade with all of the voluntarily cooperating stakeholders—including the investors. At Whole Foods we "hired" our original investors. They didn't hire us.
>
> We first announced that we would donate 5 percent of the company's net profits to philanthropy when we drafted our mission statement, back in 1985. Our policy has therefore been in place for over 20 years, and it predates our IPO by seven years. All seven of the private investors at the time we created the policy voted for it when they served on our board of directors. When we took in venture capital money back in 1989, none of the venture firms objected to the policy. In addition, in almost 14 years as a publicly traded company, almost no investors have ever raised objections to the policy. How can Whole Foods' philanthropy be "theft" from the current investors if the

original owners of the company unanimously approved the policy and all subsequent investors made their investments after the policy was in effect and well publicized?[51]

Here, without adverting to it, Mackey presses on what Ruger characterizes as Friedman's relaxed view of the social responsibilities of business. Recall that under his relaxed view Friedman maintains that businesspeople are duty-bound to conduct business in accordance with their principals' "desires, which generally will be to make as much money as possible while conforming to the basic rules of the society, both those embodied in law and those embodied in ethical custom."[52] If the company is founded by owners whose desires include engaging in even zero-sum philanthropy, and this is incorporated into its mission statement and bylaws, then on what grounds may subsequent equity owners object if they are on notice that this is the way the firm intends to conduct business? Mackey's challenge is interesting because it forces Friedman to choose between his stringent and relaxed views of the social responsibilities of business. If Friedman retreats to his stringent view in order to avoid endorsing Mackey's claim, however, he is forced to choose again between his stringent view of the social responsibilities of business and his libertarianism. For to hold that a firm founded with both profit-making and philanthropic goals is illegitimate is to hold that a form of consensual activity not harmful to others is nonetheless wrongful. Of course, there is a considerable difference between a company, like Whole Foods, *founded in part* to pursue philanthropic giving and CSR advocates' efforts to induce firms founded for other (usually profit-seeking) purposes to pursue zero-sum CSR. Thus, Mackey's challenge does more to undermine Friedman's evaluation of Whole Foods (and companies like it), in particular, than his evaluation of zero-sum CSR applied to ordinary, for-profit firms, in general.

Whether contemporary CSR is pursued more in the zero-sum or more in the Pareto-improving mode is an empirical matter. Compared to the time at which Friedman advanced the bulk of his arguments on CSR, Pareto-improving CSR has become more prominent (though it remains unclear whether it is more prominent than zero-sum CSR). However, the emergence in the academic CSR literature of "political CSR"—a doctrine embracing (among other things) the idea that large, multinational business enterprises have an affirmative duty to perform state or quasi-state functions in failed states or states where political institutions function poorly[53]—may herald Friedman's renewed relevance. For political CSR implies that business firms are and (at least in particular political circumstances) ought to be public, not private, entities. If they are public entities, however, business firms' governance structures make them accountable to only the smallest fraction of those whose fundamental rights they arbitrate. Friedman's fiduciary and jurisdictional concerns are therefore raised anew.

I end where I began: Friedman's significance in business ethics and CSR is hard to assess. That is as much a statement about his views as it is about the evolution and mutation of projects carrying the CSR label. He cannot be written off (the way he too often is) when addressing zero-sum CSR initiatives, but his arguments and concerns are less clearly relevant to (earnestly adopted) Pareto-improving CSR initiatives. Whether political CSR has the legs to change meaningfully the CSR narrative and perhaps bring Friedman a renewed, contemporary relevance remains to be seen.

ACKNOWLEDGMENTS

I wish to thank the editors for their insightful comments on the initial draft of this essay. I thank them doubly for their patience during the construction of the final version. Finally, I wish to thank Felicia Rosado for her research assistance on this project.

NOTES

1. William Ruger, *Milton Friedman* (New York: Continuum, 2011; Bloomsbury, 2013), 186.

2. Milton Friedman, "The Social Responsibility of Business Is to Increase Its Profits," *New York Times Magazine,* September 13, 1970, 32–33 and 123–26.

3. Whether one ought to take the title as indicative of Friedman's views is open to question. As Wayne Norman observes, "Despite the provocative title of the [*New York Times Magazine*] article (which may have been imposed by the magazine's editors) Friedman was concerned not so much with the social responsibility of business, but rather with the property rights of business owners, and with the contractual and fiduciary obligations of corporate leaders." See Norman, "Stakeholder Theory," in *The International Encyclopedia of Ethics,* ed. Hugh LaFollette (New York: Wiley, 2013), doi: 10.1002/9781444367072.

4. Thomas Carson, "Friedman's Theory of Corporate Social Responsibility," *Business & Professional Ethics Journal* 12, no. 1 (1993): 3.

5. Despite different terminologies and somewhat different characterizations of the intermediate level, this tripartite division of the academic business ethics field's subject matter is widely employed. See, e.g., Robert C. Solomon, "Business Ethics," in *A Companion to Ethics,* ed. Peter Singer (Malden, MA: Blackwell, 1991), 354–65 (micro, molar, macro); George Brenkert, "Entrepreneurship, Ethics, and the Good Society," *Ruffin Series in Business Ethics* 3 (2002): 5–43 (micro, meso, macro); and Richard DeGeorge, "A History of Business Ethics" (2005), http://www.scu.edu/ethics/practicing/focusareas/business/conference/presentations/business-ethics-history.html; and also DeGeorge, "Will Success Spoil Business Ethics?," in *Business Ethics: The State of the Art,* ed. R. Edward Freeman (New York: Oxford University Press, 1992), 42–56 (individual, organizational, societal).

6. For the rare, careful considerations, see Carson, "Friedman's Theory of Corporate Social Responsibility"; and John Danley, "Polestar Refined: Business Ethics and Political Economy," *Journal of Business Ethics* 10, no. 12 (1991): 915–33. Perhaps a mark of renewed and detailed interest in Friedman's views is Ignacio Ferrero, W. Michael Hoffman, and Robert E. McNulty's 2014 attack on Friedman's grounds for rejecting CSR, averring that his rejection of CSR is incompatible with his (implicit) embrace of limited liability for corporate shareholders. See Ferrero, Hoffman, and McNulty, "Must Milton Friedman Embrace Stakeholder Theory?," *Business & Society Review* 119, no. 1 (2014): 37–59.

7. See, e.g., Norman, "Stakeholder Theory."

8. This is perhaps a controversial claim. For example, in his *Milton Friedman*, 147, Ruger (following John Hasnas) credits Friedman with advancing the stockholder (sometimes referred to as shareholder) theory. In Alexei Marcoux, "Business Ethics," in *The Stanford Encyclopedia of Philosophy*, ed. Edward N. Zalta, Fall 2008 ed., http://plato.stanford.edu/archives/fall2008/entries/ethics-business/, I deny that there is a stockholder (or shareholder) theory. Instead, the locution "stockholder (shareholder) theory" is only a shorthand used by stakeholderists to refer to whatever they oppose (e.g., the shareholder primacy norm, the status quo). On stakeholderism and the denial that it, too, constitutes a genuine *theory*, see Norman, "Stakeholder Theory."

9. Like "business ethics" itself, "CSR" is a term applied by its partisans to a dizzying array of divergent, and sometimes even conflicting, projects. Some see CSR as an umbrella concept, encompassing everything included in business ethics (e.g., the avoidance of harm) and much else besides; others deny this, claiming that "CSR" refers properly only to beneficent action aimed at improving the larger society; see, e.g., Chris MacDonald, "Down with CSR! Up with Business Ethics!," *Business Ethics Blog*, February 14, 2009, http://business ethicsblog.com/2009/02/14/down-with-csr-up-with-business-ethics/. It would be remarkable if Milton Friedman, or anyone else, could characterize CSR in a way that anticipates all of the theses and projects to which the name is applied, and respond to them all. Friedman directs his arguments to the then-prevalent approach to CSR.

10. "Rethinking the Social Responsibility of Business" (debate featuring Milton Friedman, John Mackey, and T. J. Rodgers), *Reason*, October 2005, http://reason.com/archives/2005/10/01/rethinking-the-social-responsi.

11. For a succinct explanation of the concept of political CSR, see Jeffery Smith, "Corporate Human Rights Obligations: Moral or Political?," *Business Ethics Journal Review* 1, no. 2 (2013): 7–13.

12. Friedman, *Capitalism and Freedom* (Chicago: University of Chicago Press, 1962), 119–36.

13. John McClaughry and Milton Friedman, "Milton Friedman Responds" (interview), *Business & Society Review* 1, no. 1 (1972): 5–16.

14. "Rethinking the Social Responsibility of Business."

15. Friedman, "Social Responsibility of Business," 33; McClaughry and Friedman, "Milton Friedman Responds," 6. In advancing this view, Friedman anticipates the later debate over corporate moral agency. Peter French, for example, argues that through internal decision structures firms possess all of the prerequisites of moral agency. See Peter A. French, "The Corporation as a Moral Person," *American Philosophical Quarterly* 16 (1979): 207–15. Manuel Velasquez, by contrast, argues that the firm is the sum of the individual moral agents who compose it and not a moral agent in its own right. See Manuel Velasquez, "Why Corporations Are Not Morally Responsible for Anything They Do," *Business & Professional Ethics Journal* 2 (1983): 1–18.

16. Friedman, "Social Responsibility of Business," 33.

17. Friedman, *Capitalism and Freedom*, 134.

18. Ibid., 133.

19. See Ruger, *Milton Friedman*, 148.

20. Friedman, "Social Responsibility of Business," 33.

21. See Ruger, *Milton Friedman*, 150. Carson argues that the stringent formulation of Friedman's position advanced in *Capitalism and Freedom* is not coextensive with the relaxed formulation advanced in "The Social Responsibility of Business." Carson identifies five cases in which action permissible under one of Friedman's formulations is impermissible under the other one. See Carson, "Friedman's Theory of Corporate Social Responsibility," 7–10.

22. Friedman, *Capitalism and Freedom*, 133, emphasis added.

23. Elinor Mason, "Value Pluralism," in Zalta, *Stanford Encyclopedia of Philosophy*, Fall 2011 ed., http://plato.stanford.edu/archives/fall2011/entries/value-pluralism/.

24. See, e.g., Nien-hê Hsieh, "Incommensurable Values," in Zalta, *Stanford Encyclopedia of Philosophy*, Fall 2008 ed., http://plato.stanford.edu/archives/fall2008/entries/value-incommensurable/.

25. Bernard Williams, *Problems of the Self* (Cambridge: Cambridge University Press, 1976), 172–74.

26. McClaughry and Friedman, "Milton Friedman Responds," 6, emphasis added.

27. Kim Severson, "Chick-fil-A Thrust Back into Spotlight on Gay Rights," *New York Times*, July 26, 2012, http://www.nytimes.com/2012/07/26/us/gay-rights-uproar-over-chick-fil-a-widens.html?_r=0.

28. The Southern Poverty Law Center maintains that "the intention [of the Family Research Council] is to denigrate LGBT people in its battles against same-sex marriage, hate crimes laws, anti-bullying programs and the repeal of the military's 'Don't Ask, Don't Tell' policy"; http://www.splcenter.org/get-informed/intelligence-files/groups/family-research-council. Of course, there is no consensus on what constitutes "hate," as opposed to a legitimate difference of opinion. Therefore, it is not surprising that the Southern Poverty Law Center has been criticized for smear tactics against and the vilification of those who disagree with, say, the *New York Times* editorial page. See, e.g., Patrik Jonsson, "Annual Report Cites Rise in Hate Groups, but Some Ask: What Is Hate?," *Christian Science Monitor*, February 23, 2011, http://www.csmonitor.com/USA/Society/2011/0223/Annual-report-cites-rise-in-hate-groups-but-some-ask-What-is-hate.

29. Jon Entine, "The Myth of Social Investing: A Critique of Its Practices and Consequences for Corporate Social Performance Research," *Organization & Environment* 16, no. 3 (2003): 357–58.

30. Friedman, "Social Responsibility of Business," 122.

31. Milton Friedman, *The Counter-Revolution in Monetary Theory* (London: Institute for Economic Affairs, 1970), 24.

32. Here, perhaps, I am being charitable. Rubin's value to Citibank may be less any ability he has in effectuating banking deals and more in securing access to and favorable decisions from banking regulators. Whatever the case, Rubin is surely not *alone* in passing from the public to the private sector (and perhaps vice versa). So, it is not unreasonable to suppose that there are people skilled both in the solution of pressing social problems and in running businesses. Consequently, the personal competence of the individual businessperson may not be a persuasive ground on which to rest a claim that businesspeople are likely to be unsuccessful in pursuing socially responsible initiatives.

33. This idea is implicit in the work of law and economics scholar Henry Hansmann. He argues that durable organizational governance structures are least-cost solutions to the governance problems that recur in the organizations in which they endure. This is just another way of saying that they are well fitted to what they are there to accomplish. See, generally, Hansmann, *The Ownership of Enterprise* (Cambridge, MA: Belknap Press of Harvard University Press, 1996).

34. Prominent business ethicist John Boatright has stated in conversation that many business ethicists and CSR advocates want for-profit firms to act like not-for-profit firms. They fail to recognize that not-for-profit firms are organized to act that way competently. Meanwhile, for-profit firms are not.

35. "Rethinking the Social Responsibility of Business," emphasis added.

36. See Mancur Olsen, *The Logic of Collective Action: Public Goods and the Theory of Groups* (Cambridge, MA: Harvard University Press, 1965).

37. One of the more compelling justifications for government regulation is found in situations where collective action problems structure participants' interactions. Government decision-making is monocentric, not polycentric. That makes it a solution for collective action problems, but a problem for making the best use of local knowledge. On this latter point, see F. A. Hayek, "The Use of Knowledge in Society," *American Economic Review* 35, no. 4 (1945): 519–30.

38. See, e.g., Margaret M. Blair, "Corporate 'Ownership': A Misleading Word Muddies the Corporate Governance Debate," *Brookings Review* 13, no. 1 (1995): 16–19.

39. Friedman, "Social Responsibility of Business," 122.

40. There exists a vast literature on the nexus-of-contracts theory. The classic citation is Michael C. Jensen and William H. Meckling, "Theory of the Firm: Managerial Behavior, Agency Costs, and Ownership Structure," *Journal of Financial Economics* 3, no. 4 (1976): 305–60.

41. Jensen and Meckling, "Theory of the Firm."

42. See, e.g., Tamar Frankel, "Fiduciary Duty," in *The New Palgrave Dictionary of Economics and the Law*, ed. Peter Newman (London: Palgrave Macmillan, 2004), 2:127–28.

43. Suppose that I set up a trust for my niece, appointing a trustee to manage the assets I place into the trust for her benefit. The trustee is a fiduciary for my niece, but is not her agent. The trustee is subject to my control (as creator of the trust—unless it is an irrevocable trust), not hers.

44. Friedman, "Social Responsibility of Business," 33.

45. The antifiduciary approach is evident in, e.g., Lynn A. Stout, "Why We Should Stop Teaching *Dodge v. Ford*," *Virginia Law & Business Review* 3, no. 1 (2008): 163–90; Jeffrey Moriarty, "The Connection between Stakeholder Theory and Stakeholder Democracy: An Excavation and Defense," *Business & Society* 53, no. 6 (2014): 820–52; and Norman Bowie, *Business Ethics: A Kantian Perspective* (Malden, MA: Blackwell, 1999), 94 (where Bowie advances the "argument from citizenship" en route to concluding that corporations should "adapt to changing public perceptions of the public good").

46. Friedman, "Social Responsibility of Business," 122.

47. Ibid.

48. "Rethinking the Social Responsibility of Business," emphasis in the original.

49. Quoted in Ruger, *Milton Friedman*, 150.

50. "Rethinking the Social Responsibility of Business."

51. Ibid.

52. Friedman, "Social Responsibility of Business," 33.

53. See, e.g., D. Baur, *NGOs as Legitimate Partners of Corporations: A Political Conceptualization* (Dordrecht: Springer, 2011); Andreas Georg Scherer and Guido Palazzo, "A New Political Role of Business in a Globalized World: A Review and Research Agenda," *Journal of Management Studies* 48, no. 4 (2011): 899–931; and Florian Wettstein, "CSR and the Debate on Business and Human Rights: Bridging the Great Divide," *Business Ethics Quarterly* 22, no. 4 (2012): 739–70.

CHAPTER 19

Beyond the Difference Principle: Rawlsian Justice, Business Ethics, and the Morality of the Market

Matt Zwolinski

Open any textbook on philosophical business ethics, and you are virtually certain to find a lengthy discussion of John Rawls's work, a substantial excerpt from that work, or both. Business ethicists cite him in their scholarly papers, discuss his ideas at their conferences, and teach those ideas to their students. This should not be surprising. After all, Rawls's most famous book spent about six hundred pages articulating and defending a theory of justice. And questions of justice—distributive justice, justice in pricing, justice in contracts—are among business ethics' most important topics.

Nevertheless, despite all of the attention they have paid to it, business ethicists have yet to appreciate fully the breadth of Rawls's work, or the true nature of its implications for their field. Their work has often been marked by a certain narrowness in its incorporation of Rawls's ideas—both in the scope of ideas taken into account, and in the interpretation given to them. By way of illustration, consider just one striking fact pertaining to the issue of scope. In my own informal survey of the leading texts in philosophical business ethics, I found all of them to contain at least some discussion of Rawls's ideas as developed in his best-known work, *A Theory of Justice*, and none of them to contain any discussion of the ideas he developed in his later, equally path-breaking *Political Liberalism*.[1] But this way of describing the results actually understates the narrowness of the focus. For not only are the textbooks' presentations limited to *A Theory of Justice*, they are limited to a relatively small section of it—specifically, the section in which Rawls explains and defends his idea of the original position and his two famous principles of justice.[2] And even within that section, business ethicists have focused almost entirely on the second principle of justice (especially the difference principle) to the neglect of the first (the principle of equal basic liberties).

Partly because of the narrow range of Rawlsian ideas considered, I will argue, the business ethics literature has been marked by a rather narrow interpretation of the implications of Rawls's ideas for the central questions of the field. The narrowness has manifested itself in a tendency either to misunderstand the implications of the full range of Rawlsian ideas for questions about the regulation and possible public ownership of business, or to accept uncritically Rawls's own barely defended assumptions about those implications.

In this essay, I develop some of the implications of a more complete account of Rawls's ideas for business ethics scholarship. In the first section, I explain why Rawls actually had fairly little to say about many of the central questions of business ethics; in so doing, I explain the structure and deliberately limited scope of his theory of justice. In the subsequent section I present the standard view of the implications of Rawls's ideas for questions concerning the political regulation or control of business, drawing on both Rawls's own understanding of those implications and the interpretation presented in the contemporary business ethics literature. In the final section, I discuss three broad considerations that count against the standard interpretation, and in favor of a form of Rawlsianism that is not merely compatible with the institutions of property and exchange central to a liberal market order, but that positively demands those institutions as a requirement of justice. Rawlsian thought, I conclude, is not as hostile to market processes as Rawls's critics, and sometimes his followers, have suggested. But neither, I will argue, is it as hospitable to them as its own principles suggest it should be.

RAWLS ON BUSINESS ETHICS AS APPLIED ETHICS

Philosophers who write about or teach business ethics tend to focus on two broad categories of questions. The first deals with the moral norms that govern individuals and firms acting in the context of business. The questions explored here are ones that managers, employees, CEOs, and customers might ask in order to better understand how they themselves should behave in their roles as business actors. What constitutes insider trading, and is it permissible for me to engage in it? What sort of deception, or "bluffing," is it legitimate for me to employ in negotiations with suppliers? Does loyalty to my firm mean that it is unethical for me to "blow the whistle" on the problematic behavior of my coworkers? This sort of business ethics is what we might call applied or practical business ethics.

The second category deals with questions of institutional structure rather than individual behavior, and especially with political questions about the role of government vis-à-vis business. Rather than asking whether insider trading is morally permissible, for instance, one might ask whether it should be legal or illegal. On a grander scale, questions in this category might explore whether a system of private ownership of firms is just, or whether it ought to be replaced by a system of worker- or publicly owned enterprises. In a sense, then, this kind of business ethics is less a species of applied ethics than one of applied political philosophy.

It is the first category of questions about which Rawls was most conspicuously, and deliberately, silent. The reason is straightforward, and significant: the subject of Rawls's theory of justice is not the actions of individuals or even of firms, but rather the basic institutional structure of society as a whole. Rawls did not deny, of course, that individual or corporate actions could be just or unjust, in some sense of that term. But that kind of justice was not what *his* theory was about. His theory was about the overarching rules of the game, not about the particular moves made by particular players within that game.[3]

Rawls described the subject of his theory of justice as the "basic structure" of society, by which he meant the major social, legal, political, and economic institutions of society, such as "the legal protection of freedom of thought and liberty of conscience, competitive markets, private property in the means of production, and the monogamous family."[4] An important feature of the basic structure, and part of the reason Rawls makes it the focus of his theory, is that, taken together, the institutions that constitute the basic structure "define men's rights and duties and influence their life-prospects, what they can expect to be and how well they can hope to do."[5] Society, on Rawls's view, is a cooperative venture for mutual advantage, but it is the institutions of the basic structure that determine how the advantages of social cooperation will be divided among the separate persons and social groups of which society is made up.[6]

Famously, Rawls argued that individuals behind a suitably described "veil of ignorance" would choose two principles as criteria of justice for the basic structure. The first principle guarantees to each person an equal right to the most extensive basic liberty compatible with a similar liberty for others.[7] The second specifies that social and economic inequalities are "to be attached to positions open to all under conditions of fair equality of opportunity" and that they are "to be to the greatest benefit of the least-advantaged members of society."[8]

The justification of these principles, and their implications for the design of the basic structure, are of course matters of great complexity and dispute. I will return later to the question of institutional implications. For now, it is worth noting that Rawls was quite explicit in denying that his principles could be applied in any straightforward way to individuals or groups of individuals:

There is no reason to suppose ahead of time that the principles satisfactory for the basic structure hold for all cases. These principles may not work for the rules and practices of private associations or for those of less comprehensive social groups. They may be irrelevant for the various informal conventions and customs of everyday life; they may not elucidate the justice, or perhaps better, the fairness of voluntary cooperative arrangements or procedures for making contractual arrangements.[9]

The viability of Rawls's distinction between what we might call "macro" and "micro" principles of justice is, of course, a matter of some dispute.[10] But it is clear enough what Rawls himself thought his principles of justice implied regarding the behavior of managers, customers, employees, firms, and trade unions: essentially nothing.[11] Whatever moral principles govern those agents and entities will have to come from somewhere else.

Though it has not been widely noted by business ethicists, Rawls does actually devote a portion of *A Theory of Justice* to a discussion of moral principles that apply to individuals.[12] Rawls argues that in addition to the two principles of justice that govern the basic structure, individuals in the original position would also choose various principles that would impose moral requirements on individuals directly. These additional principles include various positive and negative "natural duties," such as "the duty of helping another when he is in need or jeopardy, provided that one can do so without excessive risk or loss to oneself [mutual aid], the duty not to harm or injure another; and the duty not to cause unnecessary suffering."[13] And they include certain "obligations," such as the principle of fidelity and the (famous) principle of fairness.[14]

Some of what Rawls has to say about these moral requirements could be drawn out in ways that might yield interesting implications for business ethics. Rawls's account of promise keeping, for instance, which explicitly analogizes the rules surrounding promises to the rules of a game, is reminiscent of Albert Carr's famous essay in which deception in business is analogized to bluffing in the game of poker.[15] And Rawls's duty of mutual aid might seem to have implications for debates over product safety and product liability, as well as for debates over the moral permissibility of price gouging in the wake of a natural disaster and the duties of pharmaceutical companies in possession of life-saving drugs.[16]

Unfortunately, Rawls does not develop his theory of individual requirements in much detail. He provides little in the way of argument for them; he does not consider possible alternative interpretations of them (in the way he does for the two principles of justice); and he does not spend much time discussing their implications. As a result, they stand little chance of settling, or even advancing, scholarly debate over the practical issues to which they might be applied. Those who defend price gouging or the rights of pharmaceutical companies to sell their products at a profit, for instance, do not generally ignore or deny the existence of a duty of mutual aid. Rather, they argue that the duty holds only in certain contexts, or that it can be overridden by competing moral considerations.[17] If, for instance, allocation by market prices both helps to allocate resources to those who need them most (relative to feasible alternative allocative mechanisms) and provides an incentive to other sellers to bring increased supply to market, then we might plausibly maintain that it is at least permitted by the principle of mutual aid, if not positively required by it. In this and in most other cases, the real argument will be about the details of how the principle of mutual aid is to be applied, not whether it is a valid moral principle.

Ultimately, then, Rawls has virtually nothing to say about business ethics as a kind of applied ethics for individuals or groups of individuals (e.g., firms). His two famous principles of justice simply do not apply to such cases. And the principles he describes that do apply are so general and unspecific as to be virtually useless in addressing questions about which there is serious philosophical debate.

RAWLS ON BUSINESS ETHICS AS APPLIED POLITICAL PHILOSOPHY

The second category of questions in business ethics, focused as it is on issues of just social institutions, is more closely related to Rawls's central project. Yet, even here, Rawls's comments are surprisingly brief and schematic in form. For instance, in *Justice as Fairness: A Restatement*, Rawls considers five different regime types to see whether they might be compatible with his two principles of justice: laissez-faire capitalism (which he sometimes refers to as "the system of natural liberty"), welfare-state capitalism, state socialism, liberal ("democratic" or "market") socialism, and property-owning democracy. As Gerald Gaus has noted, Rawls rather quickly rejects as unjust both of the systems he describes as "capitalist."[18] Only market socialism and property-owning democracy are held to satisfy the two principles of justice. The former involves public ownership of businesses and other means of production; the latter allows firms to be privately held but works "to disperse the ownership of wealth and capital," by means of progressive taxation and various redistributive policies.[19]

Earlier, in *A Theory of Justice*, Rawls claimed that a just basic structure would involve the addition of various new "branches" to government.[20] These branches would help to set up the background conditions for business activity in such a way that the net results of that activity combined with public policy would be in accord with the requirements of distributive justice. One branch would work to keep the price system competitive and to prevent unreasonable concentrations of market power, presumably by regulating and restricting proposed corporate mergers, or by breaking up excessively large corporations. A "stabilization branch" would seek to bring about near-full employment, perhaps by regulating the money supply or by creating jobs with the specific purpose of increasing employment, along the lines of the New Deal's Civilian Conservation Corps. A "transfer branch" would be charged with ensuring that no one in society falls below a certain specified "social minimum," by providing, presumably, not merely money but also food, education, medical care, housing, and other goods and services deemed essential. And, finally, a "distribution branch" would raise revenues for the operations of government and tax and limit inheritance in order to ensure the wide dispersal of property.

Achieving the Rawlsian goal of a just basic structure would require a large and interconnected system of taxes, transfers, subsidies, and "changes in the definition of property rights."[21] Rawls thus rejects those libertarian or classical liberal views that hold these kinds of interferences with property rights to be morally illegitimate. To be sure, a just basic structure will, on Rawls's view, guarantee a fundamental right to *personal* property.[22] And the particular form of economic liberty involved in free occupational choice is also highlighted as warranting special protection.[23] But more robust economic rights—involving freedom of contract, or the ownership of *productive* property, are excluded from Rawls's compendium of basic rights.[24] This does not mean that Rawls rejects such rights altogether—they could, for instance, be endorsed at the constitutional or legislative phase. But the fact that he does not regard them as philosophically *basic* rights means that they may be modified, limited, or sacrificed in order to meet the requirements of distributive justice set out in the second principle.

Nevertheless, it is important to note that Rawls sees considerable virtues in the (relatively) unfettered operation of market processes, so long as they operate within a just basic structure. Indeed, for Rawls, there is an important sense in which the outputs of such market processes are definitive of justice. A just distribution, for Rawls, is simply one that is produced by a just basic structure. Distributive justice is thus an instance of what he calls "pure procedural justice." Within a just basic structure, Rawls says, "there is no independent criterion for the right result: instead there is a correct or fair procedure such that the outcome is likewise correct or fair, whatever it is, provided that the procedure has been properly followed."[25] So, while a just basic structure will likely include progressively high rates of taxation on the rich, and generous social welfare programs for the poor, it will not be unjust that, as a result of a mix of skill and luck in the competitive marketplace, some people wind up relatively rich and others relatively poor.

Relying entirely on a competitive price system to determine people's income would be unjust insofar as such a system ignores considerations of need. Nevertheless, Rawls suggests, "once a suitable minimum is provided by transfers, it may be perfectly fair that the rest of total income be settled by the price system, assuming that it is moderately efficient and free from monopolistic restrictions, and unreasonable externalities have been eliminated."[26] Indeed, Rawls notes that a system that leaves prices, including wages, to be set by competitive pressures, and then issues transfers to meet claims of need, is likely to be more effective than policies such as minimum wage standards that seek to meet needs by interfering in the price system.[27] Market competition, on Rawls's view, is something to be harnessed and exploited in the quest for justice, not squashed as a threat to it. The efficiencies that such a system generates can be put to good use in improving the position of the least well-off. Moreover, the "impersonal and automatic" character of its operations is in many respects, Rawls claims, a virtue of the arrangement. "It seems improbable," says Rawls, "that the control of economic activity by the bureaucracy that would be bound to develop in a socially regulated system . . . would be more just on balance than control exercised by means of prices."[28]

Despite these concessions, however, the overall balance of Rawls's thought is hostile to a liberal capitalist order. And this is certainly the way that Rawls's ideas have been interpreted within the field of academic business ethics. For example, business ethicists have drawn inspiration from Rawls to argue that firms should be managed in a way that gives equal consideration to the interests of all "stakeholders," rather than exclusive consideration of the interests of the stockholders.[29] They have argued that Rawlsian principles support giving workers greater control over the companies at which they work, either in the form of workplace democracy or a somewhat more modest workplace republicanism.[30] And they have argued that Rawls's doctrine of self-respect provides grounds for holding that one of the proper functions of the state is to ensure people the opportunity to pursue meaningful work.[31]

Not all business ethicists have been convinced of the desirability of such proposals, or even of their claim to be valid extensions of Rawlsian thought.[32] But the view that Rawlsian justice is compatible with the basic institutional structures of free markets and private property that characterize market liberalism nevertheless remains a minority position among business ethicists sympathetic to Rawls. In the remainder of this essay, I will attempt to lend some support to this minority view.

THE CASE FOR RAWLSIAN MARKET LIBERALISM

In this section, I will survey three reasons for thinking that Rawlsian principles are more compatible with the traditional institutions of liberal capitalism than either he or his followers in the business ethics literature have generally assumed. The three reasons have to do with, first, the priority of liberty; second, the compatibility of the difference principle and a free market system; and finally, respect for reasonable pluralism.

The Priority of Liberty

Although parties in Rawls's original position would choose two principles of justice, most of the focus of the business ethics literature has been on the second principle, and indeed on just the second part of the second principle—the so-called difference principle, which requires that inequalities be to the maximum benefit of the least well-off members of society.[33] But for Rawls, the first principle—the principle of equal basic liberties—is lexically prior to the second: the first principle must be fully satisfied before any attempt is made to satisfy the second. Thus, any methods of satisfying the second principle that are incompatible with the first are ruled out.[34]

We have already seen that robust economic liberties, such as a right to ownership of productive property or a right to freedom of contract, were not included by Rawls on his list of basic liberties. That list includes "political liberty (the right to vote and to be eligible for public office) together with freedom of speech and assembly; liberty of conscience and freedom of thought; freedom of the person . . . and freedom from arbitrary arrest and seizure as defined by the concept of the rule of law."[35] The only economic liberty specified on the list is a right to hold personal (i.e., nonproductive) property. Other economic liberties, then, may legitimately be curtailed in order to satisfy the second principle of justice—or, indeed, for any reason at all within the legitimate discretion of the government.

Nonetheless, there are at least two avenues open to a Rawlsian to argue for the protection of a more robust form of economic liberty as a fundamental constraint on legitimate state activity. First, even if robust economic liberties are not themselves basic liberties, they might nevertheless be necessary for the protection of those liberties that Rawls does identify as basic.[36] Freedom of speech, for instance, is a basic right. But the full exercise of this right seems impossible without a wide array of robust economic liberties. Consider the fringe political group that seeks to spread its message by publishing newsletters and websites and by buying and selling books that advance its philosophy. Such an organization might also seek to rent spaces for meetings, to hire individuals to staff its operations, and so on. If these economic activities are blocked by the political system, or even if the freedom to engage in them is dependent on the prior permission of the appropriate political office, then the exercise of the basic liberties that depend on them will be substantially undermined.[37]

Even if we limit ourselves to concern for the basic liberties included on Rawls's list, then, there is good instrumentalist reason to hold that protection of a relatively robust set of economic liberties is of fundamental importance.

But this conclusion can be justified by a second route as well, one that accords special status to economic liberties based on their *intrinsic* value. The intrinsic value of economic liberties is justified by their connection with human agency.[38] As Loren Lomasky has argued, property rights can contribute to human agency by demarcating "a moral space within which what one has is marked as immune from predation."[39] Thus conceived, property rights protect and foster "persons' capacity to formulate and pursue particular conceptions of the good."[40]

Rawls justifies his list of basic liberties by arguing that they are proper ways of treating with respect persons who are free and equal, reasonable and rational. Persons such as this are marked by what Rawls describes as "two moral powers": a capacity for a sense of justice, and a capacity for a conception of the good.[41] The capacity for a conception of the good can be characterized in terms of the possibility of responsible self-authorship, and involves the capacity to realistically assess one's life options and to choose some course of life as one's own in light of that assessment. The capacity for a sense of justice, in contrast, essentially amounts to a recognition that other persons are responsible self-authors, too. The role of the basic liberties is to protect the full and informed exercise of these two moral powers.[42] Freedom of occupational choice, for instance, is represented as necessary to protect these moral powers, since one's choice of occupation is in many ways a profound expression of one's identity: it is where we spend a great deal of our time, it expresses and shapes our values, and it shapes the way our fellow citizens perceive and interact with us.

But what reason do we have for thinking that this form of argument applies only to the narrow set of economic liberties endorsed by Rawls, and not to the more robust set endorsed by thinkers in the classical liberal tradition? Rawls himself has virtually nothing to say in answer to this question— indeed it seems not to occur to him to even ask it. He simply asserts, without argument, that more expansive economic liberties are not "necessary for the development and exercise of the two moral powers," and that they are, therefore, "not basic [liberties]."[43]

But why should we believe this to be true? After all, many of the same arguments that Rawls marshals on behalf of liberties he admits to be basic could also be advanced with equal force on behalf of a more robust set of economic liberties. Consider the link Rawls draws between the two moral powers and occupational choice. As John Tomasi has argued,

> If the freedom to choose an occupation is essential to the development of the moral powers, the freedom to sell, trade, and donate one's labor looks equally essential for the same reasons. After all, one is defined by one's workplace experience not simply by what profession one pursues. One is also defined by where one chooses to work, by the terms that one seeks and accepts for one's

work, by the number of hours that one devotes to one's work, and much more besides.[44]

The same is true of Rawls's arguments regarding property. The arguments that show that personal property is necessary to form and act on a conception of the good also extend to ownership of productive property.[45] This is obviously true for entrepreneurs, for whom economic activities of ownership and investment often constitute a central part of their personal identity. But it is true for ordinary working-class people, and for persons in their capacity as customers as well. The kind of long- and short-term financial planning that individuals and families engage in, for example, "require that people think seriously about the relation between the person that each is at that moment to the person one will become many years in the future. They call on people to take responsibility now for the person each will later become."[46] That is to say, they require people to engage in precisely the sort of reflection about their most fundamental projects and commitments that Rawls seeks to protect by means of the basic liberties.

If these agency-based arguments for economic liberty are valid, then there is a strong case to be made—on Rawlsian grounds—for including robust economic liberties within the set of basic liberties. And if they are, then given the lexical priority of the first principle, the scope for application of the difference principle and the principle of fair equality of opportunity will be severely limited.

The Difference Principle and Market Liberalism

Even if the robust economic liberties are excluded from the set of basic liberties, however, it does not follow that the difference principle will require, or even permit, interference with those liberties in the name of social justice. Whether such interferences are warranted depends, according to the difference principle, on whether they contribute to maximizing the bundle of primary goods available to the representative least well-off person. And this, of course, is a largely empirical question that cannot be settled with the resources of moral philosophy alone.

We have seen that Rawls saw market competition as a force to be harnessed on behalf of the least well-off. He recognizes the efficiency and even the fairness of the price system (within a just basic structure) as a mechanism of income allocation, and the potential dangers of bureaucratic control of the economy.[47] But there is good reason to wonder whether Rawls took these considerations seriously enough. Rawls's rosy assessment of property-owning democracy suggests a failure to think through the immense problems of knowledge and incentives that seem likely to plague such a system.[48] If this is correct, then even a difference principle left unchecked by a robust set of basic economic liberties might wind up sanctioning something more like the free market of classical liberalism than the social democracy of property-owning democracy.

Consider, first, the various problems of incentives.[49] One of the distinguishing features of property-owning democracy is its commitment to the wide dispersal of productive capital within a society.[50] But the large-scale redistribution of capital will generate a very strong disincentive to the creation and accumulation of capital. In effect, capital will be taken from those who have demonstrated through market competition an ability to create and use it most effectively, and given to those who fare more poorly in this regard.[51] Similar (and familiar) incentive problems arise on the other side of the redistribution. Those to whom capital is given in the form of a cash grant or free education or a subsidized mortgage, for instance, will have less of an incentive to engage in productive work in order to earn that capital themselves. The predictable result of such a system of incentives is a significant reduction in the amount of capital produced, and a corresponding diminution in the size of the social pie, from which the shares of the least well-off (among others) must be cut.

The incentive problems discussed in the last paragraph plague property-owning democracy even at the level of ideal theory, at which virtually all Rawlsian theorizing about justice and institutions takes place. In ideal (or strict compliance) theory, all persons are presumed to act in accordance with the principles of justice.[52] Since reducing one's productive output in order to achieve a lower tax burden (or in response to subsidization) does not violate any precept of justice, these kinds of disincentive effects are problems even for the most "realistically utopian" form of property-owning democracy.[53]

But when we drop the idealizing assumptions of strict compliance theory, the incentive problems for property-owning democracy become even more serious. As we have seen, the implementation of property-owning democracy would require a massive expansion of the scope and degree of state power, in the form of four new "branches" of government. In ideal theory, these institutions would be used exclusively to serve the common good, in accordance with the principles of justice. But in the real world, firms and interest groups would have tremendous incentives to "capture" these regulatory bodies in order to turn them toward their own private interests.[54] And it would often be in the self-interest of the various individuals who administer those bodies to be complicit in that capture, if not to actively abet it.[55] The people who run the banks, who hold elected office, and who sit on government committees in a Rawlsian society would not be markedly different in their psychological or moral makeup from those who did so during, say, the events leading up to the 2008 financial crisis in the United States. The only difference is that with the expanded scope of state power, the payoffs to be reaped from capturing or misusing that power would be correspondingly greater.

Even putting all of these incentive problems to the side, however, property-owning democracy is still faced with massive problems of inadequate information. The government of a property-owning democracy is faced with a series of Herculean tasks—from deciding on appropriate price and wage levels, to determining the appropriate allocation of capital, to (possibly) the ownership and management of firms themselves. In a market system, decisions about how much someone should be paid, how much to invest in a particular project, and so on are made by private individuals under the guidance of information conveyed by the price system.[56] But in a property-owning democracy, price signals would be systematically distorted by a multitude of government interventions in the economy. And government agents themselves would be operating in many cases in a nonmarket environment in which even distorted price signals are unavailable as a possible guide to action. On what basis, then, are decisions to be made?

Both Rawls and contemporary advocates of property-owning democracy stress that they want to keep the price system as a method of *allocating* scarce resources among individuals and firms as producers. They simply want to reject the price system as a method of *distributing* wealth and income among individuals as consumers.[57] But allocation and distribution are two sides of the same coin, and the failure to recognize this is a sign that advocates of a property-owning democracy are not taking the informational problems of their system seriously enough. Income inequality—the fact that doctors make more than philosophers, for instance—is itself a kind of market signal, and one cannot eliminate the inequality without distorting that signal and thereby inadvertently modifying people's allocative behavior.

What ultimately matters, as far as the difference principle is concerned, is not whether people in the government are *trying* to maximize the position of the least well-off. Whether their hearts are in the right place is a proper question for the moral evaluation of their character, but not for the moral evaluation of the system they produce. What matters for the justice of the system is whether the position of the least well-off is *actually* maximized. The considerations set forward in this section give us some reason to doubt that Rawls's own preferred system of property-owning democracy would be successful in doing so. If this is correct, then even a Rawlsian difference principle unconstrained by a robust set of economic liberties might push in the direction of one of the two forms of "capitalist" orders discussed, but rejected, by Rawls himself.

Reasonable Pluralism

The previous two sections have treated Rawls's work as a continuous whole. But it is worth emphasizing that Rawls's second book, *Political Liberalism*, represented a major shift in the substance of Rawlsian thought. The most important element in that shift, and one that has gone mostly unnoticed by business ethicists to this point, is its overarching focus on the fact of reasonable pluralism.[58] In brief, the idea of reasonable pluralism holds that a diversity of conflicting and irreconcilable but reasonable moral beliefs is the normal result of free inquiry, and thus a permanent condition of a liberal society.[59] People have diverse views about which actions are right and wrong, what kind of life is most worth striving for, what the relationship is (if any) between God and morality, and so forth. A liberal society is thus marked by a diversity of what Rawls calls "reasonable comprehensive doctrines."[60]

Reasonable people will recognize this diversity, and acknowledge that it results at least in part from what Rawls calls the "burdens of judgment"— the ways in which our own unique life experiences and the difficult nature of moral problems make it unlikely that we will all arrive at the same conclusions. They will thus be unwilling to impose their own comprehensive doctrines on others by force, seeking instead for some kind of consensus on the basis of ideas implicit or explicit in their shared public political culture.[61]

"Political power is always coercive power," Rawls notes.[62] But if this is so, and if respect for reasonable pluralism puts sharp limits on the legitimacy of coercion, then we appear to have yet another element in Rawlsian thought pushing in the direction of classical liberalism. For, as Gaus has recently argued, the classical liberal institutions of several property and liberty of contract can be thought of not merely as instruments for the promotion of economic efficiency but as mechanisms for respecting reasonable pluralism by allowing individuals to live their lives according to their own comprehensive doctrines to as great an extent as possible.[63] Rights, including property rights, should be thought of as assigning to individuals a certain jurisdiction over which their own personal desires and beliefs are entitled to hold sway.[64] Rather than responding to reasonable pluralism by centralizing moral authority on the basis of some hoped-for overlapping consensus, the classical liberal response is to minimize the range of decisions on which consensus is needed by devolving moral authority to the lowest possible level: that of the individual.

This form of argument is implicit in Rawls's defense of freedom of religion. Because reasonable people disagree about matters of religion, we allow each individual to make his or her own decision about whether and how to celebrate it. We do not allow the state to erect a crucifix in the middle of the public square, but we allow each citizen to put one, or not, on the wall of his or her own home.

But if the arguments surveyed in the subsection above on economic liberties are correct, it is unclear why we should treat economic liberties differently. Economic activity, like private religious practice, can be and often is an expression of one's deeply held conception of the good. Just as religious liberties are necessary to protect the cultivation and exercise of diverse forms of religious belief and expression, so too are economic liberties of property and contract necessary to protect the diversity we find in that realm. Private businesses, on this view, are one way of allowing individuals to pursue their diverse purposes within a pluralistic society. Those purposes might involve what we think of as ideological aims, such as when a company like Ben & Jerry's sets its pay levels, directs its profits, and dictates its treatment of workers according to its own particular values and conception of fairness. But they might simply involve the pursuit of technical excellence, or even the pursuit of profit. That economic liberties have often seemed trivial and of merely instrumental value to intellectuals who write about justice is, if anything, even more reason to stress their importance. These liberties are basic to human agency, not because they protect people's pursuit of ends that we all regard as important, but precisely because they protect people's ability to exercise agency in ways that we might *not* think are important, and might therefore otherwise be tempted to suppress or marginalize.

CONCLUDING REMARKS

I have argued that for at least one major category of question in which business ethicists are interested, Rawls's work will be of little use. Rawls simply didn't have much to say about how customers, managers, CEOs, or other groups or individuals ought to act in the marketplace or elsewhere. His two principles of justice were designed to regulate the basic structure of society, and explicitly *not* intended to govern the various microlevel decisions individuals and groups might make within that structure. What little he did have to say about individual conduct is, though relatively uncontroversial, so vague and general as to be of almost no help in addressing any problem in business ethics about which there exists serious scholarly dispute.

Rawls's lasting legacy to the field of business ethics is his theory of the justice of the basic structure. The theoretical apparatus that Rawls brings to bear on fundamental questions regarding basic rights and liberties is elegant and sophisticated, subtle and deep. Unfortunately, the actual application of that apparatus to questions about institutional design is not so well developed. Rawls's arguments against the justice of capitalism and against the importance of robust economic liberties and property rights are based on moral and economic theory largely divorced from empirical analysis. And even in his purely moral reasoning, Rawls often seems to lose sight of or fail to take seriously some of his most foundational commitments and values when it comes to assessing questions of property and exchange.

I have argued that there are resources in Rawls's theory that render his principles much more congenial to a system of market liberalism. Rawlsian liberalism is not, and never will be, full-fledged libertarianism. But it can be, and perhaps should be, something more akin to the classical liberalism of Hume, Smith, and Hayek—a system in which property rights and economic liberty carry a heavy normative weight, and severely limit the extent to which the coercive apparatus of the state can be wielded in the pursuit of social goals.[65] Nothing in classical liberal theory—nor in the writings of the most famous contemporary classical liberals themselves—counts decisively against the maintenance of a state-financed and state-administered social safety net. And so Rawls's mistake was not simply that he thought that there is some role for the state to play in securing the advantage of the least well-off. His mistake, rather, lay in his belief that securing this advantage requires the rejection of a liberal market order and its replacement with the technocratic state of a property-owning democracy. Rawls underestimated both the instrumental and the intrinsic moral value of robust economic liberty, and thus underestimated the extent to which a system that embraces such liberty is compatible with his own fundamental principles.

NOTES

1. John Rawls, *A Theory of Justice* (Cambridge, MA: Belknap Press of Harvard University Press, 1971); Rawls, *Political Liberalism* (New York: Columbia University Press, 1993).

2. The texts I surveyed are the following: Tom Beauchamp and Norman Bowie, *Ethical Theory and Business,* 7th ed. (London: Pearson Prentice Hall, 2004); Thomas Donaldson, Patricia H. Wehane, and Margaret Cording, *Ethical Issues in Business: A Philosophical Approach*, 7th ed. (London: Prentice Hall, 2002); John Boatright, *Ethics and the Conduct of Business*, 5th ed. (London: Pearson Prentice Hall, 2007); Manuel G. Velasquez, *Business Ethics: Concepts and Cases*, 6th ed. (London: Pearson Prentice Hall, 2006); Kevin Gibson, *Business Ethics: People, Profits, and the Planet* (New York: McGraw-Hill, 2006); William H. Shaw and Vincent Barry, *Moral Issues in Business*, 12th ed. (Stamford, CT: Wadsworth, 2012).

3. Rawls draws on the analogy of games in his early paper "Two Concepts of Rules," *Philosophical Review* 64, no. 1 (Jan. 1955): 3–32.

4. *Theory of Justice*, 7.

5. Ibid.

6. Ibid., 5, 7.

7. This principle, like the second, goes through several formulations in Rawls's work. The version presented here is the earliest, appearing in Rawls's first discussion of the two principles in *Theory of Justice*, 60. The first principle remains mostly unchanged even into its final version (*Theory of Justice*, 302). By the time of Rawls's *Justice as Fairness: A Restatement* (Cambridge, MA: Harvard University Press, 2001), however, the principle had undergone significant modification, largely in response to H. L. A. Hart's influential critique in his "Rawls on Liberty and Its Priority," *University of Chicago Law Review* 40 (1973): 534–55. The revised principle states: "Each person has the same *indefeasible claim* to a *fully adequate scheme* of basic liberties, which scheme is compatible with the same scheme of liberties for all" (*Justice as Fairness*, 42, emphasis added).

8. *Justice as Fairness*, 42–43. The version of the second principle presented here is virtually identical to the final version presented on p. 302 of *Theory of Justice*, but more specific than the initial version presented on p. 60 of that book.

9. *Theory of Justice*, 8; see also 129. Rawls's language here seems to leave open the possibility that his two principles *could* be applied to the rules of private associations, informal conventions, etc. His point is to signal his uncertainty about the justifiability of such an extension of his theory, and to point out that it would require further argument than Rawls himself provides.

10. Nozick famously objected to this distinction, arguing that the two principles ought to be testable by microlevel counterexamples, in his *Anarchy, State, and Utopia* (New York: Basic Books, 1974), 204–5. More recently, and from a different direction, G. A. Cohen has challenged the distinction, arguing that the egalitarianism that underlies Rawls's theory of justice ought to govern not merely the basic structure, but individual actions by means of a more general "egalitarian ethos." See G. A. Cohen, *Rescuing Justice and Equality* (Cambridge, MA: Harvard University Press, 2008). For one argument that Rawls's distinction between states and corporations is overstated and that, therefore, principles of political justice ought to apply to both, see Jeffrey Moriarty, "On the Relevance of Political Philosophy to Business Ethics," *Business Ethics Quarterly* 15, no. 3 (2005): 455–73.

11. At least, they have essentially no implications for the behavior of these individuals qua managers, customers, employees, etc.

12. *Theory of Justice*, secs. 18 and 19, pp. 108–17.

13. Ibid., 114. Natural duties are distinguished from obligations in that the latter arise from voluntary acts, are owed to specific individuals, and are defined in part by social institutions or practices, whereas the former apply to us without regard to our voluntary acts, are owed to all persons regardless of institutional relationships, and have their content defined independently of social institutions or practices. *Theory of Justice*, 113, 114–15.

14. *Theory of Justice*, 112–13. The principle of fairness holds, roughly, that people are required to do their part to support just institutions from which they have voluntarily benefited. This principle has been deployed mostly in debates concerning individuals' duties to support just *political* institutions. But it would appear to be a fruitful potential source for business ethicists who seek to explore other, nonpolitical duties between firms and stakeholders. For one attempt to develop such an account, see Robert A. Phillips, "Stakeholder Theory and a Principle of Fairness," *Business Ethics Quarterly* 7, no. 1 (1997): 51–66.

15. See *Theory of Justice*, 344; and Albert Carr, "Is Business Bluffing Ethical?," *Harvard Business Review* 143 (Jan.–Feb. 1968): 143–53.

16. *Theory of Justice*, 114, 338.

17. Matt Zwolinski, "The Ethics of Price Gouging," *Business Ethics Quarterly* 18, no. 3 (2008): 347–78; Ian Maitland, "Priceless Goods: How Should Life-Saving Drugs Be Priced?," *Business Ethics Quarterly* 12, no. 4 (2002): 451–80.

18. See Gerald F. Gaus, "Coercion, Ownership, and the Redistributive State: Justificatory Liberalism's Classical Tilt," *Social Philosophy and Policy* 27, no. 1 (2010): 237. Rawls devotes his most extensive argument to rejecting a system of laissez-faire capitalism on the grounds that it "secures only formal equality and rejects both the fair value of the equal political liberties" and that it secures only a "rather low social minimum," thus failing to protect the prospects of the least well-off. See *Justice as Fairness*, 137; see also *Theory of Justice*, 65–72. Even "welfare-state capitalism" fails to satisfy the requirements of the two principles of justice, since the "very large inequalities in the ownership of real property" that it allows permit "control of the economy and much of political life" to rest in relatively few hands, and since the inequalities it permits are not regulated by any principle of reciprocity (*Justice as Fairness*, 138). Rawls's claim here is puzzling given its inconsistency with his earlier assessment in *Political Liberalism*. There, he staked out a more agnostic position, claiming that

"the question of private property in the means of production or their social ownership . . . are not settled at the level of the first principles of justice, but depend on the traditions and social institutions of a country and its particular problems and historical circumstances" (*Political Liberalism*, 338). These questions must therefore be left to "later stages" of justification where more information about these circumstances is available (298).

19. *Justice as Fairness*, 139, 160–61. See, for an extended discussion and defense, Martin O'Neill and Thad Williamson, eds., *Property-Owning Democracy: Rawls and Beyond* (Oxford: Wiley-Blackwell, 2012).

20. *Theory of Justice*, 274–84. Rawls sometimes refers to these branches as "functions," suggesting that they need not be implemented as distinct organizational structures.

21. *Theory of Justice*, 276.

22. Ibid., 61.

23. Ibid., 271.

24. *Political Liberalism*, 298; see also *Theory of Justice*, 270–74, 280–82.

25. *Theory of Justice*, 86.

26. Ibid., 277.

27. Ibid.

28. Ibid., 281.

29. See, for example, R. Edward Freeman and William M. Evan, "Corporate Governance: A Stakeholder Interpretation," *Journal of Behavioral Economics* 19, no. 4 (1990): 337–59; and R. Edward Freeman, "The Politics of Stakeholder Theory: Some Future Directions," *Business Ethics Quarterly* (1994): 409–21.

30. Nien-hê Hsieh, "Rawlsian Justice and Workplace Republicanism," *Social Theory and Practice* 31, no. 1 (2005): 115–42.

31. Jeffrey Moriarty, "Rawls, Self-Respect, and the Opportunity for Meaningful Work," *Social Theory and Practice* 35, no. 2 (2009): 441–59.

32. See, for instance, John Hasnas, "The Normative Theories of Business Ethics: A Guide for the Perplexed," *Business Ethics Quarterly* 8, no. 1 (1998): 19–42; and James Child and Alexei M. Marcoux, "Freeman and Evan: Stakeholder Theory in the Original Position," *Business Ethics Quarterly* 9, no. 2 (1999): 207–23.

33. The phrase "difference principle" refers only to part of the second principle of justice, specifically that part that specifies that inequalities must be to the advantage of the least well-off. The first part of the second principle is known as the "fair equality of opportunity principle."

34. *Theory of Justice,* 43.

35. Ibid., 61.

36. This form of argument has been described by James Nickel as a "linkage argument." See Nickel, "Economic Liberties," in *The Idea of Political Liberalism*, ed. Victoria Davion and Clark Wolf (New York: Rowman and Littlefield, 2000), 155–75. Nickel categorizes various forms of linkage arguments, but the form of argument is hardly new in the liberal tradition. See, for example, Milton Friedman's *Capitalism and Freedom* (Chicago: University of Chicago Press, 1962), esp. chap. 1.

37. As further evidence of this claim, Gerald Gaus cites the Heritage Foundation's *Economic Freedom of the World: 2008 Annual Report* and Freedom House's ranking of states that protect civil rights. Those states that Freedom House ranks as the best at protecting civil liberties are also marked by robust protection of property rights and economic liberties. Existing socialist regimes not only do a poor job protecting property rights and economic freedom; they also score as "not at all free" in the protection of basic civil and political liberties. Gaus concludes: "There has never been a political order characterized by deep respect for personal freedom that was not based on a market order with widespread private ownership in the means of production." See Gaus, "Coercion, Ownership, and the Redistributive State," 252.

38. See, for a brief discussion of this general form of argument, Gerald Gaus's entry "The Idea and Ideal of Capitalism," in *The Oxford Handbook of Business Ethics*, ed. George L. Brenkert and Tom L. Beauchamp (New York: Oxford University Press, 2010), 80–81.

39. Loren E. Lomasky, *Persons, Rights, and the Moral Community* (New York: Oxford University Press, 1990), 121.

40. Loren E. Lomasky, "Libertarianism at Twin Harvard," *Social Philosophy and Policy* 22, no. 1 (2005): 183.

41. *Political Liberalism*, 18–19.

42. *Justice as Fairness*, 113.

43. *Political Liberalism*, 298; and Rawls, *Theory of Justice*, rev. ed. (Cambridge, MA: Harvard University Press, 1999), 54.

44. John Tomasi, *Free Market Fairness* (Princeton, NJ: Princeton University Press, 2011), 77.

45. Ibid., 78–79.

46. Ibid., 79.

47. *Theory of Justice*, 277, 281.

48. Indeed, Rawls notes that his discussion of property-owning democracy, as an "ideal institutional type," "abstracts from its political sociology, that is, from an account of the political, economic and social elements that determine its effectiveness in achieving its public aims." *Justice as Fairness*, 137. It is unclear why Rawls thinks his beliefs about the concentration of wealth and its influence on political power under capitalism do not count as the kind of political sociology from which his analysis should abstract. But even more fundamentally, it is not clear why he believes that the defensibility of an institutional type *could* be assessed apart from considerations pertaining to "its effectiveness in achieving its . . . aims."

49. I am grateful for discussion with Kevin Vallier for many of the points that follow in this section. See his "A Moral and Economic Critique of the New Property-Owning Democrats: On Behalf of a Rawlsian Welfare State," *Philosophical Studies* 172, no. 2 (2015): 283–404.

50. See, for a discussion, Martin O'Neill, "Liberty, Equality, and Property-Owning Democracy," *Journal of Social Philosophy* 40, no. 3 (Fall 2009): 379–96; and Thad Williamson, "Who Owns What? An Egalitarian Interpretation of John Rawls's Idea of a Property-Owning Democracy," ibid., 434–53.

51. This claim assumes that there is no large-scale market failure in the market for capital. Neither Rawls nor other defenders of property-owning democracy make any allegations of such a failure.

52. *Theory of Justice*, 8.

53. Rawls describes ideal theory as "realistically utopian" in *Justice as Fairness*, 13.

54. See George Stigler, "The Theory of Economic Regulation," *Bell Journal of Economics and Management Science* 2, no. 1 (Spring 1971): 3–21.

55. This, of course, is one of the main conclusions of "public choice" economics. See James Buchanan and Gordon Tullock, *The Calculus of Consent: Logical Foundations of Constitutional Democracy* (Ann Arbor: University of Michigan Press, 1965).

56. See Friedrich Hayek, "The Use of Knowledge in Society," *American Economic Review* 35, no. 4 (1945): 519–30.

57. See Williamson, "Who Owns What?," 435.

58. Joseph Heath et al. make a similar point in their survey article "Business Ethics and (or as) Political Philosophy," *Business Ethics Quarterly* 20, no. 3 (2010): 433: "If the difference principle has had perhaps too much influence on the thinking of business ethicists—given that it is not obviously applicable within the firm—another aspect of Rawls's view has arguably had too little influence. This concerns what Rawls called 'the fact of reasonable pluralism.'"

59. *Political Liberalism*, 36.

60. Ibid., 13.

61. Leif Wenar, "John Rawls," in *The Stanford Encyclopedia of Philosophy*, ed. Edward N. Zalta, Winter 2012 ed., sec. 3.2, http://plato.stanford.edu/archives/win2012/entries/rawls/. On "public political culture," see *Political Liberalism*, 13–14.

62. *Political Liberalism*, 136.

63. Gaus, "Coercion, Ownership, and the Redistributive State," 233–75. See also Gaus, *The Order of Public Reason* (New York: Cambridge University Press, 2011).

64. See Gaus, *Order of Public Reason,* chap. 18. See also Gaus, "Recognized Rights as Devices of Public Reason," *Philosophical Perspectives* 23, no. 1 (2009): 111–36.

65. On the difference between libertarianism and classical liberalism, see Matt Zwolinski, "Libertarianism," in *The Internet Encyclopedia of Philosophy* (2007), http://www.iep.utm.edu/libertar/; Jason Brennan and John Tomasi, "Classical Liberalism," in *The Oxford Handbook of Political Philosophy*, ed. David Estlund (New York: Oxford University Press 2012), 115.

CHAPTER 20

Commitments and Corporate Responsibility: Amartya Sen on Motivations to Do Good

Ann E. Cudd

Amartya Sen has made wide-ranging and seminal contributions to both ethics and economics, and may be regarded as one of the most important and influential economist-philosophers since John Stuart Mill. In economics, he has made crucial interventions in the fields of social choice theory, welfare economics, feminist economics, and development economics, and as a philosopher he is widely recognized for his original contributions to consequentialist ethics, political philosophy, identity theory, and the theory of justice. Included in his prolific oeuvre are just two papers published in business ethics journals,[1] but several aspects of his work can nonetheless be applied to issues of concern to theorists and practitioners of the field. There are also a variety of topics in business ethics to which Sen's work could be usefully applied, such as (to name just a small number of topics) the constitution of agency within firms, the value of market freedoms, the convergence and divergence of interests within firms, the need for trust in market economies, and the role of markets in avoiding famines.

Sen is also a good theorist to apply to business ethics because he is pro-market, liberal, cosmopolitan, and pragmatic (in the sense of favoring a non-ideal approach to justice). He is an economist who takes seriously the notion that people are motivated by their identity and their ideals, as well as by their needs and desires for material wealth, and he is a philosopher who does not villainize the market or private property rights.[2] He understands deeply and appreciates the contributions and limitations of both economics and ethics, and he is critical of the standard economic model of human motivation in a way that brings those two fields closer than most theorists of either one would typically imagine. Most significant for business ethics, I believe, is what he has written about how the impoverishment of the model of behavior as self-interest maximization confuses the discussion of the role of ethics in business.[3]

In this essay I will apply Sen's theories to this basic question of business ethics: Do businesses have social or moral responsibilities that compete with and may override the goal of wealth creation for the owners or shareholders? I mean this question to be a normative one, which is to ask whether businesses *ought* to attend to such responsibilities, not in the descriptive sense of whether there is some social, ethical, or legal code that assigns them such responsibilities and with which it is in their interest to comply. In some sense this is the most basic question of business ethics, since it determines whether businesses—their owners or managers—themselves must deliberate about ethics or whether they are obligated only to comply with the prevailing codes and norms.[4] This debate in the business ethics literature offers at least four competing models of appropriate corporate behavior, which I will discuss below. But there is a more basic distinction between two types: the instrumental theory on the one hand and socially or morally oriented models of corporate behavior on the other.

The fundamental issue in this debate is whether there are social or moral obligations of for-profit businesses[5] over and above the obligation to maximize profits for shareholders within the externally imposed legal and customary social rules.[6] The shareholder model says no, there are not; the others say yes, there are moral obligations for corporations. Sen's work on agency and motivation illuminates this debate by offering a critique of the instrumental theory on both descriptive and normative grounds. I shall argue that Sen's work shows the instrumental view of corporations—that the sole responsibility of corporations is to maximize profits within the "legal framework and ethical custom of society"[7]—implies a vision of corporations and their role in society that is impoverished descriptively and morally. Descriptively, economic analysis suggests (though does not logically imply) that wealth creation is the only purpose of the (for-profit) corporation, but Sen's work shows that inference must be false. Wealth creation, he notes, is not the only goal of human agents or their instruments. Other appropriate goals and purposes include coordination of activity and creation of identity. Normatively, the instrumental model common among economists and businesspersons suggests that the ethical customs of a society ought to be upheld regardless of how they affect other goals or of whether the social, ethical, or legal "customs" are themselves morally acceptable. For example, if the social custom is to segregate men and women in the workplace, the instrumental model suggests that businesses should follow that custom. Accepting constraints because they are customary is a mere compliance with the rules perspective. But surely corporations (or their managers) should not themselves behave immorally. Corporations must make ethical decisions that they can stand by, even if only to justify their reasons for working within their society's legal and social framework. Sen's recognition of the entanglement of economics and ethics shows that the Friedmanian formula of "legal framework and ethical custom" is ethically naïve and theoretically flawed.

DO BUSINESSES HAVE MORAL OBLIGATIONS?

Perhaps the most basic question of the field of business ethics is whether businesses can be said to have any moral obligations. Some might argue that there is a more basic ontological question of whether businesses or corporations are moral agents at all. But for the purposes of this essay that is an issue that we can bypass by using "corporation" as a shorthand for the agents of the corporation, whether they are the corporate officers, acting together or individually in their fiduciary responsibility to command the resources of the company, or the business or corporation considered as an agent itself.[8] The shareholder model holds that corporations, or corporate officers who determine what the corporation does, should act on behalf of the shareholders. In addition, the shareholder model assumes that the goal of the shareholders in for-profit corporations is to maximize profits. In the case of nonprofit corporations, there is some other explicit goal that the officers have a duty to pursue, which may well be a moral or social goal. Since this debate primarily concerns for-profit businesses, I will ignore nonprofits for the rest of this essay.[9] Since the shareholder model takes the corporation to be instrumental to achieving the ends of the shareholders it is sometimes called the instrumental model.[10] On the instrumental model, then, corporations or their managers qua managers do not have any obligations to consider other than those internal to the stated goals of the corporation; they are simply the instruments of the owners—the shareholders—of the firm, whose motivations are assumed to be simply to maximize their private wealth. This is not to say that the shareholders do not have moral obligations as individuals, and owning a share in a corporation may be either instrumental to or contrary to a particular individual's fulfilling her moral obligations. But the corporation is not to be seen as itself having moral duties other than to pursue profit maximization.[11]

The stakeholder model holds that corporate officers ought to manage the business for the benefit of all stakeholders, which include the employees, suppliers, consumers, and local communities, as well as the stockholders. Stakeholders will have differing and in some ways opposing interests, but there are other interests they will share at least in part, such as, for example, the interest that all have in reducing the carbon footprint of production, all other things equal. Thus, the moral obligation of the firm just is to act in ways that properly balance the interests of the various stakeholders. Sometimes the interests of the other stakeholders will require the interests of the shareholders to be sacrificed. Hence the stakeholder model contradicts the instrumental model.

The social contract theory in business ethics applies contractualism to the relationship between business and society, positing "an implicit contract between the members of society and businesses in which the members of society grant businesses the right to exist in return for certain specified benefits."[12] The original version articulated by Thomas Donaldson appeals to hypothetical consent and imagines a contract between persons and potential businesses.[13] The agreement forms the terms under which persons and corporations could mutually benefit. The theory ultimately "asserts that all businesses are ethically obligated to enhance the welfare of society by satisfying consumer and employee interests without violating any of the general canons of justice."[14] Hence, the social contract theory is also a model on which there exist other-directed corporate social or moral obligations. In requiring mutual benefit rather than maximization of shareholder benefit, the social contract model conflicts with the instrumental model whenever the latter's interests could be furthered at the expense of other stakeholders.[15]

Finally, the corporate moral responsibility (CMR) model "refers to obligations a firm has as a result of its existence, reasons for existence, its scope and nature of operations, and its various interactions or relationships."[16] According to its major proponent, Patricia Werhane, the model derives corporate moral obligations from the background moral obligations that we all have to others in society when our actions affect them. She concludes that corporations have obligations to all those affected by the company's actions. Although Werhane claims, "This formulation connects corporate expertise with a broad sense of responsibility without diminishing its abilities to be profitable,"[17] the CMR model posits moral obligations beyond the interest or welfare of the shareholders, and thus is in conflict with the instrumental model.

The latter three models of corporate obligation derive the particular moral and social obligations of corporations differently, but they all hold that there are such other-directed obligations, which can conflict with the interests of shareholders. In this way they can be fundamentally distinguished from the instrumental model, which holds that there are not. I will call these latter three models "corporate moral obligation models."[18] In the next section I will examine the arguments for the instrumental model as presented by Milton Friedman and John Hasnas. In the two sections that follow the next section I will examine Sen's work, first with regard to business ethics specifically and then with regard to preferences or motivation in order to show that the instrumental model has a naïve and mistaken theory of motivation. Then I will examine work by Sen on how commitments motivate behavior, including commitments to various identities that persons embrace, in order to elaborate his reasons for rejecting the instrumental model.

ARGUMENTS FOR THE INSTRUMENTAL MODEL

Instrumental theories understand the only obligation of (for-profit) business to be to act in the interest of the shareholders, and this is often taken to mean maximizing profits for the shareholders. The classic defense of this latter position is that of Milton Friedman, who says that the responsibility of the corporate executive is "to conduct the business in accordance with [the shareholders'] desires, which generally will be to make as much money as possible while conforming to the basic rules of the society, both those embodied in law and those embodied in ethical custom."[19] On Friedman's view, the executives of a corporation are the instruments of the shareholders, whose goal "generally" in holding stock is to maximize profits, constrained only by law and social custom. I take it that profit maximization is essential to the instrumental model for all for-profit firms; the exceptions noted by "generally" are those firms that have explicitly stated nonprofit goals. As John Hasnas puts it in a defense of the instrumental view, "This fiduciary relationship implies that managers cannot have an obligation to expend business resources in ways that have not been authorized by the stockholders."[20] Only those actions that maximize profits (subject to the constraints of law and custom) are warranted. To pursue any other goal is to use someone else's capital for purposes of which they may not approve. But that is tantamount to "taxation without representation," as Friedman writes at one point, or socialism, at another. Literally, it is a misappropriation of private property, hence not permissible.

The argument just presented is a deontological one resting on the ideas of contract and the individual rights and autonomy of the shareholders. The shareholders have a contractual relationship with the corporation's executives to use the shareholders' capital in ways that will maximize profits, and not in ways that they do not expressly approve. This argument depends on two assumptions that Sen's work questions. First, that the only common goal that shareholders (or business owners) have in their market interactions is the creation of wealth. Second, that the background legal and social rules in such a pure system can be presumed to be morally acceptable, so that acting within their constraints is sufficient for normatively acceptable behavior.

Friedman and Hasnas also allude to a consequentialist argument, related to the invisible hand argument that each attributes to Adam Smith, which is that the aggregate interests of all are best served if each seeks his or her own self-interest in the market. Thus, by seeking the interest of the shareholders, corporations are simply the instruments of the invisible hand of the market, which results in an outcome that is better for some, and just as good for each, than any other outcome, that is, a Pareto efficient outcome. Sen is also critical of this argument, especially as it is put to use in the service of the instrumental theory of corporate responsibility. This argument relies on there being a clear line between the market, where self-interest is sufficient for bringing about the optimal outcome, and the rest of life, where moral considerations beyond self-interest may be relevant at every choice point. Sen's work questions this,[21] and suggests that our social and moral values are intimately connected with our interests, well-being, and identity, and that all things considered our self-interest is not so neatly separable from these.

SEN'S WRITINGS ON BUSINESS ETHICS

Sen's articles on business ethics confront the instrumental model, though not by name. In "Does Business Ethics Make Economic Sense?" Sen argues that ethical behavior is both necessary for a well-functioning economy and intrinsically rewarding for many if not all persons, and therefore is in some sense in their self-interest to perform. The latter argument might be seen as supporting the instrumental model, but that would be a misinterpretation of Sen, because the sense of self-interest that he has in mind is complex and not reducible to the motivation of profit maximization. More important, the argument for the necessity of ethics cannot easily be accommodated in the instrumental model.[22]

First, Sen argues that widespread ethical behavior in society is needed in order to develop the general sense of trust without which exchange and production cannot efficiently proceed.[23] For instance, the baker has to trust the householder to pay for the bread for which she placed an order. In production, the manager needs to trust the worker to exert effort and care in her work because the manager cannot constantly monitor or measure the effort and output of the worker, or at least it will cost considerably if he must. The instrumental model suggests that it is sufficient for each to consider her own interest, constrained only by custom, but where custom does not supply a rule, self-interested behavior may destroy the general sense of trust. In societies where there is no general sense of trust, organized crime typically takes the place of implicit assurances of promise keeping or fair dealing.[24] The fact that the existence of organized crime is preferable to there being no ability to trust in promises shows just how essential such assurances are to social life. While the instrumental model can recognize the value of a general sense of trust in society, its recommendation to individuals to pursue their self-interest constrained by custom does not imply that the individual herself should always act in trustworthy ways. If her self-interest constrained by custom conflicts with ethical behavior, the instrumental model recommends the former as against the latter.

It can be worthwhile to a firm's profit-making performance to encourage ethical and pro-social rather than narrowly self-interested behavior. Within a firm its overall success derives in part from effort that workers and managers contribute and from which all benefit. A public good is a good that is nonexcludable (those who do not pay for it cannot be excluded) and nonrivalrous (one's enjoyment of it does not take away from another's). For each individual, the effort she expends is private. There is some amount of effort that is good enough to keep her job or to achieve the reward for which she aims. If an individual expends more effort than this, then the firm does better. Others in the firm also benefit from the improved performance of the firm. If individuals choose to seek their narrow self-interest and maximize their own reward while minimizing effort within the firm, then they will not contribute as much as they would if there were a way of precisely measuring their inputs. But precisely measuring effort or the contribution that results from it is costly and will take away from the overall performance of the firm. If all or most work only as hard as they must to earn their paycheck, the firm is bound to underperform, and all the individuals in the firm will suffer. "The over-all success of the firm, thus, is really a public good, from which all benefit, to which all contribute, and which is not parceled out in little boxes of person-specific rewards strictly linked with each person's respective contribution. And this is precisely where the motives other than narrow self-seeking become productively important."[25] It is in the interest of firms to encourage in all of their workers and managers such pro-social behavior, where individuals are not concerned only with their narrow self-interest but committed to the goal of the firm's success, and so put forth their best effort even when it is not directly rewarded. Once such behavior becomes ingrained, however, managers will find it difficult to adopt the sort of calculating and amoral attitude toward others that the instrumental model encourages.[26]

Sen argues that it can also be both instrumentally and intrinsically valuable for firms to be concerned about fairness and equity in distribution. The instrumental value is indirect: workers are likely to be loyal and put forth more effort if they feel they have been treated fairly and not simply as inanimate inputs into a system. One might argue that the instrumental model can grant this and treat workers fairly *in order to* maximize profits. Although that is valid, here the most that can be said is that the instrumental model recommends actions consistent with what morality demands, and therefore the claim that firms ought to be moral is not being tested. The intrinsic value is the value attached to contributing to making society better overall, both by acting in ways that help others and by contributing to a general sense that people behave ethically in a society.[27] Seeking this value is not compatible with the instrumental model if the shareholder's wealth can be increased even while society is not benefited overall. Hence the intrinsic value of contributing to making society better overall can contradict the instrumental model's exclusive value of wealth creation.

Not only do shareholders value things other than wealth creation; they also recognize as reasonable decisions made using principles other than self-interest maximization. In "Economics, Business Principles, and Moral Sentiments," Sen observes how businesses constrain the set of actions that they consider as options: "Business principles cannot escape being influenced by conceptions of 'good business behavior,' and thus involve the standard complexities connected with multiple goals."[28] Persons also have multiple constraints, which "include not only the 'feasibility constraints' that reflect the limits of what one can do, but also 'self-imposed constraints' that the person chooses to obey on moral or conventional or even strategic grounds."[29] By "constraint" Sen means grounds for ruling in or out particular actions prior to applying any other decision principle. The particular self-imposed constraints that persons accept depend to some extent on the social and moral norms that are accepted in their cultures, but there is room for local and individual difference here, as Sen often points out. We are socially enmeshed agents, but agents with freedom to choose among (or reject or criticize) diverse interests, commitments, and identities.[30] We are motivated and constrained by far more than profit maximization or even self-interest more broadly construed. "Indeed, the inter-regional and inter-cultural variations in business behavior, which we actually observe, illustrate well the fact that business principles can take much richer and very diverse forms, with differently structured multiple objectives."[31]

In his writings on business ethics, Sen argues for both a broader notion of self-interest as a motivation than that implied by the instrumental model's imperative to maximize profits, and a wider set of business principles than maximization of self-interest. In much of his work in economic and normative ethical theory, Sen elaborates these points through a critique of the model of human agency as narrowly self-interested and aimed at maximization of that self-interest. I turn now to that broader discussion.

SEN ON THE SOURCES OF HUMAN MOTIVATION: SELF-INTEREST, SYMPATHY, AND COMMITMENT

As an economist, Sen is first of all a descriptive scientist of human behavior. Contemporary theories of economic behavior begin by assuming that choice behavior approximates what the normative theory of instrumental rationality, as elaborated in economic theories of consumer and producer behavior, prescribes. Sen has offered critiques and refinements of the theory of rational choice, beginning with some of his earliest work. Through this work he has sought to show that the purely instrumentally rational agent is a reductive caricature of a human agent, a "rational fool." The first problem with the theory is that it presumes that humans are only self-interested, and second that what self-interest comprises, according to the theory, is too restricted. Sen offers a more complex (and realistic) account of self-interest and a description of motivation that goes beyond self-interest even in that more complex account.

Sen's critique of the economic theory of behavior, centering on preference theory and rational choice theory, has two broad targets. The first, his critique of so-called revealed preference theory, aims to refute the behaviorist attempt to derive preference from choice behavior. Revealed preference theory purports to avoid mentalistic constructs, such as agency, intention, and motivation, by deriving preference from observations of individuals' externally verifiable choice behavior. Yet, he shows that some choices by agents will appear to be irrational unless we understand the agent's intentions in so acting. Because of economists' behaviorist aversion to mentalistic constructs, Sen first had to critique revealed preference in order to make a case for examining the internal motivations for behavior and understanding them as more complex than simple self-interest. The second aim was to present a theory of commitment as an alternative source of motivation. The two aims are thus related, and he treats both of them in his influential essay "Rational Fools" (1977).

Neoclassical economics defines rational action as the maximization of satisfaction of preference given budget constraints. Interpretations of preference imply theoretical and ontological commitments. Influenced by the behaviorist commitment to observables, economists, beginning with Paul Samuelson in the mid-twentieth century,[32] developed revealed preference theory, which derives preference (an apparently mentalistic construct) from choice behavior, which is at least in principle observable, thereby avoiding commitment to the underlying reality of mental states. Revealed preference theory is based on the simple, operational idea that if an agent chooses x when y is available (within his budget constraint), then he prefers x to y. Choices revealed in behavior imply a choice function. Thus, preference can be inferred from choices.

Sen has criticized this theory on several levels. Most relevant to the issue at hand, he argued that the choice act itself is meaningful to agents, not only the outcome of the choice. The choice act is important, he argued, because human choosers are situated in a social context of norms that constrain their options beyond just the physical constraints of the material situation at hand and make the choices meaningful to agents. This means that interpreting my choice as a preference for mangoes over apples requires that an observer know not only the material options available to me, but also how I interpret the options socially. If I choose the mango over the apple, it may be because I prefer mangoes over apples in every circumstance, but it may also be that I choose the mango this time in order to leave the next person with a comparable choice (say, when there are two mangoes but only one apple in the bowl). We care not only about what we achieve with our choice—the "culmination outcome"—but also about how our choosing behavior affects our entire situation—the "comprehensive outcome."[33] Since there are indefinitely many ways that the choice situation can matter to agents, revealed preference theory logically cannot infer the preference from the observed choice, and so cannot serve the positivistic purpose of avoiding getting into the heads of agents. Shareholders and firms make choices in dynamically changing and normatively rich situations, where the information available or the norms that are taken to be governing the choices are not observable. Thus, it is not a simple matter to interpret shareholder preferences from their behavior, let alone that of their corporate instruments. So the claim that the whole purpose of the corporation must be to maximize the preferences of the shareholders for maximal profits (within the constraints of social custom), insofar as it is based on observations of choice outcomes of shareholders, can now be questioned.[34]

Sen's second target is the assumption that all rational action is self-interested, which he critiques in two ways, first by analyzing the notion of self-interest and second by offering an additional type of motivation. He begins with an analysis of the meaning of self-interest, by proposing three separable "aspects" to the assumption that agents are self-interested, which aspects may be assumed in combination or separately. The first is what Sen calls "self-centered welfare," which is the assumption that the agent's welfare depends only on her own consumption. The second is what he calls "self-welfare goal," which is the assumption that the agent's goal is to maximize the expected value of her own welfare, and no one else's welfare matters, though her own welfare can be affected by others' consumption. The third is "self-goal choice," which is the assumption that the agent maximizes the satisfaction of her goals irrespective of others' goals, though the agent's goal might include raising another agent's welfare as she conceives it, or indeed, any other sort of goal, including collective goals or conforming to social norms. For example, if a mother has as a goal that her son go to a good college because she thinks that doing so will raise his welfare, and she acts to maximize the satisfaction of this preference, she is satisfying the assumption of self-goal choice. This assumption is often thought to be a necessary condition of autonomous agency, since acting autonomously requires an agent to act on her own goals.[35]

Although all three aspects are assumed in some economic models, including, as I shall argue, the instrumental model of corporate obligation, self-centered welfare is fairly easily and readily given up in economic models of behavior. It is not only extremely unrealistic to assume that people do not get any welfare from anyone else's consumption bundles, but, as Sen shows,[36] it is also unnecessary for the formalization of most of economic theory. There may be some good reasons to incorporate this assumption into one's ethical theory, but descriptively it seems clearly false and misleadingly so. It would not allow us to make sense of any sort of other-directed behavior, whether positive or negative. However, the assumption of self-welfare goal is more commonly defended as necessary for economic models. Sen agrees that much altruistic behavior can be made sense of as a kind of maximization of self-interested behavior if we suspend the assumption of self-centered welfare and allow concerns for others to play a role in agents' utility functions, that is, in their self-goal choices.

Sen distinguishes between sympathy and commitment, two types of other-directed motivations that violate self-centered welfare. Sympathy involves one's own feelings about the experiences of others; it is "the case in which concern for others directly affects one's own welfare."[37] Thus, admitting sympathy as a type of motivation does not violate the self-welfare goal assumption, which allows the economist to model behavior as maximizing a well-behaved (albeit not aimed at selfish consumption) utility function. Commitments, however, sometimes motivate agents to set aside their own goals in the interest of a different goal. When one acts on a commitment, one does something for the sake of a principle, a promise, a group norm, or the anticipation of future welfare.[38]

Although a commitment may motivate action that also maximizes one's personal welfare, commitments sometimes require one to sacrifice personal welfare for the sake of adhering to the commitment. Take voting in a large, democratic contest, for example. In such a situation there is a vanishingly small probability that any one person's vote will determine the results of the election. So the motivation for voting cannot be to bring it about that one's preferred candidate will win. But that is the natural interpretation of the motivation, if we assume that one acts to maximize one's personal welfare. If we drop the assumption of self-welfare goal, then commitments to political or moral principles, or to an identity as a member of a political community, emerge as possible motivations to explain voting behavior.

One might object that adhering to a commitment should be interpreted as itself welfare maximizing, thus preserving self-welfare goal. But we can readily imagine cases where it is highly doubtful that the voter's welfare is enhanced, such as when voting puts the voter in obvious great personal danger. In such cases it is far simpler to admit that the motivation is not the person's welfare but rather the adherence to an external norm for which the person is willing to sacrifice. This point can be made even more forcefully from an advice-giving perspective. If we want to advise someone on what he ought, morally or prudentially, to do when it is very dangerous or costly to vote in a particular election, we would not recommend that he vote if his only aim is to make sure his own welfare is enhanced or that his preferred candidate wins. Instead, we should ask him whether he thinks there is some higher principle or other consideration at stake in voting that would make such a risk or cost worthwhile.

In order to incorporate commitments into his formal theory of preference, Sen proposes that persons rank options differently according to different principles to which they are committed. For example, consider a typical faculty member thinking about how to vote in a departmental hiring decision. One might rank A over B when considering only what is in one's own research interest, but B over A when considering the best thing to advance the department's teaching mission. Sen proposes what he calls meta-rankings to model decision making given the plurality of motivational principles. A meta-ranking is a ranking according to the preferences one has for the various principles and their orderings. A meta-ranking for departmental hiring, for example, might be to rank advancing the teaching mission above advancing one's research interests. Modeling persons as choosing according to meta-rankings will allow the model to express commitments to a variety of things, such as deontic obligations, morality, or other non-self-interested principles, by the meta-ranking, which can then be treated as a preference ordering that can fit into a maximizing model. This account of meta-rankings allows multiple theories of motivation that are not simply self-interested in the sense of self-welfare goal. Applied to business ethics, a corporate board member might choose to rank order actions that avoid child labor above those that improve the bottom line, for instance.

Finally, and most controversially, Sen argues that commitment may involve violation of self-goal choice. To understand just what is at stake with this claim, Philip Pettit distinguishes between goal-modifying commitment and goal-displacing commitment.[39] A goal-modifying commitment is a commitment that alters the agent's own goals based on recognition of others' goals and how the agent's behavior affects them. The meta-ranking model can reflect the overall goal that an agent pursues in light of competing goals, such as one's desire to affect others for good or ill. A goal-displacing commitment is a motivation that replaces the agent's goals with another's goals or the goal of a group, or possibly an impartial moral norm. This latter sense of commitment as goal displacing violates the assumption of self-goal choice and cannot be incorporated into a model of the *agent's own* ranking or meta-ranking. While some such behavior is clearly robotic or slavish (such as crowd behavior in a riot), some instances of such behavior are shaped by social norms that guide behavior but are not questioned or considered.[40] The agent's goals might involve the goals of a group with which the agent identifies. However, autonomous action requires acting on one's own goals rather acting on behalf of a principle or goal that one does not oneself endorse.

Friedman's argument for the instrumental model must assume all three aspects of self-interest for his arguments to work. He argues that shareholders qua shareholders are concerned only about their own private ownership of wealth, and the corporation is simply an instrument of (that conception of their) self-interest. While they may constrain their behavior by social custom, profit maximization remains the goal within those constraints. Of course what motivates the desire for wealth can be complex in any given individual's case, but the point Friedman is making is that such complexities can be abstracted from and modeled as self-interested welfare, where welfare is measured by financial profit. Yet this is what Sen's analysis of self-interest and theory of commitment compel us to deny. First, Sen shows us that there is no reason to assume that behavior is always self-centered. Acting from sympathy as a kind of self-interested behavior may fit into the instrumental theory generally, but not Friedman's version, which takes profit to be the only kind of self-interest for shareholders qua shareholders. We can see this clearly by considering the consequentialist version of the argument. If each firm pursues profit maximization, it is argued that a Pareto efficient outcome will be secured. But if welfare depends on something other than profits, then the outcome that is Pareto efficient when measured only by profits will not be so when welfare depends on something other than profits. Second, if self-welfare goal does not hold of the motivations of shareholders, then Friedman cannot conclude that all shareholders seek to maximize profits.[41] It may be that many or most of the shareholders do seek this, but it is not the only goal pursued by agents, as Sen argues. I will elaborate on Sen's theory of commitment to argue that there are other legitimate and likely goals of shareholders below. Third, Friedman also has to assume that the goals of the agents are their own for the deontological version of the argument to hold. The deontological version holds that the shareholder has a right to be treated as autonomously contracting with the managers of the firm. On the assumption that the goal of the shareholder is profit maximization, that is what the firm must do. But if self-goal choice does not hold, then the shareholder is not acting on a goal that is his own, and hence there is no imperative to uphold the goal in order to respect the shareholder's autonomy, where autonomy is taken to be the shareholder's authentic choice. For example, if the shareholder chooses to invest in a company because he is simply following the lead of his union buddies, then his autonomy is not at stake in determining the actions of the company, since his investing was not an autonomous decision.

Sen's theory of motivation thus gives us additional reasons to reject Friedman's and Hasnas's arguments for the instrumental model of corporate behavior. First Sen's critique of revealed preference shows that we should question the descriptive connection between choice behavior and preference that may underlie their assumption that shareholders are generally seeking to maximize profit within the constraints of social custom. Second, Sen's analysis and critique of the assumption of self-interest show that although some motivations can be captured by some notion of self-interest, they cannot all be reduced to self-centered welfare, let alone to the latter being identified with, or reduced to, profit maximization only. In addition, agents are sometimes motivated by commitments that lie beyond thoughts of their own welfare or even their own non-self-centered goals.

Sen claims that commitments can play at least four kinds of roles in motivating behavior. First, adopting a commitment can be a means of building a reputation or a way of restraining oneself and thereby achieving some longer-term goal that involves one's own consumption, such as putting away funds for retirement, or throwing away the full pack of cigarettes. We might call this a "strategic commitment." This sort of commitment is like a long-term investment, but it has implications for the rejection of the instrumental model. Shareholders and owners invest for different time horizons, different life plans or priorities, and different phases of life. Even if they were concerned only with profit maximization, different time horizons will imply different and conflicting strategies for a business. Perhaps the Friedman supporter will respond that these complications can be avoided by pursuing a simple strategy of overall profit maximization. But even the business that aims simply to pay a consistent and dependable dividend will need to consider for how long it intends to do this, and adjust the strategy according to that time horizon. For example, coal companies right now should be considering diversifying their product into other energy sources and so forth, if they hope to still be paying out dividends in twenty years. Thus a commitment to profit maximization is not as clear a strategy as the instrumental model seems to suggest.

Second, acting on a commitment can serve to project an image for an agent. This kind of commitment, which I will call an "identity commitment," motivates actions that are typical of identity formation, such as buying a share of the local football team when the share neither maximizes the agent's expected profits nor brings any other direct benefit. Identity commitment can thus clearly conflict with the goal of profit maximization, and therefore with the instrumental model's recommendation to maximize profit subject only to the constraints of custom.

Commitments motivate behavior in two additional ways that point away from self-interest as the general or common goal that motivates actions. Persons can act out of social or "ethical commitments" that they embrace as at least in part their own goals, even when the outcomes of abiding by such commitments are not self-welfare enhancing. Sometimes agents choose on the basis of principles that are recognized in their communities, or that they recognize as socially beneficial or morally good. As I pointed out earlier, Sen argues that shareholders may value just communities intrinsically. If shareholders have such commitments, then for the corporation to act only in the interest of profit maximization can require it to act contrary to these ethical commitments.

Finally, Sen argues that persons sometimes act on commitments that replace their own goals, that is, goal-displacing commitments. Such commitments can help explain the fact that people often cooperate in Prisoner's Dilemma (PD) situations even though standard rational choice theory recommends defection in the one-shot game. By recognizing that the only way to "solve" the PD is to commit to cooperate, despite the fact that doing so entails sublimating their own goals to that of the community, persons can act rationally on a commitment to a goal that is not their own. According to Sen, this is a kind of social thinking, "part of living in a community,"[42] and a non-self-interested way of adopting a group identity. Thus, according to Sen, persons can act rationally on group-based preferences that are not their own but from which they rationally act as if they were.

Recognizing these four kinds of commitments as possible motivations for business or corporate behavior allows us to consider ways that businesses may deliberate about strategies for investment and about their social and moral obligations.[43] That is, commitments represent ways that a variety of ethical, political, or other normative concerns are to be ordered in the corporation's meta-ranking. Minimally, corporations must order the welfare of different shareholders with different time horizons, choosing to set some time horizon as the goal for profit maximization. They must also consider what social and moral commitments are necessary to preserve relationships of trust within their firm, at least, and arguably throughout society.[44] Finally, if corporations are to be responsive to shareholders, then they must consider the commitments that shareholders consider important, which will include commitments to their communities and the individuals within them. In sum, as Sen has argued, businesses ought to consider a much wider variety of values and commitments than that recognized by the instrumental model (which assumes that profit maximization is the sole interest of the shareholder) if they are to serve the deeper, and more realistic, interests of their owners.

One might suggest that the instrumental model can be salvaged by jettisoning the assumption, which Sen has cast in doubt, that shareholders qua shareholders are motivated only by profit maximization. Then the instrumental model would hold that businesses should operate to fulfill the aims of the shareholders, whatever they are, subject to the constraints of law and custom. This suggestion saves the instrumental model at the cost of making it both vague and implausible as an ethical theory. It is vague because it would not supply any particular ends other than whatever ends the shareholders happen to have. It is also implausible as an ethical theory, since the particular ends that the shareholders happen to have are not guaranteed to be ethical ones.

CONCLUDING REMARKS

As we have seen, Sen's work on self-interest and commitment opposes the instrumental model for descriptive and normative reasons. Descriptively, Sen shows that our interest and commitments may conflict with the sole goal of profit maximization. Normatively, Sen argues that widespread ethical behavior in society is necessary to develop the general sense of trust, without which exchange and production cannot efficiently proceed. Similarly, ethical behavior within firms is valuable to their bottom line. While the instrumental model can recognize the value of a general sense of trust in society or of ethical behavior in firms, its recommendation to individuals to pursue their self-interest constrained only by custom does not imply that the individual herself should always act in ethical ways.

It is less clear which model of corporate moral responsibility Sen would uphold, but I will offer some tentative inferences. In his recent work on justice, Sen eschews what he calls transcendental arguments for justice that are comprehensive theories designed for ideal conditions, in which the starting point is a perfectly just world.[45] Sen argues for taking a more pragmatic and piecemeal approach, which focuses on outcomes that can be realized in this world. It seems likely, then, that he would not favor the methodology of the *hypothetical* social contract model for use in the decidedly nonideal world of business.

Nonetheless, a social contract model recognizes that businesses provide benefits that give us reason to encourage their existence and to create a climate of trust in which they can operate. Sen's remarks on the role of commitments in creating an open and trusting community suggest that the social contract model is right to emphasize the benefits of businesses (as was the instrumental model). Both the stakeholder and corporate moral responsibility theories (unlike the instrumental model) focus on the interests of those affected by the decisions of businesses, which Sen would also consider important. However, they each rely on a background moral theory to determine who is affected and why that matters morally, questions that the social contract model addresses. Thus, although no one of the existing models would be sufficient in itself to be Sen's favored model of corporate moral obligations, a realization-focused contractualist model that takes the real or actual commitments as well as the interests of those affected by businesses into account may speak to his most important concerns. Such a model would need to provide a descriptive account of actual needs, interests, and commitments (perhaps along the lines of his capabilities approach).[46] The contractualist element of the model would show how businesses, within constraints derived within the model, could be operated to optimally achieve those needs, interests, and commitments given their partially conflicting and partially overlapping nature.

Ann E. Cudd

ACKNOWLEDGMENTS

This article has benefited greatly from the careful reading and copious suggestions for revision by the editors of this volume, Byron Kaldis and Eugene Heath. I am very grateful for their help. Of course, they must not be blamed for any remaining errors or confusions.

NOTES

1. Amartya Sen, "Does Business Ethics Make Economic Sense?," *Business Ethics Quarterly* 3, no. 1 (January 1993): 45–54; Sen, "Economics, Business Principles, and Moral Sentiments," *Business Ethics Quarterly* 7, no. 3 (July 1997): 5–15; and Sen, "Business Ethics and Economic Success," *Notizie di Politeia* 16 (2000): 3–13. See also his conference lecture "Ethical Challenges: Old and New," International Congress on "The Ethical Dimensions of Development: The New Ethical Challenges of State, Business, and Civil Society, " Brazil, July 3–4, 2003, http://www.exclusion.net/images/pdf/623_duvub_bra_sen_desaf-i.pdf.

2. Amartya Sen, *Development as Freedom* (New York: Alfred A. Knopf, 1999); Sen, *The Idea of Justice* (Cambridge, MA: Harvard University Press, 2009).

3. Amartya Sen, "Rational Fools: A Critique of the Behavioral Foundations of Economic Theory," *Philosophy & Public Affairs* 6, no. 4 (1977): 317–44; and Sen, "Economics, Business Principles, and Moral Sentiments."

4. It is of course possible that ethical deliberation will result in compliance with prevailing norms. But the point here is that ethical deliberation may lead one to the conclusion that complying with the prevailing norms is immoral.

5. What I will claim Sen is arguing for with respect to the moral responsibilities of businesses applies equally to corporate and noncorporate businesses, and includes social responsibilities as well. Others I discuss here, such as Milton Friedman and Thomas Donaldson, sometimes refer more specifically to corporations. Friedman uses the term "social responsibility" in a way that I will construe as a type of moral responsibility that concerns society generally rather than simply individuals. The distinction between moral and social will not play a role in this essay—what is important is that they are alleged responsibilities. I will use both "business" and "corporation" depending on whether I am discussing these more specifically aimed arguments or Sen's. However, the debate over moral/social responsibility applies mutatis mutandis to businesses more generally, as it does to corporations.

6. By moral obligation or responsibility I mean an obligation arrived at through moral deliberation and supported by demonstrably moral norms. Social responsibilities are those that are supported by social norms and may or may not be morally obligatory. I use "responsibility" and "obligation" basically interchangeably.

7. Milton Friedman, "The Social Responsibility of Business Is to Increase Its Profits," *New York Times Magazine,* September 13, 1970, 32.

8. For an instantiation of the debate over the ontological status of corporations and whether they are agents, see Jan Garrett, "Unredistributable Corporate Moral Responsibility," *Journal of Business Ethics* 8, no. 7 (1989): 535–45; and Patricia H. Werhane, "Corporate and Individual Moral Responsibility: A Reply to Jan Garrett," *Journal of Business Ethics* 8, no. 10 (1989): 821–22. Since Sen has little to contribute to this debate, I will pass over it for the purposes of this essay.

9. Such firms could have goals that are antisocial or immoral, raising the question of

whether such goals should be pursued if they do not fall within the laws and social norms of society. Although this is an interesting question, I shall leave it for others to ponder.

10. Marcel van Marrewijk, "Concepts and Definitions of CSR and Corporate Sustainability: Between Agency and Communion," *Journal of Business Ethics* 44, no. 2 (2003): 95–105.

11. Recall that I am distinguishing actual moral obligations from any supposed duty to comply with custom.

12. John Hasnas, "The Normative Theories of Business Ethics: A Guide for the Perplexed," *Business Ethics Quarterly* 8, no. 1 (1998): 29.

13. Thomas W. Dunfee and Thomas Donaldson, "Contractarian Business Ethics: Current Status and Next Steps," *Business Ethics Quarterly* 5 (1995): 173–86.

14. Hasnas, "Normative Theories of Business Ethics," 29.

15. The mutual benefit contractarian, such as David Gauthier, *Morals by Agreement* (Oxford: Oxford University Press, 1986), might object that in fact such a conflict would not occur. But this could only be true if the instrumentalist is a constrained maximizer, and if the social contract model is taken to be a mutual advantage contractarian theory, which has not been true of theories articulated to date.

16. Patricia H. Werhane et al., *Alleviating Poverty through Profitable Partnerships: Globalization, Markets, and Economic Well-Being* (New York: Routledge, 2010), 71.

17. Ibid., 71.

18. I have omitted discussion of virtue ethics theories because moral or social responsibility is only indirectly derivable from such theories.

19. Friedman, "Social Responsibility of Business," 33.

20. Hasnas, "Normative Theories of Business Ethics," 21.

21. Sen, "Does Business Ethics Make Economic Sense?," 45–46.

22. Ethics cannot be accommodated by the instrumental model as the *source* of moral obligations. The instrumental model allows social, ethical, and legal customs to be taken as constraint, but does not require or allow ethical reasoning, which might conflict with custom, to determine the aim of business transactions.

23. On this point, see also Sen, "Ethical Challenges."

24. Sen, "Economics, Business Principles, and Moral Sentiments," 10.

25. Sen, "Does Business Ethics Make Economic Sense?," 51.

26. The instrumental model encourages a calculating, amoral attitude if that is conducive to self-interest. Where it is not—for example, if others can detect those attitudes and penalize persons who have them—then it recommends hiding those attitudes or eliminating them if necessary to maximize satisfaction of self-interest.

27. Sen, "Economics, Business Principles, and Moral Sentiments."

28. Ibid., 6.

29. Ibid.

30. Amartya Sen, *Identity and Violence: The Illusion of Destiny* (New York: W. W. Norton, 2006).

31. Sen, "Economics, Business Principles, and Moral Sentiments," 8.

32. Paul Samuelson, "A Note on the Pure Theory of Consumers' Behavior," *Economica* 5 (1938): 61–71.

33. Amartya Sen, "Maximization and the Act of Choice," in *Rationality and Freedom* (Cambridge, MA: Belknap Press of Harvard University Press, 2002), 749.

34. Accepting Sen's critique of revealed preference means that any theory that interprets preferences from behaviors can be questioned as well.

35. However, it is not clear that Sen accepts this conception of autonomous agency. See Philip Pettit, "Construing Sen on Commitment," *Economics and Philosophy* 21, no. 1 (2005): 19.

36. Pettit, "Construing Sen on Commitment," 19.

37. Sen, "Rational Fools," 326.

38. Although "commitment" has a positive connotation in ordinary speech, Sen does not assume that all behavior that takes commitment as its goal is morally worthy, or in the interest of most or all others. For example, a commitment in the form of group loyalty may involve sacrifice of one's "purely personal" interests for the sake of the group or the group's cause, yet the cause may not be a morally good one. Furthermore, some forms of commitment are morally suspect because of the way that the self is sublimated, as often happens with oppressed persons who come to believe that they are naturally or deservedly treated as second-class citizens.

39. Pettit, "Construing Sen on Commitment," esp. 18–20.

40. Sen discusses the rationality of such commitments in *The Idea of Justice* (Cambridge, MA: Harvard University Press, 2009), 191–93. He argues that we can see such commitments as reflecting self-imposed behavioral constraints. Elsewhere I have argued for a model of agency that takes the foundational notion to be acting according to norms that one accepts in order to include such goal-displacing commitments as self-motivated if not autonomous actions. See Ann E. Cudd, "Commitment as Motivation: Sen's Theory of Agency and the Explanation of Behavior," *Economics and Philosophy* 30, special issue no. 1 (2014): 35–56.

41. Although it is true that Friedman says this is "generally" the motivation of shareholders, to the degree that it is not the motivation of shareholders it follows even less from his arguments that the obligation of corporations is to maximize profits.

42. Sen, "Goals, Commitment, and Identity," in *Rationality and Freedom*, 212.

43. I. B. Lee, "Implications of Sen's Concept of Commitment for the Economic Understanding of the Corporation," *Canadian Journal of Law & Jurisprudence* 21 (2008): 97–127.

44. I have not provided this argument here, admittedly, and doing so would take us too far afield.

45. Sen, *Idea of Justice*.

46. Ingrid Robeyns, "The Capability Approach," in *The Stanford Encyclopedia of Philosophy*, ed. Edward N. Zalta, Summer 2011 ed., http://plato.stanford.edu/archives/sum2011/entries/capability-approach/.

Christopher J. Berry is Professor Emeritus and Honorary Professorial Research Fellow, University of Glasgow, Scotland.

Norman Bowie is Professor Emeritus, Strategic Management and Entrepreneurship, and former Elmer L. Andersen Chair of Corporate Responsibility, Carlson School of Management, University of Minnesota, Minneapolis.

Todd Breyfogle is Director of Seminars for the Aspen Institute, Aspen, Colorado.

Nicholas Capaldi is Legendre-Soulé Distinguished Chair in Business Ethics and Professor of Management, College of Business, Loyola University New Orleans, New Orleans, Louisiana.

Henry C. Clark is Visiting Professor, Political Economy Project, Dartmouth College, Hanover, New Hampshire.

Ann E. Cudd is Dean of the College and Graduate School of Arts & Sciences and Professor of Philosophy, Boston University, Boston.

Douglas J. Den Uyl is Vice President of Educational Programs, Liberty Fund, Indianapolis, Indiana.

David Elstein is Associate Professor of Philosophy, State University of New York at New Paltz, New York.

Timothy Fuller is Professor of Political Science, Colorado College, Colorado Springs, Colorado.

Eugene Heath is Professor of Philosophy, State University of New York at New Paltz, New York.

Alan S. Kahan is Professor of British Civilization, Université de Versailles/Saint-Quentin-en-Yvelines, France.

Byron Kaldis is Professor of Philosophy and Dean of the School of Humanities, Hellenic Open University, Athens, Greece.

Eric Mack is Professor of Philosophy and Faculty Member of the Murphy Institute for Political Economy, Tulane University, New Orleans, Louisiana.

Alexei Marcoux is Professor of Business Ethics and Society and Senior Scholar in the Institute for Economic Inquiry, Heider College of Business, Creighton University, Omaha, Nebraska.

Deirdre N. McCloskey is Distinguished Professor of Economics, History, English, and Communication Emerita, University of Illinois at Chicago.

Fred D. Miller Jr. is Research Professor, Department of Philosophy and Center for the Philosophy of Freedom, University of Arizona, Tucson, and Professor Emeritus of Philosophy, Bowling Green State University, Bowling Green, Ohio.

Mark S. Peacock is Professor, Department of Social Science, York University, Toronto, Canada.

Munir Quddus is Professor of Economics and Dean, College of Business, and Associate Provost, Northwest Houston Center, Prairie View A&M University, Prairie View, Texas.

Salim Rashid is CIMB Professor, Universiti Utara Malaysia, and Professor Emeritus of Economics, University of Illinois, Urbana-Champagne.

Martin Schlag is Professor of Social Moral Theology, Pontifical University of the Holy Cross, Rome.

William H. Shaw is Professor of Philosophy, San Jose State University, San Jose, California.

Qing Tian is Associate Professor of Business Ethics, School of Business, Macau University of Science and Technology, Macau, People's Republic of China.

Karen I. Vaughn is Senior Fellow, F. A. Hayek Program for Advanced Study in Philosophy, Politics, and Economics at the Mercatus Center, George Mason University, and Professor Emerita of Economics, George Mason University, Fairfax, Virginia.

Matt Zwolinski is Professor of Philosophy and Co-Director of the Institute for Law and Philosophy, University of San Diego, California.

aesthetic perspective on commerce, of Adam Smith, 7, 242, 258, 261n30

agency problem, 27, 280n20, 371

agriculture: in ancient Greece, 33; evolution of market order and, 348; Ibn Khaldun on, 125, 127; Locke on property rights and, 165–66; Tocqueville on, 284

Albert the Great, ix, x, 99

altruism: Comtean, Mill's rejection of, 304, 305; Confucian virtue and, 56; Hayek's market order and, 352, 354

ambition: Hobbes on, 139, 150; Hume on, 226; Ibn Khaldun on, 120; Montesquieu on, 204, 210, 211; Smith's example of poor boy with, ix, 247–48, 250, 251, 260n14, 260n17; Tocqueville on, 284

Ambrose, bishop of Milan, 79–81

Annenkov, Pavel, 322

Aquinas. *See* Thomas Aquinas

Aristophanes, 34

Aristotelian business ethicists, 263

Aristotle, 31–52; as ambiguous critic of business, 31–32, 48–49; business world at time of, 32–36, 49n5; on commerce, 36, 39–40, 42–43, 46–47, 48, 207, 231; denigration of craftsmen and laborers, 23, 35–36; early modern displacement of, 224; Homer and Hesiod compared to, 23, 24, 25, 26; Ibn Khaldun's influences from, 126, 132n4, 132n8, 133n27, 134n36; on justice, 37–39, 40; on the "natural," 132n4; on practical wisdom, 252, 254; on profit, 39–40, 43, 45, 47, 48; on sale of land, 29n67; teleological

reasoning of, 302; Thomas Aquinas's reasoning based on, 98, 99, 104, 107, 108, 109; on wealth, 24, 25, 26, 29n92, 46, 47

Aristotle's virtue ethics, 2, 5; conflicting views of capitalism and, 32; critique of business based on, 38–42; critique of his critique of business, 42–45; Friedman on businessperson's responsibility and, 51n33; Hartman on social capital and, 52n36; insights for the businessperson derived from, 45–49; principles of, 36–38; virtuous mean in, 37–38, 42–44

Asabiyah (Ibn Khaldun's notion of social cohesion), 120, 122–23, 130–31

associations, Tocqueville on, 285, 286, 298n7; business ethics and, 289–90, 292, 297, 298; collective individualism and, 290; enlightened self-interest and, 288, 292; stakeholder theory and, 292–93, 294; stockholder theory and, 295–96

Augustine: *City of God*, 78, 85–86; Manichaeanism of, 79, 81; monastic community of, 81–82, 83–85; personal history of, 77, 79, 81

Augustine's ethics of exchange, x, 5; business ethics and, 89, 91–92; commerce and, 76, 88, 103; human questions underlying, 76–77; late Roman empire and, 77–79; law and, 76, 86, 88, 89–90; love and, 75, 77, 82–83, 85, 86, 88, 89–91; slave trading and, 75–76; social and spiritual economies in, 75; unity of the social order and, 6, 75, 86–88, 89,

Augustine's ethics of exchange (*cont.*)
90, 91, 92; value and, 76, 83–85, 86;
wealth and, 75, 76, 79, 81, 82, 84, 85,
86, 87–90, 91
autonomy: instrumental model of corporations and, 413; Mill on, 304, 305,
306, 311–12, 313, 314, 315, 316, 317,
319n11; Sen on self-interest and, 410.
See also freedom or liberty
avarice. *See* greed or avarice

balanced reciprocity: Hesiod's world and,
21; Homer's world and, 14
bankers, in classical Greece, 33, 34, 50n9.
See also lending money at interest
Barbon, Nicholas, 224
barter: Aristotle's analysis of, 38–39; in
Homer's world, 14, 16; Locke on transition to money instead of, 165
B corporations, 275
Ben & Jerry's, 394
beneficence, duty of: duty of corporate
managers to seek profit and, 274, 275,
276–79; Kant on, 276
benevolence (goodness): as Confucian virtue, 56–57, 60, 61, 62, 64, 67; as virtue
for Smith, 250
Bentham, Jeremy, 302, 304, 305, 310, 319n13
Berry, Christopher J., 7
Blanc, Louis, 310
Boatright, John, 379n34
borrowing, Hesiod's view of, 20–21. *See also*
lending money at interest
Bowie, Norman, 7
Bragues, George, 196n3
Breyfogle, Todd, x, 5
British Petroleum, 268
Brown, John, 222, 235n9
Brown, Peter, 77
Buffett, Warren, 156n12
business associations, Tocqueville on, 285,
286, 289–90
business ethics: abstract philosophical reasoning applied to, 3; applied questions
vs. institutional structure questions in,
382–83; Augustine's relevance to, 89,
91–92; Confucianism and (*see* Confucian business ethics); dictum "Good
ethics is good business," 265, 267, 269,
271, 275; fundamental disciplines required by, 155n4; Hobbes's relevance to,
135–36, 140, 153–55; Hume on virtues
and, 230, 233–34; main themes in,
312; Mandeville's insights relevant to,
179–80, 190–96; Marxist analysis and,
331–36; Mill and, 304, 312–17; Montesquieu's list of virtues and, 216; negative

model in contemporary scholarship of,
199n33; philosophers' limited interest
in, 263–64; Rawls and, 381–85, 387,
394; Sen and, 401–3, 406–8; Smithean
reputational sensitivity and, 257–58;
Thomas Aquinas's relevance to, 104–5,
106, 108, 110; three levels of academic
analysis in, 360; Tocqueville's relevance
to, 284, 289–98. *See also* commerce;
corporate social responsibility; wealth
business judgment rule, 278, 281n32

Capaldi, Nicholas, viii–ix, 8
capitalism: exploitation of labor in, 327,
328, 329, 335; Flew's defense of, 31–32;
Freeman on philosophical assessment
of, 136; Freeman's stakeholder theory
and, 292; Kantian, 264, 266, 275–79;
MacIntyre's critique of, 31; Marx on,
322, 323, 324–31; Marx's relevance to
business ethics and, 331–36; Rawls on,
385, 387, 392, 394, 396n18, 398n48;
Weber on Confucianism as obstacle to,
53. *See also* laissez-faire
Carr, Albert, 384
Carson, Thomas, 360
catallaxy, 347, 355
categorical imperative: Kant and, 264, 266,
275; Mill's incorporation of, 303, 305;
misunderstandings of, 264; stakeholder
theory and, 266, 293, 294; three formulations of, 275; in treating all affected
by the firm, 276; to treat others as ends,
not means, 2, 266, 275
Cathy, Dan T., 365
Chan, Joseph, 61
character: in Confucianism, 55–56; Smith
on, 244, 246, 248, 250, 254, 255, 256,
258, 261n29
Chick-fil-A, 365
Christensen, Clayton, 258
Christian ethics: Augustine's relevance to
business ethics and, 91–92; central role
of avarice in, 96–97; common values
with Islam, 130; in late Roman Empire,
79–81
Cicero: on community of interest, 86; Hume's
rejection of values of, 223, 227–28; on
wealth, 77–78, 79, 80
Citizens United decision, 297
Ciulla, Joanne B., 156n11, 199n33
civil society: Hobbes and, 136, 149; Montesquieu and, 203
Clark, Henry C., ix, x, 7
class distinctions: Augustine's world and,
77, 78, 80–81; Marx on, 321, 322, 323–
24, 325, 336; Mill's aim to dispose of,

314, 317; in Smith's analysis, 309–10; utopian socialists and, 310

classical liberalism: Confucian government more activist than, 59; Rawlsian thought and, 391, 393, 395

codes of conduct, and practical know-how, 193

Cohen, Edward E., 50n9

Cohen, G. A., 396n10

coin: in classical Greece, 26; of gold in late Roman Empire, 78; Thomas Aquinas on abuse of king's power and, 108

collective individualism, 289–91, 293, 294, 295

commerce: Aristotle on, 36, 39–40, 42–43, 46–47, 48, 207, 231; Augustine on, 76, 88, 103; classical Greek prejudice against, 11, 27n26; Hesiod and, 11, 21–23, 25, 29n70; historical antipathy to, 11, 27n26, 103, 221, 222–24, 225–26; Hobbes on, 136, 146, 149, 154–55; in Homeric society, 11, 14–15, 16–19, 25; Hume's defense of, 221–22, 225–30, 234–35; Ibn Khaldun on, 115–16, 117, 124–30; in Islam, 130; Locke on, 158–59, 175–76; Mandeville's conception of, 179–80, 181, 182–88, 190, 195–96; medieval moralists on, 103; Montesquieu on humanity and justice in, 213–15, 216; Montesquieu on laws required by, 203; Plato and, 11, 25–26; Smith on beauty of, ix, 242, 246, 247, 248, 250–52, 254, 255, 256, 258–59; terminology related to, 27n26, 235n1; Thomas Aquinas and, ix, 95, 97, 102–5; Tocqueville on democratic societies and, 284; Xenophon on, 11, 26. *See also* industrialism, Mill on transition to; trade

Commercial Revolution, 95

commercial society: Hume on, 221, 222, 225, 228, 229, 231, 234–35; Locke's defense of, 158, 175–76 (*see also* Locke, John); Mandeville on, 179, 185, 193; Smith on, 222, 229, 244, 250, 251–52

commitment, Sen on, 409, 411–16, 419n38, 419n40

commodity speculation, Aristotle on, 41–42, 44–45, 48

common good: Hume on commercial society and, 222; Thomas Aquinas on, 6, 99–102, 105, 111, 114n71. *See also* public good

Communism: Hayek's response to, 354; Mill on, 307–8, 309. *See also* Marx, Karl

competition: Confucian view of, 59, 61, 65; Friedman on proper role of business executives and, 363; in general equilibrium theory, 343, 344, 345; Ibn Khaldun

on cunning traders and, 127–28; Ibn Khaldun on prosperity deriving from, 116; Marx on, 332; in Mill's market economy, 314, 316

Confucian business ethics, x; balancing different interests in, 67; decision-making and, 63–64, 68; general principles for, 58; leadership and, 58–62, 68; limitations of, 54–55; nepotism and, 61; not a substitute for institutional measures, 68; organizational citizenship behavior and, 62–63, 71n58; requiring extrapolation from original sources, 53–54, 55, 67–68; roles of individual and organization in, 54

Confucian ethics: government promotion of, 58–59; polarized positions on, 54, 67; social environment and, 57; virtues in, 5, 55–58, 60, 61, 62, 65, 66, 67, 68

Confucianism: current business practices in China and, 53–54, 66, 67; difficulty of defining, 54; focused on practice rather than theory, 53; harmonious society and, 64–67, 68; historical significance of, 53; two most significant thinkers of, 55 (*see also* Kongzi; Mengzi)

consumer protection laws, in spirit of Ibn Khaldun, 130

consumptibility, Thomas Aquinas's argument from, 109

consumption: Augustine on unlimited desire for, 88, 89; Thomas Aquinas's understanding of, 97

contract: classical liberalism on liberty of, 393, 394; Hayek on laws of, 349, 351, 353; Locke on moral right of, 157–58, 168, 173, 174, 175. *See also* social contract

contracts: Hobbes on, 146, 154, 156n13; Hume on justice and, 233; implicit, 156n13; of Mill's firm or corporation, 313, 314, 315. *See also* promise keeping

contractual duties of corporate management, 265–66, 272–73, 274–75, 405

cooperation: Confucian focus on, 64–65; Mandeville on, 182, 183, 189, 192, 196; in Prisoner's Dilemma, 415; Smith's "aesthetic perspective" and, 258

cooperatives of workers, Mill and, 310, 313–15

corporate legitimacy, principle of, 291

corporate moral obligation models, 404

corporate moral responsibility (CMR) model, 404

corporate social responsibility: Augustine's ethics and, 89, 90, 91; Kantian capitalism and, 275–77, 279; Mandeville on incompatibilities in, 194–95; Marxist

corporate social responsibility (*cont.*)
analysis and, 334; Mill's political
economy and, 316–17; mutual funds
based on, 275, 365–66; profit and, 194,
273, 274, 361, 371, 374–75, 379n34,
402; scholarship before 1970s on, 263;
Sen's theories and, 402; three different
approaches to, 361–62, 376–77. *See also*
Friedman on corporate social responsibility; philanthropy, corporate
corporations: *Citizens United* decision and,
297; codes of conduct vs. practical know-
how in, 193; Confucian thought and, 5,
58, 60, 64, 67, 68; informal norms vs.
governance mechanisms for, 257; Kantian position on seeking profit, 265–66,
272–73; Marx's analysis and, 333–34;
Mill's political economy and, 313–16;
models for moral obligation of, 403–4,
416 (*see also* instrumental model of
corporate behavior); narrow focus on
shareholder value in, 257–58; nonprofit,
403, 405; Sen's theory of commitment
and, 415; Tocqueville on associations
and, 285, 286–87, 294; Tocqueville on
collective individualism and, 290.
See also firms
Cudd, Ann E., 9

Dawood, N. J., 119
Dayton, Kenneth, 267
debt: in Hesiod's view of community, 21;
Ibn Khaldun on decay of society and,
120, 121, 131. *See also* lending money
at interest; public debt
deception in business: Carr on bluffing and,
384; vs. failure to disclose, 187–88
Decretum Gratiani, 103
DeGeorge, Richard, 263
democracy: condemned by Aristotle, 35;
Confucian critics of, 70n30; Hobbes
and, 144; Rawls on, 385, 390–92, 395,
398n48; in Thomas Aquinas's mixed
polity, 107; Tocqueville and, 283–84,
285–87, 291–92, 297, 298, 311
democratic socialism, Rawls on, 385
Demosthenes, 34
Den Uyl, Douglas J., ix, 7
deontology: Confucianism as form of, 56;
instrumental model and, 405, 413; of
Kant, 301
Dicey, A. V., 303
difference principle, 381, 388, 390–92,
397n33
dignity: Augustine on, 75, 82, 83; Mill on,
ix, 8, 305–6; Thomas Aquinas on, 97,
104, 108

distributive justice, Aristotle on, 37–38.
See also redistribution
diversity, Confucian harmony in, 65.
See also pluralism
division of labor (specialization): Hayek on
prehistory of trade and, 348; Hume on,
232–33; Ibn Khaldun on, 119, 123; in
Mandeville's commercial society, 186;
in Marx's analysis, 327–28; Mill on danger of, 309; Smith on, 254, 255
Dobson, John, 48
Donaldson, Thomas, 263, 404
doux commerce, 213–15, 218n52
Dover, Kenneth, 34
Dunfee, Thomas, 263
Duns Scotus, 103, 109
Duska, Ronald, 268–69
duties specified by Rawls, 384, 396n13
dutifulness as Confucian virtue, 56
duty within Kantian ethics: of beneficence
by corporate manager, 274, 275, 276–
79; imperfect duties, 274, 275, 276–77,
278, 279; perfect duty for manager to
seek profit, 272, 274, 276–79; purity
of the will and, 264, 265, 268–70, 271;
Tocqueville on enlightened self-interest
and, 289

economic growth: Hayek on conditions for,
351, 354; Mill's endorsement of, 309,
310, 311; Smith's invisible hand and,
346
economic planning: Hayek's arguments
against, 341, 343–46, 352; Lockean
liberty narrative and, 306
economics: Ibn Khaldun's contributions
to, 119; interwar sentiment for central
planning in, 343; labor theory of value
abandoned by, 327; neoclassical, 99, 346,
409; subjectivist revolution of 1870s in,
171; Thomas Aquinas on ethics and,
95, 98–99, 104–5, 110
Elstein, David, x, 5
empathy, as Confucian virtue, 56, 62
employer-employee relationships: Augustinian ethics and, 89; Confucian virtues
and, 63, 64, 67
Engels, Friedrich, 321, 325, 329, 330, 332
enlightened self-interest, Tocqueville on,
287–89, 291, 292, 293, 294, 296, 298
Entine, Jon, 365
entrepreneurship: in Hobbes's commonwealth, 150; Rawlsian principles and,
390; social, 90, 91
environmental concern: Augustinian ethics
and, 89; Confucian values and, 66;
technological project and, 307

equal basic liberties, principle of, 381
equality: economic planning and, 343; Locke on, 162, 306; Mill on, 303–4, 311, 316; Rawls on justice and, 383, 388, 389; Rousseau/Marx narrative of, 306, 307, 311; Tocqueville on democracy and, x, 283, 285, 286, 287, 288, 294
equality of opportunity: Lockean liberty narrative and, 306; Mill on, 311, 316; Rawls on, 383, 390, 397n33
Evan, William, 266
executive compensation, in Mill's cooperative, 314
extended market order, 351–52, 353, 355
extrinsic titles to interest, 109–10

Fable of the Bees, The (Mandeville), 128, 179–82, 186–87, 188–89, 191; in background to Hume, 225; Montesquieu and, 202, 208–9
fair dealing: Mandeville on market prices and, 187–88; Sen on trust and, 406
fair distribution of wealth, as Confucian value, 60
fairness, Rawls's principle of, 384, 396n14
fair pricing, Thomas Aquinas's principles for, 106
feminist economics, 401
feminist theorists, 263. See also Mill, J. S.: on emancipation of women
Ferguson, Adam, 189
feudalism: abolished in French Revolution, 211; condemnation of commerce in, 103; Hume on collapse of, 228, 231–32; Marx on, 323; Mill's interest in transition from, 302, 309, 310, 313, 316; Smith on decline of, 208
fidelity, Rawls's principle of, 384
final causality: Hobbes on civil peace and, 143–44; Thomas Aquinas and the Scholastics on, 98, 100. See also teleological reasoning
Finley, Moses, 14, 27n26
firms: created to serve human needs, 52n39; Mill's political economy and, 313–16; as moral agents, 378n15. See also corporations
Flew, Antony, 31–32
Forman-Barzilai, Fonna, 261n24
Fourier, Charles, 310, 313, 325
four-stages theory, 203
freedom of speech, and Rawlsian economic liberties, 388
freedom or liberty: Cicero on public involvement and, 227; empirically correlated with property rights, 397n37; Hayek on, 343, 350, 351, 352, 354, 355, 357n37,

358n44; Hobbes on, 135, 141–47, 152, 153; Hume on, 222, 231, 232, 234, 235; Locke on, 157, 161–63, 173–74; in Mandeville's commercial society, 185; Marx on, 331; Mill on, 303–4, 306, 309, 311–12 (see also autonomy); in modern moral philosophy, 302; Rawls on, 383, 386, 388–90, 393–94, 395; Scholastic teachings on the common good and, 111; Smith's norm of freedom of choice, 255; Smith's "system of natural liberty," 137, 242, 249, 260n7, 346; Tocqueville on democratic societies and, 286, 287
Freeman, R. Edward: Kantian capitalism and, 266, 293; stakeholder theory and, 266, 267, 268, 291, 292; on theoretical frameworks, 136, 263
free trade: Hume's argument for, 227, 234; Mill's favorable view of, 316
French, Peter, 378n15
Friedman, Milton, as important economic thinker, 359
Friedman on corporate social responsibility, 8–9, 359–80; Aristotle's virtue ethics and, 51n33; consistent with Mill's position, 312, 317; different types of CSR and, 361–62; epistemic concern in, 363–66, 369; fiduciary concern in, 369–72, 377; four main concerns in, 362, 363–73; instrumental model and, 404, 405; jurisdictional concern in, 370, 372–73, 377; Kantian duties and, 272–73, 274; New York Times Magazine article and, vii, 359–60, 361, 362, 371–72, 377n3; Pareto-improving version and, 361–62, 374–77; political version and, 362, 376; published sources on, 360–61, 362; Sen's ideas and, 403, 413, 414; stockholder theory and, 295, 374–75, 378n8; summary of his views on, 362–63; technocratic concern in, 366–69; zero-sum version and, 361, 362, 366, 371, 372–73, 374, 375, 376, 377. See also corporate social responsibility
Fromherz, Allen, 122
frugality: Hume on, 228; Mandeville on, 181–82, 183–84; Smith on prudent man and, 244, 245, 246, 249, 250
Fukuyama, Francis, 123
Fuller, Timothy, x, 6

Gandhi, Mahatma, 32
Gaus, Gerald, 385, 393, 397n37
Gellner, Ernest, 122, 132n12
general equilibrium theory, 343, 344–45
generalized reciprocity: Hesiod's community and, 21; in Homeric society, 15

general will, 307

generosity, Thomas Aquinas on, 107–8

gift giving: in Hesiod, 12, 20; in Homeric society, 12, 13, 15, 18, 24, 27n29, 27n31

global economy: Mill's favorable view of, 316; Montesquieu on, 206–7; Smith and, 255, 256–57

gold: Commercial Revolution and, 95; in late Roman Empire, 78, 80

Golden Rule: Confucian virtue and, 56, 62; Hobbes on, 147; Mandeville's example of, 187

"Good ethics is good business," 265, 267, 269, 271, 275

government: bailouts of businesses by, 351; business ethics questions related to, 382–83; Confucian concern about, 57, 58–60, 61, 64, 68, 70n30; Hobbes on representative government, 150–53; Hume on stability of commercial society under, 232, 234; Ibn Khaldun on, 116–17, 128–30; Locke's radical limitation of, 157, 306; Mill's opposition to interference by, 319n37; Montesquieu on, 201, 205, 210–11, 215; in Rousseau/Marx equality narrative, 307; Smith on economic interventions by, 242; theorists of the modern state, 136, 140. *See also* law; state ownership of means of production; taxation

government regulation: in ancient Greek economy, 33–34; Hayek on, 351, 357n35, 380n37; Ibn Khaldun on, 116, 122, 130; justified for collective action problems, 380n37; Mandeville on alternatives to, 190–91; Rawls's goal of justice and, 385–86, 391; Tocqueville on, 296

Gravina, Giovanni, 205

Greece of classical period: business world in, 32–36, 49n5; changes from archaic period, 11, 23–26; unfavorable view of business in, 34–35

greed or avarice: Ambrose on, 81; vs. appropriate self-interest, 111; Augustine on slave traders and, 76; in Augustine's earthly city, 85, 90; historical opposition to commerce and, 224, 226; Hume on, 226–27; Ibn Khaldun's toleration of, 128; Islamic caution on perils of, 121, 124, 130; Marx on capitalists and, 332; not peculiar to commerce, ix; Thomas Aquinas on, ix, 96–97, 103, 104, 107, 108, 110; Tocqueville on, 286

Grumbling Hive, The (Mandeville), 128, 179, 180, 186, 187, 193

Hanley, Ryan, 260n14

happiness: Aristotle on, 25, 36–37, 46–48; Duns Scotus on commerce and, 103; freedoms conducive to, 311; Hume on, 225, 227, 229, 235; Locke on pursuit of, 157, 159, 160–61, 162–63, 167, 173, 306; in Rousseau/Marx equality narrative, 307; Smith on, 244, 247, 248, 250, 252, 254; Thomas Aquinas on, 96; utilitarianism and, 305–6

harmony, Confucian idea of, 64–67

Hartman, Edwin M., 31, 52n36

Hasnas, John, 374, 404, 405, 413

Hayek, Friedrich, ix, 8, 341–58; on cultural and political context of markets, 341–42, 351; economic planning and, 341, 343–46, 352; extended market order of, 351–52, 353, 355; on freedom, 343, 350, 351, 352, 354, 355, 357n37, 358n44; on historical evolution of markets, 346–48; on inequality of wealth, 352–54, 357n42; on knowledge in markets, 342, 345–46, 349, 350, 351; Lockean liberty narrative and, 307, 311; overview of scholarship of, 341–42; on rules in social interaction, 348–51, 353, 355, 357n40; "Socialist Calculation," 355n5, 356nn7–8; on social justice, 351–54, 357n42; on society conducive to wealth, 341, 342, 348, 349–50, 351, 354; on spontaneous order, 345, 346, 357n40

Heath, Eugene, 6–7

Hegel, G. W. F.: Marx's debt to, 324; Mill's ethics and, 302, 303, 304; moral imagination and, 140

Hendry, John, 137

Henson, Richard, 270

Herman, Barbara, 270, 271–72

Hesiod's *Works and Days*: as advice to small, independent farmer, 11, 19–23; archaic Greek context of, 11; commerce and, 11, 21–23, 25, 29n70; as historical source, 12; labor in, 19, 23; season for sailing in, 21–23, 25, 29n92; wealth in, 20–21, 22, 24, 25

Hobbes, Thomas, x–xi, 6, 135–56; on commerce, 136, 146, 149, 154–55; commercial activity in time of, 136, 156n5; on contracts, 146, 154, 156n13; Hume's thought in relation to, 224; on individual's relation to society, 302; on justice, 136, 148; laws of nature (maxims) of, 136, 138, 143, 145, 146, 147–48, 149, 153, 155; *Leviathan*, 135, 136, 138–39, 140, 147, 150, 153, 154; on liberty and authority, 135, 141–47, 152, 153; Mandeville's view of value and, 184; moral imagination and, 135, 136, 138–40, 145–46, 147, 149, 154, 155; relevance to modern business ethics, 135–36, 140, 153–55; representative government and, 150–53; on rule of law, 135, 136, 139, 140, 142–44, 145, 147–50, 151, 152; on social contract, 149, 302; on wealth, 139, 140, 143

Hofstede, Geert, 72n59

Homer's epics: archaic Greek context of, 11; aristocratic focus of, 11, 13, 15, 19; commerce in, 11, 14–15, 16–19, 25; external movement of wealth in, 15–19; as historical source, 12; internal movement of wealth in, 13–15; monetary economy in, 17; "professional" vs. "occasional" trade in, 16, 17, 29n70; status of laborers in, 18–19, 23; wealth in, 12–19, 24, 27n21

human capital: Ibn Khaldun on, 119, 123; Locke on, 166, 167, 168, 175. *See also* labor

humanity, Montesquieu on, 202, 204, 212–15, 216

humanomics, vii, viii

Hume, David, 7, 221–39; context of his defense of commerce, 224–25; defense of commerce by, 221–22, 225–30, 234–35; defense of luxury by, 222, 225–26, 227, 229–31, 234; on freedom, 222, 231, 232, 234, 235; on justice, 230, 233–34; Lockean liberty narrative and, 306; Mandeville and, 189, 224–25; on value of refinement, 228–29, 230–31

Hutcheson, Francis, 226

hypernorms, 263

Ibn Khaldun, xi, 6, 115–34; on commerce, 115–16, 117, 124–30; on the cunning vs. the unethical, 125, 127–28, 130; on justice, 116, 129, 130; life of, 118; on "natural" commercial activities, 116, 117, 125, 126, 127, 130, 132n4; policy prescriptions of, 116–17, 128–30; as precursor to modern thought, 115, 116, 119, 129, 130; on productive vs. unproductive activities, 125–26, 130; on rise and fall of civilizations, 115–16, 117, 119–23, 130, 131; on "unnatural" activities, 126–27. *See also* Islam

imagination, Smith on, 242, 247, 250, 255. *See also* moral imagination

immigrants, Locke on value of, 168

import-export business: of ancient Greek city-states, 32, 33, 34, 35; criticized in Plato's *The Laws*, 35

incentive problems, for property-owning democracy, 391–92

incentives, reduction of ethics to, x

individual in relation to society, the, 302, 318n3; Mill on, 304, 306

individualism: collective, 289–91, 293, 294, 295; of Locke, 157, 158; MacIntyre's critique of capitalism and, 31; of Mill and Hayek, ix; Tocqueville on, 285–87, 289, 297

industrialism, Mill on transition to, 302, 309, 310, 313, 316

inequality: in archaic Athens, 24; Augustine on the social order and, 87–88; Confucian concern for inequality of wealth, 58; in great republics of antiquity, 216; Hayek on inequality of wealth, 352–54, 357n42; inevitable in Lockean economy, 306, 307; Locke's theory of property and, 166; as market signal, 392; Marx's critique of capitalism and, 328; Mill on, 308, 311, 313; Plato's aversion to, 24; power distance and, 63, 72n59; Rawls on, 383, 388, 392, 396n18, 397n33; Tocqueville on ambition leading to, 283–84

inflation: corporate social responsibility and, 367; as hidden form of taxation, 108; Ibn Khaldun on, 121

instrumental model of corporate behavior, 402, 403, 404; arguments for, 405–6, 413; defined, 402; self-interest and, 405–6, 413, 418n26; Sen's arguments against, 405–8, 410, 413–16. *See also* stockholder theory

Integrated Social Contracts Theory, 263

investments, Ibn Khaldun on, 116. *See also* shareholders

invisible hand of Adam Smith, 256, 261n27, 261n33; Friedman and Hasnas on interest of shareholders and, 405; Hayek's spontaneous order and, 345, 346; Montesquieu on honor or vanity and, 211; Tocqueville on enlightened self-interest and, 290

Islam: critical of market excesses, 130; friendly to commerce, 124, 130; Ibn Khaldun's reliance on, 124; modest living emphasized by, 119, 121. *See also* Ibn Khaldun

Jevons, W. S., 306

Jews, in commerce of medieval Europe, 207–8

Johnson, Samuel, 2

justice: Aristotle on, 37–39, 40; Hayek on inequality of wealth and, 352–54; Hesiod on prosperity and, 22; Hobbes on, 136, 148; Hume on, 230, 233–34; Ibn justice (*cont.*)

Khaldun on, 116, 129, 130; ideal theory of, 391, 398n53, 416; in Mandeville's commercial society, 185, 186; Marx on capitalism and, 329–30; Marx on communism and, 339n42; Montesquieu on, 202, 204, 212–15, 216; Rawlsian principles of, 381, 383–84, 385, 388, 395n7, 396nn8–10, 396n14, 397n33 (*see also* Rawls, John); Sen on, 414–15, 416; Smith on, 249, 250, 255; Thomas Aquinas on (*see* Thomas Aquinas on justice); Wittgenstein's language games and, viii. *See also* social justice

just price: Locke on, 169–71; Thomas Aquinas on, 6, 99, 105–6, 111

Kahan, Alan S., x, 7–8

Kant, Immanuel, 7, 263–81; avoided by many business ethicists, 263; deontology and, 301; fundamental misunderstanding about, 264; moral imagination and, 140; multiple motives for an action and, 269–72; profit and, 264, 265–69, 271–79; purity of the will and, 264–66, 268–72; relation of individual to society and, 302; shopkeeper example of, 265, 269; stakeholder theory and, 266–68; Tocquevillean perspective and, 289, 293, 294, 298. *See also* categorical imperative; duty within Kantian ethics

Kantian capitalism, 264, 266, 275–77; Freeman's early version of, 266; residual problem for, 277–78; summary of, 279

Kay, John, 257

Keynes, John Maynard, 343

know-how, Mandeville on, 191–93

Kongzi (Confucius), x, 5, 55–57, 59–60, 64, 65, 66

labor: Aristotle on degradation of, 23, 35–36; in Hesiod's *Works and Days*, 19, 23; in Homer's epics, 18–19, 23; Ibn Khaldun on value of, 116, 119, 125, 127; Islamic thought on fair compensation for, 124; Locke on opportunity and, 167–68, 171; Locke on property and, ix, 101, 163–64, 165–66, 168; Locke on treatment of the poor and, 171–72; Locke on value created by, 168, 176n10, 177n21; Marx on, 322, 323, 326; Plato on, 24; Rawlsian principles and, 387, 389–90; Thomas Aquinas on merchant's profit for, 103, 104; Xenophon on, 23–24

labor theory of value: abandoned by mainstream economics, 327; abandoned by Mill, 311; of Marx, 326–27

laesio enormis, 105–6

laissez-faire: Mill and, 319n37; Smith and, 242, 259n6

laissez-faire capitalism, Rawls on, 385, 396n18

land: in ancient Greek city-states, 33; Aristotle on sale of, 29n67; Augustine on divine law and, 88; in Hesiod's *Works and Days*, 19, 21; in Homer's epics, 13; Locke on, ix, 88, 165–66, 176n10; Roman currency increasingly divorced from, 78; Tocqueville on independence from government and, 296

Lange, Oscar, xi, 343–44

Langholm, Odd, 106

Laum, Bernhard, 27n21

law: ancient Greek economy and, 34; Augustine on, 76, 86, 88, 89–90; Confucian ideals and, x, 61–62, 66, 68; Hayek on, 349, 350, 351, 357n30; Hobbes on rule of, 135, 136, 139, 140, 142–44, 145, 147–50, 151, 152; Hume on, 222, 231–32, 234; Ibn Khaldun on, 116, 124, 129, 130; Lockean "laws of liberty," 157, 168, 175; Lockean liberty narrative and, 306; Mandeville's framework of, 185, 186, 196; Marx on, 323; Montesquieu on, 202–3; Thomas Aquinas on, 99, 100, 101, 102

laws of nature (maxims) of Hobbes, 136, 138, 143, 145, 146, 147–48, 149, 153, 155

leadership: Confucian business ethics and, 57, 58–62, 68; Ibn Khaldun on *Asabiyah* and, 123, 131; Thomas Aquinas on *magnificentia* and, 108

left Smitheans, 242

lending money at interest: in ancient Greece, 33, 34, 50n9; Aristotle's objections to, 36, 41, 43–44, 48; Augustine on, 89–90; modern business ethics and, 110; Roman law and, 109, 114n66. *See also* usury

letters of exchange, Montesquieu on, 204, 207, 208

Leviathan (Hobbes), 135, 136, 138–39, 140, 147, 150, 153, 154

liberal capitalism, Rawlsian principles compatible with, 387–94

liberal individualism, of Locke, 157, 158

liberal socialism, Rawls on, 385

liberty. *See* freedom or liberty

Livy, 223, 224, 227, 228

Locke, John, 6, 157–78; on assistance to the poor, 171–72, 178n30; commercial society as endorsed by, 158–59, 175–76; "enough and as good" proviso of, 159,

164–65, 166, 167, 168, 171, 177n17; equality and, 162, 306; fundamental moral and political principles of, 159–63; Hume's thought in relation to, 224; individual's relation to society and, 302; on just price, 169–71; on labor, ix, 101, 163–64, 165–66, 167–68, 171–72, 176n10, 177n21; liberal individualism of, 157, 158; monarchical authority and, 159, 172; on money, 78, 164, 165, 166–68, 177n18; moral imagination and, 140; mutual gains in prosperity and, 158–59, 166, 168, 171, 175; on property rights, ix, 101, 157–58, 159, 163–68, 173, 174–75, 176; on religious toleration, 157–58, 172–75, 176, 178n32; restraints on trade and, 159; virtues rewarded by commercial society and, 159

Lockean liberty narrative, 306–7, 309, 311–12

Lomasky, Loren, 389

love: Augustine's ethics of exchange and, 75, 77, 82–83, 85, 86, 88, 89–91; Thomas Aquinas on common good and, 101

luxury: becoming necessity, 230–31; historically negative view of, 222–24, 228, 229–30, 234; Hume on supposed link to military weakness, 229–30; Hume on "vicious" type of, 231; Hume's defense of, 222, 225–26, 227, 229–31, 234; Ibn Khaldun on corrupting influence of, 119–20; Mandeville on, 181–82, 183–84, 224–25, 230, 231; Montesquieu on, 209, 210

Machiavelli, Niccolò, social contract and, 149

MacIntyre, Alasdair, 31, 48, 201

Mack, Eric, 6

Mackey, John, 362, 368, 374–76

Macy, Jonathan, 257

Malthus, Thomas, 310–11

Mandeville, Bernard, 6–7, 179–200; anticipated by Ibn Khaldun, 128; conception of commerce, 179–80, 181, 182–88, 190, 195–96; Hume and, 189, 224–25; justice and, 185, 186; on know-how vs. theoretical knowledge, 191–93; on luxury, 181–82, 183–84, 224–25, 230, 231; maxims gleaned from, 180, 188–95; Montesquieu and, 202, 208–12, 215–16; on moral ideals and empirical reality, 193–95; overview of, 179–80; pluralism of, 180, 182, 184–85, 186, 195; on the poor, 229; relevance to business ethics, 179–80, 190–96; on unintended beneficial outcomes, 188–91, 196; virtue as represented by, 179, 180–82, 185, 193,

196nn2–3, 196n7; writings of, 180–82 (see also *Fable of the Bees*; *Grumbling Hive*)

Marcoux, Alexei, 8–9, 294

Marcus Aurelius, 207

market economies: central planning and, 343; Lockean liberty narrative and, 306; Mill on, 309, 310, 311, 314, 316; personal freedom in regimes with, 397n37; Rawls and, xi, 382, 386, 387, 390–91, 394–95; Rousseau/Marx narrative and, 307; Sen on trust in, 401

market prices: Augustine on value and, 83–85; Ibn Khaldun on, 116; Locke on, 169–71; Mandeville's example of fair dealing about, 187–88; Rawls on, 386–87, 390, 392; Scholastics' discovery of laws of, 99

markets: depersonalized in economics, 99; Hayek on, 341–42, 345–48, 349, 350, 351; Ibn Khaldun on, 116; nonjudgmental logic of, 104; Sen and, 401

market socialism: of interwar pro-planning economists, 343, 346; Rawls on, 385

Marx, Karl, 8, 321–39; business ethics and, 331–36; on capitalism, 322, 323, 324–29; equality narrative and, 306, 307; historical materialism of, 321–24; on justice, 329–30, 339n42; normative dimension in thought of, 329–31

materialism, Tocqueville on, 286, 295, 296

McCloskey, Deirdre, on virtues, 201, 261n20

Mele, Alfonso, 22, 29n70

Melon, J.-F., 230

Menander, 34

Mengzi (Mencius), x, 5, 55–57, 58, 59–60

mercantilism: of aristocratic landlords, 310; Mandeville and, 183, 197n19; Montesquieu and, 206

Mill, James, 302

Mill, J. S., 8, 301–20; autonomy and, 304, 305, 306, 311–12, 313, 314, 315, 316, 317, 319n11; business ethics and, 304, 312–17; on emancipation of women, 302, 310, 316; on human condition, 302–4; liberty vs. equality and, 306–7; political economy and, 301–2, 306–12, 313; utilitarianism of, viii–ix, 2, 301, 303, 304–6

Millar, John, 203

Miller, Fred D. Jr., viii, 5

Millett, P., 50n9

minimum wage, Rawls on, 387

money: Aristotle on abuses of, 108; Aristotle on just exchange and, 38–39; Aristotle's criticism of commerce and, 39, 46, 47; Aristotle's highest ends and, 48;

money (*cont.*)

Augustine on use of, 86; four standard functions of, 17; in Homeric society, 17; Locke on property rights and, 164, 165, 166–68, 177n18; Locke on value and, 78; Mandeville on, 183, 184; Thomas Aquinas on, 96, 97, 104, 107–10. *See also* coin; lending money at interest; wealth

monopoly: aristocratic landlords and, 310; Aristotle's disapproval of Thales and, 41–42, 44; Confucian values and, 59; in England of Locke's time, 159, 176n3; Hume's opposition to patents and, 234; Rawls on, 387; Smith's concern about, 116; Tocquevillean stockholder theory and, 295

Montaigne, 288

Montesquieu, ix, x, 7, 201–19; ancients vs. moderns and, 203–4, 213, 214; commercial morality as subject of, 202; on communications and commerce, 204, 206; conquest vs. commerce and, 204–5, 207, 210, 214; on *doux commerce*, 213–15, 218n52; on Dutch spirit of commerce, 215; four-stages theory and, 203; historical perspective on commercial morality, 202–8; on honor and vanity, 209–11, 215–16; on justice and humanity, 202, 204, 212–15, 216; on letters of exchange, 204, 207, 208; Mandeville as context for, 202, 208–12, 215–16; relevance to business ethics, 216; *The Spirit of the Laws*, 201, 202, 207, 210, 213; usury and, 202, 207–8; virtue ethics and, 201, 202, 211–15, 216

moral free space, 263

moral imagination: Buffett and, 156n12; Ciulla on, 156n11; defined, 138; Hobbes and, 135, 136, 138–40, 145–46, 147, 149, 154, 155

Moriarty, Jeffrey, 396n10

multinational corporations in failed states, 376–77

Mun, Thomas, 224

Muqaddimah, 115–17, 118, 119, 132n10. *See also* Ibn Khaldun

mutual aid, Rawls on duty of, 384, 385

natural law: Locke's invocation of, 160, 163; Thomas Aquinas on private property and, 97–102; Thomas Aquinas on usury and, 108

nature: Ambrose on wealth and, 80; Confucianism and, 65–67, 68; teleological reasoning of Scholastics and, 98; transformed for humans by technology, 306, 307, 309

Neale, Walter, 22

neoclassical economics: depersonalization of market in, 99; maximizing utility in, 346; preference and, 409

neoliberalism, Mill and, 317

nepotism, and Confucian business ethics, 61

nexus-of-contracts theory, 313, 370

nonprofit corporations, 403, 405

Nozick, Robert: Locke and, 4, 164; on Rawls's principles of justice, 396n10

Oakeshott, Michael, 318n3

occupational choice, Rawls on, 389–90

opportunity costs of liquid funds, Thomas Aquinas and, 109–10

organizational citizenship behavior: in China vs. Western countries, 63; Confucian values and, 5, 62–63, 71n58

organized crime, and trust, 406

Osborne, Robin, 22

Owen, Robert, 310, 325

Pareto efficient outcome, and instrumental model, 405, 413

Pareto-improving corporate social responsibility, 361–62, 374–77

passions: Aristotle on, 37, 43; Hobbes on, 138–39; Hume on, 224, 225, 226; Mandeville on, 128, 181, 185, 186, 192, 193, 196n7; Montesquieu on, 208, 215; Smith and, 261n24; in Thomas Aquinas's system, 107

paternalism, and Confucian theories of government, 60, 61

peace: Hobbes on motive of, 142–43, 144, 145–46, 147, 148, 150, 153; Hume on commerce as conducive to, 230; Montesquieu on commerce leading to, 214; Thomas Aquinas on the common good and, 101

Peacock, Mark S., 5

Pelagius, 81

Pericles, 26

Pettit, Philip, 412

philanthropy, corporate: motives for, 270; stakeholder theory and, 267; stockholder preferences and, 275. *See also* corporate social responsibility

Physiocrats, 201

Plato: on commerce, 11, 25–26; on Greek city-states, 32; Homer and Hesiod compared to, 23, 24–26; on inferiority of laborers, 24; on profit, 25–26, 35; unfavorable view of business in *The Laws*, 35; on wealth, 5, 24–25

pluralism: Hume on commercial society and, 222; of Mandeville, 180, 182, 184–85,

186, 195; Rawls on, 392–94; about socially responsible values, 364–66. *See also* diversity, Confucian harmony in

political corporate social responsibility, 362, 376

poor boy, Smith on, ix, 247–48, 250, 251, 260n14, 260n17

Porter, Jean, 102

poverty: Ambrose on, 80; Augustine on, 78; Confucian ethics and, 60; Hayek on, 354–55; Hume on benefit of commercial society and, 228–29, 231, 232; Locke on assistance to the poor, 171–72, 178n30; Mandeville on management of, 229; Mill on, 309, 310, 311, 312, 313; in Rousseau/Marx equality narrative, 307; Smith on, 232, 238n81, 242; Thomas Aquinas on, 96–97; usury as exploitation and, 110

power distance orientation, 63, 72n59

pragmatism, business ethicists with perspective of, 263

preference theory, Sen's critique of, 409–15

price gouging, 42, 384–85

price system, Rawls on, 386–87, 390, 392. *See also* just price; market prices

principle of corporate legitimacy, 291

principle of equal basic liberties, 381

Prisoner's Dilemma, commitment to cooperate in, 415

private property: Hayek on laws upholding, 349; Ibn Khaldun on, 116, 125; in Lockean liberty narrative, 306; Mill on, 308–9, 310, 311, 313, 314; Rawlsian justice and, 387, 396n18; Thomas Aquinas on, ix, 97–102. *See also* property

profit: Aristotle on, 39–40, 43, 45, 47, 48; Confucian view of, 57, 58, 63–64, 65, 66, 68; corporate social responsibility and, 194, 273, 274, 361, 371, 374–75, 379n34, 402; Dobson on virtue consistent with, 48; Hesiod on, 21, 22, 23; in Homeric society, 17–18; Ibn Khaldun on, 116, 117, 124–25, 126, 127, 128; in Islam, 130; Kantian ethics and, 264, 265–69, 271–79; liberty for pursuit of, 394; MacIntyre on virtue crowded out by, 48; Marx on, 326–27, 328, 332, 333, 334, 338n26; Plato on, 25–26, 35; shareholder goal of maximizing, 403, 405, 407, 410, 413–14, 415, 416; Thomas Aquinas on, 6, 102–3, 104

promise keeping: Hobbes on, 146; Locke on, 163; Rawls on, 384; Sen on trust and, 406. *See also* contracts

property: Aristotle's arguments for, 99; Augustine on, 76, 84, 88–90; Hayek on laws of, 349, 350, 351, 353; Locke on, 101; Montesquieu on laws related to, 203; Montesquieu's virtue of justice and, 216; Roman law of, 76. *See also* land; private property

property-owning democracy, Rawls on, 385, 390–92, 395, 398n48

property rights: classical liberalism and, 393, 394; empirically correlated with personal freedom, 397n37; human agency protected by, 389; Hume on, 227, 233; Ibn Khaldun on, 116, 129; Locke on, ix, 101, 157–58, 159, 163–68, 173, 174–75, 176; in Mandeville's commercial society, 185; Rawls on, 386, 388, 390, 394, 395; Sen and, 401. *See also* private property; property

Proudhon, Pierre-Joseph, 310

prudence: in Kantian ethics, 269, 270, 272, 273; McCloskey and, 261n20; Smith on, 243–50, 251, 254–55, 256, 258, 260n14, 261n20, 261n25

public debt: Hume on, 235; Thomas Aquinas's summons to simplicity and, 110

public good: Augustine on, 78, 80, 89, 92; corporate social responsibility and, 373, 380n45; Hume's defense of commerce and, 223, 224, 225, 226; Ibn Khaldun on, 116, 130; Mandeville on, 182, 184, 189, 196n3, 198n22, 199n31; Montesquieu on, 212; Sen on, 407; Thomas Aquinas on, 104. *See also* common good

Quddus, Munir, xi, 6
Quesnay, François, 201

Rachels, James, 264
Rashid, Salim, xi, 6
Rasmussen, Douglas B., 155n4
rational choice theory, Sen on, 408–9, 415
Rawls, John, xi, 9, 381–99; applied business ethics and, 383, 385, 394; basic structure of society and, 383, 385–87, 394–95; business ethics scholarship and, 381–85, 387, 394; on capitalism, 385, 387, 392, 394, 396n18, 398n48; case for market liberalism and, 387–95; classical liberalism and, 391, 393, 395; on equality, 383, 388, 389; on equality of opportunity, 383, 390, 397n33; on inequality, 383, 388, 392, 396n18, 397n33; liberty and, 383, 386, 388–90, 393–94, 395; on moral principles applying to individuals, 384–85; *Political Liberalism*, 9, 381, 392–93, 396n18; principles of justice of, 381, 383–84, 385, 388, 395n7, 396nn8–10, 396n14, 397n33; on property-owning

Rawls, John (*cont.*)
    democracy, 385, 390–92, 395, 398n48;
    regime types and, 385; *A Theory of
    Justice*, 9, 381, 384, 385
Reagan, Ronald, 131n2
reason: classical disparagement of commerce
    and, 225; in Hobbes's argument, 135,
    137, 139, 141–42, 147, 150, 154, 224;
    Hume on the passions and, 224; Smith
    on usefulness of, 245; Thomas Aquinas's
    employment of, 95, 98
reasonable pluralism, Rawls on, 392–94
reciprocity, as Confucian virtue, 5, 56, 62–63
redistribution: Augustine's ethics and, 89;
    Hayek's arguments against, 352–54,
    357n42; in Homer's world, 14, 16;
    Rawls and, 385, 391; in Rousseau/
    Marx equality narrative, 307
regulation. *See* government regulation
religious beliefs, Hobbes on, 153
religious freedom, Rawls on, 393
religious toleration, Locke on, 157–58, 172–
    75, 176, 178n32
rent seeking: Confucian values and, 59;
    Smith and, 261n30
revealed preference theory, Sen's critique of,
    409–10, 413–14
Ricardo, David: critique of landlords, 309–
    10; as forebear of Marx, 327
Richard of Middleton, 113n45
righteousness as Confucian virtue, 56, 57;
    profit seeking and, 57, 58, 63–64
right Smitheans, 242
risk: Ibn Khaldun on cunning traders and,
    127; Scholastic objection to usury and,
    109; Smith on prudent man and, 244–
    45; Thales's profits from assuming, 45,
    51n30; Thomas Aquinas on *magnifi-
    centia* and, 108, 114n60
Roberts, John, 52n39
Rodgers, T. J., 362
Rollin, Charles, 205
Rorty, Richard, 263, 266
Rothbard, Murray, ix
Rousseau, Jean-Jacques: conjectural history
    and, 189; defects of commercial order
    and, 250; equality and, 306, 307; moral
    character of natural man and, 214
Rubin, Robert, 368, 379n32
Ruger, William, 359, 376
rules in social interaction, Hayek on, 348–
    51, 353, 355, 357n40
Ruskin, John, 32

safety in business decisions, 268
Sahlins, Marshall, 14, 21
Saint-Simon, Henri de, 310, 325

Sallust, 223, 225, 229, 231
Samuelson, Paul, 409
Sandel, Michael J., 104
Schaps, David, 24
Schlag, Martin, ix, 5
Scholastic philosophers: commerce and,
    104, 207; economic laws of, 98–99; just
    exchanges and, 105, 111; on usury,
    108–9. *See also* Thomas Aquinas
Scipio Africanus, 78
Searle, John, viii
self-interest: English commerce of eigh-
    teenth century and, 181; Hobbes on,
    137, 139–40, 148, 150, 154, 155; Ibn
    Khaldun on societal welfare deriving
    from, 116, 117, 119; instrumental
    model and, 405–6, 413, 418n26; Kant-
    ian ethics and, 270–71; of Mandeville's
    bees, 179, 208; Marx on capitalists and,
    333; in modern economics, 98; Mon-
    tesquieu on, 209, 214; Scholastics on
    appropriate limits of, 111; Sen on, 402,
    406–9, 410–16; Smith on, 137, 140,
    197n18, 259n6; Tocqueville on, 284,
    297 (*see also* enlightened self-interest)
self-liking, Mandeville on, 182, 189, 192,
    195, 197n8
self-love: Mandeville on, 181, 197n8; Smith
    on, 211
self-ownership, Locke on, 163, 177n12
self-preservation: Locke on, 161–63, 167;
    Mandeville on, 181, 197n8
self-sufficiency: Hesiod's advice on, 20, 22,
    23; Hobbes on self-restraint and, 145;
    prized by ancient Greeks, 32; Thomas
    Aquinas on, 103–4
Sen, Amartya, 9, 401–19; arguments against
    instrumental model, 405–8, 410, 413–16;
    models of corporate moral responsibility
    and, 416; relevance to business ethics,
    401–3; scope of scholarship of, 401; on
    sources of human motivation, 408–15;
    writings on business ethics, 406–8
Seneca, on luxury, 230
separation thesis, in stakeholder theory,
    267–68
Shaftesbury, Earl of, 185
shareholder model. *See* instrumental model
    of corporate behavior; stockholder
    theory
shareholders: Mill and, 313, 314, 315, 316;
    Sen on commitments of, 414–15; with
    sole goal to maximize profit, 403, 405,
    407, 410, 413–14, 415, 416
Shaw, William H., 8
Sidgwick, Henry, 304
Simon, Julian, 168

slavery: Ambrose on greed as form of, 81; in ancient Greek city-states, 33; in ancient Rome, 213; Aristotle comparing craftsmen to slaves, 35; Augustine's concerns about, 75–76; in Hesiod's *Works and Days*, 19; in Homeric world, 13, 14, 16, 17, 19, 24; Hume on commercial society and, 222; Ibn Khaldun on profit from, 125; Marx on, 329, 330

Smith, Adam, ix, 7, 241–62; advantages of commercial society and, 140; Augustine's inverse position and, 89; beauty of commerce and, ix, 242, 246, 247, 248, 250–52, 254, 255, 256, 258–59; on character, 244, 246, 248, 250, 254, 255, 256, 258, 261n29; commercial success and, 252–54, 257–58; on extended prudence, 249–50, 251, 254–55, 258; as forebear of Marx, 327; four-stages theory of, 203; global economic order and, 255, 256–57; Hume on commercial society and, 222, 229; Ibn Khaldun's anticipation of, 116, 119; on imagination, 242, 247, 250, 255; Lockean liberty narrative and, 306, 311; Mandeville's anticipation of, 183, 189, 196n5; misconceptions about, 241–42; Montesquieu on virtues and, 214, 215; on mutual benefit, 137, 346; negative comments about businesspeople, 116, 241–42, 255; on pathologies of commercial order, 254–55; on "poor boy" with ambition, ix, 247–48, 250, 251, 260n14, 260n17; on the prudent man, 243–49, 254, 256, 260n14, 261n20; Ricardo and, 309–10; on superior prudence, 249, 251, 261n25; "system of natural liberty," ix, 137, 242, 249, 260n7; *Theory of Moral Sentiments*, 241, 243–47, 249–54, 258, 261n24; *Wealth of Nations*, 116, 197n18, 241–42, 255

social capital: corporate governance and, 257; modern theorists of, 123

social cohesion (*Asabiyah*), 120, 122–23, 130–31

social contract: between business and society, 372, 373, 404, 416; Hobbes on, 149, 302; inequality in Lockean worldview and, 307; Mill and, 304, 306; rejection of teleology and, 302

social contract theory, 404, 416

social democracy. *See* property-owning democracy, Rawls on

social entrepreneurship, Augustine and, 90, 91

socialism: Hayek's arguments against, 341, 344, 352, 354; limitation of liberties in regimes with, 397n37; of Marx, 324,

325, 328, 330–31; Mill on, 307, 308, 309–10, 315; pro-planning economists and, xi, 343, 344, 346; Rawls on, 385; utopian, 310, 325, 331

"Socialist Calculation" (Hayek), 355n5, 356nn7–8. *See also* economic planning

social justice: Hayek and, 351–54, 357n42; Thomas Aquinas's perspective and, 106–7

socially responsible investment (SRI) funds, 275, 365–66

social responsibility: Augustine's ethic of, 88, 89; Hume on human nature and, 233–34. *See also* corporate social responsibility

social safety net, Rawls and, 386, 395

Solomon, Robert, 31, 263

Solon, 24

specialization. *See* division of labor (specialization)

Spirit of the Laws, The (Montesquieu), 201, 202, 207, 210, 213

spontaneous order: Confucian "heaven" and, 66; Hayek on, 345, 346, 357n40; Hobbes on, 149

stakeholder fiduciary principle, 291

stakeholder theory, 403–4; Friedman and, 378n8; Kant and, 266–68; Rawls and, 387; Tocqueville and, 283, 291–94, 297–98

state of nature, Locke on, 163

state ownership of means of production: pro-planning economists and, 343–44; Rawls on private ownership vs., 385, 396n18, 397n37; stakeholder theory and, 294

state socialism, Rawls on, 385

Steele, Richard, 182

Steiner, Hillel, 177n17

stewardship, Ambrose on, 80, 81

Stillingfleet, Edward, 182

stockholder theory: Friedman and, 295, 374–75, 378n8; Tocqueville and, 283, 291, 295–98. *See also* instrumental model of corporate behavior

stock options, to motivate managers, 273

Sufism, asceticism in, 119

sumptuary laws, 222, 227, 229

supply and demand, law of: Ibn Khaldun's appreciation of, 119; ideal conditions required for, 106; Scholastics' discovery of, 99; Thomas Aquinas's understanding of, 110

sympathy: Sen on, 411, 413; Smith on, 140, 247

system of natural liberty: Rawls on, 385; of Smith, 137, 242, 249, 260n7, 346

Tandy, David, 22

Target Corporation, 267, 275, 278

taxation: absent in archaic Greece, 14; Confucian disapproval of excess in, 59; excessive in late Roman Empire, 78, 79; Hobbes on, 153; Hume's argument for consistency of, 234; Ibn Khaldun on, 116, 120, 121, 125, 129–30, 131n2; inflation as hidden form of, 108; Montesquieu on Dutch government and, 215; progressive, Rawls on, 385, 386; Tocqueville's enlightened self-interest and, 287

Taylor, Harriet, 303

technological change: Hayek on market order and, 346, 350; Ibn Khaldun on, 123; nonexistent for hunter-gatherers, 348

technological project of Lockean narrative, 306, 307, 309

teleological reasoning: of classical and medieval ethics, 302; displaced in Hume's philosophy, 224, 228; of Thomas Aquinas, 98, 100. *See also* final causality

Thales of Miletus, 41–42, 44–45, 47, 51n30

Thomas Aquinas, ix, 5–6, 95–114; central moral considerations of, 96; on commerce, ix, 95, 97, 102–5; on the common good, 6, 99–102, 105, 111, 114n71; economic and social expansion in time of, 95; extrinsic titles to interest and, 109–10; on greed or avarice, ix, 96–97, 103, 104, 107, 108, 110; life of, 95; natural law and, 97–102, 108; persecution of heresy justified by, 112n31; on private property, ix, 97–102; relevance to modern business ethics, 104–5, 106, 108, 110; significance of economic thought of, 110–11; on wealth and poverty, 96–97

Thomas Aquinas on justice: approach to economic questions and, 111; as central virtue, 95–96; the common good and, 6, 101; economic laws and, 98–99; exchange and, 105–7; money as measure of, 107; natural law and, 98; private property and, 97, 99

Thomism, virtue ethics in, 201

Tian, Qing, x, 5

time preference: Aristotle's objection to moneylending and, 44; Turgot on, 51n28

Tocqueville, Alexis de, x, 7–8, 283–99; on associations (*see* associations, Tocqueville on); business ethics and, 284, 289–98; democracy and, 283–84, 285–87, 291–92, 297, 298, 311; on individualism, 285–87, 289, 297; Kantian ethics and, 289, 293, 294, 298; Lockean liberty narrative and, 307, 311; Mill on freedom and, 311; on self-interest, 284, 297 (*see also* enlightened self-interest);

stakeholder theory and, 283, 291–94, 297–98; stockholder theory and, 283, 291, 295–98

Tomasi, John, 389–90

"too big to fail," 351

Toynbee, Arnold, 119

trade: Confucians on purpose of, 58; Flew on exploitative nature of, 31–32; Hayek on civilizing function of, 347–48; Mandeville on public benefits of, 185; Montesquieu and, 204, 206–7, 214; mutual gains from, 43; terminology related to, 27n26. *See also* commerce

trade unions, Mill's opposition to, 315–16

trust: Hobbes on, 136, 146; modern courses on business ethics and, 136; modern social theorists and, 123; Sen on need for, 401, 406, 415, 416

trustworthiness, as Confucian virtue, 56, 62

Turgot, A. R. J., 51n26, 51n28, 203

understanding, as Confucian virtue, 5, 56, 62–63

unintended outcomes: Hayek's spontaneous order and, 346; Mandeville on, 7, 188–89, 192, 196

usury: Aristotle's objections to, 41, 51n24, 207; Hume's condemnation of laws against, 234; Ibn Khaldun on, 121; Islamic thought on, 124; Montesquieu and, 202, 207–8; Scholastic philosophers on, 108–9; Thomas Aquinas on social benefits of, 102; Thomas Aquinas on vice of, 108–10. *See also* lending money at interest

utilitarianism: Aquinas's ethics compared to, 96; of Mill, viii–ix, 2, 301, 303, 304–6; social responsibility of business and, 194; Tocqueville on enlightened self-interest and, 289

utility: justice and, viii; maximized in neoclassical economics, 346; Smith's priority of beauty over, 242, 246, 247, 248–49, 250–51, 252, 255–56

value: altered by gold coinage, 78; Aristotle on means vs. ends and, 36; Augustine on, 76, 83–85, 86; Ibn Khaldun on demand and, 119; Ibn Khaldun on labor and, 116, 119, 125, 127; labor theory of, 311, 326–27; Locke on accumulation of gold and, 78; Locke on labor in creation of, 168, 176n10, 177n21; in mutual gains from trade, 43, 51n26; Thomas Aquinas's conception of money and, 107; virtue in production of, 43, 48. *See also* wealth value pluralism, 364; corporate social responsibility and, 364–66; of Mandeville, 184–85, 186, 195

Vaughn, Karen I., ix, xi, 8

Velasquez, Manuel, 378n15

vices: Mandeville on, 179, 180–81, 186, 190, 193, 195, 208, 210; Montesquieu on, 204, 210, 215–16. *See also* greed or avarice

virtue ethics: Montesquieu and, 201, 202, 211–15, 216; recent revival of, 201. *See also* Aristotle's virtue ethics

virtues: Cicero on wealth and, 78; Confucian, 55–58, 60, 61, 62, 65, 66, 67, 68; Hayek on markets and, 352; Hume on luxury and, 225; Ibn Khaldun on *Asabiyah* and, 123; Locke on prudence and self-responsibility as, 159; Mandeville on, 179, 180–82, 185, 193, 196nn2–3, 196n7; Mill on, 305; Smith on, 250 (*see also* prudence); Thomas Aquinas on, 95, 96, 98 (*see also* Thomas Aquinas on justice); Thomas Aquinas on money and, 107; Tocqueville on enlightened self-interest and, 288, 289. *See also* justice

Voltaire, on English commerce, 181

war: Montesquieu's historical analysis and, 204; as source of wealth in Homer, 14, 15, 24; supported by the wealthy of ancient Greece, 35

wealth: Ambrose on, 79–81; archaic sources on, 25; Aristotle on, 24, 25, 26, 29n92, 46, 47; Augustine on, 75, 76, 79, 81, 82, 84, 85, 86, 87–90, 91; Cicero on, 77–78, 79, 80; Confucian values and, 58, 59, 60, 64, 68; in fourth-century Christianity, 79–81; Hayek on central planning and, 343; Hayek on inequality of, 352–54, 357n42; Hayek on society conducive to, 341, 342, 348, 349–50, 351, 354; in Hesiod's *Works and Days*, 20–21, 22, 24, 25; Hobbes on, 139, 140, 143; in Homer's epics, 12–19, 24, 27n21; Ibn Khaldun on corrupting influence of, 119–21; Ibn Khaldun on rightful acquisition of, 125, 130; Kantian

capitalism as generator of, 277; in late Roman empire, 77–79; Lockean liberty narrative and, 311; Locke on labor and, 166, 168; Locke on money and, 166; Mill on unequal distribution of, 310–11, 313; Montesquieu on, 201; Plato on, 24–25; as shareholder goal, 402, 405, 407–8, 413; Smith on images leading to pursuit of, 247–48; stakeholder theory and, 267; Thomas Aquinas on, 96–97; Thomas Aquinas on unproductive hoarding of, 110; Tocqueville on pursuit of, 284, 286; Xenophon on, 25. *See also* money; value

Wealth of Nations, The (Smith), 116, 197n18, 241–42, 255

Weber, Max, on Confucianism, 53

welfare-state capitalism, Rawls on, 385, 396n18

Wennerlind, Carl, 232

Werhane, Patricia, 263, 404

West, M. L., 22, 25

Whole Foods, 374–76

will, Kant on purity of, 264–66, 268–72

Williams, Bernard, 364

Wilson, Bart, viii

Wittgenstein, Ludwig, viii

Wood, Allen, 270–72

Wood, Diana, 103

work. *See* labor

Xenophon: on commerce, 11, 26; on degradation of labor, 23–24; on wealth, 25

Xunzi, 66

zero-sum corporate social responsibility, 361, 362, 366, 371, 372–73, 374, 375, 376, 377

zero-sum game: Augustine on creation of wealth and, 88; Confucian concept of harmony and, 65; Locke on commercial society and, 168, 175; MacIntyre on modern business as, 48; Mill on freedom and, 304; Montesquieu on international trade and, 206

Zwolinski, Matt, xi, 9